The Nonconformist's Memorial

THE

NONCONFORMIST'S
MEMORIAL;

BEING

AN ACCOUNT OF THE LIVES, SUFFERINGS,

AND

PRINTED WORKS

OF THE

TWO THOUSAND MINISTERS

Ejected from the Church of England, chiefly by the Act of Uniformity,
Aug. 24, 1662.

ORIGINALLY WRITTEN BY

EDMUND CALAMY, D. D.

Abridged, Corrected, and Methodized, with many additional Anecdotes
AND
SEVERAL NEW LIVES,

BY SAMUEL PALMER.

The Second Edition.

IN THREE VOLUMES.

Embellished with Heads of the principal Divines, chiefly from original Pictures.

VOL. II.

For the Levites left their Suburbs, and their Possession, and came to Judah and Jerusalem; for Jeroboam and his Sons had cast them off from executing the Priests Office unto the Lord.—— And after them, out of all the Tribes of Israel, such as set their Hearts to seek the Lord God of Israel, came to Jerusalem to sacrifice unto the Lord God of their Fathers.
2 *Chron.* xi. 14, 16.

BARTHOLOMEW-DAY was fatal to our Church and Religion, in throwing out a very great number of worthy, learned, pious, and orthodox Divines.   LOCKE.

LONDON:

PRINTED BY J. CUNDEE, IVY-LANE,

FOR BUTTON AND SON, AND T. HURST, PATERNOSTER-ROW;

Sold also by

CONDER, BUCKLERSBURY; AND JAMES, BRISTOL.

1802.

THE
NONCONFORMIST'S
MEMORIAL.

MINISTERS EJECTED OR SILENCED

IN

DEVONSHIRE.

ANSTY§. JOHN MAUDUIT, B. D. *Of Exeter Col: Oxford.* He was the son of Mr. *Isaac Mauduit*, a respectable merchant in the city of Exeter. Mr. Wood, in his *Fasti Oxonienses,* mentions him as being senior Proctor of that university in the year 1649. But takes no further notice of him, though it is evident that he sided with the Royalists, and appears to have been held in good estimation at Oxford, from the circumstance of his name being subscribed, in connexion with that of Mr. *Hierome Sanchy*, a fellow proctor, and Dr. *Edward Reynolds*, Vice chancellor, to a letter addressed to *John Selden*, Esq. dated *April* 1649, most earnestly recommending the university of Oxford to his care and protection, under the dangers which at that period sorely threatened it. A copy of this letter may be seen in the life of Mr. *Selden*, prefixed to the splendid edition of his works in six volumes folio, page 43.

Dr. *Walker*, in his *Sufferings of the Clergy*, though he casts so much abuse on so many others of the Nonconformists, does not attempt to bring any accusation against Mr. *Mauduit.* He takes care, however, not to pass any encomium upon him, even for his loyalty, and only mentions

§ It appears from the INDEX VILLARIS, that there are two places of this name in Devonshire, the one called *East Ansty*, the other *West Ansty:* the former is a Rectory, and the latter a Vicarage. Both of them are small livings, rated at but little more than 10*l. per ann.* At which of them Mr. Mauduit preached doth not appear, or whether statedly at either.

him as ejected from *Exeter* college upon the visitation of the parliament, consequently as a sufferer among the Royalists; and says, that his name was crossed out of the buttery-book *Oct.* 20, 1648. He preached however publicly at *Oxford* before the lord general *Fairfax*, at whose desire the sermon was published. He afterwards had the sequestered living of Dr. *Hammond* at *Penshurst* in Kent. Being obliged to quit it at the Restoration, he went to his relations at *Exeter*, and preached occasionally about the country : probably more frequently at *Ansty* than at other places. He afterwards continued at Exeter till the Corporation-act drove him and other ministers from thence. He then removed his family to *St. Mary Ottery*, ten miles from Exeter, and frequently preached as he had opportunity at several places ; freely giving his labours to those who were not able to maintain a minister. Upon the Indulgence in 1672, he licensed a meeting-house, and preached in it as long as liberty for so doing was continued. On Saturday, *March* 4, 1674, he told his family that he should die on the Monday following; which accordingly he did, with full assurance of faith, triumphantly entering on another and happier life, after he had with holy longings expressed his joyful waiting for the Lord Jesus to receive his spirit. He was a man of an exemplary conversation, and of a very chearful disposition; and for his learning and affability he was much respected by the gentry of his neighbourhood.—His son died pastor of a congregation of Protestant Dissenters in *Southwark*. [He was the father of the late worthy *Jasper Mauduit*, Esq. of *Hackney*, Chairman of the Committee of deputies for managing the affairs of the Dissenters; a zealous friend, and a distinguished ornament to the dissenting interest. It deserves to be mentioned here, that he always observed *Bartholomew-day* with some special marks of veneration and grief.]

WORKS. A Sermon at Oxford, mentioned above.—A Warning-Piece to afflicted England, 1659.—Letter to Gen. Monk on the Causes of the Ruin of Governments and Commonwealths.

ASHBURY [R. S. 37*l.* 11*s.*] Mr. DANIEL MORTON. Dr. *Walker* has nothing worse to say of him than that he had no education but in a private school : He had made the same assertion with respect to some others, whom Dr. *Calamy* proves to have been brought up at the universities. § But admitting the fact, he might have been better qualified for the ministry than some who had spent many years in a college,

college, and if he could have conformed he would not have been ejected.

ASHPRINGTON [R. 160*l*.] JOHN BURGESS, M. A. The son of a minister in this county. When he was a boy he was bit by an adder, and remarkably preserved from the fatal effects of it by the sagacity of his mother, who had no other help at hand. And his life was retrieved for good purpose; for he proved a judicious, laborious, and useful minister of Christ. About the time of his ejectment, such was the respect which the patron of this living had for him, that he made him a present of the next presentation, which he afterwards disposed of for *jool.* He removed to *Dartmouth,* and resided about four months with Mr. *Geare,* after whose death he was a great support to his widow. From thence he removed to London, where his daughter was married to Mr. *Tho. Brook,* and he retired to *Hackney,* where he and some other ministers united in carrying on a private lecture, and other exercises of religion, to a society of about thirty families. He was much tempted to conform, by the offers of preferment in the church; but he refused them all, and contented himself with boarding the sons of citizens, who went to school to Mr. *Singleton,* who had a flourishing school at Islington. And there he died about 1663[*]. He was a very polite man, of a graceful presence, and a charitable generous temper; well beloved in his parish, greatly respected by his brethren, and much followed by many in adjacent places; being a person of extraordinary abilities, and very eminent both in prayer and preaching.

AXMINSTER [R.] Mr. BARTHOLOMEW ASHWOOD. A judicious, godly, and laborious divine; ejected by the Act of uniformity. Probably the person whom Dr. *Walker* mentions at *Bickleigh* in this county. [He had a son in the ministry, who died at *Peckham* in Surrey, whose life was published by Mr. *Reynolds.* He often said of his father, "If there was a good man upon earth he was one, being strictly pious, and much devoted to prayer." He related this remarkable circumstance of him (the like to which also happened to his great-grandfather) that being under extraordinary solicitude about his children, those words were strangely impressed upon him as by an audible voice, ' I will be a God to thee and to thy seed.' His family shared in the sufferings of the

[*] If this date is correct, it seems most probable he was ejected before 1662.—The chapel at *Brook-house* was lately in being.

times,

times, and he died 40*l*. in debt; but God graciously appeared in opening the hearts of strangers for their relief. *Reynold's Life* of Mr. *John Ashwood*, p. 54 and 99.]

WORKS. The Heavenly Trade.—The Best Treasure.

BARNSTAPLE [V. S. 47*l*.] NATHANIEL MATHER, M. A. One of the four sons of Mr. *Richard Mather* of Dorchester, who, on account of the severity of the times, took him when he was young into New England, where he was educated at *Harvard* college. He succeeded his brother *Samuel* as pastor of a church in Dublin. He was afterwards in the living of Harberton, near *Totness*, and was presented to this at Barnstaple by *Oliver*, in 1656. Mr. *Martin Blake*, the sequestered minister, a learned, pious, and moderate man, was treated exceedingly ill; but Dr. *Walker*, who relates the particulars, does not even insinuate that Mr. *Mather* was any way chargeable with it. Upon his ejectment he went into Holland, and became minister at Rotterdam. He afterwards returned to London, where he was pastor of a congregational church, and one of the lecturers at *Pinners-Hall*. He died *July* 26, 1697, aged 57, having been in the ministry forty-seven years, and was buried at Bunhill-fields, where there is a long Latin inscription upon his tombstone, [which represents him as a man of great mental endowments and literary accomplishments, which he consecrated to the service of God: one every way qualified for his office; who, while he sincerely published the gospel, adorned it by his life; being particularly eminent for modesty, patience and piety. He was a ready and laborious preacher, a faithful and vigilant pastor; who in his ministrations had the sacred art of concealing the MAN, that God alone might be seen and exalted. " *In sacræ functionis exercitiis, arte pia celavit* Hominem, *ut solus conspiceretur* DEUS."] See WATT's Lyric Poems.

WORKS. The Righteousness of God by Faith; two Sermons at *Pinners-Hall*.—Twenty-three Sermons preached at that Lecture, and at *Lime-street*, [taken in short-hand as they were delivered, but most of them corrected by himself.]—A Discussion of the Lawfulness of a Pastor's officiating in other Churches. § A Fast Sermon, 1711, on 1 Cor. xi. 30.

BERRY POMREY, [V.] Mr. RANDALL.

BIDEFORD, [R. S.] Mr. WILLIAM BARTLET. Of *New Inn Hall, Oxford*. Brother to Mr. *John Bartlet* of Exeter.

Exeter. He was congregational in his judgment, but loved peace with his brethren. He was one of the assistants to the commissioners of Devonshire and Exeter. A man of considerable note in that part of the country: eminent for humility, strictness of life, gravity, authority and experience: a very solid and useful preacher, whose labours were attended with very signal success. He discovered great courage in the cause of his God, for which he became a considerable sufferer; for he was the chief object of the malice and fury of the enemies to strict godliness in those parts, some of whom, it is said, appeared to suffer the rebukes of providence on his account. He was once imprisoned, and at another time he escaped only by the mistake of the officer, who took another person for him. Dr. *Walker* brings some heinous charges against him, which Dr. *Calamy* largely considers, and clearly refutes; § particularly respecting his conduct towards Mr. *Gifford* the sequestered minister, whom he represents Mr. Bartlet as treating with great injustice and cruelty. As one among many striking instances of gross misrepresentations in that writer, (which we shall generally pass over,) it may not be improper here to introduce the substance of Dr. Calamy's defence of Mr. Bartlet against this accusation alone. " I have been informed (says the Dr.) by several aged persons, living in 1718, of as good characters as any in the town, that there were scarcely any two ministers of different persuasions to be met with, that lived and died in greater friendship than Mr. Gifford and Mr. Bartlet; and that Mr. Gifford was so far from reckoning Mr. Bartlet his greatest enemy, that he has often, with great warmth declared, that the reproaches cast upon him by such as were enemies to every thing good, upon his account, were altogether undeserved. Nay, he always gave Mr. Bartlet a good character, and would often say, he was a better man than himself." Upon Mr. Gifford's readmission to this living, when a zealous woman of the parish told him, that she had never been at church during his absence, he replied, " The verier wretch thou." And upon his death-bed he expressed a desire to see Mr. Bartlet, but those about him prevented his being sent for. With regard to this writer's reflection on Mr. Bartlet as having had no university education, there is one testimony against him that will not be contested: it is that of Mr. Anthony Wood, who mentions him among the authors educated at Oxford. He lived to a good old age, and died in 1682. A grandson

B 3   of

of his was very useful among the Dissenters in *Bideford*, and was much respected, but he died young.

WORKS. The Model of the Congregational Way.—Sovereign Balsam for healing such Professors as Satan hath wounded.

BISHOP'S TAWTON, [V.] JONATHAN HANMER, M. A. Of *Eman. Col. Camb.* Born in Barnstaple about 1605; ordained *Nov.* 23, 1632, by Dr. *Field,* Bp. of St. David's, in St. Margaret's church, Westminster. He was first presented to the living of *Instow,* by John Speccot, Esq. and had institution from Bp. *Hall* in 1632. In 1635 he was ordered by the said bishop to preach at Barnstaple at his visitation. He sent his lordship a very modest and respectful answer, begging to be excused; which shews that he was far from being such a person as Dr. *Walker* represents him. (*Cal. Contin.* p. 300.) Mr. *Hanmer* afterwards had the living of *Bishop's Tawton,* and the lectureship of *Barnstaple:* and was cast out of both places *Aug.* 24, 1662. After his ejectment, very distant parts of the kingdom enjoyed the happiness of his labours, *viz.* Barnstaple, London, Bristol, Pinner, and Torrington. The troubles he met with for his Nonconformity occasioned frequent changes as to the place of his abode, which were sorely afflictive to himself, but the cause of great joy to those who, by this means, sat under his instruction. He was a ' scribe thoroughly instructed ' to the kingdom of heaven :' a preacher of the first rank, in regard to matter, method and elocution. He had a wonderful talent in composing sermons, and a manner of delivering them to which few attain, whereby they were rendered uncommonly impressive. Few ministers in his time, were instrumental in doing more good in the conversion of souls. From the places where he preached, he often received letters from ministers, as well as private christians, thanking him for his labours, and blessing God for the great success of them. His lectures at *Barnstaple* were greatly thronged, numbers attending who lived many miles distant, and some of them persons of character and distinction. Good Mr. *Blake,* the vicar of Barnstaple, (contrary to Dr. *Walker*'s account) shewed, by his whole conduct, that he was well pleased with him. This Mr. *Blake* had a great esteem for others of his brethren who were ejected, several of whom then lived in the town. They frequently visited each other; and he would often say, " My heart bleeds whenever I see you, " to think that such worthy persons should be silenced and " cast

"cast out, and your places filled up by such as are sadly ig-
" norant and scandalous." Among Mr. *Hanmer's* papers
there is a strict order from the bishop, signed *Seth Exon*,
1665, to several of the parishioners, requiring them to pay
him what was due of tithes, at the time of his removal, and
severely threatening such as refused.

His works, both from the pulpit and the press, shewed him
to be a learned man, and his other works, a very good man.
He was full of devotion in all the solemnities of worship;
and a vein of piety towards God, and of zeal for the spiritual
benefit of men, appeared in him wherever he was. These
graces manifested themselves in a hearty concern to propa-
gate the gospel in foreign parts, particularly among the poor
Indians; and he earnestly recommended the same concern to
others. Among his papers there are many letters under the
hand of Mr. *John Elliot* of New England, in which he returns him hearty thanks for his readiness to help forward the
cause of the gospel, by the generous supplies which he procured and sent over. He died at Barnstaple, *Dec.* 18, 1687,
aged about 81. The spirit of this good man may be seen in
his letters; some extracts from a few of those which he sent
to his son while at the university, are here added.

——" I understand you are well settled in the college. I
take notice of the goodness of God towards you therein, and
desire to bless him for it, as I hope you do too. How much
doth it concern you to look to it, that you answer expectation! So will you occasion great credit to your godly tutor,
joy to your parents and friends, and glory to God; which
should chiefly prevail with you. Oh! remember what sweet
fruit you will reap from a few years well spent there, wherein
you may lay up that which will make you serviceable all your
days. Grudge not any pains and industry: 'tis but your
duty; and the issue will be such as will sweeten your life,
and make you amiable in the eyes of God and man. But the
loss of time, and of what may be got now, will be irreco-
verable, and the remembrance of it exceeding bitter. Time
and opportunity are precious talents: account so of them,
and improve them accordingly: which the Lord help thee to
do for his Christ's sake. Apply yourself to study, with an
eye to him for his blessing; and *acquaint thyself* more
with him; thereby good, all manner of good *shall be unto
thee.* Keep close to God daily. Find out some pious,
studious, ingenious youths, and make them your familiar
acquaintance.—I give thee up to the Lord. May he own
thee

thee in his Son, and make thee instrumental for his glory, which will occasion thanksgivings to him from thy tender father."

He was much concerned for his son's proficiency in human as well as divine knowledge. In one letter he writes thus:— " Strive to be a good logician What you read, thoroughly understand: if you cannot by your own study, then use the help of others: ask and confer. Daily ply the Greek; and be still on the gaining hand. Neglect not the Hebrew. Labour after a good style in the Latin tongue, and a graceful pronunciation. Imitate *Tully* as near as you are able: and for this end read him often, and write as he. Converse much with the Greek Testament, &c." He drew up several MS. tracts for his son's use while he was at *Cambridge*, one of which was a sort of commentary upon this distich;

" Surge, precare, stude, meditator, currito, prande;

" Lude, stude, cæna, meditare, precare, quiesce."§

He was admirably qualified to give advice, and greatly sought to for it, on many occasions, by persons of very different characters and stations in the world. Dr. *Calamy* has preserved his solution of one particular case, sent him by Mr. *Flavel*, respecting an argument produced by a certain author to prove, " That it is justifiable in Rulers to prescribe " some things more in the worship of God than he him- " self has instituted:" taken from *Solomon*'s conduct, 1 *Kings* viii. 64. and *Hezekiah*'s, 1 *Chron.* xxx. 23. (See *Contin.* p. 310—314.) Mr. Flavel expressed much satisfaction on the perusal of it.

WORKS. An Exercitation upon Confirmation, (much admired.)—A View of Antiquity.—He wrote a piece against the Papists, which could not obtain an Imprimatur, in the Reign of K. James. Besides this, he left a great many other MSS. of which Dr. Calamy gives an account; particularly—The Life of Paul— and a Translation of Nic. Machiavel's Florentine History.

BRAMFORD SPEKE [V.] Mr. HALLER.

BRATTON FLEMING [R.] Mr. ANTHONY PALMER. He was a person of a good estate. He succeeded Mr. *Gay* in this living in 1645, and left it for the sake of Nonconformity in 1662. Dr. *Walker* says, He administered the Lord's

§ Of the above distich, an ingenious correspondent has communicated the following translation:
" Rise, pray, then study, meditate, run, dine,
" Play, study, sup, think, pray, to rest resign."   I. J.

Supper,

Supper but once in fourteen years. This cannot now be disproved, § though the thing is highly improbable. If it were true, there might be something peculiar in the case sufficient to justify him. He died in *September*, 1693.

BRIDSTOW [R. S.] Mr. WILLIAM KNAPMAN. The only account we have of him is from Dr. *Walker*, who says, He settled here by an order of the House of Commons, in 1647, but has not a word to offer against him.

BRIXHAM [V.] JOHN KEMPSTER, M. A. Of *Christ Church*, *Oxf.* and chaplain of the college. At his first coming to Brixham he lived at Lupton, and there married one Mrs. Nicholls, a pious, prudent, charitable gentlewoman, one of whose brothers was minister of *Leskard* in Cornwal, and another was mayor of that corporation. After he was ejected he continued a while at Lupton, and then removed to Dartmouth, where he preached occasionally in his own house. From thence he was obliged to depart, by the Five-mile act, and went to London, where he was well known, and lived in good repute. Though he had not the most agreeable delivery, and had no pastoral charge after his ejectment, his occasional preaching in London had the approbation of many judicious ministers and people ; and his life was unblameable. He died of an apoplexy in *July*, 1692. His funeral sermon was preached by Mr. *J. Howe.*

BRIXTON [C.] JOHN QUICKE, M. A. Of *Exeter Col. Oxf.* Born at *Plymouth*, A. D. in 1636, of parents in the middle rank, and eminently pious. God wrought a saving change on his heart, when very young, which inclined him to devote himself to the work of the ministry. He went to *Oxford* about 1650, and left it 1657, when he returned to his native country, and preached for some time at *Ermington.* He was ordained at Plymouth, *Feb.* 2, 1658, being called to be minister of *Kingsbridge* and *Churchstow*. From thence he was called to *Brixton*, where the Act of uniformity found and ejected him. Though upon the most serious consideration he could not comply with the terms which the law imposed, yet the people being earnestly desirous of his labours, he continued preaching to them after Bartholomew-day, till he was seized in the pulpit, in the midst of the morning sermon, *Dec.* 13, 1663, and by the warrant of two justices committed to jail, for preaching without episcopal ordination, and that after excommunication.

Being

Being brought to the quarter-sessions for the county, *Jan*. 15, he passed under a long examination from the justices. The court asked him, by what authority he durst preach in spite of the law? He answered, that "He did it in despite of no authority, but from a sense of duty, and of a necessity laid upon him by his ordination, to preach to his flock, which had otherwise been wholly destitute." They then asked him, who were his ordainers? He mentioned four who had then conformed. His counsel urging that there were errors in the indictment, the bench allowed the plea, and unanimously declared his commitment illegal. But upon a motion made for his discharge, the court insisted on sureties, for his behaviour, or else his promise to desist from preaching. After a long altercation, he freely told them, He *must obey God rather than them;* and that he could not look God in the face with comfort, if he should make such a promise after that at his ordination. Upon this he was remanded to prison, where he lay in close confinement eight weeks longer, till discharged at the assizes by the lord chief baron *Hale*.

Afterwards Bp. *Ward* ordered two indictments to be laid against him for preaching to the prisoners in jail; and he was tried upon them, but acquitted. He used to observe the goodness of God to him, in and after that confinement, in many respects. He had but five pounds in the world, besides his books, when he was seized; but a kind providence supplied him: and though he was consumptive when he went to prison, he was perfectly recovered when he came out.—— At another time, he and several other ministers, by the order of the Earl of *Bath*, were imprisoned for twelve weeks in the Marshalsea at *Plymouth*, without any cause of commitment alledged. Being released, and finding other difficulties obstructing his being any farther serviceable in the West of England, he came to *London*, and in 1679 was unanimously chosen pastor of the English church at *Middleburgh* in Zealand; which he accepted upon condition that he might be at liberty to return, if he should be called into his own country. He there however met with some angry contests which he did not expect, upon which he returned to *London, July* 22, 1681, where he preached privately, with good acceptance, during the remainder of the troubles of K. *Charles's* reign, and gathered a congregation. He afterwards made use of K. *James's* Indulgence, thinking that an unjust law from the first, which deprived him and his brethren

thren of the exercise of their ministry. He refused several preferments offered him if he would conform, and one of 900*l. per annum*.

He was a good scholar, and a lively preacher. He had a great facility, freedom, and fervency in prayer. His ministry was successful to the conversion of many. His labours, as a preacher, were abundant; and he was all his life a hard student. In his health he used to be in his study at two o'clock in the morning. For the last six years of his life he was racked with the stone to a very uncommon degree, and had it almost daily returning; but he was very seldom diverted by it from his work, in which indeed he often found present ease.—He was very compassionate to persons in distress, and was at great pains and expence for the relief of the poor *French* protestants, on account of the noble testimony they bore to religion by their sufferings. He was much concerned for a learned ministry, and eminently forward in encouraging hopeful young men who were disposed to devote themselves to that office: He was a serious Christian, who conversed much with his own soul, and spent much time in meditation and prayer. He had been in great despondency and temptations, but was enabled to overcome them, and had a confirmed hope of his own state; which, upon the strictest examination, in the views of eternity, he retained unshaken to the end. The warmth and eagerness of his temper (which was the greatest imperfection that appeared in him) was his grief and burden; though it had its advantages to make him the more active in his work. He had several signal providential deliverances, and sometimes by warnings in his dreams, of which he recorded some instances. His racking pains quite broke his happy constitution; [but he had signal supports and consolations under them. When a justice told him, to what remote prison he would send him, he replied, " I know not where you are sending me, but this I am sure of, my heart is as full of comfort as it can hold."] He died in the 70th year of his age, *April* 29, 1706; Dr. *D. Williams* preached a sermon at his funeral; and Mr. *Thomas Freke*, his successor, another afterwards, which are both published. Dr. *Evans* married his only daughter.

WORKS. Synodicon in Gallia Reformata, 2 vol. folio.—A Relation of the poisoning of a whole Family in Plymouth.—A Funeral Sermon for Mr. John Faldo.—Another for Philip Harris, Esq. —The Young Man's Claim of Right to the Lord's Supper.—On
that

that Case of Conscience, Whether it be lawful for a Man to marry his deceased wife's Sister? [§ The Triumph of Faith, a sermon at Bartholomew close, Jan. 16, 1697, on the death of Mrs. Rothwell. In this discourse on *Rom.* viii. 38, 39. (now before the editor) consisting of 36 pages 4to, are introduced anecdotes of several persons who died in triumph, particularly of old Mr. Hieron, of Modbury.] He left in MS. Icones Sacræ, or the Lives of several worthy Divines, both French and English, in 3 vol. fol. The old Duke of Bedford was so well pleased with it, that he resolved to have it published, though at his own expence, but was prevented by death.

BROAD HEMBURY [V.] Josiah Banger, M. A. Fellow of *Trin. Col. Oxf.* He was imprisoned in Exeter upon the Five-mile act. He afterwards lived many years at *Mountacute* in Somerset, where his preaching was instrumental of much good. The wives of two justices in that neighbourhood were hearers of Mr. *Banger.* One of them, being ill, sent for him in her husband's absence to visit her. The husband, who was a violent persecutor of those whom she most highly esteemed, having private notice given him of the affair, returned sooner than was expected, and found Mr. *Banger* at prayer with his wife. Upon which he took him by the collar, and pushed him down stairs, asking him what business he had in his house, and soon after sent him to *Ilchester* prison, upon the Five-mile act. His people often visited him, and he had liberty to preach to them in the prison. When he was released, he returned to them and preached with more freedom. He soon after removed to *Sherborn,* where he was near his estate, and there he died. He printed *A Serious Item* to secure sinners. § A great grandson of his now lives on the same estate, and another, of his own name, at Hackney, where he has long been a deacon in the Independent church.

West BUCKLAND [R.] Mr. Josiah Gale.

CAVERLEIGH. Mr. Horseford.

CHERITON Fitz Pain, [R.] Nathaniel Durant, M. A. He was born near *Plymouth,* where his father lived as a gentleman. He was esteemed a learned man, and a good linguist. He was a person of a most agreeable conversation, and was much respected by the neighbouring gentry. He gave orders in his will, that what he left should not be put out to usury. But his children went contrary to it, and some persons observed, that they did not prosper. Probably he
might

might be influenced in this matter by a tract of Mr. *Jellinger* of this county, who wrote against Usury, and signified, with no small appearance of pleasure, that other ministers in those parts were of his opinion. Mr. *Durant* died *Oct.* 6, 1698.

CHESTON. Mr. ELLYOT.

CHYDDECK. See CHIDIOCK in *Dorsetshire.*

CLAYHADON [R.] Mr. MATTHEW PEMBERTON, Upon his ejectment he spent some years in London, and was afterwards minister of a dissenting congregation at *Marlborough.* He and Mr. *Thomas Vincent* wrote a small piece, entitled " The Death of Ministers improved;" occasioned by the decease of Mr. *H. Stubbes,* and bound up with Mr. *Baxter's* funeral sermon for him.

COLUMPTON; [V.] WILLIAM CROMPTON, M. A. Son of Mr. *W. Crompton,* a useful minister in *Barnstaple;* upon whose exclusion (occasioned by a division between Mr. *Blake,* the rector, and him) it was observed, that town dwindled both in riches and piety. This son of his continued with his people after his ejectment, and spent many years among them without that encouragement he deserved. For some time before he died, which was in 1696, he was disabled from his beloved work by a fistula in his breast.

WORKS. A Remedy against Superstition.—A brief Survey of the old Religion.—Foundation of God for the Salvation of the Elect. —Sovereign Omnipotency the Saint's Security.—A Treatise on Prayer; on *James* v. 16.—A Wilderness of Trouble leading to a Canaan of Comfort.

COMB RALEIGH [R. S.] Mr. WILLIAM TAYLOR. He left this living in 1660; when Mr. *S. Knot,* the sequestered minister, was restored. Though we cannot say of Mr. Taylor as Dr. Walker does of Mr. Knot, " That he was " by the generality of the people, looked upon as a con- " jurer," it may be truly said, He was a very honest man, and qualified to be useful to the parish as a minister.

CULLITON* [V. 200l.] Mr. JOHN WILKINS. He was presented to this living in 1654, upon the resignation of Mr. *T. Collins,* and was deprived of it by the Act of uniformity. He was a man of eminent piety; an excellent preacher; and remarkably affectionate; so that he seldom quitted the pulpit without shedding tears. Though he had several children, he

* Now usually spelt COLYTON.

quitted

which fell upon Mr. *Geare.* Mr. Joseph Cubit, then mayor, and Mr. Barnes, one of the magistrates, took a journey to Wooburn to invite and treat with him. He accepted their call, and sent Mr. *Ford* to officiate in his room, till such time as he could remove thither. In about six months Mr. *Geare* went to Dartmouth with his family, and was highly respected by the inhabitants of the town, and by the neighbouring ministers, having the character of a universal scholar, an able preacher, and an eminently pious man.

After his ejectment in 1662, he had offers of great preferment if he would conform, but he could not be moved by any solicitations, judging the terms required unlawful; and he expressed great satisfaction in his Nonconformity on his death-bed. He met with hard measure for preaching a sermon on a Lord's day after the public service was ended. Some of the magistrates informed against him, whereupon he was summoned, and appeared before the commissioners at *Exeter,* in very severe weather; whereby he got such a grievous cold as threw him into a violent fever, which in a fortnight put a period to his valuable life, towards the end of *December* 1662, when he was about forty years of age. He left a widow and five children. His being buried in the church-yard was much opposed by some; but at length, with no small difficulty, it was obtained. Mr. *Flavel* was his intimate friend.

WORKS. He was concerned with Mr. Calamy and others, in a Preface to some of Mr. Christopher Love's Posthumous Works. He translated the Dutch Annotations on the Bible, for which he was paid 60l. He left behind him a fair MS. against the Baptists, dated at Leyden.

*** TOWNSTALL, [alias ST. CLEMENTS, R.] JOHN FLAVEL, B. A. of *University Col. Oxford.* He was a native of *Worcestershire,* where his father was an eminent minister, first at *Bromsgrove,* and afterwards at *Hasler.* He was first assistant to Mr. *Walplate* at *Diptford* in Devonshire, in 1650, and ordained with several others at Salisbury, *Oct.* 17, in the same year. On Mr. *Walplate's* death, he succeeded in this rectory; but, upon an unanimous call, he removed to *Dartmouth,* where there was a larger sphere of usefulness, though the benefice was smaller. He was settled here by the Commissioners for the approbation of public preachers, having an order from *Whitehall,* dated *Dec.* 10, 1650, in conjunction with Mr. *Allan Geare.* Mr. *Flavel* preached every Lord's-day at *Townstall,* (which is the mother

Rev.d John Flavel

from an original Picture in D.r Williams's Library.

Published by Button & Son, Paternoster Row.

ther church, standing on a hill without the town) and every
fortnight at the Wednesday-lecture in Dartmouth. He here
laboured with great acceptance and success, till the Act of
uniformity ejected him. But, not thinking his relation to his
people thereupon at an end, he took all opportunities of ministering the word and sacraments to them in private. About
four months after his ejectment his colleague died, when the
whole care of the flock devolved upon him. When the Oxford act took place, he removed from Dartmouth, (his people following him to *Townstall* church-yard, where they
took a mournful farewell of each other) and went to *Slapton,*
about five miles distant, where he met with signal instances
of God's providential care, and preached twice every Lord's
day ; making frequent visits to his friends in Dartmouth, and
preaching to them as the watchful diligence of his enemies
would admit. A manuscript account says, The house to
which he retired was called *Hudscott,* a seat belonging to
the family of the *Rolles,* near *South-Molton ;* and that there
he preached at midnight, for the sake of secrecy, when the
great hall was thronged with an attentive and deeply-affected
auditory. Probably both these accounts may be true, as he
might preach privately by night at first, and find encouragement to preach publicly in the day-time afterwards. Here it
was that he laid in his materials for his *Husbandry Spiritualized,* from the observations he here made on the scenes of
rural life. Being once at *Exeter,* he was invited by many
good people of that city to preach to them in a wood about
three miles distant, where their enemies disturbed them ; but
Mr. *Flavel,* through the care of his hearers, escaped, though
many of them were taken. The rest however, not being discouraged, took him to another wood, where he preached
without any molestation.

On K. *Charles's* first Indulgence, he returned to *Dartmouth,* and kept an open meeting in the town. When that
liberty was recalled, he continued to preach more privately.
Being at last in great danger here, through the malice of his
enemies, he resolved to retire to London, where he hoped
for more safety. He went by sea, and met with so terrible a
storm, within five leagues of Portland, that both the master
and seamen concluded they must of necessity be wrecked, if
the wind did not quickly change. When things were in this
posture, he called all that could be spared to prayer, and recommended himself and them to God. No sooner was
prayer ended, than the wind changed, and one came down

from the deck, shouting, " Deliverance! God is a God
" hearing prayer!" Mr. Flavel got safe to London; where he
found much work, and much encouragement in it.   Here he
married his fourth wife. Having narrowly escaped being apprehended with Mr. *Jenkyn*, (See Vol. I. p. 111.) he resolved
to return home; but was soon confined close prisoner to his
house, where many of his people used to steal in late on Saturday night, or early on the Lord's day morning, to enjoy
the benefit of his prayers, his preaching, and conversation.
On Mr. *Jenkyn*'s death, his people gave Mr. *Flavel* a call to
succeed him, and Mr. *Reeves*'s congregation did the same;
but he was not to be persuaded to leave Dartmouth.

Upon K. *James*'s liberty in 1687, his people provided him
a large place, in which it pleased God to bless his labours for
the good of many.   He preached twice every Lord's day, a
lecture every Wednesday, and on Thursday also before the
sacrament.—He was not only zealous in the pulpit, but a
sincere lively christian in the closet, as appears from his Diary,
part of which is inserted in his life. His intimate and delightful intercourse with heaven is manifest from a remarkable
story which he relates in his *Pneumatologia* (p. 210, 2d edit.
4to) though with great modesty, using the third person, as the
apostle Paul did when speaking of his extraordinary revela-
tions. The following is the substance of the narrative. Being
on a journey, he set himself to improve his time by meditation;
when his mind grew intent, till at length he had such ravishing tastes of heavenly joys, and such full assurance of his interest therein, that he utterly lost the sight and sense of this
world and all its concerns, so that for hours he knew not
where he was.   At last, perceiving himself faint through a
great loss of blood from his nose, he alighted from his horse
and sat down at a spring, where he washed and refreshed himself; earnestly desiring, if it were the will of God, that he
might there leave the world. His spirits reviving, he finished
his journey in the same delightful frame.   He passed all that
night without a wink of sleep, the joy of the Lord still over-
flowing him, so that he seemed an inhabitant of the other
world.   After this a heavenly serenity and sweet peace long
continued with him; and for many years he called that day
" one of the days of heaven," and professed he understood
more of the life of heaven by it, than by all the discourses he
had heard, or the books he ever read.

Mr. *Flavel* was a person of good natural abilities, of unwearied application to study, and had acquired a great stock

1   both

both of human and divine learning. He had an excellent
gift in prayer, being never at a loss for matter or words, and
was always warm and affectionate. Those who lived in his
family remarked, that he seemed constantly to exceed himself,
and rarely used the same expressions twice. His preaching
was plain and popular, but at the same time methodical and
judicious. He was remarkable for the practical applications
of his discourses, and particularly for his pertinent inferences.
[A late judicious minister used to recommend to students for
the ministry, the style of his printed sermons, as a good model for pulpit discourses.] He was a person of great humility,
free to communicate what he knew, and ready to learn from
every body. He was very benevolent and charitable to the poor.
He was a great encourager of young men designed for the
ministry; some of whom he educated himself, and maintained
one at his own expence. He was ever ready to forgive injuries. In 1685, when the populace of Dartmouth carried
his effigy through the streets in derision, and burnt it, he only
prayed for them, saying, " Father, forgive them; for they
" know not what they do."—Among the many instances of his
usefulness, the two following, recorded in his life at large, are
very remarkable:—Being sent for to a young man who had
attempted to murder himself, his conversation and prayers
were the means of his conversion.——A profane person coming into a bookseller's shop to inquire for a play-book, the
bookseller recommended to him Mr. *Flavel's* Treatise *On
Keeping the Heart*, as likely to do him more good. After having grossly abused the author and ridiculed the book,
he was prevailed upon to promise that he would read it. He
accordingly did so; and about a month after, came and thanked the bookseller for putting it into his hand; telling him, it
had saved his soul; and bought a hundred copies of it to give
away.

Mr. *Flavel* died somewhat suddenly, *June* 26, 1691, aged
64, in the city of Exeter, whither he went to preach before the
assembly, (in which also he was moderator) with a view to
a union between the *Presbyterians* and *Independents*, which
he was very zealous to promote. His funeral sermon was
preached by Mr. *Tross*, on 2 *Kings* ii. 12. He was buried
in Dartmouth church, where there was a Latin inscription to
his memory upon a brass plate, which was taken down by
order of the magistrates, and is preserved in the meeting-
house, where this circumstance is recorded.

c 3 WORKS.

WORKS. Πνευμαΐολογια, a Treatise on the Soul of Man.—The Fountain of Life, in 42 Sermons.—The Method of Grace, in 35 Sermons. [In both vols. the Sermons are on various Texts.]—England's Duty, in 11 Sermons, on Rev. iii. 20.—A Token for Mourners.—Husbandry Spiritualized.—Navigation Spiritualized.—A Treatise on Providence.—Another on Keeping the Heart.—Repentance enforced by Arguments from Reason only.—The Balm of the Covenant—Sacramental Meditations. And several other Pieces, collected, since his death, in 2 vol. fol. with his life prefixed. N. B. They may also be had in 8 vol. 8vo.

DEAN PRIOR, [V. 21l.] Mr. JOHN SYMS. Some years after he was ejected he lived at *Water*, in the parish of Ashburton, and afterwards at *Metley*, in West Ogwell. He preached in his own house as often as he could. He was a man of eminent piety, and a great sufferer for Nonconformity; often exposed to dangers, and sometimes reduced to straits; but he trusted in God, and experienced his goodness in delivering and providing for him. He once hid himself in a hay-loft; when some of his enemies, in searching for him, thrust their swords into the hay, and yet he escaped unhurt. Sometimes when his wife went to market to get necessaries for her family, tho' she went out empty and sorrowful, she met with unexpected supplies, and came home full and joyous. *Hugh Stawel*, Esq. of Heerabeer, and others, one Lord's-day broke open his door while he was preaching, and disturbed the congregation. Soon after this, as that persecutor was going to London, he met Mr. *Syms*, and threatened him, that when he returned, he would do his business. Mr. *Syms* replied, " Sir, you should ask God's leave." Mr. *Stawel* went to London, but it was remarkable, he never returned.—Mr. *Syms* on his death-bed foretold the very hour of his own dissolution. After he had lain for some time silent, he cried out, " Tell my friends I have overcome, I " have overcome." Mr. *Whidden*, of *Totness*, preached his funeral sermon.

DENBERRY [R.] Mr. RICHARD BICKLE. Dr. *Walker* says, he came to this living in 1646, and lost it for Nonconformity in 1662. It was reported that he afterwards conformed, but this was a mistake: He died a Nonconformist at *Totness*, and received twenty pounds *per ann.* during his life, from Mr. *Godson*, his successor in the living of Denberry.

DITTESHAM [S.] Mr. EDMUND TUCKER, of *Trin. Col. Camb.* He was born at *Milton-Abbot*, near Tavistock, in

1627.

1627. His father had a good estate. He was settled at *Dittesham* about the year 1651; and was ordained *May* 24, 1654, by Dr. G. Kendal and four other ministers. He was a man of good natural abilities, and of a chearful temper. His preaching was solid, till age and bodily disorders impaired him. He suffered much for his Nonconformity. He was once convicted for a conventicle, and fined 30*l.* for praying with three gentlewomen who came to visit his wife, and comfort her upon the death of her only child, who was drowned at sea. In his case there was a remarkable instance of the partiality of the famous justice *Beer* (or *Bear*) and the barbarity of the informers; who tore down all the goods in Mr. *Tucker's* house; seized not only his bed and bed-clothes, but the poor children's wearing apparel, and the very victuals in the house, and left no corner unsearched for money. He had a wife and ten children, and had nothing of his own to subsist upon; but God provided for him and them. He was much afflicted with the gout, stone and diabetes; by which disorders, and the failure of his intellects, he was taken off from preaching more than a year before his death, which was, at last, somewhat sudden, *July* 5, 1702, in the 75th year of his age. His funeral sermon was preached by Mr. *John Cox*, who succeeded him at Kings-bridge.

DREWS-TEIGNTON [R. S.] RICHARD HERRING, M.A. Younger brother to Mr. *John Herring*. After he was ejected, he lived on an estate of his own, called *Perridge*, in the parish of *Kenn*, three miles from Exeter. He preached in his own house on the Lord's-day; and many went from Exeter to hear him. He also, for some time, preached in the house of Mr. *John Mayne*, in the city. Having undertaken to instruct a few boys in grammar-learning, a prosecution was set on foot against him for it, in the spiritual court; but by the favor of Bp. *Ward*, who was acquainted with him in the university, and had a kindness for him, he was discharged. He died about the year 1675. He was an excellent preacher, a pious man, well beloved by his parishioners, and very kind to the widow of Dr. *Short*, the sequestered minister; notwithstanding what Dr. *Walker* says to the contrary. This living was worth several hundreds a year; and, the patron, Sir —— *Carew* of *Anthony*, would have continued him in it if he would have conformed.

DUNCHIDIOCK

DUNCHIDIOCK [R. S.] Mr. Hunt. He had a legal right to this living; for Dr. *Walker* owns, that the sequestered minister, whom he succeeded, died in 1645. When he was deprived for Nonconformity in 1662, he lived near Exeter, and afterwards removed to *South Molton*, where he died minister of a dissenting congregation.

DUNSFORD [V.] Mr. William Pearse, of *Exeter Col. Oxf.* Son of Mr. *Francis Pearse*, of Ermington, Gent. Baptized *Jan.* 26, 1625. He was presented to this living; void by the death of the former incumbent, *Dec.* 25, 1655, from whence the Act of uniformity ejected him. He afterwards removed, with his family, to Stretchleigh-house, in Ermington parish, and preached privately in *Tavistock.* Upon the Indulgence in 1672, he took out licences for himself and his house, but afterwards met with great trouble. He was grievously harrassed and threatened; and at length, thro' the restless malice and unwearied diligence of his enemies, was forced to make over his goods, and leave his family for several months together, living in London and elsewhere, to escape their rage, who sought his ruin and his very life. The *Conventicle Courant* of *Jan.* 31, 1683, had this article. " On Sunday the 21st of *January*, several " loyal and worthy justices and constables, went to Mr. " Lobb's meeting, where they seized one Mr. Pearse, and " one Marmaduke Roberts, both preachers, who were both " committed to New Prison."—Six times, in one year, the bailiff came to Stretchleigh-house, to warn Mr. *Pearse* and his wife, with his son and daughters, to appear at the assizes at Exeter, to answer for riots, routs, keeping seditious meetings, and not obeying the laws. But he never was seized above once. Notwithstanding all his dangers, he did not waver; and God spared him till the cloud was dissipated. He survived the tribulation of those days, and saw our civil and religious liberties restored by the happy Revolution; after which, he set up a public meeting in *Ashburton*, where he continued for the remainder of his days. He died *March* 17, 1691, aged 65. Dr. *Walker* relates several things to his disadvantage, which Dr. *Calamy* proves to be notorious falshoods. *(Contin.* p. 342.)

WORKS. A Present for Youth, and an Example for the Aged; being some Remains of his Daughter *Damaris Pearse.*

EAST

EAST DOWN [R. 140*l*.] JOHN BERRY, M. A. Fel. of *Exeter Col. Oxf.* Son of Mr. *John Berry*, minister of a neighbouring parish. Dr. *Walker* says, " I am obliged to mention this gentleman, because he was dispossessed of his fellowship by the visitors *(viz.* in 1648) but he was afterwards a Nonconformist." From a Latin certificate, signed *Rob. Say, S. Sheldon*, &c. dated Oxon, *June* 17, 1653, it appears he was afterwards of *Oriel Col.* and that he bore an excellent character. After this, he was episcopally ordained, and was for some time minister of *Lankey.* He was settled in this rectory of *East Down* in 1658 (being presented by the Protector *Richard)* which he lost for his Nonconformity. He had ten children, and little or nothing whereon to subsist; but most of them afterwards lived in good repute and in comfortable circumstances. After his ejectment, he preached in several places, as he had opportunity ; and felt, in a high degree, the severe usage of those days. Once (if not oftener) he lay in the common jail at Exeter, for several months. He was advised by some, who would have borne the charges, to prosecute those who committed him, for false imprisonment, but he would not do it. After the Dissenters had liberty granted them, *Ilfracome* and *Puddington* enjoyed the chief of his labours.

God had furnished him with good abilities for his office, tho' they were not a little concealed by his modesty and humility. His preaching was very serious and affectionate, and in all his ministerial exercises he gave abundant proof of his earnest desire to do good to souls ; and many had reason to bless God for him. All that knew him esteemed him as a very sincere christian ; and he shewed himself a man of a very tender conscience, in all the transactions of his life. Whatever difficulties he met with, he maintained constant communion with God in his providences, as well as ordinances ; which appears in the diary he kept, both of public and private occurrences, respecting the state of his own body and soul, his children and friends, their actions and behaviour, their troubles, their mercies, &c. with pious reflections. The deaths of his friends, and especially of ministers, were more particularly observed by him, and piously reflected upon, in such a manner as this :

" *Dec.* 8, 1691, that holy and great luminary of Christ's church, Mr. *Richard Baxter*, deceased. O that due impressions might hereby be made upon the hearts of christians, and that the Lord would raise up some more such shining healing

healing spirits among us !"——" *June* 19, 1701. Heard
of the death of that very useful, excellent friend, Mr. *John
Flavel*, of Dartmouth. What a loss and stroke is this ! O
that it may awaken! A sudden stroke it was. The Lord
pity poor Dartmouth, and preserve that interest of serious
religion which he and others have, I trust, been instruments
to set on foot and promote there, &c. &c."

As the natural consequence of a heavenly conversion, he
died with great calmness and serenity of spirit, resigning his
soul into the hands of his Saviour, *Dec.* 1704, aged near
80.—Mr. *Baxter* gives him the character of " an extraor-
" dinary humble, tender-conscienced, serious, godly, able
" minister."—He was moderator of the Assembly at Exeter,
Sept. 8, 1696.

EDE [C.] Mr. ROBERT GAYLARD. Upon his eject-
ment he retired to *Exeter*, and was one of the public Nonconformist ministers in that city. He was twice imprisoned:
once upon false information against him ; *viz.* for some dangerous words in a sermon, which he never uttered : the
other time, upon the Corporation-act.—His funeral sermon
was preached by Mr. *George Trosse.* He was highly valued for his ministerial abilities by the most discreet and judicious professors in Exeter, and was generally reckoned a
very wise man. He was observed to have a very happy way
of using scriptural expressions, both in his preaching and
praying, and always a pleasing variety.

EXBOURN [R. 27*l.* 11*s.* 8*d.*] Mr. FINNEY, sen. He
had been about forty years minister of this parish before
Bartholomew-day, 1662, when he was ejected. He was a
very grave, solid divine, generally reputed a very good
scholar, and an extraordinary preacher. A man extremely
mortified to the world, and in a manner entirely taken up
about his studies, and his ministerial services. He and his
wife lived comfortably upon his own estate, several years
after his ejectment, and continued in the parish to his dying
day.—He brought up three sons to the ministry, who all
conformed, but were worthy men, of great temper and
moderate principles. The second son succeeded him in this
living.

EXETER. At the CATHEDRAL, THOMAS FORD, M. A.
of *Magd. Hall. Oxf.* He was born at *Brixton*, 1598, of
parents in good repute, who left his eldest brother above
200*l. per annum.* His father dying when he was young, his
                                          mother

mother took care of his education. In his childhood he had a strong inclination to learning, and discovered serious impressions. Mr. *Durant*, schoolmaster at Plympton, judged him fit for the university at the age of fifteen; but for some reasons he was not sent till the year 1620. He made great proficiency, and became as celebrated a tutor as any in the university. His inclinations were to the Puritan way; and some public expressions of it by him and some others, drew on a case which then made a considerable noise, and deserves to be remembered. Dr. *Frewen*, President of the college, changed the communion-table in the chapel, into an altar, which was the first that was set up in the university after the Reformation. Several of the preachers at *St. Mary's* inveighed against this innovation; particularly Mr. *Thorn* of Baliol College, in a sermon on 1 *King's* xiii. 2. about the altar at Bethel. And Mr. *Hodges* of Exeter College, in another, on *Numb.* xiv. 4. ' Let us make a ' captain, and return into Egypt.' Mr. *Ford* also in his turn preached on 2 *Thess.* ii. 10, 11. *June* 12, 1631. He made some smart reflections on the innovations then creeping into church; the magnifying tradition; making the eucharist a sacrifice; setting up altars instead of tables, and bowing to them, &c.

The Laudensian faction took fire; and the next Saturday the Vice-chancellor called Mr. *Ford* before him, and demanded a copy of his sermon. Mr. *Ford* offered to give him one, if he demanded it *statutably*. The Vice-chancellor ordered him to surrender himself prisoner at the castle. He offered to go if he would send a beadle or servant with him. That not being complied with, he refused to surrender himself. The next Saturday the Vice-chancellor, much irritated, sealed up his study, and afterwards searched his books and papers; but found nothing that could be urged against him, as he had the precaution to remove out of the way whatever his enemies could lay hold of. In the mean time an information was sent to Abp. *Laud*, then their Chancellor, who returned orders to punish the preachers. A citation hereupon, in his name, was fixed on St. Mary's, *July* 2, commanding Mr. *Ford's* appearance before the Vice-chancellor on the 5th. Appearing on the day appointed, he was pressed to take an oath, *ex officio*, to answer any questions about his sermon; but he refused it, because there were no interrogatories in writing. He again offered a copy of his sermon, if demanded according to the statutes;

and

and the next day delivered a copy, which was accepted. But, on pretence of former contumacy, the Vice-chancellor commanded him again to surrender himself prisoner. Mr. *Ford* appealed from him to the congregation, and delivered his appeal in writing to the two proctors, Mr. Atherton Bruch and Mr. John Doughty : (" two men, says *Fuller,* in his *Church Hist.* B. ii. p. 141. of eminent integrity and ability.") They carried it to the Convocation, who referred the cause to delegates ; the major part of whom, *viz.* ten out of sixteen, upon a full hearing, acquitted him of all breach of peace. From them the Vice-chancellor appealed to the Convocation, who appointed delegates also ; but the time limited by statute expired before they came to sentence.

Hereupon *Laud* brought the whole matter before the king and council at *Woodstock.* Mr. *Ford* appearing there, the king asked him, 1. " Why he refused a copy of his sermon ?" He answered, he had not denied it, but offered it according to the statutes. 2. " Whether Dr. *Prideaux* dissuaded him from giving it ?" (the king, it seems, being made to suspect him). He assured his majesty he had never consulted the Dr. about it. 3. " Why he did not go to prison, when the vice-chancellor commanded him thither upon his faith ?" He gave him the same answer as before to the vice-chancellor ; adding, " that he hoped his majesty's poor scholars " in the university should not be in a worse condition than " the worst of felons, who were imprisoned by a *mittimus,* " and with legal officers to conduct them." The king said no more ; and *Laud,* tho' present, interposed not one word. But the result was, the three preachers were expelled ; for the rest made appeals as well as Mr. *Ford*: the proctors were deposed for receiving their appeals, tho' legally they could not refuse them ; and Dr. *Prideaux* and Dr. *Wilkinson* were checked for meddling on their behalf.—Mr. *Thorn* and Mr. *Hodges,* upon a recantation and a year's suspension, were fully restored, and afterwards promoted to be archdeacons. But Mr. *Ford* by the final sentence, was obliged to quit the university within four days, and was conducted out of the town with much honour, by a vast multitude of scholars in their habits ; and he was soon afterwards invited by the magistrates of *Plymouth* to be their minister. But Abp. *Laud* obtained a letter to them from the king, signed with his own hand, accompanied with another from himself, forbidding them to admit him, on pain of his highest displeasure ; which obliged them to recede from their choice.

Mr.

Mr. *Ford* finding the bishop set upon excluding him from all preferment in England, embraced an opportunity of going abroad as chaplain to an English regiment, under the command of Col. George Fleetwood, in the service of *Gustavus Adolphus*, King of Sweden. He travelled with the Colonel into Germany, and lay some time in garrison at Stode and Elbing. His merit recommended him to learned men of all professions in his travels. He was invited by the English merchants at *Hamburgh*, to be their minister, with the promise of a salary of 200*l. per annum*. But he grew weary of a foreign country, and chose to return home. Whether the bishop's prejudice was abated, or length of time had worn out the remembrance of him, on his return he met with no opposition in a presentation to the rectory of *Aldwinckle*, in Northamptonshire. There he performed his ministerial work with great assiduity for some years, and married the daughter of — *Fleetwood*, Esq. of Gray's Inn, by whom he had several children. He was chosen proctor for the clergy of the diocese of Peterborough, to the famous convocation, in 1640, who framed the *Et cætera* oath. When the war broke out he retired to London, and was chosen minister of *St. Faith's*, and a member of the Westminster Assembly.

He afterwards settled at *Exeter*, where he found the city and country overspread with a swarm of errors, and under the influence of those enthusiasts who pretended to be above ordinances. He set himself vigorously to preach against these wild notions, and with wonderful success. The whole city was mightily reformed, and a good relish of the best things appeared in the generality. He preached in the choir of the cathedral (as Mr. *Stucley* and Mr. *Mall* did in the body of it) but was once put out of it, in 1649, by major-general *Desborough*, who quartered there, for refusing the Engagement. He had not only the greatest respect from the body of the people, but was highly esteemed by the magistracy and neighbouring gentry, and maintained a very friendly correspondence with the ministers of the city. He induced them to set on foot a Tuesday's lecture, where they all took their turns, and were well attended; he brought them also to have the Lord's Supper once a fortnight in each church alternately, at which the members of any of the other congregations might communicate. These methods prevented all jealousies among them, and united the people firmly among themselves.

Thus

Thus the ministers of Exeter enjoyed, for about thirteen
years, great quiet and comfort in the exercise of their ministry, till Bartholomew-day, 1662. Then Mr. *Ford* was
cast out with his brethren, but still he resided among his
people. Upon the coming out of the Oxford-act, he and
twelve other ministers who resided in that city, not satisfied
with all the particulars of the oath prescribed, and yet knowing that misconstruction would be made of their refusal,
thought it advisable to present a petition to the magistracy of
Exeter, honestly begging leave to declare, that they could
make oath—"·that they were so free from all thoughts of
raising a new war, or resisting the powers which by Divine
Providence were over them; that they were fully resolved
never to take up arms against the king's person or authority,
or to countenance others in any tumultuous endeavours to
the disturbance of his majesty's kingdoms; but to behave
themselves peaceably in all things and at all times, under his
majesty's government in church and state." Adding, that
" this they humbly offered, not as expecting to escape the
penalties of the Act by it, but that they might not be represented as disloyal or disaffected to his majesty's person and
government." But the present magistrates being such as
had no favour for men of their stamp, rejected the petition,
and they were forced for a time to leave the city †.

Mr. *Ford* retired to *Exmouth*, about nine miles from
Exeter, and there lived privately in those evil days. When
the Indulgence came out, though he liked not the persons
who obtained it, nor their design in it, yet it was his judgment that they should take the opportunity of preaching the
gospel; and though his health was greatly impaired, he returned to *Exeter*, but was incapable of preaching any more
than two sermons in public. However he was serviceable to
many by private counsel at home, and fervent prayer for them.
While numbers were flattering themselves with flourishing
times approaching, he told them, there was a sorer storm
behind, that would unavoidably fall upon the churches. He
declined in his health daily, after his last sermon, and was
soon confined to his bed, so that he could now speak but
little to visitors. Yet when two ministers of the city came
to see him, he spoke much of his own unworthiness, and
the all-sufficiency of Christ, saying, " That he would re-

† N. B. Several in this county took the oath, with a declaration concerning the sense of it, *viz.* Mr. Howe, and eleven others.

pose .

pose himself upon that rock in the storms of approaching death." When his ancient colleague, Mr. *Bartlet*, recited those words of the apostle, 'The sting of death is sin, and the strength of sin is the law,' he stopped him short, and added, ' But thanks be to God, who giveth us the victory, through Jesus Christ our Lord :' which were his last words. He died in *Dec.* 1674, in his 76th year, and was buried in *St.* Lawrence's church in Exeter.

WORKS. Two Sermons; one before the Lords, and the other before the Commons.—A Treatise on singing of Psalms.— The Sinner condemned of himself; being a Plea for God against all the Ungodly, proving them alone guilty of their own Destruction.—Scripture's Self-evidence, proving it to be the only Rule of Faith; against the Papists.

—— Mr. LEWIS STUCLEY. A gentleman of an ancient and honourable family in this county, the seat of which was at *Afton* in West Worlington. It is said that there were formerly thirteen manors belonging to it, within sight of the gate-house. One of his ancestors was standard bearer to Queen *Elizabeth.* Sir *T. Stucley* was his brother. Where he was born and educated, or where he first preached, doth not appear. In *July* 11, 1646, the standing committee of Devon ordered him into the rectory of *Newton Ferrers*, but whether he possessed it or not is uncertain. Dr. *Walker* says, " Mr. *Powel* was turned out of Great Torrington about 1646, and was then succeeded by the famous Independent Mr. *L. Stucley* ;" and mentions his having been before at Tiverton, and as being " thrust upon Mr. *Newte* as his assistant by the *godly*," (as he in derision calls them) " whom they compelled him to hire at 100*l.* a year; and afterwards, as succeeding him at Tidcombe and Clare." From Great Torrington he came to Exeter, and began to gather a church in the congregational way, about the year 1650. Soon after the Restoration, he was obliged to quit the cathedral; and on Bartholomew-day, 1662, he was silenced. He might indeed have obtained considerable preferment, if he would have conformed, by his interest with General *Monk*, who was his kinsman; but he refused upon a principle of conscience. He was very laborious in his ministerial work; and after his ejectment he did not lie idle, but discharged his duty to his people in private, when he could no longer do it in public. In the latter part of his time he lived and preached at *Bideford.* He died in *July*, 1687.

1687. See *Watkins's* History of Bideford. Dr. *Walker*
brings some heavy charges against him, which Dr. Calamy
shews to be malicious and ill-founded. *Contin.* p. 242.

WORKS. Manifest Truths against Mr. Tobie Allein.—A Gos-
pel-glass, representing the Miscarriages of English Professors.—
This last he wrote with uncommon activity and self-denial, under
the sentence of death.

—— THOMAS MALL, M. A. He was the son of a minister,
and was educated at *Pemb. Hall, Camb.* where he was
very studious, and soon became Fellow. Going into *Cornwall*, with some others, to preach the gospel, he met with
such encouragement, acceptance and success, that he returned
no more to his college. He was afterwards called to Exeter,
and was joined with Mr. *Stucley*, at the cathedral.

WORKS. The Opinion of the old Nonconformists, in a Controversy that fell out in his Congregation.—A Cloud of Witnesses;
being an Epitome of the History of the Martyrs, alphabetically
disposed, with a Preface by Mr. Flavel,—An Exhortation to holy
Living—The Axe at the Root of Professors' Miscarriages.

—— ST. JOHN'S. ROBERT ATKINS, M. A. of *Wad. Col.
Oxf.* Fellow. Born at *Chard* in Somerset, 1626. Of fifteen children he was the youngest son. He was designed for
a merchant, and had a master provided for him in *London*:
the day was fixed, and all things were in readiness for his
journey; but he was not to be found. His father [afterwards
learning the cause, and finding him averse to business] altered
his purpose, and sent him to Oxford. When he first appeared in the pulpit at St. Mary's, being but young, and looking younger than he was, from the smallness of his stature, the
hearers despised him, expecting nothing from " such a boy,"
as they called him, worth hearing. But his discourse soon
turned their contempt into admiration. After having spent
twelve years in the university, he became one of *Cromwell's*
chaplains; but soon growing weary of that situation, by
reason of the insolence of the sectaries, he removed to
Coopersale in *Essex*, a benefice of 300l. *per ann.* He found
the place over-run with sects; but his solid doctrine, joined
with a free and obliging conversation, so convinced and gained
upon them, that after a while he had not one Dissenter left
in his parish. Judge *Archer* was his parishioner and friend,
and continued such to his death. He was forced to quit this
place on account of his health, to the great sorrow of his
people. He assured them, that if he could have lived with
                                                        them

them he would not have left them ; but declared that he would not again accept of so great a benefice. He was invited by Mr. *T. Ford* to Exeter. At his first coming thither he preached at *St. Sidwell's*, while the choir of the cathedral was preparing for him. When it was finished it was a most convenient and capacious place, (commonly called *East- Peters*) where he had a vast auditory, being generally es- teemed an excellent preacher. His voice was clear, and his pronunciation very agreeable. He was so happy in his ex- pressions, as at once both to instruct and charm his hearers. His tutor Dr. *Wilkins*, used to say, That three of his pupils (of whom Mr. *Atkins* was one) were some of the best preachers in *England*.

In *September*, 1660, he was expelled from *East-Peters*. " Church music" (to use his words in his Farewell sermon upon that occasion) "justling out the constant preaching of the word ; the minister being obliged to give place to the choristers, and hundreds, yea thousands, to seek where to hear a sermon on the Lord's-day, rather than singing-service should be omitted, or not kept up in its ancient splendor and glory." Hereupon he was chosen at *St. John's*, from whence he was again ejected by the Act of uniformity. Great offers were made him, if he would have conformed, particularly by the earl of *Radnor ;* but being dissatisfied as to some of the terms imposed, the offer of a mitre could not move him to act contrary to his sentiments. However, his principles were moderate and loyal, and his charity truly catholic, so as to draw on him the censure of some rigid people, as if he was inclined to conform. In his Farewell sermon at *St. John's*, (*Aug.* 17,) he says. " Let him never be accounted a " sound Christian, that doth not both fear God and honour " the king. I beg that you would not interpret our Non- " conformity to be an act of unpeaceableness and disloyalty. " We will do any thing for his majesty but sin. We will " hazard any thing for him but our souls. We hope we " could die for him ; only we dare not be damned for him. " We make no question, however we may be accounted of " here, we shall be found loyal and obedient subjects at our " appearance before God's tribunal."—He frequently attend- ed the public worship, and exhorted others to do the same ; but continued to discharge his duty to his own people in pri- vate, as opportunity offered, and he discovered an undaunted courage in it, tho' he was naturally timorous

A little before his second ejection, as he was preaching against the growing vices of that time, one of his hearers (a gentleman of great quality) stood up just before him, and stared him in the face; but knowing on whose errand he came, he proceeded with his discourse, not fearing the frowns of the greatest. The very next morning his clerk brought him a libel, full of reflections on this gentleman, and some others, which he found sticking upon the church door. On reading this paper, he left it in his study, and went into the country. He was no sooner gone, but a messenger was sent after him, with an order for him to appear immediately before several justices of the peace in Exeter. He appeared, and was charged with this libel. Tho' he professed his innocence, he was menaced, and without any proof was committed to prison; but the next day Bishop. *Gauden* procured him his liberty. Some of the magistrates of the city, who were very severe against other dissenting ministers, favoured and connived at him. Three meetings were discovered in his house, and the names of many persons taken; yet neither he nor the house were fined. The mayor and a justice, who were far more busy than their brethren, once fined his house 20l. tho' the people were not found in his, but in a neighbour's house. Hereupon they came and broke open his doors, to distrain for the fine; but finding his books and best goods removed, they seized on him, tho' he was then very ill of the gout; brought him down from his warm chamber in a chair into his court; exposing him some hours to the cold air, (by which his health was much impaired) and made his *mittimus* to send him to prison for this fine. But of all the multitude gathered about this house, the mayor and justices could not, either by promises or threatenings, get any to carry him to prison. At length some of his friends paid his fine. The rest of the justices utterly disliked this severity.

Mr. *Atkins* was once taken at another house, where he intended to have preached. The mayor excused himself, telling him, that he thought he had been another man, and dismissed him, on his promise to appear the next day at the *Guildhall*, if sent for. But he heard no more of the matter. One of his hearers was prosecuted in the spiritual court, for having his child baptized by a Nonconformist. When Dr. *Lamplugh*, then Bp. of *Exeter*, understood that Mr. *Atkins* was the person who had baptized it, he put a stop to the proceedings, dismissed the man, without his paying any costs, and spoke very honourably of Mr. *Atkins*, for his
learning

learning and moderation ; on account of which, and the facetiousness of his conversation, many persons of quality had a great esteem for him.—He had a large heart and an open hand. He devised liberal things, and often gave in charity beyond his ability. His own and his wife's relations, as also his brethren in the ministry, who were in low circumstances, had a large share in his bounty. Towards the latter end of his life he was much afflicted with the gout ; yet would he not neglect his work, but often preached in his own house as he sat in his chair.

The affairs of the church and people of God lay near his heart. On the death of *Charles* II. the dismal prospect of the return of popery, upon *James's* declaring himself a Papist, made a very deep impression upon his spirit, and was supposed to have hastened his death, which happened *March* 28, 1685, aged 59. His funeral sermon was preached by Mr. *George Trosse*.—Such was his modesty, that notwithstanding his great stock of learning and ministerial abilities, and the repeated importunity of his friends, he could never be prevailed upon to print so much as one single discourse. Great numbers of his sermons however were transcribed, and handed about among his friends, of which six were afterwards published, *On the sin and danger of Popery*. Also his Farewell-sermon at *St. John's*.—An aged and worthy clergyman expressed a high idea of the author, in the following Letter to the Editor of them.

" I am willing to give encouragement for the publishing
" the Rev. Mr. Atkins's works, because he was my cotem-
" porary in Wadham College, though six years my senior ;
" and he was then esteemed a person of eminent parts, of
" exemplary piety, and an excellent preacher. But I wish
" the person who undertakes to publish his sermons would
" not omit one which I heard him preach before the mayor
" and aldermen, on *Mat.* vii. 12. with great approbation ;
" nor another, on 2. *Cor.* iii. 6,—*able ministers of the new*
" *testament*, a few days before the fatal Bartholomew, when
" Bishop *Gauden* and a multitude more were his hearers. I
" yet well remember he affirmed, and by 1 Cor. iv. 15.
" proved, That those ministers who beget converts to Christ
" may most properly be called *Fathers in God*."

—— St. Sidwell's Thomas Powel, M. A. After his ejectment here, he removed to London. He was a good preacher, very active in the ministry, and much esteemed for his piety. He was of the congregational persuasion.

—— St. Mary's in the Moor. Mr. John Bartlet. Brother to Mr. *William Bartlet* of *Bideford*. When he was at the university, Dr. *Sibbs* was his intimate friend. He was a great student in anatomy, till observing the straitness of the passage in the throat, he grew so melancholy as to be almost afraid to eat or drink; he therefore, on the advice of his physician, laid this study aside. He was a very laborious constant preacher, and had an excellent copious gift in prayer. His voice was low, but his matter very solid and acceptable. In his younger days he was minister of *St. Thomas*'s near Exeter, and was then much beloved by Bishop *Hall*. He was chosen by that good Bishop to preach an assize sermon before the judges, when the plague was in that city. His text was *Numb.* xvi. 46-48. The sermon much affected the auditory; and was owned, by an ancient religious person, many years after, to have been the means of his conversion. When the *Book of sports* was sent down, he was prevailed on by the Bishop (who was naturally very timorous) to read it; and at the same time (as his lordship also advised him) he preached on the fourth commandment. He continued in Exeter after his being silenced, and preached there as he had opportunity. He died in a good old age.

WORKS. Meditations.—An Explication of the Assembly's Catechism.—The Duty of Communicants.—The Use and Profit of Afflictions.—The Practical Christian; or a summary View of the chief Heads of practical Divinity.—Directions for right receiving the Lord's Supper, in Question and Answer, for the benefit of the young.

—— St. Mary Arches. Ferdinando Nicoll, M. A. A man of considerable learning, a grave divine, and a laborious minister in this city about forty years. Though he wrote his sermons he commonly preached without using his papers, but always took them with him into the pulpit. Being once called to preach before the judges, he went to church without his notes. But perceiving his mistake before he began, he went back and fetched them, as the very thought of being without them, he said, would have thrown him into confusion; but he preached with great freedom, without once looking upon them. At one time, while he was preaching, he saw several of the aldermen asleep, and thereupon sat down. Upon his silence, and the noise that was presently made in the church, by the people getting up, they awoke, and stood up with the rest. Upon which he

rose

rose up again, and said, "The sermon is not yet done, but now you are awake, I hope you'll hearken more diligently;" and so went on. — He often expressed a great desire to die in sight of his congregation, to which he had so long been pastor : and he had his request. For in the *November* after his being ejected and silenced, going towards his church on a Lord's-day in the afternoon, he met a brother minister in the street, with whom he exchanged a few words, and took a solemn farewell of him. He was observed to walk towards the church more briskly than usual. He found the people singing, and he joined them with a louder and more chearful voice than ordinary, but stopped on a sudden. Some who observed this, went up to him, and found him dead before the psalm was done.—There is no writing of his extant, but *The Life of Ignatius Jordan,*, a pious alderman of that place, which was transcribed into Mr. *Clark's* Lives.

—— ST. EDMUND'S. THOMAS DOWN, M. A. He was a diligent and useful preacher, and eminent for zeal and affection. He had the parish of *St. Mary Step* united with this, both of which were the most ignorant and profane part of the city; but he wrought a great reformation among them. He was grievously afflicted with the stone and gout, which he bore with wonderful patience. Under severe fits, when asked how he did, he would say, " I am upon my father's rack." He at last died of these disorders, just before the Oxford act took place. A young minister taking his leave of him, said, " Sir, you are now going into the haven, and we into the storm;" referring to the *Oxford* act. " No ; (said he) you are in the haven, and I in the storm : Oh ! my pain and grievous torments ! but the Lord will end them speedily." He died an hour after. He had two daughters, the one of whom married Mr. *Whidden* of *Totness;* and the other, Mr. *Flavel* of *Dartmouth.*

—— ST. PETROCK'S, MARK DOWN, M. A. Brother to the former. He was a judicious preacher, and remarkable for introducing texts of scripture, not commonly thought of, but most aptly applied, and clearly interpreted. He generally insisted on the most heavenly and melting subjects, and had an excellent gift in prayer. He died, and was buried at Exeter, in *Oct.* 1680; but his reason was impaired some time before.

—— ST. THOMAS'S. ALEXANDER HODGES, M. A. Some time Fellow of *Wadh. Col. Oxf.* Mr. *Gould,* his

patron,

patron, had such a respect for him, that he obliged his successor to pay him 20*l. per ann.* for seven years. Soon after
his ejectment he went to *Holland*, to visit some relations of
his wife. Having spent some time there, he took shipping
with a view to return to his family; when a violent storm
arose, which made such an impression upon him, that he
resolved to spend the remainder of his life in whatever
country he should first be set on shore, and not expose himself to the danger of the sea again. The ship was driven
back to the haven from whence it set out. His friends rejoiced at his return, and he was soon after invited to *Delf;*
from whence, after preaching a while, he removed to *Amsterdam*, where he continued minister of the English church
to the day of his death, in *Dec.* 1689.

FALCONBRIDGE. Mr. Coslin.

FINITON. SAMUEL HIERON, M. A. Of *Merton
Col. Oxf.* He was grandson to Mr. *Samuel Hieron*, minister of *Modbury*, and was born at *Honiton.* He was a
good scholar, a very agreeable preacher, and an excellent
expositor. He was ejected soon after the Restoration, and
the former incumbent was restored.   Upon which he returned to *Honiton*, and preached publicly as he had opportunity,
till *August* 1662. He was a man of peace, and of great
moderation ; he kept a good correspondence with the conforming minister of the town, and frequently attended the
public worship, When that was over he preached in his
own house *gratis*, but he was often disturbed, and suffered
greatly for Nonconformity. At one time his house was
violently broke open, by the order of several justices,
when his goods were seized, his plate and his very bed
were taken from him ; and they would have rifled his study,
had not his mother interposed, and produced her own plate
to satisfy their demands. His goods were exposed to sale
in the public market-place, but he employed a friend to buy
them. He was excommunicated for baptizing some children, and was imprisoned upon the Five-mile-act in Exeter
jail, with Mr. *F. Soreton*, but was released by the order of
Sir *W. Courtney*, high sheriff of the county.—He was a
very charitable man, kept many poor children at school, and
gave them books, as he did to many other persons; nor was
he confined to a party, in this or any other of his charities.
Wherever he saw real want, he was ready to shew his compassion.

passion. His house was a common receptacle of poor ejected ministers and private Christians, who were forced from
their homes by the rigor of the times. He was ready to his
utmost to compose differences between neighbours, and always free to give his advice when desired, either in spiritual
or civil matters; and all his carriage was so obliging, that it
forced the good word of many who were enemies to his
cause. A female neighbour of his, who was zealous enough
for the church, seeing Mr. *Hieron's* house so closely beset by
the officers that he could not escape them, invited them to
her house, with the offer of a treat, and then sent him notice
to make his escape.—Though he suffered much, he still kept
on preaching, taking nothing for his services, till after the
Indulgence in 1672, when he assisted Mr. *Soreton*, the ejected minister of the town; and then he gave away his whole
stipend in charity; as he had been accustomed to do, when
he was in the living of *Finiton.* He was a man of great
temperance, and yet was sorely afflicted with the gout. He
often preached and prayed when he was not able to stir out
of his place, not so much as to hold a book in his hand; but
he was eminent for his patience.—He kept very good order
in the family; and though his mother was a shop-keeper,
and had great business, the house and shop were shut at
eight o'clock on *Saturday* night, and all business laid aside.
He continued in *Honiton* till about the time of the duke of
Monmouth's landing, when he was forced out of the country.
He offered all the yearly income of his estate, which was
considerable, (reserving but a competency for himself), to be
disposed of for the common benefit of the town and parish
as the price of his peaceable continuance at home; but the
offer was rejected. He therefore removed to *London*, and
soon afterwards died at *Newington.*

FREMINGTON [V.S.201.] Mr. JOHN BARTLET, of *Exet.*
Col. Oxf. Son of Mr. *Wm. Bartlet*, ejected from *Bideford.*
He was a man much respected by all parties, for the sweetness of his temper, his affability and courteousness; but most
of all for his ministerial abilities. He was a most acceptable
preacher, and had a surprising felicity of address in persuading sinners, and winning souls to Christ, which God eminently succeeded. His very enemies spoke well of him, and
owned him to be an accomplished man. But this could not
screen him from the fury of the times; in which he suffered
considerably by bonds and imprisonments, and other har-

D 3   rassing

rassing difficulties. He was made a gazing-stock in *Stoke-Cannon* and *Exeter*. However, he rejoiced in it, as appeared remarkably in one of his consolatory addresses, which he left in writing, to one of his fellow-prisoners. It was not a little to his honour that he had contracted a most endearing intimacy with that great man Mr. *Howe*, who once lived near him, as appears from a great number of affectionate letters which he received from him. He died in 1679, aged but about 44.

HABERTON [V. S. 160l.] Mr. GEORGE MORTIMER. He had the character of a good preacher, and of an affable and courteous, as well as pious man. He freely parted with a good living, rather than wound his conscience, and never discovered the least inclination to conform. After his eject-ment he and his wife were entertained for several years at *Lupton*. He also lived some time at *Totness*. He died at Exeter, *Feb.* 27, 1688. Mr. *George Trosse* preached his funeral sermon.

HALBERTON [R. 31l.] Mr. JAMES HADDRIDGE. He kept a public meeting in this town after his ejectment.

Little HEMPSTON. JOHN KNIGHT, M. A. He had his education under Mr. *Hoppin*, Fel. of *Exeter Col. Oxon.* He was a very correct man in wording his sermons, but had such an impediment in his speech, as not to be acceptable in his preaching. After his ejectment he lived in Exeter. He was so kind as to send the author some hints with respect to the ministers of this county, of which proper use has been made.

HENNOCK. Mr. ROBERT LAW. He was said to have conformed: but from the papers of Mr. *Quick*, it appears, that tho' he did so for a time, and practised physic, he after-wards renounced his conformity, and died a Nonconformist.

HOLSWORTHY. HUMPHREY SAUNDERS, M. A. He was eight years in Oxford; yet *Wood* takes no notice of him. He had the character of a good scholar, and a very worthy man. He disgusted some of the gentry while he was in his living, by not admitting them to the sacrament: but he looked upon that affair, not as a matter of civility, but of conscience. He was moderator of the general assembly at Exeter, May 12, 1658. He had several chil-dren who were all comfortably provided for.

WORKS.

WORKS. An Apology for administering the Lord's Supper to a Select Company only, in answer to a Piece by Mr. (afterwards Sir Wm.) Morrice, for a promiscuous Admission.

HONITON [R. 250l.] Mr. FRANCIS SORETON. Educated in the free-school at *Plymouth*, and Fel. of *Exeter Col.* A man of great learning, a close student, and surprizingly humble. He was an excellent preacher; and his labours were successful to the good of many. His sermons were kept as a treasure in several hands in that town, and were sometimes repeated to the satisfaction of many. He had always such a reverent and awful sense of God upon his soul, that it gave a majesty to his presence. When the rabble of the town were guilty of any rudeness, he would go and reprove them, and they would retire at the sight of him. Besides a monthly preparation sermon, he set up a weekly lecture in the town, and had the assistance of several neighbouring ministers in it; which he continued till the act of uniformity ejected him. He then retired to the house of Sir *Wm. Courtney* of Poderham, whose aunt he married, and who presented him to this living. Upon the Indulgence in 1672, he returned to his flock. Upon the Five-mile act, he was imprisoned in Exeter jail; but Sir *Wm. Courtney*, being then high-sheriff of the county, got him released and conveyed him in his coach to his own house, where he continued till his death. While he was incumbent, he never troubled any with law-suits for his tithes, lest it should hinder the success of his ministry. None of his worst enemies had any thing to lay to his charge, but the crime of Nonconformity. He had been formerly cast out of his fellowship by the parliamentary visitors. He printed nothing but a Translation of Monsieur *Dailly's* Sermons on the epistle to the *Colossians*.

ILSINGTON [V. 180l.] WILLIAM STUKE, M. A. of *Oxf. University.* Born at *Trusham* near Chudleigh. He was settled in this living about the year 1653. After he was turned out he removed to *Whitcombe* in the parish of Trusham, where he had a good estate; and when the times admitted, he built a meeting-house upon his own land, and preached in it for some years to a large congregation. He died of a pleurisy, after three days illness, about the year 1677. Mr. *Saterleigh*, rector of Trusham, preached his funeral sermon, and spoke of him to this effect: "Now 'tis "expected I should say something of the deceased. He "was

" was well known to all of you. He was a man that would
" preach well, but pray better. And he lost a good living
" to preserve a good conscience." He was generally
esteemed a good scholar, an excellent preacher, and a very
pious man ; who was exceedingly beloved. Large offers
were made him if he would have conformed, but he could
not come up to the terms required, and always expressed
great satisfaction in his Nonconformity.

INSTOW [R. 45*l*] Mr. WILLIAM CLYD. He was chaplain to King Charles in his expedition at *Worcester*, where
he was taken prisoner. He was afterwards presented to this
living by —— *Speccot*, Esq.

INWARDLEIGH [R. S.] Mr. THOMAS BRIDGMAN.
He was ejected from this living at the Restoration, when
Mr. *F. Nation*, who had been dispossessed of it in 1657, returned to it. Dr. *Walker* says that Mr. *Bridgman* never
administered the sacrament there. Perhaps the parishioners
were not in a fit disposition for it ; which there is reason to
believe was the case in some other places where this complaint was made.

IPPLEPEN. Mr. JOHN NOSWORTHY, M. A. Of *Oxford
University*. He was born at *Manaton, Nov.* 15, 1612,
of religious parents, who put him to the grammar-school,
where he did not make the progress that was expected ; upon
which they were for bringing him up to a trade. To this
however he was greatly averse ; and from this time he
applied himself to learning with such diligence, that Mr.
Wm. Nosworthy, master of the high school at Exeter, hearing of his capacity and industry, took him under his care till
he was fit for the university, and sent him to *Oxford*, where
he continued nine or ten years. He married the daughter of
Mr. *Irish*, of Dartmouth, by whom he had sixteen children. He at first preached in Northamptonshire. When
the war broke out, notwithstanding his learning and piety,
he was exposed to no small share of suffering. He was
driven from his home, and with above forty others was
imprisoned at *Winchester*, where he met with very cruel
usage. Being removed from prison to prison, the rest went,
two by two, chained together ; and Mr. *Nosworthy*
marched single before them, with his hands so fast bound
with a cord, that the blood burst out at the ends of his
fingers. When his wife came to visit him, she found him

2   and

and his brethren comfortable and chearful in the prison, and in a short time he was discharged.—He was several times reduced to great straits ; but he encouraged himself in the Lord his God, and exhorted his wife to do the same. Nor did they do it in vain. Once, when he and his family had breakfasted, and had nothing left for another meal, his wife lamented her condition, and said, " What shall I do with my poor children ?" He persuaded her to walk abroad with him ; and seeing a little bird, he said to her, " Take notice how that bird sits and chirps, tho' we can't tell whether it has been at breakfast ; and if it has, it knows not whither to go for a dinner. Therefore be of good cheer, and do not distrust the providence of God : for are we not *better than many sparrows ?*" Before dinner-time, they had plenty of provision brought them.

From Northamptonshire he returned to *Devon*, and preached at *Seaton*, in 1655, where he met with great respect from the neighbouring gentry. In 1659, Mr. *J. Hill*, of *Manaton*, being sequestered for drunkenness and debauchery, Mr. *Nosworthy* was put into that rectory, and continued there till the Restoration ; when he gave it up to Mr. *Hill*, who died (as some people say) the very night after his return to this living, when Mr. *Nosworthy*, took out the broad seal for it, *Sept.* 29, 1660 : but the patron presenting Mr. *Eastchurch*, he was obliged to resign it to him. He then preached at *North Bovey*, till one Mr. *Ball* got him removed from thence ; and after that at *Ipplepen*, where the Act for uniformity silenced him. Upon which he returned to *Manaton*, and did what good he was able in private. When the Five-mile act drove him thence, he lived at *Ashburton*, where he met with many enemies, and much opposition. Mr. *Stawel* of Heerabeer distinguished himself in his furious zeal against him. He once came into the meeting with —— *Bogan*, Esq. who required Mr. *Nosworthy* to come down. An attorney, who was present, advised him to keep his place. But they threatened to pull him out of the pulpit, and at length obliged him to come down. The same person more than once disturbed his meeting afterwards ; and one time, on a week-day, with drums and muskets ; which so frightened Mrs. *Nosworthy*, that it was thought to occasion her death. Mr. *Stawel* at length had a mind to live in *Ashburton* ; and no house would please him but Mr. *Nosworthy's*, which, though he had taken it for a term of years, he quietly resigned to him. But

But this did not satisfy him. He and Mr. *Bogan* convicted this good man for holding a conventicle, and imposed a fine of 20*l.* upon him, and 20*l.* upon the house. Mr. *Stawel,* upon taking a journey to London for the cure of a disorder in his mouth, threatened, that at his return, he would effectually hinder old *Nosworthy* from preaching; who said, " I fear him not.; nor do *I fear what man can do unto me.*" At London this persecutor was taken sick and died. Upon which Mr. *Nosworthy* lived in peace, and departed this life, *Nov.* 19, 1677, aged 66. .

He was reputed a considerable scholar. Besides Latin and Greek, he understood the Hebrew, Chaldee and Syriac languages. He instructed three of his sons till they were fit for the university. The neighbouring ministers paid a great deference to his judgment, and often made him moderator in their debates. Mr. *Eastchurch,* who succeeded him at *Manaton* (a very worthy man) often made honorable mention of his talents and piety. After his death, several of his enemies were troubled on account of the disturbance they had given him; and sent to his children (who were eminent for their piety) begging their prayers, and desiring forgiveness of the injury they had done their family. One *Reap* particularly sent for Mr. *Sam. Nosworthy,* to pray with him and for him; and discovered much compunction for abusing his father. His eldest daughter was very kind to one *Mary Ford,* who used to join the mob at her father's meeting, and preserved her from perishing for want.

JACOBSTOW. Mr. PETER OSBORN,

Little KEMPSTON [V. S.] Mr. THOMAS FRIEND. In the subscription to the *Joint testimony* of the ministers of *Devon* in 1648, a person of this name is stiled minister of *Blackanton.* Dr. *Walker* gives him the character of " a very honest sober man, against whom no exception was to be made, the intrusion only excepted, and his not administering the sacrament (as far as appears from the parish-books) for nine years." Probably the expence of the administration might be privately provided for, and so not brought into the parish-accounts. [Or the same reason for the omission might have been alledged, as in some other cases. See *Inwardleigh.*]

KENTON [V. 33*l.* 13*s.* 4*d.*] *George Kendal,* D. D. Of *Exeter Col. Oxf.* Born at *Cofton,* in Dawlish parish, near Exeter. He was a disciple and great admirer of Dr. *Prideaux.* When the Dr. was promoted to the bishopric of Worcester, Mr. *Kendal* stood fair to succeed him in the rectory of his college, for he was zealously recommended by K. *Charles;* but was disappointed. He became fellow of his college ; and in 1646, a prebendary of the cathedral, thro' the favor of Bp. *Brownrigg.* At the Restoration he recovered the prebend, but lost it again in 1662, for Non-conformity. He was moderator of the first general assembly in Exeter, *Oct.* 18, 1655. In 1647, he became rector of *Blissland,* near Bodmin, in Cornwal. Thence he removed to London, where he had a living in Grace-church-street. Upon K. *Charles's* restoration he left the city, and became rector of *Kenton,* from whence he was ejected at the fatal Bartholomew. After which he retired to *Cofton,* the place of his birth, and the seat of his family, where he died in less than a year ; *Aug.* 19, 1663. He had the general reputation of a considerable scholar, a ready disputant, and a good preacher. He was all his days remarkable for his great contempt of riches.

WORKS. A Vind. of the Doctrine generally received concerning God's special Grace to his Elect in the death of Christ.—Doctrine of Perseverance against John Goodwin.—Fur pro Tribunali, Examen Diologismi qui inscribitur, Fur Prædestinatus.—De Doctrinâ Neo Pelagianâ : Oratio habita in Commitiis.—Twissii Vita and Victoria, &c.

LITTLEHAM [V.] Mr. JAMES WOOLSEY. [Probably this is the person intended in the next article, which is transposed from *Dorsetshire,* there being no such place in that county.]

LITTLEHAM (near *Exmouth*) Mr. OWSELEY. He died a few years after his ejectment, leaving a son, who came into the ministry after the Bartholomew-act passed.

LOCKBEAR. Mr. RICHARD SAUNDERS, M. A. Born at *Peyhembury* near Honiton, of a reputable family. His father, Mr. *Lawrence Saunders,* had a good estate. Major Saunders, and Mr. Humphrey Saunders of Hollsworthy, were his brothers. At about sixteen years of age he went to *Oxford,* and continued there till 1642, when K. *Charles* came thither. Upon which he and several others were carried off as prisoners, and committed to Exeter jail. He entered upon the ministry at this place. When he gave up this living at
the

the Restoration, (which was worth 200*l.* a year) he was presented to *Lockbear* by Zechariah Cudmore, Esq. of that parish; from whence he was ejected on Bartholomew-day. He risided a while with his brother-in-law Mr. *R. Land* of Plymptree; and afterwards lived and preached at *Honiton,* where he met with favour and connivance from several of the neighbouring gentlemen, on account of the civilities they had received from his brother the Major, before the Restoration.

In 1672, he had a public meeting in *Tiverton,* where he spent the remainder of his days. About 1681 he was disturbed in preaching at Mr. *Wood's,* carried before the mayor, and convicted for a conventicle. Tho' the fines for the preacher and the house were levied, he was bound over to the sessions at Exeter. When he appeared, the Oxford-oath was tendered him, which he offered to take in a qualified sense, and pleaded that in so doing he should answer the law, which admitted of such an explication. He said also, that it was against the law, that he should be bound over for one offence, and prosecuted and punished for another. To which the judge of the sessions (Sir *E. S.)* replied, " We must stretch the law to meet with such cunning fellows as you." So he was committed to prison. There he found two Popish priests, who were soon discharged after he came thither : but he was kept there six months; in which time he received great civilities from the inhabitants of the city.—After the liberty in 1687, he again held a public meeting in *Tiverton.* He presided as moderator of the first assembly of the ministers of Devon, at Tiverton, *March* 17 and 18, 1691. He died *July* 1692. Mr. *Robert Carel* of Crediton preached his funeral sermon, in which he speaks of him thus: ?. " As to his intellectuals, he was a man of rare parts. His fancy was high, his invention rich and copious, and his judgment deep and solid. He had the philosopher's Αγχινοια, the sagacity of a piercing and quick spirit. He was a diligent, methodical, and successful student. As to his morals, so prudent was he, that his enemies rather feared and envied, than despised him. He had a very equal temper; still keeping the scales even, neither elevated nor depressed. I who have known him above thirty years, never saw him angry; nor have I ever heard of any one that did. When he hath been highly provoked, he hath not been ' overcome of evil, but hath overcome evil with good.' He had his troubles, ecclesiastical and civil; but he was eminently composed under

der

der them. His contentment with his daily bread was singular; and so was his love, his peaceableness and moderation. His humility was admirable. He had the art of giving a soft answer, so as not to exasperate. Few, if any, less degraded others, or less exalted himself in his discourses. He disdained not the society, friendly converse and labours of those who were far inferior to him in age and learning. He was in his whole course a *Jonathan*, amiable and pleasant. He was chearful but not vain; serious, but not sullen; of good behaviour, vigilant, modest, 1 *Tim.* iii. 2. He was a good polemical divine, and in a religious sense, a man of war from his youth, fighting the Lord's battles: an excellent disputant, who made truth his triumph. He had a body of divinity in his head, and the spirit and soul of that divinity in his heart. Tho' he was a great school-divine, he rather chose to shoot at the peoples hearts, in plain and practical, tho' very rational divinity, than shoot over their heads in high and seraphic notions. His style was clear and strong, flowing from a full soul. He was an *Ezra*, a ready and eminently instructed scribe in the law of his God: clear and solid in resolving cases of conscience: in all things 'a workman that needed not to be ashamed.' And the Lord crowned his labours with success, &c."

He was also of a chearful and obliging temper. If he appeared over modest in the presence of learned strangers, he was free and communicative to his acquaintance, and especially to younger ministers; "which, for my own part, (saith Mr. *Jacob Sandercock*, minister of Tavistock) I must thankfully acknowledge, having profited more by occasional conversation with him in two years, when I was his assistant, than during any two years of my life besides." He was one of those who were at that time called *New Methodists*, and highly approved of Dr. *Williams's Gospel Truth stated*, &c. But he shewed a great deal of candour towards those of different sentiments, and earnestly wished for more charity among the several parties of Protestants,—" He was solicitous to promote the strict observation of national fasts and thanksgivings, expecting happy consequences from them, And, as he was a great observer of providence, he would give divers instances to confirm this opinion and expectation.—He had an excellent talent at expounding the scriptures; and took great pains in studying them. He made a large collection of the interpretations of particular texts, from various writers, adding his own observations. He
made

made frequent use of these in his sermons, which rendered them entertaining and profitable. Several ministers who have seen this work, have thought it deserved to be printed." Some who had been concerned in persecuting this good man, after his death were constrained to acknowledge, that he had not left many equals.

WORKS. An Assize Sermon at Exeter,—A Balm to heal religious Wounds, in Answer to Collier.—Since his death; a Discourse of Angels, with a Preface by Mr. G. Hammond.

LODDESWELL [V. 26l. os. 1d. ¼] Mr. HIND.

LUPPIT [V.] Mr. THOMAS WELLMAN, of *Oxf. Univ.* Born at *Ilchester* in Somerset, about the year 1606. After seven years spent at *Oxford*, he was episcopally ordained, and served as a curate to Mr. *Eedes*, at Honiton, a considerable time; being greatly beloved for his useful labours, and exemplary conversation. There he married the daughter of Mr. *Isaac Northcot* of that town, a pious woman, who lived with him almost fifty years, and survived him about twelve. From Honiton he removed to *Luppit*, four miles distant, having the vicarage bestowed upon him by —— *Southcot*, Esq. a gentleman of the parish. In 1644 or 1645, when Sir *R. Greenvil* apprehended, imprisoned, and murthered men at pleasure; and *Goring*'s forces infested the borders of Dorset, Somerset, and Devon, by unheard-of rapine; when his horse lay upon free quarters, plundering the very gates of Exeter ‡, to avoid their rage and cruelty, Mr. *Wellman* fled to Taunton, where there was a garrison for the parliament, with his wife and two children. There he continued during the blockade and strait siege, being highly esteemed by the governor, and well respected by the religious people of the town, whom, by his prayers and sermons, he encouraged to trust in God in the greatest dangers and difficulties; telling them that he was fully persuaded that God would deliver them. Nor had he cause to be ashamed of his confidence: for one day as he was preaching in *St. James*'s church, on *Mal.* iii. 6; insisting on this doctrine, that "God's immutability is the ground of the stability of his church and people," before the sermon was ended, some persons ran into the church, crying out *Deliverance!* For, on the appearance of a party of the parliament forces, under Col. *Welden*, the cavaliers raised the siege, after they had

‡ See *Clarendon's Hist.* vol. ii. p. 667, 668.

entered

entered the line, and burnt a third part of the town. The
people were running out of the church, on this unexpected
good news; but the preacher prevailed with them to stay and
join with him in returning thanks to almighty God for so
great a mercy. This happened on *May* 11, 1645: a day
which was afterwards observed as a day of rejoicing and
thanksgiving unto God. Mr. *Wellman* staid some time after
this in Taunton; for he could not with safety go to his own
house, while (as the noble historian informs us) "General
Goring's horse committed intolerable insolences and disorders
in Devon." And while Sir *Rd. Greenvil*, whom he calls
"the greatest plunderer of that war, did, at his pleasure,
without law or reason, send parties of horse to apprehend
honest men, and hanged up several only to enrich himself."
But as soon as the country was free from the ravages of these
men, Mr. *Wellman* returned to *Luppit*, where he was well
beloved, and settled there, tho' he had offers of better preferment; and there he continued his labours, till Bartholomew-day, 1662.

The following story is recorded by Dr. *Walker* concerning him and Mr. *Joshua North*, of *Church-Taunton;*
"Who had, on all occasions, expressed a great deal of zeal
against conformity. As he was riding with Mr. *Wellman*,
a little before the Act of uniformity was in force, he vehe-
mently dissuaded him from complying with the terms to be
imposed; professing that he would not conform, tho' for
refusing he should be hanged on the next tree. However,
when the day came, he chose rather to comply, than to part
with a fat benefice, worth about 200*l. per ann.* But it was
observed, that in reading the liturgy, he would tremble so
very much, that he could scarcely hold the book."—It is
not improbable, that it was on the same account that he was
(as the Dr. was informed) "much disturbed in his mind,
some considerable time before his death; and that he died, in
all appearance, much dissatisfied, tho' he left his family
rich."—Mr. *Wellman*, on the other hand, was true to his
principles, and left his place to keep a good conscience, tho'
he had at that time seven children, and no large estate to
maintain them. And he professed that, if he had had nothing to leave them, he would rather commit them to the care
of divine providence, than act against the conviction of his
own mind. Nor was he at all disturbed in his mind, or
dissatisfied with what he had done, but lived and died a
Nonconformist, with a great deal of comfort, tho' he did

not " leave his family rich." There were many weeping
eyes when he preached his farewell sermon ; and the great
affection of the inhabitants of *Luppit*, encouraged him, after
he was ejected, to continue preaching among them in his
own house, as he had an opportunity. He was a sickly man,
having broken his constitution by his ministerial labours and
hard studies at Honiton. He died in 1685, near 80 years of
age.

He concerned himself very little about worldly affairs ;
but was an excellent preacher, and had an extraordinary gift
in prayer. Such was his spiritual and heavenly frame, that
some who had heard him have said, " he spoke rather like
an angel than a man." His singular humility, modesty and
mildness of temper, occasioned him, when he heard of any
misconduct in his people, to write to them rather than to
reprove them to their faces ; and some of his letters on such
occasions, had very happy effects. Tho' his sermons were
well studied, he made no use of notes in the pulpit. His
sight and memory continued to the last. He was congregational in his judgment, but moderate and peaceable in his
temper, and lamented the divisions and animosities among
ministers and christians. He often advised those about him
to behave themselves so that the gospel might not be prejudiced. He was ever ready to send young scholars designed
for the ministry to the university, to direct and encourage
them in their studies, and to write to his friends on their
behalf. Many were greatly obliged to him on this account.
His cousin-german, Dr. *Simon Wellman*, a noted physician, who was intended for the pulpit, was one of that
number.

Tho' he did not desist from preaching after his ejectment,
God was pleased to secure him, so that he was never convicted or imprisoned. In difficult times, he often preached
either in the morning before day, or some hours after it was
night. Informers and soldiers endeavoured to apprehend him,
having rewards offered them for this purpose, but they were
disappointed. Some of them came near his house, but returned without entering, Others actually searched it, under
pretence of searching for arms, but with a design to seize
on him. One of them saw him in his study, but did not
attempt to take him. Others at the same time sat on horseback at the door, but never alighted. One *P—ter*, a very
bad man, was offered 5l. if he would apprehend him, but
he refused it. However, another undertook it, and endeavored

Voted to effect it, but God prevented him, by removing the good old man to a better world.

MARISTOW [V.] JOHN HERRING, M. A. Of *Camb. Univ.* Born at *Saltash*, in Cornwal, in 1602, where his predecessors lived for many generations. He had episcopal ordination, and at first preached in Lincolnshire. When he first came to *Maristow*, he was usher to Dr. *Williams*, who had the living, and kept a great school. He was also chaplain to Sir *Edw. Wise*, of that parish, who on the death of Dr. *Williams*, presented him to the benefice in 1632, and retained a very great respect for him to the day of his death. When the Act of uniformity took place, his patron pressed him very much to conform ; but not being satisfied with the terms, he was ejected, after he had enjoyed the living thirty years. He continued in the parish ten years after, on an estate of his own, and kept a school, being protected by Sir *E. Wise*, and very much beloved by the inhabitants. He afterwards purchased an estate in *South Petherwin*, near Launceston, in Cornwal, where he continued till his death. He there also taught school, and preached on the Lord's days in his own house, till he was incapacitated by the infirmities of age; he was blind six years before he died, which was in 1688, aged 86. His funeral sermon was preached by Mr. *Mich. Taylor*, of *Hollsworthy*. He was a man of exemplary piety, and great learning. He left a large collection of very valuable books. Tho' he preached so frequently, he was never imprisoned, fined, or prosecuted.

MARY CHURCH [V. S. 45*l*.] Mr. WILLIAM STIDSON. He gave place to Mr. *Ball*, the sequestered minister, on the Restoration. Dr. *Walker* calls him *Robert*, and says, " He was a very sorry canting fellow, and whether of any university, or in any orders, is wholly unknown." This will make very little impression on those who are acquainted with that writer, tho' his account cannot now be disproved.

MARY TAVY, or *Huxham*. Mr. BENJAMIN BERRY. He was afterwards at *Topsham*. He was also cast out of *Trull* in *Somerset*; but from what place he was last ejected does not appear. Mr. *George Trosse* preached his funeral sermon.

MERTON [R. 40*l*.] BARTHOLOMEW YEO, M. A. He was of a genteel extraction and an ancient family. After he

left

left his benefice he spent most of his time about those parts,
and freely bestowed his labours upon such as would attend
upon them, especially in *Hatherly* ; in the next parish to
which, and in a kinsman's house, he resigned his soul to
God, in *February*, 1693.

MONKTON. Mr. THOMAS LISLE. After his eject-
ment he lived in the family of General *Monk*, duke of *Al-
bemarle*, and was tutor to the young duke his son, and to Sir
Walter Clarges, his kinsman. He lived privately in the
latter part of his time, first at London, then at Clapham, in
Surrey, and afterwards at *Honiton*, where the author saw
and conversed with him in 1713, and there he soon after
died.

MORCHARD BISHOP [R. 36*l*] ROBERT SNOW, M. A.
Some time Fellow of *Exeter Col. Oxf.* where he continued
twelve years. He married a daughter of Mr. *Francis
Whiddon*, of Moreton Hamsted. By the death of his elder
brother, Mr. *Simon Snow*, merchant, burgess of Exeter,
an estate worth above 20,000*l.* fell to him, which he enjoyed
but a little while. After he was ejected, Mr. *Pridham*, who
succeeded him, shewed him great respect, and boarded with
him for some time. At length he removed from Morchard
to Exeter, where he preached in his own house after attending worship at the parish church. He took the Oxford oath,
and so was not prosecuted as some others were, nor driven
from his habitation. He died about 60 years of age.

MORETON. Mr. JOHN MILLS.

MORETON HAMSTED [R. 50*l.*] ROB. WOOLCOMB,
M. A. A native of *Chudleigh*, where his grandfather was
minister. He was presented to this living by the grandfather
of Sir *William Courtney*, and was ordained at Dartmouth,
Nov. 11, 1657. He was a hard student, a great philosopher, and a sound solid preacher. He was a glorious confessor for the cause of Nonconformity, losing by it not only
a good benefice, but a good estate ; for his father on that
account disinherited him, and made his son his heir, ordering
in his will that he should not have the care of his education.
However he lived comfortably and contentedly, and found
' a good conscience to be a continual feast.' He died at his
house in *Chudleigh*, 1692.

MUSBURY

MUSBURY [R.] RICHARD FARRANT, M. A. Fellow of *Brazen Nose College, Oxford.* Born at *Manchester.* He was a very modest, prudent and learned man ; eminent for humility, charity and piety ; well qualified for an exalted station, but chose to continue in this obscure corner.... Being once taken up for preaching, after his ejectment, and carried before the justices in Honiton, Sir *Courtney Poole* told him, he should be discharged if he would promise to preach no more. He replied, " he would not promise that, because he could not answer it to his great Lord and Master." He died of a consumption. Mr. *Moore* preached his funeral sermon in his orchard, on 2 *Kings* xviii. 20.

NEWTON-ABBOTS [or *Woolborough*, where the church stands] WILLIAM YEO, M. A. A native of *Totness*, brought up at Exeter school, and cotemporary, both there and at *Oxford*, with Dr. *Manton.* Having pursued his studies for some time in *Exeter Col.* he removed to *Eman. Col. Camb.* On leaving the university, he became chaplain in Col. *Gold's* regiment ; but being soon weary of that station, he settled for some time at *Brighthelmstone*, in Sussex. From thence he was removed by an order of the committee of parliament, to *Newton Abbot*, where he lived in good repute and did much service, by his serious affectionate preaching and exemplary life. He found the town very ignorant and profane, but by the blessing of God upon his labours, the people became very intelligent, serious and pious. He had a great authority among them, and was a terror to loose persons, so as to put a stop to the open profanation of the Lord's-day, by walking with a constable round the town, after the public worship was over. He was highly esteemed by his brethren in the ministry, and well respected by the neighbouring gentry, being a genteel man, and very facetious in conversation. He was of a generous spirit, an affectionate preacher, and a close student ; who had well digested what he had read.

While he was in his living, he lost an augmentation of 80*l. per annum* for refusing to take the Engagement. After he was silenced in 1662, he continued firm to his principles, and preached as the times would bear it. In consequence of an order of sessions offering a reward of 40*s.* to any one that should apprehend a Dissenting Minister, a malicious constable attempted to seize him, so that he was forced to hide himself in the fields, in a time of deep snow. He was often obliged to leave his house and family for safety, but

E 3 providentially

was never apprehended. Once it pleased
ie heart of a man who came to hear him
1, who afterwards became very serious, and
irer, and a communicant with him, to the
—His judgment, imagination, memory and
itinued to admiration, even to the last. He
the least repentance for his Nonconformity,
:tion in it. When his end drew near he had
ehensions. He was satisfied with long life,
" My soul is continually in my hand, ready
He had discharged his office in the parish,
ate, about 53 years. He died in *Oct*. 1699,
neral sermon was preached by Mr. *Richard*
n-law.

FERRERS (or *North Molton*) [V. S.
JOHN HILL, M. A. Of *Lincoln Col. Oxf.*
3ristol, about the year 1611. He was or-
·orge Cook, Bp. of *Hereford*, in 1635. In
n Pierce, Bp. of *Bath* and *Wells* (whom
imends as very vigilant and active for the
iesiastical and civil state,*) granted him a
:ll in his diocese, upon condition of his ob-
itution and injunctions, and wearing the
·ating divine service. In the same year he
id in 1643 at *Elberton*, both in the diocese
1645 he was at *Langridge*, near Bath : in
vicar of *North-Newington*, in Wilts ; in
, in Somerset ; and at last, in 1652, he
Newton Ferrers. Dr. Walker commits
n this matter. (See *Cal. Contin.* p. 293)
:er the Restoration, Mr. *Hill* was threat-
l out of his living. To secure himself he
d seal for it, *Sept.* 6, 1660, as *per Mortem*
b. *ejusdem jam vacatum*, and the king's
Lapsum. Now another game is played.
inst him for seditious words is set on foot ;
:ted, and depositions taken, at Modbury,
·efore Sir T. Hele, &c. He is summoned,
·ar at *Morley* to make his defence. In
iad testimonials, among others, from the
l clergymen of Bristol, who certified, that,
:dge, in and after the wars, he was well

of it in the account of his conduct towards Dr. Conant,
    Vol. i. p. 123. &c.

affected

affected to K. Charles I. and was for his loyalty ejected out of divers places, as Elberton and Horfield, in Gloucestershire ; and, for not taking the Covenant, out of Langridge and Cleven, in Somerset : and therefore they believed he was grossly abused by desperate swearers against him." It seems the justices or commissioners were of the same mind, for they discharged him. However these accusations and depositions served Mr. Anthony Clifford's turn ; for the duke of York being his friend, on *Feb.* 20, 1660, he got a broad seal for the living, in which Mr. *Hill's* presentation, granted not six month's before, is repealed, and this reason given, "That his words and behaviour, during the late distractions, rendered him incapable of any ecclesiastical preferment." So that on *Ap.* 23, 1661, Mr. *Hill* covenanted to yield up the living, and went to Exeter. He afterwards settled at Newton Abbot, where he died, and was buried in the chancel of Woolborough.

NORTHAM [V. 3*ol.*] Mr. ANTHONY DOWNE. He was brother to Mr. *Mark* and Mr. *Thomas Downe*, of Exeter, of whom an account was before given. He survived both of them, and lived to be about 80 years of age. He was remarkable for neatness in his compositions, and exactness of expression. These three brothers were all remembered with great respect by the good people of Exeter, both on account of their ministerial labours, and christian conversation.

East OGWELL. Mr. JOHN STEPHENS. A most eminent preacher, and a very pious man. While he continued in his living he took great pains with his people, holding meetings in the church on the week-days, to instruct young persons in the principles of religion, when he was used to propose questions to them in order to try their knowledge. He lived to a great age, and continued to preach after he was blind.

PETROCKSTOW [R. S.] Mr. WILLIAM TRIVITHWICK. Dr. Walker owns that Mr. A. Gregory, the sequestered minister, died before the Restoration, and therefore Mr. *Trivithwick*, his successor, had a legal title to the living. After being silenced he went abroad with Col. *Rolle*, as his guardian and tutor. He died in *July*, 1693. It doth not appear that he printed any thing but a funeral sermon for his patron.

PINHO.

PINHO. Mr. Grove. §He was grandfather to Mr. *Henry Grove*, an eminent dissenting minister, and, tutor of an academy, at Taunton; in the memoirs of whose life, prefixed to his posthumous works, is the following account of his ancestor: " It was Mr. Grove's happiness to be descended, both by father and mother, from families of considerable repute, and which, for several generations, had been remarkable for strict piety, sincere goodness, and a steady attachment to religious liberty and the rights of conscience: the *Groves*, of Wiltshire, and the *Rowes*, of Devon. His grandfather *Grove* was, soon after the Restoration, ejected from a good living in Devon, for Nonconformity, at that distinguished period, when so many ministers gave a noble proof that their religious profession was, not the result of secular policy, but of conscience, by giving up the most considerable worldly interests, to preserve the peace of their minds. His father [the son of the above] suffered much and chearfully in the same cause, for Lay-Nonconformity under Charles and James II.——"

PLYMOUTH. George Hughes, B.D. Of *Corp. Christi Col. Oxf.* Born in the Borough of *Southwark*, in 1603, when his mother was 52 years of age, who never had a child before, tho' she had three husbands before Mr. *Hughes's* father; and whose age was as remarkable afterwards; for she lived to her 96th year. He had so general a reputation in the university, for his proficiency in his studies, that Dr. *Clayton* being made master of *Pemb. Col.* upon the first erection of it, procured Mr. *Hughes* to be one of the first fellows. Several persons of great eminence afterwards were his pupils here. He was ordained about the year 1628. For some time he preached in and about *Oxford*; and afterwards was called to be lecturer of *Alhallows*, Bread-street, London. The incumbent being sickly and aged, Mr. *Hughes*, with his consent, performed almost all his work. After four or five years continuance in *London*, his great popularity there (being constantly attended by a very numerous auditory) and some instances of his nonconformity to the ceremonies, being complained of to Abp. *Laud*, he silenced him. Upon this, he retired for some time to Mr. *Dod's*, the famous old Puritan minister, at *Fausley*, in Northamptonshire, desiring his advice in his present circumstances, particularly about going over to New-England, which he had some thoughts of. The good old man dissuaded

suaded him from that design, and recommended him to Lord
Brook, at Warwick ; where he resided for some time, and
married a lady of Coventry. During his residence here, old
Mrs. Maynard, mother to the famous lawyer Sir John Maynard, solicited him to accept of a presentation, which she
had obtained for him of the Earl of *Bedford*, to *Tavistock*,
in Devonshire. This he accepted from a desire of more
public service, tho' he had but a very small stipend, and the
aforesaid Earl made him his chaplain. This was a very ignorant and profane place before he came ; but by the blessing
of God upon his endeavors, a great reformation was wrought,
and many persons were brought to seriousness, the fruit of
which appeared long after.—He set up a Wednesday-lecture, which was much frequented. The first serious impressions made by his ministry in this place were on three
persons who afterwards proved useful ministers ; Mr. *John
Rowe*, Mr. *Ralph Venning*, and Mr. *John Tickell*, a pious
conformist, rector of Withicomb, in Devon.

When the civil war broke out, *Tavistock* being made a
garrison for the king, the governor being his wife's relation,
gave him a pass for himself, his family and effects to Exeter,
then a parliament garrison. Soon afterwards the king's
forces besieged and took the city ; but he obtained the favor
of a safe conduct to *Coventry*, where (being a widower) he
resided for some time with his wife's relations. Not long
after his coming thither, upon the vacancy of St. Andrew's,
at *Plymouth*, the magistrates of that town, who were
before acquainted with him at *Tavistock*, presented him to
that church, and he had institution and introduction from Dr.
Brownrigg, Bp. of Exeter ; which happily prevented his
ejection at the Restoration, when one had got the king's title
to that vicarage, on pretence it was lapsed, not knowing he
had been admitted by the bishop. He came to *Plymouth* in
1664, where he found, to his satisfaction, the liturgy already laid aside, by means of Mr. *Porter*, minister of another church newly erected in that town ; though he adopted
it again in 1661, rather than lose his living. *Plymouth*
being besieged by the king's forces soon after, many of the
Puritan ministers in that neighbourhood took refuge there,
and were frequently employed in prayer and preaching, till
the raising of the siege gave them opportunity to return to
their respective charges. Here Mr. *Hughes* was indefatigable in his labours, most generous in acts of hospitality and
charity, and was universally reverenced and beloved. He
constantly

constantly maintained a good correspondence with the magistrates of the place, and an harmonious accord with people of different persuasions.

After enjoying a long calm of eighteen years, commissioners came down to Plymouth, in *August*, 1662, and after they had put out all the magistrates of the town, excepting one, the same day they summoned Mr. *Hughes* before them, and told him that he was dismissed from his ministry at Plymouth, which was a week before the fatal Bartholomew. He still continued, however, in the town; but this could not be borne where he was so much esteemed; and therefore he was summoned, with his assistant and brother-in-law Mr. *T. Martin*, his son Mr. *Obadiah Hughes* and Mr. *N. Sherwill*, to appear before the Earl of Bath, governor of Plymouth. However, they were not suffered to see the Earl, but were committed by the deputy-lieutenants of the county, tho' nothing was objected against them. Mr. *Hughes*, senior and Mr. *Martin* were sent, with two files of musqueteers, to St. Nicholas island. Mr. *Hughes*, junior, Mr. *Sherwill*, and others, were confined at Plymouth. The latter were first set at liberty; but on condition that they should not return to Plymouth without leave of the Earl of Bath or his deputy. The old gentleman and Mr. *Martin* remained in the island nine months, till at length his health was much impaired, and an incurable dropsy and scurvy were contracted, as supposed, by the saltness of the air, when he was offered his liberty, upon condition of his giving security of 2000*l.* not to live within twenty miles of Plymouth. This his friends did without his knowledge.

Hereupon he retired to *Kingsbridge;* where he continued, in great weakness, to study hard, and spend his time in private devotion, and in pious counsels and conferences with the many friends that came to visit him. He hardly cared for any discourse but what was serious and heavenly; and he had such an affecting sense of the cloud that was upon the church of God, by the ejection of so many eminent ministers, that he was scarcely ever seen to indulge any mirth after that day. When a young minister, who was much with him in this his retirement, was speaking to a person, in his hearing, of his infirm state; Mr. *Hughes* replied, " Nature would not willingly go where it must and shall go: " yet I will wait all the days of my appointed time for my " change. Oh! when will it once come, that I shall put " off this earthly tabernacle, and be cloathed with my
                                        " house

Obadiah Hughes.

from an original Picture in the Possession of M.ʳ Maundy.

Published by Button & Son, Paternoster Row.

" house from heaven! I desire to be dissolved, and at home
" with Christ. I thank God I am not ashamed to live, nor
" afraid to die." The same minister being necessitated to
leave him, when he drew near his end, upon intimation of a
warrant out against him, Mr. *Hughes* thus addressed him:
" I advise you not to faint. Hold out courageously in your
" Master's work. Take heed to yourself, and to that
" ministry you have received from the Lord by my hands
" (he being one who ordained him) and the laying on of the
" hands of the presbytery, that you do fulfil it. Be not
" discouraged on account of sufferings. The cross is the
" way to the crown. If we suffer with Christ, we shall
" reign with him. This dead cause of reformation, for
" which we now suffer, shall rise and revive again. Salva-
" tion shall come to the churches. I die, but you shall live
" to see it. (So the relator did). The very means these
" men take to suppress and destroy it, shall most effectually
" promote it. Only be cautious that you never engage in
" any indirect courses about it. Leave God to do his own
" work in his own way. Your duty is to be quiet and stand
" still. In returning and believing, you shall have rest."
He then gave him his solemn blessing. To a near relation
who asked how he did? he answered; " I never found the
actings of my faith and hope more vigorous and lively
than now."—He continued preaching privately to the last,
which he did twice the Lord's-day before he died; but concluded with these memorable words, " And now all my
work is done." The evening before he died, he ordered his
watch to lie by him, and desired a relation to observe when
it was two o'clock, " for (says he) that is my hour." And
accordingly, just at that time he expired, in 1667, in the
64th year of his age.

Mr. Hughes was a person of great natural capacity, and
a master in most parts of learning; especially a great textuary and divine. He had a thorough acquaintance with the
original languages, and was one of the most exact critics
of all his brethren in the West. He was well read in the
fathers; an acute disputant, and a judicious casuist; as a
great number of letters shewed, found among his papers,
upon the nicest cases on which he had been consulted. He
was a most skilful and faithful pastor to a very large flock.
His preaching was elaborate, but plain. He did not affect a
jingle of words, nor any quirks of wit, but his style was
chiefly scriptural. He went over many important subjects in a
course.

course. He generally preached on an average, five times in a week, and yet none of his sermons appeared hasty productions. On the Lord's-days, he constantly began the public worship with a short exhortation from some text of scripture; then prayed and expounded part of a chapter. After singing, either he or his assistant prayed and preached. In the afternoon, after a short prayer, he expounded a whole chapter, baptized the children; and after singing and a prayer in the pulpit, catechized, preached, and concluded with a prayer, a psalm, and the blessing. Notwithstanding this variety of exercise, he made the whole no longer than two hours each part of the day.

His conversation was most strict and exemplary; and unfeigned piety to God appeared in his whole deportment. He was also of a most obliging disposition. No minister in the West had a greater influence among his brethren. He and Mr. *Ford* of Exeter, prevailed with the ministers of those parts, episcopal, presbyterian and congregational, to unite in an association for mutual assistance in their ministry. They divided themselves into seven classes: each met quarterly, and subdivided themselves into lesser bodies, which met every six weeks. In their quarterly meetings, the moderator began with a Latin prayer; then there was a Thesis upon some theological question, and a disputation, wherein all the ministers present opposed the respondent. All the divisions had also a yearly meeting at Exeter, in the month of *May*. Mr. *Hughes* presided in that of 1656. These meetings promoted their mutual acquaintance and amicable correspondence, tho' they were of different sentiments about discipline. Several episcopal divines, of the best characters, joined them; and lived in great amity with them: v. g. Drs. *Hutchinson, Gandy, Fulwood, Ashton,* Messrs. *Ackland, Banks,* &c. Mr. *Hughes* was much esteemed by the generality of them. It may be worth while to mention one proof of it even after he was silenced: He happened to be at *Totness*, in 1663, on a day when Bp. *Ward* held a visitation there, without knowing any thing of it. There was a numerous appearance of the clergy, who all of them, excepting three, when they heard that Mr. *Hughes* was in the town, just as he was taking horse to go, left their bishop and accompanied him on horseback about a mile out of town (tho' he would have dissuaded them from it) and with great respect took their leave of him.

He

He died *July* 3, 1667. His funeral sermon was preached by
Mr. *John Ford*, the conformist minister, of *Totness*, on 2
Tim. iv. 7, 8: who justly gave him a high encomium, and
pressed his hearers to imitate his holy example, and live up
to his excellent sermons.—*Wood* reports several things to his
disadvantage, from which he is fully vindicated by Dr.
Calamy (Account, p. 228—231) Mr. *Tickell*, of Exeter,
in the dedication of a book to him, acknowledges him as his
spiritual father. He was interred at *Kingsbridge,* where
he died, in the same grave with his friend Mr. *G. Geffries,*
minister of that town. A handsome marble monument was
erected for him by Mr. *T. Crispin,* on which is the following inscription, composed by his son-in-law Mr. *John
Howe.*

In Memoriam suave olentem æternùm colendam Viri desi-
deratissimi *Georgii Hughesii,* S. Th. B. *Plymmuden-
sium* nuper Pastoris vigilantissimi, sacræ sensus paginæ
penitiores eruere, homines concione flectere, precibus
Deum, mirè edocti. Qui, Solis æmulum ab Oriente
auspicatus cursum (ortu *Londinas)* occidentale dehinc
sidus diù claruit, lucem in vita spargens undique,
moriens luctum: Vitæque (vere vitalis) curriculo in
annos 64 perducto, optima perfunctus, perpessus mala,
requiem tandem invenit, animo quidem in Cœlis, corpore
vero in subjacente tumulo, ipsis Julii nonis, Anno
Salutis 1667. Symmistæ longe charissimi *Georgii
Geofridi,* A. M. cujus exuviæ ante ter novem annos
ibidem sitæ nunc primum in cineres solvuntur, novis
miscendos.

> Nacta sacros cineres servato fideliter Urna,
> Hæc uterum Satio tibi fæcundabit inertem.
> O fœlix tumuli matrix, de morte renatos
> Olim tam claros hosce enixura gemellos!

Thus translated by Dr. Gibbons :

This marble is erected to the ever-fragrant and ever-honored
memory of that most excellent man, the Rev. GEORGE
HUGHES, B. D. The most vigilant pastor of the church, at
Plymouth: who was wonderfully qualified for the deepest
researches into the sacred pages, and the discovery of their
latent meaning. Alike eminent for his prevalence with men
by preaching, and with God by prayer. Like the sun rising
in the East (being born in London) his radiant orb travelled

4   to

to the West, diffusing in its course, unbounded light, and
at its setting leaving the church in night and tears.   Having
spent a life (worthy the name) of sixty-four years in our
world, in doing the best things, and in suffering the worst,
he at length attained his rest ; the rest of his spirit in heaven,
and the rest of his body in this adjacent tomb, on the 7th of
July, 1667 : and now mingles his ashes with those of his
pious fellow-labourer, and most beloved friend, the Rev.
GEORGE GEFFRIES, A. M. who was, nine years before
interred in the same place.

> Preserve, O grave, inviolate thy trust,
> This dear depositum of sacred dust.
> This fresh accession shall enrich thy womb
> Parturient when the Lord of life shall come.
> How happy then, when that blest day shall shine,
> To yield two births, immortal and divine !
> Two saints, two ministers, of prime renown,
> Whom glory with its brightest beams shall crown.

WORKS. The joint Testimonies of the Ministers of Devon
with those of London, to the Truth of Jesus Christ ; with a Confutation of the Errors, &c. of these Times, 1648, subscribed by
72 Ministers.—Sure-footing in Christianity examined : In answer
to Serjeant.§—Aphorisms concerning the Doctrine of the Sabbath.
—Exposition on Genesis and part of Exodus; printed from some
imperfect Notes.—Aaron's Rod blossoming ; the Pain and Gain
of Affliction. (Mr. Baxter esteemed this the best book of its
kind)—Sermons at Funerals ; and one before the H. of Commons.

—— Mr. OBADIAH HUGHES, son of Mr. *George
Hughes.* He was ejected from his student's place in *Christ
Church, Oxford,* 1662, when he was just about to take the
degree of M. A. He betook himself to his father at *Plymouth,* and there soon became a sufferer for Nonconformity,
being seized, and clapped up in prison with him, *Oct.* 6,
1665, tho' he could be charged with nothing but being his
son. Having been confined a considerable time he was at
length set at liberty, upon security given to leave the town,
and not return thither without leave. His father and he,
during their confinement, were not allowed to come together.; but letters continually passed between them. The following passages, out of a few of the father's letters to the
son, appear worth inserting :

§ The Papist, against whom Tillotson also wrote.

" Dear

" Dear son:

" I am the mark aimed at ; and how far God may suffer men to proceed, I know not: but free communion with God in prison, is worth a thousand liberties, gained with the loss of liberty of spirit. The Lord keep us his freemen. I am at a fixed point in heaven. The will of the Lord be done, either for liberty or restraint, for life or death. I wait for the Lord, and rejoice in him ; to which strong hold alone, I commend you also. I desire God's blessing on you, and desire you by faith to receive it from that promise, ' Blessed are ye when persecuted for righteousness-sake,' and suffering without a cause. God is wise in this bodily separation of us, and good I hope, in making us meet daily in his bosom. Keep close to him ; walk circumspectly ; be of good cheer ; and the God of comfort will be with you : and in his bosom I leave you."

At another time he wrote thus :

" I am glad to hear of your acquiescence in the will of God as to your present restraint ; and rejoice also in your aim at those holy resolutions of the saints who have suffered before. The Lord perfect, both in you and me, every grace that may enable us to do and suffer his will. Keep accounts with God every day as even as you can. Believe those promises, *Gen.* xvii. 1. *Isa.* xliii. 2, 3, and lxiii. 9. The Lord perfect faith, wisdom, holiness, and courage in you. I am well, and best of all in heaven§ : and satisfied with the will of God, which will bring us to glory. I pray for your liberty more than my own. My thoughts for myself are to keep my covenant ; and yet against all traitorous positions that are truly so, I am ready to declare. God hath suffered us to be debarred from the work of the ministry, deprived of our livelihood, shut up in prison ; and at last we are to be driven from our habitations. But this is not all intended by men, or which may be permitted by God. There is more bitterness yet to be expected, if the Lord leave the reins on the necks of violent and cruel men. But his will be done, which is to glorify himself, and perfect blessedness for his, thro' these hard ways. I hope He will deliver you from the hands of men, and from every snare."

§ There seems to have been an error here, in the copy. Probably it should have been " in the HOPE of heaven."

In another letter he thus writes :

" We have here in this island *(St. Nicholas's)* good
lectures read us every day, from heaven and earth, from seas
and rocks, from storms and calms, enough to teach us much
of God's providence in our morals as well as in naturals.
Fruitful spirits might gather much of God from them : O
that mine were so ! How might I feel out heaven this way,
as well as see it by believing ! Lord help, and I shall do it.
The everlasting arms of love and mercy keep you blameless,
and safe, to the appearance of our Lord."

Another letter has this passage :

" As to our sufferings, as ill-natured, froward, or worse,
I have passed through them, and I hope God will give you
power to despise them. I know, my son, that you suffer
at this time more immediately for my sake ; but I hope it is
on Christ's account, who will own it, and return mercy
unto you. If you are called out this day, I hope God will
give wisdom what to answer. As to myself or liberty, I
have resigned them to the good pleasure of our God. The
Lord strengthen faith, and lengthen patience : we shall then
do well, and inherit the promise. When I go forth from
hence, I shall do it in the faith of God, not knowing yet
whither I shall go.—Your father, endeared by the bonds of
nature, and grace, and sufferings. "

On *March* 9, 1670, Mr. *Obadiah Hughes* was privately
ordained to the ministry (for which his sufferings had prepared him) by Mr. *Jasper Hickes*, and five others of his
brethren. He for some time preached about *Plymouth* as
he had opportunity ; tho' he ran great risks, and was several
ways a sufferer. Finding himself no longer safe there, in
April, 1674, he removed to London, where he was chosen
pastor of a considerable part of Mr. *Well's* congregation, to
whom he ministered in holy things with great diligence and
fidelity. He was noted for his excellent gift in prayer, in
which few exceeded him. It was not long however, before
he suffered fresh persecution. He was once sent to New-
prison, and appeared at the sessions, at Hick's-hall, when
he was forced to give bail for his good behaviour ; and he
continued under it, from sessions to sessions, for a year together. Some time after he retired to *Enfield*, where, upon
                                                              the

the liberty granted in 1672, he preached publicly, and gathered a little church, composed of serious christians of various denominations, and was instrumental in preparing many of them for heaven who went thither before him. At length he was seized with an asthma, which confined him to his house and chamber, under which his patience and resignation were very exemplary. He finished his course *Jan.* 24, 1704, in the 65th year of his age, and left two sons in the ministry; the one at *Canterbury*, and the other at *Ware*, who had much of the spirit of their father and grandfather.

WORKS. Scripture Light about the Ordinance of Baptism.— A dedicatory Epistle prefixed to his Father's Aphorisms on the Sabbath, which he published.

—— Mr. THOMAS MARTYN. He was educated first at *Oxford*, but upon the breaking out of the civil war, he removed to *Cambridge*. On returning into his own country, he was chosen by the magistrates of Plymouth, lecturer of *St. Andrew's*, and was there publicly ordained by presbyters. Upon Mr. *George Hughes's* death, he succeeded him, and continued his ministry till some months before Bartholomew-day, 1662, when he was forced to desist from his public work; being, upon a rigorous interpretation of some words in private conversation, suspended *ab officio*. When it was given out that he intended to preach after this, he was threatened, by a man who carried anger in his breast and a sword by his side, that he should be pulled out of the pulpit by his ears. In 1665, he and Mr. *Hughes* were sent to the island of *St. Nicholas*, and were kept prisoners, under very hard circumstances, for ten months; in which, he, his wife, and eight children suffered much grief, and his estate much loss. He humbly petitioned for a removal, when sickness prevailed amongst the soldiers, and some of them were very near his lodging, but was denied. At length, for the sake of liberty, at the instigation of the Earl of Bath, he gave a bond of 1000l. and sureties to his majesty, not to inhabit, or to come within twenty-two miles of *Plymouth*, without his or his deputy's leave. He and his family suffered greatly in consequence of this separation from each other; for when his presence was necessary to advise, relieve and comfort them, in sickness and in death, he durst not come near them. In all this time, he was not accused of any crime or breach of law or statute; but he was never admitted to appear before the governor about this business, to make his complaint, or to vindicate his character.

—— Mr. SAMUEL MARTYN, son of the above Mr. *Thomas Martyn*. He was well known at *Plymouth* as an occasional preacher ; and tho' he was not ejected by the Act of uniformity, he was silenced, and became a sufferer by it; being apprehended upon the breaking up of a meeting at Plymouth, and sent to Exeter jail, where he lay half a year, and was excommunicated. He was at length absolved, upon receiving the sacrament according to the church of *England*. He died about 1692.

Mr. JOHN HORSEMAN, who was well known in *Plymouth*, was ejected at *Scilly* island.

PLYMPTON. ST. MARY'S [R. S.] Mr. JOHN SERLE.[*] He was presented to this living so late as 1660, when he found such dilapidations, that the repairs were more than the income for the two years he enjoyed it before Bartholomew-day, when he quitted ; and not being allowed the tithe of 1662, he was 200l. the worse for having had this living. —In all his conversation he shewed himself a very serious religious man. He ventured to preach in his own house, in the very worst of times, and was very useful. In 1685 he suffered six months imprisonment in Southgate, Exeter, for refusing the corporation-oath. Old Mr. *Hallet*, Mr. *Hoppin*, Mr. *Trosse*, and Mr. *Gaylard*, suffered with him for the same cause. Mr. *Serle* was but in low circumstances, and was chiefly maintained by friends till about the Revolution ; when he was chosen pastor to the dissenting congregation at *Plympton*. He lived to the age of 86, and preached twice a day to the last. He had such an aversion to publish any thing, that when he preached a funeral sermon, on the death of an excellent young woman, whose relations earnestly pressed that it might be printed, they at last prevailed only upon this proviso, that not so much as the first letters of his name should be inserted.

—— Mr. PITTS. [C.]. § The late Mr. Joseph Pitts, an independent minister, in the Borough, Southwark, was from this county. Probably he might be a descendant of this Mr. Pitts.

PLYMPTON MORRIS. Mr. WILLIAMS.

* Dr. Walker mentions this Mr. Serle as succeeding Mr. James Bamfield, in the sequestered living of Rattery, in this county, in which he continued till the Restoration.

POLTIMORE

POLTIMORE [R.] Mr. AMBROSE CLARE. He was brought up to trade, but afterwards went to the university. He had the character of a very good scholar, an acute disputant, and a plain, but judicious and good preacher.

PYEWORTHY [R. S. 27l. 8s. 7d.] Mr. MICHAEL TAYLOR. He was born at *Silverton*, and educated at *Cambridge*. At his coming from thence he was assistant to Mr. *Humphrey Saunders*, at Hollsworthy, with whom he lived and whose relation he married. While he continued there he was much noticed for his piety and ministerial abilities; particularly for his excellent gift in prayer. After the liberty in 1687, he had a public meeting-house, at *Hollsworthy*, where he died *May* 26, 1705. His funeral sermon was preached by Mr. *John Balster*. Dr. *Walker* says, " he would have conformed at the Restoration, could he have kept the living," which is utterly groundless. His widow writes upon this head as follows: " He quitted his living at *Pyeworthy* some time before Bartholomew-day, because there was a flaw pretended in his title, which he would not be at the charge of vindicating, when he foresaw he must quit it on the account of conscience in a little time. It was not the want of a benefice, or church preferment, that made or kept him a Nonconformist; for his interest in the gentry of his neighbourhood, and in some considerable clergymen, would have removed that difficulty : but the terms required of those that would keep any place of public service in the national church, were such as he could not comply with." She added the following certificate, declaring her readiness, if required, to swear it. " Whereas Dr. *Walker* hath published, &c. I do hereby certify, that I was married to Mr. *Taylor* some years before his ejection ; and that I never knew him signify 'any inclination to Conformity, either before, at, or since his quitting his living. But on divers occasions hath expressed his full satisfaction in his Nonconformity ; and under all discouragements did fulfil his ministry as he had opportunity ; and with patience and chearfulness did suffer for so doing, In his last sickness he spake to many of his friends who came to visit him, that Nonconformity is a good cause ; that he was intirely satisfied in it, and did rejoice in his sufferings for it."   *Mary Taylor.*

Feb. 12, 1717-8.

REW [R. 130*l.*] Mr. EDWARD PARR. He succeeded his name-sake, and probably his relation, Mr. *Bartholomew Parr*, prebendary of Exeter, in this living, which Dr. Walker intimates he lost by the ordinance against pluralities. This Mr. *E. Parr* was a fluent agreeable preacher, and a very heavenly-minded man. He every where made it his business to do good. Having no children, his great charity allowed him to lay up very little. After the Bartholomew ejection he lived at *Mary Ottery* ; when he and Mr. *Gundery* used to preach in Newton chapel, a peculiar belonging to *Ailsbeer*, the minister of which (Mr. *Cortes*, a sober, moderate, good man, and a lover of such persons as Mr. *Parr*) countenanced, or at least connived at it. The Bishop often sent to him to forbid it ; but he in excuse used to say, " If the chapel-doors were shut, the alehouse doors would " be open ; and that no body else would preach there, the " pay was so small." So that they continued to exercise their ministry there, all this time ; but his successor would not suffer it. Mr. *Parr* afterwards preached at *Buckerall* and *Aldscomb*, and took great pains, with good success, in catechizing little children and young persons grown up. He refused the parsonage of *Silverton*, worth 500*l.* *per ann.* which was offered him, if he would have conformed. So that, being above forty years a Nonconformist, he may be said to have lost above 20,000*l.* in the cause. He lived afterwards in a low condition, but died full of peace and hope. His funeral sermon was preached by Mr. *G. Trosse*.

SANDFORD PEVEREL [R. S.] Mr. STEPHEN COVEN. He was presented to this living in in 1655. Dr. *Walker* says, " It is probable he never had any orders at all of any kind." But it is at least as probable he is mistaken, as he has been proved, in many instances of this sort, to have been.

WORKS; The Military Christian ; or, a good Soldier of Jesus Christ in compleat Armour.

SATERLEIGH [R. 31*l.* 9*s.* 6*d.*] LEWIS HATCH, M. A. Of *Exeter Col. Oxf.* All that can now be learned concerning him is, that he was a good scholar.

SHODBROOK [R. 200*l.*] THOMAS TRESCOT, M. A. He was a native of *Exeter*, where his father was a fuller ; a very religious and charitable man, who left as good a character as any man in his station. This his son was many years in the university, and was a close student. [In the year 1642 he was rector of *Inwardleigh.*] Dr. *Walker* says, " In the year 1660, to secure his title to this rich parsonage he took out the broad seal for it *per lapsum ;*" most certainly therefore by the Act for ministers, which passed in 1660, he must have as good a title to his living as any clergyman in the county. The Dr. adds (without a word to his disadvantage) " He was again dispossessed in 1662 for Nonconformity." He was courted to Conformity by very advantageous offers, but chose to leave this benefice, as well as other prospects, tho' he had a wife and eight children, rather than act against his conscience. Upon his ejectment he retired to *Exeter,* and laboured there as he had opportunity. And there, after much weakness, he died, *Dec.* 16. 1684, Mr. *G. Trosse* preached his funeral sermon. He was a gentleman of good learning, great hospitality, and exemplary piety. He was much beloved by his parishioners, and much esteemed by the clergy and gentlemen all round that neighbourhood. He published nothing but an Assize sermon, at Exeter, 1642, entitled *The Zealous Magistrate.*

SHUTE[V. and COLYTON, C.] Mr. JOHN GILL. After his ejectment he continued a humble pious preacher among the Dissenters till his death, which was about the year 1688.

SIDBURY [V. 28*l.*] Mr. RICHARD BABINGTON. He was not properly ejected, but voluntarily resigned his living, some time before the Bartholomew act, to the worthy and learned Mr. *Simon Parsons,* on account of a disorder in his head, which some times disabled him in the pulpit ; but he would otherwise undoubtedly have been a Nonconformist. One reason for this supposition is, that he gave by will 100*l.* to ten ejected ministers. He had a good estate, and studied physic, which he practised only by giving advice *gratis* both to the rich and the poor. He was a learned and moderate man. He died about 1681, and ordered that there should be three Conformists, and three Nonconformists, to attend him to his grave.

SILVERTON [R. S. 51*l.* 8s. 4*d.*] Mr. NATHANIEL BYFIELD. Dr. *Walker* says, he never paid Mr. *Cotton,* the sequestered minister, his fifths ; at the same time owning. that possibly the recovery of some of his temporal estates might exclude him from a title to that benefit ; so that the circumstance ought not to have been mentioned. It is very

likely

likely that the true reason why such allowance was not made to several other persons, where the same complaint is brought, was, their being in such circumstances as not to need it; in which case they had no claim.

SOUTHBRENT [V. S. 300l.] CHRISTOPHER JELLIN-GER, M. A. He was born in the palatinate of the Rhine, near *Wormes*, in the hereditary dominions of Frederic king of Bohemia, at whose court he resided when he was in *Holland*. He studied at *Newhouse* college, in the lower palatinate, and afterwards at *Basil* and at *Leyden*. He was forced to become a soldier in the German wars, and by that means lost all he had. He was once beset by the enemy's horse in a wood, and with difficulty saved his life. He afterwards farther pursued his studies at *Geneva*, from whence he was invited into England by Mr. *White*, of Dorchester. On coming to Exeter he was liberally entertained by the magistrates and citizens. Bp. *Hall* held much free conversation with him, and preached a sermon on purpose to stir up the people to a bountiful contribution for the support of him and another exile, which he encouraged by his own example. Mr. *Jellinger* first preached in French and Dutch, and by degrees learnt to do it in English. At length he settled at *Stonehouse*, in this county, and was afterwards put into this living. After the Restoration, the marquis of Winchester offered to prefer him if he would conform, but he refused. His writings shew him not to have been a great man, but from his life which was published, he appears to have been a man of eminent piety; and Mr. *Stancliffe*, who was well acquainted with him, speaks of him as such: tho' Mr. *Prince*, a worthy neighbouring clergyman, in a letter to the author, says, " That he was not much admired for his prudence or judgment, and that he was not just to Mr. *Gandy*, the sequestered minister; a worthy man, who had a large family," Dr. *Walker* speaks of Mr. *Gandy's* wife as being cruelly turned out of doors by a party of horse; but Mr. *Jellinger* might not be answerable for this. He seems to have been of a melancholy disposition, and had some peculiarities in his conduct. Among other things, he would frequently rise at midnight to pray and sing psalms. When he left South Brent he removed to *Marldon*, not far from Totness; and at last settled at *Kingsbridge*. He continued to preach when he was very old; and died at Kingsbridge, at about 83 years of age.

WORKS,

WORKS. Disputatio Theol. de Sacra Cœna.—The Rose of Sharon.—Christ and his Saints, &c. a Disc. on Canticles.—A Cluster of the sweetst Grapes; a Disc. of Assurance.—Fifteen Conferences with Christ.—A new and living Way of dying; on *Heb.* xi. 13.—A new Canaan for the Saints Delight, &c.—Heaven won by Violence.—The Spiritual Merchant.—The invaluable Worth of Man's Soul.—The Usurer cast; on *Ps.* xv. 5.—Usury stated and overthrown.—Godliness epitomized.—Unio sacra : or a Holy Union proposed to the divided Protestants.

SOWTON [V. S.] JOHN MORTIMER, B. A. Of *Oxford University.* He was born in *Exeter;* where his father was a plain tradesman. His mother was sister to Dr. *Manton.* He was very studious and serious ; so conversant with the holy scripture, and of such a memory, that if any one mentioned a passage, he would readily tell the chapter and verse. After being silenced he was reduced to great difficulties, upon which he went to London, to his uncle *Manton,* who procured him some employment in private families, by which he earned a subsistence. In the time of the plague, he often preached in the public churches. In the fire of London, in 1666, he lost his books, together with all the notes of his sermons. On his return into the country, the plague happened to break out there ; which was ascribed to his having brought the infection ; upon which he and his wife were cruelly sent to the Pest-house, where those that had the distemper were confined : but providence preserved them both, so that they never caught it. He afterwards removed to Exeter, where he continued many years. But having a large family of children, he found it difficult to provide for them, and was at last reduced so low as to be under the necessity of absconding, thro' fear of being seized for debt. As he was walking along the road he met a man driving some sheep, whom he endeavored to avoid. But the man came up to him, and put a paper into his hand, which contained a sum of money. He immediately returned to his wife, who had been greatly dejected, and gave her the paper. On opening it, they found nothing written but these words : TO PREACH PROVIDENCE. The whole family, as might easily be supposed, were not a little affected on the receipt of so seasonable a supply, in so remarkable a manner. Mr. Mortimer died at Exeter, 1696, aged 6§.

STAVERTON [V. 32*l.* 14*s.* 8*d.*] Mr. JOHN HORSHAM. Dr. *Walker* says, he. was dispossessed of this living for Nonconformity in 1662; and intimates, " that there was one, of both these names, possessed of this vicarage before the wars." There is no reason to question his being the same person; but nothing more is known concerning him.

STOKE-CANON. Mr. JOHN JORDAN, of *Camb. Univ.* Born in St. Petrock's parish, *Exeter,* of religious parents, who lived in good repute, and were allied to considerable families. His mother was one of the founders of an hospital, in that city, to which she gave 500*l.* In his youth he went abroad, and on his return was entered a student at *Cambridge.* In 1655, the Lord Chief Baron Steel, and Sir J. Thoroughgood, Kt. presented him to this living. On *Feb.* 21, 1662, he was warned by the dean and chapter of Exeter, to leave his place. He was a very religious and charitable man, and a very laborious minister. He continued a Nonconformist to his death, tho' he was always poor. He lived to be upwards of 80 years of age.

STOKE-DAMAREL. [See SALTALSH, CORNWAL.]

STOKENHAM [V. S. 48*l.* 7*s.* 7*d.*] BENJAMIN CLELAND, M. A. He was some time at St. Petrock's, in *Dartmouth,* and removed from thence to Stokenham. He was of an advanced age when ejected, and continued a Nonconformist. On *Charles* II.'s coming to Dartmouth, in *July,* 1671, by the interest of his great friend and patron Sir *John Fowel* with the king, he was indulged the liberty again to exercise his ministry at *St. Petrock's,* without being obliged to any other terms of conformity than the bare reading of a few prayers, and such of them only as he chose. He rejoiced in this opportunity of employing his excellent talents, and faithfully discharged the duties of his ministry, till being superannuated, he was obliged to desist from his beloved work, and retire to a private life, He spent the short remainder of his days chiefly at *Pottlemouth,* about ten miles from Dartmouth, where he had an estate. As he was going to visit his son, the minister of *Ashprington,* he was taken ill on the road, and with difficulty got to the end of his journey; when he told his son he was come to die; which accordingly he soon did. He was a man of great worth; a very grave and solid divine; eminent for ministerial abilities, activity, zeal and piety. He was a *Boanerges*

in

in the pulpit, and his ministry was attended with great success ; his people, who were before very ignorant and profane, being reformed, and many of them becoming truly serious.

WORKS: The Saint's Encouragement ; shewing how to ease our troubled Hearts by believing in God and in Jesus Christ.

STOKE-FLEMMING [R. S. 200*l*.] WILLIAM BAI-LEY, M. A. Of *New Col. Oxf.* He was born of a very good and genteel family, at *Ashlington*, near Devizes. After a liberal education in the country, he was sent young to *Oxford*, where he made considerable improvements in learning. When he quitted the university, his father would have purchased a good living for him ; but he would by no means admit of it, as judging such traffic unlawful. Before the civil war he was three years chaplain to Lord *Roberts*, who always treated him with singular respect. He married a niece of Mr. *F. Rous*, provost of Eton. He was first settled at *Tamerton*, near Plymouth ; but the war breaking out soon after, he was so threatened by the neighbouring cavaliers, that he was forced, under many difficulties, to retire with his family to London by water. There he got a good living about fifteen miles from the city, and continued in it a year, when he was persuaded by some members of parliament to accept of the sequestered living of *Stoke-Flemming*, which he did, to his own injury ; for —— *Nicols*, Esq. of Cornwal (his wife's cousin-german) offered him at the same time a mort-living, which was in his gift, of 300*l. per ann.* and was displeased with him for refusing his kindness. He was induced to give *Stoke-Flemming* the preference, by the pressing solicitations of his pious wife, who knew the miserable state of that parish, which being over-run with ignorance and profaneness, wanted such a minister. There he continued discharging the duties of his office with great fidelity till the Restoration, being generally respected and beloved by the parishioners, and particularly by some of very different sentiments from his own : insomuch that upon the turn of the times, Mr. *T. Southcot*, a leading man, tho' a high cavalier, would fain have persuaded Mr. *Bailey* to conform, as the fittest man for that place ; and would have engaged, upon that condition, for his continuance in it. When his more stated labours were at an end, he did not lead an idle inactive life, but readily assisted his neighbouring brethren till *August*, 1662. when he was wholly silenced.

lenced. He afterwards grew melancholy, and was seized
with a palsy, which held him to his death, *Nov.* 23, 1672.
He was a grave solid divine, a hard student, of uncommon
learning, great ministerial abilities, a most judicious preacher,
and eminent for his meekness, humility and patience, under
all his sufferings. Dr. *Walker* lays several things to his
charge, which are confuted by Dr. *Calamy (Contin.* p. 277.)
Mrs. Burnegham, Mr. *Bailey's* aunt, by the mother's side,
was at the expence of educating the famous Abp. *Laud*, as
he himself, when at the height of his preferment, frankly
and gratefully acknowledged, On this account Mr. *Bailey*
might have expected some little favor from that prelate, but
found none.

. TALLATON [R. 32*l*, 2*s.* 9¼*d.*] ROBERT COLLINS,
M. A. After his ejectment he lived at *Ottery St. Mary*,
where he had an estate of about 100*l. per ann.* He was much
respected by the good people of the town and the places adjacent, who usually attended on his ministry in the public
church, and were now desirous to enjoy it in a more private
way. He preached therefore in his own house, between the
morning and afternoon service; and usually, with his family,
attended the public worship in the afternoon. He lived very
peaceably till the Conventicle-act took place : but then his
house was surrounded, on the Lord's-day, *(Sept.* 1670) with
the officers, and the vilest rabble of the town ; who not
daring to break open the doors till they had got a warrant from
a neighbouring justice, kept the congregation prisoners till
night, when the warrant came. When the doors were opened,
he and the people were uncivilly treated, both by the gentlemen and the mob. Getting the names of whom they pleased,
and taking some into custody, warrants were issued out for
levying 20*l.* on Mr. *Collins* for preaching, 20*l.* for his
house, and 5*s*, on each of the hearers, tho' there was no
proof that there was any preaching or praying at all. Tho'
they fined Mr. *Collins* 20*l.* for his house, yet it deserves a
remark, that there was no person found there, but in a neighbour's house adjoining. After this followed much other business of the same kind, in this neighbourhood : breaking
open of houses and shops, taking away goods and wares ;
forcing open gates, driving off cattle, and exposing them to
sale, for the raising of the fines. Many were deprived of
what they could ill spare from their families.

Some

Some time after this, when there was no service in the public church, Mr. *Collins* ventured again to open his doors to all that would come. But a warrant was soon procured from Sir *Peter Prideaux* for apprehending him ; and he, with several others, were brought before Sir *Peter*, who treated them with great inhumanity, calling Mr. *Collins* a minister of the devil, and using other scurrilous language ; and when Mr. *Collins* offered to reply, threatened him with a jail, interlacing his words with oaths and curses. When the witnesses were examined, they affirmed, that on such a Lord's-day, they heard Mr. *Collins* preach or pray, but were not certain which it was. On Saturday, *Oct.* 1, the officers came with a warrant to levy 40*l.* on him, for which they drove away sixteen bullocks out of his ground. After this he appealed from the justice to the quarter-sessions, and the record being produced and read (not till the third sessions) an error was found in it ; which was, That Mr. *Collins* was convicted of " Teaching, or preaching, or praying," but of neither, positively or certainly. His counsel insisted much on this, and Sir *T. Carew* being the chairman, said he thought it a fundamental error, and that he could not in judgment or conscience pass it over. All seemed inclined to relieve Mr. *Collins* except some few justices, one of whom said, " That Presbyterian preaching and praying was all one ; for they in their prayers would undertake to teach almighty God." Mr. *Isaac*, counsel for the prosecutor, prayed the bench to call for a dictionary, and said, there they would find that *prædicare* and *orare* were the same. This business was discussd more or less several days. Mr. *Collins* in the mean time was assured that, if he would submit to the court, he should have favor. His friends advised him by all means to submit, and accordingly he did so. Upon which, some of the court smiled, and muttered; " Now he has withdrawn his appeal, and confessed himself guilty ; which could not have been proved against him ; so that he is at our mercy." After this, not a word passed in his favor, so that he was left to pay the whole ; and they put 20*l.* more upon him, as treble costs for his unjust appeal.

On *Aug.* 20, 1675, there being no service in the parish church, many considerable inhabitants of *Ottery*, desired Mr. *Collins* to preach there, but he refused, and preached at his own house near it, which was a large handsome building, where persons of all ranks and persuasions thronged to hear him, both morning and afternoon. About five weeks after, some

some poor men of the town were sent for by justice *Hayden* ;
and being threatened and flattered, against their consciences
convicted Mr. *Collins* and several others of a conventicle,
on the 5th of *September*. Whereas there was no meeting
at all that day, but the persons convicted were at church.
However 20*l*. was laid upon Mr. *Collins*, and levied on his
goods ; 10*l*. on W. Ledgingham, Esq. for persons unable
and unknown ; 9*l*. 15*s*. on Mr. M. Streatchleigh ; 5*l*. on
Mr. Farrington, for being an officer and knowing of a
meeting, but not discovering it, when there was none at all
that month. Many lesser sums were laid and levied on other
persons, some of whom appealed, and proved they were at
no meeting that day, but at church : and yet they had treble
costs laid upon them for their appeal. The money, thus
levied, never appeared to have been applied as the act
directed.

On *Aug.* 20, 1679, Mr. *Hayden* with several officers,
upon suspicion of a meeting at Mr. *Collins*'s house, came
and broke open his gates and doors, entered his house, and
made a strict search, but found nobody there to make a meeting : however, finding afterwards that some had been there,
they got the names of twenty-three persons, and at the next
sessions indicted them for a riot, or unlawful assembly, at
Mr. *Collins*'s house : and tho' these persons were all in one
indictment, for one pretended offence, and some of them
men and their wives, yet the clerk of the peace made them
pay distinct fees ; but this was removed by a *certiorari*.—
On *May* 15, 1681, Mr. *Hayden* with several officers, but
upon mere suspicion, beset Mr. *Collins*'s house, and demanded entrance ; but being denied, broke first the great
gate, and then the door of the house. Upon search, they
found only three persons, of whom they could make no conviction ; but Mr. *Collins* had no recompence for the damage
he sustained. On *May* 25, 1681, as he and his wife were attending a funeral on horseback, a constable by a warrant
from Mr. *Hayden*, seized them both ; but at length let his
wife go, and carried him to the constable's house, and kept
him there under guard night and day, from Wednesday to
Friday ; when he was brought before Mr. *Hayden*, and had
the corporation oath tendered. Upon his refusing it, Mr.
Hayden sent him to the high jail (tho' 1000*l*. bail was
offered) where he lay six months with the common prisoners ; one of whom there was ground to hope that he was
an instrument in converting, who was condemned to be executed.   In

In 1682, Mr. *Collins* was convicted for two months absence from church, for which 16*l.* was levied on his goods; and the bailiff had 5*l.* more for taking distress. He was also often prosecuted in the ecclesiastical courts, for his Nonconformity, for fifteen years together; for not bringing his children to public baptism, nor receiving the sacrament, &c. for which he was excommunicated, and had a *capias* issued out against him. He was likewise frequently indicted at the assizes and the sessions, upon the statute of 23 *Eliz.* He and his wife and servants were also many times indicted upon 1 *Eliz.* for twelve pence a Sunday for not being at church; tho' he could not attend on account of his being excommunicated. At every sessions the justices would take no presentment from the officers, and at every visitation the court-holders would take no presentment from the wardens, unless Mr. Collins was inserted; so that both were forced unwillingly to give him disturbance. He was also prosecuted for living within five miles of the place where he had been minister. All which prosecutions bore so hard upon him, that he was at length obliged to leave his family, and at last was forced to quit the kingdom, and withdraw into *Holland*, by which he lost several hundred pounds; and he was obliged to sell a very handsome mansion-house, and a fine estate adjoining, to maintain himself and family in their distracted condition. But notwithstanding his sufferings were so great, he lived to be near 80 years of age. His funeral sermon was preached by Mr. *G. Trosse*, of Exeter. He was a grave and pious man. At his death he left 20*l.* towards building a new meeting. It was remarkable, that the high-constable was taken ill the day that Mr. *Collins* was seized, and died the Lord's-day following.

TAMERTON [V.] Mr. ROBERT WYNE. Nothing more is known of him than that he published the following

WORKS. Elysii Campi: A Paradise of Delights, in two Discourses. 1. The Confirmation of the Covenant, on Heb. vi, 17, 18. 2. The Donation of Christ, on Rom. viii. 32.

North TAWTON [R.] Mr. MAYNARD. He was an old man when he was ejected; but notwithstanding this, he met with severe usage. Soon after his ejectment he was threatened with being sent to the work-house, by justice G—, who told him that he should there hear better preaching than his own, and asked him, Who made him a preacher? Mr.
Maynard

Maynard assured him that he had been episcopally ordained. But this procured him no favor : the justice replied, " I hear you teach children to suck in rebellion : you ought to be . banished the realm, and if you return, to be cut asunder."

TAVISTOCK [V.] THOMAS LARKHAM, M. A. Of *Jesus Col. Camb.* Born *May* 4, 1601, at *Lime*, in Dorsetshire. He was first settled in the ministry at *Northam*, in this county. Being of the Puritan stamp, he was so followed with vexatious prosecutions, that, in a little time, he had been a sufferer in almost all the courts of England. He was in the Star-chamber and High-commission court at the same time. He was articled against in the Consistory, at Exeter, and under a suit of pretended slander, for reproving an atheistical wretch, under the name of an atheist ; and pursuivants came upon him, one on the back of another, till at last (to use his own words) by the tyranny of the Bishops, and the tenderness of his conscience, he was forced as an exile into New-England. Tho' he there sojourned in a land that he knew not, God was with him. After some time he returned, when he was chosen by the inhabitants of *Tavistock* as their pastor, the noble earl of *Bedford* having promised to present and pay whomsoever they chose. In this place his labours were crowned with more than ordinary success. One Mr. *Wilcox*, of Linkinhorn, in Cornwal, going to hear him on a lecture-day, merely with a design to divert himself, came away pricked at the heart, and retained a particular respect for him ever after. One Mr. *Watts*, who lived in the same town with him, published some scurrilous pamphlets against him ; but some time after, openly professed his sorrow, and begged his pardon. When Mr. *Larkham* died, this Mr. *Watts* wished his own soul in his soul's stead, and respected his memory as long as he lived ; and in his will (in which he settled an estate in the hands of trustees for pious uses) he expressed his abhorrence of his own pamphlets as " idle and wretched performances ;" adding, that " he wrote them in his " youthful years, and did not stick to cast dirt on others, for " the clearing himself."

Mr. *Larkham* met with his share of trouble after his ejectment, and at last died in the town where he had lived and laboured, confined in the house of his son-in-law, not daring to stir abroad for fear of a jail. The malice of some followed him even after his death, for they would have pre-

vented

vented his being interred in the church. But the steward of the earl of *Bedford* interposed, and he was buried in that part of the chancel which belonged to that noble family. He died 1669, aged 68, lamented by pious persons of all persuasions in those parts. He was a man of great sincerity, strict piety, and good learning. He had been chaplain for some time to Sir Hardress Waller, and the father of Mr. G. Larkham, of Cockermouth.

WORKS. Sermons on the Attributes of God——The Wedding Supper.—A Discourse on paying Tythes.

THORNCOMBE [V.] Mr. Nicholas Wakely. When the Act of Uniformity was about to pass, he was at first under great concern for fear of want, if he should refuse to comply with it, having a wife and seven children, with nothing to maintain them ; and on that account was tempted to conform. But at length, upon close consideration, he resolved to cast himself upon God and his providence ; of which he had no cause to repent, for he was remarkably provided for quickly after, by the death of a relation, upon whose decease 40*l.* a year came into his family. He was a lively, affecting preacher, and an excellent man, both in the pulpit and out of it.

TIVERTON. Theophilus Polwheil, M. A. Of *Eman. Col. Camb.* where Dr. (afterwards Abp.) *Sancroft,* was his tutor, and he became Fellow of the college. He was born in Cornwal. When he left the university he was for some time preacher in *Carlisle.* He was one of the committee appointed for ejecting scandalous ministers, &c. in 1654, for Cumberland, Durham, &c. This year he removed to *Tiverton,* where he continued till the Restoration. After the Act of uniformity took place, he had his share of sufferings with the rest of his brethren. One Mr. F——t, who had joined in communion with him, and given in his experiences before the church, afterwards became his furious persecutor. Once, when this man was mayor, he disturbed the meeting while Mr. *Polwheil* was preaching, requiring him to come down, and committing him to the custody of a serjeant. A Mr. C——n was also his great enemy, and had once formed a design to seize him as he was going out of his house, before break of day; but one *Berry,* a serjeant, discovered the plan and prevented the execution of it. But he outlived those times of persecution, and

and after K. *James's* liberty, he opened a meeting in *Tiver's ton,* and invited Mr. *Samuel Bartlet* to assist him. He died in a good old age, in *April,* 1689.—What Dr. *Walker* relates to his disadvantage is refuted in *Cal. Contin.* p. 261.

WORKS. A Treatise on Self-denial.—The evil of Apostacy and quenching the Spirit...Of Ejaculatory Prayer.—Directions for serving God on the Working-day and on the Lord's-day.—Exhortations to holy Living, in which Mr. Mall assisted.

—— Mr. JOHN CHISUL. Of *Oxf.* university. He came to *Tiverton* from *Enfield,* in Middlesex, where he kept a boarding-school (to which several eminent citizens sent their sons) and preached occasionally. One Mr. *Foot* was the chief cause of his removal. He was a very lively florid preacher, and of a courteous obliging temper. Dr. *Walker* relates some scandalous stories of him, which Dr. *Calamy* proves utterly groundless *(Contin.* p. 263.) These are told on the credit of one Mr. *Newte,* whom Dr. Walker calls *reverend and worthy.*† The following anecdote will shew what regard is to be paid to this man's word, and to some of Dr. *Walker's* stories. A certain person had charged Mr. *Newte* with inconstancy, alledging " That he was zealous for K. *James,* and had prayed for his prince of *Wales;* and that upon the Revolution he had taken the oaths to K. *William,* and had prayed for *him;* and yet, that after his death he had said, It had been well for the nation if he had died seven years sooner." Mr. *Newte* strongly denied that he had ever prayed for the prince of *Wales.* His clerk being present (an old man much respected) it was proposed that he should be asked about it. Upon which the old man replied, " Yes sure, master, you did pray for him ; and I said *Amen* to it."

WORKS. The Almost Christian, and young Man's Memento. —Seasonable Thoughts of Divine Providence. 1666.—A Word to Israel in the Wilderness; on *Heb.* iii. 8, 9.—A Poem prefixed to Dr. Teate's Poems on the Trinity.

† His father, the sequestered minister of this place, appears to have deserved this character. See Prince's Worthies of Devon, p. 476, &c.

Dr. Calamy relates that Dr. Chisul, a physician, who died at Tiverton, in 1717, wrote a Latin letter to Dr. Walker, in which he challenged him about the untruths he had published, to wound the reputation of very worthy men, and defied Mr. Newte to produce one credible witness for what he had reported of this Mr. Chisel; adding, that " Mr. Newte was a scurrilous fellow, not worthy to carry his father's books."

⁎ Great

Ridley. sc.

Mr. John Howe,

from an Original Picture in the Possession of the Author.

Published by Button & Son, Paternoster Row.

*** Great TORRINGTON [R. 64*l*. 17*s*. 10*d*.] JOHN HOWE, M. A. Of *Christ's Col. Camb.* Afterwards of *Oxford.* Mr. *Wood* says, of *Braz. Nose Col.* This great man was born *May* 17, 1630, at *Loughborough*, in Leicestershire, where his father was settled by Abp. *Laud*, but afterwards turned out by him for siding with the Puritans, and driven into Ireland ; whither he took his son, then very young, and where their lives were remarkably preserved during the execrable rebellion and massacre. In the time of the war, the father returned and settled in Lancashire, where his son had his grammar-learning. He was sent early to college, where his great attainments in literature, joined with his exemplary piety, so recommended him, that he was elected Fellow of *Magd. Col.* after he had been made *Demy* by the parliament visitors. At this time Dr. *Goodwin* was president of that college, and had gathered a church among his scholars ; of which Mr. *Howe*, at the Dr.'s own motion, became a member. (See vol, 1. p. 240.) He was ordained at *Winwick*, in Lancashire, by Mr. *C. Herle*, the pastor of that church, and the ministers who officiated in the several chapels in this parish ; on which account he would sometimes say, that he thought few in modern times had so truly primitive an ordination, for he considered Mr. *Herle* as a primitive bishop. By an unexpected event of providence he was called to *Torrington*, where, tho' young, he abundantly fulfilled his ministry, which was blessed with great success. He had a numerous auditory and a flourishing church, to which many of the inhabitants joined themselves, who belonged to an Independent church, at *Bideford*, having had a dismission from thence.

The manner in which he was used to carry on the service here, on *Fast-days* (which were frequent in those times) was very extraordinary. He began at nine o'clock with a prayer of a quarter of an hour—read and expounded scripture for about three quarters—prayed an hour—preached another—then prayed half an hour. The people then sung about a quarter of an hour, during which he retired and took a little refreshment. He then came into the pulpit again, prayed an hour more—preached another hour—and then with a prayer of half an hour concluded the service.—He was upon good terms with the neighbouring ministers, particularly with Mr. *George Hughes*, of Plymouth, whose daughter he married. With him he carried on a weekly correspondence in Latin. The following circumstance in one of them is remarkable: Mr. *Howe's* house being on fire, was extinguished by a seasonable shower. On that very day he received a letter from his father *Hughes*, which concluded with this prayer : *Sit* Ros *Cæli super habitaculum vestrum.* i. e. *Let the dew of heaven be upon your dwelling.*

The manner in which Mr. *Howe* became chaplain to *Cromwell*, was related in a former article. (See page 17.) He entered upon this office with great reluctance, and never abused the influence it gave him, to injure others, or to enrich himself ; but used it to serve the interest of religion and learning among persons of very different sentiments. His conduct in respect to Dr. *Seth Ward*, afterwards Bp. of *Exeter*, deserves particular notice. The Dr. applied, by means of Mr. *Howe*, for the Principalship of *Jesus* college; but it had been promised to another. However Mr. *Howe* so strongly recommended him to the Protector, that he gave him an annual allowance equivalent to it ; and the Dr. retained a grateful sense of the favor, when, upon the change of times, he became a greater man. Mr. *Howe* always appeared so disinterested, that the Protector once said to him, " You have obtained many favors for others, I wonder when the time is to come that you will move for something for yourself and family." This distinguished principle made him faithful in the discharge of his duty. The following is a remarkable instance of it : The notion of *a particular faith in prayer*, with respect to the obtaining of particular blessings, had prevailed much at *Cromwell's* court, and Mr. *Howe* once heard a sermon there from a person of note, designed to defend it. Being fully convinced of the ill tendency of such an opinion, he thought himself bound in conscience, when it came to his turn to preach, to oppose it ; which accordingly he did with great plainness.* *Cromwell* heard with great attention, but sometimes frowned and discovered great uneasiness, insomuch that a person who was present told Mr. *Howe*, it would be difficult ever to make his peace with him again. Mr. *Howe* replied, " I have discharged my conscience, and leave the event with God." Nothing however passed between them on the subject, tho' *Cromwell* seemed cooler towards him than before.

After *Richard Cromwell* was set aside, Mr. *Howe* returned to his people at *Torrington*. At the Restoration he met with some trouble, being informed against as delivering

* The substance of the discourse may be seen at the end of *The Memoirs of Mr. Howe*, by Dr. *Calamy*, from which this account is extracted.

something

something treasonable in the pulpit, but was honorably acquitted. When the Act of uniformity took place, he quitted his public station in the church, and became a silenced Nonconformist, after having preached two affecting sermons to his people on *Bartholomew*-day, in which he gave them some reasons why he could not comply with the act. Dr. (afterwards Bp.) *Wilkins* (with whom he had maintained a long intimacy) on seeing him some time after this, expressed his surprize that a man of Mr. *Howe*'s latitude should have stood out. Upon which Mr. *Howe* told him, that he would gladly have been under the establishment if he could have compassed it with satisfaction to his conscience; but that, having weighed the matter with all possible impartiality, he could not do it; and that his *latitude* was the very thing that made him a Nonconformist. The Dr. appeared satisfied, and advised him as a friend to stand to his principles. Mr. *Howe* continued some time in Devonshire, preaching in private houses as he had opportunity. Being acquainted that an officer of the Bishop's court had enquired after him, and left word that a citation was out against him, he rode to *Exeter*, where he met with a friend who acquainted the Bishop that Mr. *Howe* was there; upon which his Lordship expressed a desire to see him, and received him with great civility, as his old acquaintance, but expostulated with him about his Nonconformity, and desired to know the reasons. Mr. *Howe* waving others, only mentioned Re-ordination. "Why pray, Sir, (said the Bishop) what hurt is there in being re-ordained?"—"Hurt, my Lord, (said Mr. *Howe*) it is shocking: it hurts my understanding: it is an absurdity; for nothing can have two beginnings." The Bishop dropping the matter, told him, as he had done at other times, That if he would come in among them he might have considerable preferments; and dismissed him in a friendly manner, without any thing being said on either side about the process that was issued out against him.

In 1665 he took the oath required by the *Oxford*-act, upon the principle befor. mentioned (p. 30) but was this year imprisoned two months in the isle of *St. Nicholas*; tho' upon what occasion doth not appear. During this confinement he wrote the following letter to his father *Hughes*:

"Blessed be God that we shall have, and hear of each other's occasions of thanksgiving, that we may join praises as well as prayers, which I hope is done daily for one another. Nearer approaches, and constant adherence to God,

G 2   with

with the improvement of our interest in each other's hearts,
must compensate (and I hope will abundantly) the unkindness and instability of a surly treacherous world, that we
see still retains its wayward temper, and grows more
peevish, as it grows older, and more ingenious in inventing
ways to torment whom it disaffects. It was, it seems, not
enough to kill by one single death, but when that was almost
done, to give leave and time to respire, to live again, at least
in hope, that it might have the renewed pleasure of putting
us to a farther pain and torture in dying once more. Spite is
natural to her: all her kindness is an artificial disguise: a
device to promote and serve the design of the former, with
the more efficacious and piercing malignity. But patience
will elude the design, and blunt its sharpest edge. It is perfectly defeated, when nothing is expected from it but mischief: for then the worst it can threaten finds us provided,
and the best it can promise, incredulous, and not apt to be
imposed upon. This will make it at last despair and grow
hopeless, when it finds, that the more it goes about to mock
and vex us, the more it teaches and instructs us: and that as
it is wickeder, we are wiser. If we cannot, God will out-
wit it, and carry us, I trust, safe thro', to a better world,
upon which we may terminate hopes that will never make us
ashamed."

In 1671, being reduced to straits, he accepted an invitation from a person of quality in *Ireland*. Being detained
by contrary winds on the *Welch* coast (probably at *Holyhead*)
he continued there a Lord's-day. The company, being desirous he should preach to them, were seeking a convenient
place, when they met the parish minister and his clerk riding
to the town. One of them asked the clerk whether his
master preached that day? who answered, "No; my
master does not use to preach; he only reads prayers." On
being asked further, whether he would give leave for a minister, who was there, to use his pulpit, he replied, "Very
willingly;" which accordingly he did. Mr. *Howe* preached.
In the afternoon the audience was very large, and seemed
much affected. The wind continued contrary all the week.
The next Lord's-day there was a prodigious multitude gathered together; and the clergyman, having no expectation
of further assistance, was in great consternation, being not
able to preach himself, and thinking if there was no preaching it would greatly lessen his reputation. He therefore sent
his clerk to Mr. *Howe*, and begged he would come and
preach

preach again, as otherwise he knew not what to do, the country being come in for several miles to hear him. Mr. *Howe*, being much indisposed, was in bed, and in a perspiration. But considering it as a plain call of Providence, he cooled himself as speedily as he could with safety, and casting himself on God, went and preached with great freedom. He said he never saw people more moved, and that if ever his ministry was of use, it was then. Very soon after, the vessel sailed, and he felt no ill effects.

In *Ireland* he lived as chaplain to the Lord *Massarine* at *Antrim*, where he was universally respected, and enjoyed the particular respect of the Bishop of that diocese, who, together with his metropolitan, gave him liberty to preach without any conformity, in the public church, every Lord's-day afternooon. And the Abp. at a meeting of the clergy, told them, that he would have every pulpit, where he had any concern, open to Mr. *Howe*. By his preaching and conversation here he was useful to many. Upon the death of Dr. *Seaman*, 1675, he was invited by a part of his congregation to fix in *London*. After mature deliberation, and weighing the arguments on both sides, which he drew out in writing, (see *Memoirs*, p. 59, &c.) he consented to go, and made a peaceable use of K. *Charles's* Indulgence. He preached to a considerable and judicious audience, and was much respected not only by his brethren among the Dissenters, but by several eminent divines of the church of *England*, v. g. Drs. *Whitchcote, Kidder, Fowler, Lucas,* &c.

In regard to the steps taken in order to a coalition between the Church and the Dissenters, some of the dignified clergy sent for Mr. *Howe* to their houses (v. g. Lloyd, *Sherlock*, &c.) and expressed great deference to his opinion. He had a particular intimacy with Dr. *Tillotson* (afterwards Abp.) in respect to whom the following anecdote is worthy of notice. The dean, as he was then (1680) preached a sermon at court, on *Josh.* xxiv. 15. in which he asserted, that, " No man is obliged to preach against the religion of a " country, tho' a false one, unless he has the power of " working miracles." K. *Charles* slept most of the time. When the sermon was over, a certain nobleman said to him, " It's pity your majesty slept, for we have had the rarest piece of *Hobbism* that ever you heard in your life."— " Odds fish, (said the king) he shall print it then ;" and immediately called the Lord chamberlain to give his command to the dean for this purpose. When the sermon came from

the

the press, the dean, as was usual with him, sent it as a present to Mr. *Howe*, who, on the perusal, was grieved to find a sentiment which had so ill a tendency, and drew up a long letter, in which he freely expostulated with the dean for giving such a wound to the Reformation, and carried the letter himself. The dean, upon the sight of it, proposed a little journey into the country, that they might talk the matter over without interruption. Mr. *Howe* enlarged on the contents of the letter as they travelled in the chariot. The good dean at length wept, and said, This was the most unhappy thing that had befallen him for a long time; owned that what he had asserted was not to be maintained, and urged in his excuse, that he had but little notice of preaching that day, and none of printing the sermon.

When, in 1684, *Barlow* Bp. of *Lincoln*, printed a letter for putting in execution the laws against Dissenters, Mr. *Howe* wrote a free answer to it, of which a copy may be seen in his *Memoirs*, p. 104—112. The next year, the prospect of the Dissenters being very dark, he accepted an invitation of Lord *Wharton* to travel with him abroad. In the course of his travels, he had the satisfaction to converse with a number of learned Papists, and Protestant divines. In 1686, having no encouragement to return, he settled at *Utrecht*, where the Earl of *Sunderland* and his Countess, some English gentlemen, and two of his own nephews, boarded with him. During this time, he took his turn with Mr. *Mat. Mead*, and others, who were there also, in preaching at the English church; and in the evening preached to his own family. He was of great use to several English students then at the university, and was much respected by its professors, as well as by several persons of distinction from England; among whom was Dr. *Gilbert Burnet*, afterwards Bp. of *Sarum*, with whom he had much free conversation. The Prince of *Orange*, afterwards *William* III. admitted him several times into his presence, and discoursed with him with great freedom; as he sometimes did, after he ascended the British throne.

Upon K. *James's* Declaration for liberty of conscience, in 1687, Mr. *Howe's* congregation in London earnestly pressed his return, and he readily complied. He waited upon the Prince of *Orange* first, who advised him to be cautious of addressing, and not to fall in with the measures of the court. He was thankful for a little breathing-time, and endeavoured to improve it to the best purposes, and to preserve

himself

himself and others from the snares laid for them, always declaring against an approbation of the dispensing power. Upon
the glorious Revolution, he addressed the prince of *Orange*,
at the head of the dissenting ministers, in a handsome speech,
which may be seen *Memoirs*, p. 142. On the passing the
Toleration-act, he addressed a small tract both to Conformists and Dissenters, with a view to promote mutual forbearance. With the same truly christian design, he afterwards
published his sermon on the *Carnality of religious contentions*, when unhappy differences had taken place among the
dissenting ministers, occasioned chiefly by the reprinting
the works of Dr. *Crisp*, who, though a good man, was
noted for some *Antinomian* notions. These debates, however, issued in the exclusion of Mr. (afterwards Dr.) *Williams*
from the lecture at *Pinners-hall*, when Mr. *Howe*, Dr.
Bates, and Mr. *Alsop* joined him in carrying on a separate
lecture at *Salters-hall*. Warm debates soon followed, concerning the Trinity and Occasional-conformity, in which
Mr. *Howe* engaged with great moderation, christian meekness and charity; greatly lamenting the want of these in
others, and desiring to breathe a nobler air and inhabit a better region. The last thing he published was, *A Discourse
of patience in expecting future blessedness*. This was
what he himself had particular occasion for.

Having employed his time, strength and interest, in the
most valuable services, he was wasted with several diseases,
which he bore with great patience and a resigned submission
to the will of his heavenly Father. He discovered no fear
of dying, but when his end drew near, was very calm and
serene. [Having a mortification in his leg, his son, a physician, with a kind design, took the liberty to lance it without his leave; upon which Mr. *Howe* cried out, "What are
you doing? I am not afraid of *dying*, but I am afraid of
pain."] He seemed indeed sometimes to be got to heaven
even before he had laid aside mortality. He was once, during his decline, in a most affecting, heavenly frame at the
communion, and carried out into such a transporting cele-
bration of the love of Christ, that both he and the communicants were apprehensive he would have died in the service.
He was sometimes very pleasant in his last sickness, and conversed freely with the many persons of all ranks who came
to see him, and talked like an inhabitant of another world,
with the most elevated hopes of that blessedness on which
his heart had long been set; and once declared, after an un-

expected

expected revival, that were it put to his choice, whether he should die that moment or live seven years, he would prefer the former. [His hope of heaven was however accompanied with great humility, which led him to say, " I expect my salvation not as a profitable servant, but as a pardoned sinner."] Being at last worn out, he finished his course with joy, *April* 2, 1705; aged 65. His funeral sermon was preached by his fellow-labourer, Mr. *John Spademan,* on 2 *Tim.* iii. 14.

A more particular account of this eminent man might have been presented to the world, had he not, a little before his death, ordered his son to burn a large parcel of manuscripts which related to his life and times. On a blank page in his Bible were found two remarkable passages, written with his own hand in Latin, of which the following is a translation.
' *Dec.* 26. 89. After that I had long, seriously, and re-
' peatedly thought with myself, that besides a full and un-
' doubted assent to the objects of faith, a vivifying savoury
' taste and relish of them was also necessary, that with
' stronger force and more powerful energy, they might pene-
' trate into the most inward center of my heart, and there
' being most deeply fixed and rooted, govern my life ; and
' that there could be no other sure ground whereon to con-
' clude and pass a sound judgment on my good estate God-
' ward ; and after I had in my course of preaching been large-
' ly insisting on 2 *Cor.* i. 12. This very morning I awoke
' out of a most ravishing and delightful dream, that a won-
' derful and copious stream of celestial rays, from the lofty
' throne of the divine majesty, seemed to dart into my ex-
' panded breast. I have often since, with great complacen-
' cy, reflected on that very signal pledge of special divine
' favour vouchsafed to me on that noted memorable day,
' and have with repeated fresh pleasure tasted the delights
' thereof.'

. ' But what (on *Oct.* 22. 1704,) of the same kind I sensi-
' bly felt, through the admirable bounty of my God, and
' the most pleasant comforting influence of the Holy Spirit,
' far surpassed the most expressive words my thoughts can
' suggest. I then experienced an inexpressibly pleasant
' melting of heart, tears gushing out of mine eyes, for joy
' that God should shed abroad his love abundantly through
' the hearts of men, and that for this very purpose mine
' own should be so signally possessed of and by his blessed
' Spirit. *Rom.* v. 5.

Mr

Mr. *Howe* in person was tall and graceful. He had a piercing, but pleasant eye; and had that in his aspect which indicated something uncommonly great, and tended to excite veneration. To those who are at all acquainted with his writings, his intellectual accomplishments need no commendation. Even Mr. *Wood* passes a high encomium upon him; and, which is very extraordinary, upon his *style*, which is the most exceptionable of any thing in his performances. His ministerial qualifications were singular. He could preach extempore with as great exactness as many others upon the closest study. His sermons, which he always delivered without notes, were often of uncommon depth, especially at the beginning, but were plain in the sequel, and towards the close generally came home with great pungency to the consciences of the hearers. He had great copiousness and fluency in prayer. To hear him pray, upon sudden emergencies, would have been apt to make the greatest admirers of forms ashamed of the common cavils against free-prayer.* He was a person of remarkable prudence, and laid great stress upon it in others. He was very courteous to strangers, and never thought religion inconsistent with good breeding. He knew how to address himself with propriety to the greatest personages, and yet could condescend to the meanest. He was very affable to young ministers, and ever ready to offer them the kindest advice. He had a truly great soul, and seemed born to support generous principles, a truly catholic spirit, and an extensive charity. In many cases he discovered a remarkable sagacity, particularly in regard to public affairs and political manœuvres.

In conversation he was often very facetious. Some of his sudden repartees (especially against profaneness) deserve to be recorded. Being at dinner with some persons of fashion, a gentleman expatiated largely in praise of *Charles* I. and made some disagreeable reflections upon others. Mr. *Howe*, observing that the gentleman mixed many horrid oaths with his discourse, told him, that in his humble opinion he had omitted one great excellence in the character of that prince. Upon which, the gentleman pressed him to mention it, and seemed impatient to hear what it was. Mr. *Howe* then told

* An advocate for forms might object, that no argument for extemporary prayer can fairly be drawn for the manner in which Mr. *Howe* conducted it; and might naturally ask, whether it be always or generally performed in such a manner as to supersede the common arguments against it?

him

him it was this : " That he was never heard to swear an oath
" in common conversation." The gentleman took the reproof, and promised to break off the practice.—Another time
as he passed two persons of quality, who were talking with
great eagerness, and damned each other repeatedly, Mr. *Howe*,
taking off his hat, said to them, " I pray God SAVE you both,
" gentlemen :" for which they both gave him their thanks.
—At the time when the occasional conformity bill was de-
bated in parliament, he passed a noble lord in a chair in St.
James's-Park, who sent his footman to call him, desiring to
speak with him upon this subject. In the conversation,
speaking of the opponents of the Dissenters, the noble lord
said, *Damn these wretches, for they are mad*, &c. Mr;
Howe, who was no stranger to the nobleman, expressed
great satisfaction in the thought, that there is a God who go-
verns the world, who will finally make retribution to all according to their present character. " And He, my lord,
" (says Mr. *Howe*) has declared, That he will make a dif-
" ference *between him that sweareth, and him that feareth*
" *an oath*." The nobleman was struck with the hint, and
said, " I thank you, sir, for your freedom : I take your
meaning; and shall endeavour to make a good use of it."
Mr. *Howe* replied, " My lord, I have more reason to thank
" your lordship for saving me the most difficult part of a
" discourse, which is the *Application*."—As a further proof
of his happy talent for reproving this absurd vice, the following anecdote, transmitted by a nameless correspondent, is
worthy of being added. A certain nobleman with whom he
was at dinner, treated Mr. *Howe* with great respect, and requested him to say, in what manner he could effectually serve
him, strengthening his protestations of zeal with a multitude
of profane oaths. Mr. *Howe* replied, " There is one favour
" which I should be happy your lordship would grant me."
—My good Mr. *Howe*, replied the nobleman, impatiently,
with another oath, there is nothing that Mr. *Howe* can ask
but it will make me happy to grant. On which Mr. *Howe*
calmly said, " The only favour, my lord, which I have to beg
" of you, is, that your lordship will give me leave to swear
" the next oath."

In Dr. *Watts's* Lyric Poems is an admirable one addressed
to Mr. *John Howe ;* where is also an elegy on the death of Mr,
Gouge, in which is a fine encomium on that great man, then
supposed to be near his end.

WORKS.

WORKS. The Living Temple of God.—A Treatise of delighting in God.—The Blessedness of the Righteous; and the Vanity of Man as mortal.—The Redeemer's Tears wept over lost Souls.—The Reconcileableness of God's Prescience of the Sins of Men, with the Wisdom and Sincerity of his Exhortations and other Means to prevent them.—The possibility of a Trinity in the Godhead.—And many other Tracts and Sermons, collected since his death in two vols. fol.—[Also Several vols. of Sermons, taken in short-hand as they were preached, have since been published; *viz.* two by Dr. *Evans* and Dr. *Harris,* on the Spirit's Influence on the Church—and on particular Persons:—Another by Dr. *Evans,* on Family Religion, 12mo.—And two more by Mr. *Fletcher,* on the Love of God and our brother.]

TOTNESS. FRANCIS WHIDDON, M. A. of *Wadham Col. Oxf.* He was descended from an ancient and worshipful family, which was formerly posessed of some thousands a year. His grandfather was *Francis Whiddon,* Esq; of Whiddon in Chagford. His Father was that worthy divine Mr. *Francis Whiddon* of Moreton, author of *The Golden Topaz.* He was designed for the law, and placed in *Daffy's-Inn* in Fleet-street, London : but he did not stay there long, being desirous to be educated for the ministry. He continued seven years at Oxford, and took his degrees; though no notice is taken of him by Mr. *Wood.* After the death of his father, *Jan.* 5, 1656, he laid claim to *Morton Hampstead,* from whence Mr. *Robert Woolcomb* was afterwards ejected, and held it for some time : but at length, to end the competition with that good man, he preached on that text, *Let there be no strife between me and thee, for we are brethren:* and tho' his title to this living was not contemptible, for the sake of peace, he gave it up. He together with several others, was ordained to the ministry, by the laying on of the hands of the Presbytery, in the town of Dartmouth. He exercised his ministry in public for a while at *Totness* with universal approbation ; receiving great encouragement from his hearers, and being highly esteemed for his work's sake. He was very laborious in studying, preaching, catechizing, and visiting : but as for worldly affairs, he understood them little, and minded them less. God was pleased to bless him with great success in his ministry. But after the restoration of K. *Charles,* some of the people changed with the times. Thro' the illegal violence of the church-wardens, under the influence of two other persons, the church doors were shut against him, and he was ejected before his brethren, *June* 22, 1662. So that he had reason to complain, in his farewell sermon, that
" he

" he met with contempt and opposition; was shut out of the synagogue, and hindered from preaching any more in the name of the Lord:" He added, " It is somewhat my misery, that I am for the present alone in suffering. Had I enjoyed the same privilege my brethren do, you might have enjoyed my labours some weeks longer. But there is the hand of God in all this: I desire to submit, and say nothing." However he still continued in the town, and statedly preached twice on the Lord's-day, and at two weekly lectures, the one at *Totness*, and the other at *Bowden*, which is a mile distant.

In 1671, a country minister who was expected to preach at Totness-church, failing to come, Mr. *Eveleigh* the mayor, and Mr. *Gutheridge* a senior magistrate of the town, desired him to supply his place; which he did both parts of the day, to the general satisfaction of the magistrates and the rest of the auditors; and a young clergyman of his acquaintance read the prayers. Notice of this heinous crime was given to Dr. *Sparrow*, then Bishop of Exeter; to avoid whose displeasure, Mr. *Whiddon*, by the advice of friends, went to London, presented himself before the king, and begged his pardon; which he granted, and ordered the prosecution to be stopped. He was so well respected in the town, that when Mr. Gutheridge was mayor, he ordinarily attended upon his ministry in his formalities: but when Mr. T. Shapley came into that office, he disturbed him in his public meeting; and Mr. Arthur Rook did the same. The former required him to come down when he was preaching. He also frequently met with disturbance in his own and other private houses. Once having preached in his own house, he and Mr. Gutheridge, with about fifteen more of his hearers, were indicted at the assizes at Exeter for a riot. A gentleman of his name and family being foreman of the grand jury, argued that Mr. *Whiddon* being in his own house, could not be guilty of a riot, whatever the rest were: so that the bill was returned *ignoramus*. He was often put into the spiritual court, and had processes out against him; but the same gentleman, by his interest with Bishop *Sparrow*, preserved him from danger from that quarter. In times of great difficulty, he preached several times a day, only to four besides the family. Though he met with such severe treatment, yet his principles were very moderate, and his conversation inoffensive and peaceable. He lived in great amity with Mr. *Ford* (a worthy man, and of a healing spirit) as long as he was vicar of

Totness

Totness, and frequently attended the established church. He was greatly beloved by the best of the magistrates, and other inhabitants of the town, though hated and persecuted by some furious bigots.

As he was preaching in his own house, soon after a recovery from sickness, he broke a blood-vessel, and brought up such a quantity of blood as forced him to break off, to the great surprise and grief of his hearers. This was followed by a consumption, which in a few weeks brought him to his grave. He died *Sept* 21, 1679. His kinsman and dear friend, Mr. *E. Nosworthy* rector of Dipford, preached his funeral sermon, in which he speaks of his father's house as a nursery of piety and learning, and says of Mr. *Whiddon*, that, " He was a morning star, for his early shining with the light of grace and goodness. In the university he followed his studies with all commendable diligence ; and returned like another *Bezaleel*, well gifted for the service of the tabernacle. While he had the free use of his public ministry, he was a burning and shining light. For a kind neighbour and a constant friend, for his meekness and affability, sobriety, humility, &c. he may be termed another *Titus, Delicæ humani generis*. His charity was of universal extent. In giving, the bellies and backs of the poor did bless him : in forgiving, the sun of his life did not set in a cloud, The retaliation which he made to his worst enemies, was no other but his prayers and his pity. Though his sickness was long and his pain sharp, he endured both with christian patience ; never repining that God laid upon him so much, but praying, that he would lay no more than he might have strength to stand under. Of late one pulpit hath not held us ; but I trust, in due time, one heaven shall ; where there is no discord in the saints harmony ; where *Calvin* and *Luther* are made friends," &c.—Mr. *Prince* (the learned author of *the Worthies of Devonshire*) who was his near neighbour, speaks of him in a Letter to the author as " a curious preacher, and a most genteel, friendly, and courteous person."

He never published any thing : but his farewell sermons on *Zech.* i. 5, 6, were printed from the notes of a young man who wrote after him, intitled, *The last words of Mr. Whiddon.** In the close of the second sermon, he manifests his tender affection to his people in this manner ; " God is

* These are not inserted in the Country Collection of Farewell Sermons, where they might have been expected to be found.

my

my witness, whom I serve in the spirit, that I never sought
yours, but you.   I have had more comfort from my work,
than ever I had from received or expected wages; and can
still say from my soul, that I am willing to spend and to be
spent for you, since I have seen the seal of my ministry upon
the souls of many of you.   I prefer the liberty of preaching
among you, above all the profits and preferments in the world.
Take them, who love them, so I might enjoy the liberty of
my conscience, and the freedom of my ministry.   Perhaps
some of you will say, "What will he leave us for a trifle?
He might continue among us if he pleased."   O my brethren!
I could do any thing for your sakes, but only sin.   I may not
do evil that good may come of it.   I may not go against
my own light and conscience."—He left some valuable MSS.
on *John* xiv. and *Isaiah* liii.—It was observed by some of
his friends, that one of his persecutors actually destroyed
himself: another attempted it; and a third was seized with
horror on his death-bed.

Mr. JOHN GARRET.   He was fellow-labourer with Mr.
Whiddon, who, in his Farewell sermon, mentioned in the
foregoing article, speaks of Mr. *Garret* with great respect,
as having died in the same month that he himself was ejected,
viz. 13th *June*, 1662.   From his known character, there is
good reason to believe that he was, in intention and resolu-
sion, a sufferer for Nonconformity.   Mr. *Whiddon* expresses
himself thus: "It was but a few days since that God put an
end to the labours of your reverend minister, and my fellow-
labourer.   And now the Lord threatens to put an end to
mine; with this difference: He in respect of body, I in respect of office.   I have a happiness this day, which he could
not enjoy, to preach my own funeral: and I beseech you,
let the words of a dying man make some impression on your
hearts.   I look upon it as a wise providence, though a bitter
one, that we who lived together, should depart together.
You have heard many sermons from us both: never think
the worse of the word of God, because we suffer for it.   He
died to see the face of God, and is gone before to drink of
the rivers of pleasures; but I am reserved to a bitter cup.
However, shall I not drink of the cup that my Father will
have me drink of?   Well, he is gone; the Lord hath taken
him; he is better where he is, than where he was: you may
have time enough to confess his worth, and lament his
want," &c.

UXBOROUGH [V. 24*l.* 10*s.* 6*d.*] Mr. NATHAN JACOB, of *Univ. Col. Oxf.* Born in 1629. His father Mr. *John Jacob* was a major in the parliament army, and might have been a colonel under *Cromwell,* but refused all offers of preferment from that quarter. He lived many years in good reputation at *Totness,* being, after the Restoration, a captain in the militia. He designed this his son for the ministry from his cradle, if it should please God to qualify him for it; and his promising parts and early seriousness were such as raised the expectations of all that knew him. He was well furnished with grammar-learning at the age of fifteen; and continued an indefatigable student at Oxford about four years. He then went into the country to visit his friends, with a design to return. But Mr. *Garret* the vicar of Totness, and other ministers, observing his uncommon genius and improvement, persuaded his relations to use all their interest to prevail with him to enter upon the ministry immediately. Their importunity at last drew him into the pulpit, and after he had given them a proof of his great abilities, they left no means unattempted to prevent his return to Oxford, and to get him settled in the country; in which at length they succeeded. At first he assisted Mr. *Wm. Stidson* of *Mary Church,* whose daughter he afterwards married. About the year 1651, he preached at *Caffins-well,* a church which sprang from this, and was ordained by the classical Presbytery of Sarum, *June* 3, 1652. During his stay here he had an augmentation of 50*l. per ann.* but was soon presented to the vicarage of *Uxborough,* by Servington Savery, Esq. Several gentlemen of considerable estates and character had their seats in this parish, to whom Mr. *Jacob's* great learning, exemplary piety, and obliging behaviour endeared him; and after K. *Charles's* restoration, when men of his persuasion were under public marks of infamy, he was treated with a distinguished respect. The income of the place was not very considerable; but the people had gained such an interest in his affections, that he could not be prevailed upon to remove, though a good living in Somerset, and another in Cornwall, worth 200*l. per ann.* were offered him; and so he continued with them till Bartholomew-day 1662.

When he could no longer instruct them in public, he did it in private, as he had opportunity; preaching sometimes at *Shilston,* and sometimes at his own house, having the Shilston family, and other neighbours, for his hearers. His patron Mr. *Savery,* who knew how to value substantial learning and

piety,

Piety, was his hearty friend in the worst of times. He gave
him 20*l.* a year, and committed his eldest son, Christopher
Savery, Esq; and afterwards a younger son, to his care. He
rode once a fortnight to *Plymouth*, and preached to Mr.
Thomas Martyn's people, after whose death, he took upon
him the pastoral care of that congregation. There he was
convicted upon the Act against conventicles, and with Mr.
S. Martyn, about 1684, was committed to Exeter jail for six
months. He sometimes attended the established worship, and
all his days maintained a friendly correspondence with some
worthy neighbouring clergymen, who did him many good
offices. Mr. *Nosworthy* of Dipford, afforded him shelter in
his parish, when the five-mile act drove him from Plymouth.
It pleased God that he outlived those melancholy days; and
liberty being granted, he returned to the public exercise of his
ministry at Plymouth, to a numerous congregation, where he
lived beloved, and died lamented, in the year 1690; justifying
moderate Nonconformity to the last. He had generally the
character of an humble, peaceable christian; a learned, solid,
judicious minister; and his labours were crowned with great
success. His funeral sermon was preached by canon *Gilbert*,
vicar of St. Andrew's in Plymouth, who gave him a great
character for piety and learning.

.UPLIME [R. 20*l.* 8*s.* 11*d.*] Mr. THOMAS GODWINE.
A neighbouring clergyman of the church of *England* says,
" He was a grave, learned, pious divine; much broken with
the gout; and yet a constant, as well as excellent preacher."
He died in a good old age, soon after he was silenced.

UPLOMAN [R. S.] ROBERT CAREL, M. A. Dr. *Wal-
ker* is mistaken with regard to the sequestered minister of
this place. Mr. *Prince* says it was Dr. Creighton, afterwards
Bp. of Bath and Wells. Mr. *Carel* was a good scholar, an
excellent Christian, of a very tender conscience, and a solid
divine. After long preaching about the country, he fixed at
Crediton, where he died. His funeral sermon was preached
by Mr. *G. Trosse.*

UPTON HEYLON [R.] Mr. LEWIS FACY. He was
once imprisoned by a capias in Bodmyn jail, Cornwal. After
his ejeetment he was pastor of a congregation in *Falmouth.*

..WERRINGTON [C.] Mr. WILLIAM CARSLAKE. Of
Exeter Col. Oxf. He preached about in the churches in
London all the time of the plague. He was afterwards for
some

some years pastor to a congregation near Horsley-down in Southwark. He was a very good and pious man, but was in-clined to melancholy. He died soon after the Revolution.

WOODBURY Chapel. Mr. SAMUEL FONES. After his ejectment he left this country. He had the character of a very good man, and was universally beloved by his parishion-ers. There was a general weeping when he preached his farewell sermon.

WOODLAND. THOMAS PALK, M. A. Of *New Inn Hall, Oxf.* He was born in 1636, at *Staverton,* in this county. He was a hard student, and a most industrious man. Having but a small library, he borrowed many books, and abridged them for his own use. He engaged in teaching a school, but was so harrassed by the spiritual court, that he was obliged to give it up. At length he was excommunicated for his nonconformity, and died in consequence of the troubles to which it subjected him, *June* 18, 1693. Aged 56.

WORKS. The Loyal Nonconformist, or Religious subject, yielding to God his due, and to Cæsar his right: discourses on John iv. 23, 24. and Rom. xiii. 1. printed as preached in *August* 1662. —Usury stated, in opposition to *Jellinger's* Usurer cast. He left in MS. A vindication of this, and—An answer to Long's Hist. of the Donatists.

WOODLEIGH [R. S.] Mr. RICHARD BINMORE. After his ejection he was desired to preach a funeral sermon in the parish church, and leave was given by the incumbent for him to do it; but he was willing first to know the mind of some neighbouring justices. They said, the Act of uniformity was not levelled against an occasional sermon, but stated preach-ing: hereupon he ventured to preach. However notice of the sermon being soon given to Dr. *Seth Ward,* Bishop of the diocese, he sent a certificate of the offence to the justices, requiring them to put the laws in execution: which they durst not refuse upon such a charge, notwithstanding their own moderation. Hereupon he was sent thirty miles to Exeter jail. But the constable giving him leave to see the Bishop before he went to prison, after long waiting his lordship came down; and when he was told his name and his business, he thus accosted him: "*Sirrah,* how durst you preach in my diocese without my leave?" And with several more *Sirrahs,* told him, he should but inrich him by sending him to the jail: and consequently we are to suppose he dismissed him, as the greatest punishment.

WOOLFARDISHWORTHY [R.] Mr. THOMAS WALROND. He was presented to this living by the patron, and possessed it till 1662, when he lost it for Nonconformity. He was second son to *Henry Walrond*, of Bradfield, Esq. He was a person of eminent piety, a complete scholar in almost all parts of learning, a man of good breeding and estate, very exemplary to all men, and of great use in recommending religion among the gentry. He quitted this good benefice, which was in the gift of the family, and despised all preferments, for the sake of a good conscience; and not many years after made a very happy end. His elder brother, *William Walrond*, Esq. and some others of his relations (who after the Restoration ran pretty much with the stream) were not a little vexed at his relinquishing his benefice, and casting himself into a state of Nonconformity. This displeasure of his family turned out much to his detriment. But he was able to forsake all thro' faith, and adhere to Christ alone, whom he strictly followed to the death.

[For Mr. *Gay* and Mr. *Cudmore*, see *Exet. Col. Oxf.*]

Ejected at Places unknown.

Mr. JOHN POPE. Some time after being silenced he preached at or near *Crediton*, and when K. *James* gave liberty to the Dissenters he became a fixed pastor to a congregation there. He afterwards lived at *Exeter*, and there died, *July* 9, 1689. Mr. *George Trosse* preached his funeral sermon.

Mr. LAURENCE. He fell into a gross sin, and preached a public penitential sermon on account of it. Many were greatly affected to hear his discourse, and it was generally hoped he was a true penitent. But he afterwards went distracted, and continued so many years. He always had his Bible with him, and was frequently reading in it. He died about 1687.

Mr. RALPH SPRAKE. Of *Exet. Col. Oxf.* A native of *Lyme-Regis*, in Dorset, *Jan.* 1, 1627. He left the college for a time, and missed a living of 140l. *per ann.* for refusing the Engagement. When he quitted the university, he was about a Master of Art's standing, and preached at *Trull*, in Somerset, at *Bettescombe*, in Dorset, and other places; but was never settled in any living. After the ministers were ejected, he was a great sufferer for Nonconformity.

mity. He and Mr. *Samuel Chappel* were taken at a conventicle, at Capt. Cheek's, near Charmouth, in Dorset, for which they were convicted and committed to Dorchester jail, *Feb.* 27, 1666, tho' the informers owned before the justices who committed them, that they heard neither praying nor preaching. There he continued three months, preaching frequently in the prison. He declared that he never enjoyed more peace and comfort (except while he was in the university) than during his imprisonment. There he narrowly escaped having his brains knocked out with a great stone, by one who was distracted; for which great deliverance he frequently gave thanks to God. He also met with a great deal of trouble from the spiritual courts. At length he settled at *South Molton*, in Devonshire [where a church had been gathered, soon after the Bartholomew-ejectment, by several of the Nonconformist ministers, who preached here and at Torrington, Bideford and Chumleigh, in rotation : particularly Mr. L. Stucley, Mr. Palke, Mr. Cudmore, Mr. Tregosse, and Mr. Flavel, who, upon the Five-mile act, retired to *Hudscott*, near this place.] Mr. *Sprake* died here, *Jan.* 13, 1681. Mr. *H. Berry* preached his funeral sermon.

*** Mr. SAMUEL YOUNG. Dr. *Calamy* makes no other mention of him than in a list of persons who wrote against Mr. *Baxter.* He was an ejected minister, and had suffered imprisonment on account of his Nonconformity. He was a man of some wit, and a good share of classical learning; but had a wildness and irregularity in his temper, little short of madness. He was vehement and impetuous in every thing he said or did. He succeeded Mr. *Sprake*, at South Molton, where he had a fierce bigot to contend with, the parson of the parish, who was a true high-churchman, who almost distracted him—Mr. *Young* heard him preach a Thirtieth of *January*-sermon in the usual cant of the day ; which so grievously chafed him, that when the service was ended he got upon a tomb-stone, and preached *ex promptu* in answer to it, on *Matth.* iii. 10. *The axe is laid to the root,* &c. ‡ This occasioned a most violent quarrel, and a paper-war ensued. Mr. *Young* worsted his antagonist by a letter written in *Greek,* for the parson could not answer it, nor could he find any body to do it for him. Feeling Mr. *Young*'s superiority, he prudently quitted the field. But however the victory

‡ This was related some years ago by an ancient person, who well remembered this strange man, and lived in the same house with him.

might

might gratify Mr. *Young*'s vanity, the calm which ensued by no means suited his temper. His element was contention, and he could not live out of a tempest. He therefore removed to London, to enjoy it in its perfection, at the time when the republication of Dr. *Crisp*'s works occasioned that warm debate between Dr. *Williams* and others. He then wrote as violently against the Antinomians as he had done before against the Baxterians. He afterwards engaged in several other controversies, and (as the writer of this account expresses it) died before he was quite mad.

WORKS. Vindiciæ Anti-Baxterianæ.—Some political tracts; one, against his Brother the Physician, at Plymouth, who was a Jacobite.—Something against Rob. Ferguson, the noted apostate Dissenter, Roger L'Estrange and Dean Hicks.—Also a Piece in favor of Keith, the Quaker, &c.

Mr. HAYWARD. Of whom we have no account.

The following persons exercised their ministry in this county, after the Uniformity-act, *though they were not fixed at the time.*

GEORGE TROSSE, M.A. Of *Pemb. Col. Oxf.* Born in *Exeter, Oct.* 25, 1631. Son of *Henry Trosse*, Esq. counsellor at law. His mother's father, Mr. *Walter Burrow*, merchant, was twice mayor of Exeter, and a considerable benefactor to that city. Mr. Trosse, in his infancy was in danger of being starved at nurse; and in his advanced age he was much affected with this early deliverance. He was brought up in the grammar-school at Exeter, the master of which was much troubled at his being taken away too soon, saying he was the most promising child he ever had under his instruction. Being designed for merchandize, he was sent into *France*, when he was about fifteen, to learn the language, &c. which proved a great snare to him with respect to his morals. He was some time at *Morlaix*, in Lower Britanny, and afterwards at *Pontive*, in the house of Mr. *Ramet*, a French minister, where he learned to speak French readily; but grew very dissolute. In two years he returned, and covered his foreign extravagancies with falsities, which his friends were not able to disprove. From his own sad experience, he afterwards cautioned parents against sending their children abroad too young. He was sent to London, to a Portugueze merchant, in order to go over to *Portugal*, to be bound an apprentice to a merchant there.

there. During his stay in London he increased in viciousness, tho' at the same time he was zealous for the Common Prayer and ceremonies, in the love of which he had been educated; and was forward to inveigh against persons of the Puritan stamp. He sailed at length for *Oporto*, and was upon trial with one of the chief English merchants of that city. There he lived without any shew of religion, not so much as once seeing a Bible or religious book, or one act of solemn worship performed among his countrymen (who yet called themselves Protestants) during the whole time of his residence there: on which account, being in the midst of various snares and temptations, it is not to be wondered at that he still grew more profane and extravagant.

At length, not agreeing with his master, after two years he went for *Lisbon*, and from thence returned to *England*; landing at Plymouth, after a stormy passage, in which he was in no small danger; but was not at all affected with it. He brought back with him to Exeter a rampant vicious disposition, which was rather heightened than abated by the life which he led there some years after. The following are his own words: " What a life I led, what a course I took to " increase my wickedness, and to outstrip the common " (yea, those who were more than ordinary) sinners, can' " never be related or lamented by me as it ought. I had so " accustomed myself to wickedness, so blinded my mind, " and seared my conscience, that I had not the least sense of " the evil of sin, the wrath of God, or the necessity of a " change," &c. But at length, it pleased God (who had merciful purposes to serve, not only with respect to him, but by him on many others) to lay his hand upon him, and cause his own thoughts so to terrify as to overset him. Certain false steps which he had taken, the consequences of which he knew not how to bear, led him into such a hurry of spirit as issued into an outrageous distraction. He was hereupon sent to *Glastonbury* for a cure, and was wonderfully recovered; but he afterwards relapsed into his old sins. His disorder thereupon returning, and his former convictions and horrors with it, he was sent to the same place a second time, and returned home composed; but he also again returned to his vices; tho' he observes, that after this God neither suffered him to fall so foully as formerly, nor to continue long in his relapse. He soon began again to be troubled in mind, and his spirits were disturbed; upon which his friends sent him a third time to *Glastonbury*, where he was as miserable and outrageous as ever. Yet after a while, God was pleased, by the use of physic, and the good counsel and prayers of Christian friends, to deliver him from his madness and inexpressible misery, and to give him a sound mind and a healthful body; which, when he had enjoyed for some time, he returned once more to his relations at Exeter: and here it pleased God, when he was about 25 years of age, effectually to put a period to his sinful courses. Henceforward he appeared a different person from what he was before; and being delivered from his disorder and distress, he devoted himself to God thro' Christ, to walk before him in holiness and righteousness all the days of his life, and God was with him.

Having occasion to make a visit at *Oxford*, an acquaintance of his there so commended an academical life to him, that he became in love with it, and, with his mother's consent, he went thither in *May*, 1657, and entered gentleman commoner, in *Pembroke Col.* where he continued some years; Mr. *T. Cheesman*, who was blind, being his tutor. He was very studious, soon recovered his grammar learning, read many of the classics, went thro' philosophy and divinity, and got such skill in *Hebrew*, that he read over the original of the Old Testament several times. He allowed himself no recreation, and yet his mind was composed, and his health wonderfully preserved. Now he sought the kingdom of God and his Righteousness in the first place. He took competent time for secret duties, and never was absent from chapel prayers. He read many good books, and examined himself by them. He attended Dr. *Conant*'s lectures on Fridays, Dr. *Harris*'s catechetical lecture on Tuesdays, the lecture kept up by the canons of *Christ-Church* on Thursdays, Mr. *Hickman*'s ministry at *St. Olave*'s; on the Lord's-days, and heard also many excellent sermons at *St. Mary*'s. He received the sacrament, sometimes from Mr. *Hickman*, and sometimes from Dr. *Langley*, the master of his college. He attended the repetition of sermons and solemn prayer in the college-hall, on the Lord's-days before supper: and he himself repeated sermons, and prayed with a few young men in his chamber afterwards. At other times he conversed, and some times prayed, with some religious students and townsmen. He took such pains to redeem the time he had lost, that he was the wonder of all that observed him.

Upon

Upon the Restoration, he impartially studied the controversy about Conformity, and carefully read *Hooker, Sprint,*
and *Burgess,* on one side, and *Gillespy, Bain* and *Ames,*
on the other; and upon mature deliberation, determined
that he could not comply with the impositions of the church,
tho' he well knew that by such a resolution he should dis-
please his relations, and hinder his preferment. But he was
so moderate as to think, that several who were for Conformity, upon such plausible arguments as were produced for it,
might with a good conscience subscribe, and do what he
could not do without sin. At length, Dr. *Langley* being
ejected by the visitors, and the chaplain of the college dismissed with contempt, repetition of sermons suppressed, and
other good customs quite altered and ridiculed, he quitted
the college, retired to a private house, and soon after returned
to *Exeter,* where he kept close to God in duty, and farther
pursued his studies. After some time he began to preach,
but it was at first very privately, for fear of being exposed
to danger. He went usually on Lord's-days with his mother
to church, and attended on the Liturgy, in the use of which
he owned that he sometimes found the Spirit of God moving
upon his soul: but he never went to the sacrament in any
parish-church, not being satisfied with the gesture.—His first
labours met with good acceptance among serious people, but
the opposition and prejudices of his relations created him
difficulty, and made him go on with a heavy heart.

At length, in 1666, when the Oxford-act took place, by
Mr. *Atkin*'s persuasion he was set apart to the office of the
ministry, in Somersetshire, when Mr. *Joseph Allein,* of
Taunton, prayed over him. Afterwards, for above twenty
years, he preached once a week, and administered the Lord's
Supper every month, in the midst of violent persecutions.
In the time of K. *Charles*'s Indulgence he preached in a licenced house. When it was recalled, he forbore public
preaching, and went to church as formerly; but continued
preaching and administering the sacrament privately till the
Revolution. In K. *James*'s time he would not preach publicly on the Lord's-day, till the worship in the parish church
was ended. In that reign, about twenty persons, with Mr.
Trosse and some other ministers, being met to pray together,
they were informed against, disturbed, taken and abused.
When the Oxford-oath against resistance in any case whatsoever, was tendered to them, Mr *Trosse* refused it, unless
he might be allowed to qualify that expression, of " endea-

vouring

vouting any alteration of government," &c. with the word
" unlawfully," which was not allowed him. He pleaded
that the act did not reach him, because he never had had a
benefice, nor was he legally convicted for keeping conventicles : but to no purpose; for he and Mr. *Gaylard* were
sent to prison, against law, by a *mittimus*, signed with the
hands of seven justices. He continued six months in jail at
South-gate, with great satisfaction and comfort. The justices would gladly have made a riot of this meeting, that
they might have fined them at pleasure: but, upon a *certiorari*,
brought to remove the cause to *Westminster*, they stopped
the prosecution. When the Dissenters in K. *William*'s time
had a legal toleration, Mr. *Trosse*, with many others, again
preached publicly in church-time, and continued doing so
till his death.

In the account which he left of himself, he hath these
remarkable words : " Till I was four or five and twenty
" years old, I lived in a course of sin and folly, which I
" experienced to be base, unreasonable, and destructive to
" health, estate, name, rest and reason, leading to horror
" and despair, rage and hell. Ever since, for many years,
" (blessed be God for every minute of them) I have kept
" on steadily in the ways of holiness, and found them
" blessed, honourable and comfortable, both with respect to
" body and soul, and to all outward and inward concerns. I
" can say, if any can, That godliness has the promise of this
" life, and that which is to come : and must declare that I
" never heard or read of any one, so almightily saved from
" sin and hell, and so wonderfully blessed with all favors and
" mercies as I have been." This was written in *Feb.* 1693.
He lived 56 years after the change wrought in him by the
grace of God. Tho' this good man seems to have thought
he could never speak bad enough of himself, on account of
his youthful lusts, and tho' by reason of his great warmth of
imagination, he was apt to aggravate things to a great height,
(and never more than when he represented his own vileness
and wretchedness, before he was renewed in the spirit of his
mind) yet he was in reality a singular and marvellous instance
of the power and efficacy of the grace of God. He was
well furnished for ministerial service. His apprehension was
quick, his invention rich, his judgment solid, and his memory
tenacious. Tho' he set out late, yet by hard study, he arrived at a considerable degree of learning. He was as great
a reader as most. He was mighty in the scriptures, and had
them

them ready in his memory; having read over the bible in *English, Latin, Greek, Hebrew* and *French*, (as he declared himself some years before his death) a hundred and a hundred times. He had a body of divinity in his head, and could, as occasion offered, preach pertinently and profitably, without much study or preparation.

He succeeded Mr. *Hallet*, at Exeter, in 1689, in that large congregation, where his work in public and private was very great. For above twenty years, he frequently preached twice on the Lord's-day. On Thursdays in the afternoon, he had a catechetical lecture, in which he explained the principles of the christian religion, in the method of the *Assembly's Catechism*. He spent several years in explaining the attributes and works of God; and had begun to discourse on the ten commandments, but had only finished the first, when God put an end to his labours.—He preached a weekly lecture on Wednesdays, till about three years before his death; when he admitted his three colleagues to take their turns. He preached funeral sermons for no less than fourteen of his brethren in the ministry; and many other occasional discourses. So that sometimes he has preached eight sermons in a week, and that with pleasure; for his work was his delight. His discourses were methodical, and delivered with spirit and life, freedom and fluency. In his preaching he manifested such deep concern, as engaged the serious attention of the hearers; and his labours were succeeded to the good of many. He had a wonderful gift in prayer; and his administration of both the sacraments, was both judicious and affecting. He did also a great deal of work in private. He had an excellent faculty in resolving doubts, in comforting afflicted consciences, and assisting such as were going out of the world. As a good shepherd he was diligent to know the state of his flock. He shewed much love and prudence in reproving; and would sometimes do it by letter, when circumstances made it not so proper for him to do it in person. For forty-six years after his ordination, he continued with exemplary pains and diligence, to discharge all the offices of a vigilant and faithful minister.

He was regular in his devotions, and circumspect in the whole course of his life, which was an excellent comment upon his sermons. Love to God was the principle which actuated him in all. *Much was forgiven* him, and he *loved much.* He was a strict observer of the Lord's day, and took peculiar delight in thanksgiving. He kept public fasts with great

great seriousness; and a private fast in every kalendar month, with unusual strictness. He was remarkably patient and submissive under pains and sicknesses. No changes of providence could be discerned to make any considerable change in him. In dangers and difficulties, he placed his confidence in God. He had formed a noble idea of his perfections, and of the wisdom of his government, which brought him to such a calmness of temper, that sudden accidents which were shocking to others, made little impression upon him. He was cloathed with humility and with the utmost sincerity declared himself to be (as he ordered it to be engraved on his tomb-stone) " The greatest of sinners, and the least of saints."—He was very courteous and affable to all. He understood and observed the rules of conversation, and gave ' honour to whom honour was due.' Tho' he was naturally warm and hasty in his temper, he had so mastered it, as seldom to be ruffled with passion. He was scrupulously honest and faithful to his word. He had ' put on bowels of mercies and kindness ;' and was tender-hearted and compassionate to those in distress. His temperance, sobriety, heavenly-mindedness, and contempt of riches were remarkable. His mother, who died rich, would have made him her executor, but he refused it. She offered him what proportion he pleased of her estate, but he chose only a competency to provide him food and raiment, with something for books and works of charity ; and freely let the bulk of her estate go to his elder brother's son.§ He continually behaved himself as a son of peace, and was of a moderate healing spirit. While he used his own liberty, he had great charity for such as were not of his mind. His friendship was sincere, and his ' love without dissimulation.' He was a man of a public spirit, and preferred the prosperity of the church of God above his chief joy.

When zealous endeavours were used to overthrow the Protestant religion among us, and to subvert the laws and liberties of the nation ; when he saw a Romanist high-sheriff of Devon, and a mass-house opened in his native city; in order to seduce the ignorant and unstable ; he set himself strenuously to confute the errors of the church of *Rome,* and took unwearied pains to establish people in the truth, and prepare them for a day of trial. He would not join in

§ Herein, perhaps, his conduct was not altogether commendable, unless he had good evidence that his nephew would improve the property better than he himself could have done.

an address of thanks to K. *James*, for granting liberty to
the Dissenters, that he might not so much as seem to approve the dispensing power, or be at all accessary to the designs of such as were patrons of Popery, or arbitrary government. He abounded in works of charity; and took as
much delight in dispersing and giving to the poor, as others
do in heaping up riches. He laid aside the tenth part of 'all
his income for charitable uses ; to which he added much more
when need required. His charity was not confined to a
party ; nor did he consider mens opinions, but their necessities. He had such love to souls, that he never refused to
visit sick persons in the most infectious distempers; and did
not count his labour, his purse, his health dear unto himself,
when he was in the way of his duty. He also ' provoked
others unto love and to good works.' He kept a constant
watch over his heart and ways ; guarding against the particular temptations with which he was assaulted. He
' walked within his house with a perfect heart,' and filled
up all his particular relations in life with suitable duty. After
his return to God, he enjoyed settled peace of conscience,
and had a lively joyful hope, with very little interruption.

When his end drew near, his serenity was great, and his
hope unshaken. Tho' he complained much of his indisposition for some weeks before his decease, he would not remit
any thing of his public work, private studies, or secret devotions. The evening before his removal, he told his wife
very positively, that the time of his departure was at hand,
which he said without discovering any fear. The next day
being the Lord's-day, he preached as usual; but was seized
with faintness in going home ; and being carried into an apothecary's house, he said, " I'm dying." When he was a
little recovered, his friends expostulated with him for preaching under such disorders ; to which he replied, " It becomes
a minister to die preaching." He walked home, but grew
faint again; and was no sooner within his own doors, than
he fell down; his speech failed him, and in about three
quarters of an hour, he quietly surrendered his soul to God,
on *Jan.* 11, 1713, aged upwards of 81 years; and on the
Thursday following, he was interred in Bartholomew church-
yard, in *Exeter*, where, upon a black marble stone, there
is the following epitaph of his own composing:———*Hic
jacet peccatorum maximus, sanctorum minimus, conciona-
torum indignissimus,* Georgius Trosse, *hujus civitatis in-
digena & incola qui huic maligno valedixit Mundo, unde-
cimo die mensis Januarii, Anno Dom.* 1713, *Ætat. suæ* 82.
Immediately

Immediately after his interment, a funeral sermon was preached by his fellow-labourer Mr. *Joseph Hallet*, on 1 *Tim*. i. 15, a text of his own choosing. The sermon is added to Mr. *Trosse's* narrative of his own life.

WORKS. The Lord's-day vindicated, &c. in Answer to Mr. Bampfield's Plea for the Seventh Day.—The Pastor's Care and Dignity, and the People's Duty; a Sermon at the Assembly of Ministers, at Taunton.—A Discourse of Schism: designed for the Satisfaction of conscientious and peaceable Dissenters—A Defence of the former, against Aerius Prostratus.—Mr. Trosse's Vindication of himself from several Aspersions.—He also drew up the Explication of the last five Answers in Mr. *Flavel's* Expos. of the Assemb. Catech. and wrote a Preface to it.

—— JOHN HOPPIN, B. D. Fellow of *Exeter Col. Oxf.* out of which he had been ejected. He was afterwards pastor of a congregation in *Exeter.* He had been tutor to a great number of pupils, and being an acute philosopher and a solid divine, they improved much under him. He was episcopally ordained. Bp. *Lamplugh*, being desirous to gain him to the church, sent for him to his palace, in *Exeter*; and it being then a time of great rigour against the Dissenters, he promised him safe ingress and egress. When he came, his good lordship asked him, why he would not conform? He gave him a reason or two, at which the Bishop seemed a little startled, and bade him read *Hooker's Ecclesiastical Polity.* Mr. *Hoppin* replied, "That from a position in "that book, it appeared that *Hooker* himself, were he now "alive, must be a Nonconformist." The Bishop took down the book, and asked him where that position was? On shewing him the passage,§ his lordship read it, and then hastily shutting the book again, said, with his usual passion, "Go your way: I promised you indeed safe conduct out "and home, but afterwards look to yourself." Not long after Mr. *Hoppin* was apprehended, and cast into the *Southgate* prison in the sight of the palace, where he was detained six months, in a very cold chamber, and thereby got such a rheumatism, as rendered him a perfect cripple to the day of his death; so that he was carried to the pulpit constantly in a chair. He lived many years in misery; but at length died in peace, *March* 4, 1705, and was succeeded by Mr. *John Withers.*

§ It is to be wished that this curious passage had been referred to. Any reader who can point it out, is requested to communicate it to the editor.

*** NICHOLAS

⁂ NICHOLAS SHERWILL, M. A: Of *Magd. Col. Oxf.*
He was born at *Plymouth*, where his ancestors and many of
his relations lived, who were persons of the first rank.
Having spent many years in Oxford, and been legally ordained by episcopal hands, he returned to his native place,
and betook himself to his private studies, and afterwards became minister of a dissenting congregation there. On *Oct.* 6,
1665, the officers of the garrison came, as they said, from the
governor, to his lodging, and told him, the governor desired
to speak with him at the tavern. Mr. *Sherwill* hasted
thither, where he found several ministers on the same business. After they had been there a while, they perceived a guard
of soldiers set over them. *Oct* 9, Mr. *Sherwill*, with others,
was removed to another tavern, and was rudely treated by the
serjeant for offering to step to his lodging without his leave.
Two centinels were set at his chamber door, and the liberty
of the house was denied him. In the evening he was conveyed by four musqueteers, with their matches lighted, to
the colonel, who sent him to *St. Nicholas* island, with orders
from the Earl not to converse with Mr. *H.* (probably Mr.
Howe or Mr. *Hughes)* and Mr. *M.* who were prisoners
there; to have a centinel at his chamber-door, and not to go
out without a guard. He continued under this restraint till
Dec. 4. In *Jan.* he was brought before the Earl, who told
him, if he could satisfy the Bishop, He would be satisfied.
The Bishop having known him at Oxford, wrote a very obliging letter to the Earl, as much as possible in his favour.
The oath in the Oxford-act was tendered him, which he refused. His prison was changed, and *March* 30, he was released, upon his bond to quit the town within 48 hours.*
He died suddenly at *Plymouth*, where he had lived upon his
estate, *May* 15, 1696.

——— JOHN GIDLEY, M. A. Of *Exeter Col. Oxf.* He
had received episcopal ordination. He possessed excellent
abilities, but was one of the most modest men in the world,
so as hardly to be engaged to say grace at table. He lived
at *Exeter*, upon his own estate, and generally occupied the
table-pew, being with great difficulty got into the pulpit;
but whenever he did enter it, he met with good acceptance.
The other ministers in that city much esteemed him for his
learning and ministerial abilities. He afterwards settled at
Great *Marlow*, Bucks, where he died.

* The above account is taken from the Conformist's Fourth Plea for the
Nonconformists, page 65.

——— Mr.

age when he began to preach, which he did not frequently do, till after his ordination in 1682, (by Mr. *Anthony Palmer*, &c. in private) when he was near forty. He then accepted of an invitation to stated ministerial work, from the people of *Barnstaple*, among whom he laboured with great diligence, till he was incapacitated by a disorder which issued in his death, *July*, 19, 1707, when he was aged 65. He was a star of the first magnitude. His attainments in the knowledge of physic were like those in divinity, very considerable, in the opinion of very competent judges. He had also a poetic genius. Mr. *George Bowcher* of *Barnstaple*, in his funeral sermon for him, speaks of him as follows:

' He was an uncommon scholar in arts and tongues, and
' generally versed in other kinds of learning. The learned
' of different persuasions have been forward to declare him a
' great man. His custom was to rise about four or five in
' the morning, and to remain in his study till family prayer;
' soon after which, he went to his study again till about noon:
' and then, after necessary refreshment with eating and walk-
' ing, and a little discourse, he returned to his study, and
' there continued till late in the evening. His work was his
' delight: he plied it close, and on this account perhaps went
' the sooner from us. His talent at preaching was extraordi-
' nary. Most apt to instruct and persuade sinners to turn and
' live. It might as truly be said of him, as of any one, That
' solid truth, judiciously handled, was the usual entertainment
' he gave those who sat under his ministry. He took a par-
' ticular satisfaction in instructing younger persons. He had
' an incomparable way of instilling a knowledge of the great
' things of religion, into either old or young; and his private
' as well as public endeavours were very successful for the
' good of many. His love to his people was exceeding great.
' It was a great joy to him to see them go quietly hand in
' hand, in the service of their master, and their common sa-
' viour; and very grievous to him were any aberrations or
' mistakes among them. He was much of the temper of Mr.
' *Baxter*, who professed *he could willingly be a martyr for
' peace and love among christians.* He excelled in charity
' and moderation about matters of opinion. He thought true
' christianity very consistent with different sentiments of things.
' He could see and love a good christian, tho' of another com-
' munion from that which he himself thought most apostó-
' lical, and agreed best with the dictates of his own con-
' science; and was far from anathematizing or damning those
whose

' whose head was cast ·in another· mould than his; provided
' they in·their hearts and lives.tended heavenward. His mo-
' desty and humility were very conspicuous. He was an emi-
.' nent pattern, in word, in conversation, ·in charity, in spirit,
' in faith, in purity. In a word; he was remarkable for his
· piety, which is the glory of all other attainments. He had
' much acquaintance with God and converse in heaven while
' upon earth, which seemed to be uninterrupted. His pa-
' tience under ·the long affliction before his death, was great.
.' To such as asked him how he did, his common reply was,
.' Very well, blessed be God.'

Mr. Hanmer could not be prevailed on to print any thing,
tho' his ordinary performances would have stood the test of the
age he lived in, as well as most things that saw the light. His
letters, both controversial and practical, discover the excellency of his head and heart. The following is preserved as
a specimen. It was sent to a clergyman, who, in conversation, where a relation of Mr. Hanmer was present, had dropped a hint, " that in that town *(Barnstaple)* there was some
person or persons employed in instructing an assembly of
Protestants, who taught false doctrine, and· by consequence
were false teachers."

· " Worthy sir,—You were pleased, unprovoked, to charge
" false doctrine upon some certain person or persons, who are
" employed in instructing an assembly of Protestants in this
" town, under the protection and countenance of his majesty
" and the laws. You cannot rationally imagine but I must
" look on myself as concerned herein, and somewhat wounded
" with so sharp an arrow; whether shot at random, or di-
" rected point-blank at any particular person or thing, I de-
" sire to know. If on good grounds you judge me guilty,
" and liable to the crime you insinuate, I shall be so far from
" blaming, that I entreat, and shall thankfully receive, your
" admonition and reproof: only craving that this good work
" may be managed in the spirit of meekness, and with the
" wisdom and candour of a christian and a scholar. If you
" think me worthy to be smitten, do it dear sir, first in pri-
" vate, and let me particularly know my error and transgres-
" sion. Your faithfulness herein I shall value as a singular
" kindness. Such *excellent oil will not break mine head*, but
" will lay me under farther obligations to love and honour you.
" A general passionate charge without instances or proof, some
" will be apt to interpret a calumny, rather than a rational
" and christian reproof: as carrying in it continuance of ha-

tred

" tred and malice against an whole society, rather than love to
" the truth, or zeal for that religion to which we pretend.
" Some differences there have always been, and will be among
" christians, in some lighter matters and disputable points. If
" for these we censure, traduce, malign, and persecute one
" another, we shall take the readiest course to banish all peace
" out of the church for ever. If our foundation be good, and
" we agree in the main things of faith, hope, and love, this
" methinks should be counted sufficient to unite our hearts,
" and oblige and engage us to live and converse together as
" brethren. For my part I sincerely profess, that disagree-
" ment in opinions of less moment, doth not in the least abate
" my esteem and love of any. A great multitude there are of
" professed christians, who cannot comply with some things
" the church of *England* enjoins. It hath pleased God to put
" it into the hearts of the king and parliament to shew com-
" passion to them. Let not your eye be evil because theirs is
" good. What falsities have been broached in the despised
" assembly among us, which you wish for water to wash away,
" I beg that by a line or personal converse, I may understand.
" I shall wait on you when, and at any place yourself shall
" appoint. I hope you have ever found me, and I shall en-
" endeavour always to approve myself, a sincere friend to love
" and peace. Yours, &c."

Mr. SAMUEL ATKINS. He died young. His funeral
sermon was preached and printed by Mr. *Isaac Gilling*.

The following persons afterwards conformed.

Mr. BULHEAD of *King's-Ash*. Dr. *Walker* is willing to
give him up to the Nonconformists; being, according to his
account, " a sorry, illiterate, idle fellow; the jest of the whole
" parish." But Dr. Calamy is not willing to own him.—
Mr. JOHN TICKEL, of *Exeter*—Mr. JOHN LAW, of *Hinick*.
—Mr. RICHARD CONANT, of *Otterton*.—Mr. JOSHUA BOW-
DEN, of *Ashburton*.—Mr. FRANCIS COLLINS, of *St. Budax*.
—Mr. BUBEAR, of *Kinnerly*—Mr. LEONARD PRINCE, of
Ilfracombe; who continued several years a Nonconformist.
He served *St. John's* in the city of *Exeter*; and after some time
was preferred to the rectory of *Instow* near Barnstaple. He
was uncle to Mr. *John Prince*, vicar of Berry Pomeroy near
Totness, the ingenious author of The Worthies of Devon, to
whom the author thankfully pays his acknowledgments, for
several hints with respect to the ministers in this county.

MINISTERS EJECTED OR SILENCED

IN

DORSETSHIRE.

ALLINGTON. § Mr. BARTHOLOMEW WESLEY. Having applied himself to the study of physic, as well as divinity, while in the university, he was often consulted as a physician, while he was in his living; and after his ejectment, in 1662, he applied himself chiefly to the practice of physic, tho' he continued to preach occasionally. He used a peculiar plainness of speech, which hindered his being an acceptable popular preacher. He lived several years after he was silenced; but he so laid to heart the death of his son, that his health afterwards rapidly declined, and he did not long survive him.

BERE REGIS and KINGSTON [V. 25*l*. 5*s*.] Mr. PHILIP LAMB.† Of *Camb. Univ.* Son of Mr. Henry Lamb, minister at *Cern Abbey*, and there he was born. He began his ministry at *Bere Regis*, at about twenty-one years of age. He preached here one part of the Lord's-day, and the other at *Kingston*, a village, in that neighbourhood, for the convenience of some infirm people: but such as were strong and healthy attended at both places. He had, for some time, a service every day in the week, at six o'clock in the morning, at *Bere Regis*. On Monday morning he repeated the sermons of the preceding Sabbath. On Wednesday and Friday mornings he expounded the Lord's

------

§ From HUTCHIN's History of DORSET, which Mr. James has carefully examined, it appears that Mr. RICHARD SQUIB was put in here by the parliament; and it seems probable that *Allington* was not the place from which Mr. Wesley was ejected. See CHARMOUTH.

† Mr. Lamb's predecessor, *Hussey*, died March 7, 1648. Baskit succeeded Lamb, June 28, 1662, so that he was ejected before Bartholomew-day. There was no minister at Bere in 1650. *Hutchins*.

prayer, or the creed, &c. At *Kingston* he held a lecture once a fortnight, where several of his brethren assisted ; and one day in the week he had a conference. He had a strong interest in the affections of his people ; among whom there was a great and general lamentation when he was silenced. He continued for some time preaching to them in private ; but at last was forced from them by the troubles he met with, and removed to *Moredon,* where he preached and kept days of prayer in private, to the great benefit and comfort of many. Upon K. *Charles's* liberty he had a convenient place provided for him at *Kingston.* The people flocked from all parts to hear him, and much good was done by his ministry. Among other instances, there was a remarkable one in an old gentleman near eighty, who tho' he had little sense of religion, had a great kindness for Mr. *Lamb,* his old minister, having been much won by his great affableness, and nothing would satisfy him but he must be brought in a chair to the meeting. It pleased God to touch his heart, and make him sensible of his sin, and work a change upon him in his old age. Dying not long after, Mr. *Lamb,* upon occasion of his funeral, preached on *Matth.* xx. 6. *And about the eleventh hour he went out, and found others standing idle,* &c. When the licences were called in, great severity was used, and Mr. *Lamb* was forced, with his family, to London; where he had not been long before he was invited by a congregation at *Clapham,* in Surrey, where he spent the rest of his days. He died *March* 25, 1689, in the 67th year of his age. He was offered 600*l.* a year if he would have conformed ; but it did not tempt him. He was remarkable for his unaffected piety, chearful temper, and engaging deportment.

Mr. *Lamb's* Farewell Sermon, preached at Bere Regis, Aug. 17, 1662, is found in the London Collection. §It is an excellent discourse, full of sentiment, making thirty-six quarto pages, on these words, *John* xiv. 23. *If any man love me, he will keep my words ; and my father will love him, and we will come unto him, and make our abode with him.* Having largely insisted on the character described, and the promise delivered, he proceeds to exhort and direct his hearers to seek the blessing promised, and thus introduces his Farewell address : " If we would find God and Christ, we must seek all the days of our lives. They that will find what they seek, must seek till they find. Upon this work I must leave you : For now I must tell you, that perhaps you may not see my face, or hear my voice, any more in this place :

4   yet

yet not out of any peevish humour, or disaffection to the present authority of the kingdom (I call God and man to witness this day) it being my own practice, and counsel to you all, to fear God and honour the king; but rather, a real dissatisfaction in some particulars imposed, to which (notwithstanding all endeavours to that purpose) my conscience cannot yet be espoused. Wherefore I hope in this, and in all my abode with you, I may say, without ostentation, with the apostle, 2 *Cor.* i. 12. *Our rejoicing is this, the testimony of our consciences, that in simplicity, and godly sincerity, we have had our conversation in the world, especially to you-wards.* And as he said *Acts* xx. 26, &c. *I take you to record this day that I have endeavoured to be pure from the blood of all men; for I have not shunned to declare to you the whole counsel of God,* both by my life and doctrine; because I knew this very well, that, as one says, *Suadet loquentis vita, non oratio:* that the preacher's Life is the most pursuasive preaching. I shall only add this, my friends, That tho' my lips be sealed up, so that I may not speak from God *to* you, yet I shall not cease to speak to God *for* you, as ever I have done. And tho' I cannot have you in my eye, yet I shall lodge you in my heart; and asking nothing of you but your prayers, shall hope to meet you daily at the throne of grace, and that at last we may enjoy one-another in heaven. And, because they say, The words of a dying man make the deepest impression, before I am altogether civilly dead, I shall give you one exhortation more. Let it be your endeavour to keep God and Christ with you, that they may make their abode with you in your hearts and houses, that whatsoever you lose, you may not be undone.— 1. Take heed you do not slight or abuse God's providences: 2. Do not despise or neglect his ordinances. 3. Be sure you do not grieve his spirit.—Observe these ten directions, which I would leave with you, that God and Christ may make their constant abode with you. Endeavour to please God and Christ, and to walk as the gospel commands. Entertain God and Christ like themselves, &c. &c. . . . . . I conclude with the words of the apostle *Phil.* 1. 27.

WORKS. Besides the above Farewell Sermon—The Religious Family.—A Funeral Sermon for Mr. Butler.—Another for Mrs. Sarah Lye.—Another for John Gould, Esq.—A New-year's Gift; or Portraiture of a Natural Man, and a regenerate Person.

BETTESCOMB [R.] Mr. ISAAC CLIFFORD§. Of *Brazen Nose Col. Oxf.* Born at *Frampton.* He was a man of great natural abilities, an indefatigable student, and one who delighted in learning from his youth. When he was a school-boy he commonly redeemed that time for his book, which his fellows spent in play. He was a good grammarian, and a smart disputant. He also was eminent for piety, and an ingenious preacher. His heart was evidently set upon serving God, and doing good to others. Being cast into Dorchester jail, on the account of his Nonconformity, it is thought that his confinement there, tho' he was very chearful under it, laid the foundation of those distempers, which some time after brought him immaturely to the grave.

BLANDFORD [V.] WILLIAM ALLEIN, M.A.§† Of *Corp. Chr. Col. Oxf.* Younger son of Mr. R. Allein, of Ditchet, and younger brother of Mr. R. Allein, of Batcomb, in Somerset. On leaving the university, he became chaplain to a person of distinction, in London. At the beginning of the civil war he lived at *Ilchester,* and was upon some occasions consulted by great officers. For his letters to them he was proclaimed by the cavaliers a traitor in three market towns. He was often plundered, and often strangely preserved. He afterwards went to *Bristol,* where he was taken and plundered. Then he removed to London with his family. In 1653 he became the settled minister of this place, and gathered a church here, but was driven from it at the Restoration; when he freely quitted the parish, and ministered to a few people in private; but he could not be quiet, and therefore went again to *Bristol,* where he lived seven or eight years. From thence he removed to *Yeovil,* in Somerset, and there died in *Oct.* 1677, aged 63. He was a man of good learning and great piety; particularly eminent for his modesty and meekness. A true patient labourer in the gospel, and a most happy comforter of many dejected souls and wounded spirits, by a wise application of gospel-cordials. When he set himself to an immediate preparation for death, he had some regret (as it is said Abp. *Usher* had) that he had not better improved his time and talents.

§ Hutchins does not mention *Clifford,* but speaks of *Coleman,* who was his successor, as being in above a year before the Uniformity-act passed : viz. June 17, 1661. *James Strong* was here in 1650.

§† "*Blandford Forum,* William Allen, Intruder, 1653. He was allowed "55*l.* 19*s.* 4*d.* out of Lord Digby's estate." N. B. There is another Blandford, called St. *Mary.* In the Commission, 1650, it is said, "*William Allen,* a "learned, orthodox, able divine, the present incumbent."

WORKS,

WORKS. Two Books upon the Millenium, (which shew the great and good Man.) After his death, Six Discourses on the unsearchable Riches of Christ, &c.

BRADPOLE. Mr. WILLIAM SAMPSON. §In *Hutchins's* History, Mr. *Sampson* is not mentioned, but *Somers* occurs, as inducted *Nov.* 27, 1662. In the Commission, 1650, it is, " Mr. William Sampson, incumbent, for whom they " desire an augmentation."

BRIDPORT [R.] Mr. WILLIAM EATON. A very ingenious and delicate preacher. §Hutchins has it, JOHN EATON, 1650. His successor *Goodwin*, April 16, 1661.

WORKS. Two Sermons, vindicating the Ministers of Christ from the Charge of being House-creepers, on 2 *Tim.* iii. 6.

BROAD-WINDSOR [V. S.] Mr. JOHN PINNEY. The incumbent, Dr. *Fuller*, being living at the Restoration, was to have been restored to this vicarage ;§ but on coming to take possession he heard Mr. *Pinney* preach ; upon which he told the people, that he would not deprive them of such a man, [so that he for the present kept the living.] However he was obliged to leave it at the fatal Bartholomew. But he never repented of his Nonconformity, tho' he severely suffered for it. After his ejectment, he had many troubles by fines and excommunications. He was twice imprisoned ; once in England and once in Ireland, having been forced out of this kingdom by a prosecution on the statute 35 *Eliz.* He was recommended by Dr. *Harrison* to his congregation in *Dublin*, in which he succeeded him, and he continued with them near ten years, till K. *James* came thither, when most of the ministers left the city. Liberty being legally granted here in England, he returned and settled among his old parishioners. He was much of a gentleman, a considerable scholar, a very facetious, yet grave and serious companion, and an eloquent, charming preacher.

Some time before his ejectment, one *Hine*, a *Baptist*, who pretended to inspiration, and was much celebrated on that account, as well as for other uncommon gifts, came with a number of attendants to the town where he was minister, and

§ Here seems to be some mistake, as Dr. *Fuller*, author of the Holy War, Church History, &c. died *Aug.* 15, 1661. Hutchins does not rectify it, nor does he mention Pinney. He has the incumbents thus : Thomas Fuller, 1635, B. D. Francis Isaac, *Jan.* 23, 1622. (This date must be erroneous.) Edmund Sly, 25 *Jan.* 1661.

nothing

nothing would satisfy him but he must preach in the church.
On being denied the pulpit, his adherents urged Mr. *Pinney*
to preach himself; hoping by that means to get the church
doors opened. When this also was refused, they all very
freely cast out their reflections upon the ministers in general;
as "dull blockheads, and dumb dogs, that would neither
preach themselves, nor suffer others to preach that would."
At this Mr. *Pinney* was provoked to make them an offer,
that if they would give him a text, he would discourse upon
it, off hand, to all the company present, in a neighbouring
field, provided their prophet would do the like on a text that
he should propose. This was agreed to. They gave Mr. *Pinney* a text, and after offering up solemn prayer to God, he
discoursed upon it, with freedom and pertinence. When he
came to look back upon this action afterwards, he saw reason
with thankfulness to acknowledge God's assistance, though
at the same time to censure his own rashness. While Mr.
Pinney was discoursing, the prophet walked under a hedge
at a little distance, meditating upon the subject given him;
which was *Acts* xx. 30. *Also of your own selves shall men
arise, speaking perverse things, to draw away disciples
after them.* When he came to work, his prayer was short
and modest; but his discourse incoherent, rambling, impertinent, absurd, and false. Mr. *Pinney* made his objections
against what he had delivered, upon the spot, but received no
reply. His friends carried off the prophet in triumph, so that
Mr. *Pinney* had not opportunity of speaking to him, and he
never came there any more. There was this further good
effect of this management, that many persons were settled
who before were wavering, and some were recovered. He
had a son, who died a minister among the Nonconformists.

BUCLAND NEWTON [V.] Mr. JOHN WEEKS.§
After his ejectment he was many years minister of a congregation in *Bristol*, consisting of 1500 people, all of his own
gathering. He met with hardships on account of his Nonconformity, but bore them with great patience, meekness,
and courage. As he was preaching in *Froom-Woodlands*,
some informers came, who had vowed to shoot him; but he
directed his discourse to them with such majesty and boldness,
that they rode away without giving him any disturbance. He
was twice imprisoned six months, during which he preached

§ Hutchins's note here, is—"Weeks—Hally, *Intruders.* William Lyford,
instit. 1662"

out of the prison-windows, and had many of the common
people constantly to hear him. He was once carried to prison
from his pulpit: while he was in his sermon, the officers came
in and demanded, by what authority he preached? He thereupon clapped his hand on his Bible, and said, " By the authority of God and this book." They then ordered him to
come down: but he desired he might conclude with prayer;
which they yielded to, standing by uncovered. And he prayed so heartily for the king and government, that one of his
friends, after prayer, asked a clergyman who came with the
officers, What he had to say against such a man? to which
he replied, " Truly nothing; only such men eat the bread
out of our mouths." At another time the Bishop himself
came to take Mr. *Weeks*, attended by one *Hellyar*, who was
one of the most furious persecutors in that part of the kingdom. Among the persons present at the meeting, there was
one of the same name with his. When the man who took
down their names, came to him, and asked his name, he desired to be excused; and though he was pressed again and
again, he still excused himself. At last, being urged by several to inform them why he would not tell his name, he
answered, " Because I am ashamed of it." Being farther
asked, What reason he had to be ashamed of his name? He
answered, " Because it is *Hellyar*;" which set all present
à laughing at the persecutor of that name, who stood by.—It
was said of this noted enemy of the Dissenters, that when he
lay on his death-bed, he ordered this motto to be used at his
funeral, *There the wicked cease from troubling.*

There was in this place, another furious adversary of Mr.
Weeks and the Dissenters, a vintner, whose name was *Ollyffe,*
who was chosen mayor on purpose that he might exercise
severity on the Nonconformists; and he declared he accepted
the office for that reason only. But providence remarkably
interposed to prevent the effects of his fury, for he died in a
few days after he entered upon his office.

Mr. *Weeks* was a man of great piety and prudence, and
very remarkable for his courage. It has been often said of
him, " That he could bear any thing from his enemies, tho'
not from his friends." His spirits were elevated by their zeal.
He was very submissive to the divine will under severe pains
of body, and when reduced to great difficulties. He never
complained of God, but was abundant in blessing him and
admiring his dispensations; and rejoiced that he could find
his heart inclined to love God, even when under manifold
afflictions

afflictions at once. He was as popular a preacher as most in England, and remarkably fervent in expostulating with sinners. But he did not indulge in loose harrangues : he took pains with his sermons to the last. He was a minister out of the pulpit as well as in it; a most affectionate sympathising friend; one who 'became all things to all men,' and charitable even beyond his ability. He discovered a most divine temper in his sickness, and was serene and joyful in the approach of death. He exchanged this for a better life, *Nov.* 23, 1698, aged 65. His funeral sermon was preached by Mr. *Jos. Kentish* (who assisted, and afterwards succeeded him) on 2 *Kings* ii. 12. Mr. *Jos. Standen* (who married his daughter) published a funeral poem, which contained a view of his character.* His uncle, Mr. *Samuel Hardy*, was offered 500l. a year if he would have conformed.

₊ BURSTOCK [V.] Mr. HENRY PARSONS.† Born about the year 1630. He was a man of good learning, and had episcopal ordination. While he was at *Burstock*, which was but a small living, he taught the languages to several youths committed to his care, some of whom lived to shew him great respect in his old age. Soon after his ejectment by the Uniformity act, the living of *Uplime*, worth 300l. *per annum* being vacant by the death of the incumbent, the patron solicited Mr. *Parsons* to accept it ; but he excused himself, by saying that his conscience would not permit him to do it. Besides his pecuniary loss, he suffered much for his Nonconformity ; having had his house rifled and plundered ; being driven from his abode, and several times thrown into prison. He was once seized at *Taunton*, when preaching to a numerous congregation, who were desirous of enjoying his labours, and was carried to *Ilchester* jail. The persons who conducted him, obliged him, as soon as he came to the end of the town, to quit his horse, and travel through a bad road on foot ; whipping him on in a barbarous manner. His feet were so much hurt as to bleed. He took his trial at the assizes for the county, before judge *Hale*, who treated him with great respect, and found means to discharge him. He was afterwards imprisoned in *Dorchester* jail, with several of his brethren, suffering for the cause of Nonconformity. He was after that confined in the county jail of *Devon* for

---

* A farther account of Mr. Weeks may be expected from Mr. Isaac James, in his intended History of the Congregations in Bristol.

† From Hutchins, it appears that Mr. Parsons was here but a short time, " Henry Parsons, 17 Aug. 1661.—Thomas Jachol, 22 Dec. 1662."

many

many months, upon the same score. And finally, he was imprisoned in one of the *Western* jails, soon after the Duke of *Monmouth's* defeat, and thrown into a vile dungeon, from whence several of the quarters of some, who had been executed for that affair, had been carried out the preceding day to be dispersed, and hung up as monuments of *James's* and *Jefferys's* humanity.

After the Revolution Mr. *Parsons* lived many years at *Stoke under Ham* in Somerset, where he spent the remainder of a useful life, with a society of Protestant Dissenters. He died in 1717, in the 88th year of his age, full of satisfaction in his Nonconformity, and of the hope of a crown of life. He had a numerous family. One of his children. Mrs. *Mary Cole*, was living at *Dartmouth*, in a very advanced age, in *September* 1774, who gave the above account.* All that Dr. *Calamy* says of Mr. *Parsons* is, that he was a very warm and zealous man against the hierarchy, Common Prayer, and ceremonies.

CAME. (Winter-born) Mr. CHRISTOPHER LAWRENCE.† Of *Oxford* university. Born at *Dorchester*, 1613, at the time the town was in flames; so that his mother was forced to be removed into the fields, just after her delivery. He was of an ancient and respectable family in this county. On leaving the university in 1636, he was ordained by the Bishop of Bath and Wells. He afterwards lived some time at *Plymouth*, where he had an intimate friendship with Mr. *Hughes*: During the civil wars, he spent some time in London, where he assisted young gentlemen in their academical studies, among whom was Dr. *Cosh*, afterwards an eminent physician in the city, who retained a very grateful sense of the benefit he received under his instruction, which he expressed by many kind offices for his son, many years after. Mr. *Lawrence* had the living of *Odcomb* in Somersetshire, where he had some trouble from the widow and friends of the former incumbent. In 1652 he was forced to quit the place, for not taking the Engagement. He then removed his family at a great expence to London, having a prospect of some employment there as a scholar; but meeting with a disappointment, he returned to Dorsetshire, and in 1654 was presented to the living of *Langton Matravers*, in the isle of Purbeck, by Sir

* Communicated by the Rev. Mr. Reynell, of Totness.
† Hutchins says, " Christopher Lawrence Intruder, ejected 1662." N. Froncham was here in 1650. See Langton.

J   Walter

Walter Erle. In 1658 he was removed to *Came*, from whence he was ejected in 1662. He had spent a considerable sum of money in repairing, and partly rebuilding the parsonage-house, but could not get the least allowance made him for it. Many of his friends, and some persons of rank, pressed him to conform; but he could not satisfy his conscience to do it. However he was a stranger to faction, had a great abhorrence of the proceedings against the king in 1648, and was heartily desirous of the Restoration.

After his ejectment, he attended the public worship at Dorchester and at Frampton, where he was intimate with the incumbents till his death. In 1665, the militia being raised, under the pretence of a plot in the North, some soldiers were sent to Mr. *Lawrence's* to apprehend him; but missing of him, tho' he was in his study, they did a great deal of mischief in the house, particularly by destroying a great quantity of medicines which Mrs. *Lawrence* had prepared for the poor, whom she used to relieve this way with great skill and success. Going into an out-house, where they supposed him to lie concealed, they thrust their swords up to the hilts in some hay and straw, swearing they would do the rogue's business if he was there. But tho' they now missed Mr. *Lawrence*, the next day he surrendered himself to the deputy-lieutenants, and he, with other ministers, were committed to *Dorchester* jail, where he contracted an illness, from which he was never afterwards intirely free. When the Corporation-act took place, he removed to a house near *Frampton*, where, after languishing some time, he exchanged this life for a better, *May* 15, 1667, and was interred in *All-saints* church, in Dorchester.—He was a man of good learning, of a pleasant conversation, and a most inoffensive character; but his great modesty hindered him from making the shew some others did. His Nonconformity exposed him to uncommon losses; but he endeavoured to approve himself to that Being, who, he knew, could make all good to him and his, in kind or in value.

CHARDSTOCK [V. 45l. 1s. 4d.] Mr. BENJAMIN MILLS. He had a full congregation while he was in the public church, and it was observed that the parish in general was, at that time, more civilized than it was known to be either before or since. He preached privately after his ejectment, and died about the year 1693.

CHARMOUTH

CHARMOUTH [R.] Mr. Burd. §Hutchins mentions no such person here, but in another place introduces Benjamin Bird, who might possibly be the person here intended. It appears from the same work, that Mr. *Wesley* was here in 1650, and he seems to have been ejected from hence. *Hutchins's* words are " Bartholomew Wesley, In-" truder : he was ejected after the Restoration. See more " of him in Dr. *Calamy's* Continuation, p. 429."—In another place he calls him " Bartholomew Wesley, Presbyterian " minister, at *Charmouth*."—This Mr. *Wesley* is also mentioned 1650, among the Rectors of *Catherston*, which is near Charmouth. And from the next entry it is plain that Mr. Bird succeeded him here. " Benjamin Bird, 14 *Oct.* 1662." If this be the person intended by Dr. Calamy, he conformed soon after Bartholomew-day, and was ejected afterwards. But it is impossible now to ascertain the fact.

CHIDIOCK, Mr. Henry Backaller. He had been mentioned by Dr. Calamy, and in the former edition of this work, at Woodlands, in *Devonshire*, but ought undoubtedly to have been introduced in this place. The following information was sent to the author respecting a person of this name, of whom there can be no question whether he was the same that was ejected here. " One Mr. *Backaller*, an " ejected minister, lived near *Charmouth*, who was of good " conversation and of considerable parts, writes his name as " above, and says he was ejected at *Chyddeck* : a parish " either in Devon or Dorset"—[There is no such place in *Devon*]—" that he was episcopally ordained at the same " time with Mr. *Brice*, of Marshwood." [§Namely, by Dr. *Ironside*, Bishop of Bristol, in or before the year 1659. See *Marshwood*, in this county] " He died somewhere " about Exeter, in 1713, when he wanted but a few months " of being a hundred years of age. His funeral sermon " was preached by Mr. Aaron Pitts of Chard, on *Gen.* xlix. " 18. *I have waited for thy salvation, O Lord.*"

CHISLEBOROUGH. See *Somersetshire*.

CLIFTON. Mr. Richard Wyne. [So his name is written by Hutchins, who mentions him at *Dorchester*, and again at *Wraxhall*, 1 April, 1662 : his successor, April 15, 1663.] Being harrassed in his place, he left the church, and became a Nonconformist soon after the Revolution. §He is not, therefore, with strict propriety, included in the number
ber

ber of ejected ministers. According to Hutchins he was
not instituted to this living till 1687, when he must have
been a Conformist.

The following list of incumbents is an exact Transcript
from Hutchins:

Henry Dutton. [No date of his institution.]
William Oake, on the resig. of *Dutton*, instit. 7 *Jan.* 1660.
John Hayne, on the deprivation of *Oake*, instit. 12 *Feb.*
1662.
Richard Wyne, on the death of *Hayne.* instit. 26 *Ap.*
1687.
Samuel Hieron, on the resig. of *Wyne*, instit. 17 *May*,
1692.

From this register, it seems that

Mr. WILLIAM OAKE is to be inserted in the list of ejected
ministers, in the room of *Wyne ;* whose name however is
retained, as he became a Dissenter in consequence of his
being " harrassed" while in the church, doubtless for want
of strict conformity. Tho' the occasion and circumstances
of Mr. *Oake*'s leaving it, be not expressly mentioned, his
" deprivation" at the same period with so many other Nonconformists, strongly indicates that he was one of the number.
The date of his successor's institution, *Feb.* 1662, is most
probably put, as in many other cases, for 1663.

DORCHESTER. *All-Saints* [R.] WILLIAM BENN,
M. A.§ He was born at or near *Egremond*, in Cumberland, A. D. 1600 ; educated at St. *Bees*, and afterwards at
Queen's Col. Oxford ; which he left without taking any
degree, on obtaining a presentation to *Oakingham*, in Berkshire ; but upon Mr. Bateman's having got another presentation [to the same living] rather than contest it at law, they
agreed jointly to perform the duty, and receive the profits.
Afterwards Mr. *Benn* became chaplain to the Marchioness
of Northampton, with whom he lived in Somersetshire,

§ In Hutchin's Hist. *Wm. Benn* occurs, 1629.—" deprived for Noncon-
" formity, 1662."—" *Richard Wyne*, instituted 10 *Feb.* 1662.—*Toope* suc-
" ceeded *Wyne*, May 13, 1691."—This was probably the same *Richard Wyne*,
who was at CLIFTON. In that case he must have had both livings, and have
given up *Dorchester*, in 1691. (Mr. *James)* But then he must have been a
Conformist till that time.—Hutchius's account of Mr. *Benn* is pretty large,
quoted from *Athen. Oxon*, and contains some particulars which Dr. Calamy
had not, which are now inserted.

leaving

leaving Oakingham to Mr. Bateman. In 1629, the celebrated Mr. White, often called the patriarch of Dorchester, invited him to that town, by whose interest he was made rector of *All-Saints*, and was in great repute among the Puritans; and, excepting two years that he attended Mr. White, at *Lambeth*, he continued here till Bartholomew-day, when he was ejected for Nonconformity. Not satisfied with his constant labours in the church, while he held his rectorship, he preached gratis, on week-days to the prisoners in the jail, which was in his own parish : and the room not being large enough to contain the people who attended, he procured a chapel to be built within the prison walls, principally at his own expence—In 1654 he was one of the assistants to the Commissioners for ejecting such as were called scandalous, ignorant and insufficient ministers and school-masters.

When he was silenced, he continued among his people, and preached to them as he could find opportunity, so long as he lived; for which he was often brought into trouble, and sometimes fined and imprisoned. He died *March* 22, 1680; having been a painful, faithful and successful labourer in the vineyard of Christ fifty years; and was buried in *All-Saints* church-yard. He was a man of unparalleled perseverance in prayer : for he usually prayed in his study seven times in a day; and it was his custom at stated seasons daily to give God thanks for deliverance from certain imminent dangers which befel him, in the years 1630, 1643 and 1645. [The late Dr. *Theophilus Lobb*, was, by his mother's side, a grandson of his : a man eminent in piety, as well as in medical skill and benevolence.*

WORKS. An answer to Mr. Bamfield, in vindication of the Christian Sabbath, against the Jewish.—Twelve Sermons on Soul-prosperity, on iii. *John*, v. 2. published after his death.

—— TRINITY and ST. PETERS [1601.] GEORGE HAMMOND, M. A. Of *Exeter Col. Oxf.* Born in 1620. He studied some time at *Trin. Col.* Dublin, where he was once met by Archbishop Usher, who condescended to enter into conversation with him, and was so well pleased with him that the next time he came to the college, tho' it was a good

* He invented that excellent TINCTURE which bears his name, and continues its reputation, particularly as an antidote against epidemical diseases. The experience of many years induces the Editor to insert this note.

while

while afterwards, he enquired very particularly after Mr. Hammond, and expressed his apprehension, that he would prove a considerable man. It was while he was at Oxford that he first became seriously attentive to the concerns of his soul; but whether he began his studies there or at Dublin is uncertain. He was sometime minister at *Totness*, in Devon, where, just after he had been preaching with great seriousness, about patience and resignation to the will of God, he had occasion for the exercise of these graces himself, by the loss of a child, which was killed by falling out of the window of an upper chamber. [It appears from *Hutchins's* History, that he was not admitted to this living till 1660, and his successor, *June* 30, 1663.] About the year 1677, he became minister to a large congregation of Dissenters, in *Taunton*, in conjunction with Mr. *George Newton*. His excellent qualifications induced some persons of rank, (particularly the Ladies Courtney and Constantine) to send their sons to board with him.

He was faithful and diligent in his work. His sermons were plain, solid and judicious; but for want of life in delivering them, they were not valued, by the common sort of hearers, according to their merit. He had an excellent faculty at clearing difficulties, and resolving cases of conscience. His discourses on private days of prayer and conference, on various texts of scripture, with little or no previous meditation, found general acceptance, and convinced the more understanding part of his auditors, of his solid judgment and great abilities.—When the fears of Popery increased, after the Popish plot was stifled, and a sham Presbyterian plot was trumped up, he endeavored to arm his people against the attempts of seducers, and to prepare them for a day of trial. To this end, he went every Monday night to their houses, and read some part of Mr. *Poole's Dialogues against Popery;* after which he farther explained the Popish tenets, and confuted them with great strength of argument, in a very plain and familiar style; frequently citing the very words of the most celebrated champions of the church of Rome by memory, to the admiration, satisfaction and advantage of those who frequented this exercise.

The persecution which preceded, and the barbarous cruelties which followed, Monmouth's rebellion, drove him from Taunton to London; where he joined with Mr. Richard Steel, and succeeded him, after his death, as pastor of a congregation. He died *October*, 1705. He was an excellent

lent scholar, a good critic, and mighty in the scriptures; of a clear head, a faithful memory, of eminent humility and meekness, of a very even temper, and a most peaceable healing spirit.

WORKS. A Discourse of family Worship; drawn up at the request of the London ministers.—And a Preface to Mr. Richard Saunders's Discourse of Angels.—A Sermon in the last vol. of the Morning Exercise, on this question: How may private christians be most helpful to promote the entertainment of the Gospel? §He also published an excellent sermon on the death of Mr. RICHARD STEEL; entitled, A good minister of Jesus Christ. Mr. *Charles Bulkly*, in his *Christian Minister*, p. 113, speaks of it in these high terms: " It is a book written with the greatest plainness imaginable, of style and language, but yet with so much power of truth, and force of conviction, as have rendered it extremely entertaining, acceptable, and I hope useful to myself. And I venture to recommend it, not only to the perusal, but intimate familiarity of every minister. It would be worth his while to get it by heart.".

DURWESTON [R.] Mr. JOHN GALPIN. §Nothing was said of him by Dr. Calamy, who had only his surname, and that mis-spelt. The following account of him is from *Hutchins's* History of Dorset. "Richard Hooke was sequestered 1645, and his parsonage, value 100l. *per annum*, disposed of by the Committee to J. Galpin."—It follows, " *John Galpin*, Intruder. The return to the Commis-" sioners, 1650, was, that the parsonage and glebe of " *Durweston cum Knyghton*, with the annuity of 40s. " payable out of the parsonage of Stickland to it, is worth " 120l. *per ann*. John Galpin, incumbent."—His successor was inducted Dec. 3, 1664.

FORDINGTON [V. 48l. 10s.] Mr. JOSHUA CHURCHHILL. Some time after his ejectment, he assisted Mr. *Benn* at Dorchester, and succeeded him there.—He published Mr. Benn's Sermons on Soul-prosperity, with a dedication to —— Grove, Esq. of Fern, in Wiltshire.

HAMOON [R. 120l.] THOMAS MORE, M. A. Of *Trin. Col. Oxford;* where he continued eight or nine years. After his ejectment, he and his family suffered great want. The family of the *Trenchards* (in whose gift the living of *Hamoon* was) had such an esteem for him, that, as there were three vacancies at that place from Bartholomew-day, during his life, they made a free offer of the parsonage to him every time: but he still refused it, because he could not

be satisfied with the terms of conformity. Rather than
violate his conscience he chose to live in want and obscurity,
in the private exercise of his ministry; which he did till
death gave him his final release, in *August*, 1699, at Abbot-
Milton, in this county.

HASILBURY BRIAN [R.] Mr. JAMES RAWSON. He
was presented to this rectory by the Earl of Northumberland.
He was a Conformist in the time of K. *Charles* I. but
thought the terms of conformity, after the Restoration, too
rigorous. Dr. *Walker* reports, that he was cast out for
abusing the royal family in a sermon, and praying that God
would root it out. But so many false charges of this sort
were brought against the ministers of those times who did
not swim with the stream, that such a story ought not to be
credited till it be better authenticated. §Hutchins says, " In
" 1654 *James Rawson*, by order of the Committee of the
" county, officiated here, and was a preaching minister.
" Clark, the former incumbent, died during the usurpation,
" and on the Restoration the *Intruder* claimed the living,
" but was not allowed to keep it." The reason he assigns
is that above-mentioned; but it is only on *Walker's* authority.—At *Winterborn Abbas*, he has " *James Rawson*,
M. A. 1630." His successor, 1662. So that it would
seem, this last was the place from which the Uniformity-act
ejected him.

HAWKCHURCH [R.] Mr. JOHN HODDER. He
usually preached, after his ejectment, at Mr. *Henley's*, at
Colway-house, near Lyme. He was a man of excellent
abilities, and a celebrated preacher. He was so much of a
gentleman, and of such singular ingenuity, that his very
enemies admired him, and were fond of his conversation.
He was also a great Loyalist, as appears from a long epistle
of his prefixed to a sermon of Mr. *Ames Short*, on the
proclamation of K. *Charles* II. §Hutchins does not mention him, but has his successor, *Swallow*, 1662.

HOLNEST [C.†] Mr. JOHN MOORE. Of *Braz. Nose
Col. Oxf.* He was born at Musbury, and had his grammar-
learning at Colyton. Mr. *John Prince*, author of the
Worthies of Devon, mentions him with respect, as his
fellow-pupil, under Mr. Thomas Adams. He had episcopal
ordination. He was a person of a sprightly genius, and

† This is a Chapelry belonging to Long-Burton.

made

made considerable improvements. Besides officiating at Holnest, he served *Long-Burton*, five years after Bartholomew-day : and yet was at length as much silenced by the Act of Uniformity, as if he had been ejected by it at first : For falling into a close acquaintance with Mr. *T. Crane*, of Rampesham, and other silenced ministers, he was by degrees convinced of his obligation to join them, and so was rendered incapable of continuing in the church of England. But before he left it, he met with much trouble on account of his scrupling, and therefore not practising, a total conformity ; the particulars of which he committed to writing, but his papers being burnt, they cannot be retrieved.

[He afterwards retired to *St. Mary, Ottery*, Devonshire, where he had a small paternal estate. During his abode here, he was employed in preaching to the people in the country round about ; often to the great hazard of his person and of his life. However he always providentially escaped ; and once very remarkably, when he hastily fled from home in the night, in very severe weather, but a little before his persecutors entered his house with great violence, and ran their swords thro' all the beds, in expectation of either discovering or destroying him. He had at this time seven children, one of whom, being very young, innocently asked his mother, on occasion of this alarm, Whether these were not the *Philistines ?* This son lived to be his successor. While Mr. *Moore* was at *Ottery*, his goods were once seized, and publicly cried for sale, but nobody would buy them, and so they were restored. He had the greatest respect shewed him while he continued here ; the country people took the whole management of his little farm (besides other acts of kindness) so that he had a comfortable subsistence.]

In the year 1676, he became pastor to a large congregation of Dissenters, at *Bridgwater*, in Somersetshire, where he was very useful for about thirty-six years, and where many, long after his death, blessed God for him. He maintained an even chearful temper under all the hardships of the woeful times in King *Charles*'s and *James*'s reigns ; was very pleasant in conversation, and of a most peaceable spirit. He, with Mr. *Weeks*, of Bristol, and Mr. *A Sinclare* (who fled thither from Waterford, in Ireland, to escape the rage of the Papists in the reign of K. *James)* encouraged the ministers of Somerset first, and those of Devon afterwards, to assemble together in stated meetings, to maintain order, union and peace. He diligently attended the assemblies, in

Somerset

Somerset, and sometimes even in his old age travelled to
those held in Exeter. [He continued minister to a most respectable audience both for fortune and numbers, and among
them the whole magistracy of the town, till the latter end
of Q. *Anne's* reign. Once, in the reign of K. *William*,
as he came out of the pulpit, he was apprehended by a warrant from the mayor, on pretence of his keeping an academy,
tho' he only boarded the young men ; which affair cost him
30*l.* or 40*l.*]

He was afflicted many years with the stone. In his last
painful sickness, his patience and serenity of mind were
truly admirable. And so well was he fortified against what
is to nature the most terrible, that few have been known to
meet death with greater composure of spirit. He died *Aug.*
23, 1717, aged 75. His funeral sermon was preached by
Mr. *Batson*, of *Taunton :* but he could not be prevailed
with to print it. Mr. *Moore* to the last declared himself
fully satisfied in his Nonconformity, but had an extensive
charity, and a hearty esteem for good men of all persuasions. He left two sons in the ministry among the Dissenters.
One of them succeeded him at *Bridgwater;* the other was
pastor of a congregation, at *Abington*, in Berkshire.

WORKS. A Reformation Sermon, at Bridgwater, in 1698,
on Rom. xiii. 4.—An Answer to Mr. Matthew Hole's Letters,
concerning Gifts and Forms of Prayer.

HORTON [V. 48*l.*] Mr. TUCKER.

LANGTON MATRAVERS [R. 140*l.*] Mr. JOHN
MITCHEL. He was not only eminent in preaching, but he
went from house to house doing good. All the inhabitants
of the place honoured him ; and some gentlemen in the
neighbourhood, who were zealous enough for the church of
England, waited on the bishop, in order to his keeping in
his living : but nothing would do without that entire conformity in which he could by no means be satisfied. §Hut-
chins mentions *Theophilus Polewheele*, as incumbent here
in the year 1650. See *Tiverton*.

LITCHET MATRAVERS. THOMAS ROWE, M. A.
Of *Exeter Col. Oxf.* A native of North-Petherwin, in
Devonshire: Son of Mr. Thomas Rowe, an attorney. In

* He was a man of considerable learning and an eminent tutor.—He
published a learned piece, entitled, Propositions on natural and revealed
religion.—Mr. *Moore*, who published the Elegy on the death of Dr. Doddridge, was of this family.

his

his childhood, his life was remarkably preserved for future usefulness, when another child playing near him was killed by the fall of a chimney.. In his youth he was sickly, which with his great thoughtfulness about spiritual matters, made him apppear dejected; but he afterwards enjoyed a good share both of health and chearfulness. His father designed him for his own profession; but, thro' the persuasion of a good old servant in the family, together with the seriousness of his own spirit, he of all things desired to be educated, in order to the ministry. His father gratified his inclination, and placed him at Oxford, under the care of Dr. *Conant*, where he soon obtained a good character for singular piety, studiousness and integrity. He had much exercise of spirit about religious concerns, being a strict observer of his own heart, words and ways; and of a very tender conscience, as appears from his diary. He would not quit the university and enter upon public service, upon taking his first degree, tho' he was strongly urged to it, but continued the pursuit of his studies till he was M. A. He removed to *Gloucester-hall*, at the encouragement of Dr. Garbran, with a view to take pupils; and was afterwards chosen one of the state chaplains at *New-College*.

He was first settled as a minister, and ordained at *Litchet*, about 1658,* and continued there till Bartholomew-day, 1662. After the Restoration, and before his ejectment, he was twice imprisoned, with some other ministers, tho' not above a fortnight either time. After his ejectment, Mr. *Moor*, of Spargrove, in Batcomb parish, Somerset, invited him to his house, where he for some time preached every week in the family. Here Mr. *Richard Allein* was his neighbour, with whom he maintained a most intimate friendship. In 1665, he returned to *Litchet* for a year, and preached twice every Lord's-day, in Mrs. *Trenchard's* family, out of church hours; using to attend on the public preaching when the prayers were over. On the Five-mile act, he removed to *Little Canford*, near Wimborn, and preached several years in his own house, without any pro-secution or disturbance; the reason of which was supposed to be, the great number of Papists in those parts, who lived under the countenance of a considerable knight of that re-ligion; for they who were disposed, could not for shame disturb him, and leave them unmolested. Here he had a

* Hutchins has it, " Thomas Row, presented 1657," on the death of Cleves.

crowded

crowded auditory; the people coming from all parts round
the country. But he laboured gratis all the time, except for
the last half year, when they paid his house-rent.—In 1672
he removed to *Wimborn,* where he continued pastor of a
congregation for the remaining part of his life, with great
satisfaction. He had but a very slender allowance from his
hearers; yet such was his affection for them, heightened
by his usefulness, that he envied none their more plentiful
circumstances; his heart being chiefly set upon doing good.

After the licences were called in, he was often presented
and disturbed, but his christian name was mistaken, which
proved of no small service to him. There were some instances of the signal appearance of God's providence against
such as endeavored to disturb him in his ministry. In 1665,
while he lived at Mr. *Moor's,* he came to Mrs. *Trenchard's,*
at Litchet, to make a visit; intending, while he was there,
to preach in one of the poor parishioner's cottages. A person of the parish getting intelligence of it, turned informer,
and bringing a constable and another person with him, demanded the doors of the house to be opened, tho' the exercise was over. The officious informer took down the names
of all present, and the next day procured a warrant to apprehend them. Mr. *Rowe* soon got out of the reach of the
warrant into another county; but they served the warrant on
many of the hearers, and carried them before a justice, who
bound them over to the quarter-sessions. The justice to divert himself, asked some of the women, What the text was
at the conventicle? and upon being told it was *Col.* iii. 5,
Mortify therefore your members which are upon the earth,
&c. he burlesqued it, and poured forth his profane jests very
plentifully; of which, however, when he came upon his
death-bed, he bitterly repented; acknowledging that his distemper, which proved his death, was a just judgment from
God upon him for it. The busy informer had the use of his
right side taken away soon after, and died. The officer also,
who assisted in disturbing the meeting, was within a few
weeks killed by his own cart, directly opposite the house and
the very door where the meeting was held, which he assisted
in disturbing.

Mr. *Rowe* was a very humble serious man, and a close
walker with God; a strict observer of the Lord's-day, and
a daily practitioner in the art of divine meditation. Prayer
was his delight and his constant exercise. He was careful
to keep from the very borders of sin; and to abstain from
all

all "appearance of evil." He was of a most tender compassionate spirit to persons in distress, especially on a spiritual
account, and had a particular talent in administering comfort
to them ; and yet he was a most awakening preacher to secure
sinners. The *Boanerges* and the *Barnabas* met in him to
an uncommon degree; and he well knew how to be either,
as occasion required. He was a close reprover of sin
wherever he saw it, even tho' he expected the warmest resentment ; and God often rewarded his fidelity, by making
the event quite different. He once sharply reproved a gentleman of considerable figure in the world, for a particular
crime ; who not only took it in good part, but told a person
soon after, that he would have taken so sharp a reproof from
no person living besides Mr. *Rowe*, but he verily believed he
did it in the great integrity of his heart.

As a preacher he did not ' serve God with that which did
' cost him nothing,' but took much time and pains in the
composure of all his sermons ; which were not only very
methodical and exact, but had a very practical vein, and a
serious plainness running thro' them. He never began the
composing of a sermon, without piously looking upwards
for a blessing. He delivered himself with a becoming
pathos, and his heart was visible in his work. He has often
said, That he thought no king ever took more pleasure in
swaying the royal sceptre, than he did in preaching the word ;
and when he was abridged of his liberty, he declared, That
he could freely spare out of his daily bread, could it but pur-
chase liberty again to preach the gospel. He had many seals
to his ministry at *Wimborn*, especially among young persons.
He frequently visited his people, and enquired after the state
of their souls ; and he discharged the whole of his office
with great acceptance, both in the pulpit and out of it. He
was a very hard student, and most conscientiously redeemed
his time. He possessed a great serenity of mind, and sweetness of temper, mixed with a becoming gravity, which was
attractive of esteem and love from all good men. He was
entirely satisfied in his Nonconformity, and had so great a
value for the ministry in that way, under all its discouragements, that he always designed, and solemnly devoted, his
eldest son to it from the womb. God carried him thro' all
his labours and difficulties with great chearfulness and satisfaction ; and he had occasion to remark, How mercifully
God provided for him as to this world, in making the little
he had in it go farther, and afford him truer pleasure after his

K 4

ejectment,

ejectment, than a much larger income did before.—His last sickness was a violent fever, which greatly discomposed his head; but he had his lucid intervals; in which he was very serious and resigned. The night before his death, he was heard to say, " O how do I long to be in heaven!" which earnest longing was answered, *Oct.* 9, 1680, in the 50th year of his age. His funeral sermon was preached at *Litchet*, by Mr. *S. Hardy*, his intimate friend and neighbour. The church was vastly crowded, and there was scarcely a dry eye to be seen in the whole assembly. He had no fondness for appearing in print, and therefore nothing of his has been published but a little posthumous piece, entitled, *The chris-, tian's daily work*, &c. by way of Appendix to Mr. *Clif-ford's Sound words.*

LYME REGIS [V. 45*l.*] AMES SHORT, M. A. Of *Exeter Col. Oxf.* Born at *Aishwater*, in Devon, 1616; being the third son of Mr. *John Short*, a gentleman of good estate; who, having a living in his own gift, designed this son for the church. Tho' it doth not appear that he had any serious views to the ministry, he, with several other students, was brought under good impressions while at the college. When he left it he was chaplain to Lady *Clark*, of Suffolk. In 1645, he settled at *Topsham*; and March 2, 1646, was ordained by the seventh classical Presbytery at London. In 1650, he accepted an invitation to *Lyme Regis*, by the joint advice of the ministers of Dorset and Devon. Here he continued till the Bartholomew-act ejected him. He was much respected by the neighbouring gentry, who importuned him to conform; and he had considerable offers made him, particularly a Deanry, to induce him to it; but he could not come up to the terms required. He took great pains both at *Topsham* and at *Lyme*, and God was pleased to make him useful to many. While he was at *Topsham*, a very loose man who heard him preach, (to whom he was a stranger) railed at him after the sermon, for being so indecent as to publish his faults to the congregation; and threatened to kill him. Accordingly he waited for him at his return from Exeter, with a loaded pistol; but when Mr. *Short* came near him, his heart failed, and he spake kindly to him.

After his ejectment, Mr. *Short* discharged his duty to his people in private, as he had liberty and opportunity, and was many ways a sufferer for his Nonconformity, tho' he shewed so much loyalty as to preach a sermon upon the Restoration, which was printed at the request of the magistrates of the town.

town. His own father was so exasperated against him as to
leave him nothing. When the Five mile act confined him
as a prisoner at home, the county-troops often entered the
town to search for him, and rifled his house. Being several
times disappointed, they were enraged, and one of them
caught his son, held a pistol to his breast, and threatened to
kill him if he did not tell where his father was. The child
answered, " My father does not acquaint me whither he
goes." As they were searching the chimnies, chests, boxes,
&c. they threatened the servant-maid after the same manner.
Upon which she said, " My master doth not hide himself
in such places; he has a better protector." To which she
had this reply : " The devil take him and his protector too !"

Upon his first coming to *Lyme*, he drew up articles for
such as desired to join in communion with him, and rules for
the right ordering their conversation. A copy of these after
the Restoration falling into the hands of his enemies, Mr.
G. Alford, (a man famous for his furious zeal) sent them
up, as containing matters of dangerous consequence to the
government; and accused him as being seen at the head of
200 men, tho' he had scarcely been from his own house for
three weeks before. A messenger was sent down by the
king and council. Having timely notice of the design, he
rode to London some time before his arrival, and concealed
himself there till the heat was over. When the parliament
met, these dangerous papers were read in a committee ; but
none of the things whereof he was accused being found in
them, they were sent to the council-table, and the matter
died away. This was in the year 1668. About the time of
the *Rye-house* plot, the county-troops, commanded by ——
Strode, Esq. came to *Lyme* to seize Mr. *Short* and Mr.
Keridge ; when some men of the town got into the meeting-house, pulled down the pulpit, and were breaking up the
seats ; but Mr. Strode put a stop to their farther proceeding.

In 1682, Mr. *Short* was seized at Mr. John Starr's, in
Exeter, convicted upon the Act against conventicles, and
imprisoned for six months in that city. In 1685, he was
convicted at *Lyme*, upon the same act, and committed to
Dorchester jail, where he lay five months ; and upon *Monmouth's* landing at Lyme, he was removed from thence with
some others, to Portsmouth, and there laid in a dungeon.
He was for a long time summoned to appear at every assize,
and at last was outlawed. But none of these things moved
him. He was a man of an undaunted spirit, and neither

repented

repented of his nonconformity, nor was dejected at his sufferings; but often declared, That he never enjoyed sweeter communion with God, or had greater peace and comfort in his
own mind, than when his persecution was the most bitter.

During his imprisonment at Dorchester, *Solomon Andrews*, Esq. of Lyme, (a gentleman who pretended great
friendship to him before he was silenced, and urged Mrs.
Short to press her husband to conform) being at his seat in
Somersetshire, was heard to drop these words, " I will stick
as close to Mr. *Short* as his skin doth to his flesh." But as
he was returning to Lyme, in order to go to the assizes, at
Dorchester (where he was designed to be foreman of the
grand jury) he was found dead on the road.——Mr. *Short*
outlived these troubles; and after liberty was granted to Dissenters, he had a public meeting in *Lyme*, in which, *Aug.*
25, 1687, eight candidates for the ministry were ordained.
He continued to bring forth fruit in old age, having a strong
constitution, and enjoying a good measure of health. Even
in his advanced years he could and did endure hardness.
Being at Exeter, after he had prayed in the family where he
lodged, with great freedom, and dined with Mr. Pym, a
merchant in that city, he was seized with an apoplexy, and
died in a minute, *July* 15, 1697, aged 81. His funeral
sermon was preached by Mr. *George Trosse*.—He was a
genteel well-bred man, grave and serious, yet pleasant in
conversation. His wife was a gentlewoman of a good family of the name of *Arscot.* His son, Mr. *John Short*,
was a man of good learning, and very useful in educating
young men for the ministry, at Lyme and Colyton. He
afterwards died pastor of a congregation in London.

—— JOHN KERIDGE, M. A. Of *Corp. Christi Col. Oxf.*
He was born at Wooton Fitz-Pain, (a parish adjoining to
Lyme-Regis) where his father was a Nonconformist minister,
and was ejected. He for some time taught a school, at
Abingdon, in Berks, and went from thence to Lyme, where
he was ejected as a Schoolmaster. He was afterwards pastor
of a dissenting congregation at Colyton, in Devon. He
died *April* 15, 1705. An aged clergyman, who was his
pupil, gives him the character of a sober, learned, honest
man. §Hutchins mentions *Eman. Sharp*, as instit. 19 *Feb.*
1662 (perhaps 6?) on the deprivation of Mr. *Short.* This
indicates that he was ejected as a *Minister.*

MAPERTON

MAPERTON [R.] Mr. Hugh Gundery. Ejected in 1662. He continued a Nonconformist all his days ; and lived and died in a contented, tho' no very splendid condition. After his ejectment he preached mostly in Devonshire, often at Newton-chapel, a peculiar, belonging to *Ailsbeere.* He was one of those twelve in that county who took the oath required by the Five-mile act, in 1665. He was taken off suddenly by a fit of an apoplexy.

MARSHWOOD. Mr. John Brice. Of *Magd. Col. Oxf.* He was born at Neitherbury, in 1636, and had his grammar-learning at the free-school, in the same parish. Upon quitting the university, he was assistant to Mr. Thorne of *Weymouth.* He was episcopally ordained, by Dr. *Ironside,* Bp. of Bristol. In the year 1659, he settled at Marshwood, and continued there till *August,* 1662. After his ejectment he met with a great deal of trouble, and was twice in Dorchester jail for his Nonconformity. After the Revolution, he opened a meeting in *Charmouth,* and continued preaching there to the day of his death, which was *March* 15, 1716. In his latter years, he married one Mrs. *Floyer,* a gentlewoman of a good family, who had a considerable estate; by which means he lived and died in plenty. He brought up two of her nephews to the ministry ; and left about 300*l.* to pious uses.

MELBURY-BUBB [R.] Mr. Forward. §Hutchins has it, " John Forward, instit. 1648." There was a Samuel Forward, at *Gillingham,* in 1650.

MORDEN [V. 100*l.* with *Charborow*] Edw. Bennet. M.A. Of *New-Inn Hall, Oxf.* Born at South-Brewham, in Somerset, *Ap.* 18, 1618, of an ancient family, which came originally from Wiltshire. He had episcopal ordination, being ordained by the Bp. of Bath and Wells. He began his ministry at *Batcombe,* as assistant to Mr. R. Bernard, and after his decease, to Mr. Richard Allein. He was next chaplain to Sir W. Waller, and afterwards to Lord Brook, baron of Beauchamp-court. In the time of the civil war he was preacher in London, (it is supposed at *Christ-Church*) where he remained about a year and a half, and then removed to Bratton, in Somerset. After refusing two rich parsonages, of which he was offered his choice, he settled at *South-Petherton,* at the invitation of the principal inhabitants ; where he was greatly beloved, not only by his
parishioners,

parishioners, but by the generality of ministers and religious
people in those parts. He had a flourishing congregation,
was greatly followed, and had a remarkable blessing attending his labours. He was much delighted in his work, and
abhorred trifling in his study or pulpit. He preached three
times a week in public, expounded the chapters he read, and
catechized children and young persons. In the evening he
repeated the sermons in his own family, to which many of
his neighbours came for several years. He was very cautious
in admitting persons to the sacrament, and as cautious in
refusing. He used to take all occasions for pious discourse,
and had days of conference with his people. He spent
much time in visiting the sick, and resolving the doubts of
the dejected. His whole conduct was exemplary, as he
carefully practised himself what he recommended others.
By his excellent instruction and wise conduct he reduced a
great part of the town to sobriety. In 1649 he refused to
take the Engagement against the king and house of lords,
and by that lost an augmentation of 100l. *per annum*, for
five years. This was at last the cause of his leaving the
country, for he fell under the obloquy of the Cromwellians,
for crossing their designs. In 1651 or 1652 he was appointed
one of the triers for the approbation of ministers.

In 1654 he removed to *Morden*,§ being earnestly invited
by Sir *Walter Earle*, and there was ejected in 1662. He
was here much followed, and that by some persons of good
rank. He was an awakening preacher, and was an instrument of good to many. He here received some uncommon
answers to his prayers. In 1663 he returned to his ancient
flock at *South-Petherton*, being earnestly invited by the inhabitants of the town, and some of the neighbouring
parishes. There he taught school, and constantly preached,
tho' he attended, with his family, as a hearer at the parish
church, where he had been a preacher. Nor did he confine
his labours to this place : Many a weary step did he take to
serve his master and do good to souls. Many a dark night
has he been travelling with these views. On *March* 25,
1665, being the Lord's-day, as he was preaching at *T. Moor's*,
Esq. at Spargrave, the foot-soldiers came and besieged the
house. Two justices entered ; one of whom told him that
he should come off for three pounds. But he modestly
refused to convict himself, and so was committed prisoner

§ Hutchins mentions his name as occurring in the register of this parish,
from 1654 to 1657.

to the marshal, and then delivered over to the constable of
the hundred. On the Tuesday following he went to *Wells,*
and tho' treated civilly, was committed to Ilchester jail ;
where he was imprisoned two months only, because of the
respect one of the justices had for him ; and he preached to
his fellow prisoners till he was released. In 1669, upon the
death of a near relation, he removed to his native place,
where he had an estate, and there held on preaching privately
as long as he lived. He spent much of his time in writing
letters to his friends upon their spiritual concerns. Indeed
his whole heart seemed set upon promoting the work of
grace in himself and others.

When the Conventicle-act came out, which confined the
number of auditors in private meetings to four adult persons,
besides the household, he preached three times on a Lord's-
day, in different families ; admitting only four others ; but
as many under sixteen years of age as would come. He
preached also frequently on the week-days.—He was a great
recorder of the mercies of God to him and his, to which end
he wrote a ' Book of Remembrance,' wherein he carefully
inserted many particular providences in his education, and
the several stages of his life ; in his removes, in his ministry,
and in preserving him from his adversaries. He strictly adhered to his principles in all the turns of the times, and kept
a clear conscience and an unspotted reputation to the last.
Not long before his death, he particularly expressed his satisfaction both in not having taken the Engagement, and in
his Nonconformity. He died of an apoplectic fit, when he
was taking horse to preach, *Nov.* 8, 1673, aged 56. His
funeral sermon was preached by Mr. *W. Parsons,* at
Brewham.

He was a man of good learning and considerable abilities ;
an excellent *Hebrician* ; of a quick and clear apprehension,
and strong reason ; a hard student, and a ready disputant ;
able to defend the truth by argument ; of a courageous
spirit, fearing no danger in the way of his duty. He was a
strict observer of the sabbath, and frequent in secret prayer ;
a great reprover of sin wherever he saw it, whether in great
or small. Most sincere and plain-hearted in the whole course
of his conversation ; of a chearful temper, sweet and obliging in his deportment, and of a very humble behaviour.
His discourse was ingenious, innocent and instructive. He
was in his judgment a Presbyterian, but of known moderation towards those of other sentiments. He abhorred censoriousness,

soriousness, or confining religion to a party, and was respected by all parties. He had always a friendly correspondence with the neighbouring clergy, who treated him with
great civility.

MONKTON, (TARENT) [C.] Mr. RICHARD DOWN.
After his ejectment he lived at Bridport, where he did much
good. He died in *August* 1687. § There is a Vicarage
at Monkton at which Hutchins mentions *Henry Martin* as
incumbent 1650. He adds, " There is a chapel united to
it, not eight furlongs from the church, supplied by Mr. Martin." But does not mention Mr. *Down*. It was doubtless this chapel that is here intended.

NEWTON, (MAIDEN) [R. 30*l*. 4*s*. 10*d*.] Mr. AN-
DREW BROMHALL. He was one of the Triers in this county
for ejecting immoral and insufficient ministers. After his
ejectment he removed to London, where, it may be presumed, he was in good repute, as he was concerned in the Morning Exercises. There is a sermon of his in the collection,
on the discovery, and cure of Hypocrisy.§ No. 27. in the
vol. dated Nov. 14. 1661. Text, *Luke* xii. 1. An excellent and useful discourse, which shews the author to have
been a man of ability and learning.—" The return to the
" commissioners, 1650, was, that Andrew Bromhall, an
" able minister, was put in by the Parliament."—"Matthew
" Osborn was sequestered, and his parsonage 240*l*. *per ann.*
" ordered to Bromhall, a famous Trier. But he (Osborn)
" survived the Restoration, and repossessed the living.
" Bromhall died before the Restoration." *Hutchins.*

OVER-COMPTON [R.] Mr. ROBERT BARTLET.
Born at *Frampton*, where he had the advantage of a good
grammar-school. He first preached as a lecturer two years
at *Sarum*, and from thence removed, in 1654, to Over-
Compton, where he was ordained by Mr. *Butler* and others,
and where he continued discharging the office of a faithful pastor till he was ejected in 1662. He afterwards removed to *Bradford*, a neighbouring parish, having there a
small estate of his own ; and some serious people, who still
considered him as their pastor, attended on his preaching in
a private house. Here he continued about three years, till
the Five mile-act obliged him to go farther off; when he
removed to *Cadbury* in Somersetshire, where he lived with
his family about twenty years, privately exercising his ministry

nistry among some of his own people who adhered to him, of whom there were several both in *Lower* and *Over-Compton*. When the Toleration came out, he removed to *Lower Compton*, where he lived twelve years. The congregation of Dissenters at *Yeovil* (a neighbouring town) calling him to be their pastor, he removed thither, but divided his labours on the Lord's-day between the two places, which he continued to do till his death. He was much respected, and had most of the inhabitants both of *Over* and *Lower-Compton* to attend his ministry. He died much lamented, in 1710, in the 79th year of his age.

He was a judicious and learned man, of the congregational persuasion, but very moderate, and of a very healing spirit. He was humble in his deportment; a plain, affectionate, popular preacher; very laborious and constant in his ministerial service; and took great pains to speak to the capacities of his hearers. He appeared to have a great awe of the Divine Majesty upon his spirit when he was in the pulpit, and always behaved with great gravity out of it. The seriousness of his common discourse was very peculiar. There was somewhat in his mien and air that commanded respect from his very enemies. His behaviour was so inoffensive and exemplary, that many profane people were heard to declare, That if but one man in the county went to heaven, they believed in their consciences it would be Mr. *Bartlet*. But notwithstanding all this, some who were in the commission of the peace resolved to put a stop to his preaching. *Yeovil* being in Somerset, and *Compton* in Dorset, several justices in each county agreed to have him apprehended and confined. A Somersetshire justice signing a warrant against him, sent it with all expedition to the constable of North Cadbury. But he being suspected to be a friend of Mr. *Bartlet*'s, the servant had a special charge to accompany the constable, and see the warrant executed, which he did. Mr. *Bartlet* promising to appear at the quarter-sessions to be held in a few days, the constable took his word, and he appeared accordingly. As soon as he came into court, he was very warmly charged by some of the justices as a preacher of sedition, &c. to which he with great gravity and composedness replied, that " He preached " only the gospel of our Lord Jesus Christ, which teacheth " men to lead quiet and peaceable lives, in all godliness and " honesty, under those who are in authority." They asked him by what authority he pretended to preach? His an-

swer

swer was, " I am ordained to the ministry, and woe to me
" if I preach not the gospel." The last words of which
answer were spoken with such an awful seriousness, that
they were surprized, and for a while continued silent. At
length one of them asked him, " By whom were you or-
" dained ? by a bishop?" He answered, " There was no
" bishop at that time, but I was ordained by laying on of
" the hands of the presbytery." The justice then asked
him, Whether he owned the king's supremacy ? and whether he had taken the oath of allegiance? On his answering
in the affirmative, he further asked, Whether he would take
the oath of allegiance again? To which he replied, that he
was ready to do it if it was required. Whereupon the justice
ordered the oaths to be administered to him, and he took
them in court; upon which he was civilly dismissed, to the
no small disappointment of some present.

A Dorsetshire justice, who lived near *Compton*, was so
enraged, that he immediately issued out his warrant to seize
him there. The menaces and vigilance of his enemies made
him decline coming to Compton on the Lord's-day, but he
sometimes came on the week-days and preached there. As
he was once going from thence to *Yeovil*, he met the above
justice, who had often openly declared he would commit
him; when (to the amazement of his own two servants that
attended him) he spoke to Mr. *Bartlet* with great civility,
and left him without giving him any angry word. Being
thus preserved, Mr. *Bartlet* went on, with prudence and
privacy, preaching to his people, in the latter end of K.
Charles's reign, and the beginning of K. *James*'s. When
he had liberty to preach publicly, his constant method was
to begin the service with a short speech of about five or six
minutes; the design of which was to excite an awful fear
of God in the minds of his people. He usually took occasion from some providential occurrences; for instance,
the death of any of the people; any thing remarkable respecting the season, &c. &c, In this, as well as all other
performances in the pulpit, he discovered a great awe upon
his spirit, and delivered himself with such gravity and seriousness, as very much affected his people; so that no one
could go into any auditory wherein there appeared more seriousness and devotion, than might be discerned in the generality of Mr. *Bartlet*'s hearers. And they were all so desirous of hearing the preparatory introduction to public worship,

ship, that the whole congregation was generally present before he began.

Some of the chief persons in his society were, in K. *Charles's* time, thrown into Ilchester jail, and prosecuted at the assizes for 20*l.* a month, so as to be in danger of being ruined. But the judge pleaded for them, and brought them off, by telling their persecutors that the Act, upon which they were for proceeding against these persons, was made not against Protestant Dissenters, such as they were, but Popish recusants.—Mr. *Barlett* brought up two of his sons to the ministry. His son *Samuel* settled at *Tiverton*, where he had a large congregation ; and his arduous labours among them were thought to hasten his end. He died, after a short illness, *June 7*, 1701, which was some years before the death of his father, who lived to see his other children well provided for. His funeral sermon was preached by Mr. *S. Bulstrod*, on 2 *Tim.* iv. 7, 8.

OWER-MOYNE [R.] Mr. THOMAS TROIT [*or* FROYTE] Probably he was the person who afterwards practised physic in Lincolnshire, and lived near Horn-Castle.—§*Hutchins's* entry here is as follows : " Dr. Edward Thornborough, at " the Restoration, claimed and possessed Over-Moyne, and " ejected the Intruder FROYTE, who had kept him thirteen " years out of his right, which he had from his father."

PIMPERN [R. S.] Mr. JOHN WHITE. Son of the celebrated Mr. White, of Dorchester. §*Hutchins* says, " He " had the concurrence of the House of Commons for this " Rectory, *July* 11, 1646." He takes notice of the name of John White appearing in the register from 1642 to 1650, but no mention is made of a successor till 1661. —He was obliged to quit this living at the Restoration ; between which time and Bartholomew-day, 1662, he sometimes assisted Mr. *Lamb*, at Bere Regis. He was a man of eminent piety, and an exemplary conversation.

POOLE [D.] Mr. SAMUEL HARDY.* Of *Wadham Col. Oxf.* He was dismissed from the college because he

* *Hutchins* has this account of him—" Samuel Hardy, 1667. A Dissenter, born at Frampton, 1636, officiated at Charminster, and continued there after 1662, it being exempt from the episcopal jurisdiction. He was favored by the Trenchard family, and sometimes occasionally conformed. He was chosen minister of Poole, 1667. By a commission from the crown, he was ejected for not wearing the Surplice, and omitting the sign of the Cross in baptism, 23 *Aug.* 1682, and died at Newbury, 1690." At *Charminster*, he is mentioned as minister there in 1666.

could not take the oaths, when about to take the degree of
M. A. He then went to *Charminster*, which is a peculiar
belonging to the family of the Trenchards, within a mile of
Dorchester, and out of any episcopal inspection or jurisdiction. The minister there is a kind of chaplain to that family,
but neither parson nor vicar ; nor does he take any institution or induction. Mr. *Hardy* continued in this place some
years after the Bartholomew-act took place, being protected
from the Bishop's courts by its being a peculiar, and from
the justices by the favour of the Trenchards, and by a little
conformity, in reading the scripture sentences, the creed,
commandments, lessons, prayer for the king, &c.—Dr.
Bridoke, the archdeacon, once came to Mr. Trenchard, and
after saying many good things of Mr. *Hardy*, began to persuade him that he might be instituted and inducted ; which
Mr. Trenchard strongly opposed. Mr. *Kent*, this archdeacon's successor, had a peculiar respect for Mr. *Hardy*,
and proved his protector. Being himself a loose and de-
bauched man, he often used to say, " If he should die, he
had nothing to plead for himself to God, but his love to Mr.
Hardy,"—In this station Mr. *Hardy*, besides other good
services, had an opportunity of doing something towards
forming the minds of several young gentlemen in his patron's
family ; among whom was Sir John Trenchard, who was
afterwards secretary of state. He had a peculiar freedom
in addressing persons of high rank, without any thing of
rusticity. When Lord *Brook* lay on his death-bed, he went
to him, and spoke to this effect : " My lord, you of the no-
" bility are the most unhappy men in the world ; nobody
" dares come near you to tell you of your faults, or put you
" in the right way to heaven." Hereby he paved the way
for dealing closely with his lordship, without giving him any
offence.

After Mr. *Hardy* had lived at Charminster a considerable
time, the inhabitants of *Poole* invited him to that living,
which was likewise a peculiar. He accepted of it, and there
preached, and prayed, and conversed, in the same manner as
he did before. But several traps were laid for him. Once by
a person who desired him to baptize his child. If he had
used the Common Prayer, the Conformists would have glo-
ried in gaining him. If he had not used it, they would have
articled against him and got him out. But archdeacon *Kent*
happening to come to the town that day, Mr. *Hardy* applied
to him to baptize the child for him, who readily consented,
                                                       and

and so for the present the storm blew over.—At this time a member of parliament was to be chosen at *Poole.* The earl of *Shaftsbury*, then lord chancellor, was very urgent to have his son elected. Mr. *Hardy*, who had great interest there, opposed it, and brought in Mr. *John Trenchard* as a fitter man. The Chancellor was incensed, and wrote a very angry letter to Mr. *Hardy.* When he went to London, he was advised to wait upon the chancellor, and make his peace; which he accordingly did, and behaved himself so, in his honest blunt way, that the chancellor was very well pleased, and ever afterwards spoke respectfully of him. At last a commission was obtained to examine the title of Mr. *Hardy* to the living of *Poole.* Three bishops were in the commission, but they would not act in any thing that might seem prejudicial to the authority of their own courts. The country gentlemen however were willing to act. When they came to Poole for this purpose, a sermon was appointed, before which the clerk set a psalm, and Mr. *Hardy* went into the pulpit without using the Common Prayer. This was enough for them: They immediately discharged him, and he durst not appear there any more. He then went to *Badsly*, where he continued two years, but met with much trouble for not conforming to the canons; after which he never preached in public again. He then became chaplain in the house of —— *Heal*, Esq. at *Overy-Hatch*, in Essex. After spending two years in that situation, he went to *Newbury*, where he died, *March* 6, 1691, aged 54, having been much afflicted with the stone. He took great delight in doing good, and while at *Poole* was the means of redeeming many captives from slavery, having collected near 500*l.* for that purpose.

WORKS, A Guide to Heaven; (a book which has gone thro' many editions, and been remarkably useful)—Advice to scattered Flocks.

§ —— Mr. JOHN HUDDESLEY is mentioned in *Hutchins's* History, as instituted to this living of *Poole*, in the year 1647. His successor, Tho. Thackham, 1667. It is there further said of him, " That he was imprisoned at Poole, " by order of Cromwell, 1653; had 90*l.* 16*s.* allowed " him out of Lord Digby's estate, and died minister of a " dissenting congregation at Salisbury, 1699."—There seems to be reason for adding his name to the list of ejected ministers.

PORTLAND [R.] Mr. JOHN SPRINT. §Either he or his brother published something considerable. *Brader* is mentioned by *Hutchins*, as instituted here in 1660. He also mentions " One *Henry Way*, as appointed to this living to succeed Dr. Henchman, who was sequestered in 1643."

RAMPESHAM [R.] THOMAS CRANE, M. A. Of *Exet. Col. Oxf.* A native of *Plymouth*, where his father was a merchant. Upon his arrival from the university he became assistant to Mr. *Richard Allein*, and at length was put into this living by *Oliver Cromwell*, from whence he was ejected at the Restoration. He afterwards settled at *Beaminster*, where he continued till his death, which was a few days after that of queen *Anne*, 1714, aged 84. He was indicted in K. *Charles* I.'s time, at the sessions, at *Bridport*, for absenting himself from church; but the word *not* happening to be omitted, the indictment ran—"*for coming to divine service*," &c. which occasioned it to be dismissed, so that Mr. *Crane* escaped. From the known character of the officer concerned, it was plain that this was not the fruit of any design to do him service; but he viewed it as a kind interposition of that Providence in his favour, the honour of which he had so earnestly studied, and endeavoured to promote : For he was so great an observer of the steps of divine providence towards himself and others, and was so frequent in his remarks upon it, that he was commonly called *Providence*. He at length published a treatise on that subject; which is much commended by Mr. *Flavel*, in the Postscript to his own book upon the same topic. Mr. *Crane* was a hard student, and had a penetrating genius. His composures were remarkably judicious. He was a good textuary, and an excellent casuist; but much inclined to solitude. A mirror of patience, and remarkable for his charity towards his bitterest enemies, if he found them in want. He continued the constant exercise of his ministry till within a month of his death.

WORKS. Isagoge ad Dei providentiam; or a Prospect of divine Providence.—A Dedication of a posthumous Piece of Mr. Lyford's (his father-in law) upon Conscience.

SHAFTSBURY [R.] Mr. HALLET. §This is most probably the place intended by SHAFTON, as it is in Calamy : which used sometimes to be called *Shaston*. Whether the *Hallets*, of Exeter, were descendants of this Mr. Hallet, is not known, but not unlikely.

                             ** SHERBORN

. SHERBORN [V. 24*l.* 4*s.* 5½*d.*] FRANCIS BAMP-
FIELD, M. A. Of *Wadham Col. Oxf.* He was descended
from an ancient and honourable family, in *Devonshire,* and
being designed for the ministry from his birth, was educated
accordingly; his own inclination concurring with the design
of his pious parents. When he left the university (where
he continued seven or eight years) he was ordained a Deacon
of the church of England by Bp. *Hall ;* afterwards a Presbyter by Bp. *Skinner,* and was soon after preferred to a living
in Dorsetshire, of about 100*l.* per annum; where he took
great pains to instruct his people, and promote true religion
among them. Having an annuity of 80*l.* a year settled upon
him for life, he spent all the income of his place in acts of
charity among his parishioners, *v. g.* in giving them Bibles
and other good books, setting the poor to work, and relieving the necessities of those that were disabled; not suffering
a beggar, knowingly, to be in his parish. While he was
here, he began to see that the church of England in many
things needed reformation, in regard to doctrine, worship
and discipline; and therefore, as became a faithful minister,
he heartily set about it; making the laws of Christ his only
rule. But herein he met with great opposition and trouble.
About this time, the people of *Sherborn* wanting a minister,
earnestly solicited him to come thither. This place being
very populous, there was more work, but less wages.
However, as there was a prospect of doing more good, and
the people, as well as some neighbouring ministers, were
very urgent, after waiting two years, he accepted their call.
Here he continued to labour with universal acceptance and
great success, till the Act of uniformity took place. Being
in his conscience utterly dissatisfied with the conditions of
conformity, he took his leave of his sorrowful congregation
the Lord's-day before *Bartholomew*-day, 1662.

He afterwards suffered great hardships, from which it
might have been expected his character, particularly for
loyalty, would have protected him. In all the changes of
the times, till now, every party was for having a man of
such piety and learning kept in the ministry. Besides having
had the approbation of the associated ministers of the presbyterian and congregational persuasion, the licence of the
Protector, and the testimony of the Triers of public
preachers; as well as ordination from two Bishops of the
church of England, he had licences for preaching, under the
hands and seals of two Kings, *Charles* I. and *Charles* II.

And it was very remarkable in him, that tho' he joined
heartily in the reformation of the church, he was zealous
against the parliament's war, and *Oliver's* usurpation ; constantly asserting the royal cause under all changes, and
even suffering for it. Yet he was so far from having any favour shewn him on these accounts, that he suffered more for
his Nonconformity than most other Dissenters.* Soon after
his ejectment, he was imprisoned for worshipping God in his
own family ; of which the author of *The Conformist's
Plea for the Nonconformists*, gives the following account :—

   September 19, 1662. . As he was engaged, after his usual
manner, before he came to *Sherborn*, in family duty, and
expounding 1 *Thess.* v. 6, 7, some of his neighbours being
present, one *S*—— with other soldiers, entering his house,
required him in the king's name to be silent, and with the
rest to quit the room. Two deputy-lieutenants had been
consulted to know if such an exercise as Mr. *Bampfield*
used was contrary to law. But without an answer from
them, one *T*—— an apothecary, who came with *S*——
said, that he had a warrant from them to serve upon Mr.
Bampfield, Mr. *Philips* his assistant, and ten of the chief
auditors ; and thereupon they took these two worthy ministers, and about twenty-five other persons to the house of
the provost-marshal, where they all continued prisoners (except the two ministers, who were separated from the people)
in one room, which had but one bed in it, for five days and
nights. On the Saturday night, leave being obtained, the
prisoners all came together [the two ministers it is supposed
being permitted to join the rest] when, while one of them
was in prayer, the soldiers broke into the room and spoke
aloud, calling him rogue, and bidding him give over; at
length they laid hands upon him, and forced the rest of the
prisoners away. On the Lord's-day, Mr. *Bampfield*, tho'
at first refused, had leave to preach to the prisoners. Many
people of the town desired to be present ; and some, by
giving the soldiers a fee, got in, but were afterwards thrust
out again. , Some got into a back yard, but were threatened
with writs for the trespass, by the owner, tho' his wife had
given them leave, and satisfaction of ten times the value
was offered. At night Mr. *Philips* had leave to preach, but

   * The above, and some subsequent passages, are from Crosby's Hist.
Baptists, Vol. 1. p. 363, &c.

while

while he was in prayer the soldiers broke in and prevented it. On the Wednesday following, four or five of the deputy-lieutenants met, and called Mr. *Bampfield* before them first, and then Mr. *Philips.* Sir *J. S——* of *Par*, was in the chair. Mr. *Bampfield* owned that he was worshipping God in his family, and that several neighbours came in. Nothing was charged, in the prayer or exposition, as being seditious; nevertheless the chairman declared the exercise tended to sedition, and required sureties for their good behaviour, and appearance at the next assizes, which accordingly were produced. Some further instances of injustice and cruelty to these good men while in the prison may be seen in *The Conformist's Fourth Plea*, p. 46.

Mr. *Bampfield* afterwards suffered eight years imprisonment in Dorchester jail, which he bore with great courage and patience, being filled with the comfort of the Hol Ghost. He also preached in the prison, almost every day, and gathered a church there. Upon his discharge in 1675, he went about preaching the gospel in several counties. But he was soon taken up again for it in *Wiltshire*, and imprisoned at *Salisbury*; where, on account of a fine, he continued eighteen weeks. During that time he wrote a letter, which was printed, giving an account of his imprisonment, and the joy he had in his sufferings for Christ. Upon his release he came to *London*, where he preached privately several years, with great success, and gathered a people; who, being baptized by immersion, (Mr. *Bampfield* having become a Baptist) formed themselves into a church, and met at *Pinners-Hall;* which being so public, soon exposed them to the rage of their persecutors.

On *Feb.* 17, 1682, a constable, and several men with halberts, rushed into the assembly when Mr. *Bampfield* was in the pulpit. The constable ordered him in the king's name to come down. He answered, that he was discharging his office in the name of the King of kings. The constable telling him he had a warrant from the *Lord Mayor*, Mr. *Bampfield* replied, " I have a warrant from Christ, who is " *Lord Maximus,* to go on ;" and so proceeded in his discourse. The constable then bid one of the officers pull him down; when he repeated his text, *Isa.* lxiii. ' The day of ' vengeance is in his heart, and the year of his redeemed ones ' is come ;' adding, ' He will pull down his enemies." They then seized him, and took him with six others, before the Lord-mayor, who fined several of them 10*l.* and bid Mr.

Bampfield be gone. In the afternoon they assembled at the same place again, where they met with a fresh disturbance; and an officer, tho' not without trembling, took Mr. *Bampfield*, and led him into the street; but the constable having no warrant, they let him go; so that he went, with a great company, to his own house, and there finished the service.

On the 24th of the same month, he met his congregation again at *Pinners-Hall*, and was again pulled out of the pulpit, and led thro' the streets with his bible in his hand, and great multitudes after him; some reproaching him, and others speaking in his favour; one of whom said, " See how he walks with his Bible in his hand, like one of the old martyrs." Being brought to the sessions, where the Lord-mayor attended, he and three more were sent to prison. The next day they were brought to the bar, and being examined, were remitted to *Newgate*.——On *March* 17, 1683, he and some others, who were committed for not taking the oaths of allegiance and supremacy, were brought to the *Old-Bailey*, indicted, tried, and by the jury (directed by the judge) brought in guilty. On *March* 28, being brought again to the sessions to receive their sentence, the recorder, after odiously aggravating their offence, and reflecting on scrupulous consciences, read their sentence; which was, " That they were out of the protection of the king's majesty; that all their goods and chattels were forfeited; and they were to remain in jail during their lives, or during the king's pleasure." Upon this Mr. *Bampfield* would have spoken, but there was a great outcry—" Away with them: we will not hear them, &c." and so they were thrust away; when Mr. *Bampfield* said, " The righteous Lord loveth " righteousness: the Lord be judge in this case." They were then returned to *Newgate*, where Mr. *Bampfield* (who was of a tender constitution) soon after died, in consequence of the hardships he suffered, much lamented by his fellow-prisoners, as well as by his friends in general. Notwithstanding his peculiar sentiments, all who knew him acknowledged, that he was a man of serious piety, and deserved a different treatment from what he met with from an unkind world. He was one of the most celebrated preachers in the West of England, and extremely admired by his hearers, till he fell into the *Sabbatarian* notion, of which he was a zealous asserter. Dr. *Walker* says, He was collated to a

                                          prebend

prebend in the cathedral of Exeter, *May* 15, 1641, and that
he was repossessed of it at the Restoration, and enjoyed it,
with his living at *Sherborn*, till Bartholomew-day, 1662.§

WORKS. A Letter containing his judgment for observing
the Seventh-day Sabbath.— All in one; all useful Sciences and
profitable Arts, in one Book of Jehovah.—[*Crosby adds the following*—The Open Confessor, and the Free Prisoner; a sheet written
in Salisbury jail.—A Name. and a new one ; being an account of
his Life.—The House of Wisdom ; for promoting Scripture Knowledge.—The Free Prisoner; a Letter from Newgate.—A just
Appeal from lower Courts on Earth to the highest Court in Heaven.
—A Continuation of the former.—A grammatical Opening of
some Hebrew Words and Phrases in the Beginning of the Bible.]

—— HUMPHREY PHILIPS, M. A. Of both universities,
and some time Fellow of *Magd. Col. Oxf.* He was born
at *Somerton*, in Somersetshire, of a genteel family, and was
inclined to the ministry from his youth. He had a severe fit
of sickness while at the university, from which God wonderfully recovered him. He afterwards retired into the
country for his health, and became chaplain and tutor at
Poltimore, near Exeter, the seat of the ancient family of
the *Bampfields*. At the end of the year he returned to the
college, and was soon after chosen Fellow of *Magdalen*.
At the age of twenty-four he was ordained by Dr. *Wild*, Mr.
Hickman, &c. and preached frequently in the university,
and the parts adjacent. Being turned out by the visitors at
the Restoration, he retired to *Sherborn*, where he had been
two years before assistant to Mr. *Bampfield*. There he was
useful to many, and very successful till the Uniformity-act

§ *Hutchins* gives the following account of him—" Francis Bamfield, M. A.
1653, on the death of Lyford. Third son of John Bamfield, of Poltimore,
in Devon, Esq. Was admitted at Wadham Col. Æt. 16. M. A. 1638, and
took episcopal orders 1641. He was presented to . . . . in Dorset, and
collated to a prebend in the church at Exeter. He was then zealous for the
King, and publicly read the Common Prayer longer than any minister in this
county. After Mr. Baxter brought him over to the parliament party, he took
the Engagement, and in 1653, succeeded Mr. Lyford here. In 1662 he was
ejected by the Act of uniformity, and lost his preferments, and afterwards
kept a conventicle here and at London, for which he was imprisoned the
last ten years of his life, several times. In 1683 he was found guilty at the
Old Bailey, of refusing the Oath of supremacy and allegiance, and died that
year in Newgate, and was buried at the Anabaptist burying-place, near Al-
dersgate-street. *Wood* says, He was inconstant in his principles : had been
a Churchman, Presbyterian, Independent, Anabaptist, and at last a Jew
[because he was for the seventh-day Sabbath] and an Enthusiast. His writings were full of the most unintelligible bombast ; and in one piece, he
seems to have anticipated the Hutchinsonian conceit of deriving all sciences
and arts from Scripture."

took

took place; when both Mr. Bampfield and he preached their farewell sermons, and the place was a *Bochim* [A place of mourners]. However they did not leave their people, but preached to such as would hear them in a house, till they were apprehended and sent to an inn, which was made a prison for them and twenty-five of their principal bearers; which put them to a considerable expence. They were bound over to the next quarter-sessions, and to their good behaviour in the mean time. When they understood that the *good behaviour* designed, was an obligation not to preach, they openly renounced it, and returned to their work. They went to Mr. *T. Bampfield*'s, at Dunkerton, near Bath, where they preached at first to a small number, but it gradually increased. They were often threatened, but were not discouraged. After some time Mr. *F. Bampfield* was apprehended in Dorsetshire, and sent to Dorchester jail. Mr. *T. Bampfield* and Mr. *Philips*, now his chaplain, were also sent to Ilchester. The former returned in a month's time; but the latter after eleven months confinement, was brought from prison, in the depth of winter, and in a heavy snow, to the assizes at *Wells*, where he met with cruel usage, being put into a chamber, like *Noah*'s ark, full of all sorts of creatures, and laid in a bed with the Bridewell-keeper, where the sheets were so wet, as to cling to his flesh. The justice who committed him gave him harsh language; but the judge discharged him, as he had satisfied the law. Whilst he was in prison, there was another disturbance at Mr. *T. Bampfield*'s, by a person of Bath; who, in searching for his ink-horn to take down names, having a pistol in his pocket shot himself in the thigh, which endangered his life, and made him miserable all his days.

Mr. *Philips* having his liberty, went over to Holland with a son of Col. Strode's, a member of parliament, and made a visit to his old acquaintance Mr. Hickman, at Leyden; where he saw the most noted places in Holland, and conversed with many learned men, particularly the famous Dr. *Gisbert Voet*, the only surviving member of the Synod of *Dort*. Among other things, he particularly asked his sentiments about the lawfulness and propriety of the ejected ministers persisting in their work, when silenced by the magistrates, against which many so much exclaimed. His answer was, " Puerilis est Controversia. *It is a childish dispute.* * But he added, " There are many pious people dissatisfied; and you ought

* A childish answer, which shewed his ignorance of the subject.

to

to take care of them."—Upon his return to England, Mr.
Philips went back again to Dunkerton, where he continued
to preach with good success, tho' he met with great difficulties; especially from Mr. *Bampfield* and his brother, who
espoused the seventh-day-sabbath, and carried it strangely to
him, because of his different sentiments. He continued
however his respect to them, and committed his cause to
God, who in time made them more charitable to others,
tho' immoveable in their own opinion. He had afterwards
various trials and temptations; many removals from place to
place, and divers bodily infirmities. Fines were often imposed and levied upon him, and he had much trouble from
the bishop's court, which drove him from his home to Bristol, London, and other places, for several years, till K.
Charles's Indulgence. He then returned to *Sherborn*, (to
which the good people about Bath were very reluctant) and
for a year was very serviceable there. But on the expiration
of the liberty, he met with great disturbance, and was forced
away. After several removes he went to his own estate, at
Beckington, where he lived many years, preaching to various
congregations, far and near; particularly that at *Froome*,
bringing forth fruit in old age. He died *March* 27, 1707,
having been fifty years in the ministry. His funeral sermon
was preached by his son-in-law, Mr. *John England*, on
Acts xx. 24. §The following are extracts from it.

" My deceased father, who recommended these words
unto me for the present occasion, told me that this text was
his motto: a motto very becoming a gospel minister."—In
the close of the discourse he runs a parallel between the
apostle and Mr. Philips, in some particulars of which the
text speaks; observing, " 1. That like Paul he was a great
admirer of the Grace of God. 2. That he was not diverted
from preaching the gospel by bonds and afflictions. He had
his trials of this kind almost ever since he entered upon the
ministry, which is upwards of fifty years."—Having mentioned his first ejectment at Oxford, because he could not
submit to re-ordination, and his second by the Act of uniformity, with his subsequent imprisonments, &c. (related in
the preceding narrative) he adds—" After this he was vexed
in the bishop's court, and was excommunicated; and a writ
being out *de excommunicato capiendo*, this forced him, for
a time, to leave his dwelling, and to wander up and down,
having no certain abiding place. And whilst he was from
home, there was a warrant out against him for sixty pounds,
                                                    having

having' been convicted for preaching at two meetings; the
first offence being 20*l.* and the second 40*l.* Having survived
these troubles, another warrant of 20*l.* fine was out against
him for being at a meeting; which warrant was executed
and the money paid. In short, the whole time of his ministry, excepting a little at the beginning, the year of the
Indulgence, in 1672, and the present Toleration, was full of
trouble and danger . . . . yet he was not diverted from
preaching the gospel: *None of these things moved him.*—
3: Like Paul, he had the Joy of success in his labours, God
gave him many seals to his ministry. There be many at
Sherborn, and the places adjacent, that have owned, and
will own to this day, that his preaching was a means of their
conversion." [One instance is mentioned of a person converted by a sermon of Mr. Phillips's, on a text from which
he had lately desired Mr. England to preach at his funeral]
" And how useful he had been in planting of churches, and
keeping them up, is well known to you in these parts.—He
did not confine his labours to the pulpit, but imitated Paul in
teaching privately *from house to house.* His visits usually
were short, but seldom or never without some pious instruction or counsel, or some discourse of the things of God.—
I may truly say of him, He was an able minister of the new
testament : a lively affectionate preacher, having an admirable gift in prayer : under whose ministry a person could not
but profit, unless it were his own fault."—This sermon was
not printed till six years after Mr. Philips's death, and was
then published with another, by the same author, on the
decease of *John Derbie,* Esq. Receiver-general of the county
of Dorset, Mr. Philips's intimate friend: to whom the text
Psalm xxxvii. 37. seems to have been justly applied. From
a manuscript note in the title-page, it appears that Mr.
Philips was interred, under a flat stone, at *Beckington*
church.

WORKS. A Funeral Sermon for Mr. Ivyleaf.—Another for
Mrs. Anne [wife of Mr. Philip] Gibbs, entitled, God's Excellency, and his People's Preciousness, &c.

SIMONDSBOROUGH [R. S.] 36*l.* 3*s.* 4*d.*] JOHN
HARDY, M. A. Elder brother of Mr. Samuel Hardy, of
Poole. Born at *Frampton.* §*Hutchins* says, He was minister of this parish, in 1650, by order of parliament, on
the sequestration of Dr. Glemham.] He was one of the
ministers who preached at Wesminster-abbey, on the thanksgiving

giving for the Restoration. How he left Simondsbury doth not appear. He afterwards preached at *Southwick*, in Hampshire, and there lived much beloved, and died exceedingly lamented, about 1668, aged but about 35. He was a celebrated preacher; of good life and conversation; eminent for his charity and readiness to do good to all, to the utmost of his ability, nay, according to the common estimate, beyond his ability. He gave away many bibles, catechisms, and other good books; put out poor children apprentices; and helped distressed families. He had this motto continually before him in his study, written in *Greek*; *Wo unto me if I preach not the gospel.*

STAFFORD *(West)* [R.] BENJAMIN WAY, M. A. §*Hutchins* mentions him as instituted here, 27 *Feb.* 1660, —See a further account of him at BARKING, in *Essex.*

TARANT HINTON [R. 140*l.*] Mr. TIMOTHY SACH-EVEREL. Of *Trin. Col. Oxf.* Brother to Mr. *John Sackeverel,* of Wincanton, and great uncle to the famous Dr. *Henry Sacheverel.* His patron, Mr. *Moor,* of Spargrove, in Somersetshire, had such an extraordinary respect for him, that, finding he could not conform, he freely told him, That if he thought it lawful to hold this parsonage, and act by proxy, in order to receive the profits, he should readily have it; which however he honourably refused. Mr. Moor then told him, none should be presented to the living but one that he recommended: he accordingly recommended Mr. *Tyndal,* a worthy man, who was brother-in-law to Bp. *Fowler,* and who enjoyed the living to his dying-day.— Between the Restoration and Bartholomew-day, Mr. *Sacheverel* was put down at the head of a list that contained the names of several who were to be sent to prison; but Sir *Gerard Naper* being in the chair at the sessions, and having a respect for him, refused to set his hand to the commitment; and so they all escaped for that time.

Soon after Bartholomew-day, he was cited to the spiritual court, at Blandford, whither many people came, in hope of something like a public disputation; at least, expecting to hear him very severely reprimanded: but the chancellor told him, That he did not send for him to dispute with him, knowing him to be a person of great worth, temper and learning; but only desired him to weigh all matters calmly and without prejudice, and then to do as God should direct him. Hereupon, as soon as he had admonished him in form, he

dismissed

dismissed him.—Not long after, several troopers of the militia rushed suddenly into his house one morning whilst he was at prayer with his family. One of them came and held his pistol at his back, commanding him in the king's name immediately to stand up. He continued praying some time, but soon concluded; and then with great presence of mind asked the trooper, How he durst thus pretend in the king's name to interrupt him, while he and his family were presenting their petitions to the King or kings?

He continued at Tarant Hinton, after his ejectment, till the Five-mile act came out, preaching to a select number. He afterwards removed to *Winterburn*, where he opened his house to all comers, and preached to them after the public worship was over. This he continued till the Indulgence in 1672. He was then going to fit up an out-house for a place of worship ; but there happened at that time a fire in his house, which consumed all his books, papers, manuscripts, and sermon-notes, with almost every thing he had. There were many circumstances which excited suspicion that this fire was kindled by some ill-designing persons, to prevent the opening of a public meeting-house in the town. And it had the effect ; for it occasioned his removal with his family to *Enford*, in Wiltshire ; from whence he afterwards went to *Devizes*, where his wife kept a boarding-school for young ladies, by which they were very comfortably supported : and here he preached *gratis* as long as he lived. It was a frequent petition to God in his prayers, " That those might " be suffered to preach who looked upon their work to be " sufficient wages."

Mr. *Johnson*, the parish minister on his first coming hither, preached against him ; tho' he was generally his hearer, and only preached out of church-hours. One of his texts was 1 *Kings* xviii. 21. ' If the Lord be God follow ' him, &c.' One of Mr. *Sacheverel*'s hearers pressed him to answer Mr. *Johnson* publicly ; to which he replied, that he knew better things : which being reported to Mr. *Johnson*, so softened his temper, that in a little time he conceived a great respect for him, and carried it very civilly to him ever after. His principles were very moderate. The renouncing the Covenant, was a main thing he stuck at in conformity. He had great comfort in his last sickness ; rejoicing to think he was going to the marriage supper of the Lamb. He died in 1680.

§ STOKE ABBOTS

§STOKE ABBOTS (or *Abbotstock*) [R.] Mr. BRID-
GIGINS AVIANEN. *Hutchins* in his history, mentions him
from the Register, as Incumbent at this place in the year
1650. This is doubtless the person whom Calamy calls Mr.
Avien, whose place of ejectment is mentioned as uncertain.
See *Noncon. Mem.* 1st. Edit. Vol. ii. p. 648.

§WAMBROOK [R.] Mr. WILLIAM RANDAL. He is
undoubtedly to be added to the number of ejected ministers,
as appears from the following entry in *Hutchins*—" WAM-
" BROOK, 1650. Mr. William Randal, an orthodox divine
" was their minister, inducted by order of the Committee
" of the county." Afterwards it is said, " Gamiliel Chase,
" B. D. was succeeded here by *one Randal*, who lived to
" deliver it up to him again, 1660."

WAREHAM [R. S.] Mr. CHAPLYN. Of *Trin. Col.
Camb.* He was piously disposed from his youth. When
he went to the grammar-school, which was above a mile
from his father's house, while his school-fellows turned aside
to play by the way, they sometimes found him under a
hedge at prayer. At the university he improved in knowledge and piety. While he was at *Wareham*, he was well-
beloved, and did much good.§ He used to preach in an afternoon at a chapel of ease, at a place called *Earn*. He was
strict in observing the Sabbath himself, and zealous to prevent the profanation of it in others. Once, as he was returning from *Earn* on the Lord's-day evening, he saw a
parcel of boys at play in the Castle-close. It seems they
commonly did this, but thro' fear of him, used to set a
watch to observe him coming on the causeway, and then to
disperse. At this time their watch being negligent, they
were surprized and caught; and tho' they scampered away
as fast as they could, he knew several of them distinctly.
He acquainted the mayor and other magistrates with the

§ He appears to have preached at different churches in this town, from the
following account, transcribed from *Hutchins's* History :—" *Holy Trinity* Rec-
" tory, 1656. Tho. Chaplyn, M. A. with his assistants, supply the cure.
" There was a sermon every Sunday morning.—Tho. Chaplyn, Intruder,
" occurs 1648—1660. He retired to Cambridge, and dying, *Aug.* 31,
" 1667, æt. 46, was buried in St. Bennet's church there, where is a monu-
" ment for him, styling him A. M. of *Kath. Hall*, late rector of Wareham.
" St. *Martin's* Rectory, 1650. Tho. Chaplyn, incumbent, preached once
" every Sunday :——Intruder, circa 1643.
" St. *Michael's* Rectory, 1650. The present possessor Thomas Chaplyn.
" St. *Mary's* Rectory, 1650. Thomas Chaplyn officiated every Sunday
" morning.—*June* 3, 1643, certifies he had received the parish Register."

matter.

matter. The next day a hall was called, and the parents of those boys whom he knew, were sent for and reprimanded, and charged to take more care of their children for the time to come. It was observed, that this had some good effects, and some of these boys mentioned the matter with thankfulness after they were grown up; and other parents were hereby cautioned.—When Mr. *Chaplyn* was ejected and silenced, he had eight children; but the providence of God wonderfully supported him. His wife engaged in the malting business; and had relations in *London* who kept her accounts, and otherwise greatly assisted her. The family had also no small benefit from a 100*l.* which Mr. *Chaplyn*, a little before his death, put into the *East-India* Company, at its first formation. They had 40, 50, 60 and even 70*l. per ann.* profit by their dividend; and at last their stock was sold for 550*l.* to raise portions for the children.

Mrs. *Chaplyn,* when she died, was buried in the chancel; but having been excommunicated, her body was dug up again, after seven weeks, by the order of the Bishop's court, and the church was for some time suspended. She was then laid in the church-yard; but when the court understood it, they were displeased, and ordered that she should be dug up again and removed; tho' her children after her death had paid 3*l.* for taking off the excommunication. Upon which the mayor of the town and some others informed the court, That there were three burying-places in the church-yard, belonging to three parishes united; and that she was buried in the path between two of them. Upon this they answered, that if two credible witnesses would swear to that, she should lie still. This was accordingly done; and so peace was made between them. Some of the church people have since desired to be buried in the same place.

WEEK (King's) or WYKE REGIS [R.] Mr. DAMER. [A correction is here made in his name, from *Hutchins*, who has only this entry: "—— *Damer*—between 1652 and 1662.] Some time after his ejectment, he was employed as steward to *Denzil* Lord Hollis, and preached only occasionally. He afterwards lived at *Dorchester*, and was useful in many adjacent places. He brought up a son to the ministry, a very worthy person, who for some time preached at Ringwood, and died at some place in the neighbourhood of Bath. §*Hutchins* has here this note. "Wyke Regis "and Elwell. -Dr. Henchman being retired into the King's army,

army, 1643, *Henry Way* was appointed by the H. of
Commons to be his successor." *Butler* succeeded him,
1652.

WEYMOUTH [R.] Mr. GEORGE THORN. §He was
settled in this living so early as the year 1641 ; as appears
from *Hutchins*, who mentions him among the Rectors thus :
" George Thorn, &c. Intruder, 1641—1660." In the
Commission, 1650, is this entry : " Out of the impropria-
" tion of Affpuddle, about 30*l.* last year was paid to Mr.
" George Thorn, minister."—He was a person of great ministerial abilities, as well as eminent piety ; but was violently
persecuted, so as to be obliged to quit the kingdom.* And
upon his return, tho' he appears from his farewell address to
have been a peaceable and loyal subject, he was so malici-
ously prosecuted for his nonconformity, that he was obliged
to sell his estate, and fly from place to place to conceal himself. In the London collection of Farewell Sermons, there
is Mr. THORN's, at *Weymouth*, apparently from his own
copy. It is appropriate to the occasion, and affords a
strong testimony in his favour, both as a man of piety, and
an excellent preacher. The following is an epitome of it :

PSALM xxxvii. 34. *Wait on the Lord, and keep his way.*
Not knowing whether ever I shall speak to you more from
this place, being willing to leave a word in season, I shall
recommend to you what, in answer to prayer, I have received of the Lord, for directing me in my course in this
gloomy dark day ; being well assured that as many of us as
work by this rule, and sail by this compass, (however we
may be scattered by the tempestuous storms we meet with
here in the sea of this world) shall shortly arrive at, and
meet in, our desired port, the haven of eternal rest.—The
scope of this psalm is to direct the people of God, and to
encourage them, to keep on in the course of godliness, at
such times as when the wicked prosper, flourish and grow
great, and the godly are afflicted, persecuted and oppressed.
—From the text we have this profitable point of doctrine :
" However it go with the truly godly in this world, especially
" when the wicked watch them to do them mischief, it is

* The editor is in possession of a long and pious Letter from his wife, Mrs.
Martha Thorn, written to him during his exile, dated 16 *Feb.* 1663, which
was communicated by Mr. *Joseph Chadwick*, minister of Oundle, a descendant of his. But the writing is too small and too much obliterated to be
easily read.

" best [for them] to wait on the Lord and to keep his way:"
—It is here supposed—that the condition of the godly in
this world may be full of troubles—particularly from the
malice of the wicked.   So it hath ever been.   Many texts
in proof of it.   There is the same principle of hatred in the
wicked against the righteous as ever :—and there is the same
ground and occasion of their hatred to them, *John* xv. 19.
1 *John* iii. 12.

Two things recommended in the text.   I. *To wait on the
Lord :* which imports—attending him as his servants—and
patiently expecting his salvation.   ver. 7. *Ps.* 130. 5.—II.
To keep his way :—To observe the way of his providence,
Is. xxvi. 8.—To walk in the way of his precepts.   This last
inforced by several motives.   (1.) This is the most *innocent*
and *honest.*   Other ways are not so. e. g. Lying; the way
Peter took : shuffling and equivocating, as *Abraham* did ;
revengefully rendering evil for evil, as *David* would have
done to *Nabal,* if Abigal's wisdom had not prevented.
1 *Sam.* xxv. 33 :—basely deserting one's station ; which *She-
maiah* would have put *Nehemiah* upon, but he refused.
Neh. vi. 10.—acting rebelliously and traitorously, as *David*
was tempted, and *Abishai* was inclined to have done. 1.
Sam. xxiv. 4. *Ch.* xxvi. 9. That none of these ways are
just and honest, proved.—(2.) This is the *wisest* course.—
It is the way to which the wisdom of God directs. *Luke* xi.
49.   This is the way the wisest men have taken. *David, Ps.*
xviii. 21. *Daniel. Ch.* vi. 10. *Christ. Luk.* xiii. 31. 32.—
(3.) This is the *safest* way. *Prov.* x. 9 : xxviii. 18.—It is
the way to escape the mischief which the wicked devise.
Prov. xvi. 7. ' When a man's ways please the Lord, he
maketh their enemies to be at peace with them ;'—sometimes
—by changing their hearts, as he did the heart of *Ahasuerus,*
of *Nebuchadnezzar,* and of *Paul :*—by restraining their
rage and envy. *Ps.* lxxvii. 5, 6, 10. see the case of Laban
and Jacob :—by making them use his people well when in
their power. *Jer.* xv. 11.—Always by over-ruling what they
do, so as not to hurt them. *Is.* liv. 17. *Act.* xviii. 10.

Some think it is the *safest* way to comply, tho' in things
sinful :—others, to avenge themselves :—some to equivocate :
—and others to desert their stations, &c.—All these proved
dangerous and destructive.   No way so safe as that of duty.

4. This is the most *honourable* way. *Neh.* vi. 10. 11.—
It is the way of true valour and courage :—of victory and
triumph :—the way to bring the most honour to God :—
                                                        and

and to gain that true honour which cometh from him.—(5.)
This is the most *comfortable* way. It is the way to have
inward peace. *Ps.* 119, 165.—to have the Holy Ghost the
comforter to abide with us—to fill the soul with joy under the
sorest outward trouble—and to arrive speedily where the
wicked shall trouble no more ; where you shall have perfect
rest, and fulness of joy for ever.

Application. This consists of a great number of excellent cautions and directions, well worthy the attention of
christians at all times, and of all descriptions:

Among the *Cautions*, are these: Take heed lest you be
offended, at the cross :—by the falls and apostacies of hypocritical professors :—by the reproach cast on the way of the
Lord and on those that walk in it :—by the prosperity of the
wicked. *Ps.* xxxvii. 7, 8.—Take heed of such persons as
these, by whom you may be turned out of the way :—Take
heed of yourselves : beware of Satan : beware of false
teachers; beware of worldly friends, who will counsel you
to spare yourselves ; such as savour not the things of God,
but those that be of men.

Among the *Directions* are the following: 1. Let the
Spirit of Christ be your guide and principle. 2. Make the
word of God your rule. 3. Let the example of Christ be
your pattern : He always kept the way of the Lord. If you
would do so, follow him, and walk as he walked. 4. Let
the glory of God be your end.

All these particulars are admirably illustrated, and would
afford very useful extracts : But we shall only add what the
author addressed to his people, with an immediate reference
to the occasion of his leaving them :

" I call God to witness, in whose name I have preached
to you, that I have preached the way of the Lord sincerely
and faithfully. I therefore beseech and intreat you, out of
the hearty love I bear to you, as you tender the glory of
God, your own peace here, and eternal happiness hereafter,
or the eternal good of others, that you will remember how
you have heard and received, and keep the way of the Lord :
—keep it in your memories : in your judgments and consciences : in your profession : in your hearts and affections :
in your lives and conversations.—*Fear God, and honour the
King.* Let nothing but conscience towards God hinder you
at any time from yielding obedience to all the King's laws.—
And here, beloved, I shall take occasion to open my heart
sincerely to you. You know what is required of me if I

will continue a minister in this kingdom. I hope no sober person can think me such a humourous perverse fanatic as to throw away my maintenance, much less my ministerial capacity (which is much dearer to me than livelihood, yea than life) out of a proud humour and vain-glorious fancy. In brief, therefore, as I shall answer it before the great God, the searcher of all hearts, and the righteous judge, did not conscience towards God forbid me, I would willingly do all the Act requires. But seeing I cannot declare an unfeigned *assent* and *consent,* I dare not (and from your love to me I know you would not have me) dissemble with God and men. I do therefore humbly choose to submit to the penalty rather than by a hypocritical conformity (for such it must be in me, if any) to dishonour my God, wound my own conscience, and dissemble with men.; knowing assuredly that my God hath no need of my sin: and if he has any work for me in the public ministry, he will incline the king's heart to grant liberty and encouragement to me, with the rest of those who desire to be faithful in preaching the gospel: which that the Lord may grant, I promise myself the help of all your prayers who have been favoured with any spiritual blessings thro' my ministry."

WHITCHURCH [*Canonicorum* V. 30*l.*] Mr. John Salway. He was afterwards minister of Rilmington, in Devonshire. §The correction here made in his name is from *Hutchins*—" *John Salway*, Intruder."—" Samuel Locket, " sequestered *May* 17, 1643. He was ordered to receive " *Robert Tutchin,* lecturer at Bridport, to be lecturer " here on Sunday morning :" probably the person mentioned at *Newport,* Hants.

WHITCHURCH [*Winterborn*] † John Wesley, M. A. Of *New-Inn-Hall, Oxf.* Son of Mr. Bartholomew Wesley, of *Charmouth,* father of Mr. Samuel Wesley, rector of Epworth, in the diocese of Lincoln, [and grandfather to the late celebrated Mr. *John Wesley.*] It pleased God to incline him to remember his Creator in the days of his youth. He had a very humbling sense of sin, and a serious concern for his salvation, even while he was a school-boy.

† There are two places of the name of *Whitchurch,* distinguished as above. That this last was the place from whence Mr. Wesley was ejected, and not the preceding, as before supposed, appears from Hutchins, who has this entry here : " John Wesley, M. A. 1658, ejected 1662."

He

He began to keep a diary soon after God had begun to work upon him, and not only recorded the remarkable events of providence which affected his outward man, but more especially the methods of the spirit of grace in his dealings with his soul; the frame of his heart in his attendance on the ordinances of the gospel, and how he found himself affected under the various methods of divine providence, whether merciful or afflictive. This course he continued, with very little interruption, to the end of his life.

During his stay at Oxford, he was taken notice of for his seriousness and diligence. He applied himself particularly to the study of the oriental languages, in which he made great progress. Dr. *Owen*, who was at that time vice-chancellor, shewed him great kindness. He began to preach occasionally at the age of twenty-two, and in *May*, 1658, was sent to preach at *Whitchurch*. The income of this vicarage was not above 30*l. per ann.* but he was promised an augmentation of 100*l.* a year, tho' the many turns of public affairs which followed soon after, prevented his receiving any part of it. He married a niece of Dr. *Thomas Fuller*; and having a growing family he was necessitated to set up a school, that he might be able to maintain it. Soon after the Restoration, some of his neigbours gave him a great deal of trouble because he would not read the Book of Common Prayer. Dr. *Gilbert Ironside*, Bp. of *Bristol*, was informed, by some persons of distinction, that Mr. *Wesley* would not gratify those who desired him to use the liturgy; expressing their apprehension that his title to *Whitchurch* was not valid; and that for this and some other parts of his conduct, he might be prosecuted in a court of justice. Mr. *Wesley* being informed that the bishop was desirous to speak with him, took an opportunity to wait upon his lordship, and had the following conference with him, as it is recorded in his own diary:

Bishop. What is your name?—*Wesley.* John Wesley.

B. There are many great matters charged upon you.

W. May it please your lordship, Mr. *Horlock* was at my house on *Tuesday* last, and acquainted me that it was your lordship's desire I should come to you; and on that account I am here to wait on you.

B. By whom were you ordained? or are you ordained?

W. I am sent to preach the gospel.

B. By whom were you sent?

W. By a church of Jesus Christ.

M 3 *B.*

B. What church is that?

W. The church of Christ at *Melcomb.*

B. That factious and heretical church!

W. May it please you, sir, I know no faction or heresy that the church is guilty of.

B. No! Did not you preach such things as tend to faction and heresy?

W. I am not conscious to myself of any such preaching.

B. I am informed by sufficient men, gentlemen of honour of this county, viz, Sir *Gerrard Napper,* Mr. *Freak,* and Mr. *Tregonnel,* of your doings. What say you?

W. Those honoured gentlemen I have been with, who being by others misinformed, proceeded with some heat against me.

B. There are the oaths of several honest men, who have observed you, and shall we take your word for it, that all is but misinformation?

W. There was no oath given or taken. Besides if it be enough to accuse, who shall be innocent? I can appeal to the determination of the great day of judgment, that the large catalogue of matters laid to me; are either things invented, or mistaken.

B. Did not you ride with your sword in the time of the committee of safety, and engage with them?

W. Whatever imprudences, in matters civil, you may be informed I am guilty of, I shall crave leave to acquaint your lordship, that his majesty having pardoned them fully, and I having suffered on account of them since the pardon, I shall put in no other plea, and wave any other answer.

B. In what manner did the church you speak of send you to preach? At this rate every body might preach!

W. Not every one. Every body has not preaching gifts and preaching graces. Besides, that is not all I have to offer your lordship to justify my preaching.

B. If you preach, it must be according to order; the order of the church of *England,* upon an ordination.

W. What does your lordship mean by an ordination?

B. Do not you know what I mean?

W. If you mean that sending spoken of *Rom.* x; I had it.

B. I mean that: What mission had you?

W. I had a mission from God and man.

B. You must have it according to law, and the order of the church of *England.*

W. I am not satisfied in my spirit therein.

B.

B. Not satisfied in your spirit! You have more new-coined phrases than ever were heard of! You mean your conscience, do you not?

W. Spirit is no new phrase. We read of being sanctified in body, soul and spirit:—but if your lordship like it not so, then I say, I am not satisfied in *conscience*, as touching the ordination you speak of.

B. Conscience argues science, science supposes judgment, and judgment reason. What reason have you that you will not be thus ordained?

W. I came not this day to dispute with your lordship; my own inability would forbid me so to do.

B. No, no; but give me your reason.

W. I am not called to office; and therefore cannot be ordained.

B. Why have you then preached all this while?

W. I was called to the work of the ministry, tho' not to the office. There is as we believe, *Vocatio ad opus, & ad munus.*

B. Why may not you have the office of the ministry? You have so many new distinctions! O how are you deluded!

W. May it please your lordship, because they are not a people that are fit objects for me to exercise office-work among them.

B. You mean a gathered church: but we must have no gathered churches in *England*; and you will see it so. For there must be unity without divisions among us: and there can be no unity without uniformity. Well then, we must send you to your church that they may dispose of you, if you were ordained by them.

W. I have been informed by my cousin *Pitfield* and others, concerning your lordship, that you have a disposition inclined against morosity. However you may be prepossessed by some bitter enemies to my person, yet there are others who can and will give you another character of me. Mr. *Glisson* hath done it. And Sir *Francis Fulford* desired me to present his service to you, and being my hearer, is ready to acquaint you concerning me.

B. I asked Sir *Francis Fulford* whether the presentation to *Whitchurch* was his. Whose is it? He told me it was not his.

W. There was none presented to it these sixty years. Mr. *Walton* lived there. At his departure, the people desired

M 4   me

me to preach to them; and when there was a way of settlement appointed, I was by the trustees appointed, and by the
Triers approved.

B. They would approve any, that would come to them,
and close with them. I know they approved those who
could not read twelve lines of *English.*

W. All that they did I know not : but I was examined
touching gifts and graces.

B. I question not your gifts, Mr. *Wesley.* I will do
you any good I can : but you will not long be suffered to
preach, unless you will do it according to order.

W. I shall submit to any trial you shall please to make.
I shall present your lordship with a confession of my faith,
or take what other way you please to insist on.

B. No, we are not come to that yet.

W. I shall desire several things may be laid together,
which I look on as justifying my preaching. 1. I was devoted to the service from my infancy. 2. I was educated in
order thereto at school and in the university.

B. What university were you of ?—*W.* *Oxon.*

B. What house ?—*W.* *New-Inn-Hall.*

B. What age are you ?—*W.* Twenty-five.

B. No sure, you are not!

W. 3. As a son of the prophets, after I had taken my
degrees, I preached in the country, being approved of by
judicious able christians, ministers and others. 4. It pleased
God to seal my labour with success, in the apparent conversion of several souls.

B. Yea, that is, it may be, to your way.

W. Yea, to the power of godliness from ignorance and
profaneness. If it please your lordship to lay down any
evidences of godliness agreeing with the scripture, and if
they be not found in those persons intended, I am content
to be discharged from my ministry. I will stand or fall by
the issue thereof.

B. You talk of the power of godliness; such as you
fancy—

W. Yea, the reality of religion. Let us appeal to any
common-place book for evidences of grace, and they are
found in and upon these converts.

B. How many are there of them ?

W. I number not the people.

B. Where are they ?

W. Wherever I have been called to preach. At *Radpole,*
Melcomb,

Mèlcòmb, Turnwood, Whitchurch, and at sea. I shall add another ingredient of my mission. 5. When the Church saw the presence of God going along with me, they did, by fasting and prayer, in a day set apart for that end, seek an abundant blessing on my endeavours.

B. A *particular* church?

W. Yes, my lord, I am not ashamed to own myself a member of one.

B. Why you mistake the apostles' intent. They went about to convert heathens, and so did what they did. You have no warrant for your particular churches.

W. We have a plain, full, and sufficient rule for gospel worship in the New Testament, recorded in the Acts of the Apostles and the Epistles.

B. We have not.

W. The practice of the apostles is a standing rule in those cases which were not extraordinary.

B. Not their practice, but their precepts.

W. Both precepts and practice. Our duty is not delivered to us in scripture only by precepts, but by precedents, by promises, by threatenings mixed, not common-place-wise. We are to follow them as they followed Christ.

B. But the apostle said, ' This speak I, not the Lord :' that is by revelation.

W. Some interpret that place, ' This speak I now by re- ' velation from the Lord ;' not the Lord in that text before instanced, when he gave answer to the case concerning divorces. May it please your lordship, we believe that *Cultus non institutus est indebitus.*

B. It is false.

W. The second commandment speaks the same; ' Thou ' shalt not make unto thyself any graven image.'

B. That is, forms of your own invention.

W. Bishop *Andrews* taking notice of *non facies tibi,* satisfied me that we may not worship God but as commanded.

B. You take discipline, church-government, and cir- cumstances for worship.

W. You account ceremonies parts of worship.

B. But what say you ? did you not wear a sword in the time of the Committee of safety, with *Demy*, and the rest of them ?

W. My lord, I have given you my answer therein : and I farther say, that I have conscientiously taken the oath of allegiance, and faithfully kept it hitherto. I appeal to all that are round about me.

B.

B. But nobody will trust you; you stood it out to the last gasp.

W. I know not what you mean by the last gasp. When I saw the pleasure of providence to turn the order of things, I did submit quietly thereunto.

B. That was at last.

W. Yet many such men are trusted, and now about the king.

B. They are such as the on the parliament side during the war, yet disown those latter proceedings: but you abode even till *Haslerig's* coming to *Portsmouth*.

W. His majesty has pardoned whatever you may be informed of concerning me of, that nature. I am not here on that account.

B. I expected you not.

W. Your lordship sent your desire by two or three messengers. Had I been refractory I need not have come; but I would give no just cause of offence. I think the old Nonconformists were none of his majesty's enemies.

B. They were traitors. They began the war. *Knox* and *Buchanan* in Scotland, and those like them in England.

W. I have read the protestation of owning the king's supremacy.

B. They did it in hypocrisy.

W. You use to tell the poor Independents for judging folks hearts: Who doth it now?

B. I do not. For they protested one thing, and acted another. Do not I know them better than you?

W. I know them by their works, as they have therein delivered us their hearts.

B. Well then, you will justify your preaching, will you, without ordination according to the law?

W. All these things laid together are satisfactory to me for my procedure therein.

B. They are not enough.

W. There has been more written in proof of preaching of gifted persons, with such approbation, than as been answered by any one yet.

B. Have you any thing more to say to me, Mr. *Wesley?*

W. Nothing: your lordship sent for me.

B. I am glad I heard this from your own mouth. You will stand to your principles you say?

W. I intend it thro' the grace of God; and to be faithful to the king's majesty, however you deal with me.

B. I will not meddle with you.

W.

W. Farewell to you, sir.

B. Farewell, good Mr. *Wesley.*

It is to be hoped the bishop was as good as his word, and did not meddle with Mr. *Wesley,* to give him any disturbance. But there were some persons of figure in his neighbourhood, who were too much his enemies to permit him to continue quietly at *Whitchurch* till the Act of uniformity ejected him. For in the beginning of 1662, he was seized on the Lord's-day as he was coming out of the church, and carried to *Blandford,* where he was committed to prison. But after he had been some time confined, Sir *Gerard Napper,* who was the most furious of all his enemies, and the most forward in committing him, was so far softened by a sad disaster (having broke his collar-bone) that he applied to some persons to bail Mr. *Wesley,* and told them, that if they would not, he would do it himself. Thus was he set at liberty, but bound over to appear at the assizes, where he came off much better than he expected. The good man has recorded in his diary the mercy of God to him in raising up several friends to own him, inclining a solicitor to plead for him, and restraining the wrath of man, so that even the judge, tho' a very choleric man, spoke not an angry word. The sum of the proceedings, as it stands in his diary, is as follows:

Clerk. Call Mr. *Wesley,* of Whitchurch.

Wesley. Here.

Cl. You were indicted for not reading the Common Prayer. Will you traverse it?

Solicitor. May it please your lordship, we desire this business may be deferred till next assizes.

Judge. Why till then?

Sol. Our witnesses are not ready at present.

J. Why not ready now? Why have you not prepared for a trial?

Sol. We thought our prosecutors would not appear.

J. Why so, young man? Why should you think so? Why did you not provide them?

Wesley. May it please your lordship, I understand not the question.

J. Why will you not read the book of Common-prayer?

W. The book was never tendered me.

J. Must the book be tendered you?

W. So I conceive by the act.

J. Are you ordained?

W.

W. I am ordained to preach the gospel.

J. By whom?—*W.* I have order to preach.

J. From whom?

W. I have given an account thereof already to the bishop.

J. What bishop?—*W.* Of *Bristol.*

J. I say, by whom were you ordained? How long was it since?

W. Four or five years since.

J. By whom then?

W. By those who were then empowered.

J. I thought so. Have you a presentation to your place?

W. I have.

J. From whom?

W. May it please your lordship, it is a legal presentation.

J. By whom was it?—*W.* By the trustees.

J. Have you brought it?—*W.* I have not.

J. Why not?

W. Because I did not think I should be asked any such questions here.

J. I would wish you to read the Common-prayer at your peril. You will not say, " From all sedition and privy con-
" spiracy; from all false doctrine, heresy and schism; good
" Lord deliver us."

Cl. Call Mr. *Meech* (He was called and appeared) Does Mr. *Wesley* read the Common-prayer yet?

M. May it please your lordship, he never did, nor he never will.

J. Friend, how do you know that? He may bethink himself.

M. He never did, he never will.

Sol. We will, when we see the new book, either read it, or leave our place at Bartholomew-tide.

J. Are you not bound to read the old book till then? Let us see the act: Reading to himself, another cause was called.

Mr. *Wesley,* tho' bound over to the next assizes, came joyfully home, and preached constantly every Lord's-day, till *Aug.* 17, when he delivered his Farewell sermon to a weeping auditory, from *Acts* xx. 32. On the 26th of *October,* the place was, by an apparitor, declared vacant, and orders were given to sequester the profits; but his people had already given him what was his due. On *Feb.* 2d following, he removed with his family to *Melcomb;* but the corporation made an order against his settlement there, im-
poſing

posing a fine of twenty pounds upon his landlady, and five
shillings per week on him, to be levied by distress. He
waited upon the mayor and some other persons, pleading
that he had lived in the town some time formerly, and had
given notice of his design to come hither again. He also
offered to give security, which was all that their order required : but it was of no avail. For on *March* 11, another
order was drawn up for putting the former in execution.
These violent proceedings forced him out of the town, and
he went to *Bridgewater, Ilminster* and *Taunton,* in all
which places he met with great kindness and friendship from
all the three denominations of Dissenters, and was almost
every day employed in preaching in the several places to
which he went; where he also got many good acquaintance
and friends, who were afterwards very kind to him and his
numerous family. At length a gentleman who had a very
good house at *Preston,* two or three miles from *Melcomb,*
permitted him to live in it without paying any rent. Thither he removed his family in the beginning of *May,* and
there he continued (excepting a temporary absence) as long as
he lived. He records his coming to *Preston,* and his
comfortable accommodation there, with great thankfulness
and admiration.

Soon after his being fixed in this house, he had great debates in his mind about a removal abroad, either to *Surinam*
or *Maryland ;* but, after much consideration and advice, he
determined to abide in the land of his nativity, and there
take his lot. About the same time also he greatly hesitated
about hearing in the established church ; but at length, by
several arguments in Mr. *Nye's* papers, he was determined
to do it. He was then not a little troubled with respect to
his own preaching, whether it should be carried on openly
or only in private. Some of the neighbouring ministers,
particularly Mr. Bampfield, Mr. Ince, Mr. Hallet, of Shafton, and Mr. John Sacheverel, were for preaching publicly,
with open doors. But Mr. *Wesley* thought it was his duty
to *beware of men,* and that he was bound in prudence to
keep himself at liberty, so as to be in a capacity of service,
as long as he could. Accordingly, by preaching only in
private, he was kept longer out of the hands of his enemies
than the ministers above mentioned were ; all of whom were
indicted at the next assizes, for a riotous and unlawful assembly held at *Shafton.* They were found guilty by a jury
of gentlemen, and fined forty marks each, and were bound
to

to find security for their good behaviour. In the mean time
Mr. *Wesley* preached very frequently, not only to a few good
people at *Preston*, but likewise occasionally at *Weymouth*,
and other places round about. After some time, he was
called by a number of serious christians at *Poole*, to be their
pastor; in which relation he continued to the day of his
death, administering all ordinances to them as opportunity
offered.

By the *Oxford-act*, however, he was obliged, for a time,
to withdraw from *Preston*, and leave both his people and
his family. But he preached wherever he was, when he
could procure an auditory. Upon his coming to the place of
his retirement, on the above Act, in *March*, 1666, he put
this question to himself "What dost thou here? at such a
"distance from church, wife, children," &c.? And in his
answers, he set down the oath, and then added the reasons
why he could not take it, as several ministers had done; particularly this; That to do it in his own private sense,
would be but juggling with God, with the king, and with
conscience; especially as some magistrates declared they had
no right to admit of such a private sense. But after all this,
and a good deal more against taking the oath, he thankfully
mentions the goodness of God in so over-ruling the law-
makers, that they did not send the ministers farther from
their friends and flocks, and that they had so much time to
prepare for their removal, and liberty to pass on the road to
any place.

After he had lain hid for some time, he ventured home
again, and returned to his labour among his people, and occasionally among others. But notwithstanding all his prudence in managing his meetings, he was often disturbed, several times apprehended, and four times imprisoned; once at
Poole for half a year, and once at *Dorchester* for three
months; but the other confinements were shorter. He was
in many straits and difficulties, but was wonderfully supported and comforted, and many times was very seasonably
and surprizingly relieved and delivered. Nevertheless, the
removal of many eminent christians into another world, who
were his intimate acquaintance and kind friends; the great
decay of serious religion among many that made a profession
of it, and the increasing rage of the enemies of real godliness, manifestly seized and sunk his spirits. At length, having ' filled up his part of what is behind of the afflictions of
' Christ in his flesh, for his body's sake, which is the
                                        ' church,

'church, and finished the work given him to do,' he was taken out of this vale of tears, to that world ' where the ' wicked cease from troubling, and the weary are at ' rest,' when he had not been much longer an inhabitant here below than his blessed Master was, whom he served with his whole heart, according to the best light he had. The vicar at *Preston* would not suffer him to be buried in the church.

WINBOURN. *(Minster.)* Mr. BALDWIN DEACON. After his ejectment he lived and preached at *Bramfield*, in Somersetshire. Some years before his death he lost his sight. Dr. Calamy says nothing more of him than that He was a worthy person. § But the following note in Hutchins contains a further anecdote of him: " April 21, 1650, the " corporation elected Mr. *Arthur Hern* to be one of their " ministers: Mr. *Baldwin Deacon* another, with an allow- " ance of 80*l. per ann.* was appointed to preach the Friday's " Lecture. In 1660, *Deacon*, not being found in holy " orders, was discharged." By not being *in holy orders* is doubtless meant, not being episcopally ordained.

WOTTON *Fitz Pain.*   Mr. JOHN KERIDGE.   § So his name is entered in *Hutchins*, who speaks of him as Incumbent, in 1650, and *Benj. Bird*, 18 Jan. 1662 (for 1663) He was the father of Mr. Keridge, of *Lyme*. He died soon after Bartholomew-day, the time of his ejectment.

—— Mr. WILLIAM HUSSEY, ejected from the same place. § Dr. Calamy has only his surname; but most probably this was the person mentioned in the following note, in *Hutchins*.—" HINTON MARTEL. *James Crouch.* In " 1644, he was ejected [i. e. by the Committee.] In 1661, " he was with some trouble restored to his living, and was " thought to be the first sufferer [i. e. among the Royalists] " and the last restored in this county."—" WILLIAM HUS- " SEY, Intruder, 1646." Possibly he might, in like manner, *intrude* at both places.

The following ministers were ejected in this county, from places unknown:

Mr. MARTYN.—Mr. BOWYER.—Mr. LIGHT [There was a Mr. *Lyte Whynnel*, rector of Askerwell, 1638.]—Mr. FRANCIS MUTTALL.—Mr. MORGAN.—Mr. KING.

Dr. Calamy also mentions

Mr. WAY, Junior. § Most probably this was Mr. HENRY WAY, who is mentioned by *Hutchins*, as placed by the Committee in the living of *Broadway*, where Mr. Haslewood was incumbent, in 1650. This Mr. *Henry Way* is also mentioned at two other places. See *Portland* and *Week Regis.* It is presumed that he was related to Mr. *Benjamin Way,* of *Stafford,* in this county and *Barking,* in Essex.

§ Mr. THOMAS BLUNT seems to be another ejected minister, who should be added to our list, from the following entry in *Hutchins's* History.—" COMPTON ABBAS, *Tho-.* " *mas Boult,* 1647. He is supposed to have been *ejected* for " *Nonconformity,* 1664."

N. B. There are so many Inductions in the Registers of this county, in the year 1662, that it seems highly probable, there were many more ejected here than we have any account of.

The following afterwards conformed :

JOSEPH CRABB, M. A. of *Beminster.* A man of good abilities and learning, of a ready invention, and very facetious in conversation. After continuing some time a Nonconformist, he accepted the living of *Axminster,* in Devon, and continued minister there to the day of his death, when he was about 80 years of age. Tho' he was in the established church, yet in his principles, and manner of preaching and praying, he so resembled the nonconforming ministers, that he was still looked upon as one of them. He visited some of his ejected brethren, when persecuted and imprisoned ; sheltered and did good offices to others, and shewed on all occasions that his heart was with them. About 1683, he was accused to Dr. *Lamplugh,* Bp. of Exeter, for neglecting to read prayers on Wednesdays and Fridays, and for not coming up to the height of conformity ; but the Bishop after he had heard his defence, dismissed him with kindness, to the disappointment of his accusers. He joined with Mr. *Wm. Ball,* and others, in publishing a volume of Abp. *Usher's* sermons, and prefixed to them an elegant Latin epistle.

Mr. HERN, of *Winbourn.*—Mr. RICHARD DE SHUTE; of *Stalbridge.* § He was afterwards minister of *Stowmarket,* in Suffolk; and died 1688.

MINISTERS

MINISTERS EJECTED OR SILENCED

IN

DURHAM.

AUKLAND (Bishop's) [L.] RICHARD FRANKLAND, M. A. Of *Christ's Col. Camb.* Born in 1630, at *Rathmil*, in Yorkshire, in the parish of Giggleswick, in *Craven*, and educated in the famous school there. He made good proficiency both in divine and human learning, at the university, to which he went in the year 1647, when Dr. *S. Bolton* was master. While he was there, it pleased God to make him deeply in love with serious religion, by blessing to him the useful ministry of Mr. *Samuel Hammond*. On his removal from thence, he was invited to *Hexham*, in Northumberland, where his stay was short. He afterwards preached for a little time at *Haughton Spring*, and then at *Lanchester*. On *Sept.* 14, 1653, he was set apart to the office of the ministry by several ministers, which ordination he accounted to all intents and purposes valid, and durst not do any thing like a renouncing it, tho' much solicited by Bp. *Cozens*, after the Restoration, with a promise of considerable preferment. Meeting with some discouragements here, he removed into alderman *Brook's* family, at *Ellenthorp*, where he continued his ministry. From thence he went to *Sedgfield*, as assistant to Mr. *Lupthern ;* and at last settled in the living of St. Andrews, in *Aukland*, which was given him by Sir *Arthur Haslerig*, and was of good value.

When the protector *Oliver* erected a college for academical learning, at *Durham*, Mr. *Frankland* was pitched upon to be a tutor there. But that college being demolished at the

Restoration, and the Act of uniformity taking place, he not only lost his designed post, but his living too, upon his refusal to conform. While he was in it, he laid himself out to his utmost in his Master's work. He always expounded the scripture on the Lord's-day morning before sermon ; and besides preaching in the afternoon, catechized the youth, and explained to them the principles of religion in a familiar way. His conversation was exemplary and inoffensive ; and his labours successful to many souls. After the king's return he was among the first that met with disturbance. Some time before the Bartholomew-act passed, one Mr. *Bowster*, an attorney, who had formerly appeared to be his friend, was so forward as to ask him publicly before the congregation, whether or no he would conform ? He told him that he hoped it was soon enough to answer that question, when the king and parliament had determined what conformity they would require. Mr. *Bowster* told him again, that if he did not answer then, he should be turned out of his place. Mr. *Frankland* said, He hoped the king's proclamation for quiet possessions would secure him from such violence. To which the other replied, " Look you to that." Soon after which, he and one Parson *Marthwait* (a man of no character) got the keys of the church, and kept Mr. *Frankland* out. He complained to some of the neighbouring justices, who owned it was hard, but were afraid to stand by him. He indicted *Marthwait* and his adherents for a force and riot, at the quarter-sessions, and the indictment was found ; but the defendants by a *certiorari* removed the matter to the next assizes, and there his cause was the last that was heard : the clerk had mistaken *praesentatum est* for *praesentatum fuit*, in the indictment ; his council was cow'd, and he could not have justice done him.

After this Bp. *Cozens* solicited him to conform, promising him not only his present living, but greater preferment. Mr. *Frankland* told him, that his unwillingness to renounce his ordination by presbyters made him incapable of enjoying the benefit of his favour. This engaged him in a debate with the Bishop, which was managed with great calmness. His lordship asked him, whether he would be content to receive a new ordination so privately that the people might not know of it, and have it conditionally with such words as these : " If thou hast not been ordained, I ordain thee," &c. He
than..ed

thanked his lordship, but told him, he durst not yield to the proposal; at the same time assuring him, that it was not obstinacy but conscience which hindered his compliance. A little after, the Bishop preached on 1 *Cor.* xiv. *ult.* ' Let all ' things be done decently and in order.' Mr. *Frankland* within a few weeks being invited by a neighbouring minister to preach in his pulpit, insisted on *v.* 26 of the same chapter, ' Let all things be done to edification.' The bishop hearing of it, was offended, thinking it done in a way of contempt, and threatened to call him to account; but he was prevented by a sober neighbouring gentleman, a justice of peace, who was that day Mr. *Frankland's* auditor; and who told the Bishop that he did indeed, in that sermon, speak against pluralities, non-residence, &c. but that he spoke nothing but what beame a sound and orthodox divine, and what was agreeable to the doctrine of the church of England.

After his being silenced, he lived at *Rathmil*, in *Yorkshire*, on his own estate; where he was persuaded to set up a private academy. Sir *Thomas Liddal* sent his son *George* to be educated under him, and many others followed his example; so that in the space of a few years he had to the number of three hundred pupils † under his tuition; many of whom proved worthy and useful ministers of the gospel. From *Rathmil* he removed in 1674 to *Natland*, near *Kendal*, in *Westmoreland*, upon a call from a christian society there; where, besides his care in the education of those who were committed to him, he preached frequently in his own house, at *Kendal*, and at several other neighbouring places. From thence, by reason of the Five-mile-act, he removed successively to *Dawsonfold*, in the same county, to *Hartburrow*, in Lancashire, to *Calton* in Craven, in *Yorkshire*, to *Attercliff*, near Sheffield; from whence he returned to *Rathmil* again. In these parts he had a thriving congregation, whom he kept in peace by his candour and humility, gravity and piety, notwithstanding their different principles; and he was generally beloved, and exceedingly useful. In the latter part of his life he was afflicted with the stone, the strangury,

† A list of the names of all his pupils may be seen at the end of Dr. LATHAM's Funeral Sermon, for Mr. MADDOCK, of UTTOXETER, who was one of them; with the date of their commencement. This respectable list is now before the Editor. With this Sermon is also printed a Latin letter from Sir Isaac Newton.

and

and various other infirmities, which he bore with an exemplary patience. He died *Oct.* 1, 1698, aged 68. His funeral sermon was preached by Mr. *Chorlton*, of Manchester, from *Matt.* xxviii. ult.

Mr. *Frankland* was an eminent divine, and an acute metaphysician; a solid interpreter of scripture; very sagacious in discovering errors, and able in defending truth. He was a person of great humility and affability. Not a very popular, but a substantial preacher. Few conversed with him, but they respected and valued him. He was a man of great moderation; very liberal to the poor; studious to promote the gospel in all places; and good in all relations in life. And yet he met with much opposition, especially in the latter part of it. He was cited into the Bishop's court, and excommunicated for non-appearance; but lord *Wharton*, Sir *Thomas Rookby*, and others interceding with K. *William*, he ordered his absolution, which was accordingly read in *Giggleswick* church. Abp. *Sharp* some time afterwards sent for him to meet him at *Skipton*, and at first was rather warm; telling him how many complaints were made against him, and intimating that the course he took tended to perpetuate a schism in the church, and that therefore it was not sufferable. Mr. *Frankland* freely told his Grace, that they of the established church were certainly fallible in their judgments, as well as the Dissenters; and therefore he desired they might fairly argue the case about schism, before he determined any thing about it. The Abp. seeming to think there was no occasion for a debate on the subject, Mr. *Frankland* took the freedom to tell him, That he apprehended there was much more proper work for his Grace to do, than to fall upon the Dissenters. And when the Abp. asked him, what that was, he told him, It was to endeavor a reconciliation between sober Protestants, for strengthening the Protestant interest, at a time when it was so much in danger; and added, That if he thought there was need of using severity, it would be the best way to begin with those of his own clergy who were disorderly.

The Abp. freely acknowledged there was need of both, and promised to use his utmost endeavours in both the particulars mentioned; and said, He hoped they would find him an honest man. Mr. *Frankland* replied, that candour and moderation went to make up honesty. The Abp. readily granting this, he added, That if his Grace should not exer-

cise

cise moderation, he would frustrate the hopes of many worthy persons, considering the good character that was given of him, &c. Mr. *Frankland* afterwards went, by his desire, to make him a visit; when he treated him with great civility, and shewed him the petition that was drawn up against him, and the number of subscribers to it. After this, tho' a fresh citation was sent from the ecclesiastical court, a prohibition was sent down to stop the proceedings. Still however his troubles were renewed and continued. And indeed it was observed, that from the Revolution in 1688, there was scarcely a year in which he had not some fresh troubles, till by his death God delivered him out of them all.

BOWDEN. Mr. ROBERT PLEASANCE. After his ejectment he never would preach to a greater number than the Act against conventicles allowed. He had a pretty good estate, and left some considerable legacies for the support of the gospel.

COTHAM. Mr. KIPLIN.

DURHAM (City) ST. NICHOLAS, [C.] Mr. JONATHAN DEVEREAUX. He died soon after his ejectment.

—— HELVETH PARISH in the same city. Mr. HOLDSWORTH.

ELWICK [R.] Mr. JOHN BOWY. He was a native of *Scotland*, and when he was silenced here, he returned to his own country.

GATESHEAD. *St. Mary's* [R. 27l. 13s. 8d.] Mr. THOMAS WELD. His living was in the bishopric, tho' parted from the town of Newcastle only by the river. He was turned out by Mr. Ladler, who had a dormant presentation to the living from Bishop *Morton*. He had been formerly minister at *Terling*, in Essex; but not submitting to the ceremonies, the place was too hot for him, and he was forced to quit it, and go over to New-England. § Whether he returned or not doth not appear. He is not mentioned by *Cotton Mather*, otherwise than by an occasional reference to the first of his books, and in a list of Graduates, in *Harvard* College, 1671.

WORKS. The Rise, Reign and Ruin of Antinomianism, &c. in New-England.—An Answer to *W. R.*'s Narration of the Opinions and Practices of the Churches lately erected in New-

England, vindicating those Churches.—He, with three others, wrote The Perfect Pharisee under Monkish Holiness, against the Quakers.—He also, with Mr. Samuel Hammond, &c. was concerned in a tract, intit. A False Jew, &c. upon the Discovery of a Scot, who first pretended to be a Jew, and then a Baptist, but was found to be an impostor.

HARTLEPOOL [V.] Mr. Bowey.

HEIGHINGTON [V.] Mr. Squire.

JARROW. Mr. Francis Batty.

KELLOW [R. 20l.] Mr. Thomas Dixon. He was in a tumultuous manner turned out of his church by one Pearson, whom Dr. Cozens, then Bishop of Durham, had presented to the place, and afterwards continued a Nonconformist.

LAMSLEY. Mr. Thomas Wilson. § He was, as is supposed, the son of Mr. Thomas Wilson, a native of Cumberland; a very eminent minister, whose life is published in Clark's last volume of Lives, and who died in the year 1657, leaving ten children. He had several removals, and it doth not appear where this his son was born or educated.—After K. Charles's Indulgence, in 1672, he and Mr. Robert Leaver (formerly of Bolam, in Northumberland) for two years carried on a meeting for divine worship, in his house, preaching by turns to all that came.—Mr. Wilson, in the latter part of his life, was afflicted with such violent pains, either of the stone, or some other complaint about the urinary passage, that he was utterly disabled for service, and was rendered an object of great compassion.

MIDDLETON [R. 200l.] Mr. Thomas Kentish. He was betimes thrown out of his place, and severely harrassed soon after the Restoration; of which a narrative was printed in 1662. He brought up three sons to the ministry, and died in London full of years.

NORTON [V.] Mr. Brough.

Great STAINTON [R. 300l.] William Pell, M.A. Of Magd. Col. Oxf. Born at Sheffield, in Yorkshire, and sent to the college in 1650, of which he was afterwards chosen a Fellow. He had formerly been at Easington, to which the old incumbent returned in 1660, and was ejected from Stainton, in 1662. He was a tutor at Durham, when
Oliver

Oliver was attempting to set up a university there. After his ejectment, being occasionally at Durham on a Lord's-day, he preached in a house not far from a tavern, where some justices of the peace were drinking together, who overheard the people as they were singing a psalm. Thereupon one of the company made a motion to go and disturb them. To which another replied, " That if any of them thought in " their consciences, that singing psalms and hearing a sermon " upon such a day, was a more improper employment than " drinking in a tavern, they might go and make them for- " bear ; but that for his own part he would not be one of " them :" and so the proposal was quashed. However, some time after, Mr. *Pell* was imprisoned at Durham for his Nonconformity ; but removed himself to London by an *Habeas corpus*, and was set at liberty by judge *Hale*. He then retired to the northern parts of Yorkshire, and practised physic. Afterwards he preached publicly at *Tattershal*, in Lincolnshire, as Mr. *Young* had done before him ; and by being entertained in the earl of *Lincoln*'s family as a steward, he was preserved from the violence that others met with, and to which he had otherwise been exposed.

Upon K. *James*'s liberty he was called to a congregation at *Boston*. After seven years continuance there he removed to *Newcastle* upon Tyne, where he was assistant to Dr. *Gilpin ;* and there he finished his labours. His friends often urged him to teach academical learning, for which he was wonderfully qualified ; but they could not prevail with him, because of the oath he had taken at the university, at his commencing M. A. None that knew him could, without the greatest injustice, deny him the character of a very learned pious man, and a grave solid preacher. He was particularly eminent for his skill in the *Oriental* languages. He had three reams of paper bound up, purely for collections out of eastern authors ; but they were unfinished, thro' the many disturbances and avocations which attended his unsettled condition. He would repeat off hand the various readings and interpretations of scripture given by Jewish writers. Indeed he was fit to have been professor of the *Oriental* languages, in any university in Christendom. In preaching and praying he was excelled by few. He died in *Dec.* 1698, aged 63. He often preached in *London*, where he providentially became acquainted with one Mr. *Pell*, a merchant, who was very kind to him for his name's sake.

WASHINGTON

WASHINGTON [R. 130*l*.] Mr. WILLIAMSON.

WEREMOUTH (Bishop's) [R. 200*l*.] Mr. GRAVES.

WITTON GILBERT. Mr. HUTTON. ·

The following afterwards conformed :

Mr. JOHN WELD, of *Riton,* son to Mr. *T. Weld,* of *Gateshead.*—Mr. RICHARD BATTERSBY, of *Haughton.*—Mr. LUKE COATES, of *Sedberg,* who afterwards had a living in Yorkshire.—Mr. JOSIAH DOCKWRAY, of *Lanchester,* afterwards LL.D.—Mr. JOHN KID, of *Ridmarshal.*—Mr. SCOT, of *Wickham.*—Mr. JOHN BERWICK, of *Stanhope.* afterwards lecturer of St. Nicholas's church, in *Newcastle.* —Mr. BICKERTON, of *Wolsingham,* the same.—Mr. PARISH, of *Darlington,* afterwards in Yorkshire.—Mr. JOHN TIMSON, of *Hellen's Aukland.*—Mr. THOMAS BOYER, of *Mugglewick.*—Mr. DANIEL BUSHEL, of *Eglescliffe.*

MINISTERS EJECTED OR SILENCED

IN

ESSEX.

———

ABREY-HATCH. Mr. KIGHTLY. § Nothing more can now be ascertained concerning him than that, after his ejectment, he preached at *Billericay*, in this county, where there has long been, and still is, a considerable body of Dissenters. It does not appear that his name occurs in *Newcourt's Repertorium Eccles*, or that it was subscribed to either of the papers so often referred to in the accounts of the ministers in this county: viz. The Testimony of the Essex Ministers, printed in 1648; and the Essex Watchman's Watch-word, in 1649.* This however was the case with several others, concerning whom there is no doubt of their having been ejected in this county. Many came to their livings after that period, and some refused to subscribe any paper. See the account of Mr. *Cole*, at Wethersfield.

ALPHAMPSTON [R.] Mr. SAMUEL BRINSLEY. Some time Fellow of St. *John's Col. Camb.* He was a pious and laborious minister of Christ. After his ejectment he resided

---

* Dr. Calamy generally takes notice whether the ministers ejected in this county are mentioned by Newcourt or not, and whether or not they subscribed either of the above papers. The editor of this work has not generally introduced these circumstances, unless they appeared of importance to ascertain their true names, or the length of time they had been in their livings.—In this county there is an unusual number of mere names of persons and places. But this is a defect in the original work: nothing of any moment contained in that being here omitted. Some small articles are now inserted which were not in the former edition; but few additions of any moment have been communicated or could be procured.

principally

principally in and about London. But it doth not appear
that he had any stated congregation. He died about the
year 1695.

ARKESDEN [V. 43*l.* 8*s.* 9*d.*] RICHARD PEPPS, M. A.
Formerly Fellow of *Eman. Col. Camb.* A correction is
here made in his name from *Newcourt,* who mentions *T.
Paget,* as succeeding to this living upon his deprivation,
Feb. 25, 1662. Which fixes the time of his ejectment six
months before the Bartholomew act passed, unless 62 is put
(as sometimes it was) for 6½.

Great BADDOW [V.]   Mr. CHRISTOPHER WRAGGE.
He was a man of some considerable note, of good abilities,
and great acceptance. It appears from Newcourt that he
came to this living upon the death of the former incumbent,
of the name of Clerk.

Little BADDOW [V. S. 33*l.* 15*s.* 10*d.*] THOMAS GIL-
SON, M. A. Of *Eman. Col. Camb.* He was born at *Sudbury,* and was trained up in the free-school at *Dedham.*
He removed from Cambridge to Oxford, where he became
Fellow of *Corpus Christi Col.* After being silenced at Baddow, he went to London, and was chosen pastor of a Dissenting congregation in *Radcliff,* where he died, much lamented, about 50 years of age, in 1680. His funeral sermon was preached and printed by Mr. *Slater.* He was a
good scholar, and had very valuable ministerial gifts. He
was very diligent in his master's work, and zealous to advance his glory. On his death-bed he expressed his intire
acquiescence in his early removal, in words to this effect:
" When many live sixty or seventy years in the world before
" they have done the work for which they were sent hither,
" If I can dispatch mine in fifty, what reason have I to
" complain?"—Mr. *Gilson* left a son in the ministry, at Colchester.

§ BARKING [V.] BENJAMIN WAY, M. A. Dr.
Calamy here has only —" Mr. *Way.*" But this is undoubtedly the person mentioned at STAFFORD, in Dorsetshire, and
afterwards at Bristol, where he succeeded Mr. *John Thompson,* since *Hutchins* mentions his name as being in the parish
register of Stafford. The following account of him is
                                                transmitted

transmitted by a descendant, who bears both his names.*
" The Reverend Benjamin Way, M. A. was descended of
a reputable family long settled at Bridport, in Dorset, and
educated at Oriel College, Oxford. He was presented to
the living of Barking, in Essex, where he resided till he
was ejected by the Act of Uniformity. From that time he
lived at Dorchester till 1675, when he was invited by the
congregation of Protestant Dissenters, meeting at the Castle
[now called *Castle Green*] in Bristol, to be their minister;
with whom he continued till his death; which happened on
the 9th of November, 1680. As to his works, I know of
none that he published. But I have his farewell sermon to
his people at Bristol, from 1 *Cor.* xv. 19, expressive of great
seriousness and piety. In his last illness, he frequently mentioned, with the greatest satisfaction, his having quitted his
living, in 1662, which was of 400*l. per annum* value, for
his conscience-sake: using this expression to his eldest son,
on his death-bed: " I bless God that I did not submit to that
" burden of conformity."

From a subsequent account it appears that Mr. *Way* married the daughter of the celebrated Puritan minister, Mr.
White, of Dorchester, and that there is yet extant in her
own hand writing, an account of the births and baptisms of
all their children. Their eldest son *Joseph*, lived and died a
merchant, at Bristol. The second, *Benjamin* (grandfather
to the writer of this account) was a merchant, in London.
Two other sons, *Richard* and *John*, as also a daughter,
Martha, died young. Hence it appears that Mr. *Way* had
no son in the ministry. It remains to discover, who was the
Mr. WAY, *Junior*, whom Dr. Calamy mentions as ejected
at some unknown place in this county: or, Mr. HENRY
WAY, spoken of page 176.—Mrs. *Way* died in 1675, and
he married a second wife from Dorchester, of the name of
Hall, about the time he went to Bristol.

---

* BENJAMIN WAY, Esq. in a Letter to the Editor, dated *Denham*, near
Uxbridge, *June* 10, 1775: too late to be inserted in its proper place in the
first Edition. This gentleman, who has lately renewed his correspondence
on the subject, was not aware that his worthy ancestor ever had the living
of *Stafford*, and is now apprehensive that he was presented to it on the
death of *R. Russel*, 1660, to hold for *R. Russel*, presented in 1663; for on a
failure of the male line in Russel, the adjacentia aliquot prædiola, came to
Robert White, and afterwards to Richard White, who was presented to
Stafford, in 1708, to whose family Mr. Way was by marriage related, as
mentioned in the addition to the above account.

BARNSTON

BARNSTON [R.] John Beadle, M. A. From *New-court's Rep.* it appears, that he came to this living in 1632, " on the resignation of Mr. *Wright.*" He was long exercised with great weakness, which he bore with much faith and patience.

WORKS. The Journal or Diary of a thankful Christian.

BELCHAM (Water) [V.] Mr. Deersley. See the end of this county.

BELCHAM (Otton) Mr. Thomas. § This was undoubtedly Mr. Edward Thomas, who subscribed the Testimony of the Essex Ministers in the year 1648, as then " Minister of *Oaten Belcham.*"

BENTLEY (Magna) [V. 28*l.* 16*s.*] Mr. Thomas Beard. Dr. Walker says, he got this living in 1654.

BOREHAM [V.] Mr. John Oakes. *Newcourt* mentions his successor, 17 *Sept.* 1662, from whence may be inferred his ejectment by the Act of uniformity. Upon which he became pastor of a church at *Little Baddow*, which is separated only by a small river from this parish. He was afterwards invited to London, viz. upon the death of Mr. *Thomas Vincent*, whom he succeeded in his congregation. He was a man of a very chearful spirit, of a sweet even temper, of unaffected piety, of great candour and charity, and of an exemplary life and conversation. He was suddenly taken ill in the pulpit, and silenced by his great master in the midst of his work, in *Dec.* 1688. He was succeeded by Mr. (afterwards Dr.) *Daniel Williams.*

WORKS. Paul's Trial and Triumph ; a sermon on the death of Mrs. *E. King.*—A Sermon in the Morning Exercise continued, on *Prov.* xxx. 8, 9.—§ An elaborate and useful discourse, on Agur's prayer; to shew wherein a middle condition in the world is the most eligible.

BOXTED [V. 28*l.* 10*s.*] Mr. Lax.—From the same place also was ejected,

—— Mr. Carr. An able and useful preacher,

BRAINTREE [V. 48*l.*] Mr. John Argor, Of *Camb.
University.* Born at *Sayor Britton,* near 'Colchester, During part of the civil war he was minister of *Lee,* in this county; and at Braintree succeeded Mr. Samuel Collins,
who

who had been minister there forty-five years, and died in
1657. After Mr. *Argor's* being laid aside for nonconformity, he continued in *Braintree,* and kept the grammar-school there till the Five-mile-act took place, when he was
forced to leave the town. He often used to say, " He left
" his living upon no other terms than he would, if called to
" it, have laid down his life." He was exceedingly beloved,
and the loss of him was much lamented. He was a very
serious and lively christian, who had a sense of religion betimes; and in his advanced years, often had raptures of joy.
When his livelihood was taken from him, he lived comfortably by Faith. Being asked by some friends, How he
thought he should live, having a great family of children ;
his answer was, " As long as his God was house-keeper, he
believed he would provide for him and his."—He kept a diary
of God's providences towards him, and among other things,
in stirring up friends to assist him. The following are a few
instances, in his own words :

" *Jan.* 2, 1663, I received 5*l.* 2*s.* This was when I
was laid aside for not conforming. So graciously did the
Lord provide for his unworthy servant.—On *Jan.* 3, I received 3*l.* 19*s.* The Lord have the praise ! And I received
3*l.* 15*s.* which was gathered for me by my friends. This
great experience of God's gracious providence, I received
almost at one and the same time. All glory be to God
blessed for ever.—On *April* 2, 1663, I received 5*l.* 12*s.*
So graciously doth the Lord regard the low condition of his
servant. Blessed be his holy name for ever. I received likewise on the 8th day, 4*l.* So good is the Lord in stirring
up hearts, and opening hands, to the relief of his unworthy
servant." Many similar observations, and pious aspirations
are contained in his papers. In the latter part of his time he
had a congregation at *Wivenhoe.* He died at *Coptford,* in
this county, in *December,* 1679, aged 77 ; and was buried
in *Coptford* church. He never could be prevailed upon to
publish any thing.

—— Mr. FRIAR was ejected from the same place.

BUMSTED (Steeple) [V.] Mr. EDWARD SYMMES. A
very humble, modest and pious person. He appears from
Newcourt to have held this living many years, and not to
have been ejected till Bartholomew-day, for tho' his name is
not mentioned in the *Repert.* his predecessor is entered in,
the year 1606, and his successor *Sept.* 22, 1662.

BURBROOK

BURBROOK [R. S.] Isaac Grandorge, M. A. Some time Fellow of *St. John's Col. Cambridge.* After his ejectment, in 1660, he lived at *Black-Notley.* He was an excellent man, and a great scholar ; a very prudent person, and a judicious preacher.

Great BURSTED. Mr. Samuel Bridges.

CHELMSFORD [R. S. 81*l.* 2*s.* 4½*d.*] Mr. Mark Mott. He was put into this living by the House of Commons, in 1643. Dr. *Walker* relates a story concerning the intolerance and cruelty of some of his congregation towards some *Brownists,* who had a meeting at Chelmsford. If Mr. *Mott* gave them any encouragement, he had occasion to reflect upon it with regret when he himself was silenced by the Act of uniformity.. But it doth not appear that he had any concern in the business.

CHICKNEY [R.] Mr. Archer.

CHILDERDISH [V. 59*l.* 9*s.* 10*d.*] Mr. Harris.

CHISSEL *Parva* [R.] Mr. James Willet. He signed the Essex Testimony as minister of this place, in the year 1648. From *Newcourt's Rep.* it appears that he resigned this living *June* 13, 1662.

CLAVERING [V. S. 200*l.*] Mr. John Moore. Of *Peterhouse, Camb.* Born at *Burton Overy,* in Leicestershire. He was an excellent scholar, and a good preacher. When he left the university, he settled at *Bedford ;* § and from thence removed to *Clavering,* where he continued seventeen years, till the *Bartholomew*-act ejected him. He allowed 20*l.* a year to a chapel of ease, at *Newport,* in the parish of Clavering. He afterwards preached at *Easton,* in Huntingdonshire, where he had an estate. He died in 1673, at the age of about 70. He was a man of an humble spirit, and of a blameless conversation.

§ There are five parishes in that town. The editor, who is a native of it, recollects an ancient widow lady residing there, fifty years ago, of the name of *Moore,* whose husband, he was told, had been a Dissenting minister, but had conformed. Probably he might be related to the above. His character was said to be remarkably similar.

–COGGESHALL

COGGESHALL [V.] Mr. JOHN SAMS. He came from *New-England*, where he had his education. He settled first at *Kelvedon*, in this county, and afterwards succeeded Dr. *Owen* at this place, where the Act of uniformity silenced him. After the loss of his living, he and some of his people attended the parish church; but others of them not being satisfied so to do, and the minister publicly reproaching them that did, for not being present in time of divine service,§ he desisted, and set up a separate meeting there, where he gathered a church, of which he died pastor, about 1675. He was a man of good learning, and valuable ministerial abilities, but of a melancholy disposition.

COLCHESTER *St. Andrew's*. OWEN STOCKTON, M. A. Of *Christ's Col. Camb.* and afterwards Fellow of *Gonville* and *Caius Col.* He was born at Chichester, in *May*, 1630, his father being a prebendary of the cathedral, in that city; upon whose decease his mother removed to the city of *Ely*, where he had his grammar learning under Mr. *Wm. Hickes.* [He was very hopeful from his childhood; his ingenuity and inclination to learning were such as presaged more than ordinary improvement. Once looking accidentally into *Fox's Acts and Monuments*, which lay in one of the churches, he was so affected with what he read, and so desirous of a further knowledge of that history, that he importuned his friends till he procured a volume of it, and employed all his vacant time in reading it, declining all childish recreations. He was admitted to the university in 1645, where he had Dr. *Henry More* for his tutor, and where he was remarkable for his sobriety and diligence. When he commenced B. A. he still resided in the college, and applied himself to the study of divinity, which indeed was almost his principal object. With a view to his greater proficiency, he went to *London* and spent some months there, getting an account of the best writers in divinity, frequenting *Sion* college library, and *Gresham* college lectures. He also applied to several learned and worthy ministers of that city, and attended on their preaching, to observe the

§ That is, during the prayers. It is no wonder that any Clergyman should censure such persons, as guilty of a great indecency and inconsistency. There are many of the same description in the present day, whose conduct deserves severe animadversion, and the ministers whom they attend, merely for the sake of the Sermon, may justly "reproach them" for pouring contempt on the prayers of the church, and disturbing the congregation, by coming in at the close of the worship.

variety

variety of their gifts, and their several methods of preaching. By these means he found so much improvement, that
he often said, if he had a son he would advise him to do the
same.]

He began his ministry in some villages near the university,
with good acceptance and success, [though with the utmost
privacy, so that many of the people who heard him knew
not who he was, nor whence he came; and he did all *gratis.*]
In 1654 he was catechist in his college, and soon after fixed
as stated preacher in *St. Andrew's* parish, *Cambridge.* [He
had such an affecting sense of the importance and difficulty
of the ministerial office, that he for a long time declined ordination; but being at length satisfied that God had called
him to the office, he was determined to devote himself more
thoroughly to it by ordination; which he did in London,
Feb. 30, 1655: upon which he returned to his charge at
Cambridge, and applied himself to the work to which he
was devoted with the greatest faithfulness, diligence and
zeal. Nor did he confine his labours to his congregation;
he was useful as a tutor in the university, and preached a
great many lectures about the country, where he never
wanted a full auditory.] From hence he removed to *Colchester*, where he was chosen by the mayor, aldermen, &c.
to preach to them on Lord's-days in the afternoon, and every
Wednesday morning. [His very first sermon was blessed
to the conversion of one who heard it, and his second or
third to that of another, who was noted as a very profligate
sinner, and who came from mere curiosity to hear him. He
was a great blessing to the town, both in a spiritual and a
temporal view:] Of his own accord he preached on the
Lord's-day mornings at *St. James's* church *gratis.*

He laboured faithfully, diligently and successfully, till the
law disabled him. He afterwards preached three years in his
own house, to all that came to him, till the town was visited
with the pestilence; when, as other ministers fled, he offered the magistrates to stay and preach to them, if they
would allow him the liberty of a public church; which,
notwithstanding the great necessity of the people, was
denied him. Hereupon he removed to *Chattisham*, in
Suffolk, where he had for some time an opportunity of
exercising his ministry in public. When K. *Charles* published his declaration for Indulgence, he had a call from a
congregation at *Colchester*, and another at *Ipswich*. That
he

he might answer both as far as he was able, he undertook half the service of each ; and, with other ministers, divided his labours between them as long as he lived. Besides his preaching twice on the Lord's-day, he frequently expounded, catechized the youth, and resolved cases of conscience. He preached also a lecture on the week-day at *Ipswich* once a fortnight ; and scarcely a week passed, but he assisted in some other lecture, or was called to preach some funeral or other occasional sermon.

His diligence in his master's work drew upon him many enemies, but Divine Providence wonderfully preserved him ; so that notwithstanding complaints, indictments, presentments, and excommunications, he was never imprisoned, apprehended, distrained on, or brought before any court or magistrate. [He expected and desired (as he owned in his last illness) to have died a martyr ; but, says he, " God is " wiser than I, and knows my weakness." He was raised far above the fear of death, both in health and sickness. In his perfect health, considering the evil of the days wherein he lived, he would often say, " 'Tis a good time to die ; I " am content to live, and willing to die." As death was not terrible to him, neither was it unexpected : tho' he had a strong constitution, he told a friend, a year before, he thought he should not live long, and that God had been inclining his heart to study how a Christian might get above the fear of death. The substance of his thoughts upon the subject he committed to writing. On *Aug.* 31. 1680, he was seized with a fever, which proved fatal, *Sept.* 10, when he was in his full strength, being about 50 years of age. He discharged his dying office by grave exhortations and encouragements to seriousness in religion, and a readiness to suffer for it. He blessed God for Jesus Christ, and for calling him to be a minister of his gospel; for making him faithful in that office, and affording him his presence and blessing under all the difficulties of it. He rejoiced in the testimony of a good conscience and the hope of glory, and declared his full satisfaction in his Nonconformity, in which nothing influenced him but his conscience towards God.

God blessed him with a good estate, and he made a good use of it while he lived. [He disposed of the greatest part of his salary to charitable purposes, particularly in the education of some poor scholars of promising talents for the work of the ministry, and he also stirred up others to do the same. At his death he left the most valuable part of his well-fur-

nished library to *Gonville* and *Caius* college, and ordered
500*l.* to be settled on the said college for the maintenance of
a scholar and fellow for ever. And in case his only daughter
should die before the age of 21, he bequeathed 20*l. per
annum* to be settled on the college in *New-England,* for
the education of a converted *Indian,* or to any other that
would learn the *Indian* language, and preach to that poor
people. He was an excellent Christian, a man mighty in the
scriptures. His private papers, published in the account of
his life, shew that he most carefully practised himself the
things which he recommended to others. He was a man
more than ordinarily mortified to the pleasures of the flesh,
and the vanities of the world. His conversation was in
heaven; his delight in the saints; his business was religion;
his whole deportment strictly conscientious. He was a lover
of hospitality, a faithful friend, an industrious peace-maker,
a forgiver of injuries, a hearty mourner in *Israel,* a man
full of charity, eminently holy and wise in all his conversation, serious and grave, yet not melancholy. He was never
disturbed with anger, or any other passion, that could be
observed by those who were most conversant with him.
Tho' he was not very forward to speak, yet he was ever
ready for pious discourse, and would often begin it.

[His sermons§ were well studied, his matter was substantial and spiritual, his arguments strong, his utterance clear,
deliberate and grave; his words apt, and very expressive of
his conceptions. He affected not ' the words which man's
wisdom teacheth,' nor did he allow himself in an indiscreet
liberty of speech. In prayer, his deportment, his language
and utterance, always bespoke his solemn and affecting apprehensions of the majesty and holiness of the great object
of worship.] He was an eminent example of those qualifications which the apostolic canons (in the epistles to *Timothy* and *Titus*) require of a minister. In a word, he was
one of those who earnestly recommended religion to all that
observed him. [A full account of him may be seen in
Clark's last volume of Lives, from whence much of the
above is extracted.]

WORKS. A Scriptural Catechism; and a Treatise of Family
Instruction.—A Rebuke to Informers.— Counsel to the Afflicted;
occasioned by the Fire of London : (a Book excellently adapted to

§ The editor is in possession of several of them in his own hand-writing.

the afflicted in general.) [After his death was published, Consolation in Life and Death, &c. with the Life of Mrs. Ellen Asty, Widow of Mr. Robert Asty, Minister of Stratford, in Suffolk.] He left the following MSS. The Cure of the Fear of Death.— A Treatise of glorifying God.—The Best Interest.—And A Warning to Drunkards.

——— *St. Peter's,* in the same town. Mr. EDWARD WARREN. A pious and learned divine. A man of singular abilities, good elocution, and great humility. He once managed a controversy with one *Tillam,* a *Ranter,* with great judgment, and preserved the town from his poisonous errors. When he was cast out of *St. Peter's,* he continued in *Colchester,* and practised physic, still exercising his ministry, and was exceedingly useful. He was so courteous and affable to all, that he was generally beloved. And even those who hated him for his preaching as a Nonconformist, highly esteemed him for his skill and tenderness as a physician.

WORKS. The Jewish Sabbath antiquated, and the Lord's-day instituted, &c. in answer to T. Tillam.

COLN ENGAME [R.] Mr. JOHN CLARK. *Newcourt* mentions him among the Rectors of this parish.

COOPER SALE. [See THOYDON MOUNT.]

COPFORD [R.] Mr. ROBERT THOMPSON.

CRANHAM [R.] Mr. JOHN YARDLEY. So his name was spelt in Dr. Calamy's Account; but in the Continuation he proposes to alter it for HARDLEY, because *Newcourt,* in his *Rep. Eccles.* places him among the Rectors of this parish, under that name. But this is not a sufficient authority, as *Newcourt* is not always correct, and it appears that a person signed his name to the Essex Testimony, in 1648, JOHN YARDLEY, as then minister of *Sheering:* who was most probably the same. Nothing more is said of him than that he was an able and judicious divine.

DANBERY [R. S. 20l.] Mr. JOHN MAN. In 1648 he subscribed the Testimony as minister of *Rawreth.* In Newcourt he is called *Richard Man.*

DEDHAM [V.] MATTHEW NEWCOMEN, M. A. Of *St. John's Col. Camb.* where he was much esteemed for his wit; which being afterwards sanctified by divine grace, fitted

him

him for eminent service in the church of God. Dr. *Collinges*, in his preface to the sermon which Mr. *Fairfax* preached on his death, says, " That he had had thirty years ac-
" quaintance with him, and never knew any that excelled
" him, as a minister in the pulpit, a disputant in the schools,
" or as a desirable companion." His gift in prayer was incomparable. He was a solid, painful, pathetic and persua-
sive preacher. He succeeded that great man, Mr. *John
Rogers*; but their gifts were different. Mr. *Rogers*'s great
talent lay in a peculiar gesture and manner of delivering
the solid matter he had prepared : but Mr. *Newcomen*'s gifts
lay almost all ways. His worst enemies could not deny that
he shewed as much skill as piety in all his religious services.
He was a most accomplished scholar and christian. In his
ordinary converse he was pleasant and facetious, and of extraordinary humility and courtesy. His whole deportment
was pious and amiable. He was a member of the Westminster Assembly, during which time he preached with Mr.
Calamy, at Aldermanbury, and assisted Dr. *Arrowsmith* and
Dr. *Tuckney* in drawing up the Catechism. He was also one
of the commissioners at the *Savoy*. [Mr. *Baxter*, in his
own Life, frequently mentions Mr. *Newcomen* with great
respect, as one of the principal ministers concerned in the
transactions of those times.] After he had fixed at *Dedham*
he would listen to no temptation to any other place, tho' he
had many and great offers, but continued there till he was
ejected in 1662.

He was soon after invited to a church in *Leyden*, which
he accepted, for the sake of liberty to preach the gospel,
which he preferred to any thing in the world. He was there
exceedingly esteemed by Dr. *Hornbeck*, and the other professors, and by other learned men in those parts. He died of
an epidemical fever in 1668 or 9. [Mr. *Fairfax*, in his funeral sermon for him (entitled *The dead saint speaking*)
preached at *Dedham*, describes Mr. *Newcomen* as " A scribe
" well instructed to the kingdom of God; one whose gifts
" were like *Aaron*'s breast-plate, whereon *holiness to the
" Lord* was engraven; one who, like *Isaiah*, had the
" tongue of the learned, and touched with a live coal from
" God's altar, knew how to speak a word in season to the
" weary. One who was the desire of thousands: whose
" doctrine fell as the rain; whose life shined as the light;
" whose zeal provoked others : whose labours blessed the
" earth ; whose prayers pierced the heavens ; at whose pre-
          4   " sence

" sence the boldest sinners blushed ; at whose thunderings
" the hypocrite trembled ; at whose force the kingdom of
" darkness shook, and the powers of hell were vanquished :
" —as one who bound up many a broken heart ; as a spiri-
" tual father to many children ; as the happy instrument of
" life to many dead souls.]

WORKS. Irenicum (a work much commended by Dr. Collinges). —A Sermon before the Parliament, Nov. 5, 1642.—A
Sermon at the funeral of Mr. Samuel Collins, pastor of Braintree.
—The best Acquaintance ; being discourses on Job xxii. 21.—A
farewell Sermon in the London collection.—§ On *Rev.* iii. 3.
*Remember therefore how thou hast received, and heard, and hold fast, and
repent.* It is said to have been preached at Dedham, *Aug.* 20,
and is thus introduced : " I began this scripture the last *Lords-day.*"
It is plainly but a part of what he delivered from the same
text, and not very accurately taken. He himself transcribed
the whole, but did not publish it. His manuscript however
is yet in being, in the possession of Mr. *Robert Winter.* The
writer of this, has had the pleasure of perusing it, and finds it to
correspond with the copy in the London collection. The substance of it was given a few years ago in the first volume of the
Protestant Dissenters Magazine; which renders it unnecessary here
to introduce an abstract of it. The date of this MS. is *August*
17, which is doubtless correct, that being the Sabbath preceding
Bartholomew-day.

There is also another Sermon of Mr. Newcomen's in the Country collection, which is the last in the volume, and is detached
from the rest. It is not said where it was preached, or when. It
is not probable that it was in the parish church, but it is plain that
it was just before he left this country for Holland. The title is,
" *Ultimum Vale :* or the last farewell of a minister of the gospel
" to a beloved people. By *Matthew Newcomen,* M. A. late
" preacher of the gospel to the church of Christ at *Dedham,* in
" Essex: Now to the English church, at *Leyden,* in Holland.....
" London printed in the year 1663." The text is, *Acts* xx. 32.
It consists of 78 pages. Having gone thro' the several observations grounded on the words, he closes with an affectionate parting
address, of which the following is an abstract :

" I am now, by the providence of God, upon the point of
leaving not only you, but the Land, and I know not whether ever
I shall see the face of this assembly any more. I would fain,
before we part, *commend you to God,* and leave you in the arms of
his everlasting mercy. O that I could do this with confidence
concerning every one of you. Concerning some of you I profess
I can, and that on the same account that the apostles did, *Acts* xiv.
23. They commended the churches to the Lord, *on whom they had*

o 3   *believed.*

*believed.....*Such are some of you : believers, not in name and profession only, but in deed and in truth. Such I can heartily confidently and comfortably commend unto God, and leave with him, in full assurance that however things go in *Dedham*, however things go in *England*, however things go with yourselves, as to the concerns of this life, it shall be well with you to Eternity.

O that I could think thus, and speak thus, and hope thus of you all! But are there not some among you, who are sinners against the Lord? whom a minister, according to the gospel rule, should rather deliver to Satan? Are there not some of you whose characters are found 1 *Cor.* vi. 9, *Phil.* iii. 18? Do you think a minister, after above twenty years spent among such a people, in fruitless labours, can with confidence commend such unto God? O Sirs, what shall I say to you? what shall I do for you?—My heart's desire and prayer for you all is, that you may be saved. I charge you (as holy Mr. *Bolton* did his children, on his death-bed) that none of you dare to appear before me in the day of judgment, in an unconverted condition. I charge you all from the highest to the lowest, before God and the Lord Jesus Christ, who shall judge the quick and the dead at his appearing....lest these words of mine be brought in on that day as a witness against you. O that God would make this last warning, this last charge, more effectual than a thousand others have been! That as Sampson slew more Philistines at his death, than in all his life, so I might be the happy instrument to save more souls at my departure from you, than in all my life before!"

———— Mr. GEORGE SMITH was ejected from the same place, and had been fellow-labourer with Mr. Newcomen many years. In 1649 he subscribed the Essex *Watch-word*, as " minister of the gospel at Dedham."

HIGH EASTON [R.] Mr. MARTIN HOLBITCH. From the singularity of the name, there seems to be the highest reason to believe that he had been the master of the celebrated school at *Felsted*, in this county, and that he was the person to whom Dr. *John Wallis*, of Oxford refers in his account of his own life, published by Mr. *T. Hearne*, in his appendix to his preface to *Peter Langstoft's* Chronicle, 8vo. 1725. where the Dr. signifies, " that at *Christmas*, 1630, he was sent to school to Mr. *Martin Holbitch*, at *Felsted*, in Essex, who was a very good schoolmaster, who there taught a free-school, of the foundation of the Earl of *Warwick*, whose seat at *Lees*, was within that parish." [1]

parish." He further says, " that at this school, tho' in a
" country village, he had at that time an hundred, or six
" score scholars, most of them strangers, sent thither from
" other places, upon the reputation of the school; from
" whence many good scholars were sent to the university."
No notice is taken of him in *Newcourt's Rep.* But it is
possible that notwithstanding this, he might have had this
living.

EASTWOOD [V.] Mr. PHILOLOGUS SACHEVEREL.
Of *Oxford University*, where he was supported by his half-
brother, a great intimate of Mr. *William Clopton*, mentioned in this county. They were both ill at the same time,
but Mr. *Clopton* died first. Mr. *Sacheverel*, over-hearing
some persons in his room talking of his death, said, " Then
there is a good man gone to heaven ;" and laying himself
down again, died immediately, and they were both buried in
the same grave. This minister was great uncle to Dr. *Henry
Sacheverel*, the high-flying church-man.

FELSTED [V.] Mr. NATHANIEL RANEW. Of *Eman.
Col. Camb.* He was some time minister of *Little East
Cheap*, in London, from whence he removed into Essex,
where he was of great use in the association. After his
ejectment at *Felsted*, he removed to *Billericay*, where he
constantly preached in the latter part of his life, and died in
1672, aged about 72. He was a judicious divine, and a
good historian, which rendered his conversation very entertaining. He was well beloved by the Earl and Countess of
Warwick, who allowed him 20l. *per ann.* during life.
The old Earl of Radnor (some time lord-lieutenant of Ireland) had a great respect for him, and admitted him to his
intimate acquaintance. He was indeed generally esteemed
by those that knew him.

WORKS. Solitude improved by divine Meditation ; proving
the duty, necessity, excellence and usefulness of it, 8vo. 1670.
(One of the best books upon the subject.)

FERIN [V.] Mr. CONSTABLE. *Newcourt* in his *Rep.
Eccl.* mentions a person of this name at *Lindsel* vicarage.

FINCHINGFIELD. Mr. HUGH GLOVER. Of *Eman*, *Col. Camb. Newcourt* in his *Rep. Eccl.* has it *John Glover. Hugh Glover* subscribed the testimony of the Essex ministers in 1648, as minister of *Debden.* He was a facetious, genteel person, and a very popular preacher, like his predecessor Mr. *Stephen Marshal.* He did not preach after his ejectment, till the Dissenters had liberty given them, but went to church with his family. He died of a consumption at Bishop's Stortford.

FINGRINHOE [V. 36*l.* 10*s.*] Mr. GREGG.

FORDHAM [R.] JOHN BULKLEY, M. A. His grandfather was Dr. *Edward Bulkley*, who had the living of Odehill, in Bedfordshire, (in the gift of Sir *T. Alston*,) in which his son *Peter* succeeded him, and continued till the rigours of Abp. *Laud* drove him away; when he fled to *America* for shelter, where he was chosen minister at *Concord*, and wrote his book of the *Gospel Covenant.** He brought up three sons to the ministry, Gersham, Edward and John. Edward succeeded his father in New-England, and died there. John, the youngest son, took the degree of M. A. in *Harvard* college, in 1642. He afterwards came into England, and settled at *Fordham*, where for some years he exercised his ministry with good acceptance and usefulness. After his ejectment he went to *Wapping*, in the suburbs of London, where he practised physic several years with good success. He was eminent in learning, and equally so in piety. Tho' he was not often in the pulpit, after his ejectment, he might truly be said to preach every day in the week. His whole life was a continued sermon. He seldom visited his patients without reading a lecture of divinity to them. and praying with them. He was remarkable for the sweetness of his temper, his great integrity and charitableness; but that which gave a lustre to all his other virtues was, his great humility. He died at *St. Katherine's*, near the *Tower*, in 1689, in the 70th year of his age, with unusual tranquillity and resignation of mind. Mr. *James*, of *Nightingale-lane* preached and printed his funeral sermon on *Prov.* xiv. 32.

---

* See some account of him in *Mather's Hist. of New-Eng.* b. iii. p. 96.— His first wife was the daughter of Mr. *Thomas Allen*, of *Goldington*, near Bedford, whose nephew, Sir Thomas Allen, was Lord Mayor of London. Ib. p. 98.

but

· GESTINGTHORP [V. 35*l.* 5*s.* 6*d.*] Mr. Davis. *Newcourt* here has Rob. Davy, A. M. 11 *Sept.* 1661. ⸢If this was the person intended, he had not been twelvemonths in possession of this living.

HACKWELL [R.] Mr. Josiah Church. In 1649, he subscribed to the Essex *Watch-word*, as Minister of *Sea Church.*

· WORKS. The divine Warrant of Infant Baptism ; or Six Arguments for the Baptism of the Infants of Christians. 4to, 1652.

· HALSTED [V.] Mr. William Sparrow. Of *Camb.* University. Born in *Norfolk*, and of good extraction. He was first awakened by the preaching of Mr. *Stephen Marshal.* He was early in declaring for the congregational discipline ; and was a great correspondent of Dr. *Owen's.* He was a man of considerable learning, and remarkable ministerial gifts : As much reputed thro' the country for a preacher, as Mr. *Rogers*, of *Dedham*, had been some time before. He had a numerous auditory on Sabbath-days ; and kept up a weekly lecture on the Market-days, to which there was a general resort of the ministers and gentry of those parts. His ministry was blessed of God, to the conversion of many souls. He was noted for being very affable and courteous, and of a most genteel deportment. He died at *Norwich.* He is not mentioned in *Newc. Rep.* but his successor is inserted thus : *Joh. Redman,* S. T. P. 14 *Oct.* 1662, *per inconform.* ult. Vic. [This is the case with several other ministers in this county.]

＊ West HAMSTED. Mr. Green. Probably this was Mr. Edward Green, who subscribed the Testimony of the *Essex* ministers, 1648. Perhaps the place intended was West Ham.

South HANVIL [Q. *South Hanningfield* R.] Mr. Cardinal. Most probably he was the person who signed the *Essex* Testimony in 1648, Richard Cardinal.

HATFIELD Broad-oak [R. 200*l.*] John Warren, M A. Of *Oxford* University. Born *Sept.* 29, 1621. Mr. *Baxter* says, " He was a man of great judgment and ministerial abilities, moderation, piety and labour." He came to London in 1642, designing to go beyond sea with some merchants; but Sir *T. Barrington*, occasionally meeting with him, was so pleased with his conversation, that he prevailed with him to go to *Hatfield*, in 1643, to succeed their lecturer who was lately dead. There he continued till he was forced away; and tho' he had invitations to several more public places, where he might have had far greater worldly advantage, he refused to remove, being extremely delighted with the conversation of many eminent christians. He often said, that he would not leave Hatfield christians for any place in England. After some time, the minister of the place removing into *Norfolk*, the whole work devolved upon him. So that he preached constantly three times a week at home, and took his turn in several other lectures, which were kept by a combination of ministers. There was also a monthly meeting of ministers in those parts, of which he was the first promoter, which continued many years, wherein there were disputations and Latin sermons, and determinations which might well have become the divinity schools, or have entertained an academical auditory. After his ejection, Mr. *Brooksby* was put in his place, by *Trin. Col. Camb.* He was a moderate man, and there was a good understanding between him and Mr. *Warren*, who went to church to hear him; afterwards instructing a few persons in his own house. He at length removed to *Bishop Stortford*, where he continued his useful labours till his strength and intellects failed him: and he there exchanged this for a better life, in *September*, 1696.

He was a general scholar, had a great quickness of apprehension, and clearness of thought; a retentive memory, and a solid judgment. He was an indefatigable student, and had an insight into almost all parts of useful learning. He was an excellent preacher. His style was plain and neat. His words proper and significant. His exhortations and motives both convincing and affecting. He had an excellent delivery, and all the advantages of elocution. He was an admirable expositor; a mighty man in prayer; and an excellent casuist: of a very public spirit, a close walker with God, and of great humility. His conversation was always profitable. He had a perfect good-will to all mankind; seeming to be made up of love and kindness, tenderness and compassion. Tho' he was driven from his habitation as a
disturber

disturber of the peace, and by citations to the spiritual courts put to great trouble and expence, he was not at all exasperated, so as to make the least reflection on the persons concerned, and discouraged others who were disposed to reflect. He heartily forgave his enemies, and begged forgiveness of God for them. He was very charitable to man; and very submissive to the will of God in all his troubles. In short, he was a great man, a general scholar, an admirable christian, a mirrour of holiness, and a pattern both to ministers and christians, living and dying. His funeral sermon was preached by Mr. *Henry Lukin*, where the reader may find a farther account of him. He was very backward to publish any thing in his life-time: but since his death, a manuscript of his hath been printed, entitled, *The Method of Salvation*.

HEMPSTED [In *Freshwell* hundred] Mr. THOMAS ELLIS.

HENHAM [V.] Mr. SAMUEL ELY. After his ejectment he lived at *Bishop Stortford*. He was a great critic in *Greek* and *Hebrew*, and the Oriental tongues, and was a man of great worth, but humble and modest to a fault. *Newcourt* does not insert his name, but mentions his successor thus: Joh. Rous, Cl. 6 *Nov.* 1662, per inconformitatem ultimi Vic. This does not appear from Dr. Walker to have been a sequestration.

HENINGHAM (Castle) [C.] Mr. JOHN SMITH. He was first turned out at *Dunmow*, which was a sequestration; but it was here that he was silenced. He was a very able, prudent, judicious, useful divine. *Newcourt* mentions one of the same name at this place in 1664. But the name is so common that he was probably another person.

HENNY *Parva*. Mr. SAMUEL CROSSMAN. He was omitted in Dr. *Calamy*'s first Account; but from *Newcourt*'s *Rep. Eccl.* (vol. II. p. 327, 328) it appears that he was a Nonconformist, and therefore is added to the list.

HOCKLEY [V. 48*l*. 11*s*. 2*d*.] Mr. FARNWORTH.

HOLLINGSBOROUGH *Parva* [R.] Mr. WATERS.

HORNCHUCH [D.] Mr. WELLS.

INGATSTONE

INGATSTONE. John Willis, M. A. An able divine. He is thus mentioned in *New. Rep. Eccl.* John Willis, A. M. 19 *Jan.* 1630, *per cess. ult. Rect.* He was one of those who were designed by the foundress of *Wadham Col. Oxf.* to be admitted as scholars of that house, and was accordingly admitted *April* 20, 1613. He was afterwards presented by the warden, fellows, and scholars of that house, to the vicarage of *Hockley*, in this county ; but how long he continued there does not appear. Upon his ejectment from *Ingatstone* for Nonconformity in 1662, he removed to London, and settled in *Wapping ;* where, being a very acceptable and popular preacher, he had a numerous auditory, to whom he preached some time after K. *Charles's* Indulgence. Upon his decease Mr. *G. Day* was chosen pastor of this congregation.

INWORTH [R.] Mr. Robert Dod, of *Oxford* university. He was brought up in *Westminster* school, and went from thence to *Oxford*, where he was seven years under the tuition of Mr. *Joseph Allein ;* by whom he greatly profited as to serious religion, as well as in useful human learning. He is mentioned by *Newcourt* thus : Rob. Dod, *Cl.* 27 *Jul.* 1666 (doubtless for 1656) *per mortem Wharton.* He was ordained soon after the Restoration, by Bishop *Juxon*, who declared to him, That he was not for going high against the *Presbyterians.* After his ejectment he preached some time in a meeting at *Sible Hedingham*, from whence he removed to *Wethersfield*, upon Mr. *Cole's* death, and continued there till his own. His enemies had many designs against him, but God wonderfully preserved him. He was often obliged to change the place of his preaching, and sometimes preached to a large congregation in the fields. He had many severe trials in the course of his life, and used to say, That he enjoyed most of God under affliction.—In his younger days he was once supposed to be dead for seventeen hours, and the nurse would have laid him out, but his mother, apprehending there was some warmth in him, would not suffer it. It was very remarkable that he had the Smallpox and Plague both together. But God, who had wise purposes to serve by his life, preserved him amidst these dangers, and spared him to a good old age. He was a lively affectionate preacher, and zealous for Nonconformity, but moderate towards such as differed from him. He died *Ap.* 9, 1706.

—— Mr. Jenkyns, from the same place.

LAVER

LAVER *(Magdalen)* Mr. Hervey. A sincere upright person, of good ministerial abilities.

High LAVER [R.] Mr. Samuel Borfet. He was some time Fellow of *King's Col. Camb.* where he was cotemporary with Mr. *John Janeway*, to whose life he hath prefixed an epistle, by way of attestation to the truth of the relation; besides which, nothing of his ever appeared in print. After his ejection in Essex for Nonconformity, he settled at *Maidstone*, in Kent, where he was very useful and much beloved. Being driven thence by the rigors of K. *Charles*'s reign, he came to London, where he succeeded Mr. *Calamy* in his congregation after his decease. At *Morton* he was a useful preacher, and an exemplary liver. For several of the latter years of his life he was disabled for his work by manifold infirmities, and confined very much to his chamber. During his confinement he was sorely exercised in his spirit, and some times extremely depressed with fears as to his future state. Once in particular, having been for some nights deprived of his rest, he was like one distracted; his discourse was extravagant; he gave up all hopes; thought his case desperate; and apprehended hell was already begun in the horrors of his soul. But God mercifully affording him his wonted sleep, he was in a few days again revived, and sensibly found the difference between a natural disorder and a grounded despair. When his end drew near God gave him abundant comfort, so that he departed this life, with chearful hopes of a better. He was succeeded by Mr. *John Shower*. *Newcourt* mentions him among the rectors of this parish, tho' he mis-spells his name. Dr. *Calamy* received many letters from him, in which he wrote it as above.

Little LAVER. Edward Whiston, M.A. of *Trin. Col. Camb.* Brother to Mr. *Joseph Whiston*, of Maidstone, in Kent. *Newcourt* mentions him, but writes his name *Wilson*. When he subscribed the *Essex* Watch-word, in 1649, he was pastor of Norton Mandeville. He preached at *Abrey Hatch*, in this county, when he was near ninety years of age.

Little LEIGHS [V.] Mr. John Benson. *Newcourt* mentions him as coming to this living 13 *Feb.* 1662. He was much befriended by lord *Fitzwalter*'s family, near Chelmsford. His son was many years pastor of a dissenting congregation at *Sandwich*, in Kent.

Low

Low LEIGHTON [V. 33*l.* 12*s.*] PHILIP ANDERTON. M. A. Of *Eman. Col. Camb.* About the year 1651 he had an augmentation of 50*l. per ann.* out of the sequestered estates. He was ejected by the Bartholomew-act, and afterwards taught school in this parish. *Newc. Rep.* II. 382. He died *Aug.* 27, 1669.

LYNDSEL [V.] Mr. CLARK.

MALDEN [V.] THOMAS HORROCKES, M. A. Of *St. John's Col. Camb.* He descended from the *Horrockes,* of Horrockes-hall, in Lancashire, and was the only son of Mr. Christopher Horrockes, of Bolton in the Moors, whose true zeal for the Protestant religion created him many enemies among his Popish relations, so that he and his family fled from their persecution into New-England with Mr. *Cotton.* But they left this their son at *Cambridge,* where he took his degrees, and launched out into the world without any friends to help him, but under the guardianship of the divine care. He was ordained by the Bishop of *Durham,* and called to the free-shool, at *Rumford,* where he taught the sons of many eminent citizens and country gentlemen. He was invited to a great school at *Manchester,* but refused to accept it. He was afterwards presented to a considerable living in *Norfolk,* and was going to take possession, with letters of institution and induction; but travelling with a false brother, he was robbed of his papers, and supplanted in his parsonage, to which he submitted, without offering to recover his right by law. When he subscribed the Essex *Watch-word,* in 1649, he was minister of *Stapleford Tawney.* After a great variety of changes and troubles, upon the removal of Dr. Hewit, he was fixed in the living of Malden, having *All-saints* and *St. Peter's* for his cure; and there was a diligent and painful preacher for twelve years, and was an instrument in converting many souls. He was much respected by Lord Bramston, of Roxwell, the Earl of Warwick, Sir Gobert Barrington, Sir Thomas Honywood, Sir Walter St. John, and many others of the nobility and gentry in those parts. His charity was very great; and he endeavoured to do good to all.

He was ejected in 1662. He had some enemies who bore very hard upon him, but not many. He was cast into the dungeon of the town prison, where he lay ten days. His wife went to London, to wait on the king and council; and the Earl of *Manchester* and the Lord *Roberts,* who were

2   her

her friends, obtained a *Habeas corpus* to remove him, to the great mortification of his adversaries. A court being called in the town, he was accused of various crimes, and called by some of the aldermen, heretic, schismatic, traitor, &c. and when he was pleading for himself, one of them rose, from the bench, and gave him a box on the ear, so as to beat off his satin cap; when he stooped down to take it up again, and thanked the boisterous gentleman. They told him, If he must be gone, he should hire his own horse, or go on foot: but he answered, that he had done nothing against the king or government, and therefore they should take care to send him, for he could not walk, nor hire a horse. They at length sent him on horseback, with a serjeant on each side of him, thro' all the towns like a criminal; and Mr. *Hart*. who struck him, followed to prosecute him. He was brought before judge *Mallet*, who tho' severe enough of himself, as God ordered it, was favourable to him. He reproved the alderman, saying, He thought the prisoner looked like a very honest gentleman, and deserved no such treatment. To which the alderman answered, That he was a pestilent fellow, and had preached to five hundred at once thro' the grate of his prison but the *Sunday* before. The judge said, " That was a sign he was well beloved," and acquitted him. But the furious bailiff went and entered his action in the *Crown-office*, so that tho' it was eight o'clock at night, he was forced to go to *Rumford*, which cost him a violent fit of sickness.

He was harrassed from one court to another for three assizes, and his life was threatened; but some gentlemen who were his friends, soliciting Sir *Orlando Bridgman* the judge, who was his countryman, he at last was cleared; when some of the justices came down from the bench and congratulated him. After a great many fatigues, he at last settled at *Battersea*, in Surrey, where he boarded and taught young gentlemen; among whom were two of the sons of Sir Walter St. John, Alderman Howe's sons, five of the Lordels, three of the Houblands, &c. and several others of good note, who could bear witness to his learning, humility, integrity, courtesy, and loyalty. He died at *Battersea* about 1687, generally lamented, and was buried in that church. It was a distinguishing part of his character, that he loved all good people, how much soever they differed in opinion from him. He was a man of a very chearful temper, and an able divine. For labour in preaching, on Sabbath-bath-days and week-days, and going from house to house, there were scarcely any in these parts who equalled him. He is mentioned by *Newcourt*.

MORETON [R.] EDMUND CALAMY, M. A. Of *Sydney Col.* and afterwards Fellow of *Pemb. Hall, Camb.* He was the eldest son of Mr. *Calamy*, of Aldermanbury, [and father to our author.] From a MS. of Mr. Francis Chandler's, it appears that he was ordained at Moreton, *Nov.* 10, 1652, by Mr. *Chandler*, Mr. *Poole*, and five other ministers, in that neighbourhood; Mr. *Borfet* and Mr. *Roberts* being ordained at the same time. He is mentioned by *Newcourt* among the rectors of this parish, on the death of his predecessor, 1658. After his ejectment he removed to London, where he for some years kept a meeting in his own house in *Aldermanbury*. Upon K. *Charles*'s declaration for Indulgence, he set up a public meeting in *Curriers-hall*, near Cripplegate, where he continued his labours as long as the times would permit; and when the laws against the Dissenters were rigorously put in execution, he met his people privately as he could. And tho' he did it usually every Lord's-day, and sometimes twice in a day, and even several times in a week, so favourable was providence to him, that he was never once disturbed in the time of divine worship; nor was he ever apprehended, or carried before a magistrate, tho' warrants were often out against him. But he was several years in the *Crown-office*, with several others of his brethren, which was both troublesome and expensive.

He was a man of peace, and of a very candid spirit; who could not be charged, by any that knew him, with being a Nonconformist either out of humour or for gain. He abhorred a close and narrow spirit, which affects or confines religion to a party; and was much rather for a comprehension, than for a perpetual separation. He was ready to do good to all as he had opportunity; tho' such a lover of retirement, that he was for passing thro' the world with as little observation as possible; and therefore he was not upon any occasion to be persuaded to appear in print. He was as well pleased with his majesty's restoration in 1660, as any minister in the county. And in the year following, when an act passed the two houses, " to enable his majesty to send out commissioners to receive the free and voluntary contributions of his people, towards the present supply of his majesty's affairs," &c. Mr. *Calamy* advanced generously towards

wards it; as did several others of his brethren, whose loyalty however was not at all considered, but who were cast out the next year with all imaginable contempt.

Dr. *Calamy* has given a copy of the instrument by which he was presented to the living of *Moreton*, and of his bonds to the Protector *Richard*, for the payment of the first fruits. (See *Contin*. p. 461—463.) Of the former, the following is an extract. " Know all men by these presents, that the twentieth day of *April*, in the year one thousand six hundred and fifty-nine, there was exhibited to the commissioners for approbation of public preachers, a presentation of Edmund Calamy the younger to the rectory of Moreton, in the county of Essex, made to him by the right honourable Edward Earl of Manchester, John Lord Roberts, Sir Gilbert Gerrard, Bart. Anthony Tuckney, Doctor in Divinity, Master of St. John's College, in Cambridge, Simeon Ash, Clerk, and Edmund Calamy the elder, Clerk, Feoffees in trust of Robert Earl of Warwick deceased, the patrons thereof, together with a testimony in the behalf of the said Edmund Calamy, of his holy life and good conversation: upon perusal and due consideration of the premises, and finding him to be a person qualified as in and by the ordinance of such approbation is required, the commissioners above-mentioned, have adjudged and approved the said Edmund Calamy to be a fit person to preach the gospel, and have granted him admission, and do admit the said Edmund Calamy to the rectory of Moreton aforesaid, to be full and perfect possessor and incumbent thereof," &c.—He died of a consumption in *May*, 1685, and was succeeded by Mr. *Borfet*.

NASING [V. 43*l*. 10*s*.] Mr. JOSEPH BROWN. Of *Emas. Col. Oxf.* He was born at *Ware*, in Hertfordshire, in 1620, and ordained at London about 1649. When he was ejected from this living, in 1662, he undertook to teach school, at *Nasing*, which he did till he was forced away from the place by the Five-mile-act. After some time had elapsed he returned; when he met with a great deal of trouble from one Justice *Wroth*, in that neighbourhood; by whose means his goods were seized and carried off in carts. These spoils however he suffered joyfully. And so much was he beloved by many in the parish, [to whom it is presumed he privately ministered] that they persuaded him to continue with them, and he furnished his house anew. But he was such an eye-sore to the above *justice*, that he soon afterwards signed a warrant for seizing both his goods and his person; and lest the knowledge of his design should transpire, so as to prevent the execution of it, he managed the affair with such secrecy that he only spoke of it the overnight to some of his servants, who were the next morning to see the business executed. A poor gardener in the house, who over-heard the orders given, was so much troubled that he could not sleep. He therefore arose in the dead of the night, and went to Mr. *Brown*, to inform him of the matter, and then stole back to bed again undiscovered. Mr. *Brown* immediately got a waggon and moved off all his effects out of the reach of those who were to have seized them, who when they came in the morning were equally surprized and enraged. Mr. *Brown* [who remained somewhere in the neighbourhood] was forced soon to move farther off, without letting any one know whither he went.

About a month after, he appointed a day to meet his family, when it was supposed that some servant had discovered his intention: for he was way-laid in several places thro' which he was to pass; so that if he had gone, as he intended, he would have been taken. But it providentially proving bad weather, and his mind misgiving him in the morning, he did not undertake the journey, and so escaped. In the year 1683, that he might be secured against such dangers, he remove to *London*. Upon an invitation from *Nasing*, soon after the Revolution, he returned thither in 1690, where he was useful, and 'brought forth fruit in old age.' He continued preaching till he was near 80, and died about the year 1700. He appeared, to all that knew him, to be of a catholic spirit, and an extensive charity. He could by no means approve of those, by whatever name they were called, who confined religion to their own party. He was a man of great meekness and humility, modesty, temperance and self-denial. He loved retirement, and suffered himself to want in obscurity, rather than appear in public and make his necessities known. He was calm and chearful in all circumstances.

NEWENDEN [R.] Mr. DAVIS FOULIS. He was omitted in Dr. *Calamy's* first Account; but *Newcourt* mentions him as ejected for his Nonconformity (*Rep. Eccl.* vol. ii. p. 436) and therefore his name is added to the list.

NORTON

NORTON (Cold) [R.] Mr. Hubbard.

NOTLEY (Black) [R. S.] Mr. Sparrowhawk.

OCKINDEN *(South)* [R. 33*l.* 6*s.* 8*d.*] Mr. Burnaby:

OKELEY. Mr. John Hubbard.

ONGAR (High) [R. 90*l.*] Mr. John Lavender. He was a holy heavenly divine; of a very sweet disposition; much in prayer, and eminent therein ; as he also was in spiritualizing occurrences. He was full of love to Christ both in life and in death. He was very earnestly dissuaded against conforming, by a neighbouring minister, who yet conformed himself, and on Mr. *Lavender's* ejection, got into his living. Mr. *Lavender* had a son a conforming clergyman, a sober man, who died young.

ONGAR (Chipping) [R. 45*l.* 17*s.* 9*d.*] Mr. John Lorkin. So *Newcourt* in his *Rep. Eccl.* writes his name. Calamy has it *Larkin.* He was a solid divine, but not so active as some of his brethren, by reason of some bodily infirmities, which made him the more readily engage their assistance. At his church several neighbouring ministers used to carry on a weekly lecture. After his ejectment, he lived upon his estate, which was a very good one, and enabled him to entertain his brethren, which he was always ready to do.

PANFIELD [R. S.] Mr. George Purchas.

FARNDON Magna [R.] Mr. Bastwick.

PATSWICK [C. or D.] Mr. Ralph Hill.

PEDMARSH [R.] Mr. Blakely. He was very active and useful in his situation.

PENTLOW [R. S.] Mr. Henry Esday. In 1649, when he subscribed the *Essex Watch-word*, he was pastor of *Gingrave.* After his ejectment, a relation left him a considerable estate, upon which he lived privately, and died in *Hoxton-square*, London.

PRITTLEWELL [V. 18*l.* 13*s.* 4*d.*] Thomas Peck, M. A. He had been many years in this living, as appears from *Newcourt*, who mentions him in his *Rep. Eccl.* thus: —*Tho. Peeke*, cl. 2 Maii 1633 *per mortem Negus.* He was esteemed a judicious and learned divine.

WORKS.

WORKS. A Sober Guess on several Mysteries in the Revela-
tions.—A Funeral Sermon for Mrs..Dorothy Freeborne.— A Discourse upon the inseparable Union between Christ and Believers.

RADWINTER [R. S. 21*l*. 11*s*. 4*d*.] Mr. GEORGE
MOXON. Son to Mr. George Moxon, of Astbury, and
brother-in-law to sheriff *Sute*, to whom he was chaplain
when that gentleman served the office of sheriff for the city
of London; in whose house in the country he lived and
died: viz. at *Eaton Constantine*, which was the place where
Mr. Baxter's father resided. §But Mr. Baxter makes no
mention of him in his life, which is somewhat remarkable.

RAYLEIGH [R.] ABRAHAM CALEY, B. D. He had
been preacher at *Gray's-Inn*, London. He was presented
to this living by Edward Earl of *Manchester*, and ejected
from it in 1662. After his ejectment, a kinsman of his,
Mr. *Bull*, had the two livings of *Hadley* and *Rayleigh*,
which lie near together. Mr. *Caley*'s daughter was married
to a gentleman in *Suffolk*, and with him he usually resided;
but commonly once a year spent some time in a visit to his
nephew at *Rayleigh*. One day, having retired to his
chamber, and staying there longer than ordinary, Mrs. *Bull*
was afraid something might ail her uncle, and therefore desired her husband to call him, which he did; but having no
answer, he looked thro' some crevice in the door, and saw
him sitting in an elbow-chair, with his handkerchief in his
hand, and in a leaning posture. Mr. *Bull* thinking him engaged in contemplation, was unwilling to disturb him and so
retired. But going again some time after, and knocking
hard, but receiving no answer, he broke open the door, and
found him dead in the chair. He was a learned and humble
man, of an unblameable conversation.

WORKS. A Glimpse of Eternity. (A book great in value,
tho' small in bulk and price.)

RECKONDON [or Rattendon, R. 160*l*.] WILLIAM
CLOPTON, M. A. Of *Eman. Col. Camb.* He was of a
good family in *Suffolk*, and was very humble and conde-
scending. He had the offer of a much better parish than that
he was in, but he refused it because it was a sequestration. Mr.
Nathan Hewson, of Burnham, visiting him a little before

§ Mr. Baxter was not *born* here, as was before intimated, but at *High
Erchal*, where his grandfather resided.

Bartholomew-

Bartholomew-day, 1662, asked him, what he intended to do? Mr. *Clopton* answered, He did not know what he should do. "Oh, (said Mr. *Hewson* to him) never conform." But he himself acted contrary to the advice he gave; for when the day came, he declared his assent and consent. He afterwards sent Mr. *Clopton* a letter, in which he desired him to " take care what he did, for that *Reckondon* was a " good living." In answer to which Mr. *Clopton* wrote back, " that he hoped he should keep a *good conscience*." And he had afterwards much satisfaction in witnessing against ecclesiastical impositions. He died in the 58th year of his age; and was buried in the same grave, and at the same time, with his neighbour and intimate friend Mr. *Philologus Sacheverel*.

REDGWELL [V. 25*l*.] DANIEL RAY, M. A. Of *St. John's Col. Camb.* A pious person, of good learning, and of great industry, modesty and patience, tho' afflicted with much bodily weakness. He was minister of *Debden*, in Suffolk, at the time of K. Charles's restoration; which being a sequestration, he soon resigned it, and came to *Redgwell*, where he was well beloved, and held on preaching till *August*, 1662. After his ejectment, he preached privately in the same town, notwithstanding the severity of the times. Upon the Indulgence in 1672, he and Mr. *Giles Firmin* set up a meeting there together. In 1673 he removed to *Burstal*, in Suffolk, where, without any disturbance from the incumbent, who had another living, he had the liberty of preaching every other Lord's-day, which he continued to do till his death, in 1677, when he was only in the 42d year of his age. His funeral sermon was preached at *Burstal*, by Mr. *Tobias Legg*.

RIVENHALL [200*l*.] Mr. GEORGE LISLE. *Newcourt* mentions him, in his *Rep. Eccl.* among the rectors of this parish. He was one that honoured his function, by his deportment in it: but was imprisoned at *Colchester* for his Nonconformity.

ROODING (Abby) [R. S.] Mr. JOHN WOOD. This was the sequestered living of Mr. *Nicholas Burton.*—Dr. *Walker* observes (part ii. p. 200) of Mr. *Wood*, " That he " is ranked among the persecuted confessors—because he was " not permitted to devour the substance, and eat the bread of " another person, any longer than *seventeen years*." But it is obvious, he is mentioned among the rest of the sufferers by the *Act of Uniformity*, [not merely as it cast him out of *this* living, but] as it so effectually silenced him as to incapacitate him for preaching *any where* without full conformity. [This observation should be attended to in other similar cases.]

ROODING (White) [R. S. 200*l.*] Mr. SANDFORD. A good scholar, much of a gentleman, and very charitable. He quitted this living at the Restoration, when Sir Charles Leventhorp returned to it.

SANDON [R. S.] Mr. SAMUEL SMITH. A judicious divine. Probably the person mentioned at *Cresage*, in Shropshire.

SHALFORD [V. 39*l.*] Mr. GILES FIRMIN. Of *Camb.* University. He was a native of Suffolk. He was converted when a school-boy by Mr. *Rogers, of Dedham*, who observing him and some others crowding into the church on a week-day, cried out with his usual familiarity, " Here are some young ones come for a Christ. Will " nothing serve you but you must have a Christ ? Then you " shall have him," &c. This made such an impression upon him, that he dated his conversion from thence. He at first applied himself to the study of physic, and practised it afterwards several years in *New-England*, whither he retired, with several other pious persons, to enjoy liberty of conscience. He was there in the time of those troubles which were created by the Antinomians, under the conduct of Mrs. *Hutchinson*, and was present at the synod held there on that occasion, and afterwards wrote in defence of the ministers. Returning to England about the latter end of the civil wars, he suffered shipwreck on the coasts of Spain. At that very time a little child of his, then with her mother and the rest of the family in *New-England*, lay crying out by times all night, " My father! my father!" and could not be pacified ; which moved them to pray heartily for his safety.—Some time after his coming into England he brought over his family, and settled at *Shalford*, where he was ordained when he was near forty years of age. There he continued a painful labourer in the work of the ministry, till the fatal year 1662.

After his ejectment, the church-doors were shut for several months, and there was no public worship, as indeed was the case in several other places. Some time after he retired to *Redgwell*, a village about seven or eight miles distant, where he continued till his death. He practised physic many years, but still was a constant and laborious preacher, both on the Lord's-days and week-days, excepting once a month, when there was a sermon in the church, which he always heard. He held on thus, in the hottest part of K. *Charles's* reign, having large meetings, when so many others were suppressed, owing to the respect which the neighbouring gentry and justices of peace had for him as their physician. Indeed he was extremely respected by all, for there were none but he was ready to serve, which he did with great tenderness and generosity. The poor had often both advice and physic *gratis*; and of those who were more able he took but very moderate fees; whereas he might easily have got an estate. He died in *April*, 1697, aged above 80, and retained the vigour of his faculties to the last. He was a man of excellent abilities and a general scholar; eminent for the oriental languages; well read in the fathers, school-men, church history, and religious controversies; particularly those between the Episcopal Party, the Presbyterians, and the Independents.

His judgment was, That there ought to be more elders or presbyters than one in a church, instancing in eight churches mentioned in scripture, wherein there were several elders, viz. Jerusalem, Rome, Antioch, Corinth, Ephesus, Philippi, Coloss, and Thessalonica; besides those general texts that speak of many churches, *Acts* xiv. 23. *Tit.* i. 5. He thought also that one of these elders was, in the apostles' times, primate and president among them, for order sake, during life; and that from the abuse of this constitution arose prelacy, and at last the pope. In his *Vind.* of *Presb. Ordination*, he takes notice that he had read of 900 bishops in one province, in Austin's time; and says "Surely the "bishops did not then extend their power farther than some "great parishes, in some counties in England, or some of "our large towns.—If you will have such bishops and give "them no more power than Christ has given, for order sake, "I will yield to them and give them honour," &c. He esteemed imposition of hands essential to ordination.—But well skilled as he was in controversial matters, he most ex-celled in practical divinity, especially in directing a sinner how to get peace with God, and how to judge of his state. He was eminent for holiness, and zeal for God's glory; and yet he was exercised with various temptations, and very perplexing fears as to his own spiritual estate ; which made him very humble and meek, (tho' naturally a man of a very great spirit) and careful in his preaching and writing (while he did not encourage hypocrites, or embolden any in sin) not to create unnecessary trouble to truly gracious persons. Herein lay much of his excellence. He was a man of a public spirit ; not rigid and morose, but of great moderation. He went about doing good, and therein was his chief delight. Tho' in his life he had much spiritual trouble, in his death he had much comfort. His loss was generally lamented all the country round.

Mr. *Crofton* says of Mr. *Firmin*, (in his Preface to his *Liturgical Considerator considered)* " That he was a man " no less approved for his learning, modesty, piety, and " zeal for the unity of the church, and his anti-separation in " in the days of its prevalency and prosperity, than for his " loyalty and fidelity to the king's majesty in the day of his " distress." And Mr. *Hodges* observes, " that Mr. *G. Fir-* " *min* declares in one of his pieces, that he and others of " his nonconforming brethren, in the time of the Usurpa-" tion, prayed for the afflicted Royal Family."

WORKS. A serious Question stated, Whether Ministers are bound to baptize the Children of all who say they believe in Christ, but are grossly ignorant and scandalous.—A Treatise of the Schism of the parochial Congregations in England.—The real Christian ; or a Treatise of effectual Calling.—The Questions between the Conformist and Nonconformist truly stated ; in Answer to Dr. Falkner.—A Reply to Mr. Cawdrey, in Defence of the Serious Question stated——A Treatise against Separation from the Churches of England.—Establishing against Shaking ; or, a Discovery of the Prince of Darkness, working in the deluded People called Quakers. —The Power of the civil Magistrate in Matters of Religion vindicated ; a Sermon of Mr. Marshall's, with Notes by Mr. Firmin. —A Treatise of Schism, parochial Congregations in England, and Ordination by Imposition of Hands ; in Answer to Dr. Owen of Schism, and Mr. Noyes, of New-England.—Presbyterial Ordination vindicated ; with a brief Discourse concerning imposed Forms of Prayer and Ceremonies.—The Plea of the Children of believing Parents, &c. and their Title to Baptism ; in Answer to Mr. Danvers.—Scripture-warrant, sufficient Proof for Infant Baptism ; a Reply to Mr. Grantham's Presumption no Proof.—An Answer to Mr. Grantham's Vain Question, charged upon Mr. F———, viz. Whether the greatest Part of dying Infants shall be damned? —Some Remarks on the Anabaptist's Answer to the Athenian Mercuries.

Mercuries—A brief View of Mr. Davis's Vindication ; and Remarks upon some Passages of Mr. Crisp.—Weighty Questions discussed, about Imposition of Hands, Teaching Elders, and the members meeting in one Place.

SHELLY [R.] Mr. ZACHARY FINCH.

SHENFIELD [R. S.] Mr. GEORGE BOUND. He was ejected at the Restoration, and died before Bartholomew-day. But one who knew him well, says, He is satisfied that if he had lived he would not have conformed.

SHOBURY [R.] Mr. WATSON.

SOUTHWOLD, near *Brentwood.* WILLIAM RATHBAND, M. A. Of *Oxf.* University. He was brother to Mr. *Rathband,* some time preacher in the minster of York, and son of an old Nonconformist minister, who wrote against the Brownists. Dr. Stillingfleet having quoted him in proof That preaching contrary to established laws was against the doctrine of all the Nonconformists in former times, Mr. *Rathband,* in a letter to Mr. *Baxter,* assures him, " That his father was not to be reckoned among those who held such a sentiment, since he exercised his ministry, tho' contrary to the law, for many years, at a chapel in Lancashire ; and after he was silenced, he preached in private as he had opportunity, and the times would bear ; of which, says Mr. *Rathband,* myself was sometimes a witness. Afterwards, upon the invitation of a gentleman, he exercised his ministry at *Belcham,* in Northumberland, for about a year ; and from thence he removed to *Ovingham,* in the same county, where he preached also about a year ; till being silenced there, he retired into private as formerly." *(Baxter's Second Defence of the Nonconf.* p. 193.)—This his son, after many removes, settled at *Highgate,* where he continued to his death, in *October,* 1695. Mr. *Slater,* who was his fellow student, and had been acquainted with him above fifty years, preached his funeral sermon.

SPRINGFIELD [R. S.] JOHN REEVE, M. A. He was ejected at the Restoration, when the sequestered minister returned to this living. He died pastor of a congregation in London, in which he succeeded Mr. *Thomas Brooks.* He was imprisoned in *Newgate,* and probably died there.

WORKS. A Funeral Sermon for Mr. Brooks.—A metrical Paraphrase on Canticles.

STANBORN

STANBORN [R.] Mr. HENRY HAVERS. Of *Kath.
Hall, Camb.* at the time when Dr. *Brownrigg* was master.
He was born in this county, of a very ancient family, which
had continued there for several centuries. He first preached
at *Ongar,* and afterwards was chaplain to the earl of Warwick. In 1649, when he signed the *Essex Watch-word,* he
was minister of *Fyfield.* Being presented to this living of
Stanborn in the time of the Commonwealth, he was ordained by the presbytery at London, and admitted without
taking the Engagement. He was courageous in his work,
and wonderfully preserved in the most troublesome times.
He did not quit the place where he was silenced; and even
after the *Five-mile-act* took place, he never removed his habitation. He continued preaching twice a day, till he was
80 years of age; and even then held on to do it once a day.
He was a good philologist, and a substantial divine. A man
of great piety, and of a most amiable, peaceable temper, on
whom malice itself could never fasten a blot.

STANFORD Rivers [R. S. 200l.] Mr. MATTHEW EL-
LISTONE. A person of great worth, and good ability. A
friend in a letter to the author mentions one Mr. *Thomas
Ellistone* whom he knew, who preached at *Malden,* and
several other places in this county; and died old in 1684;
but whether it was another person, or the same, he is not
certain. Mr. *Whitlock,* in his *Memoirs,* p. 226, speaks of
an ordinance of parliament to make Mr. *Ellistone* parson of
Sandford, in Essex, *Sept.* 3, 1646. Dr. *Walker* says,
Dr. *Meredith,* the sequestered minister, returned to this
living in 1660.

STANSTED [V. 43l 19s. 7d.] Mr. ROBERT ABBOT.
In 1648 he signed the Testimony, &c. as minister of *Stansted Mountfichet.* Newcourt mentions Thos. Wallis as
succeeding to the vicarage, *Jan.* 1663. Whence it is supposed Mr. *Abbot* was ejected in 1662.

STAPLEFORD (Abbots) [R.] Mr. LEWIS CALAN-
DRINE, whose father had been minister of the *Dutch* church
in London. He had ten children at the time of his ejectment, and nothing to trust to for support but divine Providence, on which he cast himself and them. He met with
many difficulties and trials, but was contented and chearful
                                                    under

under them all. Soon after his ejectment he went to *Holland* for a few months, and then returned into Essex. In his old age he lived in an alms-house, at *Mile-end*, London, where he officiated as chaplain.

STAPLEFORD *(Tawney)* [R.] Mr. WARD. Most probably this was Mr. NATHANIEL WARD, who subscribed the Essex Testimony as Minister of Shenfield.

STEBBING [V.] SAMUEL BANTOFT, B.D. He was many years Fellow of *Jesus Col. Camb.* and some time President. He was a noted university-preacher. A man of profound judgment and great sense, yet of much modesty and candour in conversation: eminently pious, acceptable, and useful. He preached for some time after his ejectment in 1662, at *Braintree*, but was forced from thence to London, and there was prosecuted to an excommunication. He removed afterwards to *Ipswich*, but never undertook any pastoral charge, and there he died *Aug.* 21, 1692, in the 73d year of his age. Just as he was dying, he was heard to say, He blessed God who had kept him faithful, so that he never conformed.

—— Mr. ANGEL was ejected from the same place.

STISTED [R. 300*l.*] Mr. THOMAS CLARK. *Newcourt* does not mention his name, but has his successor thus : " *Tho.* " *Wallis*, Cl. 22 *Jan.* 1663, per inconform. ult. Vic." Mr. *Clark* was a very laborious and useful preacher. [He had ten children when he left this valuable living for the sake of a good conscience. A daughter of his was mother to the late Mr. *Thomas Woodward*, an eminent brewer in *Bedford* ; a gentleman in good repute, and of considerable influence in that town, as well as in the dissenting congregation there §; two of whose daughters were married to eminent dissenting ministers ; the one to Mr. *James Belsham*, some years minister of *Newport Pagnel*, who afterwards preached only occasionally, residing at *Bedford*; the other to Mr. *Samuel Sanderson*, who died pastor of the congregation in that town ; and afterwards to the late Mr. *Pickard* of *London*. Mr. *Belsham* left a son in the ministry, who was tutor in the academy at Daventry, and afterwards removed to Hackney.

STOCK [R.] Mr. MARTYN SYMPSON.

STOW MARY's [R.] Mr. JAMES MAULDEN.

§ At that time there was only one dissenting congregation in that town, whereas now there are three.

TAY

TAY (Much *or* Great) [V. 33*l.*] Mr. GREEN.

TAY (Marks) Mr. RICHARD RAND. He was, some
time after his ejection, pastor of a congregation at *Little
Baddow*, where he died about 1692. He was a holy, humble, learned man, and a very serious, awaking, useful
preacher. He possessed considerable abilities ; but was very
diffident of himself. He had a present made him of the
Works of *Crellius*, the Socinian, but he said he durst not
read them, having neither a call nor leisure to answer them ;
and to have read them merely to satisfy his curiosity he
thought might have done him hurt, and exposed him to fall
into error. He suffered from the persecutions of the times,
but often escaped from his enemies for want of their knowing
his christian name. Once a Quaker of the same surname
was taken for him, who being a man of honour, tho' he
knew Mr. *Rand*'s christian name, would not reveal it. God
hath many ways to protect his people, and uses various instruments for that purpose.—He had a son in the ministry, a
very hopeful young man, who died about the same time with
himself, and was buried in the same grave.

TERLING [V. 46*l.*] JOHN STALHAM, M. A. Of *Oxford*
University, and a native of Norfolk. He had held this living thirty years : for *Newcourt* thus mentions him in his
Rep. Eccl. Joh. Stalham, A. M. 5 *Maji,* 1632, *per
depriv. Weld.* He was an able preacher, and a holy liver :
of strict congregational principles. He kept up a meeting in
this place after his ejectment, and died pastor of a dissenting
congregation here in 1680, or 1681.

. WORKS. Vindiciæ Redemptionis ; a book against general
Redemption, in Answer to Oats.—A Piece against the Quakers.
—The Sum of a Conference which he, Mr. Newton, and Mr.
Grey, had at Terling with two Catabaptists, *Jan.* 11, 1643.

THAXTED [V. 20*l.*] Mr. JAMES PARKER. According
to *Newcourt*, who does not mention his name, his successor,
upon his Nonconformity, was not inducted till *Dec.* 1,
1662.

THOYDON MOUNT [R. S.] Mr. FRANCIS CHAND-
LER. He officiated both at this place and at *Garnon*, preaching at the one in the morning, and at the other in the afternoon. They were both sequestered ; and in the year 1663,
he was forced to resign them to Mr. (afterwards Dr.) *Meggs,*
who had such an esteem for him that the next day after his
induction, he desired him to be his assistant, and allowed
                                                      him

him twenty shillings per week for his services. This account is given by one of his family. . Mr. *Chandler* was a serious, bold, awakening and popular preacher. . He was humble, and yet chearful ; a man of good learning, and a good christian. His conversation was pleasant and profitable, and generally acceptable. He was very desirous of K. *Charles's* restoration ; and prayed for him as rightful king some time before. On *May* 29, 1660, he went to London with great joy to see his pompous entrance. In 1662 Dr. *Meggs* much pressed him to conform ; and tho' he could not be satisfied to comply with the terms that were fixed, he continued very kind to him, after he was obliged to part with him as his assistant. Judge *Archer* was Mr. *Chandler's* intimate friend ; and several other persons of rank and fashion in those parts, shewed him a great deal of civility and respect. In 1657 he married the daughter of counsellor *Coys*, with whom he had some houses at London, the rent of which comfortably supported him after his ejectment, till the year 1666, when the fire consumed them, by which he was reduced : but God raised him up friends whose kindness supported him.

Before his ejectment, he maintained a constant course of preaching and catechizing, and instructing those committed to his charge ; and at the same time kept a grammar-school. His Farewell sermon, preached from *Heb.* xiii. 20, 21, occasioned many weeping eyes. He afterwards commonly attended the public service of the church of *England*, and preached between the morning and afternoon service, and in the evening, privately, in his own house, or at other places, as he had opportunity. On the other days of the week he also frequently preached, and was often called in to assist on private days of fasting and prayer ; and yet it doth not appear he ever met with any disturbance. Once, after being silenced by the Uniformity Act, he preached at *Thoyden* church with Dr. *Meggs's* leave ; and he kept a good correspondence with the neighbouring clergy as long as he lived there. In the beginning of *March*, 1666, he removed to *Bishop Stortford*, and there enjoyed the agreeable conversation of good Mr. *Ely*, till about *May*, 1667, when, in the prime of his years, he exchanged this for a better life. He was much afflicted with the gout, but was a man of wonderful patience and resignation. He used to set God always before him, and took care to keep up constant intercourse with him. He would often say, *Incipienti, progredienti, et proficienti, Deus mihi sit propitius.* Mr. *Samuel Chand-*

4　　　　　　　　　　　　　　　*ler,*

ler, who was first pastor to the congregation of dissenters at *Fareham*, and afterwards to another at *Andover*, in *Hampshire*, was his son.

—— Dr. *Wells* was ejected at the same place. The name of WALTER WELLS is subscribed to the Essex Testimony, as incumbent of *Thoyden Mount*, in the year 1648.

TOPSFIELD [R. 24*l.*] Mr. JOHN OVERHEAD. In his younger time he lived in the house of Mr. *Mead*, in the parish of *Finchingfield*, where Mr. Stephen Marshal used very frequently to visit. He was an aged, grave, serious and humble man, and a very good preacher. He died between 1670 and 1680.

UGLY, (alias *Oakley*, near Stansted) [V.] Mr. LUCAS.

UPMINSTER [R. S. 26*l.* 13*s.* 4*d.*] Mr. HAWKES.

*UPPINGER. Mr. JOHN ROBOTHAM. He printed a piece entitled The Preciousness of Christ to Believers, which was reprinted 1669.

WAKERING (Great) [R. 20*l.* 13*s.* 4*d.*] Mr. CHRISTOPHER SCOTT. He was a very worthy man, and a good scholar; but very blunt in his speech. Two of his successors in this living thought it not beneath them to take instructions from him with respect to their method of preaching. He printed a Funeral sermon for Mrs. *Fisher*, entitled, The Saint's privilege, or Gain by dying. 4to. 1673.

WALTHAM *Parva* [R.] JOHN HARRISON, M. A. A very intelligent judicious person. *Newcourt* mentions him by name as coming to this living upon the death of Mr. *Aleyn*, 23d *Nov.* 1643, and as ejected for Nonconformity, being succeeded by *Tho. Aleyn*, S. T. P. 6 *Nov.* 1662.

, WANSTED [R. S.] LEONARD HOAR, M. D. Of *Harvard Col.* in *America*. Having finished his education there he came into England, where he preached the gospel in various place, and received from the university of *Cambridge* the degree of M. D. Being invited to the pastoral charge of the South church, at *Boston*, he returned to

* Dr. Calamy says, this should be *Upminster*. If so the preceding article is wrong, unless both these ministers were ejected from the same place.

New-England, having first married a virtuous daughter of Lord *Lisle*. Soon after his arrival, an invitation to preside over the college at *Cambridge* superseded the former. He was a truly worthy man, considered as a scholar or as a christian; and was generally esteemed as such, till, by some unaccountable means, he fell under the displeasure of certain persons of figure in the neighbourhood; when the young men in the college took advantage of it to ruin his reputation, as far as they were able; canvassing whatever he said or did, and aggravating every thing disagreeable to them in his conduct, with a view to render him odious. In this too many good men gave them countenance. At length, things were driven to such a pass, that the students deserted the college, and the Dr. on *March* 15, 1675, resigned his presidentship. The ill usage he met with made so deep an impression on his mind, that his grief threw him into a consumption, whereof he died the winter following, *Nov.* 28, at *Boston*. In his time, new edifices were erected in this college, for which a contribution was made thro' the colony, which amounted to 1895*l.* 2*s.* 9*d.* He was succeeded by Mr. *Urian Oakes*.

WARLEY *Parva* [R.] Mr. POWEL. A Mr. JOHN POWEL subscribed the Essex Testimony in 1648, without mentioning his place of residence. Most probably this was the person.

WEST-HAM [V. 250*l.*] Mr. WALTON. After his ejectment he kept a school, and had a very flourishing one, first at *Bishop's-Hall*, and afterwards at *Bethnal-Green*, near London.

WETHERSFIELD [V.] JOHN COLE, M. A. Some time Fellow of *Jesus Col. Camb.* He was born at *Ipswich*, in Suffolk, and was minister of *Burwel*, in Cambridgeshire, where he was a zealous preacher, and an instrument of much good. He removed from thence to this place in 1655, where he had spent about seven or eight years, when he was turned out by the Act of Uniformity. Not long after, he was cited into the spiritual court, for expounding the scripture and praying, and at length excommunicated, in February or March, 1663. Mr. *Clark*, who first had his living, died in a few months. Mr. *Pelsant*, the minister who succeeded him, was a sober, grave man; of a good conversation, tho' no great preacher. He had been so zealous for the Common Prayer, that he read it

it in *Oliver's* time; and when the large Prayer-book was
taken away, he used a small volume, which he carried in
his pocket. But when the sentence of excommunication
was to be read against Mr. *Cole*, he did it with tears in his
eyes, and said it was the bitterest pill that ever he had taken in
his life.†

Mr. *Cole* kept a diary, in which (besides a particular account of his own spiritual experiences) there are memoran-
dums of domestic providences, with his remarks upon them;
the success of his ministry among his people, &c. which
discover him to have been a serious christian, and a strict observer of divine providence, &c. He refused to sign the
Testimony of the Essex association, which Mr. *Firmin*
sent him in 1657. And he also refused taking the Engagement, being very unwilling to hamper himself by signing
papers. He preached his Farewell sermon *Aug.* 11, 1662,
when there was such a vast appearance of people as had
scarcely been seen for twenty years before, and a general lamentation. After being silenced, he preached in his own
house, whither many resorted to him; and thro' the kindness of the people and the good providence of God, he had
ample supplies sent him for the support of his family. In
May, 1663, a *Capias* was out against him, but he still
continued preaching, and yet was protected.

At length he was apprehended as he was preaching in his
own house, and sent prisoner to *Colchester*, where God
was with him, and shewed him favor in the eyes of the keeper
of the prison. His enemies perceiving it, removed him to
Chelmsford jail, where he found the like favour, and increased
his property, tho' his health was much impaired by his tedious imprisonment, of about eight years; from which he
was released on *Charles*'s Indulgence, in 1672. He was a
chearful man, and of strong faith; a very solid spiritual
preacher, and possessed fine abilities. He died *April* 11,
1673, aged about 52, and was buried in Wethersfield church-
yard. In the inscription on his grave-stone he is styled
Master of Arts.

WHITE-COLN [D.] Mr. JOHN BIGLEY. This living
being a donative, he kept it without conforming.

† Dr. *Calamy's* account of this matter is very confused. See his *Continuation,*
page 482, 483.

WICKHAM

WICKHAM *Bishop* [R. 120*l*.] Mr. ROBERT BILLIO. Of *Trin. Col. Camb.* Born at *Sibble Hedingham*, in this county. He was put to school at *Castle Hedingham*, where he attended on the ministry of Mr. *Brewer*, a most excellent preacher, whose sermons made more than ordinary impressions upon him when he was about twelve or thirteen years of age. When he came from school, he used to entertain his sisters with good and religious discourse, repeat Mr. *Brewer*'s sermons to them, and pray with them. When he entered into the ministry, he was settled at *West Bardfield*, near Colchester, and did much good there. From thence he removed to *Hatfield Peverel*, where he was seized with the gout, which took away the use of both his legs and of one arm; so that he was scarcely able to go with crutches. After he had been in this condition for some time, being one day alone in his parlour, he had an encouraging impulse upon his spirit to go to prayer, when with some difficulty he crept up into his chamber, and poured out his soul before the Lord. Whilst he was praying, he found himself strengthened, and when he rose from his knees, his pain was gone, and he walked as well as ever. He came to his wife with great joy, and told her of God's goodness to him; but at first she could hardly tell how to believe him.

About the year 1658, he removed to *Wickham*, from whence he was ejected *Aug.* 24, 1662, but he still lived there in a small house, about a year, and then removed to *Yeldam*, near Hedingham. Whilst he was here, he went on a visit to *Wickham*, where some of the chief persons of the town had been converted by his ministry. During this visit, he fell down in a swoon, and seemed dead; which was followed with a lameness, which held him many weeks. Here the good Lady *Vere*, of Hedingham (whose life Mr. *Clark* published) shewed him great respect.—He afterwards removed to *Felstead*, where he had the advantage of the school for the education of his sons. The good Countess of *Warwick*, sister to Mr. *Boyle*, (whose life was published by Dr. *Walker*, and abridged by Mr. *Clark*) sometimes joined in prayer with him, in her chamber, and in the banqueting-house in the wilderness, and allowed him 5*l. per ann.* towards the educating his eldest son for the ministry, till 1678, when she died; and he continued at *Felstead* till his death.

He never had a settled congregation after his ejectment, but preached occasionally, at a variety of places as he was invited, and was constantly employed, preaching often six or seven times a week, and did much good. In the latter part of his time he was about to remove to *Bacton*, in Suffolk, where Mr. Barnadiston, who had been a Turkey merchant, then supported a meeting; but it pleased God, just as he was about settling there, to seize him with a high fever, and call him home to his everlasting rest, *April* 19, 1695, aged 73.—In times of persecution, he was wonderfully preserved, tho' he was once very near being taken, when he was preaching at the house of Israel Mayo, Esq. at Bayford, near Hertford, being but just in time conveyed into a garret, and covered in a dark hole with billets. In the time of king *James* he, with most others, was full of fears as to the Indulgence that was granted, which he expressed in the words of *Nehemiah*, chap. iv. 11. But God then, as well as at other times, proved better to them than they feared.

He had an able body and a strong voice, and was a fervent zealous preacher. His sermons were plain and methodical, and they shewed him to be a good man; who sought the glory of God, and the holiness and salvation of his hearers: in promoting which ends, he was exceedingly useful. There were few whose preaching more affected the greatest part of the hearers than his. His conversation also was edifying, and ' such as might minister grace unto the hearers.' He was much taken up in admiring the goodness of God, and praising him for it. His youngest son (who slept with him many years after his wife's death) observed that he scarcely ever waked out of his sleep, but he immediately uttered some expressions of thankfulness to God.—He had two sons, who were both of them nonconforming ministers. The youngest, Mr. *Joseph Billio*, was at *Malden*, in this county. The eldest, Mr. *Robert Billio*, was brought up under Mr. *Samuel Cradock*. Having finished his studies, he became chaplain in the family of Sir *Francis Bickley*, Bart. of Attleborough, in Norfolk, and tutor to his children. He married a relation of that family; Mrs. Sarah Rider, daughter to Mr. Rider, who was ejected from *Bedworth*, in Warwickshire, in 1662. He first settled at *Chissel Parva*, in this county, where he taught school, and preached in his turn at *Cambridge*. In the reign of king *James* II. he went into *Holland*, to avoid the storm that threatened; and just before the Revolution, returned to England, and fixed at *St. Ives*, in the county of Huntingdon; from whence he

was

was called to succeed Dr. *Bates*, at *Hackney*,§ where he died of the small-pox, *May* 5, 1710, having much comfort in his soul; and was succeeded by Mr. *Matthew Henry*. He was a plain and useful preacher, generally acceptable to serious christians. He also left two sons, *Robert* and *Joseph*, who were educated for the ministry first in *Scotland* and afterwards in *Holland*.

WITHAM [V. S. 22*l*. 6*s*. 0*d*.] Mr. THOMAS LUDGUT-TER. Dr. *Walker* owns the sequestered clergyman, Mr. *F. Wright*, to have been a man of an infamous character; [and adds, that the House of Commons, in *April*, 1643, put Mr. *Edward Brewer* into his place: but does not mention Mr. *Ludgutter*, who most probably was ejected at the Restoration,] when the Dr. believes Mr. *Wright* was "repossessed of the living, to the dishonour of the church."

WYLEY. Mr. DOWELL. This place was before spelt *Weely*. It lies between Colchester and Harwich.

YAXLEY [R.] Mr. JAMES SMALL. He was born in the same town with bishop *Hopkins*, or at least brought up at the same school, and was well acquainted with him. After he was silenced, he lived as a chaplain in the house of Mr. *Davis*, a gentleman of a good estate in the West of England. He afterwards lived in the same capacity, in the house of Lord Massareen, in the North of *Ireland*, and preached to his family, with whom many other persons in the neighbourhood used to attend him. This most probably was after Mr. *Howe*'s removal to London. At last Mr. *Small* became chaplain in the house of Sir John Barrington, at Hatfield Broad Oak, in this county; with whom he continued as long as he lived, and after his death with his Lady, while the family resided there; which was till the year 1690. When Lady Barrington quitted this house, Mr. *Small* staid and preached in the town; and after Mr. *Warren* removed to Bishop Stortford, the people built a meeting house for him. —He was a well-bred man; very free and yet prudent in conversation; very kind and charitable. He was moreover a laborious and useful preacher. Tho' he had but little to live upon,* yet he was chearful and contented; but appeared

§ His name is engraved on the Communion-plate belonging to the church in Mare-street, dated 1700.

* It seems surprizing and not consistent with justice, that the Barrington family should not have better rewarded his services.

much

much concerned for the miseries of the poor in that neighbourhood. He often used to say, " his food would be more
pleasant to him, if others were not in such want." Not
long before his death, however, something considerable fell
to him by the death of a relation, [which enabled him to eat
his bread with greater chearfulness, by relieving those whom
before he could only pity.] He died about the year 1704.

YELDHAM *Magna* [R. 20*l.*] Mr. Robert Chadsly.
His successor, according to *Newcourt*, took possession 23
Feb. 1662. He was very poor, but was remarkably provided
for till he was taken hence by death.

Mr. Henry Lukin was a minister in this county, who
was silenced by the Act of Uniformity, tho' not ejected;
being in *France* [with Sir *William Masham*] at the time
when that act passed, where he spent about three years,
When he returned, he took his lot with the despised suffering
Nonconformists. He lived many years with Mrs. *Masham*,
(the mother of Sir *William*, as is supposed) preaching to a
small society in the neighbourhood ; no temptations being
able to induce him to conform. He was a man of great note
and eminence. His works shew him to have been a judicious
and learned divine. [They are all of them small pieces, of
a very practical nature and useful tendency] His *Chief Interest
of Man*, was translated into Latin by a clergyman of the
church of England.

§ He had a daughter who lived in the latter part of her
time at *Hackney*, who told a friend of the editor, that her
father had a particular intimacy with Mr. *John Locke*, (which
he contracted by his connection with the *Masham* family)
and that he was the last person with that great man before he
died. Mr. *Lukin* lived to the great age of 92. He died
Sept. 17, 1719. It was customary at that time to give pious
books to the company who attended at Funerals, with the
name of the deceased printed on the cover. The editor is
in possession of one of the books given at the funeral of Mr.
Lukin, which is one of his own : viz. *The Chief Interest
of Man*. It has the following inscription, inclosed in a
mourning border printed on a Ticket within the first cover :

In Memory
OF THE
Reverend Mr. Henry Lukin,
Who died
XVII. SEPTEMBER, MDCCXIX.
AGED XCII.

                                                    WORKS.

WORKS. A Funeral Sermon for the Rev. Mr. John Warren, of Bishop Stortford.—An Introduction to the Holy Scriptures.— The chief Interest of Man; or a Discourse of Religion.—The Life of Faith, with the general Use of Faith.—The Interest of the Spirit in Prayer.—A Remedy against Spiritual Trouble.—The Practice of Godliness.

The following are said to have been ejected in this county, but the places are uncertain.

Mr. BLAGRAVE. Perhaps this was Mr. WILLIAM BLA-GRAVE, the person mentioned at *Wooburn*, in Bedfordshire.

Mr. PINDAR. He died pastor of a congregation at *Little Baddow*, in 1681. Most probably this was Mr. WILLIAM PINDAR, who is mentioned in *Newcourt's Rep.* vol. ii. p. 359.—Mr. *John Pindar* is taken notice of in *Nottinghamshire.*—§ The person here intended had one daughter, who was married to Dr. *Charles Owen*, an eminent dissenting minister and tutor at Warrington, whose son was living there in 1755, and preached in the neighbourhood. Mr. *Job Orton* (who spent a year in the Doctor's family before he went to Northampton*) says, that he heard both Dr. Owen and his wife speak highly of the character and abilities of Mr. Pindar.

Mr. EDMUND TAYLOR. He preached in several places. He was imprisoned in Tilbury Fort, in the Duke of Monmouth's time; and died at *Witham*. Perhaps he was the person mentioned in *Monmouthshire.*

There was one person in this county, of whom it is hard to say whether he is to be reckoned among the Conformists or the Nonconformists, viz. Mr. *John Chandler*, of Bromley Parva. After the general ejectment he had the living of *Petto*. He had been ordained by Mr. *John Fairfax* and others, in the Presbyterian way, and would not yield to any thing that might be capable of being interpreted as casting a reflection on his former ordination. Upon his signifying this to Bishop *Reynolds*, he desired the company that were present to take notice, that Mr. *Chandler* was already as good a minister as he could make him; and told him that he might go and preach the gospel at *Petto*. He read some of the Common-prayer; and now and then wore the surplice; but did not use all the ceremonies, for which he was sometimes threatened, but never prosecuted.

* The late learned Mr. HUGH FARMER also, previous to his studying under Dr. Doddridge, was a pupil of Dr. Owen's.

The

The following Persons afterwards conformed.

Mr. THOMAS HARPER, of *Epping*.—Mr. HOWEL, of *Wickelshow*.—Mr. LATHUM, of *Orset.*—Mr. HILL, of *High Rooding*.—Mr. HOLMES, of *Writtle*.—Mr. FERRIS, of *Norton.*—Mr. THOMAS DEERSLEY, of *Belcham Water,* who subscribed the Testimony, 1648, as Minister of *Wick-ham.*

Mr. *John Deersley,* it appears was not a Nonconformist, as had been supposed. He was, however, much of that cast. He was minister of *Chattisham* when Mr. *Owen Stockton* resided there, and used to preach for him constantly once a month at *Hadleigh.* He used often to pray, That God would forgive the nation that great sin of turning out so many ministers.

MINISTERS

MINISTERS EJECTED OR SILENCED

IN

GLOUCESTERSHIRE.

────────

ASTON SOMERVIL, Mr. WOOD. § The name of the place, before doubtful, is now indentified, but nothing more than the name of the person can be procured.

BECKFORD [C,] RICHARD EEDS, M. A. After his ejectment he lived at *Cleve*. He was an affectionate, useful preacher, and one of the Worcestershire association. He was overcome with melancholy before he died, which was at *Gretton* in this county, in *April* 1686.

WORKS. The Great Salvation; a Discourse on *Heb.* ii. 3. to which Mr. Baxter wrote a Preface.

BRIMSFIELD [R.] Mr. THOMAS JENNINGS. He signed the Testimony of the ministers in this county, as minister of *Matson*. He was a moderate Baptist. § *Crosby,* in his History of the Baptists, has nothing more concerning him than this passage quoted from Calamy, tho' he takes care to give the Dr. a sarcastic stroke.

BOURTON on the Water, [R.] ANTONY PALMER, M. A. Educated in *Oxford,* and some time Fellow of *Baliol College.* Born in Worcestershire. He was forced out by some of the neighbouring gentry, before the Act for uniformity was framed. He put in a curate, who also was disturbed for disusing the Common Prayer. He had a congregation afterwards in *London,* and exercised his ministry there till his death, on *Jan.* 26, 1678. He possessed good ministerial abilities, and was of the congregational persuasion.

§ *Atkyns,* in his History of Gloucestershire, says, " 1649 Anthony Palmer, Rector of this place, was a great instrument in ejecting loyal and orthodox ministers, and after the Restora-

Q 4   tion

tion of *Cha.* II, he engaged in all rebellious plots."—But *Big-land*, in his Collections (tho' he carefully omits the puritanical preachers; putting asterics instead of their names) has the following noble testimony in Mr. Palmer's favour: " 1649 Anthony Palmer M. A. appointed by the parliament: was born at Great Cumberton, co. Warwick, admitted Fel. of Bal. Col. 1640. He is pourtrayed by the severe pencil of A. Wood with the strongest traits of party zeal, being appointed a Commissioner for ejecting ' scandalous ministers' by the parliament; and adopting their virulent and unprincipled measures. His writings were frequent in support of his religious tenets and party. *The Gospel New Creature*, which was published in 1658, is the most approved of his productions. He died in 1678. The high esteem in which his memory is held by his followers, compensates for the extreme severity with which the Royalists have marked his character. It may be candid to determine from such opposite descriptions, that he was a man of strong parts, enterprizing and undaunted in the prosecution of what he thought his duty; and it is but just to allow, that no part of his private life could justify any suspicion of his integrity."

WORKS. A Scripture Rail to the Lord's Table; against Mr. J. Humphreys's Treatise of Free Admission.—Memorials of Godliness and Christianity.—The Christian's Freedom by Christ—The Gospel New Creature.

CHARLTON (Kings) [C. or D.] Mr. THOMAS HARRISON.

CHELTENHAM [C. or D.] Mr. JOHN COOPER.

CHURCHDOWN. Mr. THOMAS MOUNT.

CIRENCESTER. Mr. ALEXANDER GREGORY. He was one of the Country Triers. When the king's army besieged this town, a cannon-ball fell upon the house where he lived, and tore a great part of it to pieces, while he was at prayer; but he was wonderfully preserved. When the town could hold out no longer, he with one other person attempted to make an escape. One of the king's soldiers pursued them, and quickly killed his companion; but tho' he ran at him several times, he parried off the blows, and got away unhurt. Upon the town's being taken by the king's army, Mr. Gregory was forced away from his people; and when the war was at an end, he settled at another place, at some considerable distance,

distance, where he was well beloved: but upón the earnest solicitation of his old friends at *Cirencester*, he returned to them again, tho' his benefice there was of considerably less value than the other. There he continued till the Act of uniformity passed; when he was much solicited to conform, by a person at that time in great power; who signified to him, that his so doing would be very acceptable to his majesty, who was inclined to prefer him, and would resent his non-compliance. But he could not satisfy his conscience with the terms, and drew up a paper, containing the reasons of his Nonconformity, which he sent to the person who solicited him.

In his last sermon in public, he told his flock, That tho' he should be deprived of his benefice, which was all that he and his family had to subsist upon, he would yet continue to minister to them, as long as the government would suffer him. But at last the Five-mile-act forced him away, when he removed to *Minching-Hampton*, and there he finished his course not long after. Upon taking leave of his friends, he told some with whom he was most intimate, that he should see their faces no more; and it fell out accordingly; for the very day on which some of them had agreed to make him a visit, he was taken ill and died. He was a very humble man, a serious and affectionate preacher, exceedingly desirous to promote the good of souls; and his unwearied labours had great success. He kept up a weekly lecture every Tuesday, and on Thursdays in the afternoon he catechized in his own house, which he did in a very acceptable manner, taking great care not to discourage such as were bashful, or had bad memories, for whom he was so solicitously concerned, that he would often follow them to their own houses, (even the meanest in his parish) to give them private instruction in a plain and familiar way. He was always very tender of giving offence to any, and was generally beloved.—After being ejected and silenced, he was much taken notice of, and respectfully visited, both by Conformists and Nonconformists.

CLAPTON [C.] Mr. THOMAS PAXFORD. Tho' he was not brought up a scholar, he had good natural abilities, and both preached and prayed well. He sometimes officiated for Mr. *Palmer* at Burton on the Water. After his ejectment he became a Baptist, and fell under some censures as to his morals. § Crosby has nothing more than this quotation from Calamy, except abuse of the author for relating this last circumstance, which he does not attempt to disprove.

COMPTON

COMPTON [R.] Mr. BECKET. He was originally a tradesman, and no scholar; but it was not on that account he was ejected. He was a good man, and useful particularly to many of the lower sort of people. §There are three Comptons in this county.

DIRHURST (or *Deerhurst*) [C.] Mr. FRANCIS HARRIS.

DUNTSBORNE [R.] Mr. EDWARD FLETCHER. It appears from Mr. *Jessey*'s tract, entitled, *The Lord's Loud Call to England*, (in which he relates the rudeness of the cavaliers in this county, in 1660) that Mr. *Fletcher* in particular was treated very inhumanly by them, and his life threatened. Upon this he returned to *New-England* from whence he came, and there he died. § He is not mentioned by *Mather* in his History.

DURSLEY [R.] JOSEPH WOODWARD, M. A. Of *Oxford* University. He was born at Upper *Cam* in this county, where his father was a tanner. He did not at first take orders, but was master of the free-school at *Wooton-under-edge*. His carriage was very obliging, but he had at that time very little seriousness, and much frequented the company of some gentlemen whose character for virtue or sobriety was not very eminent: but it pleased God, by a seemingly little accident, to awaken him to a serious consideration about the things of another world. Being out late one evening, as he was coming home, some dogs fell a fighting about him so furiously that he thought himself in great danger; which occasioned him seriously to reflect, What would have become of his soul, if he had been torn in pieces by those creatures. Hereupon he left his former company, and changed it for that of the godly professors at *Wooton*, who used to pray and repeat sermons, and sing together; which edifying society he found so beneficial, that he afterwards used to say, " Tho' *Oxford* made him a scholar, the professors of *Wooton* " fitted him for the ministry." Another person relates, That he did not so much as look into a Bible till he found one of his own scholars (Mr. *Sprint*, afterwards minister of *Andover*) reading the scripture in his chamber. The master was struck with shame to think that he should do less than a school-boy, and immediately procured a Bible, which he read and studied with care; and shortly after he set about a reformation in his school. Whereas Latin prayers only had been read in it, and those made in popish times, for a dead patroness,

patroness, he introduced praying in English, reading the scriptures, singing of psalms, and all pious exercises.

Some time after this visible change in him, being urged by many to undertake the ministerial office, he with much diffidence consented to be ordained, and became very useful. The people of *Dursley* unanimously invited him to be their minister; upon which he fixed with them. And tho' he was afterwards tempted to *Wells* with double the stipend, he would not accept it. He took a great deal of pains among his people, and after some time, he vigorously set about the reformation of many disorders in discipline and manners among them ; endeavouring to set up the Presbyterian government. In this attempt however, he met with many discouragements. Some withdrew from his ministry; others withheld their part of the stipend solemnly promised him, and others refused to pray and sing, and receive the sacrament, under pretence of [it being unlawful in] a mixed multitude. When he declared his resolution to admit none to the Lord's-supper but those who, besides a visible probity of conversation, had a competent knowledge of divine things, a certain person said, " He would not submit to examination ; " and if Mr. *Woodward* would not give him the sacrament, ", he would take it." In pursuance of his resolution, this man was coming to church on the sacrament-day, but he had scarcely set one foot over the threshold, before he fell down dead. The troubles which his people occasioned him, so much affected him, as to bring upon him disorders, from the effects of which he was never perfectly recovered. At length he determined upon a removal; and several persons came to Dursley, with a design to take him to another place, where he had better prospects; and he was much inclined to go with them. But the very persons that opposed and slighted him before, when they found he was likely to leave them, came and begged his pardon, promising a better carriage for the future ; and so he consented to stay. Some time after, however, his troubles were renewed. There were about seven men who had formed a resolution to ruin him, some by swearing against him, and some in other ways ; but it pleased God that several of them died ; and his principal enemy fell desperately ill, who upon his death-bed sent for him to pray with him, and confessing his wicked design, desired Mr. *Woodward* to preach his funeral sermon, to warn all his associates to desist from their vile purposes, as they would not provoke God to visit them with his judgments.

Mr.

Mr. *Woodward* was now delivered from his troubles, and at last had the comfort to see his people become very teachable, and conformable to the rules of the gospel. His labours among them were very great. Besides the toil of a school, he preached twice every Lord's-day, expounding in the morning, and catechizing in the afternoon, before sermon. Every Tuesday he expounded for an hour or two, and carried on a lecture every Thursday, usually without any assistance. On Lord's-day-evenings he repeated his sermons to his scholars, and many of his auditors at his own house: and at funerals, he either preached or expounded. He was very plain and zealous in maintaining the foundations of religion. Twice a year he kept a public fast, besides many in private. Every Monday after dinner he used to visit ten families, to instruct the ignorant, reprove the scandalous, comfort the dejected, &c. He was very diligent in instilling the principles of religion into the young, and collected money for teaching poor children to read. He himself also was very liberal in works of mercy. He was a very strict observer of the Sabbath; and used on that day to rise very early. He was a man of a very large soul and a public spirit; of unshaken constancy and resolution, sincerity and plain-heartedness. He took great pains to oppose the sectaries, disputing with them openly, as occasion offered, all round the country, and silenced them. He protested and preached against taking the Engagement. *Oliver*, upon some occasion, appointing a day of public Thanksgiving, he, thinking there was more need of Fasting, appointed a solemn public fast, and kept it with his people.

At length, being over-borne with labour, and his health declining by a consumption, he got Mr. *Stubbes* to officiate among his people, and he died before the Act of Uniformity took place. But in his last sickness, he sent word to Mr. *Forbes* of *Gloucester* (as he assured the author) " That, " with submission to the will of God, he desired to live a " little longer, that he might bear a testimony against episco- " pacy, and the new conformity."——Some persons in the country having a design to publish his life, Dr. *Woodward*, his son, (a worthy conformist of Maidstone in Kent,) sent the following account of his father in a letter, to be inserted in this work.

" I am assured that very few (at least in these degenerate days) are blessed with such eminency of grace as he was; which seemed always to be in the height of pious zeal, with-

4   out

out any considerable abatements at any time. In truth, such
a pitch of ardor seemed to many to be above the common state
of humanity itself, and to have a tendency to decay the health
and course of nature. But the power of God bore him up
for many years, till at last indeed the raised soul grew too big
for the body, and by degrees rent it into pieces, to make way
for a happy dissolution.

" About the 23d year of his age, he was so smitten with a
sense of the evil of sin, (thro' what particular means I do not
remember) that he has professed he thought himself the vilest
creature breathing. He fancied the very dogs in the street
were by their Maker set against him. So that he was constrained to forbear company for a while, and to retire from the
public, to set himself to the most important and absolutely necessary work of life ; viz. to spread the wounds of his soul
before the Physician of souls ; and to seek the healing balm of
his Redeemer's blood : to which he applied himself (thro' the
grace of God) with such earnestness, and to so good effect,
that all his after life shewed, that he was in earnest in the
things of salvation : there appearing little concern in him for
any thing, but the glory of God, and the insuring eternal life.
Yet he did not presently step forth into the ministry. He rather dreaded that tremendous charge, in which, above all em-
ployments, men ought to appear with the highest advance-
ments of holiness, prudence, and diligence ; and like *Nazian-
zen, Chrysostom,* and most of the primitive divines, was by
much entreaty drawn to so solemn an office ; after he had
spent a considerable time in the university of *Oxford,* passing
thro' the degrees of B. A. and M. A. having, with great applause, performed the exercises requisite to both.

" When he arrived at the age of thirty, God was pleased to
send an inward warmth into his soul, which was more com-
pulsive than all outward persuasion. He discovered such a
zeal for God, and the souls of men, as burnt like fire, and
(like that of the prophet *Jer.* xx. 9.) was no way to be made
easy, but by giving it vent; which the sermon he first preached
did very plainly shew ; which was delivered in the church of
his native village, on those words of *Peter* and *John, Acts,* iv.
20. ' For we cannot but speak the things which we have
' seen and heard.' And I have heard many who heard him
say that ' they all wondered at the gracious things which
' proceeded out of his mouth,' He had indeed such a readiness, or rather exuberance, in delivering the will of God,
upon any subject before him, that tho' he always wrote his
sermons

sermons at large, yet he has often confessed, that he has been carried into a field of doctrine, which he never had committed to writing; not in a roving and injudicious discourse, but in such melting and close argument, as seldom failed to reach the mark he principally aimed at, *viz.* the softening and reducing obstinate hearts.

" The whole course of his labours in the ministry, was suitable to his careful entrance upon it. He was earnest even as St. *Paul* (beyond strength,) and never would preach a sermon to others, but what had first warmed his own breast: for which cause he sometimes either razed out a part of a sermon, or wholly threw it by. He was most affectionate and devout in prayer, earnest in preaching, bold in reproving, kind in admonishing, ready to advise, and succour, and comfort the feeble and disconsolate: and, in a word, he ' spent, and was spent,' in his ministerial labours. He made frequent visits to all under his care at their own dwellings. He would pry into most of their failures and neglects, and would compassionate all their wants of soul, body, and estate. I know not by what peculiar impulse it was, that he particularly fixed his desires of exercising his ministry in *Dursley*; a place at that time very dissolute; insomuch that it had the name of *Drunken Dursley*: but if he found it so, it was very much altered by his labours of many years there, and became one of the most wealthy and best trading towns in the neighbourhood. Some of them having told me, that they cleared a thousand pounds a year by the trade of cloathing, in the time of his residence there. His presence in the streets, made the youth grave, and the aged circumspect. It made the sober to rejoice, and the guilty to hide themselves in corners. He seldom went to church but with a multitude with him For his house being distant from the church the length of a long street, every one got their families ready as he came by, and stood in their doors, and so fell in with those that followed; so that he literally ' went with the multitude to the house of God.' And every one's zeal seemed inflamed by the flame he beheld in his neighbour: so that I have heard that there was the most composed and affected congregation that could any where be seen.

" I can only hint his more than brotherly love to Mr. *Stubbes*, whose embraces were always like those of Jonathan and David; and his correspondence by letters with Mr. *Haviland* and other London ministers of great eminence; of which I may probably collect some, &c. His sorrow for the
death

death of king *Charles* I.; his lamenting for want of a good foundation in the Inter-regnum; and his joy at the return of king *Charles* II. ought to be inserted: and also the raptures of his death.——Thus, sir, I have complied with your desire, not to give materials for a book, so much as to give some hints to a friend. Your's, &c. *Josiah Woodward.*"

" P. S. He gave me my name in desire of Reformation: and named my younger brother *Jeremiah*, when he saw the little hopes of it."

—— HENRY STUBBES, M. A. Of *Wadham Col. Oxf.* He was born at *Upton* in this county, upon an estate given to his grandfather by king James I. with whom he came from Scotland. He was first minister of St. Philip's in *Bristol*, and afterwards of *Chew-magna.* In 1654, he preached in the city of *Wells*, and was assistant to the Commissioners appointed by the parliament to eject ignorant and scandalous ministers; but the Act of Uniformity found him at *Dursley*, whither he came as assistant to Mr. *Joseph Woodward.* Upon quitting this living, he went about preaching from place to place, with unwearied diligence and great success. Being settled in peaceable principles, wherever he came he repressed the spirit of censoriousness and unjust separation, and preached up the ancient zeal and sincerity, with a spirit suitable to it. After he had for some little time preached privately in *London*, he was allowed the public exercise of his ministry, by the connivance of Dr. *Pritchet*, then Bp. of *Gloucester*, in the parish church of *Horsley*; where the income was so small that it had been without a minister for several years. Here he read some parts of the Common-prayer. He was a plain, fervent and moving preacher: eminently successful in the conversion of sinners. He was of a calm temper; never fierce, but against sin; and had the cordial respects of good men of all persuasions. He set apart some time every day to pray for the church of God, without the narrow distinction of this, or that, or the other party.

The last Lord's-day he preached at *Horsley*, he told his auditory, he desired to see them the next morning before his journey, and take his leave of them in the church, where he preached most affectionately, from *Prov.* iii. 6. He died at *London*, *July* 7, 1678, aged 73, and was interred at *Bun-hill-fields*. Mr. *Baxter* preached his funeral sermon from
Acts

Acts xx. 24.[*] From this discourse Dr. Calamy's account is principally taken, not to the best advantage. On comparing both, it was thought advisable to give the reader the whole of what that great man has said of Mr. *Stubbes*, in his own words:

"This faithful servant of Christ hath run his race. What that was, and how he performed it, the county of Gloucester knoweth, and the city of Wells, in Somersetshire knoweth, and this city and this congregation partly know. I will speak but little of him but what I know myself, or have by unquestionable testimony. His birth, parentage and youthful life, I am not acquainted with. He was a minister of Christ about fifty years, dying at the age of 73. His studies and parts and labours lay not in the critical or controversial way. He was so happy as not to waste his time in contentious studies. He was so humble and honest as not to trouble his auditory with such matters, nor pretend to have studied what he had not; nor like many proud ignorants, to boast or contend most where they know the least. His soul was taken up with the great things of religion. His preaching was most on the Baptismal covenant, the articles of the Creed, the Lord's prayer, the Decalogue, and such necessary things which essentially constitute the christian. I never heard him meddle with controversies in public, or in his private talks; but [the drift of all was] how to know God in Christ, how to seek and serve him, how to resist temptations to sin, how to live in love, righteousness, peace, and profitableness to one another: especially how to serve God entirely, and in what state we shall live with him for ever. He was the freest of most that ever I knew from that deceit of the serpent mentioned 2 *Cor.* xi. 3. who corrupteth men by drawing them from the *simplicity which is in Christ.* His breath, his life, his preaching, his prayers, his conference, was christian simplicity and sincerity. He knew not how to dissemble or wear a mask : his face, his mouth, his whole conversation, laid bare his heart. While he passed by all quarrels, few quarrelled with him.

[*] With this was printed a piece entitled " The death of ministers improved; occasioned by the decease of Mr. Stubbes ;" by Mr. Matthew Pemberton and Mr. Thomas Vincent.—See Baxter's sermon in his Works, Vol. iv. p. 881. and an extract in Toms's Biog. Col.

Of all men that ever I knew he seemed to me one of the most humble. His preaching, his discourse, his garb, and all his behaviour, spoke pure humility. Never did I hear from him a word of ostentation, much less of envy at the precedence of others. He came to Christ as a teachable child, and he preached as a learner. He had learned of Christ to be meek and lowly; to make himself of no reputation; nor did he seek the honor that is of man. O how far was he from striving to be above his brethren, or troubling the church by a proud, imperious or turbulent spirit! He was exceedingly peaceable in his principles and in his practice; never contending with opiniators, or those that cry down this and that error of their brethren, to get the reputation of being free from errors; nor did he make himself of a sect or faction, nor preach for this party against that, except for Christ's party against the Devil's. Nor did I ever hear him back-bite any, nor exercise the too common liberty against others, in carping at their infirmities. He honored his superiors, and was obedient to authority, as far as it would stand with his obedience to God. I never heard that publicly or privately he spoke a disloyal or irreverent word of the king, or others in power.

After he had preached here awhile in London, he had a *preferment* to a parish-church in Gloucestershire, of EIGHT POUNDS *per ann.* maintenance, which had many years no minister. And by the honest connivance of the Rev. Bishop of Gloucester, he there preached for some years in peace; of which I am past doubt that Bishop hath no cause to repent. He used part of the Liturgy, not sticking at the censure of [bigots.] His judgment, his age and experience set him above all factious inducements, and taught him to please God, whoever were displeased. And when at last he was driven away, I never heard him speak of it with any bitterness. He is now where God's praises are celebrated, and whence no holy soul shall ever be cast out.

His labour was such as beseemed one absolutely devoted to God. His preaching was very plain and faithful: fitted rather to country auditors than to curious ones (and he chose accordingly) but it was wholly for faith, love and holiness. He was much in catechizing youth, and very moving in his familiar exhortations to them; setting his whole heart upon the winning and edifying of souls, and longing for success as much as covetous merchants do for rich returns. Wherever he came, he kept a private weekly meeting for the young people, to whom he used to propose familiar questions, and he much rejoiced in their willingness and his success. The greatest benefice cannot please one that worketh for the fleece, so much as he was pleased that his unwearied labour profited his flock. How thankful was he to God and the bishop's connivance for that short liberty to work. And to their honour I must say, that he praised not only the friendly peaceableness of the magistrates and gentry of the county, but also of his neighbour conformable ministers that lived by him in love, and envied not his liberty.

This holy man so little cared for the hypocrite's reward, that no reproach of man did move him ; nor did he count his great labour or life dear to him, that he might subserve him who came to seek and save the lost. If Seneca could say, " That no man more shewed himself a good man than he who will lose the reputation of being one, lest he should lose his goodness itself," no wonder if this holy man accounted not his fame too dear to preserve his conscience. His friends and physicians suppose that his labours hastened his death. He came from the country to London again to work ; and after his journey, preaching almost every day, and some days twice, even after he began to be ill, no wonder that the fever, and the dysentery which followed, dispatched him. At first he fell down in the pulpit, but recovering, he went on ; and so again till he was disabled. Some will censure him for imprudence in such labour. But they must consider, What it is to be above the inordinate love of life, and to long for the good of souls ; and withal, that which much emboldened him was, that he was wont to go somewhat ill into the pulpit, and to come better out. But the heat of the season, and seventy-three years of age, gave advantage to the messenger which God sent to end his labours and all his sufferings.

Two things especially I commend to imitation. 1. That he was more in instructing and catechizing children by familiar questions, than almost any man that I have known. 2. He prayed as constantly as he preached ; no wonder then that his labours had much success. A man of prayer is a man of power with God.

For my part, I never saw him till his coming to live in London, I think not seven years ago, tho' I long heard of his successful preaching. But to shew you how great his charity was, and what a loss I have myself, and how faulty I and others are in too much forgetting our friends, I will

4   tell

tell you that he hath often told me, that he never went to God in prayer, for above twenty years, but he particularly remembered me. But his love hath not tempted me to say a word of him which I verily believe not to be true. And I conclude with this profession, that I scarce remember the man that ever I knew, who served God with more absolute resignation and devotedness, in simplicity and godly sincerity, and not with fleshly wisdom, and living like the primitive christians, without any pride, or worldly motives, or in whose case I had rather die. And therefore, no wonder that he lived in peace of conscience, and died with Paul's words, *I have fought a good fight---henceforth there is laid up for me a crown of righteousness,"* &c.

Much of this good man's spirit and temper is discovered in the preface to his last will, which is preserved in *Turner's History of Providence*, Chap. 143, p. 99. § As that book is become very scarce, we shall here insert a copy of it:

The last Will of Mr. Henry Stubbes, *deceased,* July 7, 1678. *Published at the desire of his widow:*

" Knowing that I must shortly put off this my earthly tabernacle, I make my last will and testament. *Imprimis,* I commend my soul into the hands of God, wholly trusting in Jesus Christ my dear Lord and Saviour; thro' his all sufficient satisfaction and powerful mediation, to be accepted, *Eph.* 1. 6. *Item.* I commit my body to the earth from whence it was taken, in sure and certain hope of a resurrection to life eternal, building upon that sure word, *John* vi. 40.—I leave my fatherless children to the Lord, who hath promised to be a father to the fatherless. *Ps.* lxviii. 5. and to preserve them alive. *Jer.* xlix 11.—Commanding them to keep the way of the Lord. *Gen.* xviii. 19.— I exhort my widow to trust in the Lord, of whose care she hath had no little experience; and therefore should trust in him. *Ps.* ix. 10.—I desire her to read often *Jer.* xlix. 11. *Ps.* lxviii. 5. *Heb.* xiii. 6.—The congregations to which I have been formerly a preacher, and that with which I now am by a special hand of providence, I commend to God, and the word of his grace, which is able to build them up, &c. *Acts* xx. 32, beseeching them by the Lord Jesus, That as they have received of me how they ought to walk and please God, so they would abound more and more. 1 *Thess.* iv. 1. —And for my kindred according to the flesh, my heart's desire and prayer to God for them is, That they may be saved. *Rom.* x. 1.—And for all those yet living who have seriously

and

and earnestly desired my prayers, my earnest request to God for them is, That it would please him to do for them all as the matter shall require. 1 *Kings* viii. 50.—And for my brethren in the ministry, my prayer is, That they may take heed to themselves, and to all the flock over which the Holy Ghost hath made them overseers, to feed the church of God which he hath purchased with his own blood. *Acts* xx. 28. —And for the people my prayer is, That they may obey them that have the rule over them. *Heb.* xiii. 17.—And for professors of religion—that they may walk worthy of God, unto all well-pleasing, being fruitful in every good work. *Col.* i. 10. 11,—And for the King, my prayer is, That mercy and truth may preserve him. *Prov.* xxvi. 28.—And for him and all that are in authority, my prayer is, That they may so lead their own lives, that the people under them may lead quiet and peaceable lives, in all godliness and honesty. 1 *Tim.* ii. 2.—And for the whole land of my nativity, my humble prayer to the Lord of all grace and mercy is, That the power and purity of the gospel, together with a learned and faithful ministry to dispense the same, may be continued and preserved therein."

Mr. *Stubbes* was of a very charitable disposition, and devoted the tenth part of his income to pious uses. He settled four pounds *per ann.* on the parishes of *Dursley* and *Horsley*, for teaching poor children, and buying them books. He also gave 200*l.* to *Bristol*, and a like sum to *London*, to be annually improved for the good of the poor, to buy them Bibles, and to assist poor ministers' widows. § *Atkyns* says, " Mr. Henry Stubbes, a Nonconformist preacher, gave 50*l.* to the parish of *Uley*, to teach poor children to write."

WORKS. A Dissuasive from Conformity to this World. —God's Severity against Man's Iniquity.—God's gracious Presence the Saints great Privilege : A Farewell Sermon to a Congregation in *London.*—The great Treaty of Peace : an Exhortation to the making Peace with God.—Conscience the best Friend upon Earth ; or the happy Effects of keeping a good Conscience.—A Funeral Sermon for a Lady in Gloucestershire. —Two Epistles ; the one to the professing Parents of baptized Children ; the other to the baptized Children of professing Parents.—After his Death, A Voice from Heaven: being his last Sermon and Prayer.

ELBERTON [C.] Mr. HILTON.

FILTON

Increase Mather

from an original Painting in the Possession of M.ʳ Townsend, Holborn

Published by Dalton & Son, Paternoster Row.

.FILTON [R.] WILLIAM BLACKWELL, B. A. After his ejectment he continued to live, not at *Felton*, in Herefordshire, as before supposed, but FILTON, in this county, which is about four miles from *Bristol*, where he was so reduced, that for a time he maintained himself, by stitching of bodice, or womens stays. § *Bigland* decides the place of his ejectment, as well as the spelling of his name and his degree, in this entry : " 1645. Will. Blackwell, B. A. " ejected for Nonconformity, 1662."

GLOUCESTER. INCREASE MATHER, D. D. He was the youngest son of Mr. *Richard Mather*, who went to America, in 1635, because he could no longer exercise his ministry with satisfaction to his conscience in his native country, and became minister at *Dorchester*, in New-England; where this his son was born, A. D. 1639. After gaining a good knowledge of the languages at school, and spending some time in *Harvard* college, he lived in the family of that worthy divine, Mr. *John Norton*, several years. It pleased God to make serious impressions upon his heart betimes, by which he was fitted for great service in his church. In 1657 he took a voyage to England, and after visiting his friends in Lancashire, went to Ireland to see his eldest brother, Mr. *Samuel Mather*, then minister in *Dublin*. He entered himself in *Trinity College* there, and in 1658 proceeded Master of Arts, performing the usual exercise with great applause. He was much respected by Dr. *Winter*, then Provost of the college, and was chosen Fellow, but did not accept it. The air of that country not agreeing with him, tho' he met with great civilities, and some good offers there, he returned to England, and was for some time a preacher to Mr. *Howe*'s parish, at Torrington, in ·Devonshire, which was in the neighbourhood of another of his brothers, Mr. *Nathaniel Mather*, then minister of Barnstaple. Upon Mr. *Howe*'s return to Torrington, after *Richard* quitted the protectorship, he accepted an invitation of Col. Bingham, governor of *Guernsey*, to go into that island, in the year 1659, where he preached every Lord's-day morning at the castle, and in the afternoon at the town called *Peter's Port*.

From thence he removed to *Gloucester*, at the earnest solicitation of Mr. Forbes and his friends there; but after some time he returned to *Guernsey*, where he was at the time of the Restoration. Upon his refusing to set his hand to a paper, which was sent thither by General *Monk*, to be signed by all

commissioned

commissioned officers in those parts, by which they were required to declare, " That the times then were and would be happy ;" he was in danger of losing the arrears of his salary, which amounted to above 100*l.* but providentially he escaped that loss. And upon Sir *Hugh Pollard's* being made governor of that island, when he came to be under the necessity either of conforming or quitting the place, he left Guernsey and came into England, where he was offered a living of some hundreds a year, if he would forsake his principles. But he chose rather to trust God's providence, than violate the tranquillity of his mind ; and so he sailed again for *New-England* to his aged father, and there settled in the New Church, in the north part of *Boston.* He was ordained *May* 27, 1664, when his father gave him the charge. He married the daughter of Mr. *John Cotton,* by whom he had three sons, *Cotton Mather,* D. D. well known by his writings ; Mr. *Nathaniel Mather,* who died at the age of nineteen, whose life is printed ; and Mr. *Samuel Mather,* who had a small congregation at *Witney,* in Oxfordshire, and published several valuable writings. The old gentleman had also seven daughters ; and he and his wife had this uncommon comfort and satisfaction, of having seven of their children receiving the Lord's Supper at the same communion with them.—In 1680, when the Synod sat at *Boston,* and the confession of faith was agreed upon, Mr. *Mather* was the moderator, and drew up the preface to it.

In 1683 K. *Charles,* by a declaration, required from the inhabitants of New-England, a full submission, and an entire resignation of their charter to his pleasure ; or else signified a *quo warranto* should be prosecuted. Mr. *Mather* being desired to be present at a public assembly of the freemen of *Boston,* to give his thoughts about that matter, complied, and publicly declared against their having a hand in their own ruin ; persuading them rather to leave themselves in the hands of God, and submit to his will, in a faithful discharge of their duty, than deliver themselves immediately into the hands of men, by a full submission and entire resignation to their pleasure. The question was carried in the negative *nem. con.* And this had a great influence on the country in general. Some malicious people, in order to be revenged on him for this, forged a letter, full of impertinent as well as treasonable expressions, and dating it *Boston,* 10 M. 3*d* 1683, they subscribed his name to it, and sent it to a worthy person at *Amsterdam:* This letter being conveyed to London, was
read

read before the king and council; but it carried such evidence of its being a forgery, that tho' Sir *Roger L'Estrange* published some scraps of it, with his own comments, there was no prosecution of Mr. *Mather.* But judgment was entered against the charter of *Massachusetts* colony. K. *Charles* died soon after, and in 1686 K. *James* sent a governor, with a commission that enabled him, with three or four other men, to make what laws, and levy what taxes, they pleased.

But in a little time that king published a Declaration for liberty of conscience. Some of the ministers of *New-England,* and their churches, drew up addresses of thanks to him, for the benefit enjoyed by this Declaration; and Mr. *Mather* was desired to take a voyage to England and deliver them. A copy of the forged letter before-mentioned coming to New-England, Mr. Mather wrote to a gentleman that had it, to vindicate himself, and named a person whom he suspected to have had a hand in the contrivance. This person arrested Mr. *Mather* in an action of defamation, and 500*l.* damage, purely, as was apprehended, with a design to stop his voyage. But the jury cleared him, and ordered the plaintiff to pay costs of court, and he embarked for England, *April* 7, 1688.—He landed at Weymouth, and hastening to London, presented the addresses to the king; when he laid before his majesty the state of the country, and was favourably received.

Upon the Revolution, he waited on the prince of *Orange,* and was instrumental in preventing the sending a letter to New-England (in common with the other plantations) confirming their old governor till farther order, which would have had pernicious consequences. After the coronation of K. *William,* Mr. *Mather* frequently waited upon him, and was very much assisted by Philip lord *Wharton,* and others. His great endeavour was to get New-England resettled upon the charter foundation; but he was disappointed in his object by the unexpected dissolution of parliament. His next attempt was to get a writ of error in judgment, by which the case relating to the *Massachusett* colony might be brought out of Chancery into the King's-bench; but herein he also failed. All therefore he had left for him to do was, to petition the king for a new charter, containing all the old one, with the addition of new and more ample privileges; which, after some time, he obtained, and then, *March* 29, 1692, he set sail for New-England, in the company of Sir *William Phips,* whom his majesty sent over governor, and they arrived

rived safe at *Boston, May* 14 following. Soon after, there being a meeting of the general assembly of the province, the speaker of the house of representatives, or commons, publicly returned him thanks for his faithful and indefatigable endeavours to serve the country.

He now returned to his more pleasing employment, the care of his church, and of the college, of which he was President, and was created D. D. But in 1701 he resigned his charge in the college, because the general assembly required the President to reside at *Cambridge.* He continued at *Boston* preaching to his beloved people. He had several fits of sickness, from which he was remarkably recovered; but till he was past 80 years of age, his intellects did not appear enfeebled. He at last expired (in the arms of his eldest son) *Aug.* 23, 1723; and was honoured by his church (who ever shewed a great esteem and veneration for him) with a more splendid funeral than ever had been seen for any divine in those parts. His funeral sermon was preached by Mr. *Foxcroft,* on 2 *Chron.* xxiv. 15. And the ministers of *Boston,* for nine or ten weeks successively, supplied his pulpit, and expressed their condolence with his church. He kept a constant diary, in which he inserted remarks upon the most eminent dealings of God with him, both in a way of providence and grace.

WORKS. A Discourse on the Mystery of Israel's Salvation.— The first Principles of New-England, on the Subject of Baptism and Communion of Churches.—A brief History of the War with the Indians in New-England, from *June* 24, 1675, to *Aug.* 12, 1676. —Some important Truths about Conversion.—The Divine Right of Infant Baptism.—Practical Truths, tending to promote Godliness in the Power of it.—Diatribe de signo Filii Hominis, et de secundo Messiæ adventu.—An Essay for the recording illustrious Providences.—The Mystery of Christ opened and applied, in several Sermons concerning the Person, Office and Glory of Jesus Christ.—De successu Evangelii apud Indos in Nova Anglia. Epist. ad Cl. Virum, D. Joh. Leusdenum.—A Discourse on Comets, 1683.—A Call to the rising Generation.—A Funeral Sermon for Mr. John Bailey.—The Doctrine of Div. Providence.—Sermons on Ezek. ix. 3.—The Folly of Sin.—The Excellency of a public Spirit.—A Disc. on the Truth of the Christian Religion.—A Disc. concerning Angels...The Life and Death of Mr. Richard Mather. ...A Sermon against Drunkenness...The Day of Trouble, &c... A Disc. on the Subject of Baptism, &c....The Wicked Man's Portion...The Times of Men in the Hand of God...A Relation of the Troubles of New-England from the Indians, from the
Beginning,

Beginning...A Disc. on the Prevalence of Prayer...Renewal of
Covenant, &c...Of praying for the rising Generation...The great
Concernment for a Covenant People, &c...Heaven's Alarm to
the World...The Church a Subject of Persecution...Against promiscuous Dances...The greatest of Sinners exhorted, &c...A
Testimony against Superstitions...The Unlawfulness of swearing
on a Book, &c...Several Papers relating to the State of New-
England...The Revolution in New-England...The Blessing of
primitive Counsellors...Cases of Conscience concerning Witch-
craft, &c...An Essay on the Power of a Pastor for the Administration of the Sacraments...On the Case, whether a Man may
marry two Sisters...Solemn Advice to young Men...A Disc. on
Man's not knowing his Time...Concerning eating of Blood...
David's serving his Generation...The surest Way to the highest
Honour...Discourse on Hardness of Heart...The Order of the
Gospel vindicated...The blessed Hope...Remarks on a Sermon of
G. K. The Glory departing, &c...The Duty of Parents to pray
for their Children...Gospel Truths...The Voice of God in the
stormy Winds...Practical Truths to promote Holiness...Medita-
tions on the Glory of Christ...A Disc. concerning Earthquakes...
A Testimony against Sacrilege...A Dissertation concerning a Right
to the Sacraments...Meditations on Death...A Disquisition concerning the State of Souls departed...A Dissertation concerning
the future Conversion of the Jews, &c...A Disc. concerning Faith
and Prayer for the Kingdom of Christ...A Sermon at the Artillery
Election...Awakening Truths...Meditations on the Glory of
Heaven...Concerning the Death of the Righteous...The Duty of
the Children of godly Parents...Burnings bewailed; Remarks upon
an Answer, &c...Of Sanctification of the Lord's-day...A Disc.
shewing who shall enter into Heaven...Believers gain by Death.
...Resignation to the Will of God;...Jesus Christ a Saviour...Dis-
quisition concerning ecclesiastical Councils...There is a God in
Heaven...The Duty and Dignity of aged Servants of God...
The Duty of praying for Ministers...A Sermon at the Ordination
of his Grandson...Sermons on the Beatitudes...An Ordination
Sermon...A Birth-day Sermon...Advice to Children of godly
Ancestors...A dying Pastor's Legacy,...Besides several Prefaces
to books written by divines in New-England, and to two of Mr.
Flavell's.

——— JAMES FORBES, M. A. He was of an honourable
Scottish family, and was pious betimes. He had his education at *Aberdeen*, and being Master of Arts there, was admitted at *Oxford, ad eundem*. When he came to England,
he was full of serious thought; and most earnestly desirous
that God would choose for him a useful station, and bless
his ministry, to the conversion of souls. He entered upon
the

the pastoral office with extraordinary seriousness and fervent prayer. Not being satisfied to accept a parish that was offered him, he was in 1654 sent by the powers that then were, to the cathedral of *Gloucester*, where he preached with great success, but to the apparent danger of shortening his life. He gathered a church, which was chiefly made up of his own converts; and after six years he was ejected from the cathedral, when dean *Brough* took possession of it; but he still continued at *Gloucester*, ministering privately as he could. Dr. *Frampton*, who was first dean, and afterwards bishop of Gloucester, courted him to conformity in vain. In consequence of *Yarrington's* plot, (or *Packington's* rather) he was committed to *Chepstow* castle, where he was long kept in a strait and dark room; as also was Col. *Overton*. When he was discharged, he returned to his pastoral care, in the pursuit of which he suffered several imprisonments in *Gloucester*, one of which was for a whole year.

In the reign of K. *Charles* II. he was indicted upon the Corporation-act, the penalty of which was imprisonment. He was also indicted on 23 *Jac.* I. the penalty of which was 20l. a month; and upon 35 *Eliz.* of which the penalty was to abjure the realm, or suffer death. At the same time also he was excommunicated, and the writ *de excom. capiendo* was out against him. In *Monmouth's* time he retired to *Enfield*, in Middlesex, and there continued unmolested in his ministry. He was afterwards recalled, and returned to his own people, tho' to his disadvantage : and he continued with them to his death, living in a respectable manner, but mostly upon his own property. He was on the whole fifty-eight years minister in this city; abundant in labours, both there and in the country round about. In his judgment he was a strict *Calvinist*, and congregational, but of a catholic temper. He was a holy, humble, serious, learned man; blessed with much success in his younger days; deeply wounded at later decays of ministers and professing christians, and greatly concerned that the rising generation of ministers should adorn their doctrine by an excellent holy conversation. He was a man full of good works; liberal even beyond his ability in life; and at his death he left many gifts to charitable uses, especially his library, which was of considerable value. He died *May* 31, 1712, aged 83, and was buried under his own communion-table. His funeral sermon was preached by Mr. *Isaac Noble*, of Bristol.

WORKS.

WORKS. Nehushtan; in Answer to J. Elliot, a Quaker....
The Christian directed in his Way to Heaven...God's Goodness
to Israel in all Ages...His Remains, prefixed to his Funeral Sermon. *viz.* A Letter to his People, to be communicated to them
after his death...Sermon before the Assembly at Stroudwater....
Some Instructions, &c. for Youth concerning their Souls.

HASLETON [R. S.] Mr. JOHN DUNCE. Dr. Walker
says, this was the sequestered living of Dr. Whittington,
and after him of Mr. Dobson, who was dispossessed of it
by Mr. *Dunce*, who obtained the seals for it from the then
keeper *Lysle*, and that upon the Restoration Mr. *Dobson*
was reinstated. Mr. *Dunce* however was silenced by the
Act of uniformity, tho' not ejected. He continued to preach
privately some years after he was blind. He died chaplain to
Mrs. Beck, of Batcot, near Farrington. —— *Dunch*, of
Pisie, Esq. allowed him twenty nobles a year during his
life. He was a pious man, and an affectionate preacher.

HEMPSTED [R.] Mr. JONATHAN SMITH, jun. After
his ejectment he continued to preach privately, and taught
school at *Ross*, in Herefordshire.

KEMPLEY. Mr. PAUL FREWEN. He was of the Bap-
tist denomination, a good preacher, and very popular. After
his ejectment he was minister to a congregation at Warwick.
§ *Crosby* has nothing to add to this account.

LEMINGTON [C. augmented 50*l.*] Mr. EDWARD
FINCH. Dr. Walker says, he had been a cobler; which
may be as true as some of his other stories. Be this as it
may, this was not the cause of his ejectment.

LEONARD STANLY [C.] Mr. WILLIAM HODGES.
He lived and died a Nonconformist, at *Wooton under Edge.*
He was a learned, able preacher, and a great enemy to the
sectaries.

LONGHOPE [V. 44*l.* 7*s.* 10*d.*] Mr. THOMAS SMITH.
Dr. Walker says, he got this vicarage in 1655. He lived
afterwards at *Bristol*, without *Lawford's Gate*, and continued preaching at several places in the county, till he was
near 90 years of age. He died in *Bristol*, very poor, about
1705. § His wife, whom he long survived, was buried in
the Baptist Ground, *Mar.* 15, 1695.

MISERDEN

MISERDEN [or MINSTERWORTH] Mr. WILLIAM MURREL. It is uncertain which of these two places he was at. He died soon after the Restoration.

MORTON VALANCE [Prebend.] Mr. ANTHONY COLLIER. He quitted *Morton upon Lugg*, in Hereford-shire, at the Restoration ; and afterwards preached one part of the Lord's-day at *Morton Valance*, in Gloucestershire, and the other at *Whitminster*, in the same county, and was ejected from both places in 1662. § In the latter part of his life he settled with a Dissenting congregation at *Rosse*, in Herefordshire, where he died.

NAUNTON [R.] Mr. HOODS. § He was ejected at the Restoration, 1660.

NOTGROVE [R.] Mr. WILLIAM DAVISON. A warm and useful preacher. He lived at *Tewkesbury*, after he was ejected, and there had his goods plundered. His house was made his prison ; as he durst not stir abroad, because of the writ *de excommunicato capiendo*. He was afterwards pastor of a congregation in *Cambden*, in this county. He died on the 25th of *December*, 1711. He had a son many years pastor to a congregation in *Winchester*.

ODDINGTON [R: 130*l.*] WILLIAM TRAY, M. A. Of *Christ. Church* and *Magd. Col. Oxford*. Born at *Gloucester*. He was master of seven languages, and educated many young gentlemen ; several of them for the ministry. When he was ejected he had a wife and seven children, with but thirty pounds *per ann.* of his own, to maintain them ; which obliged him to set up a school. He removed afterwards to *Leonard Stanley*, where he preached in his own house. Mr. *Henley*, the minister of the parish, who lived at the next door, informed against him, and got him excommunicated. But the Bp. of *Gloucester* wrote to him twice, and offered, if he would conform, to give him as good a parsonage as any in his diocese. Mr. *Tray* thankfully acknowledged the Bishop's kindness, but said, That he was too old to conform. He then went to *Horsley*, in this county, and preached at the house of Mrs. *Willowby*, where there was a great resort to him, so that a very large place was soon provided, which was afterwards called *Nails-worth* meeting. He continued preaching there, while he had liberty, and after that went to *Chipping Norton*, in Oxfordshire, where he finished his course, and made a comfortable

able exit, aged 59. He was a person very exemplary in his life and conversation; and was particularly noted for being exceedingly charitable and hospitable; very modest, humble and peaceable.

In the year 1653, there was a public dispute at Winchcomb, in which Mr. Tray joined with Mr. Helmes and Mr. Welles, of Tewkesbury, against Mr. Clement Barksdale, [who was rector of *Naunton*] and Mr. William Towers; and it was observed that none in all the company was more candid and ingenuous than Mr. Tray. An account of this disputation was published in 1654. There is added to it a letter or two of Mr. *Tray*'s, which shew him to have been both a scholar and a gentleman.

OLVESTON [C.] Mr. HENRY HEAN.

PUCKLECHURCH [V.] Mr. JOHN FOX. He did a great deal of good in this country. After his ejectment he was pastor of a church at *Nailsworth*. From the little he wrote, he appears to have wanted neither affection nor judgment; *viz.*

WORKS. Two small Tracts. One on Redeeming the Time. [a very excellent little piece, ED.]..The other, The Door of Heaven opened and shut, on *Matt.* xxv. 10.

RISSINGTON MAGNA [R. 22*l.* 0*s.* 2½*d.*] Mr. DRYE{ An ancient grave man. After his ejectment he preached at Burford, Brice-Norton, and other places thereabouts.

RUDFORD [R.] Mr. THOMAS SARE. Some time after his ejectment he went to London, and exercised his ministry privately. As he was once preaching for Mr. *Doolittle*, whose place he chearfully undertook to supply, at a dangerous time, when that good man was prudently advised to absent himself, a party of soldiers came in and disturbed the meeting. On their being ordered to fire, Mr. *Sare*, opening his breast, bid them to shoot if they pleased, for he was ready to die for his master; at which they were so struck as to desist, and he got away in the croud unhurt. This circumstance is referred to in the account of Mr. Doolittle (Vol. I: p. 87) but Mr. *Sare*'s name is not there mentioned.

SAPERTON [C.] Mr. APPLEBY.

SHIPTON MOIGNE [R.] DANIEL CAPEL, M. A. Some time Fellow of *Magd. Col. Oxf.* He was a native of Gloucestershire, and the son of the eminent Mr. Richard Capel. Dr. Walker mentions him as ejected by the Oxford visitors. He was successively minister of *Morton, Alderly,* and *Shipton,* in this county. On parting with this living at the latter of these places, in 1662, he practised physic at *Stroud,* as long as he lived.

SLAUGHTER [R. there are two places of this name, *Upper* and *Lower*] Mr. JOHN KECK. It does not appear that he preached after his ejectment. He had a place in the Custom-house, in London.

SLIMBRIDGE [R. 28*l.* 2*s.* 4*d.*] Mr. PETER GUILLIAM. He was ejected at the Restoration, and died soon afterwards.

STOW in the *Would* [R.] Mr. WILLIAM BEAL. He died in London not long after his ejectment.

STOWEL [R.] Mr. THOMAS JORDAN.

STROUD. Mr. BUTT.

TEWKSBURY. Mr. JOHN WELLES. Of *Gloucester Hall, Oxford,* where he was colleague with Mr. Clement Barksdale, to whom he was a most eager opponent in the disputation (before mentioned, in the preceding page) at Winchcomb, in 1653. § It is to be wished that something better could have been related concerning him. ED.

THORNBURY [V. 25*l.* 15*s.* 8*d.*] Mr. HAINE. He was brother to Major General Haine.

WESCOT [R.] Mr. EDWARD ROGERS. He was ejected also at *Medley,* in Herefordshire. Probably one of the two was a sequestered living; but it is uncertain which of them. He was afterwards at *Chelmsford,* in Essex, and died pastor of a congregation there.

WESTERLEIGH [C.] Mr. RICHARD FOWLER. He was father to Dr. *Fowler,* Bishop of *Gloucester.* He had another son who lived and died a Nonconformist minister. He was a great man, both in ministerial abilities and labours.

WESTON

WESTON (Sub-edge) [R. S.] Mr. RICHARD COOPER. In the year 1648, he subscribed the testimony of the ministers in this county, as minister of *Tewkesbury*. § He is mentioned by *Atkins*, at this place.

WHITMINSTER [V.] See MORTON VALANCE.

₊ **WILLERSLEY** [R. S.] Mr. RICHARD FLAVEL. Father of Mr. *John Flavel*, of Dartmouth. He was an eminent and laborious minister, first at *Broomsgrove*, and then at *Hasler*, in Worcestershire; from whence he removed to this place, where he continued till 1660, when the old incumbent was restored. The loss of this living did not so much affect him as his want of a fixed place for the exercise of his pastoral function. He lived some time with his son at Dartmouth. A little before the Bartholomew ejectment, being near *Totness*, in Devonshire, he preached on *Hos.* vii. 6. ' The days of visitation are come; the days of recompence ' are come; *Israel* shall know it.' The application of this sermon was so close, that it offended some of his hearers, and occasioned his being carried before a justice of the peace; but they could not convict him, so that he was discharged. He afterwards quitted this country, and came to London; where he continued in the faithful and acceptable discharge of his office, till the time of the plague in 1665.; when he was taken and imprisoned in the manner following:—He was at Mr. *Blake's* house, in Covent-garden, where some good people had met privately for worship. While he was at prayer, a party of soldiers broke in upon them, with their swords drawn, and demanded their preacher; threatening some, and flattering others; but in vain. Some of the company threw a coloured cloak over Mr. *Flavel*, and in this disguise he was carried, with his hearers, to *Whitehall*. The women were dismissed; but the men were detained, and forced to lie all night upon the bare floor; and because they would not pay five pounds each, were inhumanly sent to *Newgate*, where the plague dreadfully raged. Here Mr. *Flavel*, and his wife, who went with him, were seized with this distemper. They were bailed out, but they both died.*

---

* The above account of Mr. Richard Flavel is extracted from the Life of his Son, Mr. John Flavel.

, Of thirty-eight persons taken and committed at the same time, nine died of the plague in *Newgate*, and nine or ten more after their discharge. In the same year, while the king and parliament were at Oxford, many of the old officers were clapped up, and several Nonconformists with them, (of whom old Mr. *Flavel* was one) upon pretended suspicion of a plot. It was suggested to the court, that while the city was forsaken by reason of the sickness, and the parliament on that account sitting elsewhere, the malecontents might take that as an opportunity to give some disturbance to the government; and that therefore it was adviseable to be beforehand with them. But neither in Mr. *Flavel's* case, nor the case of others, who suffered at that time, and on that occasion, was there any thing like a proof of guilt.

He was an affectionate preacher; [and a man of such extraordinary piety, that those who conversed with him said, they never heard a vain word drop from his lips.] He had another son besides him of Dartmouth, viz. Mr. *Phineas Flavel*, who was chaplain in the family of the right honourable *Edward* Lord *Russell*. It doth not appear that he ever had any settled congregation. He preached occasionally about London, and died in Westminster. He printed, *The deceitful Heart tried and cast.*

WINCHCOMB. Mr. CAMSHAW HELMES. After his ejectment he came to London, and died pastor of the church which was formerly Mr. *Freak's*. Dr. Walker relates something to his disadvantage, which may be as true as some other of his stories, which, upon enquiry, are found not to have the least shadow of a foundation.

WITCOMB. Mr. GRETORIX. There are two Rectories in this town.

WOOTON *under Edge* [V.] Mr. BODIN. After his ejectment he for some time preached privately at *Bath.*

YANWORTH (A Chapelry to *Hasleton*) Mr. FISHER.

—— Mr. JOSHUA HEAD. The place of his ejectment is uncertain. He afterwards preached at *Bourton* on the Water. He was a worthy man, of the *Baptist* denomination. § *Crosby* has nothing to add to this short account, which he quotes from Calamy, nor any reflection to make upon it.

The

The following persons afterwards conformed :

Mr. WILLIAM MEW, of *Easington.* He preached his farewell sermon, as the rest of the ejected ministers did; but on the Lord's-day following, he read, " I *A. B.* do declare " my unfeigned assent and consent, &c." without mentioning his own name. A minister (from whom the author had it) discoursing afterwards with him, told him that he must also go to the bishop, and *subscribe* as well as read ; to which he replied, That by his subscription he should only declare that he did read, " I *A. B.* &c." This [shameful equivocation] brought in him, who had been one of the Assembly at Westminster. Mr. BRITON, of *Biesley,* and several others of this county, to their great reproach, followed upon like grounds.

Mr. ALWAY, of *Upper-Grayling.*—Mr. FIDO, of *Cold-Aston.*—Mr. HALL, of *Beverston.*—Mr. NATH. HALL, of *Avening.*—Mr. SHENE or SHEVE, of *Old-Sodbury.*—Mr. C. SUMNER, of *Alveston.*—Mr. BARNSDALE, of *Frampton.* Mr. JOHN LEE, of *Barnsley,* all conformed.

MINISTERS EJECTED OR SILENCED

IN

HAMPSHIRE.

ALRESFORD [R.] Mr. TAYLOR. Whose character and history are now irrecoverably lost.

BADDESLEY. Mr. LANCASTER. All that is now known concerning him is, that he was a person of eminent skill in the Oriental languages. N. B. There are in this county two places of the name of Baddesley.

WORKS, Vindiciæ Evangelicæ ; or a Vindication of the Gospel, yet with the Establishment of the Law, &c.

BEADLEY. Mr. SAMUEL JEFFERSON.

BINSTED [Chap. to *Alton.*] Mr. JOHN YATES.

BISHOP'S STOKE [R. 200*l.*] Mr. HENRY COXE. Of *Pemb. Col. Oxford.* He was cast out to make way for Mr. T. Gawen, who is owned by Dr. Walker, to have been a Papist : *(Attempt,* part ii. p. 77.) Whether it was in 1660 or 1662, the Dr. and Mr. Anthony Wood are not agreed. Mr. *Coxe,* after his ejectment, retired to a farm-house called *Boyctt Farm,* in the parish of South Stoneham, where his old friends and hearers resorted to him, and there he preached to them some years. Upon the Five-mile-act, he removed to *Botly,* and afterwards to *Southampton.* While he lived in this latter place, he preached about a mile out of town, towards Stoke, and there also many of his old people attended him, among whom he continued his labours to his death. He was buried at Stoke church. From the inscription on his grave-stone, it appears that he died *June* 13, 1679, aged 56. He was an agreeable preacher, a courteous man, of good address, and congregational in his judgment.

BRAMSHOT

BRAMSHOT [R. 200*l.*] Mr. JOHN CORBET. Of *Magd. Hall, Oxf.* Born and brought up in the city of Gloucester. He was a great man every way. He began his ministry in his native place (where he lived some years) under Dr. Godfrey Goodman, a Popish bishop of the Protestant church. † Here he continued in the time of the civil wars, of which he was a mournful spectator. His account of the Siege of Gloucester, is, reckoned to give as good an insight into the rise and springs of the war, as any thing extant in a narrow compass. He afterwards removed to *Chichester,* and thence to *Bramshot,* were he was ejected in 1662. He then lived privately in and about London, till K. Charles's Indulgence, in 1672, at which time a part of his old flock invited him to *Chichester,* where he continued his labours with great assiduity and success. During his residence there, Bp. *Gunning,* out of his abundant zeal, gave a public challenge to the Presbyterians and Independents, the Baptists and the Quakers, and appointed three days for the disputation : the first for the two former, and the other two for the two latter.

On the first day, a considerable congregation being present in the church, and Mr. *Corbet* and others being ready to make their defence, the Bishop came and took the pulpit, having a heap of books about him, and from his fort fired very fiercely, his whole harrangue being full of sharp invectives. Schism and rebellion were the ball he shot, poisoned with the strongest venom ; forgetting that ' A bishop should ' be no brawler.' Mr. *Corbet,* who was known to have a great command of himself, earnestly but modestly offered to interpose by way of defence ; but the Bishop would hear very little, and told him. He should answer by writing, and take another time and place. Mr. *Corbet* desired, as was most reasonable, that their defence should be at the same time and place with the crimination. When his Lordship would hear nothing, Mr. *Corbet,* turning to the mayor and his brethren present, desired that they would be pleased to assign some convenient time and place for the hearing of his vindication ; but they declined it.

When the Baptist's day came, the Bishop treated them with greater civility. It may be he was the cooler now, for

---

† This the bishop himself owned in his last testament, which is in print. *Wood* in his account of him quotes his very words ; and yet gives a more favourable character of Him than he does either of *Wilkins* or *Tillotson.*

the heat he had let out the day before. The Quaker's day
being the last of the three, they had time to summon in their
friends from all quarters, and several came from Hampshire
and Surrey, as well as the remote parts of Sussex. When
the Bishop fell to railing, they paid him in his own coin, and
with interest too. And when, in some surprize, he left the
pulpit and the church, some of them followed him home,
and one of them, as he passed along, plucking him by the
sleeve, said, " The hireling fleeth, the hireling fleeth."

After this, Mr. *Corbet* drew up his defence in writing,
and taking with him some substantial citizens, went to the
Bishop's palace, to make a tender of it to his lordship, but
he refused to receive it. Mr. *Corbet* intreated him to read
it; and when he refused, began to read it himself; but the
bishop would not suffer him to proceed, and urged him to
write now, offering him pen, ink, and paper. Mr. *Corbet*
replied, That was needless, for he had written already, what
he now tendered, at home, where he could be more composed.
The Bishop persisting in the refusal, Mr. *Corbet* finally told
him, Since nothing else would do, he must take some other
method for his vindication ; intimating that he would use the
press. When Mr. *Corbet* went away, the Bishop followed
him to his palace-gate with bitter railing ; but He, under all,
expressed the greatest temper and meekness, returning good
words and good wishes for very evil ones.

Mr. *Corbet* was for many years afflicted with the stone,
which at last proved the cause of his death. While the pain
was tolerable, he endured it, and did not desist from preaching, till within a fortnight of his being brought up to London in order to be cut. But before that operation could be
performed, death put an end to his sufferings, *Dec.* 26, 1680.
His funeral sermon was preached by Mr. *Baxter*, who gives
him this character :† " He was a man of great clearness and
soundness in religion, and blameless in conversation. He
was of so great moderation and love of peace, that he hated
all that was against it, and would have done any thing for
concord in the church, except sinning against God, and
hazarding his salvation. He was for catholic union, and
communion of saints, and for going no further from any
churches or christians than they force us, or than they go
from Christ. He was for loving and doing good to all, and

† See *Baxter's* Works, vol. iv. p. 911. or *Tong's* Biographical Collections.

living

living peaceably with all, as far as was in his power. Something in Episcopacy, Presbytery, and Independency he liked, and some things he disliked in all. He was true to his conscience, and valued not the interest of a party or faction. If all the Nonconformists in England had refused, he would have conformed alone, if the terms had been reduced to what he thought lawful. He managed his ministry with faithfulness and prudence. He had no worldly designs to carry on, but was eminent in self-denial. He was not apt to speak against those by whom he suffered, nor was he ever pleased with ripping up their faults. He was very careful to preserve the reputation of his brethren, and rejoiced in the success of their labours as well as of his own ; and a most careful avoider of all divisions, contentions, or offences. He was very free in acknowledging by whom he profited, and preferring others before himself. He was much in the study of his own heart, as is evident from the little thing of his that is published, called *Notes for Himself*, &c. He had good assurance of his own sincerity, and yet was not altogether without his mixture of fears. He had the comfort of sensible growth in grace. He easily perceived a notable increase of his faith, and holiness, his heavenliness, and humility, and contempt of the world, especially in his latter years, and under his affliction, as the fruit of God's correcting rod; and died at last in great serenity and peace."—There is no occasion for wonder that such a man should fall under the censure of Mr. *Wood*. His commendation had really been a disgrace.

WORKS. An Historical Relation of the military Government of *Gloucester*, from the Beginning of the Civil War to the removal of Col. Massie to the Command of the Western Forces, 4to. 1645; (which Mr. Baxter much commends in his Preface to his Confession of Faith.)..A Vindication of the Magistrates of Gloucester from the Calumnies of Robert Bacon; to which is added, The Discussion of ten Questions, tending to the Discovery of close Antinomianism...The Interest of England in the Matter of Religion; in two Parts, 1661, 8vo. (an admirable book, where any man may clearly see the spirit and design of those called Presbyterians, at and after the Restoration.)..The Kingdom of God among Men ; a Tract of the sound State of Religion: to which is added, A Discussion of the Point of Church Unity and Schism. ..A Discourse of the Religion of England...Self Employment in Secret, containing Memorials for his own Practice, his Evidences

s 3   upon

upon Self-Examination, &c.†...And his REMAINS; containing a Discourse of the Church, of the Ministry, of Certainty and Infallibility; and the true State of ancient Episcopacy; a Consideration of the present State of Conformity in the Church of England. A Discourse of Divine Worship. An Exposition of Jonah, ii. 1—4. An Exposition of John xvi. 33. An Enquiry into the Oxford oath; A Plea for Communion with the Church of England, &c. With a modest Defence of his ministerial Nonconformity, and the Exercise of his Ministry, in Answer to the Bishop of Chichester's (Gunning's) Charge against him. An Explication of the Decrees and Operations of God, &c. And an Account of the Principles and Practices of the Nonconformists; shewing that their Religion is no other than what is professed in the Church of England...He had also a considerable hand in compiling Mr. Rushworth's first Volume of Historical Collections; which, by competent judges, is reckoned a master-piece of the kind.

BROKENHURST [C. or D.] Mr. ROBERT TUTCHIN. Second son of Mr. Robert Tutchin, of *Newport*, in the Isle of *Wight*. After his ejectment he had a separate church in the New Forest, and a lecture at *Lymington*, where he died, and was buried in the chancel of the church.

CALBOURN [R. 202*l*.] Mr. EDWARD BUCKLER. He was much the gentleman, a good preacher, and a good writer. He had been one of *Oliver Cromwell*'s chaplain's, and preached before him four times a year, for which he received 20*l*. After he was ejected he lived privately at *Bradford Abbis*, in Dorset, where he followed the business of malting, and preached but seldom; except in and about the year 1672, at a gentleman's house, where few if any were admitted besides the family. He frequently attended at the public church.

† A very small, but excellent piece, recommended by Mr. *Howe*, of which there has been a new edition, by the Rev. Mr. UNWIN, a respectable clergyman, in consequence of the character given of it by Mr. *Job Orton*, in a letter to Mr. Steadman, communicated by the late Sir James Stonehouse. "There is no book (says Mr. Orton) I have so often read as *Corbett's Self Employment*. It is always upon my desk: my vade mecum in travelling: by my bed-side in sickness. I can read a little in that, when I can read nothing else. It is the best manual I know for a christian minister. His prudential maxims are excellent, founded on much experience and knowledge of mankind. And, excepting a few phrases common in those days, there is great sprightliness and strength in it. It is indeed (as Mr. Howe in his preface calls it) the anatomy of the heart: and happy the heart that can trace his image in itself. It will furnish excellent materials for addressing conscience, and directing your hearers to judge of their spiritual state, and for preaching experimentally, which is the life and soul of preaching."—This letter has lately been published in a Collection of Mr. Orton's Letters to a young clergyman.

WORKS.

WORKS. A Catechism.—A Treatise, entitled, God All in All.—And an Assize Sermon.—He also left some things in manuscript.

CHRIST-CHURCH [V.] Mr. John Warner.

CLANFIELD [two parishes] Mr. Dyman.

COWES West (Isle of Wight) Mr. Simon Pole. Of Oxf. University. He was born in Somersetshire, and after his ejectment he went thither, where he was seized as he was preaching, and imprisoned seven years. This long confinement brought distempers upon him, which, it was believed, shortened his days. He was a bold spirited man, and an excellent preacher. He had a large family, and was very poor. Samuel Dunch, Esq. (who was a great friend to all the suffering ministers whom he knew) often relieved him.

CRAWLEY [R. 300l.] Samuel Tomlyns, M. A. Of Trin. Col. Camb. He was born at Newbury, in Berks, and was qualified for the university at thirteen years of age. When he quitted it he officiated some time as a chaplain; and at length was presented to this living of Crawley, in 1655, from which he was ejected with his brethren in 1662. He afterwards preached privately as he had opportunity, till he was called by a congregation to the city of Winchester: where, for nine years, he continued exposed to great hardships and difficulties, on account of his nonconformity. From thence he removed to Hilcot, in Wiltshire, and there he preached to a few people in his own house, till K. James published his Declaration for liberty of conscience; upon which he was chosen by a congregation in Andover, with whom he spent a few years. In the beginning of the reign of K. William and Q. Mary, he removed from thence to Marlborough, where he continued his ministry for many years. And there, after having been for several months under great pains and bodily infirmities, he at length finished his course, June 18, 1700, in the 68th year of his age. His funeral sermon was preached by Mr. Benj. Flower, of Chippenham, on Isa. lvii. 1. He was a good critic in Greek and Hebrew, and an excellent textuary: A man of great gravity and wisdom, and a good casuist. He was mighty in the scriptures; for his head, memory, heart, and tongue were full of them. And he had a general reputation, as a scholar, a preacher, and a divine.

s 4   WORKS.

WORKS. A Funeral Sermon for Mr. Walter Marshal, of Hursley...Another for Mr. Richard Moor, of Hungerford...The Justification of Believers by the Righteousness of Christ only... The humble Sinner's Supplication for Pardon...The preaching of Christ, and the Prison of God, on 1 *Pet.* iii. 19...The necessity of breaking up our Fallow-ground, &c...The great Duty of Christians to go forth without the Camp to Jesus ; on *Heb.* xiii. 13. ...Supplication to the Sovereign Judge, the Duty of the best of Men...Christ's second Coming, and the Purging of his Kingdom ; two Sermons, on *Matt.* xiii. 41...And a Discourse on 2 *Cor.* iii. 6, at a Meeting of Ministers.

CRUNDEL [V.] Mr. HUMPHREY WEAVER. Of *Oxford* University. After his ejectment from this valuable living, he continued preaching in his own house, in the parish of *Crundel*, to the time of his death, to an auditory of serious Christians, of whom he would take nothing for his labour ; God having blessed him with a large increase of his estate, after his ejectment. But he met with a great deal of trouble from his enemies, on account of his Nonconformity, and his preaching so constantly. At the time of the Five-mile-act they sought to take him up ; but he bought an house at a little above five miles distance, whither his auditory followed him: and he continued preaching to them to the very last Sabbath of his life. He died in 1696. He was a good scholar, a great preacher, a zealous Nonconformist, and a man of a generous and a very public spirit.

DROXFORD [R. S. 300*l.*] Mr. ROBERT WEBB. The former incumbent, immediately upon the Restoration, came to take possession of this living, and thrust out Mr. *R. Webb* and his family with their goods in a rough and violent manner. A gentleman in the neighbourhood, tho' a Roman catholic, was so concerned at such severity, that he humanely received them for the present into his own house, till in a little time the wife of Richard Cromwell, Esq. sent a coach for them, and brought them to a house of theirs. Mrs. *Webb*, being big with child, fell in labour in the carriage. Mr. *Webb* had a large family, and was very poor. *S. Dunch*, Esq. of *Badsly*, was kind to him as long as he lived ; and at his death left him 10*l.* a year during life. He was a good scholar, and an eminent preacher. He died *Aug.* 14, 1675, aged 42.

N. B. For Mr. NOAH WEBB, see *Upton Grey.*

ELLINGHAM

ELLINGHAM (or *Milbrook*) Mr. THOMAS BROWN. A man of great piety and learning, who died soon after he was ejected.

EWHURST [Chap. to *Basingstoke*] JOHN HARMAR, M. A. Of Winchester-school, and *Magd. Col. Oxford*. He was Greek professor in that University, and was ejected soon after the Restoration. He was so excellent a scholar, that even *Wood* gives him this character : " He was a most " excellent philologist, a tolerable Latin poet, and was happy " in rendering Greek into Latin, or Latin into English, or " English into Greek or Latin, whether in prose or verse." Upon his ejectment he retired to *Steventon*, in this county, where he died in 1670.

WORKS. Praxis Grammatices : Verum et genuinum Declinationum et Conjugationum usum liquidò indicans, &c...Janua Linguarum ; sive Methodus et ratio Compendaria et facilis ad omnes Linguas ad Latinam verò maxime aperiens...Eclogæ Sententiarum et Similitudinum, e D. Chrysostomo decerptæ: Gr. et Lat, cum Annot ..Protomartyr Britannus ; seu Elegia Sacra in Conversionem et Martyrium S. Albani...Lexicon Etymologicon Græcum, junctim cum Scapula...Epistola ad D. Lambertum Osbalstonum, Cui intexitur Apologia pro honoratiss. illustrissimoque viro ac Domino, D. Johannæ Williams Archiep. Eborac. et Angliæ Primate. ..Oratio Oxoniæ habita, in Schola Publica Linguæ Græcæ assignatâ, 15 Aug. 1650...Oratio, Serenissimi Protectoris Elogium Complectens, Oxoniæ habita 30 Kal. Maii 1654, 4to. Ad Protectorem Carmina de Pace, cum Belgis sancitâ. Vindiciæ Academiæ Oxoniensis ; sive Oratio Apologetica qua Exercitiorum Academicorum in Trimestre vacat. a Crimine vindicatur, 8vo. 1662. ..M. Tulli Ciceronis Vita, ex optimis quibusque Scriptoribus delibata, et in Compendium reducta, 8vo. 1662. Oratio Panegyrica in honor, Car. 2. &c. in Angliam, Plaudente Orbe Britannico, remigrant. Habita Ox. 27 Maii, 1660. He also translated the Assembly's Shorter Catechism into Greek and Latin, &c.

EXTON [R.] Mr. JOHN RIDGE.

FARLINGTON [R.] Mr. ROBERT LECESTER.

FORDINGBRIDGE [V. S.] Or some place near it. Mr. CROSSIN. Mr. Cuff, the old incumbent, was reinstated at the Restoration ; tho' he was a person of so little seriousness, that he took the liberty to jest in the pulpit. Mr. Crossin afterwards went into *Devonshire*, where he found so much favor with the Bp. of *Exeter*, as to be continued in a living there some time after 1662, without re-ordination.

FRESHWATER

FRESHWATER [R. 300*l.*] JAMES CRESWICK, B. D. Fellow of *St. John's Col. Camb.* He was a native of *Sheffield*, in Yorkshire. On *Aug.* 24, 1662, and for some months before, he preached on those words, *Heb.* x. 34. ' And took joyfully the spoiling of your goods, knowing in ' yourselves that ye have in heaven a better and an enduring ' substance.' He continued to preach two Lord's-days beyond the time to which the law confined him, unless he had conformed; for which, two of his parishioners, his great enemies, informed against him, and complained of him to Dr. *Morley*, Bishop of *Winchester*, who was holding a visitation. Mr. *Creswick*, understanding their intention, made application himself to the Bishop, and told his Lordship what he had done; alledging, that his continuing to preach was, because he was willing the parish should be supplied till another incumbent came. He added, that he conceived himself sufficiently justified in what he did, as he was yet Fellow of *St. John's Col.* which gave him a privilege to preach in any church or chapel, &c. And producing his licence, he took the freedom to ask the Bishop, Whether that was invalidate by the Act of uniformity? The Bishop replied, He thought not. Whereupon Mr. *Creswick* farther said, Then he thought he might still preach, tho' he did not expect any recompence. But on the Sabbath following, his lordship ordered the churchwardens to keep the doors shut against him, and there was no preaching at all.

Mr. *Creswick* was a man of great abilities; well skilled in the learned languages, and an accurate preacher, tho' he was sometimes so afflicted in his eyes as to be incapable of using notes. He was a man of great piety, and of very exemplary patience under the tormenting pains of the stone. He used frequently to say, " Lord, I am thine, and thou " canst do me no wrong. I had rather have health of soul, " in a body full of pain, than health and ease of body in a " distempered soul." He died in *Feb.* 1692, aged 75, at *Beal*, in Yorkshire, where he had purchased an estate of 300*l.* a year, and preached to a poor ignorant people.

WORKS. Mr. Oliver Heywood published a posthumous Tract of his, entitled Advice to an only Child; where his character may be seen. He also had prepared for the press another tract, concerning Man's Fall, and his Recovery by Christ.

GODSHIL (in the Isle of *Wight*) [V.] Mr. THOMAS CLARK. He was one of the ministers who preached the lecture at *Newport.* Soon after he was ejected his wife died, and left him only one daughter, who was entertained in the families where he was chaplain. In that capacity he lived with Sir *Anthony Irby,* ten years. He there became acquainted with Sir *Philip Harcourt,* Lady *Irby*'s nephew. who came often to visit her, and who was so extremely pleased with Mr. *Clark*'s conversation (which was very facetious) that he greatly importuned him to come and live with him, at *Stanton Harcourt,* in Oxfordshire, to which he at length consented. In 1675 he removed thither, and took his daughter down with him. Not long afterwards, Sir *Philip*'s only son, Simon Harcourt, Esq. (afterwards Lord Harcourt) clandestinely married her. Upon this, Mr. Clark soon quitted the family [being most probably *ejected*] and went to *Portsmouth,* where he spent the remainder of his days. But in what manner doth not appear.

GUERNSEY Island. Mr. Le Marsh.

HARTLEY WASPIL [R. 120*l.*] Mr. John Jennings. Of *Christ-Church, Oxf.* He was born in the parish of *Oswestry,* in Shropshire, A. D. 1634. Having enjoyed his living about four years, he resigned it in 1662. He was afterwards tutor to Mr. *Noyes,* of Tuckwell, and then chaplain to Mrs. Pleasant, of *Langton,* in Leicestershire. While he lived here, he gathered a church out of that neighbourhood, and for some years after this Lady's death, he continued in her house, in which his congregation used to assemble. At length he moved both his habitation and his meeting to *Kibworth,* a village two miles from *Langton,* where he bought a little estate. There he died in the year 1701. He was a serious and laborious preacher, who spent much time in his study. He was of a cheerful temper, and was well respected both by his people and by the neighbouring ministers; and was very easy in that retired course of life which he led in the latter part of his time, in this obscure situation. He left two sons, who were brought up to the ministry among the Dissenters, [and were both of them eminent tutors of dissenting academies. The one, Mr. *John Jennings,* was minister at *Kibworth,* and afterwards at *Hinckley,* in Leicestershire. He was tutor to the celebrated Dr. *Doddridge,* (who succeeded him in that office) and was the author of two excellent tracts, on Preaching Christ, and on Experimental preaching. The younger son was the late Dr. *David Jennings,* pastor of the congregation (now Mr.

Noah

Noah Hill's) in Old Gravel-lane, Wapping, and tutor of the academy, afterwards removed to *Hoxton,* but now extinct.]

HACKFIELD. Mr. Goss.

HAYLING Isle [V.] Mr. JOHN ROWEL.

*** HOUGHTON [R. 900*l.*] THOMAS WARREN, A. M. He was presented to this rectory by the parliament in the year 1650. The presentation (which passed the seal *Feb.* 6,) represents the vacancy as occasioned *per relictionem ultimi incumbentis ;* but whether this is to be understood of a voluntary resignation, or of a sequestration, may admit of a doubt. The latter is most probable. Mr. *Warren* appears to have been one of those Presbyterian divines who did not scruple conformity upon the terms of K. Charles's Declaration, of *Oct.* 25, 1660; for at the close of this year he went to Scotland, and was ordained both deacon and presbyter the same day *(Dec.* 22.) by the Bp. of *Whithern.*† On the 1st of *Feb.* following he received episcopal letters of institution and induction to his rectory from Dr. *Bryan Duppa,* Bp. of Winchester, and was accordingly inducted into it by Mr. Anthony Hilary, rector of Broughton, *Feb.* 7.—After his ejectment in 1662 he might have had great preferment in the church, (the king offering him the bishopric of Salisbury, and that of Winchester;) but he could not conscientiously accede to the new terms. However he lived unmolested in the worst of times. He was pastor to a private congregation at *Rumsey,* in this county; and upon K. Charles's Indulgence, in 1672, he took out a licence as a Presbyterian minister, to preach in the house of Mr. *Tho. Burbank,* in that town, which is dated *July* 1, and is signed by lord *Clifford's* own hand, and likewise by that of the king himself. It appears from this licence, that the ministers who complied with the terms of it, were allowed to preach, not only in the place therein specified, but in any other allowed by the king's declaration of *March* 15, 1672. When K. *James* granted the Indulgence, Mr. *Warren,* being desirous to know the sentiments of the London-ministers con-

† The testimonials are signed *Thomas Candidæ Casæ Episcopus.* The original, as also the parliament's presentation, and the other papers and instruments referred to in the above account, are now in the editor's hands, by the favour of the Rev. Mr. *Henry Taylor,* late of *Croydon,* who, by the mother's side, is a great-grandson of Mr. *Warren's.*

cerning

cerning it, and what part it was most adviseable to take, wrote
to one Mr. *Leigh* in London for information, who gave him
an answer, of which the following extract seems worth
preserving:

" Worthy sir,——The sentiments of ministers here in relation to the king's Declaration, are best explained by their
practice. I find all make use of it freely.—The Presbyterian
ministers have presented a gratulatory address to his majesty,
with about thirty hands to it. Mr. Hurst, Veale, Rosewell,
Chester, Reynolds, Turner, and three more, as I hear, did
attend his majesty. *Hurst* delivered it. The pleasant coun-
tenances of the courtiers, as also his majesty's courteous words,
looks and behaviour, did bid them welcome. After it was
read, I am informed, his majesty thus expressed himself, or to
this purpose: " Your address is very acceptable. I am well
" pleased to see so good an issue of my Declaration, as the
" ease and peace of my subjects. It is my judgment, that
" conscience is under God's empire, and not to be forced in
" matters of religion. Go home; make your hearers good
" christians, and then they will be good subjects. You have
" a *magna charta* for your property; I would you had it
" also for this liberty. But do not surmise that I have any
" unknown design, for my Declaration is a true interpreter
" of my mind." I find that most, if not all, judge it *good
manners* to thank his majesty for this great favour. Many.
I find are not well pleased with this liberty, much less with
the addresses. That God would give us assistance, direction,
courage, and perseverance in the way of duty, is the request
of

  London, April 30, Your obliged friend and servant,
    1687.   *William Leigh*."

Mr. *Warren* continued preaching at *Rumsey* eighteen
years, and gathered a large congregation, which continues in
a flourishing condition to this day. He ceased not from his
labours in the latter part of his life, tho' he was almost blind.
The day before his death he discoursed freely with a friend,
and gave him a short history of his earthly pilgrimage; which
he concluded with these words: " And now I am neither
" afraid to die, nor unwilling."—From the inscription upon
his grave-stone in *Rumsey* church, it appears that he died *Jan.*
27, 1694, aged 77. He is there stiled " a learned, pious,
" and faithful minister of Christ; a solid and nervous assertor
" of discriminating grace and FREED will." He was suc-
                  ceeded

ceeded in his congregation at Rumsey by Mr. *John Goldwire, junior.* He was a man of considerable note for ministerial abilities, and of an uncommonly mild and gentle spirit. He was engaged in a controversy with one *Eyre* of Salisbury, in consequence of a sermon which he preached before that corporation, on the subject of Justification, and he appears to have been a thorough master of his subject, and to have greatly the advantage of his adversary. He writes not only like a scholar, and an able disputant, but as a zealous advocate for truth and holiness. The following is the title of the book at length, which contains all his

· WORKS. Unbelievers not Subjects of Justification, nor of mystical Union to Christ; being the sum of a sermon preached at New-Sarum; with a vindication of it from the objections and calumniations cast upon it by Mr. *W. Eyre* in his *Vindiciæ Justificationis;* together with animadversions upon the said book, and a refutation of that anti-fidian and anti-evangelical error asserted therein, *viz.* The justification of infidels, or the justification of a sinner before and without faith. Wherein also the conditional necessity and instrumentality of faith unto justification, together with the consistency of it with the freeness of God's grace, is explained, confirmed and vindicated, &c. *Prov.* xvii. 15. Dedicated to the mayor, the court of aldermen, &c. of New-Sarum.

*** HURSLEY [V.] Mr. WALTER MARSHAL. Of *New Col. Oxf.* Of which he became Fellow. He was also chosen Fellow of the college at Winchester. In regard to church government he was esteemed a Presbyterian. After his ejectment he was pastor of a congregation at *Gosport,* where ' he was a burning and shining light.' He was much exercised with troubled thoughts for many years; and had, by many mortifying methods, sought peace of conscience, but his troubles still increased. Whereupon he consulted others, particularly Mr. *Baxter,* whose writings he had been much conversant with, who told him that he took them too legally. He afterwards consulted Dr. *T. G.* an eminent divine, [probably *Thomas Goodwin*] giving him an account of the state of his soul, and particularizing his sins which lay heavy on his conscience; who told him " he had forgot to mention the greatest sin of all, that of unbelief, in not believing on the Lord Jesus for the remission of his sins and the sanctification of his nature." Hereupon he set himself to the studying and preaching CHRIST, and attained to eminent holiness, peace of conscience, and joy in the Holy Ghost. The book he published, mentioned below, was the fruit of his experience.

perience. A little before his death he said to those about
him, that he died in the full persuasion of the truth, and in
the comfort of that doctrine which he had preached. His
dying words were ‘ The wages of sin is death, but the gift
‘ of God is eternal life thro' Jesus Christ.’ Mr. *Tomlyns*
preached his funeral sermon.

WORKS. The Gospel Mystery of Sanctification opened, &c.
to which is added, a Sermon on Justification. [*Note.* This book
was abridged, and many passages in it, which were liable to
abuse, very judiciously guarded against an Antinomian construction, by the late pious, sensible, and useful Mr. *Benjamin Forfitt*,
who died at *Hackney*, in *March*, 1773.]

*** KINGSWORTHY. Mr. JOHN HOOK. After his eject-
ment he was pastor of a dissenting congregation at *Basingstoke*.
Mr. *Joseph Barber*, of London, who was some time minister
at that place, gives the following acount of him, which he gathered from some elderly people there. He lived here many
years in reputation and usefulness. He was a holy, humble
man ; of exemplary life and conversation. His memory
was very precious to his people after he was dead. His preaching was sententious, and they treasured up many of his
sayings, among which they related the following :—“ A
“ new heart consists of an enlightened mind, a renewed will, a
“ tender conscience, and sanctified affections.—An hypocrite
“ is in the worst condition of any man upon earth ; for he is
“ hated of the world because of his profession, and hated of
“ God because he has no more than a profession.” As an
encouragement to christians to ‘ fight the good fight of faith,’
he would often say, “ The conflict may be sharp, but the
“ victory is sure; the reward is great, and the crown is
eternal.”

§ In addition to these, the following have since been received, with some further account of Mr. *Hook* :*—“ Live
“ by the spirit of Christ, and aim at the glory of Christ.”
—“ 'Tis grace to be *in* him, and glory to be with him.”—
“ Some are condemned to an estate; others are exalted to
“ poverty.” *James* i. 9. 10.—“ When the root is bitter-
“ ness, the blossom will flie up as dust.”—“ It will go hard

* From Mr. Joseph Jefferson, the present minister of Basingstoke, who
selected them from a number of papers put into his hands by a descendant of
Mr. Hook, who also presented to him a Bible, containing marginal notes
and references, chiefly in short-hand : likewise a volume of manuscript Sermons, written by Mr. Hook's father.

“ with

" with men if they be found in the guilt of the least sin, or
" [only] in the worth of the best duty."—" We should learn
" to do natural things in a spiritual way, and spiritual things
" in a natural way."—" By Faith we enjoy God, by Love
" we enjoy our neighbours, and by Patience we enjoy our-
" selves."

Mr. *John Hook* was the son of Mr. *Wm. Hook*, of whom
an account is given, Vol. I. p. 184. He continued to preach
after he was blind, and died in peace, at the age of 76. In
the burying ground at Basingstoke, is the following inscription on his tomb-stone :

M. H. T. Virum verè reverendum Johannèm Hook,
Evangelio salutofero Dudum devotum Present. ΘΕΑΝΘ-
ΡΩΠΟΥ vivificam Sperantem Sacris Libris admodum versa-
tum Eximiè doctum nec non Insigni Pietate ornatum.
Obiit Anno C. S. 1710. ÆT. S. 76.

His funeral sermon was preached by Mr. *Ball*, on *John*
xiv. 3. A MS copy of it is preserved, of which the following is an extract.—" To you among whom our Rev.
Father lived, it need not be told what his excellences were ;
and to others, so brief an account as I am able to give is not a
sufficient tribute to his memory......I have within the space of
ten or twelve years had an opportunity of frequent converse
with him. As a scholar, no man could call him in question.
I remember an ingenious and learned gentleman, who was a
very capable judge, gave him the character of being learned
in the oriental languages ; and yet he told me himself, he
was near thirty years of age before he had any acquaintance
with the Hebrew—an evident argument that he thought it
his duty to cultivate his own mind....This made him a great
scribe in the kingdom of heaven ; able to bring out of his
treasury things new and old. He had the Greek Text of the
New Testament very much at command, and could readily
recite it upon any occasion. He did not only read the modern
systems of divinity and philosophy, but studied the holy
scriptures, those living oracles, from whence the man of God
is to fetch all his fulness. With these he was so well acquainted, in our English translation, that he could carry
them almost in his head. When his eye-sight failed him,
he could tell by feeling the book he generally made use of,
how many chapters were contained within such leaves, that
were offered to him : I can truly speak it, because I made
the experiment myself. His ministerial course was thro' the

4　　　　　　　　　　　　　　.good

good providence of God lengthened out among you to a con-siderable period. You must bless God, that he was continued to you so long. The great thing that he delighted in, was to convince men of their wretchedness by nature, and their need of Christ and his sufficiency to save sinners, and the wonderful display of God's love, wisdom and grace in the method of our redemption. The self-justiciary he laboured to convince of his erroneous apprehensions ; and he bent his endeavours to that noble end of exalting God, and the riches of his grace ; and to lay corrupted man as low as possible, that he that glories, may glory in the Lord. In his prayers he was humble, devout and affectionate. Sometimes I have been much moved with those expressions which have savoured of a deep self-abasement, flowing from an uncommon sense of God's awful majesty, and his unspotted holiness. His prayers did always abound with pithy sentences, and expressions of God's grace and man's unworthiness.

We in the ministry have lost a real friend ; those of us especially who are of the younger sort. I cannot forbear to mention to the honour of his memory, that he was very ready to encourage young men ; he used to pray much for us, and would give us good advice, and exhort us to study hard, to pray often, and to preach a crucified Redeemer. Tho' he was an ancient and able divine, yet he would not disdain the benefit of the prayers of the younger. I, do not know whether ever I parted with him without such a request on his part : " Pray for me, as I do for you." He would often enquire concerning the state of our church ; whether the gospel prevailed in the hearts of our hearers. Indeed all places sustain a considerable loss by his departure from us. We lose the benefit of his prayers to God, both ministers and people ; and if I mistake not, every man under his care he recommended to the divine blessing. He did not only teach you from the pulpit, but also his converse among you was instructive, by expounding difficult places of scripture, or propounding or answering profitable questions. He continued in his ministry and calling as long as his strength held out. When his service was done, he waited for his dissolution. He bore the weakness of old age with a becoming patience, desiring in God's time and way to be released. He was a blessed and faithful minister of Christ ; he endeavoured and desired the welfare of your souls ; and I will say it to your honour, that you have shewed yourselves to be a respectable people, in endeavouring his comfortable support,

during

during his continuance among you, when he became not
able to carry on his wonted service among you. What you
have done to him, you have done to a prophet of the Lord."

LONGSTOCK [V.] Mr. JOHN PINCKNEY. Of *Magd.
Hall, Oxford.* He was of the ancient family of the Pinck-
neys, of *Russel,* near Marlborough. His father Mr. Philip
Pinckney, was minister of *Denton,* in Wilts, between twenty
and thirty years, having a small maintenance, but a large
family. He had thirteen children, who lived to be men and
women. From Denton he removed to *Bemerton,* near
Sarum, (a good parsonage) and there he died, leaving behind
him a good reputation for piety and learning. This son of his
was observed in his tender years to be very religiously inclined. When he went to school, he was so diligent, that
he attained to more than common skill in the Latin and Greek
tongues, and especially the latter; insomuch that his master
used often to boast of his young Grecian. He went to Oxford
at the age of fourteen, where he studied so hard, that he
often allowed himself but four hours sleep. This however
impaired his health, and brought him into an ill habit of
body, which was afterwards a great hindrance to him in his
work. When he first entered on the ministry, he succeeded
his father at *Denton,* and afterwards at *Bemerton :* from
whence, about half a year before the Restoration, he removed
to *Longstock,* where he was much beloved, and found his
preaching very successful. And here, in 1662, he was
ejected.

He was very diligent in all the parts of ministerial service,
and would not have left his place, if he could have satisfied
his conscience as to the terms of conformity; for what estate
he had, would do but little towards the maintaining himself,
a wife and three children. After he was silenced, he continued with his family at *Longstock,* and attended on the ministry of his successor, whom he found to be an honest
good-humoured man, but not very able to study two sermons
a week; he therefore advised him one part of the day to adopt
some good printed sermons, and lent him a volume for this
purpose, the whole of which he delivered. While Mr.
Pinckney was in this place, he not only taught his people by
public preaching and catechizing, but instructed them privately
from house to house; and in this way he continued to endeavour to promote serious piety, when he was denied the liberty
of preaching in the church. They that were often in his
company

company observed, that he took a singular pleasure in talking, of heaven, and in such discourse as might help men forward in the way to it. The points which he chiefly insisted on, were not the comparatively little things that unhappily divide the christian church, but the essentials of religion; and particularly the divine original and authority of the holy scriptures, in the belief of which, he urged all to take care to be well established; and he endeavoured to help them in it, by discoursing in a manner suited to the capacities of those with whom he conversed. His extraordinary humility and exemplary meekness, procured him the good opinion of many from whom he dissented. He was very seldom seen in any heat or commotion; and when he was, the affairs of religion were always the occasion. He ever discovered a most compassionate concern for the *Jews*, and upon all occasions prayed earnestly for their conversion. He died *May* the 6th, 1680, being about 67 years of age.

MICKELMARSH [R. 300*l.*] Mr. JAMES TERRY. He was a very popular preacher, and continued the exercise of his ministry at *Odiham*, in this county, gratis, till sickness disabled him. He died *Sept.* 29, 1680, aged 71. He left many children; the eldest of whom, Mr. *Peter Terry*, conformed, and was minister in New-Sarum, a prebendary in the cathedral there, and rector of Upper-Clatford, near Andover.

MILBROOK [See *Ellingham.*]

MOTTON. Mr. JOHN CROFTS. After his ejectment he was chaplain to Lady Fiennes, at *Newtontony*, in Wiltshire.

NEWPORT (in the Isle of *Wight*) Mr. ROBERT TUTCHIN. He was so well beloved by the inhabitants of this town, that when he was turned out, they allowed him the same stipend as when he was their minister: so that they paid two ministers till his death. He had three sons, John, Robert and Samuel, all considerable men, and all silenced on the same day with himself. His successor, Mr. *Goldsmith,* preached his funeral sermon, and such was his respect for him, that he would not suffer him to be interred in the common burying-place, but ordered a grave for him within the church. § It is supposed that this Mr. *Tutchin* is the person referred to in *Hutchins*'s Note, as having been lecturer at *Bridport.* See WHITCHURCH.

T 2   ODIHAM

ODIHAM [V.] Mr. Samuel Tutchin. He was the third son of Mr. Robert Tutchin, of Newport. After his ejectment he went to the East-Indies, and was chaplain to the factory, at Fort St. George. He died there, and was buried by the factory, and his grave was adorned with a monument. The company also settled an annual pension upon his widow after his death.

OVERTON [R.] Mr. Thomas Kentish. Of *Pemb. Col. Oxf.* He was the son of Mr. Thomas Kentish, who was cast out of *Middleton*, in the bishopric of Durham, soon after the Restoration. Upon his ejectment, he came to London, and was pastor of a society in *Canon-street*. He was taken at Mr. Janeway's, and for some time confined in the *Marshalsea.* He was a very serious, useful, friendly, candid person. He died in 1695, and was succeeded in his congregation by Mr. *Thomas Reynolds.* He left two sons in the ministry; the one in *Southwark*, and the other at *Bristol;* who neither of them long survived their father.

PORTSEY [V.] William Bicknel, M. A. Of *Oxford* University. He was born at *Farnham*, in *Surrey.* When he left the university, he became assistant to Mr. *Robert Tutchin*, at Newport, in the Isle of Wight, and afterwards preached in *Porstey* island, from whence he was ejected in 1662. He lived afterwards at *Farnham*, and preached many years there and at *Alton*, as he could. Upon the Act of Toleration, he was chosen by the Dissenters of *Farnham* to be their pastor, and continued labouring among them till his death, in *Feb.* 1696. His funeral sermon was preached by Mr. *Prince*, of Ockingham. He was a man of good learning, and serious religion. A laborious, methodical, but plain preacher. He carefully watched over his flock, and would wisely and seriously rebuke their miscarriages. He was a faithful friend, and in his whole deportment very sincere and upright. He was free in discourse, and ready to give his advice wherever he thought it might be of use. He was a great sufferer for conscience-sake, which he bore with much patience. 'When he was reviled, he reviled not again.' He behaved like one who was very desirous that his 'moderation might be known unto all men.'

PORTSMOUTH [V.] Mr. Benjamin Burgess. A wise man, and very active, especially at the time of the Restoration. He preached a famous sermon before the Parliament, at Westminster-abbey, in that juncture, which discovered remarkable prudence.

—— Mr.

—— Mr. THOMAS BRAGG was also ejected at the same place.

*REANER [Q. Rowner.] Mr. GEORGE WHITMARSH.

RIPLY Mr. UP-JOHN.

ROCKBORN [C. or D. 200*l.*] JOHN HADDESLEY, M. A. Of *Corp. Chr. Col. Cambridge.* He was born at *Ward*† in Hertfordshire, in 1624. He was first minister of *Poole* in Dorsetshire, where he was committed to prison by Col. *Read* the governor, for refusing to observe a Thanksgiving-day appointed by *Cromwell.* After he had been some time confined, there came down an order of council, requiring him to leave the town. Hereupon he went to Sir Thomas Trenchard's, and lived in his family till *Rockborn* parsonage was given him by Sir Wm. Darrington. Here he was ejected by the Act of uniformity, but he continued for some time to live in the parish. At the coming out of King Charles's Indulgence, he was chosen by the Dissenters at *Salisbury* to be one of their ministers; and there he continued the remaining part of his life. Soon after the Declaration was called in, he was seized in his own house, and committed by the mayor and recorder of the city to the common prison; but one of his friends very confidently asserting in all companies that Mr. *Haddesley*'s imprisonment was illegal, a person who had a principal hand in it, was induced to consult with some who understood law better than himself, by whom he was told, that he could not answer for what he had done. Whereupon he sent privately to the keeper of the prison, and ordered him to let Mr. *Haddesley* out; which was done very silently, for the sake of those who committed him. This was a very seasonable deliverance; for his health was so much impaired by his confinement, that it is likely, if he had continued there much longer, it would have proved fatal.

Being set at liberty, he preached to his people as he had opportunity for several years; but in the latter end of K. Charles's reign, he very narrowly escaped being taken again, as he was preaching on a Lord's-day; but he was privately conveyed away, just before the assailants had forced open the doors of the meeting-place. Being disappointed, they vented their rage on the pulpit and seats, which they broke to pieces. After this he concealed himself, and was so nar-

† WARD is in *Hampshire.* Perhaps the place intended is WARE.

rowly

rowly watched, that he was forced to leave his house for
several months. But upon the liberty in 1687, he returned
to his people and to his work. He usually preached twice
every Lord's-day, and sometimes on the week-day also, till
about eight months before his death; when the congregation
called another minister to be co-pastor with him; after which
he preached once a day, till within a week of his death. On
June the 4th he preached with a very remarkable animation,
and died the next Lord's-day morning, *June* 11th, 1699, in
the 76th year of his age. He was very much of Mr. *Baxter's*
sentiments in the quinquarticular points, and of a catholic
healing spirit, with reference to church controversies. He
was pious, prudent, and humble; had an excellent gift in
prayer; and was a very useful preacher. But so excessively
modest, as to be under some restraint when any of his brethren were present, tho' they were much his inferiors.

RUMSEY [V.] Mr. JOHN WARREN. [Probably a relation of Mr. Thomas Warren, who was ejected from
Houghton, and who afterwards preached at this place.]

SELBORN [V.] JOHN FARROL, M. A. Fellow of
Magd. Col. Oxford. He was a humble, peaceable, laborious
divine; prudent and inoffensive in his conduct: Of a healthful constitution of body, and of a meek and even temper of
mind. He did not much resent the injuries of his adversaries,
nor was he soon cast down under the apprehension of trouble
attending his duty. He was of an active disposition; and
made his garden his diversion, when his labouring mind called for a relaxation from his studies, so as to become a noted
botanist. After the Restoration, he voluntarily resigned this
living to the former incumbent, as he was advised to do, and
retired to *Guilford* in Surrey, where he boarded young gentlemen who went to the free-school. When the Corporation-oath was imposed, not being satisfied to take it, he removed to *Farnham.* On *June* 14, 1669, he was taken up
near Godalming, and sent to the Marshalsea in Southwark,
for being found within five miles of a corporation, and for
preaching at *Godalming.* He continued six months in prison,
and sometimes said, " That was one of the most comfortable
" parts of his life, thro' the kindness of friends whom God
" raised up to administer relief to him in his troubles." His
enemies said, that they would not send him to prison again,
because he lived better there than at home. Perhaps this
might be one reason why the religious meetings in his own
house

house were afterwards so much connived at. His custom was to go to the public church, as his people also did, and either before or after to preach in private.

In the latter end of Bp. *Morley*'s days, he was frequently desired to visit his lordship; and upon repeated assurances of being welcome to him, he went, and was very respectfully entertained by him several times at his table. His lordship was free in discoursing with him upon past times; and when he spoke of Mr. *Dod* (who taught him *Hebrew*, and was other ways helpful to him) made this addition, " who is now in heaven." Surely therefore he could not (as some did) hold Puritanism to be a damning sin.—Mr. *Farrol* afterwards removed to *West-Horsley*, where he lived upon what he had of his own; till K. *James*'s liberty, when he removed to *Guilford*, and bestowed his labours between that place and *Godalming* and *Farnham*. § At last he removed to *Lymington* in Hampshire, where he was not idle; but preached frequently as opportunity offered, and Providence greatly favoured him; till by a gentle decay, the candle of life burning down to the socket, he expired, with a sweet savour. The morning before he died, his son, at his desire prayed with him; and no sooner had he ended, but with all the composure of mind imaginable, he himself began to pray to God and praise him, with a strong and articulate voice; which he continued doing for eight hours, without intermission, till, thro' want of strength, his speech failed; but his active and unwearied soul, even then discovered its continued exercise, by the motion of his lips and hands, till insensibly he fell asleep in Jesus, in the 80th year of his age.

SOMBORN [V.] Mr. JONES.

SOUTHAMPTON. *All-Saints*. Mr. NATHANIEL ROBINSON. After his ejectment, he was imprisoned for Nonconformity, with Mr. *Giles Say*. He continued preaching to a congregation of Dissenters in *Southampton* to the day of his death.

—— *St. Michael's*. Mr. GILES SAY. He was ordained at *Bishop's-Stoke* in this county, *May* 8, 1660, by Mr. H Cox, minister of the place, Mr. R. Symons of Southweek.

§ It is remarkable, that all these three places were endowed by a Clergyman, and were for many years united. Mr. *Ring*, lately deceased, supplied them all, the interest in each being sunk very low.

&c. After his ejectment in 1662, he preached in several places as he had opportunity, for which he met with trouble, and was sometimes imprisoned. After K. James's liberty, he was chosen pastor of a dissenting congregation at *Guestwick* in Norfolk, of which Mr. *Worts* had before been pastor; where he continued till his death, *April 7, 1692.* A son of his being at *Southweek*, where he had been at school, conversing with some of the Dissenters of that place, met with a woman of good repute for piety, who told him with great joy, That a sermon preached by his father thirty years before, on these words, ' The entrance of thy word giveth light, it ' giveth understanding to the simple,' was the means of her conversion. This his son, Mr. *Samuel Say*, was brought up to the ministry, and was useful among the Dissenters at *Ipswich* [from whence he was called to *Westminster*, where he succeeded Dr. Calamy, in the place where Dr. Kippis afterwards preached. The late Mr. *Isaac Toms*, minister of *Hadleigh*, married a daughter of his: an excellent woman, who died but a little before him.] §

SOUTHWEEK Mr. RICHARD SYMONS.

** TICHFIELD [R.] Mr. URIAN OAKES. In his childhood he was taken to *New-England*, by his pious parents, who were blessed with several worthy sons, by whose education in the college there at *Cambridge*, the family was rendered considerable. He was noted, from his infancy, for the uncommon sweetness of his temper; and his ready abilities, adorned by the grace of God, encouraged high expectations from him. When a lad of small stature, he published a little parcel of Astronomical calculations, with this apposite verse in the title-page;

Parvum parva decent, sed inest sua gratia parvis.

Having taken two degrees in the college, he preached his first sermon at *Roxbury*. He soon after returned to England,

§ Mr. Toms informed the Editor, that Mr. SAY wrote a full account of his father, for Dr. Calamy's use, but that it was too late to be inserted. This is much to be regretted, as such a piece of biography from his pen must have been valuable. Mr. DUNCOMBE, late of Canterbury Cathedral, says in a letter to the Editor, " I wish some more notice had been taken of Mr. *Samuel* " *Say*, as his abilities were very distinguished and his two Prose Essays, pub- " lished soon after his death, in 1745, were particularly admired." Some account of him, with copies of Letters to and from him, were inserted in the *Prot. Diss. Magazine*, where it was intimated that his Life and correspondence would probably be published. See Mr. Ray's Funeral Sermon for Mr. Toms.

where

where he grew in favour with God and man. After he had been a short time chaplain to one of the most noted persons then in the nation, he settled at *Titchfield*, where his preaching and and his living were such as became a minister of the gospel. There he might challenge the device and motto of Dr. *Sibbes*, a wasting lamp, with this inscription, *Prælucendo pereo* : " I perish by giving light " When he was ejected by the Act of uniformity, Col. *Norton* received him into his house, where his presence and prayers produced a blessing like that on the house of *Obed-Edom*. When the persecution was a little abated, he returned to the exercise of his ministry, in a congregation where Mr. *Symonds* was his colleague. Upon an invitation from Cambridge in New-England, he removed thither, and the church there was so sensible of the divine favour to them in giving them such a pastor, that they kept a day of thanksgiving on the account; when, being desired to preach, he took for his text, 2 *Cor*. xii. 11. *1 be nothing*. He was here very useful for many years. At length the college in Cambridge, languishing for want of a president, invited him to that office; but he would not, for some years, admit any title to this place but *pro tempore*; and soon after he had accepted the presidentship, he was arrested by a malignant fever, which quickly proved fatal.

He was on all accounts, a truly admirable person. Considered as a christian, he was full of all goodness; and, like a full ear of corn, he stooped with a most profound humility. Considered as a scholar, he was an eminent critic in all the points of learning. Considered as a preacher, he had few equals. Mr. *Increase Mather*, in a preface to a discourse of his, published after his death, says of him, " An age doth seldom produce such an one, so many ways excelling. Considering him as a divine, a scholar, and a christian, it is hard to say in which he did most exceed. I have often in my thoughts compared him unto *Samuel* among the prophets, inasmuch as he did truly fear God from his youth, and was betimes employed in holy ministrations, and was at last called to be the head of the sons of the prophets.—It may, without reflection upon any, be said, that he was one of the greatest lights that ever shone in this part of the world." He was of the Independent denomination, and discovered a very high opinion of that discipline, as being more scriptural and rational, and attended with much greater advantages than any other. He died *July* 25, 1681, aged 50.

WORKS.

WORKS. The conquering and unconquerable Christian-Soldier; a Sermon to the Artillery Company in Boston.—Another on the like Occasion at Cambridge, on Eccl. ix. 11.—A Fast Sermon on Is. xliii. 22.—A Sermon to the Gen. Court of the Massachuset-Colony, on Duter. xxxii. 22.

South TIDWORTH [R. 120*l*.] Mr. SAMUEL SPRINT. Of *Trin. Col. Camb.* He was son to the famous author of *Cassander Anglicanus*, and much of the same judgment, as to ecclesiastical controversies. He was born at *Thornbury* in Gloucestershire, about 1624. In the university he had Dr. *Isaac Barrow* for his chamber-fellow. They studied in concert, and went both together to Mr. *Abraham Wheelock*; to discourse with him about the *Arabic* language, which they were desirous to learn; but upon hearing how great difficulties they were to encounter, and how few books were in that language, and the little advantage that could be got by it, they laid aside their design. Upon Mr. *Sprint's* leaving the university, he was chosen master of the free-school at *Newbury* in Berkshire, where he continued several years, till he was called to *Tidworth*. He was an intimate friend of Mr. *Woodbridge*, and of the same pacific, healing, catholic spirit. A complete scholar, a very useful preacher, and a man of strict piety; of wonderful modesty and humility; and therefore contented to live in an obscure corner, tho' he had large offers elsewhere. His conversation was equally pleasant and profitable. His preaching was very instructive, but his delivery was not popular. His behaviour was such as recommended him to the esteem of all the neighbouring gentry. One of them (a noted justice of peace) invited him to his house, and desired his acquaintance, telling him, That he thought him a man of the most universal good character of any in the county; for he never heard any one speak ill of him: but they who most freely loaded other Nonconformists with reproaches, spoke very well of him.

And yet he was not secure from the ill-will of some of the neighbouring clergy, who were so severe and violent in prosecuting him, that he was to be excommunicated, for not receiving the sacrament in his parish church at *Christmas*, tho' his wife lay upon her death-bed at that very time. To prevent such a proceeding, Mr. *Sprint* rode to *Farnham*, to Bp. *Morley*, and told him his case; when his Lordship was pleased to assure him, That his chancellor should not treat him so severely as he expected: accordingly the prosecution was stopped. The Bishop made him stay to dine with him,
                                                                    and

and discoursed with him about his Nonconformity. Mr,
Sprint told him, That the declaring unfeigned *assent* and
consent was what he could not be satisfied to yield to. Upon
which his lordship said, He must not philosophize upon the
words *assent* and *consent*; nor suppose, that the parliament
did by *assent* mean an act of the understanding, and by *consent* an act of the will; for no more was intended, than
that the person so declaring, *would read the book*; and
therefore, if he would make the declaration in the words prescribed in the act, and then say, that thereby he meant no
more than that he would read the Common-prayer, he would
admit him into a living.

Mr. *Sprint* thanked his lordship, but could not think such
an expedient warrantable. He afterwards mentioned the
cross in baptism, as what he could not comply with. To
which the Bishop replied, " This was honest Mr. *Dod*'s
scruple," but gave no other answer than this: " That the
cross was only a visible profession of our believing in a crucified Saviour, in conformity to the practice of the primitive
christians who crossed themselves; declaring by this action,
as by words, that they were christians." But it did not appear to Mr. *Sprint*, that it might lawfully or safely be made
a term of communion: and for this reason among others, he
could not submit to use it. How the conversation issued,
doth not appear, but we may suppose it was amicably.
Mr. *Sprint* was very temperate and abstemious; which being
once taken notice of at a gentleman's table, one then present, who had lived in Bp. *Hinchman*'s family, told him,
" That if he became a Conformist, he must expect no great
preferment; for he once heard Bp. *Hinchman* recommend a
person to Abp. *Sheldon*, as one very fit for some ecclesiastical promotion; of whom the Abp. said, " I believe your
lordship is mistaken in the man: I doubt he is too puritanical:" to which the Bishop replied, I assure your grace he
is not; for he will drink a glass of wine freely."

With great thankfulness Mr. *Sprint* observed, and frequently mentioned, the care that divine providence took of
him and his numerous family, for he had six sons and two
daughters when he was cast out of his living. It was very
remarkable, that when he put the lives of three of his children into the little estate that he took at Clatford, near Andover, he was directed to pitch upon those two sons, to be of
the number, who were the only ones of all his eight children
that survived him. After he removed from *Tidworth*, which

was about the year 1665, he spent the remaining part of his life, which was about thirty years, in that obscure village ; preaching as opportunity offered at *Andover* (a mile from thence) and also at *Winchester.* He had but a very inconsiderable allowance from his people ; but was used to say, " If " the bottle and satchel held but out to the journey's end, it " is sufficient." He was exercised with a very lingering sickness, previous to his dissolution, thro' the whole of which he discovered earnest longings to be at rest. On his deathbed he declared his full satisfaction in the cause of Nonconformity.

UPTON-GREY. NOAH WEBB, M. A. Before his ejectment from this place, he had been cast out of *Chevely*, in Berkshire, which was a sequestration. He was a man of an excellent conversation, and a pattern of holiness : of great devotedness to God, and an ardent zeal for the good of souls. An excellent, plain, practical, useful preacher. After he left *Upper-grey*, he settled somewhere near *Frimly*, and afterwards removed to *Saunders.* He went about doing good, preaching almost continually in several places; neglecting no opportunity of service, tho' exposed to the greatest danger. He rode forty miles from his own house every week, for three quarters of a year together, to preach at *Auburn*, in Wilts. He died of a consumption in 1676, aged but about 43; having quite worn himself away with studying and preaching. His funeral sermon was preached and printed by Mr. *Daniel Burgess.*

WALLOP. Mr. MARRYOT. Three places of this name : *Upper, Nether* and *Middle.*

WEEK § [50*l.*] Mr. THOMAS NEWNHAM. Of *Oxford* University. He was the son of Mr. Thomas Newnham : born about 1631, at *Gotton*, in the Isle of Wight, an ancient family seat. His education in the island was first at Kingston school, and afterwards at the free-school at Newport, where he made some proficiency in grammar learning, with a brother of his who was designed for the university. But he refusing to go, the father asked his son *Thomas*; Whether He was willing to be a minister ? And he discovering an inclination to the office, was sent to *Oxford*, where he continued some years. He returned from Oxford to the

_____
† The former note here seemed not necessary to be repeated.

Island

Island with Dr. *Pettis*, who afterwards conformed, and was first rector of Gatcomb, in the Isle of Wight, and then of St. Botolph's without Bishopsgate, and they were both ordained together, by presbyters, in *Newport* church. Mr. *Newnham* being ejected from his living in 1662, for his Nonconforty, some of his parishioners shewed a particular respect for him, by carrying in their corn before Bartholomew-day, on purpose that he might have the tythe of it ; while some others, not so well affected to him, would not carry in theirs till afterwards, which it was observed, was in great part spoiled by excessive rains.

After his ejectment, (being persuaded that he was called of God to labour in the word and doctrine) he took all opportunities that offered to do good to souls. As he sometimes went to Whitwell church to hear Mr. Harrison, one Lord's day when he was there, Mr. Harrison not coming, the people desired Mr. *Newnham* to officiate ; who, that they might not be wholly disappointed, preached to them from the seat in which he was sitting. For this however, Mr. Harrison put him to a great deal of trouble and expence. He preached the word in season and out of season. In troublesome times, when many were sleeping in their beds, he was engaged in his master's business. God had given him a strong constitution of body, and he possessed great natural and acquired abilities for ministerial work. And such a gracious presence of the Spirit was with him while he was ministering in holy things, that he was never more in his element than when thus employed. He sometimes preached at *Roslin*, and *Yard*, and other places ; but more constantly to the church committed to his care at *Road, Bridge-Court* and *Stroud-Green*. His chief and most earnest desire was, to pluck sinners ' as brands out of the burning.' To this end did he ' reprove and rebuke with all authority,' endeavouring ' by the terrours of the Lord to persuade men.' He was in his sermons a *Boanerges*. With what an emphasis would he often close with those words, *Psalm* l. 22. ' Now consider ' this, ye that forget God, lest he tear you in pieces, and ' there be none to deliver you.'

He was blessed with a quick apprehension, a solid judgment, a tenacious memory, warm affections, and a ready utterance. Once at a meeting of the ministers at *Stroud-Green*, the person expected to preach not coming, several of the ministers present pleaded their unpreparedness for supplying his place. At length Mr. *Newnham* was prevailed

4

on to undertake it; and tho' he had no notes, as he commonly had, nor any expectation of preaching when he came thither, his performance was such, that he had the applause of those that heard him; and, it was said, he did not use notes in preaching afterwards. At another time, being to preach at his usual place on the Lord's-day, the Prince of *Orange's* fleet appeared that very day near the island, when he was coming to save the nation from popery and slavery in 1688. Upon this occasion he left the subject which he intended to have preached upon, and took another, suited to such an event of providence, on which his extemporaneous discourse greatly affected his people.

Mr. *Newnham* met with much trouble on account of his Nonconformity, being prosecuted, fined, &c. but he bore all with invincible patience, courage, and constancy of mind. Being threatened by a justice of peace, that his books should be taken from him, he replied to this effect: " That he " blessed God, if he had no book but the bible, he questioned " not but he should be able to preach the gospel."—When the Conventicle-act passed, he for some time preached in a house by the road side, where the auditory, without fear of incurring the penalty of that act, came boldly to hear him, standing in the high-way, during the time of the service.—As his preaching was acceptable and useful, so his conversation was ' a living epistle, known and read of all ' men.' He was a man of great seriousness and exemplary piety, and his words did continually ' minister grace unto the ' hearers.' He died of the small-pox, at *Whitwell*, and was interred in the parish church there, in 1689, about the 58th year of his age. On his death-bed his faith was lively and strong, and he manifested a remarkable degree of resignation to the will of his heavenly Father.

WELD. MARTIN MORELAND, M.A. Fellow of *Wadham Col. Oxford.* He was eminent in the university and afterwards. In his younger years he was *Terræ filius* in the Oxford-act, as his brother (who was afterwards Sir Samuel Moreland), was *Prevaricator* in the Cambridge commencement. Both of them came off with honor and esteem for their ingenious performance, and their innocent and pleasant entertainment. He was a man of a clear understanding and great reading; an accurate and affectionate preacher; moderate in his principles, charitable in his temper; serious and remarkably upright in his life and conversation. He spent the latter part of life at *Hackney*.

WINCHESTER

WINCHESTER. FAITHFUL TEATE, D. D. In a discourse which he published, entitled, *Right Thoughts*, he has the following passage, accommodated to his own ejected and destitute state: " The righteous man, in thinking of his present condition of life, thinks it his relief, that the less money he has, he may go the more upon trust; the less he finds in his purse, seeks the more in the promise of him that has said, ' I will never leave thee, nor forsake thee. The ' Lord is his shepherd, and he shall not want; and therefore ' he will trust in the Lord, and do good, [believing that] ' verily he shall be fed;' or (as some read) truth shall be his feeding; so that he thinks no man can take away his livelihood, unless he can first take away God's truth."

WORKS. A Scripture Map of the Wilderness of Sin; and Way to Canaan...Ter Tria; or the Doctrine of the Sacred *Persons*, Father, Son and Spirit: Principal *Graces*, Faith, Hope and Love: Main *Duties*; Prayer, Hearing, and Meditation...Right Thoughts, the righteous Man's Evidence; a Discourse on Prov. xii. 5. *The thoughts of the righteous are right.*

—— Mr. COOK. Ejected from the same place. As also was

—— Mr. THEOPHILUS GALE. See the account of him in the university of *Oxford*. He died minister of *Moston*, in the Isle of *Wight*.

WORTLINGTON. Mr. JOHN HARRISON.

YARMOUTH (Isle of *Wight*) Mr. JOHN MARTYN. He had been Fellow of *Exet. Col. Oxf.* He was an eminent preacher, and a great scholar. The old incumbent (a mere reader of homilies) had the profits of the living, amounting to 18*l.* a year; but Mr. *Martyn* had 100*l. per ann.* allowed him. When he was ejected, he offered to have continued preaching for nothing. He afterwards frequently preached at *Newport*, where he lived, and in several other places, in the Island, till he went into *Wiltshire*, which was his native county, and there died at about 70 years of age.

YAVERLAND [R.] Mr. MARTIN WELLS. He was a man of great integrity, tho' not reckoned so eminent as the other ministers ejected in the Isle of Wight. He afterwards continued to exercise his ministry here in private. He brought up his son Mr. *Samuel Wells* to the ministry, who was chaplain to Mr. *Grove*, of Fern, in Wiltshire, and died in in that family. He was one of those who signed the *Address* of some ministers in the Isle of Wight, and county of Southampton, to the people of their respective charges, to discharge their duty in catechising, &c. Mr. *Martin*, last mentioned, was another.

It does not appear that any of the ministers ejected in this county afterwards conformed, except Mr. HUMPHREY ELLIS, of *Winchester*.

MINISTERS

MINISTERS EJECTED OR SILENCED

IN

HEREFORDSHIRE.

———

ASHTON. Mr. J. BARSTON. Of *Oxford* university. Born in this county. He was an Israelite indeed; a good scholar; an able, solid divine; a judicious, methodical, practical preacher, and a good casuist. He was also a man of exemplary conversation; a great pattern of self-denial, humility, submission, resignation and patience under all his afflictions, of which he had a large share. He was esteemed by all that knew him for his learning and piety, especially by that ornament and support of religion Sir *Edward Harley*. Nothing could be objected against him by his enemies, but his Nonconformity. He had a small estate, which he spent, as he did himself, in the service of his Master. He had but very little from the poor people among whom he laboured; but he laid by a tenth part of all his income for charitable uses. He died pastor of a congregation in *Ledbury*, A. D. 1701.

ASTON. Mr. FARRINGTON. Too well known about London, for the scandal he brought upon religion by his immoralities.

HEREFORD CATHEDRAL. Mr. WILLIAM VOYLE, Mr. WILLIAM LOW, Mr. GEORGE PRIMROSE, and SAMUEL SMITH, sen. M. A. These four were all joint pastors, who administered the Lord's-supper by turns. They lived in great peace among themselves, and with great unanimity carried on the work of the gospel in that city. They ordained many ministers both for England and Wales, in the cathedral. Four mornings in every week they publicly expounded in same place, beginning between seven and eight o'clo

They also kept up a constant weekly lecture on Tuesdays, with the assistance of the most eminent ministers in the county, and stemm'd the tide against the sectaries of those times, till the Restoration, when they were all cast out.—Mr. SMITH, after his ejectment here, had a living in Berkshire, and was cast out by the Act of uniformity in 1662, and silenced at *Stamford-Dingley*, where Dr. Pordage had been before. He afterwards mostly resided in Gloucestershire. After the turn of the times, he met with great unkindness from several of the episcopal party, whom he before had screened, and to whom he had shewn great kindness.—He died in Herefordshire in 1681.

Mr. PRIMROSE had his education in Scotland. His mother was nurse to prince *Henry*. He studied also at Saumur, in France. He was an excellent scholar, and a judicious, successful preacher. He was of a grave, even, and composed temper. Once as he was discoursing with Bp. *Crofts*, after he had been released from imprisonment, the Bishop attempted to persuade him to conform; but when he heard his objections, his lordship told him, He wished the church-doors had been wider. He retired for some time from *Hereford*, but preached constantly about the country; and when K. James gave liberty, he returned to Hereford again. But his growing weakness forced him back into the country, and there he died.

LITTLE-HEREFORD [V.] Mr. GARNONS.

LANTWARDINE [100*l*.] RICHARD HAWES, M. A. Of *Camb.* University. His father, a religious man, dying when he was very young, his mother soon after married a man wholly carnal, intent upon nothing but the profits of this world, and utterly negligent about instilling the principles of religion into his family, who remained grossly ignorant of God and his will. However, he put this youth to school, when he was about nine years of age, at *Ipswich*; where he happened to hear the famous Mr. *Ward*, on a lecture-day, and was so affected, as to request leave from his master constantly to attend that lecture, which he was permitted to do; and by this means he received lively impressions of religion in that early age. Having a very strong memory, he was able to repeat good part of the sermon, which he commonly did to his father-in-law's mother, with whom he lodged at Ipswich; and this happily proved the means of her conversion.

Being determined upon the work of the ministry, he went to Cambridge, where he studied some years, but lost that deep

sense

sense of religion which he possessed in his childhood, which he did not recover for a great while after he left the university. When he finished his studies, a living of considerable value fell void, the advowson of which his father-in-law laid claim to, who would have put him into it, and contested it in a law-suit, with the then Lord-keeper *(Coventry)*, who pretended it to be in the King's gift, and consequently at his disposal. But Mr. *Hawes*, chusing rather to rest satisfied in the Lord-keeper's promise of presenting him to the next living in the king's gift which should become void, so disobliged his father-in-law, that he cast him off. After this, he was for a while reduced to such straits, that his life became a burden to him; so that he would sometimes go, in the close of the evenings, to places where robberies and murders were wont to be committed, in hope of having an end put to his misery. But God extricated him out of his difficulties, by opening a door for his settlement at *Humber* in this county, to which the Lord keeper presented him; from whence he soon removed to *Kenchurch* in the same county.

For many years after he entered into the ministry, he continued much addicted to vain company, and was sometimes guilty of excessive drinking. But it pleased God to rouze him out of this security, by bringing him into some hazard of his life. For *Hereford* being garrisoned by the king's forces, he was, upon a false and malicious accusation, presented to the governor, fetched away a prisoner thither, and a council of war ordered to try him for his life; which was by an extraordinary providence secured, by the removal of the governor, a man of a violent temper, and the substitution of another; who being a person of more sobriety and candour, upon examination, discovered the prosecution to be wholly grounded on malice, and courteously dismissed him. From this time there was an observable alteration in his behaviour, and such an air of seriousness appeared in him, as procured the respect of all pious persons that knew him; and he became a plain, earnest, and useful preacher.

During the civil war, he had his house frequently plundered, and received many abuses from soldiers, particularly from one *Burk* an Irishman, who forced him to walk thro' the dirt by his horse's side, holding his pole-ax over his head, and locked him up in a gentleman's house in the parish, designing after he had done plundering there, to carry him away; but on going off, he forgot him, and left him behind. —About a year before the Restoration, he was presented, by the truly religious Sir Edward Harley, to *Lantwardine :* which he was the rather induced to accept, on account of the small success of his labours for twenty years, at *Kenchurch,* a Paganish and brutish place.—Shortly after the Restoration, upon the noise of plots, he was made a prisoner at *Hereford,* and very much threatened by Sir Henry Lingen, a fierce royalist, with severe usage upon his return from London, whither he was then going ; but he died at Gloucester, on his way home.

When the Bartholomew-act came out, such was Mr. *Hawes's* moderation, that some apprehended he would have conformed ; particularly one of his neighbour ministers, Mr. *C——y,* of *W——e,* who complained that he himself was likely to stand alone, on that side of the country, and professed to be so resolved against yielding to any of the terms required, tho' it were but to read some small part of the Popish Mass-book (as he termed the Common-prayer) that he would sooner suffer himself to be torn in pieces. However when they both went together to the Bishop, this man, (having been importuned by his wife) soon yielded ; tho' to his death he detested what, for lucre-sake, he practised, always declaimed against it, and never thrived afterwards.†
But Mr. *Hawes* maintained his ground in a conference with the Bishop, who civilly allowed him to preach a month after Bartholomew-day, and professed it to be contrary to his inclination to have such men as be removed, saying, " It was the Law that turned him out, and not he." After this Mr. *Hawes* boarded, as long as he lived, with his son-in-law and daughter Billingsley ; first at Webley, then at Abergavenny, and lastly at Awre. During his abode at the second of these places, the Bp. of Landaff (Dr. *Hugh Lloyd,* a very moderate man) allowed him to preach in public without subscribing ; which licence he made use of occasionally, and to his death enjoyed the same liberty, upon his removal into another diocese, by the connivance of Dr. *Nicholson,* Bp. of Gloucester.

. In his last sickness (occasioned by a journey to Kidderminster, for Mr. *Hieron)* he seemed not be uneasy at any thing, but his disability to preach God's word, which he said he hungered after as a hungry man after his food, and

---

† A relation of his, however, assured Dr. *Calamy,* that the above reflection was unmerited, and that Mr. W. was a great and worthy man ; but he did not give the Dr. such a satisfactory account of him as he desired, with a view to publication. *Contin.* p. 523.

complained

complained that he was then more useless than the stones in the street. He died in *Dec.* 1668, in the 65th year of his age, in the comfortable sense of God's favour, and the assurance that he was going to the enjoyment of him in glory. His countenance was most composed and chearful. He expressed, in his last hours, great satisfaction in his Nonconformity; declaring that if he had complied, he should have been afraid to die; whereas, he said, as the case now stood, he no more dreaded to die, than to go out at the door; and that, were the thing to be done again, he would rather chuse to suffer the greatest hardships, than to yield to what was required. His last words were those of the apostle, 'We know that if our earthly house of this tabernacle were dissolved, we have---'. He could say no more, but instantly expired. He desired that nothing might be said of him by way of commendation, in his funeral sermon, and that if he were spoken of at all, it might be only as a great sinner, who had obtained great mercy: which request was scarcely complied with by the preacher, Mr. *Jordan*, a worthy conformist, who highly esteemed him, and who did not long survive him. His text was *Psalm* xxxvii. 37.

*** LEOMINSTER [V.] JOHN TOMBES, B. D. Of *Magd. Hall, Oxf.* Born at *Bewdley*, in Worcestershire, 1603. His parents designed and educated him for the ministry. Such was his proficiency in grammar-learning, that he was fit for the university at the age of fifteen, where he was under the famous Mr. *William Pemble*, and soon gained a reputation for incomparable abilities and learning; so that upon the decease of his tutor, in 1624, he was chosen to succeed him in the catechetical lecture in this hall. He held his office about seven years, with great reputation, and then went to *Worcester*, where he was very popular as a preacher; but it doth not appear that he had any settlement there. He was soon after possessed of the living at *Leominster*, which he enjoyed several years. Tho' the parish was large, the income was very small; but Lord Viscount *Scudamore*, from his great respect for him, made an addition to it.

Mr. *Tombes* was among the first of the clergy of these times who endeavoured a reformation in the church, by purging the worship of God of human inventions. He preached a sermon on the subject, which was afterwards printed by an order of the House of Commons. This exposed him to the rage of the church-party, so that, at the

beginning

beginning of the civil war, some of the king's forces coming into that country; in 1641, he was driven from his habitation, and plundered of all he had in the world. Upon
this he fled to *Bristol*, which was in the parliament's possession, and General Fiennes, who had then the command of
that city, gave him the living of *All-saints* there. He had
not been there above a year before the city was besieged by
prince *Rupert* and his army, and a plot formed by their friends
within to deliver up the city, to burn the houses, and massacre the inhabitants. But this was seasonably discovered
and prevented. Mr. *Tombes*, on the day of thanksgiving
observed by the city on this occasion, preached two suitable
sermons, which were printed by an order of parliament,
with a short account of this bloody plot, and the means of
deliverance. This had like to have cost him dear; for the
next year the city was taken by the king's party, when his
wife and children were plundered, and a special warrant was
out for apprehending him; so that it was with great difficulty
he and his family got safe to *London, Sept.* 22, 1643.

While here, he took an opportunity to divulge the scruples
which he had long entertained, respecting *Infant Baptism*,
to several of the ministers who were now come from all
parts to form the assembly at Westminster. There was a
meeting of the London ministers on the occasion in *Jan.*
1643, but it ended without affording Mr. *Tombes* satisfaction. He then drew up in Latin the chief grounds of his
doubts, and sent them to Mr. *Whitaker*, the chairman of the
Assembly of Divines. But it must be owned he did not
meet with that respectful treatment which his own character,
or the nature of the affair deserved.† Being now minister
of *Fenchurch*, his stipend was withheld because he did not
practise the baptism of infants. How far he had just matter
for complaint on this head is left to the reader's own judgment. It deserves however to be mentioned, that he avoid-
ed introducing this controversy into the pulpit. He was then
chosen preacher at the *Temple*, on condition of his adhering
to this resolution : but after four years, he was dismissed,
for publishing his first treatise on Infant Baptism. He printed
his apology in 1646, of which Mr. *John Batchiler* says,
" Having perused this mild apology, I conceive that the in-
" genuity, learning, and piety therein contained, deserve
" the press."

† See a more particular account of this matter in *Crosby's* Hist. of the
Baptists, (vol. i. p. 282..295.) from whence this article is taken.

After

After this, the people of *Bewdley* chose him for their minister. He there publicly disputed against *Infant Baptism*, and gathered a separate church of persons of his own persuasion, in which were trained up three Baptist ministers, *viz.* Mr. *Richard Adams*, Mr. *John Eccles*, and one Capt. *Boylston :* But still continued minister of the parish. While he was here, he held a public disputation with Mr. *Baxter* about *Baptism*, as he did at other places with other ministers; and persons of different sentiments from his own, acknowledged that he appeared to great advantage, both with respect to learning and argument. This living being small, he had the parsonage of *Ross* given him, (which Dr. *Walker* says is worth 250*l. per ann.*) which he resigned upon having the mastership of the hospital at *Ledbury*. At length, the affections of his people being alienated from him, on account of his difference from them about baptism, he was restored to his first living at *Leominster*. In the year 1653 he was appointed to be one of the Triers of ministers. Upon the Restoration, he readily fell in with the monarchial government, and wrote for taking the oath of supremacy. But finding the spirit of persecution revived, and the former government and ceremonies of the church imposed, and having married a rich widow, he quitted his places, and laid down the ministry, resolving to live at rest and peace in his old age. He conformed to the church, as a lay-communicant, but could not be prevailed upon to accept any benefice or dignity in it, tho' he had very considerable offers.

Many testimonies may be produced to his character, learning and abilities. The Earl of *Clarendon*, soon after the Restoration, spoke to the king in his favour, by which he was protected from any trouble on account of any thing he had written or acted in the preceding times; and, when made Lord Chancellor, he introduced him to his majesty to present his book, which was dedicated to him, entitled, *Saints no Smiters*. Bp. Sanderson, and his successor Bp. Barlow, had a great esteem for him, as likewise had Dr. Ward, Bp. of Salisbury; whom, while he lived there, he often visited. Mr. *Baxter*, tho' he had engaged in disputes with him, calls him " the chief of the *Anabaptists*," and publicly asked God and him pardon for some unhandsome things, which, in the warmth of debate, he had said against him. *Wood*, the Oxford biographer, owns, " There were few better disputants than he was ;" and Mr. *Nelson*, that zealous churchman says, " It cannot be denied that he was esteemed a

person

person of incomparable parts." Mr. *Wall*, in his History
of Infant Baptism, says, " Of the professed Antipædobaptists, Mr. *Tombes* was a man of the best parts in our nation,
and perhaps in any." And in the free conference between
the Lords and Commons, on the Occasional-conformity-bill,
Bp. *Burnet*, to shew that receiving the sacrament in the
church does not necessarily imply an intire conformity, observed, " There was a very learned and famous man at *Sa-
" lisbury*, Mr. *Tombes*, who was a zealous Conformist in
" all points but one, Infant-baptism." Dr. *Calamy*'s character of him is this : " All the world must own him to have
been a considerable man, and an excellent scholar, how dis-
inclined soever they may be to his particular opinions." He
died at *Salisbury, May* 25, 1676, aged 73.

WORKS. Christ's Commination against Scandalizers ; two
treatises...Fermentum Pharisæorum ; or the Leaven of Pharisaical
Worship ; a Sermon on Matt. xv. 9...Jehovah-Jireh ; a thanksgiving sermon...Anthropolatria ; or the Sin of glorying in Man...
Animadversiones quædam in Aphorismos R. Baxteri de Justificat.
..True old Light exalted above pretended new Light ; against the
Quakers...Romanism discussed ; recommended by Baxter...Se-
rious Consideration of the Oath of Supremacy...Suppl. to ditto...
Sepher Sheba ; a treatise on Swearing...Saints no Smiters ; against
the Fifth Monarchymen...Theodulia ; in defence of hearing Ministers in the church of England...Emanuel ;against the Socinians.
..Animadversiones in Librum G. Bulli, cui titulum fecit, Harmo-
nia Apostolica...The following upon BAPTISM : An Exercit. about
Infant Bapt. presented to the Chairman of Committee of Assemb.
of Divines...Examen of Mr. S. Marshall's Sermon...Apology for
the foregoing...Addition to ditto against Bailie...Antidote against
a Passage in Dedicat. of Baxter's Saint's Rest...Præcusor ; or, a
Fore-runner to a large Review of this Dispute...Antipædobap-
tism ; or, no plain or obscure scripture proof, &c...Ditto, Part II.
..Ditto, Part III...A Plea for the Antipædobaptists ; an Answer,
&c. to *The Anabaptists silenced*..Short Catechism about Baptism...
Felo de se ; against Baxter...Just Reply to Wills and Blinman.

MORTON. Mr. ANTHONY COLLIER, § See *Gloucestershire*.

§ In MAITLAND's History of London is the following copy of an inscription upon a grave-stone, in Bunnhill-fields : ABEL COLLIER,
minister of the gospel, and pastor of a congregation, at HALSTED, in
Essex, who died *May* 29, 1695, in the 66th year of his age. Query,
Whether he was an ejecteted minister, or related to the above. ED.

SILLECK

SILLECK and CAPLE. Mr. ROBERT TAYLOR. He preached alternately at both these places, which are in the same parish, the income of which was very small. He was a very affectionate and earnest preacher ; using frequently to weep in his public administrations. After his ejectment in 1662, he never took the pastoral care of any people, but preached as he had opportunity, in this and the neighbouring counties, and frequently at Col. Kirle's, who lived near *Rosse*, where he for the most part resided. He died about 1678, at the age of 45.

WEBLEY [V. 8*l.*] Mr. NICHOLAS BILLINGSLEY. He removed from this place to *Abergavenny*, where he taught a free-school, till, by the good offices of Sir Edward Harley, he was settled at *Blakeney*, in the parish of *Awre*, in Gloucestershire, a privileged place : the maintenance of it (which was at least 50*l. per annum)* depended upon an impropriation, which, by the generosity of a gentleman, had been annexed to a chapel of ease, in the above village. The vicarage, which was worth 8*l. per annum,* was offered him, but he refused it on the same principle which made him leave *Webley*. Here he lived very peaceably, while Dr. *Nicholson* was Bp. of Gloucester, and Mr. *Jordan* (a moderate and pious man) was vicar of the parish. Mr. *Jordan* dying in or near 1668, and the Bishop not long after, two succeding vicars were perpetual thorns in his side ; nor was Dr. *Frampton*, the succeeding bishop, his friend ; much less Mr. Richard Parsons, the chancellor. After his preaching a visitation-sermon, in which he took great freedom in reproving the clergy for their vices, that *gentleman* immediately, and in the open street, discovered his resentment, by pulling him by his hair, and uttering these words, " Sirrah, " you are a rogue, and I'll bind you to your good behaviour." After this, Mr. *Billingsley* had frequent suspensions, for want of that conformity to which his place did not oblige him ; and was put to no small trouble and expence to take them off. He complied so far as to read more or less of the Common-prayer, and to wear the surplice, after the Bishop had given it under his hand, that it was not required to be worn upon the account of any supposed holiness in the garment, but only for decency and comeliness. His Lordship would sometimes treat him with great civility ; but yet would send a suspension after him to be read the next Lord's-day.

He once ordered him to read prayers, and not preach at all for a quarter of a year. A person who stood by, saying, " I hope your lordship is not against preaching the gospel," he replied, " Well, let him go on with his beloved preaching."

He continued in this place till the Revolution, when the Bishop was turned out as a Nonjuror, and was succeeded by the valuable Dr. *Fowler*. Before he actually came from London to the palace, the chancellor had again used his authority to suspend Mr. *Billingsley*, whom he still accounted his enemy, for having once told him the truth. At length, wearied out with the troubles he met with, he resolved to quit the place. The Bishop blamed the chancellor for what he had done, and expressed his desire to have Mr. *Billingsley* return; accordingly the place was kept vacant for a year. But he determined to return no more, and from that time he employed his ministry among the Dissenters in different places in Gloucestershire. He at length became very feeble thro' his great age, and died at *Bristol, Dec.* 1709. His elder son *Richard*, died minister at Whitchurch, in Hampshire, a very worthy man: father of Mr. *Samuel Billingsley*, late of Peckham. See Vol. I. p. 402. His younger son *Nicholas*, was minister at Ashwick, in Somersetshire.

WESTON. Mr. JOHN SKINNER

WHITCHURCH (or RICKARDS CASTLE.) Mr. WILLIAM WOODWARD. A great and good man; much respected by Sir E. Harley and E. Littleton, Esq. of the Moor, to whom he dedicated a sermon or two. He was a tutor, in *Oxford*, and educated Mr. *Flavel*, of Dartmouth. After his ejectment he travelled to *Turkey*, and visited Smyrna and Aleppo. He at last settled at *Leominster*, where he was pastor of a considerable congregation till his death in 1691 or 2. Dr. *Walker* relates a story concerning his cruelty to the wife of the sequestered clergyman, which cannot be credited without better evidence, as it no way agrees with the character given of him by all that knew him. Probably this is the person mentioned in the university of *Oxford*, Vol. I. p. 221.

Mr. BOYLE and Mr. WOTTON were ejected in this county, but at what places is uncertain.

Mr.

Mr. BROSTER, of *Wormbridge*, afterwards conformed. As also did Mr. MALDEN, of *Sapy*, tho' not to the satisfaction of his conscience; for he used afterwards often to say, It repented him that he did not let his wife and children go a begging, rather than that he had conformed. However, he continued in his living till his death, and always paid a great respect to the Nonconformists.

MINISTERS EJECTED OR SILENCED

IN

HERTFORDSHIRE.

ST. ALBANS. St. *Peter's* church. Mr. WILLIAM HAWORTH. Of St. *John's Col. Camb.* He was well skilled in the Latin, Greek and Hebrew languages. After his ejectment here* he was desired on occasion of the death of some friend, to preach a funeral sermon. Accordingly he had assembled a congregation for this purpose, at some place in the town, but was hindered by some malicious persons who obliged the people to disperse. Upon this, they went to the Cloisters in the abbey, where Mr. *Haworth* had resolved to perform the service. While he was in his sermon, a party of soldiers came in with a view to apprehend him; when one of the hearers interposing to prevent it, was shot dead on the spot. Mr. *Haworth* was taken up, and on account of this affair was tried at the assizes: when, tho' he was discharged, he was heavily fined, while the soldier who committed the murder escaped with impunity. He afterwards lived twenty years at *Hertford*, and preached to a society of Dissenters there.

§ The congregation at *Hitchin*, of which Mr. *Holcroft* had been pastor, being dismissed to Mr. *Haworth's* charge, he used to preach to them about once a month, in a barn belonging to the other society in that town, according to an

* He could not have had the living of St. PETERS, but must have been only a preacher there, as John Retchford succeeded William Retchford as vicar, in 1661, and was living till 1700.—N. B. The original account of Mr. Haworth is so confused and imperfect as to require being drawn up afresh, and some words supplied, to render it intelligible. The additions to it, and to several other articles in this county, are communicated by Mr. Isaac James, a native.

agreement

Nathaniel Partridge.

from a scarce & valuable old Print, in the possession of M.ʳ Simco.

Published by Button & Son, Paternoster Row.

agreement made in 1687. They used generally to go to *Hertford* on communion-days, but sometimes met, from both towns, at *Bragbury-end*, which is about half way. Mr. *Edward Hitchin* (author of *The Infant's Cause pleaded*, who was grand father to the late minister of *White Row*, Spital-fields, London) left the society which now meets in Tyler-street, *Hitchin*, in 1688, and joined Mr. *Haworth's* church.—The following little anecdote is found in *Maurice's Monument* of *mercy to the Church at Rowell*. Mr. Haworth being present at a meeting of ministers in a neighbouring town (probably *Kettering*) and disapproving of their proceedings, relative to Mr. *Davis* of Rowell,* questioned their authority, crying out, *Quo Jure, quo jure?* This unexpected attack produced a sudden silence, upon which some person answered, *Nullo Jure.* Then, replied Mr. *Haworth*, " It is *Injuria.*"

———. Mr. NATHANIEL PARTRIDGE. Probably he was at *St. Michael's* church, for it appears that one was ejected there in 1662, from *Newc. Rep. Eccles.* (vol i. p. 778), where we have this entry: *John Cole*, A. M. 3 *Mar.* 1662. *per non subscriptionem ultimi Vicarii.* Mr. *Partridge* having once preached at *St. Albans*, upon those words, *Rev.* iii. 18. ' Anoint thine eyes with eye-salve, that thou mayst see ;' a poor man who was as blind in mind as he was in body, went afterwards to his house, and asked him very gravely, " where he might get that ointment to cure his blindness ?" [Doubtless Mr. *Partridge* improved the occasion for saying something to this ignorant creature, with a view to open the eyes of his mind, tho' we have no information concerning it.] After his ejectment, he preached in *Old-street*, London, many years, and suffered six months imprisonment in Newgate for his Nonconformity. He took a great deal of pains with the condemned prisoners there, not without some good success ; and died, in a good old age, *Aug.* 6, 1684. Mr. *Christopher Nesse* published an elegy upon him, some lines of which were so severe, [against court measures] that he was forced for a time to hide from the messengers who were very busy in hunting after him.

ALBURY [V.] Mr. FRANCIS COMYNG. It appears from *Newc. Rep.* that he was admitted to this living before the

* See the account of Mr. Davis under the article DISBOROUGH, Northamptonshire.

civil

civil war began; *viz.* in 1637, and therefore had an unquestionable title to it. §There is a Mr. *Cummen* among
the fifteen Tuesday lecturers appointed by Parliament, at
Hitchin, July 19, 1642. Probably this was the same person.

ASHWELL [V.] JOHN CROW, M. A. Of *Kath. Hall,
Camb.* He was born in *Kent,* and was half-brother to the
famous Mr. *Herbert Palmer,* whom he succeeded at this
place; where, for about sixteen years, he faithfully discharged
the ministerial office in all its parts, and kept up the piety
which Mr. *Palmer* left in that large parish. After being
silenced, he continued with his family several years at *Ashwell,* living in great amity first with Mr. *Milburn,* (a man
of a different spirit from his nephew) [Mr. *Luke Milburn*]
and afterwards with Mr. *Bland,* both of them men of great
moderation and good temper, curates to Dr. *Cudworth,* who
was Mr. *Crow's* immediate successor. With them he cheerfully united in the several parts of public worship, and assisted them all he could, in subserviency to their public
ministry, by pious conference with his neighbours, and repeating and reinforcing their sermons to such as would come
to him at his own house. He afterwards removed to London. If he was inferior to Mr. *Palmer* in learning and controversial skill, he was equally eminent for piety, simplicity,
humility and moderation. He was indeed of a most sweet,
mild, and peaceable temper, and very charitable to the poor;
to whom, when he was minister of *Ashwell,* he used to sell
corn below the market-price. His life was so unblameable,
that he was universally beloved. But he was not without his
trials, and some of them considerable and shocking too, in
his old age.

BALDOCK [L.] and WALLINGTON [R. 160l.] Mr.
WILLIAM SHERWIN. These two places are about two
miles distant. He kept an assistant in his house to preach at
Wallington on Lord's-days in the afternoon, when he
preached at *Baldock;* casting his net where there was plenty
of fish. And he did it to good purpose; for God blessed his
ministry to that great congregation very much. In the latter
part of his life he lived with his daughter, Mrs. *Crackinthorp,*
whose husband was minister at *Foulmire* in Cambridgeshire,
and there died in a good old age; *viz.* about 80. He had a
venerable aspect, was a considerable scholar, a hard student,
and of an unblameable life. He bent his studies very much
to

to the obscure prophecies of scripture, and was very fond of
the Millenarian notions. § His portrait is prefixed to some
of his pieces, and was engraved by his son.

WORKS. Several small Treatises on the prophecy of *Daniel,*
and the *Revelation* ; commonly bound up together. § The following
is a more compleat account of his principal treatises. The world
to come.—The word written concerning the word ever-living.—
The fore-runner of Christ's kingdom.—Christ's peaceful kingdom.
—The first and last preacher.—The new Jerusalem.

BARLEY. See ROYSTON.

BARNET [R.] Mr. SHAW.

BUSHY. Mr. WARD is mentioned here in Dr. Calamy's
account, but ought to be omitted ; for, as Dr. *Walker* says,
" being possessed of this living in 1660, he got a presentation
to it from his majesty, *per lapsum,* and disusing the surplice,
he mangled the prayers here until his death, in 1684."

CHESHUNT [V.] Mr. WILLIAM YATES. He was
ejected either here or at *Barn-Elmes* in Surry. In the time
of *Charles* II.'s Indulgence, it is certain he lived here, and
preached at *Theobalds* in the same parish ; and here he died,
leaving a worthy name behind him, in August. 1679, being
near a 100 years of age.

COTTERED [R.] Mr. THOMAS GARDINER. An ingenious and learned divine. The father of Dr. *Gardiner,*
who lived and died in Abchurch-Lane, London. § *Chauney's*
entries here are, " 1627, *Thomas Gardiner,* A. M. 1661,
John Gardiner, D. D." *(Hist. of Hertfordshire.)* Hence
it seems that the father was ejected at the Restoration, and
that the son being a conformist, succeeded him.

ESSINGDON. Mr. SKINGLE. See *Hadham parva.*

GILSTON† THOMAS MOCKET, M. A. Of both uni-
versities, first of *Queen Col. Camb.* Born about the year 1602.
He was sometime chaplain to the Earl of Bridgewater, when
he was lord president of the Marches of Wales, in the reign
of K. *Charles* I. and by him was favoured, and promised
preferment. He was preacher at *Holt* in Denbighshire, before he was settled at *Gilston,* viz. about 1639. This last

† This was before called GADESDON. It is sometimes spelt GELDESDEN.

place

place he resigned to *Christophsr Webb*, the former incumbent in 1660. He was a very pious and humble man.

WORKS. Gospel Duties and Dignity.—A Discourse on the Covenant and Protestation.—The Church's Trouble and Deliverance.—Christian Advice to old and young, rich and poor. § This piece has his portrait prefixed, engraved at the expence of Edward Brewster.—He also published, in 1651, Christmas the christians grand feast, its original growth and observation : also, of Easter, Whitsuntide, &c.

GRAVELEY [R.] Mr. CARTER. § *Chauney* enters his name ANDREW CATER. Edwards, in his *Gangræna*, P. iii. p. 105, has this passage, which is supposed to refer to him. " There is one *Carter*, having but one eye, a sectary at *Watton* in Herts, and a great preacher, who keeps conventicles on the Lord's day, there being great resort to him, never coming to the public assemblies." After his ejectment, he lived some time in the family of Sir *Robert Josseline*, near Sabridgeworth. When he died, he left a charity, of which the heir of that family is one of the managers in course.

*** HADHAM *Magna* [R. 300*l*,] DANIEL DYKE, M. A. Of *Camb*. University. He was born in 1617, at *Epping* in Essex, where his father, the good old Puritan, Mr. *Jeremiah Dyke*, was minister. He was nephew to the famous *D. Dyke*, B. D. who wrote the treatise *Of the deceitfulness of the heart*. He had episcopal ordination. When he appeared in public he was soon taken notice of for his great learning and useful preaching, and was preferred accordingly. Besides having this valuable living, he was made one of the chaplains in ordinary to *Oliver Cromwell*, and in 1653 was appointed one of the Triers of ministers, for which office he was well qualified by his learning, judgment, and piety. He was of the Baptist persuasion, and appears to have been the only one of that persuasion, besides Mr. *Tombes*, in that commission. Upon the Restoration, he shewed his integrity by refusing to conform to the episcopal government, and to the ceremonies of the church established, and voluntarily resigned his living soon after; foreseeing the approaching storm. When his intimate friend Mr. *Case*, (who was one of the ministers deputed to wait on the king at the *Hague*, and one of the commissioners at the *Savoy*) endeavoured to persuade him to continue, and told him what a hopeful prospect they had from the king's behaviour, &c.
Mr.

Mr. *Dyke* very wisely answered, " That they did but de-
" ceive and flatter themselves: that if the king was sincere
" in his shew of piety, and great respect for them and their
" religion, yet when he came to be settled, the party that had
" formerly adhered to him, and the creatures that would
" come over with him, would have the management of
" public affairs, would circumvent them in all their designs,
" and in all probability not only turn them out, but take
" away their liberty too."

After he resigned his living, he preached as often as he had
opportunity, and was generally preserved by some kind appearance of Providence from the rage and malice of his persecutors. Tho' he lived in two or three great storms, and
had several writs out against him, he was never imprisoned
more than one night. He was at length chosen and ordained co-pastor with Mr. *William Kiffin* to the congregation of Baptists in Devonshire-square, London, where he
continued a faithful labourer to his death in 1688, when he
was about 70 years of age. He was buried at Bunhill-fields,
and Mr. *Warner* preached his funeral sermon. He was a man
of so much modesty, that he could never be prevailed upon
to publish any thing. His name, however, stands with some
others in two or three printed papers, in the composing of
which it is supposed he had some concern; *v. g.*

WORKS. The Baptist's Answer to Mr. Willis's Appeal.—A
Recommendation of Mr. Cox's Confut. of the Errors of T. Collier.
—Relation of a Meeting at Barbican between the Baptists and
Quakers.—He was the editor of several select sermons of his
father.

HADHAM *Parva.* Mr. DANIEL SKINGLE. § This
was most probably the person mentioned at *Essingdon,* of
whom the following anecdote is related. He was once invited to preach at a chapel of ease belonging to *Hitchin* (called Minsden, or Minzell, now in ruins) which he accordingly did, and a prosecution was immediately set on foot;
but no one of the auditors would betray him. At length a
person waited on him hypocritically pretending to be under
deep conviction of sin, and by this method, drawing Mr.
Skingle into free discourse, got out of him the particulars of
his preaching at the said chapel. Upon this he was thrown
into the Spiritual court, and after expending about 300*l.* he
and the chapel-warden were glad to get clear, by making the
following submissions:

" I Daniel

" I Daniel Skingle, of the parish of Minsden magna in
the county of Hertford, do acknowledge and confess to have
committed a great fault, by taking upon me to preach contrary to law, in the chapel of Minsden, within the parish of
Hitchin—and do beg the right rev. father in God, James
lord bishop of Lincoln his pardon, and all others offended
thereat; and do promise that I will not commit or do the
like for the future. Witness my hand this 20th day of *Dec.*
A. D. 1700, Daniel Skingle." *Concordat cum orig. Testi-
bus nobis,* Fr. Bragge *Vicar de Hitchin.*   Thomas
Harris.

The other is given in the Note below *

HARDEN [Chap. S.] Mr. Nathaniel Eeles. Of
Eman. Col. Camb. He was born at *Aldenham* in this
county, in 1617, of good parentage. Having prosecuted
his studies till he was senior batchelor, in order to his greater
improvement he studied two years at *Utrecht,* under the
celebrated *Gisbert Voet*; and being judged competently
qualified for the ministry, was there ordained a Presbyter, and
then came into England, and preached at *Caddington* in Bedfordshire. In 1643, he was called by the people at *Harding*
to be their pastor. There he continued preaching with great
satisfaction, and good success, till 1661, when he was ejected
by the succeeding incumbent Dr. *Killigrew.* For that being
a chapel of ease to *Wheathamstead,* (both belonging to the
dean and chapter of Westminster,) and being a sequestered

* *The Submission of* John Heath, *made in* Hitchin Church, *Sunday* Nov. 23,
1701.——" Whereas I John Heath, Chapel Warden of Minsden, a member
of this church, have contrary to the duty and dignity of my office, which I was
sworn to observe and execute, permitted and suffered Daniel Skingle, a mere
Layman and in a Lay-Habit, to preach or rather profane the holy word of
God, in the chapel of Minsden; and did also invite and encourage him to the
repetition of such his illegal and unwarrantable practices, and have thereby
violated the solemn oath I took, for the performance of my office, and have
given great offence to the church in general, and to this church, and the
minister and parishioners of this parish in particular: I am therefore, by the
command of my ordinary's own letter, to make this acknowledgment,
which I heartily and willingly submit to, and do, in the presence of Almighty
God and this congregation, unfeignedly confess my said fault, and the great
sin I have thereby committed against God, and the offence I have given to
the church in general, and to this church, and minister, and people, in particular; and I beseech God and you all to forgive me, and to join with me in
prayer for the assistance of his holy spirit that I may have a due regard to my
duty for the future."—Then he repeated the Lord's prayer.—*This is a true copy.
Witness* Fr. Bragge, *vicar of* Hitchin.

place

place, it was restored to the dean before the Act of uniformity. At the time that act took place, he had a wife and seven children. When the Corporation-act had passed, he left his family, and lived some time at *Borington*. Before and after which, as he had opportunity, he preached in private, sometimes at his own house, and sometimes at *St. Albans* and other places, till K. Charles's Declaration for liberty of conscience in 1672, when he took out a licence for his own house at *Harding*, where he preached, gratis, to all that would come. When the licences were recalled, he continued to expose his house and person to the fines and penalties that were then recoverable of him, and still continued his ministry till his last sickness: and providence so ordered it, that he never was disturbed, tho' often threatened. He had little trouble, except what was given him by citations from the spiritual courts. Having a call from the people of *Codicote* (a village near Welwyn) he preached there twice every other Lord's-day, still providing a supply (Mr. *Robert Tory* for the most part) for his own people at *Harding*, without any expence to them.

He was a man of considerable parts, great prudence, good judgment, admirable temper, and a candid disposition; much respected and beloved by persons of all ranks, having a good mien and a grave presence. He was an excellent textuary, and well acquainted with the scriptures; strict in the observation of the Lord's-day, both for himself and family; very tender of offending any, and had a good report of all. No occasion could be found against him, even by his worst enemies, except in the matter of his Nonconformity; concerning which, being enquired of by Mr. *Tory*, when he was very near his end, What he thought of it, and whether he apprehended it worth while for a man to venture his estate, liberty, and good name for it? He answered, with a voice and earnestness beyond his strength, " That he would not be with-" out the comfort of it for ten thousand worlds." He was afflicted several years with a sciatica, he had also a bloody flux and the piles to a great degree. Tho' his pains were often severe, he was never heard to speak a hard word of God; but always justified him, and begged patience under his afflictions, rather than deliverance from them. His weakness was such, by reason of these disorders, that for some time he was forced to preach sitting, which he continued to do till about a fortnight before his death, *Dec.* 18, 1678, aged 61, when he left a wife and ten children. § He is mentioned

tioned

tioned among the lecturers at *Hitchin* and *Dunstable* in 1642. He was also one of the Triers for this county in 1654.

§ HERTFORD [R.] St. Andrews. Mr. JEREMIAH BUR- WELL. He was born about 1624, and died of an apoplexy, at the house of George Poyner, Esq. at *Codicote*, near Wel- wyn, where there is the following inscription on his grave. "Here lieth Jeremiah Burwell, late minister of St. Andrews, Hertford, who departed this life, Feb. 11, Ann. 1668 Ætatis suæ 44." *Chauncy.* He had the character of a pious, heavenly, humble, moderate, friendly man; as also of a good preacher.

HITCHIN. Mr. BENJ. KING. See OAKHAM, *Rutland.*

KIMPTON. JOHN WILSON, M. A. Of *Kath. Hall, Camb.* A worthy, pious and contented man; who was pos- sessed of considerable learning, as appears from his Answer to *Philosophia Scripturæ Interpres*, and to *Wolzogen.*

§ KERSHALL [R.] Mr. WILLIAM JANEWAY. Of *King's Col. Camb.* He was the eldest son of Mr. William Janeway, of *Lilly*, Herts; who, about 1644 removed to *Aspeden*, and afterwards became minister of *Kelshall*, where he died, leaving a widow and eleven children; of whom William, John, James, and Abraham, were ministers, and all of them (excepting *John)* were ejected. *William* was admitted at Cambridge about 1650. He probably preached at *Kelshall* after his father's decease, as he resided there, and was a preacher in 1657; when his brother *John* finished his short but holy life at his house. It does not appear that he had this Rectory; if he had, he could have held it but for a short time, for John Franklyn was presented to it Sept. 25, 1660. Bp. *Kennett*, in many instances, endeavours to invali- date Dr. *Calamy's Account*, and observes, that "A trans- cript of the several presentations, and especially of the epis- copal collations and institutions, both in the time of the usurped powers, and from and after the Restoration to the end of 1662, would make up the best comment on the *Ac- count* and *Continuation* of the ejected or silenced minis- ters——" *Kennet's Register and Chronicle*, p. 879. Quot- ing the register of Bp. *Wren*, he says, " Ann. 1662, Dec. 5. Presentatus est Ricardus Salmon, A. M. ad Rect. de Kel- shull, in Com. Hertf. vacantem per Cessionem cujusdam GULIELMI JENOWAY, ultimi Incumbentis ibidem." He then observes that; " If Dr. Calamy's assertion, *that he was*
EJECTED,

EJECTED, * had been true, the register would not have run, *per cessionem.*" In p. 883, quoting the *same* register, he has it: "Janeway ult. Incubatoris," and calls him " the last intruder ;" thus sufficiently answering his own objection, and proving that incorrectness was not confined to Dr. Calamy.

LANGLEY (Abbots) [V.] Mr. JOHN KING. In *New-court Rep.* his successor is mentioned thus: Tho. Wright Cl. 29 *Jan.* 1662, *per inconform.* King.

MUNDANE *Parva* [R.] Mr. WILLIAM GRAVE. § So *Chauncy* enters his name, with the date 1659.

ROYSTON [V. S.] NATHANIEL BALL, M. A. Of *King's Col. Camb.* Born at *Pitminster*, near Taunton-Dean in Somersetshire, 1623, of pious parents, who gave him a very religious education, which by the grace of God was successful to his conversion very young. He made a good progress in school-learning, and when he was entered at Cambridge, he spent his time conscientiously. He was noted for his accuracy in the Latin, Greek, Hebrew, and French languages. The latter he spoke so well as to be often taken for a native of France. When he left the university, he settled at *Barley*, about ten miles from Cambridge. Here he employed himself indefatigably in his Master's service, and was an instrument in turning many to righteousness. This being a sequestered living, he punctually paid a fifth part of the income to Dr. *Thorndike*, whom he succeeded. He preached much upon the necessity of regeneration, upon faith and holiness, and the great truths of the gospel. It was generally his way to continue upon a text for a considerable time. He took great pleasure in expounding the scriptures, and catechizing. He endeavoured to be acquainted with every family in his parish, and spent much time in visiting his people, discoursing with them about the state of their souls, and the great things of their salvation. He earnestly put them

* The word " ejected" is not strictly applicable to the nonconformists of 1662: the term "*per cessionem,*" as often used in the registers, is certainly more accurate, since they were voluntarily in quitting their livings. But they were thus far *compelled* to it; they could not conscientiously keep them; new terms of conformity being imposed on purpose to drive them out, and such as it was known many hundreds of worthy, able, and learned men, who had a legal title to their preferments, would not submit to, from a principal of integrity. See Pref. vol. 1. p. 1. note.

upon

upon performing family duties; and when any objected their
want of gifts for prayer, he furnished them with directions,
both as to matter and manner, with such success, that many,
before unaccustomed to this exercise, arrived at a great
ability in it.

When he entered upon a married state, and his family increased, he was very exact in the government of it. He was
indulgent to his children and servants, in every thing but
what was sinful, where he was always severe. Some servants
of his had reason to bless God that ever they knew him.
He was very strict in observing the sabbath; and his piety was
observable in his whole conduct. He had an admirable talent of introducing pious discourse at his table, and in all
companies. He was much respected by several students at
Cambridge, and particularly by Mr. *Tillotson*, afterwards
Abp. of Canterbury. He instructed several, both Nonconformists and others, in various branches of learning, especially
in the *Oriental* languages, in which few equalled, and
scarcely any exceeded him. With the greatest ease would
he, at first sight, render any part of the *Hebrew* Bible into
proper English. He compiled a *Chaldee* grammar, which
was unhappily lost, as many valuable things of his have
been.

Tho' he scarcely ever used a note in preaching, his sermons
were so exactly penned as to be fit for the press; but such
was his humility, that he thought nothing of his worth printing. His natural abilities, great learning, and close application, qualified him for great service; but his grand study was
to *know Christ, and him crucified.* He so studied plainness
in preaching, that he often used to say, It cost him more
pains to bring down every word in his sermons to the under-
standings of the meanest hearers, than if he were to preach
in Latin.—He quitted *Barley* in 1660; and was chosen the
public minister of *Royston.* That being a town of great
profaneness, and but little religion; his zeal for God, and
love to souls, made him lay out himself in an extraordinary
manner. He set up a lecture on the market-day, which was
blessed with great success. The trade of wickedness was
spoiled, and some of the worst of sinners were wrought upon,
who proved eminent in grace. He had a public hour of
prayer daily, between twelve and one; to which many christians resorted. He was through life a great redeemer of his
time, scarcely allowing himself any recreation, which seemed
to shorten his days. He rose very early in the morning, and
if

If the service of God did not call him away, he was by a moderate computation, not less than ten hours out of twenty-four in his study, for thirty years together. He loved a private life, and went but little into company, where he had not the prospect of usefulness; and was not fond of making visits to London, where, he said, people were mad upon the world.

On Bartholomew-day, 1662, he quitted his public ministry, to the great grief of his parish, and the christians of that neighbourhood. Though he had a wife and several children, with the prospect of more, (who increased at length to thirteen,) yet the tenderness of his conscience kept him from conformity. He continued however for some time in the town, going about, many miles, preaching as oportunity offered, and exhorting such as came in his way. This he did with great success, till the Oxford-act took place, &c.; then he removed five miles off, where he lived peaceably, and won upon many by his holy life, his great moderation, and sweetness of temper. For though he was very zealous for the purity of Christ's institutions, against all impositions and human inventions, so as never to comply in what he thought but doubtful, yet he was very candid, and full of respect to all such as differed from him, who discovered any regard to real religion.

He lived above seven years in a small village in *Essex*, where he was screened by Mr. *Parr* his brother-in-law, a worthy, serious, conforming minister; and having a convenient house to preach in, of a pious widow-lady. Many judicious christians attended on his ministry, some coming five miles, and some even ten, on Lord's-day to hear him. He preached also occasionally in *Cambridge, Epping, Beyford*, and several other places, with great success. He was contented with any mean way of living, so that he might but bring some glory to God. He lived in a cottage of forty-shillings a year rent, and never received above 20l. a year for all his labours, after he was ejected; but he relied on providence, and would often say, to the praise of divine goodness, " That he never lived better than when he knew not how to " live; nor ever enjoyed more of God's presence than in that " poor place." He kept a diary of God's providences to him and his, which excited his thankfulness, and encouraged his hope and trust in difficulties. From many of his paper, it appeared, that he was strict and frequent in self-examination. He was also faithful to others; reproving sin where-

ever

ever he observed it; and when any told him of their great experiences, he would say, "It is good news, but take heed "that it is true." He held a correspondence with many worthy ministers and valuable christians by letter, in which he took great pleasure, and was very useful. When his goods were seized for his preaching contrary to law, he took it joyfully, and heartily prayed for his enemies.

His last removal was to *Epping*, to which place however he did not wholly confine himself. He was of a strong constitution, but at length was worn out by labour, study and travels. He was very charitable to the poor, and much concerned for the public, especially for the church of God. His patience in his last illness was exemplary, while he languished some months in a consumption, and in much pain. He still gave serious counsel to such as visited him, and was much in prayer for the church, particularly in England, and heartily lamented the great breaches among Protestants. To a neighbouring minister who was with him, he said, "I bless God "I never conformed: I have now the comfort of it." He told a friend who enquired what his thoughts were when he was turned out of his living, "That he was then supported "by God's promises, and ever since by his providences." He died, as he had lived; as penitent as if he had been the greatest sinner upon earth, but in the exercise of a lively faith; relying only upon Christ the mediator for pardon and acceptance with God. And he had this character from all that were acquainted with him, That he was one who laboured much for God, walked closely with him, and lived in great contempt of the world. He died *Sept.* 18, 1681, in the 58th year of his age.

WORKS. Spiritual Bondage and Freedom; (a good, serious, practical book.)..He left his papers with his good friend Mr. Thomas Gouge, who did not long survive him.

SHENLEY [R.] ISAAC LOEFFS, M. A. Fellow of *Peter-house, Camb*. Mr. Stephen Jones resigned this living, in the year 1650, when Mr. *Loeffs* succeeded him, being presented by three of the parishioners, upon whom the patron *(John Crew*, Esq; of Crew in Cheshire) had conferred the right of presentation for that time. Dr. *Calamy* has given a copy of Mr. *Jones*'s resignation of the living, of Mr. *Loeffs*' presentation to it, &c. which are too long and too uninteresting to be here inserted. After the Act of uniformity passed, Mr. *Loeffs* came to London, and was assistant to

Dr. *Owen*. [Dr. *Savage*, the late pastor of that church, writes, That from his church-book, Mr. *Loeffs* appears to have been some time co-pastor with Dr. *Owen* or Mr. *Clarkson*; standing in the list of pastors after the latter: and that he died *July* 10, 1689. Nothing more particular appears concerning his character than what is contained in the following recommendations of him.] The first is, that of Mr. (afterwards Dr.) Lazarus Seaman, *Sept.* 9, 1648. " These are to certify whom it may concern, that *Isaac Loeffs*, M. A. of the last year, and Fellow of Peter-house, Cambridge, is of a godly life and conversation, orthodox in judgment, and well-affected to the parliament. In witness whereof I have subscribed my hand. *La. Seaman, Magr.* C. S. P." After this follows a Latin testimonial of Henry Rich, Earl of Holland, &c. &c. one of his Majesty's most honourable privy-council, and Chancellor of the University of Cambridge: and of the Masters and Scholars of the said University; certifying, that Mr. *Isaac Loeffs* was admitted to the degree of M. A. at the appointed time, and annual commencement in the year 1648; and that he was a discreet person, whose learning, good life, and laudable conversation, qualified him for that degree, and could not be called in question by the envy of slanderous, or malice of insidious persons, &c. Given at Cambridge, *Dec.* 9, 1648.

§ WORKS. The soul's ascension in a state of separation, 8vo. 1690.

STORTFORD Bishop's [V.] Mr. JONATHAN PAINE. He is mentioned in *Newcourt's Rep. Eccl.* § It is uncertain where he preached after his ejectment. But a congregation of Dissenters was gathered in this place, of which the eminent Mr. *Craddock* became pastor, and it continues in a flourishing state to this day. The worthy Mr. *Angus* lately died there, having been pastor above half a century. See his funeral Sermon by his colleague, Mr. W. *Chaplin*, which contains a just character of him.

THERFIELD [R. 350*l*.] Mr. MARMADUKE TENNANT. He was an acceptable preacher, and an exemplary liver; eminent for piety and charity. He prefixed an epistle to the life of Mr. *John Janeway*, who died in his neighbourhood in 1657.

THORLEY [R. S.] Mr. WARREN. A very hopeful young man. § In 1654 Mr. *John Warren* was appointed one of the Triers of this county.

TOTTER-

TOTTERIDGE. William Tutty, M. A. He was ordained by Dr. *Curle* Bishop of Winchester, in 1640. Dr. Calamy produces a copy of the testimonials of his ordination, in which however there appears to be nothing singular. Mr. *Tutty*, after his ejectment, went first into a farm; but soon became chaplain to Col. *Markham*. He afterwards preached at Newgate-street, in the parish of *Hatfield* in this county, and died in 1678. He was a man of great abilities, good learning, and eminent piety; a follower of love and peace. He had great satisfaction in his Nonconformity, from his ejection to his grave. § In 1642, Mr. *Tuttey* (so his name is sometimes spelt) was vicar of *South Mymms*, not six miles distant from *Totteridge*, where *Chauncy* mentions him as curate in 1646. In 1654, he was appointed one of the Triers of this county.—He published a funeral sermon, and something on Sol. song, in prose and verse.

WALDEN (Paul's) [R.] Mr. Peachy. Dr. Calamy supposes him to be the person of that name who practised physic in London, and wrote several medical pieces. § But according to *Wood*, John Pechy M. D. who wrote the medical tracts, was only six years of age when the act of uniformity passed.

WALLINGTON. Mr. Sherwin. See *Baldock*.

WARE [V.] Mr. John Young. He kept up a considerable meeting for some years at *Kimpton*, in this county, where his name was long remembered with respect. § He was one of the *Hitchin* Lecturers in 1642, and a Trier for this county in 1654.

WATFORD [V.] Philip Goodwin, M. A. Of St. *John's Col. Camb.* He was among the Triers appointed in this county. He most probably quitted this living at the Restoration, as *Newcourt* enters his successor June 1661, tho' *Chauncy's* date is 1659. He is supposed afterwards to have conformed, as one of this name was rector of *Liston* in Essex in 1673, and there died in 1699. But as this might possibly be another person, and if it was the same, he might have been twelve years a nonconformist, his name is retained in our list.

WORKS. Family religion revived; a discourse on Family prayer.—The Lord's day revived.—Evangelical communion; a treatise on the Lord's Supper.—The History of Dreams.

§ WELWYN

§ WELWYN [R.] Nicholas Greaves, D. D. of *Oxford* university. He is not mentioned in Dr. Calamy's account, but there is the best authority for placing him among the ejected ministers, and his name will do honour to the list. He was the son of Mr. John Greaves, rector of *Colmore*, near Alresford, Hants. His elder brother, Mr. John Greaves, was the celebrated mathematician and traveller. His younger brothers were also men of eminence: Thomas in divinity, and Edward in physic. Nicholas was first a commoner of St. *Mary's Hall* Oxford; elected fellow of *All Souls*, 1627, and junior proctor of the university, in 1648. He took his degree of B. A. Nov. 1, 1642. and was created D. D. in the year following. He was afterwards promoted to the Deanry of *Dromore* in Ireland. It is probable that he fled into England in the time of the rebellion. *Chauncy* has his name at *Welwyn* in 1651. Bp. *Kennet*, in his Register and Chronicle, has the following extract from the Lincoln Registers, from whence it is plain that he was deprived of this rectory by the act of uniformity.—" 1662. " Die ult. Octob. Gabriel Towerson, clericus. A. M. ad- " miss. ad Rect. Eccl. de Wellwyn, Com. Hertford. per " privationem Nicolai Greaves, S. T. P. ult. Incumb. " virtute Actus Uniformitatis legitime vacantem, ex " Pres. Custodis et Sociorum Coll. Omn. Animarum. Oxon." N. B. This is the valuable living of which the celebrated Dr. *Young* was many years Rector.

WILLIAN [V.] Mr. Isaac Bedford. He was the son of an excellent father of the same name, who was first a school-master at *Sutton* in Bedfordshire, and afterwards many years minister of *Clifton*, four miles distant. This his son, after his ejectment, retired to *Clifton*, and lived upon a small farm of his own. He took scholars to board, and employed a Conformist to teach them. He died there about the year 1667. § He was one of the Triers in 1654, and a Lecturer at *Hitchin*. His name in the list is spelt Bedforde.

The following afterwards conformed.

Mr. Halsey, of *Broxborn.*—Dr. Hicks, of *Hertingford-bury*, afterwards rector of St. Margaret-Pattens in London.—Mr. Owen, of *Brandfield.*—Mr. Stallybrasse, of *Essingdon.*—Mr. Thornton, of *Hempsted.*—Mr. Godwin, of *Eastwick.*

MINISTERS

MINISTERS EJECTED OR SILENCED

IN

HUNTINGDONSHIRE.

BLUNTISHAM [R. 200*l.*] JAMES BEDFORD, B. D. The worthy son of Mr. Isaac Bedford, the excellent minister of Clifton in Bedfordshire; and there he was born. Mr. Bedford of *Willian*, in Hertfordshire was his brother. He was much applauded for his ability and faithfulness in the work of the ministry. [There was a Mr. *Bedford* a dissenting minister at *Royston*, early in the last century, who was probably a relation of his. There was also a clergyman of the same name, who held the living of *St. John's* in the town of *Bedford*, who was supposed to be of the same family.]

WORKS. A Sermon on Heb. ix. 27, at the funeral of a daughter of his eldest brother Samuel Bedford, Esq.

BOTTLEBRIDGE. Mr. SIMON KING. He was some time a schoolmaster at *Bridgnorth* in Shropshire, where Mr. *Baxter* and he lived together in the same house: they were afterwards fellow-labourers in *Coventry*. Mr. *King* was minister of Trinity parish in that city from 1642 to 1645. After 1662, he lived at *Long-Orton* near Peterborough. It pleased God to try him by many afflictions; and among others, with the burning of his house to the ground, in *August* 1689, by which he was in a manner deprived of all his substance, and that at a time when he and his wife were both of them above eighty years of age. He was an able scholar, a man of a solid judgment, of an honest heart and unblameable life; inclined to no extreams.

ELTON. Mr. COOPER. He was the patron of this valuable parsonage, which he held till 1662, when being
unable

unable to keep it himself, on account of the new terms of conformity, he gave it to Mr. *Ball,* who married his daughter, the son of the worthy Mr. *Ball* of Northampton; and a son of his afterwards possessed it. Mr. *Cooper* was a grave, venerable person, of the Puritan stamp; and a man of great note in this country, for the piety of his life, the prudence of his conduct, and his ministerial abilities.

HEMINGFORD. Mr. HEATH. There are in this place two Rectories and a vicarage.

HUNTINGDON. SAMUEL BROOKS, B. D. Many years Fellow of *Kath. Hall. Camb.* He was turned out for refusing to take the *Engagement.* He was a learned man, a great school-divine, and a laborious tutor, who always had a numerous company of pupils of good rank. He died at an estate of his own in *Essex.*

OVERTON Longvill. Mr. EDWARD SPINKS. He was also ejected at *Castor* in Northamptonshire, (a living reckoned worth 300*l. per ann.*) most probably at the Restoration, as it seems that living belongs to the Bp. of Peterborough. Which of the two was the sequestration doth not appear. Mr. *Spinks* was an able preacher, and a man of great note. After he was silenced, he lived near Mrs. *Elmes,* his wife's mother, who had a good estate, and made all nonconformist ministers welcome at her house.

＊ORTON (Cherry). Mr. GIBSON, M. A. He was many years Fellow of *Pemb. Hall, Camb.* and was presented to this parsonage, by that college, and it is one of the best belonging to it. It lies near Peterborough. Mr. *Gibson* was a good scholar, and an eminent preacher.

——Mr. SCOTT. The place of his ejectment is uncertain.

Mr. RICHARD KIDDER of *Standground,* after some time conformed, and was made Bishop of *Bath* and *Wells.* § He is well known as the author of a valuable work entitled "The Messiah."

MINISTERS EJECTED OR SILENCED

IN

KENT.*

. **A**DDISHAM [R.] Mr. CHARLES NICOLS. A clergyman in a MS. note says, " He only had some
estate in this parish, but never was Rector. Dr. *Du Montin*
had the living before the Restoration, and was collated a-new
by Abp. *Juxon*. *Nicols* settled there after the Restoration,
and held a meeting." § Probably the place of his ejectment
was *Barming*, as a person of this name is there mentioned.

ASH. Mr. WILLIAM NOKES. Of *Camb*. University,
where he was cotemporary, and very intimate, with Dr. Stillingfleet. After his ejectment he continued preaching here
and there as opportunity offered, but died in a few years, . He
was esteemed a man of good abilities. § *Hasted* spells his
name *Noakes*, and has the date 1659.

ASHFORD [V.] Mr. NICOLAS PRIGG. (*Hasted* writes
it SPRIGG.) He was a man of eminen tabilities, and a celebrated preacher. He married one Mrs. *Scott*, with whose
marriage-portion he bought some land, which maintained
them after his ejectment. He was so melancholy for many
years afterwards, that he was unable to preach. But he grew
better, and at length died in comfort.

BARHAM [Chapel, to the R. of *Bishopsbourn*.] Mr.
JOHN BARTON. In the diary of Mr. Thoroughgood of
Monkton, there is an account of some members of parliament,

---

* Several additions, in this county, are communicated by Mr. Isaac James,
particularly from HASTED's History of KENT.

and

and other well-disposed persons about this neighbourhood, who agreed to unite together in religious meetings. The former were Mr. *John Boys* of Betteshanger, Col. *John Dixwell* of Broom, in Barham, and Mr. (after Sir) *Harry Oxenden* of Dean in Wingham, with their relations. The ministers were, Mr. *Quinton* of Addisham, Mr. *Thoroughgood*, and Mr. *Barton*. Other persons also joined them, from several adjacent parishes, who had not the sacrament administered where they lived. They met at first once a fortnight on Fridays, and afterwards, once a month, they had a sermon, in some private house. They also met every month, upon the Lord's-day, to receive the Lord's-supper, after hearing a sermon in the church, and the three ministers above mentioned took their turns in officiating. They also kept many days of fasting and prayer together, and held on in this course very comfortably and profitably, for several years.

East BARMING [R.] Mr. NICOLS. § Possibly he might be the person mentioned at ADDISHAM. *Hastead* has this entry. " Richard Webb, 1624. Ob. Oct. 20. 1667. He " seems to have been displaced by the fanatics; for one " *Nicholls* held it at the restoration, and was ejected by the " Bartholomew-act,"—He mentions a Mr. *Nicholls* as ejected at LINTON in 1662, and refers to *Cal. Life of Baxt.* p. 286. 1 Ed.

BENENDEN [V.] Mr. JOSEPH OSBORN. One *Austin* being turned out of this living for insufficiency, the people got Mr. *Osborn* to preach among them for half a year, during which time he had an invitation to a place in *Sussex*. The people of *Benenden* having notice of it, met together, and united in an earnest request to Mr. *Osborn* to continue with them. As the income was but small, they readily entered into a subscription to encrease it to 60*l*. The patron of the living being then abroad with K. *Charles*, it fell into the hands of the Committee at London to provide for the place. The people promised to use their utmost interest with that Committee to get Mr. *Osborn* settled among them. They renewed their subscription for another year, and after that for three years more, and then for five. They also moved for an augmentation of 40*l. per ann.* which was obtained; and still cheerfully continued their own subscriptions.—When the Protector took upon him to place and displace ministers, Mr. *Osborn* was tried by the Committee of his appointing; and when he appeared before them, he brought a certificate from

4   the

the people, and another from the neighbouring ministers, as to his abilities and behaviour. He satisfactorily answered all the questions proposed to him, fifteen commissioners being present, Mr. *Caryl* in the chair. He afterwards obtained the Protector's order for the living, and the vicarage-house being gone to decay, the committe agreed to repair it.

At the Restoration in 1660, when all the ministers whom *Oliver* put in, were to be immediately turned out,— *Hendon*, Esq; the patron, who came over with K. *Charles*, finding Mr. *Osborn* greatly beloved by the people, and knowing the living to be but small, would not present any one in his room. His brother also (afterwards Sir *John Hendon,)* desired him to continue there, and, if he possibly could, to conform. Another of his acquaintance (a very considerable man) earnestly pressed him likewise to conformity. But he told him, That faith and a good conscience would stand him in more stead than a hundred livings; and so he quitted this vicarage in 1662. Mr. Buck, the Dean of Rochester, came to him soon after, and offered to enter into a bond of 500*l.* to put him, within a month, into a better living than *Benenden*, provided he would conform. To which he answered, That if he could have conformed at all, it should have been at *Benenden* rather than for any other place whatever; because he should never meet with a more affectionate people, or a place where he was likely to do more good. His integrity was the more remarkable, as he had six children when he was silenced; and his wife was then lying-in.

After his ejectment, he lived for some time at *Staplehurst,* and then went to *Hathfield* in Sussex, where he had four children more; and there he continued several years. He afterwards preached nine years at *Brighthelmstone.* About the year 1681, he was sued for 20*l.* a month, on account of his Nonconformity. Upon this he came to London, and preached some time at *Peckham.* He afterwards went to *Ashford* in this county, and from thence to *Tenterden*, where he continued about nine years. He spent about nine years more at *Barsted* near Maidstone, where he concluded his ministry, by reason of his infirmities, and then returned to *Staplehurst*, where he finished his course, *Dec.* 28, 1714, aged 85.—A kind providence attended him in all his removes. He lived in friendship with the established clergy; and at his death he left something to the poor in all the places in which he had resided.

. **BETTES-**

BETTESHANGER [R.] " John Dod, A. M. Nov. 9. " 1661, ejected 1662." *Hasted.*

BIDDENDEN [R.] Mr. William Horner.

BIRLING [V.] Mr. Thomas Gunns. He died about the year 1666.

BROMLEY [R.] Mr. Henry Arnold. " 1656, ejected 1662." *Hasted.*

CANTERBURY. The Cathedral. Mr. John Durant. He was born in the year 1620, but where, and how long he' lived, are unknown. He was an excellent practical preacher, as sufficiently appears from his

WORKS. Consolation for weak believers.—A Discovery of the glorious love of Christ to believers...Comfort and counsel for dejected souls...The Woman of *Canaan* ; Sermons on *Matt.* xv. 22, &c...Silence the duty of saints under every sad providence; a Serm. on the death of his daughter...[The salvation of saints by the Appearances of Christ : 1. Now in Heaven. 2. Hereafter from Heaven.]

—— John Player, M. A. He was born in this city, and educated in the free-school there. He was brother to Sir Thomas Player, chamberlain of London. After the fall of Abp. *Laud,* he became public preacher in the cathedral, and gave great satisfaction by the seriousness and beneficial effects of his labours. He was of a very peaceable and healing temper, and kept a good correspondence with all his brethren in the city. He was pious and devout towards God, and plain and honest in his conversation with men.

—— St. Margaret's [R.] Thomas Ventress, M. A. Of *Bennet Col. Camb.* He was born in St. Alphage parish in this city, and brought up in the King's school there. At the College (where he had *Erasmus's* chamber) he made remarkable progress in good learning ; and after taking his master's degree, devoted himself to the sacred ministry, and was ordained by Abp. *Laud.* He first began the stated exercise of his office in this city, where he was curate to Archdeacon *Kingsly* ; and afterwards settled in *St. Margaret's* ; § where he so behaved himself in those difficult times, when

§ " August 10, 1639 : ejected 1662. He was presented to the Hospital of " poor priests in Canterbury, and the parish church of St. Margaret annexed " to it, and in the patronage of the crown by lapse." *Hasted.*

there were so many changes in the state, that upon the king's return in 1660, he found more favour from the gentry and clergy than most of his brethren. He could not, however, be spared in 1662, and was ejected with the rest. But not thinking himself thereupon discharged from his work by his Lord and Master, he preached privately, as he had opportunity: and at last gathered a congregation, to which he became pastor, and laboured, tho' under great disadvantages, yet with great acceptance, for several years. At home he spent much of his time in his study, and in the instruction of several gentlemen's sons who were committed to his care.

Thus he continued to be employed till the latter end of K. *Charles's* reign; when he was not a little oppressed by the violent endeavours of two great informers, one of whom had once given great hopes as to his piety and seriousness. These two men (whose names were well remembered in this city) gave great disturbance to such as only desired liberty to serve and worship God according to their consciences. One of them, it was said, received some hundred of pounds out of the exchequer, for the good service he had done the church (or rather the Papists) in this affair; besides what he extorted by false indictments, &c. The other died miserably. Many nonconformists were imprisoned, and Mr. *Ventress* among the rest: but he found so much favour, as to be permitted to go home every night, upon his parole of returning to prison in the morning. He died soon after, with uncommon serenity. Laying himself down on his bed, dressed as he was, and taking his Greek Testament in his hand, he kissed it, laid it on his heart, and soon fell asleep in the Lord, in the 73d or 74th year of his age.

He was a person of no small learning, especially in history; a very pious man, and very careful in redeeming his time. He had his fixed hours for visits, which he would not exceed, nor must his friends. Indeed, he walked very much by rule in all things; tho' he did not desire to tie up others to his rules. He kept to one method of preaching, thinking that the most profitable to his hearers; and he was often elevated in it. He was a great enemy to divisions, as well as to every thing irreligious and immoral, especially among ministers, who should teach others by example as well as word. He followed peace with all men, as much as he could; but found that to obtain it was not *possible.* He greatly admired the

discipline

discipline of the French churches [as exercised in this city] and often expressed his great desire of their prosperity. Tho' he had not much of this world, yet he loved and desired it less. He sometimes partook of the generosity of others, but used it as a man that had set his heart upon better things, liberally imparting to those who looked no further than these, from an apprehension that they had more need of them, as well as more love to them than himself. Sir *Robert Hales* and his family at *Beaksbourn* were his constant attendants and great friends. He was prudent in all changes, and died in the hope of good things designed by God for these nations.

—— ST. ALPHAGE [R.] FRANCIS TAYLOUR, M. A. Of *Bennet Col. Camb.* Son of the famous Mr. Francis Tay-lour, a member of the Assembly, and well known by his works. He was born in this city, and there also received the first rudiments of learning. At Cambridge, it pleased God, by the small-pox, to deprive him of his sight. But he did not on that account lay aside his studies; and having the charitable help of others, who read to him, he improved greatly. He settled in his native city, where his ministerial labours were very acceptable and useful, till the fatal Bartho-lomew, 1662. He could not bear being idle; and therefore endeavoured to be useful afterwards, by preaching to, as well as conversing with, many who were disposed to en-courage his labours; and God wonderfully provided, not only for him, but also by him, for his brother and sister. His brother was blind as well as himself. But he not only main-tained him, but also took great pains to instruct him, and make him in love with serious religion: tho' not with all the success he desired.—Such were his gifts and graces, that, to-gether with his blindness, they greatly engaged the hearts of many to him; but could not move the compassion of some church-zealots, who seized and carried him to prison. How-ever God remembered him there; tho' he did not long sur-vive the cruel treatment he met with. He was buried in *St. Alphage*-church. He was a man of good abilities, and was noted as an eloquent preacher. He endeavoured to live in love with all parties of serious christians; and his ministry was much valued and well attended. He was chearful in all his afflictions.

WORKS. Grapes from *Canaan*; or the Believer's present Taste of future Glory...Also a Piece in Verse.

—— St. Stephen's [V.] § Robert Beak (or Beck.) M. A. He was born in or near Canterbury, and there had his first education, which was afterwards compleated at *Cambridge*. When he was silenced in 1662, he assisted Mr. Ventress, and others of his brethren in their work, preaching usually once every Lord's-day. God having blessed him with an estate, he took nothing for his services. He had a share in the troubles of K. *Charles's* reign; but bore them with great evenness of mind, and at length quietly resigned his soul to God, *Aug.* 31, 1679, aged about 59. His remains lie in *St. Mildred's* church. He was of an excellent temper, and could easily overlook slights and injuries. He was a diligent reader, making remarks on all that he read. He was a pious and devout man, and a plain serious preacher. He abounded in hospitality, and all manner of good works, to ministers and others. As he lived, so he died, in the exercise of charity.

CHALLOCK [Chap.] Mr. Corker. After his ejectment, he taught school in this parish for a livelihood.

CHART *Magna* [R.] Mr. Edward Line.

§ CHARTHAM [R.] Thomas Woodruff, A. M. Dr. Calamy has not his name, but from the following entry in *Hasted's* Hist. of *Kent*, v. iii. p. 157, it is unquestionable that he is to be added to our list. "Patron, the King: sede vac. Thomas Woodruff, A. M. instituted Oct. 3, 1646, ejected 1660. He was an inoffensive man, *tho'* a Presbyterian. He was chaplain to the earl of Warwick, by whose interest he obtained this Rectory, and when ejected, retired to the earl's house. He frequently affirmed in discourse, that he made 280*l.* of this Rectory."

CHATHAM [R.] † Thomas Carter, M. A. Of St. *John's Col. Camb.* A fine scholar, and an excellent preacher; much esteemed and loved by Dr. Stillingfleet Bp. of Worcester to his death: and often assisted by him. They were

§ Alias *Hackington*. Robert Beek was ejected here at the Restoration, for his successor John Gough, who had been sequestered in 1643, died Nov. 20. 1661. *Hasted*.

† This had been corrected in the *Errata* for CHARTHAM, on the authority of Mr. Duncombe of Canterbury; but from the preceding article it seems to have been right. From *Hasted*, who quotes Lambeth Surveys, it appears that Walter Rosewell was sequestered at Chatham, and restored in 1662.

cotem-

cotemporaries at the university. Mr. *Carter*, when silenced, practised physic, and lived at Newington-Butts, where he died, about the year 1685.

CHATHAM-DOCK. Mr. LAWRENCE WISE. [A man of a learned education, and in Oliver's time a preacher at *Aldgate* church. He afterwards became a Baptist, and preached latterly in Goodman's Yard in the *Minories.* He was one of the five ministers *Charles* II. sent for, when about to grant the Dissenters liberty.] He was imprisoned in Newgate for his Nonconformity in 1682, when his friends collected 50*l.* for him; he died in 1692, aged about 70. *Crosby*, vol. iii. p. 3ª.

WORKS. Select Hymns for the Sacrament. To which are added some of his last Sermons, apparently taken from broken Notes.

CHADDINSTON. Mr. THOMAS SEYLIARD, § or SILLYARD. See after DEAL.

CHILHAM [V.] SAMSON HERNE, M. A. Of *Camb.* university. *(Hasted* writes his name *Horne.)* After his ejectment he was kindly entertained by Sir *John Fagg*, at his house in Chartham parish, where he was not only lodged, but supported by that worthy baronet. He sometimes preached, and at last died there. He was a man of great learning, a very curious preacher, and pious liver. He had the sight of but one eye.

CLIFFE. Mr. HENRY HOLCROFT. Son to Sir Henry Holcroft; a learned and pious gentleman, some time Fellow of *Clare-Hall*, and cotemporary with the learned Mr. *Daniel Clarkson*, who married his sister. There were ever great endearments between Mr. *Clarkson* and him; and he obtained a good report in the church for his labours and his exemplary piety and charity.

CRANEBROOK [V.] Mr. WILLIAM GOODRIDGE. There were no less than ten ministers ejected from this town, and the places adjacent; at which the good people in that neighbourhood, being much affected, met together on a week-day, for prayer, that God would sanctify such a melancholy providence to them. For this they were prosecuted by a neighbouring justice of the peace, and by him and another were fined; and for non-payment they were sent to *Maidstone* jail for three months. Amongst the rest there was one *Harman Sheafe*, who was very kind to his parish-minister,

and

and usually attended upon public worship in the church of *England.* This severe method of proceeding, instead of diminishing the number of Dissenters in those parts, rather increased it.

DEAL [R.] Mr. HEZEKIAH KING. Of *Cambridge* University. He is said to have been ejected from this place on Bartholomew-day. His funeral sermon was preached by Mr, *Vinke,*

—— Mr. SAMUEL SEYLIARD was silenced somewhere in this neighbourhood. He was younger brother to Mr. Thomas Seyliard of Chaddingston. He was an acceptable preacher. § Hasted has his name SILLYARD,

DENTON. Mr. CLEMENT BARLING. "Rector, Sept." "23. 1644, presented by Sir Ant. Percival, Knt. ejected 1662." *Hasted.*

§ DEPTFORD. St. *Nicholas.* Mr. THOMAS MALLORY. Hasted mentions him here as "ejected for Nonconformity by the Act, 1662." This is the person of whom a short account is given vol. 1. p. 167, as Lecturer at St. *Michael's,* Crooked-Lane, London. § His sermon in the Morning Exercises at Cripplegate, before mentioned, is on *Gen.* xviii. 27, and affords proof of considerable ability.

DOVER. Mr. NATHANIEL BARRY ; who came hither in 1655. He was turned out in 1660, and departed this life 1675. § *Hasted's* entry is, "St. *Mary's.* Nath. Barry in 1654: salary 100*l.* He was ejected after the restoration, in 1661."

—— "St. *James's.* JOHN DAVIS, in 1656, ejected "1662. He seems to have been no settled incumbent. See "*Cal. Life Baxt.* p. 286. *Wood's Fasti,* p. 241."

EGERTON [Chap.] Mr. WALTER PALMER. After the Uniformity-act took place he continued preaching till he was forced to desist, by being beset with a troop of horse and two or three hundred men.

ELTHAM [V.] Mr. OVERTON,

FAIRLANE. Mr. DARBY,

FEVERSHAM [V.] Mr. NATHANIEL WILMOT. By his labour in preaching and catechizing, &c. he wrought a great reformation in this town, and brought the Lord's-day
to

to be very strictly kept. After he was ejected he endeavoured to carry on the same good work, by preaching from place to place, as God opened a way for him. At length he was fixed pastor of a church at *Dover*, where he had Mr. *Starr* for his assistant. God was with him there, and he was much beloved. He was esteemed a good scholar, and an excellent preacher. He was very laborious in his work. § *Hasted* mentions him as being ejected both here and at PRESTON, in 1662.

FOLKSTONE [V.] Mr. BAKER. After his ejectment he became very poor, and his understanding was impaired. He lived for some time in a very afflicted, distressed state, and at length died at *Dover*.

—— Mr. *Rolles* was ejected from the same place.

GODMARSHAM [V.] Mr. ROBERT FERGUSON. One as much known as most men, and best able to give his own character. Some time after his ejectment he taught university-learning at *Islington*, and was assistant to Dr. *Owen*; but at length he ran so far into political matters as to fall under general censure. He was very intimate with lord Shaftesbury, when he was run down by the court, and followed him into Holland. He came back with the duke of *Monmouth* in 1685, and was with him in the *West*; but made a shift to escape after his defeat. He came again with the prince of *Orange* in 1688, who, when he was king of Great-Britain, gave him a good place; but being disgusted, he fell in with the malecontents in his reign, as he had before done in the reign of K. *Charles* II. He was indeed a man by himself; and behaved so that the ministers were ashamed of him. He was always plotting, and yet still found a way to escape. He was in the first proclamation that was published in K. Charles's time, upon occasion of what was called the *Presbyterian plot*; but when Mr. Legat, the messenger, had warrants delivered to him to seize other accused persons, a strict charge was given him by Mr. Secretary Jenkyns not to take Mr. *Ferguson*, but to shun him wherever he met him; and in whatever company he might be, to let him escape. This is a mystery that is not to be unriddled, without believing him to be a state-intelligencer, employed to betray others.

The duke of *Monmouth*, speaking of him when he was upon the scaffold, called him " a bloody villain." Bp. *Burnet*, in his *History of his own Time*, says, " He was a hot

and

and bold man, whose spirit was naturally turned to plotting. He was always unquiet, and setting people on to some mischief." He adds, that " He knew a private thing of him, by which it appeared that he was a profligate knave, and could cheat those that trusted him entirely." By which probably he refers to the affair of the lady *Vere Wilkinson*, of which the author had a particular account from that good lady's own mouth. The Bishop farther adds, " He was cast out by the Presbyterians, and then went among the Independents, where his boldness raised him to some figure, tho' he was at bottom a very empty man. He had the management of a secret press, and of a purse that maintained it, and he gave about most of the pamphlets writ on that side, and with some he passed for the author of them. And such was his vanity, because this made him more considerable, that he was not ill pleased to have that believed, tho' it only exposed him so much the more." He died in 1714, very poor and low, tho' he had some persons of rank often resorting to him.

WORKS. The interest of religion; with the import and use of scripture metaphors, and some reflections on Mr. *Sherlock*'s writings, particularly his Discourse on the knowledge of Christ. (A good useful book.)—A sober Inquiry into the nature, measure, and principle of moral Virtue.—A Discourse on Justification...And many political Tracts. § Among the rest, The Duke of MONMOUTH's MANIFESTO, on his landing at *Lime*, A. D. 1684.

GOUDHURST [V.] Mr. EDWARD BRIGHT. He had the character of a very good man, and was endowed with a great deal of patience, which indeed he much needed, having the affliction of a very froward and clamorous wife. On this account many thought it a happiness to him to be dull of hearing.

GRAVESEND [R.] Mr. SHARP.

HAWKHURST [R.] Mr. EPHRAIM BOTHEL. " From 1657 : ousted by the Bartholomew-act." *Hasted.* He was no great scholar, but he was a very plain, honest, and good man.

HEVER. Mr. JOHN PETTER. He was descended from a religious and reputable family in this county. In his whole

§ Concerning this piece Bp. Burnet thus writes. " The Duke of Monmouth's " Manifesto was long, and ill penned : full of black and dull malice. It was plainly FERGUSON's style, which was both tedious and fulsome." *Hist. of own Time* Vol. ii. p. 325, 8vo. 1743.

deportment

deportment he was an example to his flock. and was kind and beneficent to all. After his ejectment he removed to *Sevenoak*, where he died, about 60 years of age. Mr. Burrowstone, his curate, succeeded him § in this living from whence he was ejected in 1662, having possessed it twelve years.

WORKS. He wrote a Preface to a large Commentary on St. MARK, in two volumes folio, written by his brother *George Petter*, M. A. which he published in 1661, with some account of the author.

HORSMONDEN [R.] Mr. EDWARD RAWSON. Dr. Walker says, He was presented to this living in 1655; and adds, " He was a New-England man, and a violent Presby-" terian :" which, if true, was a little peculiar [his country-men being warm Independents.] He was esteemed a man of great piety. Mr. *Elliston* had formerly been in this place, and could have cut down timber there, to the value of 200l; but he declared, It should not be said that *Horsmonden* had made him rich. *Hasted* has " Edward Rawson 1653, ejected 1662."

HUNTON [R. 180l.] Mr. LATHAM.

ICKHAM [R. 250l.] Mr. JOHN SWAN. He afterwards commenced physician.

LAMBERHURST [V.] Mr. STEEL. He was a man of eminent piety, who was far advanced in years when he was ejected.

LANGLEY. Mr. TILDEN.—" 1653, ejected 1662." *Hasted.*

St. LAWRENCE. See Isle of *Thanet*.

LEE [R.] WILLIAM HICKOCKS, M. A. A small work of his was published after his death, in the preface to which it was said to be " A taste of the fruit, under the weight " whereof the tree that bore it did bend and break and fall." The title of it is, *Strength made perfect in Weakness*; in 4 sermons, 1674.

LENHAM [V.] § THOMAS SHEWELL, M. A. Of *Camb.* university. He was born at Coventry, where his father was

§ Hasted, who spells his name *Shewell*, does not place him among the vicars here but at the curacy of LEEDS, above mentioned. He notices his ejectment in 1662 and quotes *Cal. Life Baxt.*

a rea reputable citizen and clothier. He was a pupil of that learned and excellent person Mr. James Cranford. His first settlement in the ministry was at this place, and he was ejected from it by the Act of uniformity. He afterwards kept a private school at *Leeds* in this county. He married a niece of the Rev. Mr. *Thomas Case.* After many years, he returned to his native city, and continued preaching there to the last. There was something extraordinary in the circumstance of his death. He had been for some time preaching upon the subject of original sin, from *Rom.* v. and had not finished it. On the Lord's-day before he died, tho' in perfect health, instead of going on (as was expected) with his former discourse, to the great surprize of all his auditors, he took for his text, *Rev.* xxii. 21. ' The grace of our Lord Jesus ' Christ be with you all, Amen:' on which he preached a most excellent sermon. The people were under very great concern, and some of them being afraid he had a design to leave them, enquired of his daughter whether she knew the occasion of his changing his subject. She told them, that on the Saturday evening she perceived him walking about in his chamber, and as he did not come down to family prayer at the usual time; she went up to him, and enquired how he did. He told her that he found his thoughts in such confusion, that he could not go on with his subject, but must preach the next day on something else. However, he appeared to continue very well till Wednesday, which was his lecture-day, and went to the meeting-house in perfect health. He prayed as long and consistently as usual. But having opened his bible, and named his text, he began to falter in the reading of it, and immediately dropped down in an apoplectic fit. He was carried into the vestry, and never spoke one word after, but died in about two hours, *Jan.* 19, 1693. Mr. *Tong* preached and published his funeral sermon.

LOOSE. Mr. WILLIAM LOCK. He was a diligent and faithful minister of Christ ; much beloved by his people, towards whom he also bore a tender affection. Just before his ejectment in 1662, he preached his last sermon to them, from *Acts* xx. 32. Telling them in his introduction, " That those words, which were part of *St. Paul*'s farewell sermon to the *Ephesian* elders, he had chosen for the subject of his to them ; but with this sad difference in the case, that St. *Paul* was but called by Providence to service elsewhere, whereas he and a considerable number of his brethren, must be laid by in silence. They (the *Ephesians*) it is true, were no longer to hear him ; but, saith he, our mouths must be stopped from
speaking

speaking in a ministerial way any more. In this situation he said, He knew nothing he could better do for them, than, according to his text, to ‘ commend them to God, and to the ‘ word of his grace.’ &c.’’ Many were the proper, useful, and affecting things he left with them. He reminded them of the uncertain terms of enjoying ministerial advantages; of the affection which good ministers bear to a people they have any time had relation to; and their concern at parting. In many other particulars did he instruct, encourage, and exhort them, suitably to the occasion, and the import of the text; chiefly insisting upon this proposition : “ That God is the great refuge of his people, who will take care of them in all times and conditions.” In the close of all he reminded them, as *Paul* did the *Ephesians*, of the time he had been with them, and made the same appeal, that he ‘ had not shunned to declare to them the whole counsel of God;’ that he had studied more to profit, than in a sordid way to please; sought more to gain their souls to Christ, than to make a worldly gain of them to himself. And now, since his public ministry must end, he commended them to God, who so takes care of his church and children, as they had heard; and to the word of his grace, which, thro’ mercy, they yet had in their hands, and which, studied and used aright, would ‘ build them up, ‘ and give them an inheritance among all them that are sanc- ‘ tified.’

LYDD [V. 300*l.*] Mr. HEMMINGS.

MAIDSTONE [*Abp.* C.] Mr. JOSEPH WHISTON. After his ejectment, he continued some years in this county, till he was called to the pastoral charge at *Lewes* in Sussex, where he continued to the time of his death, which was for near twenty years. He was congregational in his judgment; a man of great wisdom, self-denial, and moderation, who endeavoured to promote unanimity among Christians of different denominations. Upon K. James’s liberty, he declared, that where there was a congregational minister, he was for having the people who were presbyterians to acquiesce in him; and where there was a presbyterian minister, he was for having the people who were congregational to acquiesce in him. He had a considerable hand in promoting an association of ministers of both descriptions, which died with him. Tho’ he had no children, yet he wrote much, and to good purpose, on the covenant-privileges of the infant-seed of believers. Mr. *Baxter* said, that hardly any man had written with more judgment upon that subject. When he drew near his end, being

being asked, what his thoughts were as to that point upon which
he had written so much, he said, "He was not conscious to
himself, that he had discoursed or written any thing on that
subject, but what was according to the mind of our Lord
Jesus Christ, the consideration of which was a great consolation to him then in a dying hour §." He frequently expressed
his apprehension that the sword was to pass thro' the land.
He died in *January* 1690. in the 63d year of his age, and was
interred in the church-yard of St. Michael in *Lewes*, where
are deposited the remains of several ministers who were
ejected for Nonconformity, *e. g.* Mr. *Jones*, Mr. *Stani-
nough*, Mr. *Earle*, Mr: *Postlethwait*, Mr. *Beecher*, Mr.
Crouch, &c. besides Mr. *Bunyard* and *Osborn*, who died
before, and who were of the very same spirit and opinions.

WORKS. Infant-Baptism from Heaven. Part I... Ditto
Part II...An Essay to revive the primitive Doctrine and Practice of
Infant-Baptism...Infant-Baptism plainly proved...A brief Disc. of
Man's natural Proneness to, and Tenaciousness of Error...The
right Method of proving Infant-Baptism.

———Mr. JOHN CRUMP, was ejected from the same place.
He was a considerable divine, and a useful preacher; blessed
with a most agreeable temper, and remarkable for his affable
deportment, which much recommended him to those with
whom he conversed. He was of so moderate a spirit, that
after his ejectment, the conforming minister of *Boxley* (two
miles from *Maidstone*) often admitted him into his pulpit.
He died and was buried at *Maidstone*, where his memory
was long precious. He succeeded the eminent Mr. *Thomas
Wilson* in this parish, and was strongly recommended by him
to it. §This circumstance is mentioned in the Life of Mr.
Wilson, where is the following passage: "Being sensible
"of his approaching death, he was exceedingly solicitous
"for the town and parish whereof he was minister, and sent
"for some of them, who were prudent and gracious, and ad-
"vised them to consider of some able and godly minister to
"succeed in his place. He recommended unto them Mr.
"*John Crump*, a worthy minister, as the fittest that he knew
"to be their pastor. And accordingly Mr. *Crump* did suc-
"ceed him, not only in his place, but also in his faithfulness
"and diligence and serviceableness, to the great comfort and
"advantage of the people." This must have been about

§ This was a proof of his great integrity, but nothing more. Many a Baptist author has been able to say the same. ED.

the

the year 1653, for Mr. *Wilson* is said to have been born in 1601, and to have died at the age of 59.*—It doth not appear that Mr. *Crump* published any thing but a Discourse on the Parable of the great Supper.

Town MALLING [V.] Mr. SAMUEL FRENCH. After his ejectment, for the better maintaining his family, he betook himself to trade, for which few were better capacitated. But in the midst of a great currency of business, he found himself considerably reduced, and left off in good time. He was an ingenious man, and a chearful christian. He was troubled for his Nonconformity, both by the ecclesiastical and civil courts. In 1684, he at once had his goods distrained, for the great crime of preaching the gospel, and his person imprisoned in Maidstone jail for six months, upon the Five-mile-act, having neither fire nor candle in the winter-time, nor yet a chamber allowed him for privacy. He had no company he could delight in, but his God, and his wife who would be his fellow-sufferer. He had once taken the Oxford-oath, but had no certificate of it; so that he was required to take it a second time; when, having studied the matter more fully, he was dissatisfied to do it, and suffered imprisonment. During his confinement, some christian friends from Staplehurst made him more than a bare visit, which he gratefully remembered afterwards; and as soon as he was released, he went and spent a Lord's day amongst them, preaching upon that text, *Acts* iv. 23. where it is said of *Peter* and *John* who had been imprisoned, that ' being let go, they went to their own company.' This proved the happy occasion of his fixing in a pastoral relation there, among a kind people, of whom he even boasted, and with whom he spent both his labours and himself. He died *August* the 20th, 1694, and was buried at Staplehurst. It is memorable, that at that time when Mr. *French* came to Staplehurst, being in a remarkably cold winter, when yet the fire of persecution burnt outrageously throughout England, that place, with Cranbrook and Tenterden, enjoyed a considerable degree of public liberty; which continued even to the time of the Indulgence.

MINSTER and MUNCTON. See Isle of THANET.

* See CLARK's last vol. of Lives, 1683. page 39. N. B. There must be a misprint in the date either of his birth or of his death.

NET-

NETTLESTED [R.] Mr. Deacon § The chapel of *Barmingjett* was annexed to this rectory.

NEW-CHURCH [V.] Mr. Spencer.

NORTHBORNE. Mr. Lane. § Hasted mentions him as ejected *Aug.* 1662.

§ PENSHURST. Mr. John Mawdell. Hasted mentions him as ejected in 1662, and refers to the Parliamentary surveys, vol. xix, as also to *Calamy's* Life of *Baxter*. But his name is not in the *Account*, or *Contin.* and consequently not in the former edit. of the Noncon. Mem.

PLAXTED [Q. *Plaxtole.*] Mr. Matthew Darby.

RAINHAM [V.] Mr. Carter.

ROCHESTER. Mr. Ackworth.

ROLVENDEN [V.] Mr. Richard Gyles. After being ejected and silenced, he was desired, by a messenger from the parish-minister of *Sandhurst*, to preach for him one Lord's-day ; which he did. But this minister, being threatened for suffering a person not episcopally ordained to preach in his church, joined with the informers, and prosecuted Mr. *Gyles* and some of his hearers for a conventicle. Upon which about 80*l.* was levied upon them ; *viz.* 60*l.* for the minister's preaching twice, (which, because he was judged unable to pay it, was fixed upon the hearers) and 5*l.* a man upon several officers, for their neglect to suppress the said conventicle ; besides what some of them were fined as hearers. An appeal was made by many of them to the quarter-sessions at Maidstone ; when all the impannelled jury, who were not known to the court to receive the sacrament at church, were challenged upon the motion of the justices. They therefore were set aside and more fit men taken in, who found the morning-meeting a conventicle, tho' contrary to the judgment of several lawyers. Hereupon the appellants' council moved, that the matter of the afternoon-meeting might be found specially, and argued at the next session before the court, which was agreed to ; and when it was argued, the appellants had the judgment of the court in their favour, and the money levied for the afternoon was restored,

SANDWICH. Mr. Robert Webber. He was one of the commissioners in this county for ejecting scandalous ministers ; and five others were joined with him, who were
all

all afterwards sufferers for Nonconformity. See *Culmer's Looking-glass*, p. 38, 39.

SHOREHAM [R. 150*l*.] Mr. DUKE.

SMARDEN [R.] Mr. THOMAS VAUGHAN. " July 19, 1644, ejected 1662." *Hasted.*

SMETHE [Chap. to *Aldington*] Mr. SINGLETON. Mr. *Lewis*, of Margate, says, " Mr. *Singleton*, whether he conformed or not, could not keep *Smethe* without the rector's consent;" and asks, " With what justice or propriety of speech, can any man or men be said to be ejected from places for their Nonconformity, which they could not, according to the constitution of the government, have held had they conformed ?" It is sufficient to reply, That they may justly and properly be said to have been *silenced;* and therefore it is agreeable to the plan of this work to mention them. By the Act of uniformity Mr. *Singleton*, with multitudes more, was not merely removed from a particular station, but disabled for service in any other.

SOUTH-FLEET [R.] HENRY SYMONS, M. A. All that is known of him is, that he published an assize-sermon at Maidstone, *March* 17, 1657.

SPELDHURST [R.] Mr. DRAPER.

STAPLEHURST [R. 200*l*.] Mr. DANIEL POYNTEL. Of *Camb. University.* He was born at Chisselhurst, and was famous in all the county for his extraordinary abilities natural and acquired, his eminent piety, sweetness of temper, and great moderation; for his generous principles, his great acquaintance with, and interest in, the clergy; for his rational and yet earnest way of preaching, and learned expositions of difficult texts of scripture; in a word, for being an honour and ornament to the church, and her champion too, excepting her hierarchy, against which he was always vehement. His peaceable spirit was troubled with some unquiet Baptists and Quakers. Having at one time severely reflected upon the latter, in expounding *Matt.* vii. 15. *Beware of false prophets, which come to you in sheep's clothing,* &c. one of them came to his church the next Lord's-day, and declared he was sent of God. But Mr. *Poyntel* being then upon the following verses, the Quaker

4   expressed

expressed his disappointment, expecting something farther on the former subject. Upon this Mr. *Poyntel* took occasion with advantage to argue, That the Quaker could not be sent of God who certainly knew the subject he would be upon, and would doubtless have better informed his messenger—His Tuesday lecture in this place was much frequented by people from the neighbouring parishes, to hear his explication of the principles of religion, and the obscure passages of the prophets.

· Mr. Poyntel often expressed his wish to be satisfied with the terms of conformity; which made some zealots say, He wanted to blind his conscience for a fat benefice. But he could never bring himself to swallow the oaths, or dispense with the obligations he must have brought himself under. The weighty sense he had of his ordination-vow, his desire of doing good to souls, and the woe he expected if he did not preach the gospel, induced him to comply farther than some persons of narrower principles thought warrantable, and sometimes brought him into the pulpit, at *Staplehurst*, after *Bartholomew*-day, to preach to his own flock. But it was plain he was not covetous of the fleece, for he generously told the succeeding incumbent, that he desired nothing of the income, if he could but have the pulpit one part of the day ; who said, he was willing to grant it, provided he could get leave of the archbishop. Mr. *Poyntel* then waited on his grace, with whom he was very intimate, and readily got his permission. But the incumbent, having been in the mean while, otherwise advised, absolutely refused it. And therefore, as soon as the licenees came forth in K. *Charles* II.'s reign, he opened a meeting at *Staplehurst*. which was greatly crowded during the remainder of his life: and once, so much as to prove the cause of his death. The windows being taken down to let in air, upon a funeral occasion, he took so violent a cold as threw him into a fever, and carried him off, delirious, in a few days, 1674. Thus lived and died " the learned Mr. *Poyntel*," (for that was his common name in this county) an honour to the party with whom he suffered, a bright ornament to the catholic church, and a reproach to the spirit of bigotry and ignorance, which triumphed in his ejectment His ministry appears to have been very useful, for he had scarcely a prayerless family in his parish.

WORKS.

WORKS. A Discourse at the *Dutch* Church in Maidstone against the Hierarchy; for which he was like to have had much trouble from the bishops....Moses and Aaron; or the Minister's right, and the Magistrate's duty vindicated: an Answer to a piece against Tythes, by R. Kingnoth, a famous Baptist, who acknowledged his fault and begged him to call his book in, promising to do the same by his.--He left some MS. sermons against Regicide principles, in the hands of his son-in-law, Dr. *Groombridge* of *Cranbrook*. Also a piece against the Infallibility of the Light within.

STONE [S.] Mr. HENRY PRICE. Dr. Walker writes his name *John*, and says he came to this living in 1657. §*Hasted* has it, "Henry Price 1657, ejected 1662."

STOURMOUTH [V.] Mr. RICHARD BURES. Of *Chr. Ch. Oxf.* Born in *Nov.* 1629, at *Northall* in Middlesex, where his grandfather had been minister, and educated at St. *Paul*'s school in London, under Dr. Tong. It doth not appear that he had any other living than this of *Stourmouth*, from whence he was ejected in 1662. He had some disturbance there from the Quakers, as several of his neighbours also had. Some time after his ejectment he removed to *Guildford* in Surrey; and from thence went to *Farnborow* and *Frimley*, in all which places he preached as occasion offered, but never took a pastoral charge till the year 1692. While he was at *Guildford* he was twice imprisoned for preaching; first in the Marshalsea in Southwark, and next in Windsor-Castle. His deliverance from this latter confinement was remarkable. Lord Mordant being then governor, was one day visited by Dr. *Lewis*, who had been his tutor at Oxford. Mr. *Bures* hearing of it, and having himself been a pupil of the Dr.'s, he prevailed with the keeper to convey a note into his old tutor's hand. The Dr. upon this interceded with the governor for his discharge; and, upon his arguing against it, offered to be bound for his appearance upon summons, if needful; and being very importunate, he at length prevailed. Some years after, Mr. Price when he lived at *Frimley*, was again taken up at Guildford, by means of Mr. Thornbury, a clergyman, who had professed a great kindness for him. The very next day, this Mr. Thornbury came to him, and pretended to be much concerned at what had befallen him, assuring him, that he had not either directly or indirectly the least hand in it. Soon after this, he was seized with such a disorder, that he first attempted the life of one of his children, and afterwards went into a wood

and hanged himself.—Mr. *Bures* came to London about the
year 1677. He succeeded Mr. *Turner* in Hatton-Garden
in 1692, and died *May* 7th, 1697. He was a very valuable
man, of the old Puritan stamp : of great gravity, and an excellent preacher. He was succeeded by Mr. *Christopher
Taylor.*

STROUD [2.] Mr. DANIEL FRENCH. He was the son
of Mr. Samuel French of Town Malling, and was reputed a
very pious man.

TENTERDEN [V.] Mr. GEORGE HAWES.

ULCOMB [R.] WILLIAM BELCHER. A. M. § Instituted 1643, ejected 1662. He was also ejected from the
Rectory of BIRCHOLT. *Hasted.*—Dr. Walker relates something to his disadvantage respecting tithes. Supposing this
story true, all the inference that can be justly drawn from it
is this ; that there have been ill men on all sides : which no
wise man ever questioned. But probably Mr. *Belcher* may
be herein considerably wronged ; for one who was nearly related to him assured the author, that he was a person of
great piety and probity, and very useful : nor can it be easily
supposed that, if his character had been so stained, the excellent Mr. *Wilson* of Maidstone would have suffered his daughter to marry him.—§ Mr. *John Belcher* is supposed to have
been a son of his. He was a Sabbatarian Baptist, and died
about 1696. Mr. Joseph Stennett preached his funeral sermon, which may be seen in his works. *Crosby* has no account of him.

WICKHAM [R.] EDWARD ALEXANDER, M.A. He
was born at Canterbury and educated at Cambridge. His
living was of considerable value. Dr. Walker says he was
admitted to it in 1654. After his ejectment, he gave his labours freely in and about Canterbury till he died. He was
inclined to melancholy, especially after he was cast out of
his church, but he maintained such a behaviour, that he was
respected by persons of various persuasions. Tho' he was
not insensible of the injuries done him, he was ready to overlook them. He strove against every thing like malice and
revenge, and denied himself at last to his own prejudice. He
greatly excelled in prayer. § *Hasted* has one of his name at
Ightham. Doubtless the same.

WOOLDHAM [R.] Mr. SHEWEL.

WOOLWICH [R.] Mr. John Hawkes. § *Hasted's* entry is " *William Harney, or* Hawkes, 1650, ejected Aug. 1662."

WOOTTON [R.] Edward Coppin, M. A. Of *Bennet Col. Camb.* He was born at *Beaksbourn,* and educated partly in a country-school, and partly at Canterbury. At Bartholomew-day 1662, he did what the act required in order to his continuance in his public charge; but was very uneasy afterwards, and therefore gave up his living, and betook himself to his native village, where he lived upon his own estate. He was there in great esteem with Sir *Robert Hales* and his family, who were his neighbours. There also, when liberty was given, he preached in his own house to any that would attend, but frequented the established worship. He died at this place, and was buried at *Wootton.* He was esteemed a good scholar, a devout and prudent man, who preached well, and sought peace both for himself and others: desiring not to trample upon any, nor to be trampled upon by any. [He had an uncommon fear of the pains of death, and it was mercifully ordered that he died suddenly. MS. note.] § *Hasted* says, in 1619. He mentions him as instituted in 1646, and ejected 1662.

In the Isle of THANET.

The Rev. Mr. Lewis of *Margate,* in his MS. observations on the *Account of the ejected Ministers,* which he drew up for Dr. Walker, and afterwards sent to Dr. *Calamy* for his use, takes some particular notice of the ministers ejected here. As to those ejected from *St. Peter's, St. Lawrence, Monkton,* and *St. Nicholas,* he says, " they have all left very good characters behind them." With respect to those said to be ejected at *St John's* and *Minster,* he makes some objections to the Dr.'s account, to which the Dr. replies. The editor has been favoured with a copy † of *Calamy,* in the margin of which are manuscript notes, which appear to be the remarks of this Mr. *Lewis* on the Dr.'s vindication.]

St. John's.—— Mr. *Lewis* says, there was no settled minister, and consequently none ejected. [It appears how-

† This is that referred to in the Preface, page 16, vol. 1. and is the property of Mr. *Thomas Lomas,* of Islington. The quotations marked MS. are from those notes.

ever

ever that one who preached some time in this parish was silenced there, *viz.* Mr. *Stephen Street,* the person mentioned at first by Dr. Calamy at St. Margaret's. Mr. *Lewis* says, " no such person was ever vicar here." But he might have been a preacher here, tho' not vicar. It afterwards appeared that he was at *St John's* just before the Uniformity-act took place. In Mr. Thoroughgood's Diary (mentioned below) is this note.—" 27 *July,* 1662, Mr. *Street,* at St. John's in this island, was silenced and put by preaching, by Capt. Rook, by special order from the king himself, because the book that was set out concerning the execution of Col. Oakey and two others was seen at his house." His daughter says, he is the person mentioned at *Buckstead* in Sussex ; [See there] and that he only preached in this island for some time occasionally. [The MS. note here in the *Contin.* p. 548, is, " Thomas Stephens, S. T. B. was admitted to this vicar-" age *Sept.* 18, 1660, and buried here *Jan.* 2, 1661, John " Rice, curate here, was buried *Oct.* 26, 1661. John " Overing vicar 1661, who died 1665. By this it appears, " that if *Street* was here, he was a curate or assistant to " *Stevens,* and was removed before the Act of uniformity."]

ST. MARGARET'S. § [Dr. *Calamy* having remarked in his *Contin.* that Mr. *Lewis* denies Mr. *Street* had ever been here ; the MS. note, p. 547, is, " One *Edward Rigs* came " hither from *Deal,* 1657. He had been chaplain to vice-" admiral Blake. In 1660, he was forced to remove, and " was afterwards a clerk to a brewhouse in London, and in " 1661 concerned in a conspiracy against the government." Qu. *Was there any legal proof of this fact?*]

ST NICHOLAS. Mr. WILLIAM JACOB. He is mentioned in several lists, sent to the author, as being the person ejected here ; but nothing more is said concerning him. § *Hasted's* entry is, " Wm. Jacob, about 1653, ejected 1662."

ST. PETER'S. Mr. WILLIAM WINGFIELD, Mr. *Lewis* owns that he left a very good name there.

MONKTON [V. 100.] Mr. NICOLAS THOROUGHGOOD. Of *New-Inn Hall, Camb.* The following account of him

___

§ Hasted calls this " St. *John Baptist,* alias MARGATE." He is doubtful whether there was any settled minister here from 1655 to the restoration, but confirms the above account of Mr. Stephens.

is

is extracted from his Diary.—He was born of a good family at *Deal*, in 1620. Besides what learning he got at the grammar-school, he had the assistance of a gentleman who was a considerable traveller and scholar, (who lodged in the house with him,) who, out of school-hours, instructed him in Latin, Greek, French, Spanish and Italian. When he was about sixteen years of age, he took a fancy to travel, and went a voyage to *Spain, Italy*, &c. carrying goods and money with him, with which he traded to advantage, and spent some time in the university of *Padua*, where he had for his tutor a Scottish Doctor, who was a Papist, and but loose in his morals. While he was abroad, he was in great perplexity of spirit about religion, and often under great temptations to question the main foundations of it: but applying himself to God by serious prayer, and diligently consulting his word, he at length obtained satisfaction that religion was a great reality: and on his return, (after being absent two years and an half) he had so warm a sense of it, that others could not but observe it. He now thought merchandize or any other employment mean, in comparison with the honourable work of the ministry, which he most earnestly desired to be fitted for, and useful in. In order to this, he determined upon a close application to his studies, and entered himself in *New-Inn-Hall*, where he had Mr. *Cooper* for his tutor. Here he was very studious, and made great proficiency; taking care to choose the soberest associates, that so the seriousness of his spirit might increase instead of abate.

In the time of the civil war, the house was pillaged, and he being absent, lost his books, cloaths, and other things, which he never could recover. He afterwards pursued his studies at home, and had the assistance of one Mr. *Vahn*, and other learned men. At length he went and took his degree at *Cambridge*; tho' what it was doth not appear. Afterwards, living with an uncle who was purser of the ship called the *Happy Entrance*, which was going out under the Earl of *Warwick*, lord-admiral, on the recommendation of Mr. *Calamy* and Mr. *Cornish*, he became chaplain to the Earl, and went in the same ship with his uncle, The officers, and all on board, were very civil to him; he prayed with them daily, and preached and catechized every Lord's-day. They seemed to attend, and he was useful to them. After his return, upon the pressing invitation of the parishioners, he went to *Hawhurst*, in Kent, *Dec.* 12, 1644, and settled there. They promised to make the living an 100*l. per ann,* which they paid him duly for a year and a half: but, upon obtaining an augmentation from government, their additions were withdrawn. On *June* 20, 1645, he, with nine other ministers, was ordained in St. Magnus church at London-Bridge, by Mr. *Richard Lee*, Dr. *Wm. Gouge*, &c. Mr. *Cook* prayed over him. He then returned to *Hawkhurst*, much strengthened in spirit for his work, and was useful till the Engagement came out, for not taking of which he was discharged, *April* 30, 1651, and at the same time lost a whole year's augmentation, of 50*l.* which his successor received.

The 13th of *June* following, he went to *Monkton*, on the invitation of Major Foch and Mr. Thomas Paramor, who were both in the commission of the peace, and lived in that parish. Those two gentlemen entertained him very civilly, and gave him his board, and the keeping of a horse, tho' he could not yet be settled as minister there, because of the Engagement. The state of the living at that time stood thus: Two of the inhabitants of *Monkton* were made sequestrators, and impowered to collect the income, and to satisfy such as should from time to time supply the place. They paid Mr. *Thoroughgood* the income, till the Engagement was taken away. They also paid him the arrears that were due from the death of the former minister, which was more than the 50*l.* he lost at *Hawkhurst*. "Herein (he observes in his " diary) was the promise made good in the very letter, in " finding what is lost for Christ's sake, as (says he) I reckon " that was, which was lost for conscience sake." He obtained also an augmentation by means of the Recorder, Steel, Sir John Thorowgood, &c. trustees; tho' opposed by Mr. Farrington, an officer under them. On *May* 10, 1654, the Engagement having been taken away the preceeding year, and he having appeared the very month before at *Whitehall* before the commissioners, called Triers, was settled at *Monkton* and *Birchington*; and the trustees, took care to have his augmentation continued; so that the living was to him worth better than 100*l.* per annum, besides a good vicarage-house, &c.

July 7, 1662, as he was riding to Canterbury, he was arrested near *Sar*, and forced to give two bonds of 40*l.* each, to appear at the assizes at Maidstone, and the sessions at Canterbury, on account of his not reading the Common-Prayer. The 17th of the same month, he put in a demurrer at Maidstone, and on the 23d, at *Canterbury* sessions, he traversed the matter, and heard no more of it. This was at the instigation

gation of Mr. *Rook* his neighbour, who laboured to get him out, notwithstanding his former readiness to serve him in his necessity; and that he might have somewhat against him, sent him the prayers to read. *Aug.* 27, 1662, Mr. *Thoroughgood* preached his farewell sermon at Monkton, in the morning, from 2 *Sam.* xv. 25, 26; and in the afternoon at Birchington, from *John* xiv. 27. He removed from Monkton, *Sept.* 3, 1662, and lived at Stockbury. *Sept.* 17, 1667, he removed to Canterbury, and continued there some years. At first he preached only to his own family, and afterwards to some others. *Nov.* 27, 1668, he set open his doors on the Lord's-day, for all to come in who chose it. He also set up a weekly Wednesday-lecture in his house; and conducted his ministerial service in concert with Mr. Ventrice, Mr. Beak and Mr. Taylor, tho' much opposed by Mr. Hardress, the recorder, and others. When the proclamation against the meetings was published in Canterbury, on Saturday, *April* 4, 1668, he and the other three ministers consulted what to do the next day, and they all agreed to preach, whatever was the consequence. On so doing, they were all four apprehended and imprisoned in West-Gate, upon the Corporation-act, for half a year. All the time of their confinement, they preached every Lord's-day morning and afternoon, and once every week on Wednesdays, to their people; the keeper conniving at them, as he found that was most for his own advantage. After their release, he and two of his brethren preached in their turns, twice every Lord's-day at *Sandwich*, and carried on a Friday lecture there, till the Act that passed in *May*, 1670, which hindered them every where.

Mr. *Thoroughgood* was cited once and again into the Bishop's court, but for some time escaped, by reason of his christian name not being known. At last it was found out, and he not appearing, was excommunicated. But he rejoiced that he was counted worthy to suffer for his Lord.—In *June* 1672, he removed to *Rochester*, where he got a house licenced, and preached every Lord's-day twice, and once on a week-day. The mayor forbidding him, he riepled, That in all lawful things he might command him; but in the cause of his Great Master, he would not obey. He afterwards preached privately about the country and at length was indicted at the assizes at Maidstone, upon the Act, for 20*l.* a month, to the value of some hundred pounds. He endeavoured to keep off a conviction, and several times by interest got the trial put off; but at length the judge, who could not

be

be prevailed with to delay any longer, told him, that on the morrow he should be convicted. But that very night, it pleased God, that Mr. *Thoroughgood* was seized with the gout in his arm, which was so very painful, that oath was made in court that he was not able to bear his cloaths on. The judge then gave him till Lady-day assizes, before which the king died; and so he happily escaped this trouble, and saved his estate, which would have been seized had they proceeded to a conviction. His last remove (which was occasioned by the unkindness of some people at Rochester) was to *Godalming* in Surrey, where he had not continued long before death silenced him, on *November* 17, 1691. His funeral sermon was preached by Mr. *John Buck*, and printed.

In his diary he recorded various interpositions of providence, in the course of his life, with great expressions of thankfulness. In particular, he there notices some very remarkable things attending the faithful discharge of his duty in reproving sin, which he always did with fidelity, but with great meekness. At one time, while he was at *Monkton*, when he had preached against swearing, one of his hearers, sensible of his guilt, and thinking he was the person particularly intended, resolved to kill him; in order to which he hid himself behind a hedge by which he knew Mr. *Thoroughgood* would ride, to preach his weekly lecture. Accordingly, when he came to the place, this man attempted to shoot him; but his piece failed, and only flashed in the pan. The next week he went again to the same place with the same intent. When Mr. *Thoroughgood* was come up, the wretch offered to fire again, but the gun would not go off. Upon this his conscience accusing him for such a wickedness, he went after him, and falling down on his knees, with tears in his eyes, related the whole to him, and begged his pardon. This providence proved the means of this man's conversion. Mr. *Thoroughgood* was much in fasting and prayer; and had many remarkable returns of prayer, which he carefully noted. He was eminent for humility; and made conscience of visiting the poorest of his flock. He was unwearied in his studies; and constantly rose at four in the morning. He was a very strict observer of the Lord's-day; and had a wonderful art of sliding in good discourse wherever he came. He constantly laid by two shillings out of every twenty for the poor. He was naturally very timorous; but in the cause of God he was as bold as a lion, He was a most hearty lover of all that he thought loved the Lord Jesus; received all injuries
juries

juries with great meekness; was most ready to forgive, and to do good to those that had done him wrong; and he was beloved even of the high church-party for his peaceable behaviour.

ST. LAWRENCE. PETER JOHNSON, M. A. He was of a very reputable family in this island. He was minister of *Marsfield* in Sussex, before he came to settle at this place, where he was ejected in 1660. He was ordained at London in 1654. The certificate of his ordination may be seen in Dr. *Calamy's* Account, signed by *Edm. Calamy, Simeon Ash,* and three more. After his ejectment he taught some scholars, and now and then preached at *Ramsgate,* where he first gathered a dissenting congregation; but he did not altogether absent himself from the established worship. He was a man of good learning and very useful gifts. But at last he lost his sight, and for several years was confined, by various afflictions. He died in 1704, and was buried in *St. Lawrence* church,

MINSTER [V. 200l.] RICHARD CULMER, M. A. Of *Magd. Col. Camb.* He met with unusual opposition in this parish, of which a particular account was published, by his son Richard Culmer, in a pamphlet entitled, *A Parish Looking-glass for Persecutors of Ministers,* &c. 4to. 1657. From thence it appears, that he continued at Cambridge about eight years. Being settled minister of *Goodnestone* in East-Kent, he was driven from thence by Abp. Laud, because he would not read the Book of Sports. He then continued three years and a half silenced. He was afterwards assistant to Dr. *Robert Austin,* at Harbledown near Canterbury, where he preached several years. But many clamoured against him, for his opposition against drunkenness, and prophaning the Sabbath by cricket-playing, &c. He afterwards preached in Canterbury, and was one of those appointed by parliament to detect, and cause to be demolished, the superstitious inscriptions and idolatrous monuments in that cathedral. It was he that broke the great window there, § for which many were enraged against him. Soon after he published a book entitled, *Cathedral News from*

§ It is presumed that this was not meant to be recorded as matter of approbation, but merely as matter of fact. Mr. Culmer, with many good qualities, appears to have possessed too much of that false zeal which is injurious to any cause, and which naturally excited the prejudices against him, hereafter mentioned. ED.

Canter-

Canterbury, Anno 1643. The mayor, some principal in-habitants of that city, and the Earl of Warwick, recom-mended him to the committee appointed by parliament for plundered ministers, who placed him in the living of *Minster*, after the Assembly of divines had sent them a certificate of his being a fit person for that place. But still he was much opposed, and one person resolved he would spend 500*l.* to drive him from thence. Many stories were raised to preju-dice people against him, some refused paying him their tithe of corn, and played him various tricks. Upon which he printed two books concerning the frauds in tithing. But notwithstanding all their ill usage, God was pleased to own him, and the parish was much reformed.

Mr. *Lewis* objects to the above account of Mr. *Culmer*, and says, " He left but a very bad character behind him." † Perhaps prejudice may have much contributed to the badness of it. He adds, " You *know* Abp. *Laud* charged him with offering to bribe his servants, to procure *Chartham* for him." Whereas I must declare (says Dr. *Calamy*) I had not heard it. I doubt not but that Archbishop was against § him ; but as for evidence ‖ with which such a charge is supported, I am yet to seek. " However it is certain, says Mr. *Lewis*, he acted more the part of a bully, than of a christian minister. He was often engaged in broils, and being a very strong man, cared not whom he fought with.—I have now a letter by me from the principal parishioners of *Minster* to Dr. *Casaubon*, [the sequestered minister] wherein they tell him, that for the three last Sabbaths they had tumults in their church between the poor people and Mr. *Culmer*." That there were tumults among them has been owned. But the question is, who was the occasion of them ? Mr. *Lewis* thinks it too favourable an account of him " that God was pleased to own him :" but if what immediately follows be true, *viz.* that the parish was much reformed, * which Mr. *Lewis* doth not deny, this may safely enough be said. Mr. *Lewis* adds, " After his leaving *Minster*, on account of Dr. *Casaubon's* being repossessed of it, he went to a little village in the parish of *St. Peter's*, in

† " He was of a very warm and violent temper, and had a zeal which was not according to knowledge : broke the church windows, &c." MS.
§ " *Culmer* was evidence against him at his trial, having been disobliged by him." *Id.*
‖ See Abp. *Laud's* diary and trial, published by Mr. *Wharton. Id.*
* " This does not appear, nor that the people here were worse than their neighbours." *Id.*

the same island, called *Broad Stairs,* where he led a useless vicious life, ‡ giving himself in a manner up to drinking." This seems to be a misrepresentation, for Mr. *Thoroughgood,* of whom Mr. *Lewis* gives a very good character, writes in his diary thus: " *March* 20, 1662. My loving faithful friend, old Mr. *Culmer,* died in my vicarage-house at *Monk-.ton,* where he was since he was put by as minister at *Minster* (the next place,) having been ill some time. before; and on the 22d, I preached his funeral sermon from *Rev.* xiv. 13. ' Blessed are the dead which die in the Lord,' *&c.*"

Mr. EDMUND TRENCH. See HACKNEY, *Middlesex.*

Mr. DANIEL HAYES, of *Preston,* afterwards conformed.; as also did Mr. OSMANTON, of *Ivy-church,* who was after- wards parish-minister at *Little-Horsted* in *Sussex.*

§ There are so many Inductions in this county, in the year 1662, that there is reason to believe there were many more ministers ejected here than we have any account of.

‡ " *Bradstow.* This Mr. *Lewis* was told, and he wrote it to Dr. *Calamy,* who desired his observations, &c. in a private letter, which should not have been made public without *L.'s* consent." [To this note is added, apparently written since,] " It is a mistake, for *Culmer's* son, who was afterwards mas- ter of the free-school at *Sandwich.* Abp, *Juxon's* papers, MS." *Id.*

MINISTERS

MINISTERS EJECTED OR SILENCED

IN

LANCASHIRE.

N. B. *Most of the Places in this County not otherwise distinguished are* Chapelries.

ALKINGTON. Mr. ROBERT TOWN.

ALTHOME. Mr. THOMAS JOLLIE. Of *Trin. Col. Camb.* His first stated preaching was at *Althome*, to which place he was unanimously invited by the parishioners. There he continued near thirteen years with great success. Before his ejectment he was seized by three troopers, according to a warrant from three deputy-lieutenants. When he was brought before them, he was accused of many things, but nothing was proved. They then required him to take the oath of supremacy, with which he readily complied, and was discharged. In the same month he was again seized and confined; and when he was released, his enemies would by violence have prevented his preaching in public; but not succeeding in their attempt, he was cited into the Bishop of *Chester*'s court, and obliged to attend there three times, tho' he lived at forty miles distance. He was at last censured by the court for refusing the service-book, and his suspension, *ab officio & beneficio*, was to have been published the next court-day, but the death of the Bishop prevented it. Some time after, however, the suspension was declared, but not published, according to their own order; and yet they thereupon proceeded to debar him the liberty of preaching one Sabbath before the Act came to be in force. When the day came, in which he must either submit to what he thought unlawful, or resign his place, he preferred the latter.

Upon

M.ᶜ Kennit. ſc.

Thomas Jollie.

from an original Painting in the Poſſeſſion of
Mᴿ Thornthwaite. Paternoſter. Row.

Publiſhed by Button & Son, Paternoster Row.

Upon his leaving *Althome*, he remained for a time in an unsettled condition. At length he retired to *Healy*, where he had not been long, before he was apprehended by Capt. Parker's lieutenant-serjeant and two soldiers, and brought before two deputy-lieutenants, by whom he was examined, and obliged to find sureties for his good behaviour, without any reason alledged for it, and by their order confined in a private house. The family were religious, and as he and they were engaged in family worship, Capt. Nowel broke into the house, and with blasphemous expressions snatched the Bible out of his hands, and dragged him away to the guard, pretending they had kept a conventicle. The captains obliged him to sit up with them all night, whilst they drank and insulted him. In the morning, they let him lie down upon a little straw in the stable; and the next day, tho' it was the Lord's-day, and excessively wet, they sent him to *Skipton* in Craven, where he was committed into the marshal's hands. He had not been long released from this imprisonment, before he was again seized by three troopers, who told him they must carry him to *York*. He demanded their warrant for taking him out of the county. They laid their hands upon their swords, and taking hold of his horse's bridle, obliged him to go with them. He was there committed close prisoner at the castle, in a small room, and allowed no fire, tho' it was winter. The window was much broken, and the stench of the stable came into the room, which had two beds in it, with two in each bed. In this miserable place he was confined for some months. At length, as they could find nothing against him, he was discharged.

In 1664, he and some others were taken at a meeting, and committed to *Lancaster* jail for eleven weeks. In 1665, he was arrested again, by an order from the lord lieutenant, and very roughly treated by Col. Nowel. In 1669, he was committed to jail for six months, having preached within five miles of *Althome*, and refused to take the oath required by the Oxford-act. At *Preston* the justices who committed him refused to release him, tho' their illegal proceedings were plainly proved to them. Nay, they suffered him, with some others, to be indicted as a rioter, for the very same supposed crime for which they had committed him. In 1674, he was apprehended by justice Nowel at a meeting in *Slade*, and fined 20*l*. In 1684, he was apprehended by order of the lord chief justice, and brought before him at Preston, where he was obliged to find sureties, who were bound in 200*l*. each

(Judge

eminent professor of the Puritan stamp, who was much
vexed in the days of the former bishops, and put to great expences'in the ecclesiastical courts. He had several sons, but
John was the flower of the family, who was educated with
great care, both at school and in the university. He exercised his ministry for some time at *Walmsley* chapel ; but
when Mr. Henry Fairfax quitted the living of *Ashton*, Sir
George Booth gave him the presentation, which he resigned
in 1662. Lord Delamere continued his kindness to him, and
offered to put his son *Maurice*, who was a conforming
minister, into his place; but Mr. *Harrison*, fearing his son
might not be fit for that charge, and preferring the advantage of his people's souls to the advancement of his own
family, he conscientiously waved it, and made use of his interest on the behalf of Mr. *Ellison*, a man of great worth
and a good preacher, who enjoyed the living till his death.
Mr. *Harrison*, living privately, was his usual auditor, till he
was banished by the Oxford act, when he retired to *Salford*;
where he was soon afterwards deprived of the use of his limbs,
which was thought to be the consequence of his indefatigable
labours, fastings, and night studies. Finding some benefit at
Bath, he returned to *Ashton*, but his disorder increased, till
it put a period to his life, in 1669, aged 57. He was an excellent preacher, and a man of great devotion. He constantly
kneeled in prayer in the pulpit. He was eminent for holiness,
humility, industry, zeal for God, and stedfastness in his principles. When some gentlemen of the episcopal party opposed the classis at *Manchester*, and wrote several papers,
the ministers of that presbytery appointed Mr. *Harrison* to
answer them, which he did very largely and learnedly, in a
piece entitled, *Censures of the Church revived*, 4to, 1659.
His funeral sermon was preached by Mr. *Ellison*, who gave
him a great character, but not beyond his desert. Tho' his
merits were great, his circumstances were mean; but his
spirit was always easy.

ASHTON in *Macclesfield*. Mr. JAMES WOODS. An
indefatigably laborious man, who was in his study, even to
the last, both early and late. He died in 1688, aged 63.
He was an excellent preacher, and had great success. §As
a proof of the estimation in which he was held, the following
anecdote is related. On the sabbath after Bartholomew-day,
the new minister preached : when the people came out of
the

the church, a good old woman remarked "I think if Mr.
Woods had only gone into the pulpit and shook his grey beard
over us, it would have done us more good." J. O.

BILLING, JOHN WRIGHT, M. A. Of the college in
Dublin. Dr. *Calamy* produces a testimonial of this, signed
Nath. Hoyle Vice præc. *Gilbert Pepper*: dated 1641. The
testimonials of his ordination, by fasting and prayer, with imposition of hands, *Aug.* 13, 1645, (when he was about 28
years of age) are signed by Mr. *James Hyet*, Mr. *Alex.
Horrockes*, Mr. *Isaac Ambrose*, and eight others. When
he was silenced he lived privately, prayed much, but preached
little, having but a poor state of health. In the time of K.
Charles's Indulgence, in 1672, he lived at *Prescott*, and
preached at the house of Mary Lyon, which he had licensed
for that purpose. Being gone one morning, according to his
common custom, to walk in a field near his house, and not
returning at his usual time, a person sent to look for him
found him dead; it was supposed of an apoplexy: *Feb.* 1,
1685, when he was 70 years of age. His life was exemplary,
and he did much good in his place. He left a son, Mr.
James Wright, who was educated at Oxford, where he
took his degree of B. A. as he afterwards did that of M. A.
at *Cambridge.* Dr. *Samuel Wright*, of Carter-lane, London, was son to the latter, and grandson to the former.

BIRCH Chapel. Mr. ROBERT BIRCH. After his ejectment he commenced physician and surgeon.

BLACKLEY. Mr. THOMAS HOLLAND. A gentleman
by birth, but an able and diligent preacher. He was some
time minister at *Ringley* chapel. When he was silenced at
Blackley he removed to a house of his own, and lived privately, [tho' not without preaching occasionally.] He had
sore afflictions in body and estate, and was laid aside from his
work some years before he died, in 1675, aged 57. He left
several children. There was a Mr. *Robert Holland*, of
whom there is some account in Mr. *Matth. Henry*'s life;
who died in 1709, aged between 50 and 60, probably a relation.

BLACKRODE. Mr. RICHARD ASTLEY. Born near
Manchester, and brought up in the public school there. His
early good inclinations and solidity, were very observable
where he boarded, so that when his father came to take him

from school, intending him for trade, some discerning persons in the family earnestly recommended his continuance at school, expressing their hope that he might be useful in the ministry. His father yielded to their advice, and found his son's proficiency in learning answer his expectation. Upon his going to the university, some of his pious friends met together, without his knowledge, to seek a divine blessing upon his studies. One of them, a good solid christian, when prayer was over, said, " I believe God will do great things for this lad, tho' I shall not live to see him leave the university. When he returns, acquaint him with what I say, to excite his thankfulness." They accordingly did so : and Mr. *Astley*, upon giving them a sermon in private, fully satisfied them that the expectation was just. He proved an excellent preacher. After his ejectment from *Blackrode* he became pastor of a dissenting congregation in *Hull*, where he died about the year 1691. Mr. *Astley* of Chesterfield is a descendant of his.

BOLTON [V.] Mr. RICHARD GOODWIN, M. A. Of *Eman. Col. Camb.* He was born in *Sussex*, and was very providentially brought into this country, where God had much work for him. He was ordained by Bp. Bridgman at *Great-Leaver*, and preached some time at *Cockey* chapel; but in the civil war, when the town of *Bolton* was taken by prince Rupert, 1645, he fled to *Hull*, and from thence to London, where he was recommended to a parsonage at *Hargraves* in Northamptonshire, which was a pleasant and advantageous situation. But the temper of the people not suiting him, he had not much satisfaction among them, and therefore in a little time he removed back into *Lancashire*, and accepted the vicarage of *Bolton*, where he continued preaching with great success for twenty years, till he was ejected in 1662. He afterwards lived publicly or privately, preaching to many or few, as the times would allow. When the Five-mile-act took place he removed to *Manchester*, and there lived retired, studying chemistry, in which he was a great proficient. In 1672 he took out a license, and preached twice every Lord's-day at a private house in *Bolton*, where he died, *Dec.* 12, 1685, aged 72. He wrote much, but printed nothing. One of the MSS. which he left was, on the lawfulness of eating blood. He was a plain practical preacher, and had an excellent gift in prayer. Such was his usefulness, that he will have a great retinue of souls to present

to

Samuel Mather.

from an original Painting in the Possession of Mr. Townsend, Holborn.

Published by Button & Son, Paternoster Row.

to his Master at the last day. He was succeeded in his meeting-place at *Bolton*, by Mr. *John Leaver*.

—— Mr. ROBERT PARK. Of *Eman. Col. Camb.* a native of *Bolton*. He was vicar of this parish before the civil war, upon the approach of which he withdrew into *Holland*, and was assistant to Mr. Symmonds, in the English congregation at *Rotterdam*. Mr. Gregge, vicar of *Bolton*, dying in 1644, the people sent to Mr. *Park*, and earnestly solicited him to return. After some time he did so, and was lecturer there while Mr. *Goodwin* was vicar. He had the benefit of Mr. *Gosnold*'s donation, as well as the free contribution of the people, by whom he was much beloved. He was a person of incomparable ability, learning and piety, and a very correct preacher. He was also a man of a ready wit, and very facetious in conversation. When he was ejected, he for a time lived privately, and on the passing of the Five-mile-act he removed to *Braughton* in this county. But he at length returned to *Bolton*, and preached as he had opportunity. He died in 1669, aged 70. He had a very good library, which was sold for the support of his wife and children.—A correspondent of the author, near *Bolton*, writes as follows : "This neighbourhood has been an ancient and famous seat of religion. At the very first dawn of the Reformation, 'the dayspring from on high visited' this town and the adjacent villages ; and by the letters of those brave martyrs, Mr. *Bradford* and Mr. *George Marsh*, which we have yet remaining, it appears, that a number of persons and families in that neighbourhood betimes received the gospel in its purity and simplicity. And a good relish of it appears remaining to this day."

BURTON-WOOD. SAMUEL MATHER, A. M. Born in this county in 1626. He was the eldest son of Mr. *Richard Mather*, whose life may be seen in Mr. *Clark*'s collections. He went with his father in 1635, to New-England, where he had his education in *Harvard-College*, and was the first Fellow who took his degrees there. Having spent some time in the exercise of his ministry in those parts, he returned into England in 1659. He met with a most violent storm in his passage ; the ship also was in great danger of being burnt ; but God who had considerable purposes to serve by him, kept him in safety. He spent some time both at *Cambridge* and *Oxford*, where also he took his degrees. He was chap-

lain in Magdalen-College, and preached frequently at St.
Mary's. He went with the English commissioners into Scot-
land, and preached the gospel publicly at *Leith* two years.
In 1655, he returned to England, and soon after attended
Lord Harry Cromwell into *Ireland*, with Dr. Harrison, Dr.
Winter, and Mr. Charnock. He was there made a Senior
Fellow of *Trinity-College*, where he again took his degrees.
He was chosen colleague with Dr. *Winter*, and preached
every Lord's-day morning at the church of St. Nicholas in
Dublin; besides his turn, once in six weeks, before the lord-
deputy and council. His preaching there was much esteem-
ed, and very successful. There he was publicly ordained by
Dr. Winter, Mr. Taylor of Carrickfergus, and Mr. Jenner, of
Tredagh, *Dec.* 5, 1656.—Even *Wood* scruples not to own, that
" Tho' he was a congregational-man, and in his principles
a high Nonconformist, yet he was observed by some, to be
civil to those of the episcopal persuasion, when it was in his
power to do them a displeasure. And when the lord-deputy
gave a commission to him and others, in order to the displa-
cing of episcopal ministers in the province of *Munster*, he
declined it : as he afterwards did the like matter in *Dublin* ;
alledging, that he was called into that country to preach the
gospel, and not to hinder others from doing it,"

But notwithstanding this, soon after the restoration, he was
suspended for two sermons which he preached against reviving
the ceremonies, from 2 *Kings* xviii. 4. He was represented as
seditious, and guilty of treason; tho' he uttered not a disrespect-
ful word of the king or government, but only set himself to
prove that the ecclesiastical ceremonies then about to be restored, had no warrant from the word of God. Being now disabled
from any further service in Ireland, he returned to England,
and continued his ministry at *Burton-wood*, till the Bartholomew-act took place ; and then he went back again to *Dublin*,
and preached to a gathered church in his own hired house.
After he had continued there some years a Nonconformist,
he had a pressing invitation from a church at *Boston* in New-
England, to be their pastor; but he was not willing to leave
his own church without their consent, which was not to be
obtained. Their meetings were at first more favourably connived at in Ireland than in England. But as Mr. *Mather*
was preaching privately, *Sept.* 18, 1664, he was interrupted
by an officer, who carrried him to the main guard. He rea-
soned with the officers and soldiers about their disturbing a
                                                        meeting

meeting of Protestants, when they suffered the Papists to say mass without any interruption. They told him, that such men as he were more dangerous than the Papists, &c. The mayor having consulted the lord-deputy, told Mr. *Mather* that he might go to his lodgings, but that he must appear the next day before his lordship, for which he and some others gave their word. Accordingly they appeared, when the mayor told him, that the lord-deputy was much incensed against him for his conventicle, being informed there were many old discontented officers there. Mr. *Mather* denied that he saw any such persons, and gave him an account of his sermon, on *John* ii. 15—17. which could not give any reasonable offence. However, that evening he was seized by a pursuivant from the lord-deputy, and the next day imprisoned; but he was soon released.

About this time he had an interview with one *Valentine Greatarick*, who pretended to cure diseases by stroking; a man of a stong imagination, whom he found to have read *Cornelius Agrippa*, and had got his *Abracadabra*. Dr. *Stubbes* having printed some letters in his favour, the people of Dublin crowded after him.[*] Mr. *Mather* therefore wrote a piece to expose his pretences. But tho' it was read with approbation by some persons of figure, he was not allowed to publish it.—A certain lady afterwards sent him a discourse drawn up by some Popish priest, entitled, *The one Catholic and Roman Faith*, to which he drew up an answer which was published, and met with good acceptance. He continued labouring to do good, in all ways within his power to the last. He had generally the character of a good scholar and a generous spirited man. He left this life for a better, in 1671, and was succeeded by Mr. *Nathaniel Mather* his younger brother.

WORKS. Besides the above...A Treatise against stinted Liturgies.—An *Irenicum*, in order to an Agreement between Presbyterians, Independents, and Anabaptists...A course of sermons upon the Old Testament Types, with some discourses against modern superstitions; published by his brother after his decease.

BRADSHAW. Mr. DRURY.

[*] Dr. *Henry More* had a very high opinion of this man as a man of piety. See his *Scholia* on *Atheismus Triumphans*. A particular account of him may be seen in *Wood's Athenæ Oxon.* vol. ii. p. 365.

CARTMEL. Mr. PHILIP BENNET. He subscribed * the *Harmonious Consent* of the ministers in this country, in 1648, as minister of *Ulverston.*

—— Mr. CAMERFORD, before mentioned as ejected in this neighbourhood. His name was *Gabriel.* See STAVELY, *Westmoreland.*

CHORLEY. Mr. HENRY WELSH. A very humble, mortified man. Tho' he did not excel in gifts, it was made up in grace. His very enemies had nothing to say against him. He was of so blameless a conversation, that most gentlemen had a good word for him ; and was esteemed so faithful, that Mr. *Standish* of *Duxbury* (a person of great estate) left the tuition of his children to him, after his own and his wife's death. And he discharged his civil as well as ministerial trust so faithfully, that the most critical adversary had nothing to lay to his charge. He died in 1665, aged 64.

CHOWBENT Chapel, in *Leigh* parish. **Mr. JAMES WOODS.** He was the son of Mr. JAMES WOODS of *Ashton.* He followed his father's steps, and imbibed his spirit. § He continued pastor to a congregation of dissenters here many years, and had a son who succeeded him. The *Woods* preached here above a century. J. O.

COCKEY Chapel. **Mr. JOHN LEAVER.** Of *Braz. No. Col. Oxf.* Born in *Bolton*, and brought up in the free-school there. His father was a Papist. How he himself became a Protestant does not appear. He was a man of great integrity, and a useful preacher. In 1672 he preached to a good number in his own house; and after K. *Charles's* Act of indulgence, he kept an open meeting in *Bolton*, where he administered the Lord's-supper every month to some hundreds. He was silenced in 1662, and died *July* 4, 1692, aged 58. He was succeeded by Mr. *Robert Seddon.*

CROFTON. Mr. LAW. He was only an Assistant here or at *Ecclestone.*

CROSBY. Mr. JAMES HIET. He was a native of *London*, and was educated at *Cambridge.* He had been minister

* *N. B.* Dr. *Calamy* in the *Contin.* observes of most of the ministers in this county, that they subscribed this paper; which circumstance is here omitted, except when, as in the case above, their subscription discovers the place they were in at the time.

here

here many years when he was ejected in 1662. He had been, before ejected for refusing the Engagement, which was the case of many others in this county. He died in 1664, about 70 years of age, leaving no children. He was an able preacher, had a considerable estate, and was given to hospitality.

DALTON, near *Lancaster*. [V.] Mr. THOMAS WHITE-HEAD. A pious, laborious and faithful minister, who studied to do good in his place, and preached as often as he could to his people after his ejectment. He died in *Feb.* 1679, aged 73; and Mr. *Benson* succeeded in his congregation.

DEAN. [V.] JOHN TILSEY, M. A. Of the university of *Glasgow*. He was born in Lancashire. When he left Scotland he preached with Mr. *Horrocks* at *Dean* church, and was to him like Timothy to Paul, a son in the gospel. He possessed uncommon abilities: a retentive memory, which made whatever he read his own; a solid judgment, a ready invention, a fluent delivery, and warm affections. He was very strict in his life, free and familiar in conversation, and eminently charitable: Of a bold and active spirit, fearing nothing when once satisfied as to the grounds upon which he proceeded. When the assembly of *Boston* had suspended a prophane and dissolute preacher at *Rochester*, and most others were afraid to preach at the place and declare the suspension, Mr. *Tilsley* readily went, and did it with great courage, yet with a becoming candour and meekness. He succeeded Mr. *Horrocks* at *Dean*; where he was ejected no less than three times. The first, for refusing the Engagement, but he was soon restored. The second, by the Act of uniformity in 1662. After which, tho' he forbore preaching, he continued in the house adjoining to his church, which being in the hands of trustees, was still allowed him. When the excellent Dr. *Wilkins* became Bp. of the diocese, he allowed him to preach in his church again as lecturer, when the new vicar read the prayers. When the Bp. was dead, he was indicted at the assizes for his Nonconformity, and by the influence of several gentlemen in the neighbourhood, ejected a third time, in 1678. He spent the rest of his days in a private life at *Manchester*, where he died, *Dec.* 12, 1684, aged 60. Tho' his abilities were such as seldom meet in one man, such was his modesty, that he was not sufficiently satisfied with his own performances to print any thing. He preached funeral

sermons

sermons for Mr. Rathband, Col. Bradshaw and Mr. Horrocks, but could not be persuaded to publish either of them.

DENTON. Mr. JOHN ANGIER. Of *Eman. Col. Camb.*
He was born at *Dedham* in Essex, and lived some time with
Mr. John Cotton at Boston in Lincolnshire. His first settled
ministerial work was at *Ringley.* He had episcopal ordination from Dr. Lewis Bayly, author of *The Practice of Piety*,
who ordained him without subscription. Being a Nonconformist to the ceremonies, he had some adversaries, who
brought many complaints against him to Dr. Bridgman, Bp.
of *Chester*, who lived near him at *Great Leaver.* Upon
which he sent for Mr. *Angier*, and gently expostulated with
him, expressing great respect for him. The Bishop's wife, being at that time under great trouble of conscience, frequently
conversed with Mr. *Angier*, who was an instrument of much
good to her by his counsels and prayers. His lordship however, on the pressing solicitations of Abp. *Laud*, was forced
to suspend him. After continuing a year and a half at *Ringley*,
he removed to *Denton*, in 1632. When the Act of uniformity
took place he continued in his public station without conforming. Warrants were sometimes issued to apprehend him, but
even the worst men had no heart to meddle with him. Some
times they searched for him, but professed they would not
see him for a hundred pounds. The Bp. of *Chester* often
enquired of his son, "How doth the good old man, Mr.
Angier do?" Most of the justices had a great respect for
him, some of whom were nearly related to his wife: and by
the special providence of God, he continued preaching in his
public chapel to the last. It was the common saying, "He
is an old man, and cannot live long; let him alone while he
does live." He died *Sept.* 1, 1677, aged 72, having been
pastor of this people 46 years. He was of a sweet, moderate,
catholic, healing spirit; an excellent casuist; a man mighty
in prayer; a hard student; of an exact conversation; very
affable and courteous; full of charity and good works; and,
in general, a pattern of holiness. He had been an instrument of great good to many. Some remarkable passages of
his diary, and his judicious resolution of some cases of conscience, are added at the end of his printed life.

WORKS. A treatise concerning God's worship, entitled, A
Help to better Hearts, for better Times; recommended by Mr,
Calamy and Mr. *Case*...An Epistle prefixed to Mr. *Newcome's.*
Sinner's Hope...Another to Mr. *Bell* on Patience.

—— Mr.

—— Mr. JAMES HOLM. He was assistant to Mr. *Angier*, and lived with him. He often changed his habitation, and at last had a call to *Kendal* in Westmoreland, where he died in 1688. He had a son brought up for the ministry, with whom he went into *Holland*; who, having finished his studies, was some time pastor of a congregation at *Uxbridge*, but died young.

DOWGLES. Mr. JONATHAN SCHOLFIELD. He had many years been minister at *Haywood* chapel, from whence in 1659 he removed to this place, where he was ejected in 1662. In the course of his life he met with a great variety of family afflictions. When he was silenced he had many children, and no visible way of subsistance for them; but God raised up friends to him and his, so that they were never brought to extremity. He died in 1667, aged 60. Mr. *Scholfield* of Birmingham, is a descendant of his.

DUCKENFIELD. Mr. SAMUEL EATON. Of *Oxford* university. The son of Mr. Richard Eaton, vicar of *Great Budworth* in Cheshire, [and brother to Mr. Theoph. Eaton, the renowned governor of *New-Haven*. *Wood* says of him, "After he had left the university, he took orders according to the church of *England*, and was beneficed in this country; but having been puritanically educated, he did dissent in some particulars thereof. Whereupon, finding his place too warm for him, he revolted and went into *New-England*, and preached among the brethren there."—But upon his dissent from Mr. *Davenport*, about the narrow terms and forms of civil government then imposed upon that infant colony, his brother advised him to a removal. Calling at *Boston* in his way, the church there gave him a pressing invitation to settle with them; but he was fully bent upon coming back to *Old-England*, where God had most work for him to do.] Upon his return, he gathered a congregational church at *Duckenfield*, and afterwards removed to *Stockport*, where he preached in the free-school. Some of the people here ran things to a great height, and grew wiser than their minister, so that they occasioned him much difficulty. After he was ejected in 1662 he attended on the ministry of Mr. *Angier* at *Denton*, as did many of his old hearers; who by difficulties and sufferings were wrought into a better temper. Mr. *Eaton* died *Jan.* 9, 1664, aged 68. He left no children, but left a good name among persons of all persuasions. [He was a very holy man; a person of great learning and
judgment,

judgment, and a most incomparable preacher; of eminent note and influence in this and the neighbouring counties.] *Mather's Hist. New-Eng.* p. 213.

WORKS. The Mystery of God incarnate; against Knowles... A Vindicat. of it against the same...-[He assisted Mr. Tim. Taylor in writing The Congregational Way justified.]

ECKLES. [V.] Mr. EDMUND JONES. His father had been vicar of this place many years, and brought up three sons to the ministry, of whom this was the only Nonconformist. He was one of the first classis of Manchester. A man of excellent abilities, and an able scholar, naturally very rhetorical. When he was ejected, he preached in private; and when authority allowed it, more publicly. He died *May* 2, 1674, aged 48.

ELHILL Chapel. Mr. PETER ATKINSON, sen. A man of such singular ability and general interest, influence and usefulness, that he was called the apostle of the North. He had so much favour with the gentry, that he preached quietly at his chapel for a considerable time after the Act of uniformity took place. His income there indeed was but small; but his encouragement, in the success of his ministry, very considerable. He died *July* 17, 1677, aged 75.

—— Mr. PETER ATKINSON, jun. Son of the former.

GARSTANG [V.] Mr. ISAAC AMBROSE. He was some time minister of *Preston*; from whence he removed to this place, where the Act of uniformity found him in 1662. Soon after the Restoration, there was a meeting of above twenty ministers at *Bolton,* to consult what course to take. Mr. *Ambrose* and Mr. *Cole* of *Preston* declared before them all, that they could read the Common-Prayer, and should do it, the state of their places requiring it, in which otherwise their service was now necessarily at an end. The ministers, considering the circumstances of their case, approved their proceeding. Mr. *Cole* (afterwards Dr. *Cole*) declared that he had got to his *Ne plus ultra,* and could comply no farther. Accordingly he was turned out of *Preston*; but found some stronger motives in other parts, for he afterwards conformed, and was lecturer at *Dedham* in *Essex.* But Mr. *Ambrose* lived and died a Nonconformist; and was a man of such substantial worth, such eminent piety, and such an exemplary life, both as a minister and a christian,

that

that it is to be lamented the world should not have the benefit of particular memoirs concerning him from some able
hand. One thing peculiar to him deserves to be mentioned
here. It was his usual custom, once in a year, for the space
of a month, to retire into a little hut in a wood, and avoiding
all human converse, to devote himself to contemplation. Possibly by this practice he was the fitter for his sacred ministrations all the rest of the year. He spent the latter part of his
life at *Preston*; and when his end drew near, was very sensible of it. Having taken his leave of many of his friends
abroad with unusual solemnity, as if he foresaw that he
should see them no more, he came home, and set all things
in order. When some of his hearers came from *Garstang*
to visit him, he discoursed freely with them, gave them good
counsel, told them he was now ready whenever his Lord
should call, and that he had finished all he designed to write;
having the night before sent away his *Discourse concerning
Angels*, to the press. He accompanied his friends to their
horses, and when he came back, shut himself in his parlour,
the place of his retirement. Being thought to stay long, the
door was opened, and he was found just expiring. This was
in the year 1664, aged 72. * He was holy in his life, happy
in his death, and honoured by God and all good men.

His WORKS were printed altogether in folio, in 1639. One
of the most celebrated is, On looking to Jesus.

GORTON Chapel. WILLIAM LEIGH, M. A. Fellow
of *Christ's Col. Camb.* A serious, single-hearted man ; of
good abilities, and very laborious in the work of the ministry.
He was one of the classis of *Manchester.* For some years he
was grievously afflicted with the stone, which at last cut him
off, in 1664, about 50 years of age. He wrote an elegy on
the death of Dr. *Samuel Bolton,* and another in *Latin* on
Mr. *Bright.*

HAMBLETON. Mr. BULLOCK.

HORWICH. Mr. JAMES WALTON. It is certain he
was some time minister at this chapel, which is in *Dean*
parish; but it is doubtful whether he was ejected here or at
Shaw chapel near *Oldham.* He was provided with no subsistence when ejected, and had several children. He died in
1664, aged 64. He was a laborious faithful minister.

* At the bottom of his picture it is 59, 1663.

HARWOOD

HARWOOD. Mr. SANDFORD.

ST. HELEN's Chapel. Mr. THOMAS GREGG. *Of Camb.* University. His father was minister of *Bolton,* and died about 1644. *Bradley-Hall,* an estate of 100l. *per annum,* was his right by inheritance; but he quitted it, because of some incumbrance upon it, and would not entangle himself in the affairs of this life. He was very undaunted and courageous in his Master's work; preaching mostly in the chapel, or openly in houses, in the face of danger, and yet was never imprisoned. He was a man of great integrity, and kept close to his people in the worst of times. He died in 1681, aged about 44, exceedingly beloved, and much lamented.

HAYWOOD Chapel. Mr. GEORGE THOMASSON. A diligent, laborious preacher, who earnestly longed for the good of souls, and was very useful in promoting it. He died in 1672, aged 58.

HINDLEY. (in the parish of *Wigan*). Mr. JAMES BRADSHAW. *Of. Corp. Christ. Col. Oxf.* Born at *Hacking,* in the parish of Bolton, of very pious parents. Few families were better known in those parts than the Bradshaws. On his mother's side he sprang from the *Holmes's,* who were the first on that side of the county who became Protestant, and whose posterity have all along been zealous for Reformation and gospel purity. He had his grammar-learning at the free-school at Bolton, and was esteemed a good critic in it. Thro' the influence of his uncle *Holmes* (a worthy divine in Northamptonshire) he left the university without taking any degree. Having pursued his studies for some time under his direction, he returned into his native country, fixed in this place, and there was ordained by the classis of which Mr. *Earl* was moderator; where he continued till he was ejected. In conjunction with many others, he had a concern in the rising of Sir *George Booth,* with a design to make way for the Restoration; for which he afterwards had very unsuitable returns. After *Bartholomew*-day, 1662, he suffered some months imprisonment for the crime of preaching, thro' the malignity of a neighbouring justice of his own name; but he was not to be frightened from his master's service, or discouraged in it.

When K. *Charles* granted indulgence he removed to *Rainford,* a consecrated chapel in *Prescot* parish, at a greater

distance

distance from his old neighbour, and there held an amicable correspondence with several of the established clergy, who sometimes preached for him ; which was one means of his keeping his chapel. The chapel-wardens were obliged, at the visitation, to make their appearance ; and he having a friend in court, the question was commonly proposed to them in this manner : " Have you Common Prayer read yearly in your chapel ?" To which they could safely answer, *Yes* ; because once or more in every year, some of the neighbouring clergy read the service. The Bp. of *Chester* discharged informations against peaceable and sober persons ; and so, without being prosecuted, he continued his ministerial service in the chapel aforesaid. Nor had he any molestation, except at the time of *Monmouth*'s rebellion, when he and many other worthy persons, were imprisoned in *Chester* castle. But even there he was kindly treated, and upon *Monmouth*'s defeat was released.

He preached frequently where others of his brethren durst not, and met with good acceptance. He had a numerous family of children, and having a poor people, was in strait circumstances ; but he bore up with great chearfulness. He was often employed in arbitrations amongst neighbours, of different persuasions, in which he had such good success, as often to prevent vexatious law-suits, and have thanks from both sides. He was also frequently concerned in ordinations. He was a hard student, and a smart disputant ; very lively in his family exercises, and ever zealous for the national interest and the public good. He was one of the *Bolton* lecturers. As he was once riding several miles to preach, he bruised his leg, which for want of due care, proved the means of putting a period to his valuable life, A. D. 1702, in the 67th year of his age. His son, Mr. Ebenezer Bradshaw, was pastor of a dissenting congregation at *Ramsgate* in Kent.

WORKS. Two practical treatises : The Alarum to the Sleepy Spouse...The Trial and Triumph of Faith.

HIGHTON [V.] WILLIAM BELL, M. A. A great scholar, and a good orator. He was ordained by Dr. *Bridgman* Bp. of *Chester*. He was one of those who had 50*l.* per. ann. bequeathed by queen *Elizabeth* to four itinerant preachers in Lancashire, who were called the king's or queen's preachers. But both this and his living he left in 1662, for the sake of his conscience. After his ejectment he lived

lived privately, at *Sinderland* in the parish of Ashton under
Line, being a constant hearer of Mr. *Angier* of Denton. In
1672 he returned to his old people at *Highton*, and preached
among them by virtue of a licence. He died in 1681, aged 74.
He left several children; and among them, two sons who
were conforming ministers. Mr. *Bell* was a learned and
pious man, of very considerable ministerial abilities; noted
for his neat and sententious preaching.

WORKS. A Discourse on Gen. v. 24. intitled, Enoch's Walk.
--The excellency, necessity, and usefulness of Patience...The Patience of Job, and the end of the Lord; in two little Treatises, with
a Preface by Mr. Baxter: and some other small pieces.

HOLCOMB Chapel. HENRY PENDLEBURY, M. A.
Of *Christ's Col. Camb.* Born and brought up in these
parts. He preached his first sermon at *Ahsworth* chapel, in
1648, and continued there some time as Probationer. He
was set apart to the office of the ministry, *Oct.* 3, at *Turton*
chapel near Bolton, with Mr. *James Lievesey*, after performing their preparatory exercises before the second classis
in Lancashire, who met ordinarily at *Bury*. He afterwards
preached some time at *Horridge* chapel; and thence, in
1651, removed to *Holcomb*, where he diligently applied himself to his studies, preaching, discipline, and administering all
ordinances, till he was ejected in 1662. He still continued
in the exercise of his ministry, and was instrumental for the
good of many. He died of a languishing disease, *June* 18,
1695, aged 70, with these words in his mouth: "Father,
come, and take me to thyself." He was a man of great
learning, strict godliness, and every ministerial qualification.
He was beloved and reverenced by all that knew him, and
especially by his brethren in the ministry. All the adjacent
parishes were very desirous of his labours after his ejectment
as well as before. He continued a diligent and zealous labourer in the Lord's vineyard 44 years. He had read over
most of the ancient fathers, and had fully studied the controversies betwixt Protestants and Papists, as appears from his
writings. His piece on *Transubstantiation* was carried privately, by a friend, to Abp. *Tillotson*, who so much approved
it as to cause it to be printed.

WORKS. Besides the above Treatise.—Another, on the Sacrifice of the Mass, [lately republished.]—The barren Fig-tree.—
The Books opened; a Disc. on *Rev.* xx. 12.—Since his death; In-
visible Realities, &c. containing an Account of his Life.—Several
Sermons

Sermons of his on Christ's Transfiguration were abroad in MS. which many wished to be printed.

HOUGHTON Chapel. Mr. PETER NAYLOR. Of *St. John's Col. Camb.* He was born in this county, and preached much in *Peniston* parish in the time of Mr. Swift's confinement, and removed thence to *Alverthorp* near Wakefield in 1672. He preached in the meeting-place there and at *Pontefract* as long as he lived. He died *June* 2, 1690, aged 54. § His funeral sermon was preached by his friend and fellow-prisoner Mr. *Whitaker* of Leeds, on *Zech.* 1. 5.—A son of his, Mr. James Naylor, was some years assistant to Mr. John Nesbit, but died young, of a consumption.

KIRKBY [V.] Mr. NEHEMIAH AMBROSE.

KIRKBY LONGSDALE [V.] Mr. JOHN SMITH.

LANCASTER [V.] Dr. WILLIAM MARSHAL. After his ejectment he travelled abroad for some time, and then settled at London, where he practised physic.

LINDHAL Chapel. Mr. THOMAS DRINCHAL.

LONGRIDGE Chapel. Mr. TIMOTHY SMITH. Formerly minister of *Bradshaw* chapel. Tho' he did not conform, he often preached in the chapel after his ejectment; for this being an obscure place, with a small salary, there was no great striving for it. He died very poor, in 1679, aged 60.

*LUN Chapel. Mr. JOSEPH HARRISON. A good scholar and a methodical preacher; fixed in a dark corner, where he was wonderfully followed, and very useful. He died in 1664.

MANCHESTER. HENRY NEWCOME, M.A. Of *St. John's Col. Camb.* A hard student, and of great proficiency there in philosophy and theology. He was first rector of *Gausworth* in Cheshire, from whence, in 1656, he removed to Manchester, upon a unanimous invitation, to succeed Mr. Richard Hollingworth, having at the same time a like invitation from *Shrewsbury.* He had not been here long, before Sir George Booth raised the country for Charles II. in which affair Mr. *Newcome* was heartily engaged, for which he continued in great esteem and friendship with that honourable person. He here exercised his public ministry till 1662, joining with Mr. *Heyrick* in classical meetings with the rest of the neighbouring ministers, and dispensing all ordinances
in

in that numerous congregation; and afterwards preaching privately at home and abroad. When he could preach no longer, he wrote many excellent papers upon practical subjects, and dispersed them among his hearers, who contributed liberally towards his support, and shewed great kindness to him and his family. The Oxford-act forced him to remove into *Ellenbrook* chapelry; but he returned, as soon as he could with safety, to his family and flock. He preached privately till the year 1672, and afterwards in a licenced place. At length, the people built him a large stately chapel on the south-side of the town called *Ackers*, which he had not used long before it pleased God to remove him by death, and he was one of the first that were buried in it, *Sept.* 20, 1695, aged about 68. His funeral sermon, (containing his character at large) was preached by Mr. *Chorlton*, who succeeded him.

He was a person of good natural abilities, cultivated by an extraordinary industry, which began very early, and continued all his life: witness the many volumes left behind him,. written with his own hand. He possessed a large stock of solid learning and knowledge, which was always ready for use, but never for ostentation; and he had an admirable fitness for friendship and conversation, in which he was amiable above many. His temper was sincere, candid and generous. His discourse ingenuous, innocent, facetious and instructive. His deportment grave, yet sweet and obliging. A most sincere and unartificial humility at once hid and adorned his other excellencies. His moderation was known unto all men that ever knew or heard of him. He had an extensive charity, and a great veneration for such as differed from him, who were men of real worth, and he held an amicable correspondence with many of the conforming clergy, to whom his society was as grateful, and his memory as dear, as if he had been one of their own class. But his peculiar excellence was in preaching. His sermons were practical, plain and discursive; full of holy zeal and fervor, and a natural inimitable eloquence. He had a singular way of insinuating himself into the bosoms of his hearers, whose only regret hath been that the sermon was so short. An eminent divine who once heard him, said, "If I had this man's tongue, I could not help being proud of it." Among other lectures abroad in which he assisted, there was one instituted by Mr. Nath. Hilton of London, at *Bolton*, his native place, in which Mr Newcome took his turn once a month for many years, with Mr. Baldwin, Mr. Pendlebury, and Mr. John Walker.—§ He

was

was the ancestor of the Newcomes of Hackney, whose school has long been celebrated. The late Abp. of *Armagh* was of the same family.

WORKS. The Sinner's Hope; a Discourse on Ezra x.——Usurpation defeated, and David restored; a Sermon on the Restoration of Charles II.—The Covenant of Grace effectually remembered.—A discourse on Psalm cv. 8. with 1 Chr. xvi. 15... An Help to duty in, and right Improvement of, Sickness...A Discourse on Job v. 6, 7, 8...A Treatise on rash and sinful Anger, on Prov. xxv. 28. (an excellent piece, worth reprinting. ED.)

—— Mr. RICHARDSON. A competent scholar, and pious man. He preached the sermon at six o'clock on Lord's-day mornings at Manchester. By virtue of a licence in 1672, he preached at *Chorton*, and was very laborious in his Master's work. He died in 1680.

—— Mr. WIGAN. He was at the time of the ejectment a candidate for the ministry, as yet unfixed.

MAYHALL [or *Maghall*] Mr. W. ASPINWALL. See MATTERSEY in *Nottinghamshire*.

MELLING [V.] Mr. JOHN MALLINSON. Of *Oxford Univ*. Born at Rastrick in Yorkshire, and ejected here in 1662. He was esteemed an excellent scholar, but not a very celebrated preacher. His family was numerous, and he died very poor, in *May* 1685, aged 75.

—— Mr. WHITE was ejected at the same place.

ST. MICHAEL's upon *Plyer* [V.] Mr. NATHANIEL BAXTER, M. A. Of *Jesus Col. Camb*. Born at *Astle* near Chelford, in Cheshire. When he left the university he went and boarded with Mr. Newcome at Manchester, and sometimes preached for good old Mr. Angier. At length Mr. Isaac Ambrose was instrumental in settling him here at *St. Michael's*, where he remained till his ejection by the Act of uniformity. Providence afterwards removed him into Yorkshire, where he was chaplain to Sir *William Middleton* of *Aldwark* near Rotheram; where he fell into the company of Mr. Pegg, of Beauchief-hall, in Derbyshire, who requested of him a sermon in an old abbey-church, about half a mile from that place, called *Beauchief-Abbey*. He readily complied, and the next Lord's-day he preached there again, at the request of the same gentleman, who then invited him to continue, and offered him 16*l*. *per ann*. the place having no endowment. ·Mr. *Baxter* being then a single man accepted the offer, and afterwards, when married, he purchased a small estate in that neighbourhood and lived within a mile of the abbey several years. But at length, on account of the education of his children, he removed to *Sheffield*, about three miles from the abbey, still however continuing to preach there every Lord's-day, and he usually repeated his sermons at night, to a room full of people, in his own house. Having preached at this place seventeen years, the young heir, *Shelly Pegg*, Esq; on his father's death, desired him to desist, not out of disrespect to him, but from fear, because of the severities that were then used with the Nonconformists.

· When K. *James* granted his Indulgence some time after, the same gentleman desired Mr. *Baxter* to return to his preaching in the abbey, offering him 30*l. per. ann.* But he refused, saying, He could now exercise his ministry without reading the Common-Prayer, as he before had done. The young gentleman offered him a reader, but Mr. *Baxter* declined it, nor did he ever settle with any congregation afterwards, but preached either at some neighbouring meeting or at some gentleman's house; *v. g.* Major Taylor's of Walling-Wells, Mr. Riches of Bull-House, &c. where some other ministers took their turns.—For the last five years of his ministry at the abbey Mr. *Baxter* received no salary; but when the young gentleman died, he left him a handsome legacy, on account (as he expressed it) of his pious and charitable service at Beauchief-Abbey.—Mr. *Baxter* died at *Attercliffe* near *Sheffield*, in *Sept.* 1697, aged about 65. He was a true *Nathaniel*. His sense of religion was early, and became habitual, lively and persevering. He was both personally and relatively good and virtuous. His pulpit gifts and performances were very acceptable: he was fervent in prayer, and affectionate in preaching. In his family worship his method was, to begin with a short address for the divine presence and assistance and then sing part of a psalm. —He had five sons, of whom he brought up four to the ministry. Mr. *Samuel Baxter*, his eldest son, was for many years pastor of a congregation of Dissenters at Ipswich in Suffolk. His son *Nathaniel* lived to finish his studies, and to compose a sermon, but never preached it. His son *Thomas* preached with great acceptance several years as assistant to Dr. *Colton* at York. His son *Benjamin* preached for a few years in some private houses, to the dissenting magistrates at

    Notting.

Nottingham, in the latter part of Queen Ann's reign, when excluded from public worship in the way that they preferred.

NEW-CHURCH in *Rossendale*. Mr. KIPPAX. §*Whitaker* has this entry at Haslingdon. " *J. Kippax*, 1658, sep. apud [i. e. *buried at*] Colne, *Dec.* 27, 1679.

NEWTON-HEATH Chapel. Mr. WILLIAM WALKER. He was one of the preachers of the *Bolton* lecture. Upon the turn of the times, just before the Restoration, he was sent up to *London* with some others, to procure an augmentation to some poor livings, but without success. After his ejectment he preached at *Rivington* chapel to a good old age. He was a considerable man, and a good preacher. A nephew of his, Mr. John Walker, was many years a dissenting minister at Brentford in Middlesex, and was succeeded by Mr. John Baker.

OLDHAM [C. or D.] Mr. ROBERT CONSTANTINE. He had been many years minister of this parish. In 1650, he refused the Engagement for which justice Ashton, of Chatterton, vigorously prosecuted him, so as to force him to remove, when upon an invitation, he went to *Burstal* in Yorkshire, where he was succeeded by Mr. John Lake, afterwards Bp. of Chichester. But after three or four years he returned to *Oldham*, where he continued till his ejectment in 1662. He afterwards lived privately till the time of *Charles's* Indulgence in 1672, when he took out a licence, and preached to a considerable number of people at *Greenakers*, about three miles from Oldham. He was a member of Manchester classis, and was often chosen chairman. In the prime of life he was a man of a clear head, fruitful abilities, solid learning, and a pleasant conversation. He was also a well-accomplished preacher, having a good method, an audible voice, and an agreeable delivery. But living to be very old, his faculties decayed, and he was superannuated with respect to his work. He died however as he had lived, in good credit both with ministers and private christians.

ORMSKIRK [V.] Mr. NATHANIEL HEYWOOD. Of *Trin. Col. Camb.* Brother to Mr. Oliver Heywood. He was born at *Little-Leaver* in Bolton parish, and baptized in that parish church *Sept.* 16. 1633. He dated his first fixed seriousness of spirit from the ministry of Mr. S. Hammond, who was preacher at St. Giles's when he was at the university. On leaving Cambridge, he was some time with Mr.

Edward

Edward Gee of Ecclestone. He first settled at *Illingworth*
chapel, in the vicarage of Halifax. From thence he removed, in 1657, to *Ormskirk*, where he was ejected in
1662. [But he continued preaching in the church after
Bartholomew-day, till the place was filled with a new vicar.
He was much beloved, and his loss lamented by the whole
parish, both good and bad.] When he was about quitting
his living, a poor man came to him and said, " Ah ! Mr.
Heywood, we would gladly have you preach still in the
church." Yes, said he, and I would as gladly preach as you
can desire it, if I could do it with a safe conscience.—" Oh
sir," replied the other, " many a man now-a-days makes a
great gash in his conscience; cannot you make a little nick
in your ?"—Tho' he could not do this, he staid in the
parish, and was abundant in his labours among his old hearers. As his successor, Mr. *Ashworth* [a school-master,
lived six or eight miles off, and was absent all the week, Mr.
Heywood seemed to have still the charge of the whole parish]
visiting the sick &c. He also preached privately as he had
opportunity: usually twice on the Lord's day, and often
several times on week-days; ordering his labours in several
parts of the parish, both in the day and night. Nay, in
times of great danger, he hath preached at one house the beginning of the night, and then gone two miles on foot over
mosses, and preached towards morning at another. Upon
the Indulgence in 1672, he licenced two places; the one at
Bickerstaff, and the other at *Scaresbrick*, both in Ormskirk
parish, and preached on the Lord's-day at each alternately..

[After the licences were called in, he met with much
trouble and frequent interruptions in his work, even at *Scaresbrick*, tho' the chapel belonged to a great person, lady
Stanly, who, at the advice of a member of parliament, had
the Common-Prayer read in it. On the Lord's-day, *Dec.*
20, 1674, three men came while Mr. *Heywood* was in his
prayer before sermon, and when he had ended, they went
up to the pulpit, (tho' lady Stanly interposed) and said, " Sir,
you are our prisoner : come down, and go along with us."
Mr. *Heywood* desired he might be suffered to preach, and
promised then to submit. But the wretch held a pistol to
his head, and with dreadful curses and threatenings ordered
him down †. However, persons of character and influence

† Conformist's Plea for the Noncon. iv. p. 52, where is a fuller account of
his troubles.

espousing

espousing his cause, he was kept from prison, and his goods
from distress, but his spirit was overwhelmed with grief on
the account of his people, whom he loved as if they had been
his children. He afterwards wrote to his brother thus : " I
wish neither you nor any faithful minister that minds and
loves his work, may ever know what I have felt in the want
of people and work : other afflictions are light, compared to a
dumb mouth, and silent Sabbaths, &c." And not long before his death, he said to a friend, " I think this turning us
out of our licensed places will cost Mr. *Yates* and me our
lives. This goes heavily. Our casting out of our great
places was not so much as casting us out of our little places."
However God gave him favour in the sight of those with
whom he conversed ; and he had no adversaries but for *the
matters of his God*, wherein his principles carried him to
practices different from theirs ; and even they would commend his preaching, and at their death, some who had
been his bitterest enemies, were reconciled to him. One of
them was Mr. Brownlow, an old gentleman who lived at
Ormskirk, who conceived a grudge against Mr. *Heywood* after the Restoration, because he would not read the Common-
Prayer ; but when he lay upon his death-bed, he sent for him,
and intreated his prayers. And when Mr. *Ashworth*, the vicar,
would have come to read the common-prayer to him, he refused, and would not part with Mr. *Heywood* as long as he lived.

Mr. *Heywood* died on the Lord's-day morning, *Dec.* 6,
1677, in the 44th year of his age. He was a man of great
piety, and an excellent preacher. He was very useful in
saving many persons and families in these parts from being
perverted by the Papists. A few hours before his death, being asked by a minister whether his Nonconformity was any
trouble to him, he with great chearfulness answered, "No,
it is a great comfort to me ;" and signified his full satisfaction
in what he had done and suffered in opposition to rigorous
impositions, and in pursuit of further reformation. He was
succeeded by his son. His life was published by Sir *Henry
Ashurst*, Bart. in 1695, and dedicated to Lord Willoughby
of Parham. The following are a few additional anecdotes
from it :—

§ Mr. Heywood in his infancy was so weakly, that
his parents several times gave him up for dead, and when a
youth, was taken from school as incapable of prosecuting a
course of study for the ministry. But he afterwards recruited
his strength, and with good natural abilities, and close application, he made great proficiency in academical learning. He

B b 3   spent

spent two years in the family of Mr. Gee, which proved of great use to prepare him for ministerial service. Here he became acquainted with Mrs. E, *Parre*, nearly related to Dr. *Parre*, Bp. of the Isle of Man, whom he in due time married. —He met with great opposition at Illingworth, where he first settled, on account of which one of his adversaries said to him, "Mr. Heywood, you have raised differences and disurbances since you came." To whom he answered, "I have not sought the *peace* of the place, but the *good* of it;" alluding to *Mat.* x. 34.—The income at *Ormskirk* being but 30*l. per ann.* there was an augmentation of 50*l.* from the revenue settled by Q, Eliz. on four itinerant preachers. This, one Mr. Stanninghaugh, parson of *Augham*, surreptiously obtained for himself, at the Restoration, tho' he had no child, and his own living was worth 140*l.* a year. Mr. *Heywood*, who was a great loyalist, preached a thanksgiving sermon for the King's return, on 2 *Sam.* xix. 30.—*Yea let him take all...as the king is come again in peace*; by which some supposed he intended an allusion to the above circumstance. It was very remarkable that this unjust man's gains did not prosper, for at his death he left nothing but debt, and a wife in poverty; whereas Mr. Heywood had *the blessing of God which maketh rich and addeth no sorrow.* Tho' he had some debts to discharge after his ejectment, and had nine children, two of his sons at school at Holland [*Lancashire*] (which cost him 14 pounds a year!) and one at Mr. Frankland's academy; besides much sickness in his family; and had to pay, 6*l.* for the lease of a house, of which he built a good part, and some other expences, yet such was the blessing of God upon him, that he waded through all without contracting any debt, and rather encreased his substance, which often excited his thankful admiration.

' When he was first apprehended, being faint on the road, he desired to stop at an ale-house for a little refreshment, when the landlady (tho' he did not know her,) was very kind to him, and said " He should have any thing she had in the house, but those rogues that took him shall not have a morsel."—Several respectable persons, and some intimate with the justices, offered to be bound for his appearance at the next quarter sessions at *Wiggan*. Accordingly he appeared, when a number of his friends came forward on his behalf, among whom were old lady *Stanly* and Mr. *Henry Houghton*, a justice of peace, and another justice then on the bench said, If Mr. *Heywood* was sent to jail, he should

be

be as comfortably maintained, and as honourably released, as
ever any prisoner was; upon which some of his enemies
slunk away and rode home. Mr. *Heywood* was then dismissed,
to the great joy of his friends, and the amazement of all.—
Snares were laid to entrap him upon the Five-mile-act, but
nobody would swear that he lived in the town, tho' he was
often seen in it, and when a warrant was issued to distrain
his goods for 20*l.* the officers said, the doors were shut, and
they had no orders to break them open.—He was once seized
with a malignant fever, when Dr. Fife, a boisterous and
prophane man, on looking into his mouth, pronounced, with
a horrid oath, that he was a dead man; but he from that
time began to mend, and the Dr. himself was taken ill of the
same fever, of which he died before he could get home.—Mr.
Heywood, by his arduous labours, his frequent and long
preaching, in which he sometimes stood two, and even three
hours, and his neglect to take due care of himself, brought
on him the most painful disorders, which shortened his days.
He was often on the rack with the strangury, but manifested
wonderful patience, and chiefly lamented his inability for
public usefulness. In his memoirs are contained extracts
from several of his letters, written in the time of his affliction, and an account of his death-bed conversation, which
our limits do not allow us to insert. He was frequently repeating those words *Come Lord Jesus, come quickly.*
About four hours before he died, being asked how he did,
he answered, Very well. The last words he was heard to
utter were, " *Come away, Lord,* come, come." His funeral
sermon was preached by Mr. *Starky*, a Nonconformist minister, in the parish church at *Ormskirk*, with the consent
of all concerned. The text was *Col.* iii. 4. Signal honour
was paid him on his death : the chief magistrate carried the
staff before the corps, and the other officers followed in order.
The body was laid in the chancel, in the vault belonging to
the ancient family of *Stanlys* of *Bickerstaff*, knights and
barons, at the desire of that family. At the close of the life,
is the character of Mr. Heywood at large, and the copy of a
letter written by him to a christian friend on the death of his
godly wife, *May* 1, 1675.

WORKS. Since his death have been printed two Discourses :
the one on John iv. 10, entitled, Christ the best Gift, and the other,
Christ the best Master, on John xiii. 13. Neither of them intended for the press, for he would never consent to publish any thing.

RADCLIFF

RADCLIFF [R.] Mr. THOMAS PYKE. He at first preached at *Walmsly* chapel in Bolton parish; and after his ejectment, on the Indulgence in 1672, at *Blackley* near Manchester, where he was very useful. When his end drew near, he
said to those about him " that he found the best preparations
of the best men were little enough when they came to die."
He died in *July* 1676, about 54 years of age. He left several
volumes of his own sermons, fairly transcribed for the use of
his children.

RAYNFORD. Mr. ROGER BALDWIN. See PENRITH,
Cumberland. Being ejected at *Raynford* in 1662, the account of him would have been more properly placed here.

RIVINGTON. Mr. SAMUEL NEWTON. Being turned
out in 1662, he lived at *Crompton*, and preached there as the
times would admit. He afterwards removed back again to
Rivington, and consented to read some of the prayers, as he
had liberty to preach in the church without disturbance. He
died in *March*, 1682, not above 40 years of age, when his abilities and graces were in their full maturity. His funeral sermon was preached by Mr. *John Walker*, his neighbour and
successor, on 1 *Sam.* xxv. 1.

ROCHDALE [R.] Mr. ROBERT BATH, He was born
in *Kent*, and sent down into Lancashire by Abp. *Laud*,
who was his wife's uncle, and who was mightily disappointed by his proving a Puritan. He heartily fell in with the
ministers of the county, and joined with the second classis at
Bury. He freely left his vicarage, tho' considerable, after
holding it above thirty years, rather than ensnare his conscience. The Oxford-act forced him to leave his family;
but upon the king's indulgence he returned home, and
preached to a numerous assembly, in a place called *Under-
hill*. He was a gracious, humble, meek, and peaceable
man, and a solid divine, tho' he had not a ready utterance.
He was a faithful friend, and good in all relations. He spent
much time in visiting the sick, advising his neighbours, and
writing serious letters to distant friends. He died in 1674,
aged 70. § *Whitaker* says, " He complied with all the
changes of the times but the last, and retained his benefice
till *Aug.* 24, 1662; when he retired to a small house at
Deepleach hill, in Castleton, where he frequently preached
to crowded auditories. He was interred *March* 12, 1674."

—— M.

—— Mr. ZACHARIAH TAYLOR. Tho' he had been a chaplain in the king's army in the civil war, he joined with the classical Presbytery at Bury. He was Mr. *Bath's* assistant, and was ejected with him in 1662. He afterwards taught school, first at Rochdale, and then at Bolton, being the first master of the school erected there by Mr. James Leaver of London. From thence he removed to a celebrated school at Kirkham in the Field. He died in *Feb.* 1692, aged 74. He was a very good scholar, a useful school-master, a solid orthodox preacher, and a pious man. He was father of Mr. Zachariah Taylor, who wrote the *Lancashire Levite.*

SALFORD. RICHARD HOLBROOK, M. A. Of *Trin. Col. Camb.* He was born in Manchester, [to which this place is contiguous.] When he was silenced, he applied himself to physic. He was a man of good ability, learning and piety. He died *July* 1676, aged about 40.

SEFTON. Mr. JOSEPH THOMPSON. Of *Oxford* University. Born in *Wigan.* He had a pleasant seat and a rich parsonage, at Sefton, which he quitted in 1660 ; and it seems was not in any other living in 1662. He was a good scholar, a man of wit, and great ingenuity. He was possessed of a considerable estate, with which he did much good. He spent the latter part of his life at *Ormskirk,* where he died about 1669.

SINGLETON. Mr. CUTHBERT HARRISON. Of *Camb.* University. He was born at *Newton* in the parish of Kirkham in this county. On *Nov.* 27, 1651, he was ordained at Kirkham, to officiate at the chapelry of *Singleton* in the said parish, by *Richard Briggs,* and the other ministers of the 7th classis. From thence he in a few years removed to *Lurgan* in the county of *Armagh* in Ireland, where the Uniformity-act found him, and separated him from a loving and beloved people, and a place above 100*l.* per ann. He then returned to England, and settled at *Bankefield* near Singleton. Having obtained a licence from Bp. *Wilkins,* he preached in his own house ; and in 1672 he obtained the king's licence for the chapel in *Elswicke Lees* in the parish of *St Michael,* for the use of such as did not conform to the church of *England,* commonly called Congregational. He there in a short time met with a storm of persecution, for the great crimes of preaching the gospel, baptizing, and marrying, which pursued him to the grave. He died comfortably, tho' reported

to

to be under church censure for the said crimes, in *Oct.* 1680. Such as knew him spoke of him as a man of good sense, whose ministrations discovered both learning and piety.

STANDISH. Mr. PAUL LATHUM. He was some time chaplain to Col. *Ashton* of *Middleton.* He had a good estate, and lived in a manner suitable to it. He was a man of good abilities, exemplary piety, and unwearied diligence in the ministry. He readily forsook this rich parsonage in 1662, rather than hurt his conscience, and died in the year following, aged about 54.

TEATHAM. Mr. NICHOLAS SMITH.

TORKSCATH-PARK Chapel near *Liverpool.* THOMAS CROMPTON, M.A. Of *Oxford* University. Born at Great Leaver, and brought up in Manchester school. After the Act of uniformity took place he continued to enjoy the liberty of the public chapel, being some way privileged. He and Mr. *Briscoe,* who lived in the neighbourhood, supplied it alternately. Mr. *Crompton,* was a man of excellent abilities and good elocution. After Mr. Baldwin's death he removed to *Eccles.* He died at Manchester, *Sept.* 2, 1699, aged 64.

TURTON. Mr. TAYLOR.

ULVERSTON. Mr. LAMVET. A warm and lively preacher. After his ejectment he lived obscurely beyond the Sands, and died in 1677.

WALTON [V.] Mr. HENRY FINCH. Born in the parish of Standish in Lancashire, and baptized *Sept.* 8. 1633. He was at Wigan and Standish schools, where he acquired a considerable exactness both in Latin and Greek : and from thence went to the university, where by diligent study he so improved his fine natural abilities, that he returned to his native country well furnished with substantial learning for the work of the ministry. He preached in the field-country till called to the vicarage of *Walton,* vacant by the death of the former incumbent. On this charge he entered, by the consent of both patron and people, in the year 1656. In that considerable station he laboured with great zeal and diligence, and with eminent success, till *Aug.* 24, 1662. He studied the point of conformity with great care, and would gladly have continued with his beloved people, if he could have satisfied his own conscience about the terms imposed. Not being able

to

to remove the scruples of his mind, he chose to follow his judgment against his affections, and with a growing family cast his care upon divine providence. He retired to *Warrington*, where some of his wife's relations dwelt; and there lived in great esteem with them and many others. His catholic and healing temper led him to a peaceable attendance on the established worship on Lord's-days, improving the evenings, either in repeating and inforcing what had been delivered at church, or in preaching to his neighbours and friends at home. He kept many private fasts in the neighbourhood, praying and waiting for an opportunity to fulfil his ministry in a more public and extensive way. By the Corporation-act in 1665, he was forced to remove again, and a kind providence brought him to *Manchester*, tho' he was a stranger to the place and the people. That not being a corporation town, several other ministers fled thither, who lived in great harmony, and much usefulness to the town and adjacent country. Here also he ordinarily joined with the established church, till the liberty in 1672; when he renewed his beloved work of public preaching at *Birch* chapel, with great diligence. His prudent management kept him employed, when his brethren were silenced by the recalling of their licences. Many and signal were the providences which concurred to keep him in safety in those days of trouble and darkness. Many threatening clouds were in a wonderful manner scattered, and he had a numerous auditory for a long time. His opponents once thrust a conformist into his place, but for want of maintenance, that project dropped, and Mr. *Finch* continued with his flock in that chapel till the chief proprietor died, whose heir took it from him. Under this necessity, he joined with his hearers in the expence of building a meeting-house, where he continued his labours and charities till the sickness of which he died, *Nov.* 13, 1704, in the 72d year of his age.

He was a great blessing to younger ministers, who loved and honoured him as a father; his behaviour to them being full of condescension and tenderness. He greatly resented any thing that either broke in upon order, or tended to the reproach of the ministry; particularly the bold intruding of forward young men, without examination and trial: with respect to which, he and his brethren made a very good rule, which was observed in that district, and ought to be in others. He was a bright ornament to his profession, as he was not merely inoffensive and peaceable, strictly just, and sincere, without stratagem or affectation, but extensively benevolent.

Tho'

Tho' cautious and prudent, he was free and communicative. Above all, he lived a life of devotedness to God, with whom he had closely walked many years. He feared nothing so much as sinning against his maker, whose interests were always dear to him. His preaching was clear and methodical ; adapted to convince the judgment as well as to move the passions. He absolutely refused the Engagement, and was desirous of . K. Charles's Restoration. After the defeat of Sir *George Booth*, the sequestrators seized all his effects that they could meet with, which he had certainly lost, for his love to the king, if the speedy turn of affairs had not prevented. He rejoiced however at the Revolution in 1688, and entirely fell in with it ; but had a great tenderness for those who refused the oaths and lost their places for conscience-sake, to some of whom he was a charitable contributor as long as he lived.

—— Mr. ROBERT EATON. Of *Camb.* University. He was born in Cheshire, and settled first in *Essex* ; from whence he removed to this place, where he was ejected in 1660. After some time, he was chaplain to the Lord *Delamere.* When the liberty of the Dissenters was established by law, he preached to a congregation in the parish of *Prestwich*, where they built him a handsome chapel. He was a solid divine, a good scholar, and a judicious christian ; of great moderation, and exemplary in his behaviour. He died at Manchester, in *August* 1701 ; and his funeral sermon was preached by . Mr. Finch.

WALMESLY Chapel. Mr. MICHAEL BRISCOE. Of *Trin. Col. Dublin.* He was pastor of a congregational church in this chapel. He afterwards removed thence to *Toxtoth-Park*, where he preached in the chapel jointly with Mr. *Thomas Crompton*, and continued there till he died, which was in *Sept.* 1685, aged 96. He was a good scholar, and a fine orator. His sermons were judicious, but his voice was low, which was more than compensated by his pleasing delivery.

WARRINGTON [R.] Mr. ROBERT YATES. An able orthodox divine. A very useful laborious minister in that populous parish. In the time of the Commonwealth, he was tried for his life at Lancaster, for speaking against the Engagement, and matters were carried so far against him, that he had prepared his last speech ; being fully resolved not to retract what he had preached. But by the unexpected

clemency

clemency of the judge (supposed to be *Twisden*) he was pardoned. When he was afterwards ejected for his Nonconformity, he had several potent enemies, who brought him into some trouble by the Five-mile-act. In 1672, he took the opportunity of preaching in a public meeting-house, but was violently disturbed. He was not long after seized by a palsy, which affected his intellects, and rendered him incapable of his work a year before he died; which was in November 1678, aged 66. He was succeeded by his son Mr. Samuel Yates.

§ WHALLEY [V.] Mr. WILLIAM MOORE. Another ejected minister who should undoubtedly be added to our list, as appears from the following note in *Whitaker's* History of *Whalley.*—" 1656. *William Moore.* From the parish ac-" counts it appears that he resigned his vicarage, and went " out upon the Bartholomew-act, tho' he is not mentioned by " Calamy."

WIGAN [R.] Mr. CHARLES HOTHAM. Some time Fellow of *Peter-house* in *Cambridge*, and Proctor of the university. He was son to Sir *John Hotham*. After his ejectment he went to the *West-Indies*, but returned to *England*. He was an excellent scholar, both in divine and human literature. A great philosopher who loved to search into the secrets of nature, and was very fond of chymistry. In his younger years he had studied judicial astrology, but gave express orders in his will that all his papers and books relating to that art should be burnt.

THERE were several candidates for the ministry in this county, not fixed any where when the Act of uniformity took Place, who continued Nonconformists, and therefore should be mentioned here; *v. g.* Mr. THOMAS WADDINGTON.—Mr. JAMES HADDOCK.—Mr. CUTHBERT HALSALL.— Mr. JOHN EDDLESTONE—Mr. THOMAS KAY; afterwards at *Houghton-Tower.*

Mr. JOHN CROMPTON. He died, in *August* 1703, minister of *Cockey* chapel. [Mr. *Mat. Henry*, speaks of him thus : "He was a man of great worth and great humility. Indeed it were easy to enlarge upon the characters of Mr. *T. Jollie* and Mr. *Crompton*: men of the first rank both for ministerial gifts and graces : steadfast to their principles in trying times, and ornaments to their holy profession. But I

4   forbear ;

forbear; their praise is in all the churches of that country."]
Mr. Henry's *Life*, p. 279.

Mr. JOHN PARR. He preached sometimes at *Preston*, and sometimes at *Walton*, about a mile off. His conversation was strictly pious and regular; his temper meek and peaceable; and his preaching affectionate, searching, and useful. He met with many sufferings and hardships. Preaching once at a chapel not far from *Preston*, before he had concluded, there came two neighbouring justices, who took his name, and the names of several hearers. Some of them made friends and got off; but he and four more were bound over to the quarter sessions, and proceeded against as rioters. The jury for some time refused to find the bill; but being threatened by the justices, it was at last found. The others submitted, and were fined; two of them in 10*l*, and two in 5*l*. each. When he was called, and refused to submit, the justices roared upon him like lions, threatening that it should cost him 200*l*. He attended the next sessions, and took a lawyer with him, who with much difficulty obtained a writ to remove his farther trial before a judge of assize. He did not attend the next assizes, being informed that the writ was then only to be filed; but his neighbour and prosecutor was there, tho' very lame and gouty. The following assizes he attended, and when called, after waiting three or four days, there was not a man that opened his mouth against him, and so he was acquitted. At another time, about the end of Charles II.'s reign he and his wife being invited by a neighbour to come and stay a night at his house, a few friends were got together in expectation of some religious exercise. But before he began, a neighbouring justice, came in and took his name, and the names of all he could find, either in or about the house. They were proceeded against upon the act to suppress conventicles; and soon after, an officer was sent to levy 20*l*. upon him as the minister, and 4*l*. upon his wife as a hearer. Rather than venture to contest the matter in those discouraging times, he paid two thirds of the fine, and the rest was remitted, by means of a friend. Not long after, upon the landing of the Duke of *Monmouth*, he was kept prisoner, five or six weeks, without knowing the reason, first at Warrington, and afterwards at Chester; where he and eight other ministers were thrust into the common jail, the lodgings in the *Castle* being taken up by prisoners out of several counties.

Dr.

Dr. *Calamy* closes his Account of the ejected ministers in this county, with answering the Remarks made upon it by the compilers of the large work, entitled, *Magna Britannia & Hibernia, & Antiqua Nova.* The greater part of what the Dr. has advanced, is applicable to the ejected ministers in general, and is therefore here omitted. The following, which is the concluding passage, may properly be retained.

" As for the ejecting and silencing so many useful Protestant preachers in this county, where, as these gentlemen observe, *Papists abound more than in any other part of England,* this was most certainly a very impolitic step, in any who had the Protestant interest at heart. And after this, to complain, *that the Protestants did not get ground in this county so fast as might be wished,* is just as if, upon a country's being invaded by an enemy, a considerable number of the able inhabitants should be disarmed, and they that did it should afterwards find fault that the enemy should take advantages of it."

The following afterwards conformed.

Mr. BRADLEY HAYHURST, of *Leith.*—Mr. ASPINWELL, of *Heaton.*—Mr. JOSHUA AMBROSE, of *Derby.*—Mr. WILLIAM COLE, of *Preston.*—Mr. WILLIAM COLEBURN, of *Edinburgh.*—Mr. LOBEN, of *Oldham.*—Mr. JAMES BOCKER, of *Blakely.*—Mr. WILLIAM ASPINWELL, of *Formeby.*—Mr. BRIARS, of *Heapy.*—Mr. FISHER, of *Kirkham.*—Mr. JAKEYS, of *Bolton.*—Mr. JESSOP, of *Winwick*; who died at *Coggeshal* in *Essex.*—Mr. ROBERT DEWHURST, of *Whitmouth* chapel. § One of this name (probably the same person) is mentioned by *Whitaker* as being at *Newchurch, Rossendale,* 1650: " An able divine, who received no allowance but what the inhabitants gave. He seems to have gone out upon the Bartholomew-act."

*** The account of Mr. JOLLIE of Attercliffe, was received too late to be inserted in its proper place. It will be given, with the *Addenda,* at the end of the volume.

MINISTERS

MINISTERS EJECTED OR SILENCED

IN

LEICESTERSHIRE. *

———

BLABEY [R.] Mr. THOMAS BOSSE. He and Mr. *Swayne,* and Mr. *Stephens* of Fenny-Draton, were engaged in a dispute about Infant-baptism, against Mr. *Robert Everard* and other Baptists, in 1650; as appears from Mr. *Swayne's* answer to Mr. *Everard,* at the end of Mr. *Stephens's* Precept for Infant-baptism, p. 64,

BOWDEN *Magna.* Mr. THOMAS LANGDEN. § Inducted 1656.

COLE-ORTON [R.] Mr. SAMUEL OLDERSHAW. Dr. *Walker* says he got this living in 1654. After his ejectment, he lived as chaplain in the family of —— *Spademan,* Esq. at Roadnook in Derbyshire. He afterwards commenced physician.

CONGERSTON [C. or D.] Mr. GEORGE WRIGHT. A man of great piety, and an awakening and useful preacher. He had an extraordinary gift in prayer, and was favoured with some uncommon answers to his prayers. He had a great felicity in discoursing warmly on spiritual things, by which means God made him instrumental of good to many. After his ejectment he took a farm at King's-Heath, in the parish of King's-Norton; which he managed with great care and labour to maintain his family.

COTSBATCH [R.] Mr. JOSEPH LEE.

* Several additions in this county are communicated by Mr. Isaac James, from NICHOLS's History of Leicestershire, in which are frequent quotations from the Nonconf. Mem.

DRAYTON

DRAYTON (Fenny) [R.] NATHANIEL STEVENS, M. A. Of *Oxford* University. His father was minister of Staunton-Barnwood in Wilts. This living of *Drayton* was not, as *Wood* reports, a sequestration; Mr. *Stevens* was duly presented by the patron, Mr. *Purefoy* of Berkshire. Here he lived till the violence of the cavaliers, who threatened plunder, imprisonment and fire, drove him to seek sanctuary in Coventry. There, during the civil war, he preached on Lord's-day morning in the great church. At his return to Drayton he had trouble from some Baptists. The noted Quaker, *George Fox* came out of his little parish. Mr. *Stephens* had much discourse with him, but with little effect. He thought his time better spent in instructing a teachable people; which he did very diligently. He took much pains in studying the book of the *Revelation*; and some apprehended that few ever did it to better purpose. Besides what he published himself, some few of his thoughts, being communicated to Mr. *Poole*, are to be found in his *Synopsis*. After his ejectment for Nonconformity in 1662, he continued in the town for some time, preaching privately, but was afterwards so molested, that he was forced to remove seven times for peace. At last he fixed at *Stoke-Golding*, where he exercised his ministry, as he had opportunity, till his death, in *Feb.* 1678, aged 72. He was a good scholar, and a useful preacher. In his younger days he was a very hard student, often spending sixteen hours a day in his study. His thoughts were sometimes so intent, that he would strangely forget himself. In his old age he was pleasant and chearful. As an instance of it, one acquainted with him relates that he went with a friend to his house, and knocked at the door; when, no one being within but himself who was lame, and his wife who was blind, he called to them to come in, and then asked them, which of the two they would have had open the door for them, the blind or the lame? He was a man of a generous catholic spirit, but had a great aversion to that ceremoniousness which was carried so high in the reign of Charles I. and would often tell a story of what happened in the West, when he was young. A clergyman coming into the church, went up to the chancel to bow to the altar. It happened that there was no altar there, but the communion-table stood against the East-wall, and a boy sat upon it. The boy seeing him coming, slipt down and stood before the table. The priest made a low bow, and the poor boy thinking it was to him, bowed as low; and the bows were repeated three times

on each side; but the boy was surprized at the priest's wonderful complaisance. "In this case (said Mr. *Stephens*) the
boy knew well enough who it was he himself bowed to; but
whether or not it was so as with the priest is questionable:
for the God whom Christians worship, is no more in the East
than in the West; no more in the chancel than in the church;
nor any more there than in the house or field, unless when
his people are there worshipping him in spirit and truth. Before the coming of Christ, the Jews in the Western parts,
worshipped towards the East, because Jerusalem and the temple stood that way (1 *Kings* viii. 48. *Dan.* vi. 10.) This
might be the reason why some Christians in the primitive
times prayed towards the East. But now Mount *Sion* is no
more holy than Mount *Gerizim*, or the mountains in *Wales.*
Happy were it for the world if *John* iv. 20—24, were generally understood."

WORKS. A Precept for the Baptism of Infants, out of the N.
Test.—A plain and easy Calculation of the Number of the Beast;
Rev xiii. 17, 18.—His [MS.] Treatises on the Revelation were,
after his death, in the hand of Sir Charles Woolsley. Mr. *Caldwell,*
of *Cambridgeshire,* had his leave to copy one of them, on the Slaughter of the Witnesses. Of this some account is given in *Cal. Contin.*
p. 579.

DUNNINGTON (Castle) [V.] Mr. THOMAS SMITH.
He was born at *Kegworth* in this county, of good parentage.
He became the minister of this parish about the year 1657,
and continued there till the fatal Bartholomew. His preaching and praying were very affectionate, and his life was exemplary. He was well beloved by his parish, and much lamented when silenced. His very enemies had nothing to
say against him. When K. Charles gave a Toleration, he
preached once a month freely at *Dunnington,* but lived not
long after; having spent himself in his Master's service.

EDMONTHORPE [R.] Mr. JOHN WRIGHT. "In-
ducted 1651." After his ejectment he retired to *Lessingham* near Sleaford in Lincolnshire, where he had a small
estate. There he spent the remainder of his days, and was
beloved and honoured by his neighbours, especially by Sir
William York and his family, for his prudence, moderation,
and usefulness, in promoting knowledge and piety amongst
them.

FOXTON [V.] Mr. JOHN WILSON.

§ GLOOSTON

§ GLOOSTON [R.] Mr. Samuel Smith. His name
is not mentioned by Dr. *Calamy*, but is undoubtly to be
added to the list of ejected ministers, on the authority of
Nichols, who in his *History of Leicestershire*, Vol. II. p.
586, has the following entry at this place. "Samuel Smith,
" 1657. He was one of the Nonconformist ministers, who
" signed the representation to parliament in 1659, and was
" ejected at the restoration."—See the list of all those ministers at the end of this county.

GUMLEY [R. 120*l*.] Nicholas Kestyn, M. A. "Rector in 1644." (*Nichols.*) He was a man of eminent piety.
After being silenced he went to Leicester, where he was pastor of a congregation several years. He died at about 76
years of age.

HALLATON [R.] Mr. Mauritius Bohemus. A native of Germany, and nephew to Dr. *Burgius*, who was
chaplain to the elector of Brandenburgh. He had a brother
in the ministry, who was ejected from *Sleaford*, in Lincolnshire. After his ejectment from Hallaton, he returned to his
own country. He was in good esteem for learning and piety. § Nichols mentions him as rector here in 1654. In
the parish registers are the following entries, which give some
account of his family. "Jane, wife of Mr. *Bohemus* [proba-
" bly the father of the minister] buried *Dec.* 14, 1647.—Anne,
" daughter of Mr. Boheme, and Eliz. his wife, baptized
" March 12, 1652.—Eliz. wife of Mauritius Bohemus, mi-
" nister, buried July 10, 1654.—Mauritius Bohemus, mi-
" nister, and Hannah Vowe, published Jan. 13, 20, 27.
" Married Feb. 27, 1656.

WORKS. Exercises on several Scriptures, (recommended by
several learned divines.)—A Christian's Delight: or Scripture Meditations, in one century: with an Appendix against promiscuous
admission to the sacrament, and a Latin Dedicat. to Sir Arthur
Haslerig.—An English Translation of a Work written in High-
Dutch, entitled, The Pearl of peace and concord; a treatise of
pacification between the Dissenting churches, by Dr. Burgius.

HARBOROUGH [C. or D.] Mr. Thomas Lowrey.
He was a native of Scotland, and had a living in Essex be-
fore he came hither. § *Nichols* mentions him as inducted,
Feb. 24, 1649, and says, " The moiety of the rectory of
Whitwick was appointed to be given to Mr. *Lowrey* for an
augmentation of his salary, the profits of Harborough not

being sufficient. He was appointed lecturer of *Malden* in Essex, June 12, 1649, but being the settled minister of Harborough, he did not accept of the same."—A large society of dissenters was formed here, of which Mr. *Matthew Clark* was afterwards pastor, and after him, the excellent Mr. *David Some*, who was succeeded (not immediately) by the late Dr. *Stephen Addington.* See Mr. *Some's* funeral sermon, by Dr. Doddridge.

HINCKLEY [V.] Mr. THOMAS LEADBEATER. Of *Camb.* university. He was a native of Cheshire. In his younger days he was chaplain to the pious Lady Wimbledon. His ministerial labours were very acceptable and useful in this town. After his ejectment he retired into his own country, *viz.* to *Namptwich,* where he had a very good correspondence with the public minister, which some others who came thither for shelter, were denied. He was a grave, learned, judicious man, and had a good estate. He preached privately in his own house, and elsewhere as he had opportunity, till the Indulgence in 1672, when he took out a licence for his house at *Armitage* * a large hamlet near *Church-holme* in *Cheshire.* But, that he might give the less offence, he went to church first, and preached at home afterwards. At length he fixed with a private congregation in *Wirral*, and there he died suddenly, by vomiting blood, *Nov.* 4, 1679, aged 52.

HOUGHTON on the Hill [R.] § Sir JOHN BURROW. A man of great worth and eminence. *Nichols* places him here in 1651. He was also vicar of *Thornton.* He was the son of *Erasmus Burrow,* rector of *Burrow,* and his pedigree is traced up to *Henry de Stockton,* who lived in the reign of HENRY II.

⁎ HUMBERSTONE § [V.] Mr. RICHARD ADAMS. After his ejectment in 1662, he married a wife at Mountsorrel, and there set up a meeting in his own house. At first many persons were afraid to appear at it, but afterwards it

* In my copy of the Index Villaris, against the word *Armitage*, is put in MS. —— *Leadbeater,* Esq. so that this seems to be the family seat. ED.

§ The late Mr. Ryland of Northampton, in a letter to the editor, observes, that Mr. HANSERD KNOLLYS is omitted in this work, who should have been mentioned as ejected from *Humberstone.* But this is evidently a mistake, as that very respectable and worthy man, after he became a Baptist, voluntarily left the church, A. D. 1636. See *Crosby's Hist. of Bapt.* Vol. I. p. 334—44, where there is an excellent account of him.

greatly

greatly increased, and he continued it about fourteen years·
Justice Babington, who, tho' a sober man, was very zealous
against the Dissenters, and oppressed them more than all the
other justices in that county, was very severe against him.
He fined him twelve-pence per day, and sent to the officers
of the parish to make distress for it. The poor men were so
troubled in conscience, that they knew not what to do. At
length, upon the justices threatening them, they seized his
pewter, and sent it to the pewterer's, who refused to buy it.
After this, the justice sent for Mr. *Adams*, and told him he
was not against his keeping school, but if he would not leave
off his meeting he must expect to be troubled. Soon after this
the justice died of excessive bleeding. Mr. *Adams* went to
London, and being of the Baptist denomination, succeeded
Mr. *Daniel Dyke* at Devonshire-square. He was a man of
great piety and integrity. He lived to a great age, and some
years before his death was disabled from preaching. Mr.
Mark Key, his assistant, succeeded him. *Crosb. Hist.
Bapt.*-vol. iii. p. 37.

HUNGERTON [V.] Mr. Samuel Muston.

IBSTOKE [R. S.] William Sheffield, M. A. of *Trin.
Col. Camb.* In the time of the civil war, he preached several
years at *Great-Bowden.* The committee of *Leicester* offered him his choice out of three rich parsonages in the county, then vacant, viz. *Lancton, Kibworth* and *Loughborough,*
but he refused them all, and accepted *Ibstoke,* upon the invitation of the principal inhabitants (after the sequestration of
Dr. *Lufton*) tho' it was near 50l. *per ann.* worse than any of
the others. During his ministry there, he was greatly respected and beloved, not only by his own parishioners, but
by the generality of ministers and religious people in the adjacent parts: of which, among many others, there was this
remarkable proof; that when Dr. *Lufton,* the former incumbent, was dead, and Mr. *Job Grey,* brother to the Earl of
Kent, obtained the presentation of *Ibstoke* parsonage from
the lord-keeper, several gentlemen, ministers, and other
principal persons in the neighbourhood, sent a petition to
court, signed by above a thousand hands, begging that Mr.
Sheffield might be continued; and accordingly he was confirmed in the living, by a broad-seal; which however soon
became useless, when the Act of uniformity took place, at
which time he resigned.

cc3   He

He once held a public dispute with one *Samuel Oates* (father of Dr. *Titus Oates*) a popular Baptist preacher, who came into that country, and disturbed several congregations, dispersing challenges, to dispute with any minister upon the point of baptism. Several justices of peace desired Mr. *Sheffield* to accept the challenge. He yielded to their request, and Sir *Tho. Beaumont* was moderator. At the entrance of the dispute, which was held in Leicester castle, Mr. *Sheffield* protested, that it was truth and not victory he aimed at; and that therefore, if he could not answer the arguments brought against him, he would publicly acknowledge it. Mr. *Oates* also agreed to do the same. The dispute continued three hours, and was managed with great fairness and temper. At length Mr. *Oates* being pressed with an argument, was loudly called upon, by the people present, either to answer it, or to confess he could not. Upon which he frankly confessed that at present he could not answer it. The justices, at the breaking up of the meeting, obliged Mr. *Oates* to promise, that he would no more disturb the congregations in that county §.

Mr. *Sheffield*, after being silenced, went to *Kibworth*, where he had a small estate; having also in view the benefit of the free-school there for his children. He there lived privately till his death, in 1673. During this time of his retirement, he constantly went in the morning, with his family, to the parish-church, and preached in his own house in the afternoon. His son was pastor of a church in *Southwark*.

KIBWORTH [R. 300*l.*] Mr. JOHN YAXLEY.* Of *St. John's Col. Camb.* Dr. Walker says he had this living in 1654. He was not only turned out of it, soon after the restoration, but robbed of his goods, and also arraigned for his life, for saying in his pulpit, that "he thought hell was broke loose." His enemies would have made those words treason against the king and government; but God would not suffer them to take away his life. His wife was miserably

§ However intemperate this Mr. Oates might be, he met with cruel and shameful usage in other places; See *Crosby's Hist. Bapt.* vol. i. p. 236. Such disputes as that related above, and others mentioned in this work, are but a sort of spiritual duels, which can no more decide the equity of any cause, than an appeal to the sword or pistol, and ought to be as much discountenanced among christians.

* See a further account of him at the end of this county.

abused

abused by the soldiers, who pushed her down stairs headlong, turned her out of doors with the servants, and took possession of every thing. In her fright she forgot a grand-daughter that lay in a cradle; upon which she went back, but could not get in. Looking thro' the hall-window, she saw the child in the cradle, and the soldiers by it; when in an agony she cried out to them, "You villains, will you kill my child?" For which they shot at her thro' the window, and so wounded her in the face, that she lost her sight to the day of her death. Mr. *Yaxley* lived to be between 70 and 80 years of age, preaching near West-Smithfield in London. He was a sincere, plain-hearted, humble, pious man; a faithful friend, and very communicative. While he was in the church he was very zealous in promoting reformation, both in his own parish and in the whole country.

KINGCOTT [R.] Mr. BENJAMIN SOUTHWOOD. Dr. Walker says "He got himself possessed of this living in 1655;" but, for any thing that appears, he got it honourably, and might legally have kept it if he could have satisfied his conscience with conformity.

Church LANGTON [R.] Mr. OBADIAH MUSSON. *Nichols* has it, "*Richard Muston* 1659." (See the list at the end). He was all his life time a lover of good men, and a follower of that which was good. What he wanted in ability, he made up in serious affection. He left his living when he was very aged, and unprovided of other supports. He retired to *Coventry*, where he found God and good people kind to him, till worn away by age. Dr. *Bryan* preached his funeral sermon, on *Job* v. 26. ' Thou shalt come to ' thy grave in full age, like as a shock of corn cometh in ' his season:' Which he afterward turned into a poem, and printed under the name of *Harvest-home;* with a further account of him. (*See the end of this county.*)

LAUGHTON. WALTER HORNBY, M. A. only an Assistant. § *Nichols* mentions no incumbent here from 1562 till *Jan.* 10, 1662. It seems doubtful whether R. *Muston,* or one of the name of OB. MUSTON, was not ejected here.

LEICESTER. Mr. WILLIAM SIMMS.

LEARE [R. 200*l.*] Mr. JAMES FARMER. A very holy spiritual man, and zealous in his ministry. He preached but seldom after his ejectment, and lived but a few years.

LOUGHBOROUGH [R. 300*l.*] Mr. OLIVER BRUM-SKILL. He was a judicious solid divine, an excellent preacher, and an holy liver. His deportment was grave and serious, his temper mild, humble and peaceable ; in general somewhat reserved. He lived with the eminently pious old lady Bromley, widow to judge Bromley.

LUBBENHAM [V.] Mr. WESTON. § *Nichols* mentions him as inducted 1659, and ejected 1662.

LUTTERWORTH [R.] Mr. JOHN ST. NICOLAS. He was an able scholar, and had a good estate. He married the daughter of the Earl of Kent, who was an old Puritan minister : and who, when the title came to him as heir of that noble family, was not to be prevailed upon, tho' pressed by many, to quit the ministry, but held on officiating as usual, without being molested, as he had often been before, on account of some failures in point of conformity. In a short address to the governors and ministers of the colonies in New-England, prefixed to his History of Baptism, he speaks of himself as " An adventurer in the first plantation, as well as a sympathizer in their joys, fears and sorrows." He lived to a good old age, and was used to the last to stile himself, A Student in St. Paul's Epistles. He went to the public church as long as he was able to go abroad, tho' he was for many years so deaf that he could hear nothing. When asked the reason, he said, It was to give an example to others, who, if he should stay at home, might be encouraged to do so without a like excuse. He died at *Burbage* in this county, *May* 27, 1698, in the 95th year of his age.

WORKS. The History of Baptism.—The Widow's Mite.—A Help to Beginners in the Faith ; containing explicatory Questions upon the Creed, Lord's Prayer, &c...An English Translation of Dr. Ame's Marrow of Divinity ; printed by order of Parliament.

NARBOROUGH [R. 120*l.*] MATTHEW CLARK, M. A. Of *Trin. Col. Camb.* He was a younger brother of a genteel family in Shropshire, where his father was a minister near Ludlow. His grandfather also was a minister, and beneficed near Ely. He was born about the year 1630, and educated first at the Charter-house, and afterwards under Dr. *Busby* at Westminster. When he was in the college (where Dr. *Hill* his uncle was the master, and Dr. *Templer* his tutor) he associated with several students who were remarkable for religion, and used to spend much time together in such exercises

ercises as tended to further their preparation for the work which they mainly designed. He was an indefatigable student, and well versed in the classics, and oriental learning; his fondness for which was such, that he learned the modern *Persic* after he was 66 years of age. He was moderator of his year in the sophisters schools, and came off with credit. He went into North-Britain, as chaplain to Col. Hacker's regiment; and afterwards waited upon General *Monk*, as he passed thro' Leicester in his march from the North to London; but could not at all judge of his intentions.—He was presented to the living of *Narborough* by Mr. Stratford, the patron, in 1657, and was ejected in 1662; when one who had been his competitor for this living, and had appeared before the triers, became his successor; having changed with the times. Mr. *Stratford*, much pressed Mr. *Clark* to conformity upon the Restoration; but he could not bring his conscience to comply with the terms. He had an estate of 50*l.* a year in Shropshire, which he gave to his sister, never intending to marry; tho' he afterwards saw occasion to change his mind. He was no sooner married, than he gave notice of it to his college, not desiring those profits which were no longer his due; and they dealt as honorably by him, in voluntarily returning some considerable arrears, which he did not know to be due to him.

After his ejectment he continued preaching in and about *Leicestershire*, readily embracing all opportunities of usefulness. And tho' there were some furious justices about the country who watched him narrowly, he had the happiness for some time to escape them. But at length it came to his turn to suffer for Nonconformity, and he was three times imprisoned in Leicester jail for the crime of preaching. He first lived, after being silenced, in a very lonesome house in Leicester forest; but was driven from thence by the Five-mile-act, and went to *Stoke-Golding*, where he had the agreeable company of Mr. *Stephens*, Mr. *Shuttlewood*, and Mr. *Southwell*, in his neighbourhood. From thence he was invited to *Harborough*, where he settled a meeting about the year 1673, and had a large congregation. At the latter end of K. *Charles's* reign, Mr. *Clark* was excommunicated, and prosecuted upon the act for 20*l.* a month, and his goods were seized. When K. *James* gave liberty to the Dissenters, he as well as others, was much pressed to sue for a reparation of damages, and had a fair prospect of succeeding; but

but he forbore, lest such an attempt, as circumstances then stood, might do more hurt than good.

His judgment was congregational; but nothing of party could alienate his affection from true piety, in whomsoever he beheld it: nor would he speak evil of any man without a notorious cause. He was very remarkable for modesty and humility. He always discovered very low thoughts of himself and his own performances; which made him very backward to censure the weaknesses of others; and when any who did so, asked his opinion of them, he would often say, He thought the person censured preached better than himself. If at any time he jocosely related the foibles of any, he carefully concealed their names. At the same time, he, was patient in bearing, and ready in forgiving, censures passed upon himself; and such as had shewed a slight of him for some time, afterwards valued him the more, when they came to be better acquainted. His carriage was so inoffensive, and his charity so large, that he was generally beloved by those who had not an inveterate malice against true goodness; and he had the good word of many whose opinions he could not countenance. When Mr. *Richard Davis* † made such a stir in his neighbourhood, and created some disturbance among his flock, many of his censorious followers would speak of Mr. *Clark* with respect. He was intimate with Mr. *Maidwell* and Mr. *Browning*, two worthy ministers * not far from him, and in his mild and peaceable way concurred with the former, in opposing the turbulent proceedings of [a strange set of people in those parts.]

His preaching was very plain, and suited to the capacities of his people. He was an instrument of good to many souls, and the country round about had reason to bless God for him, as a promoter of true piety. When he settled at *Harborough*, he used every Lord's-day morning, in all weathers, to ride to *Ashly*, four or five, miles off; and having preached there, and taken a hasty dinner, to return and preach at *Harborough* in the afternoon. His constitution being strong, he bore this fatigue many years. Tho' he had very advantageous offers from other places, nothing could draw him from his people, as long as he was able to serve them.—He was naturally generous, and had been very liberal to strangers who

---

† Concerning this Mr. Davis, see *Desborow* in Northamptonshire.
* Mr. Maidwell was at Kettering, and Mr. Browning at Rowell.

solicited

solicited charity: but finding he had been often imposed upon, he prudently retrenched those expences. The following instance of his regard to Liberty is worth recording. The assessors being put upon rating him to the king's tax for his salary from his people, a relation suggested to him, that if the act of parliament had not taxed him, for him to pay to his assessment would be betraying the rights of subjects. He therefore resolved to stand it out; for which some angry justices threatened to 'send him to Leicester jail in a cart. But when they had thought a little on the matter they became cooler, and 'sent to request him to pay the money that time, promising it should be repayed him. But he still refused; and they who were bent upon giving him trouble, thought it the safest to make up the sum among themselves. He continued his arduous labours till he was seized with the palsy on one side; and then, thinking his work done, he removed to *Norwich*, to live with his daughter, Mrs. *Allen*; where he died about 1708, near 80 years of age. He left a son in the ministry, who had a good congregation in *Miles's-Lane*, London, who died in 1726.

PACKINGTON [V.] Mr. WILLIAM SMITH. Born in Worcestershire, and educated in *Oxford*. His first labours were in this county, as assistant to Mr. Blackaby, of *Langton*. From thence he removed to *Packington*, near Ashby de la Zouch. After his ejectment in 1662, he went to *Diseworth-Grange*, where he continued many years, teaching school, and preaching constantly, either in his own house or in places adjacent, as opportunity offered. He was a worthy man, and a plain useful preacher. He enjoyed a greater measure of health than most students and laborious preachers do; but in his 63d year, hypochondriacal disorders put a period to his valuable life, *Oct.* 20, 1686.

⁎ RAUNSTON and HOOSE. JOHN SHUTTLEWOOD, A. B. Of *Christ's Col. Cambridge*. He was born at *Wymeswold* in this county, *Jan.* 3, 1631, of respectable parents, and had his grammar-learning at a school in *Leicester*. On *Ap.* 26, 1654, he was ordained to the ministry, in the congregation of *Raunston*, with an honourable testimonial from the classical presbytery of *Wirksworth*, in the province of *Derby*. With what profound humility, dependance upon divine assistance, and fixed resolution to promote, to the utmost of his ability, the everlasting welfare of the souls intrusted to his charge, he entered upon the ministry, will
appear

appear from his solemn Dedication of himself to God, drawn up in Latin, of which the following is a translation :—

"O my God, on the account of my sins thou hast afflicted me with thy judgments. Thou art just, O Lord, in all thy dispensations towards me, because I have grievously offended against thee. I have followed the world, I have too much indulged the flesh, and I have been very often overcome by Satan. To thee I give up myself, to live to thee. And now before God, the searcher of hearts, I promise and engage to leave my worldly concerns to the companion of my life †, to renounce the flesh with its affections, and to study the good of the souls which thou art committing to my care. Now, O Lord, do thou so strengthen and fortify me, by the spirit of grace, against all these my enemies, that I may obtain the victory over them : And that I may seriously perform these my good resolutions, let this paper, signed by my name, be a witness against me if I lie before thee."   *John Shuttlewood.*

He was a great sufferer for his Nonconformity, not only by the loss of a very comfortable subsistence, but by the seizure of his goods, and the imprisonment of his person. In 1668 he was taken, with many others, as they were singing a psalm, by *M. B.* and 30 or 40 horsemen with swords drawn and pistols cocked. Several of both sexes were beaten and driven into the field, and dismissed upon promise of appearing the next day before some justice. Mr. *Shuttlewood* was asked by justice *Streete* "When he had been at his parish-church to hear divine service?" Mr. *S.* answered, " that he did not know any who charged him with being absent." He then asked him, " if he would promise to go the next *Sunday?*" Mr. *S.* replied, " that he did not know how divine providence might dispose of him before that time." Upon this the justice made his *mittimus* for a breach of the 35th of *Elizabeth,* and delivered him to the custody of one *Charles Gibbons,* a quarter-master in a troop of the trained bands, to convey him to Leicester jail. It being too late that night, they rested where they were. As Mr. *S.* was asking a blessing upon their food, *Gibbons* came into the room, swore a bloody oath, and said, "What, are you a preaching?" Soon

† He married, *April 26,* 1652, Elizabeth, daughter of the pious Mr. Humphry Carter, of Dreycot in Derbyshire. An excellent woman, whose Diary is still remaining. She survived her husband several years, and died *July 3.* 1705, aged near 71.

after

after a neighbouring gentleman came and requested that Mr.
S. and the rest of the prisoners might go for that night to
their own houses, and offered a bond of a thousand pounds
for their appearance.   Upon the gentleman's pressing the
matter hard, *Gibbons* girt his sword about him, and desperately swore, " That since he loved them so well he should go
with them," and continued swearing all night, that if the
gentleman stirred he would run him through.   The next
morning *Gibbons*, staying with the gentleman, sent the prisoners to the jail ; and glad they were to go ; esteeming their
late situation worse than that of a prison.   They continued
in confinement till *Feb.* 24, and were then dismissed.   In
1670, soon after the Act against conventicles came out, the
said *Gibbons* came with armed men, and took Mr. *Shuttlewood*, with six or seven others, at a house in *Theddingworth*,
and carried them to an alehouse ; but after some time dismissed them, upon promising to appear the next morning at 4
o'clock at the same place.   The next day he took them to
three different places in Leicestershire and Northamptonshire,
keeping them a considerable time in each place, and at last
brought them to *C——* in Leicestershire, where justice *C.*
would have extorted some confessions from them.   *Gibbons*,
commonly a desperate swearer, told the justice, in their presence, " That he could not swear there was a conventicle,
" and he would not damn his soul for any of them."   Upon
which the justice was about to dismiss them ; but a lawyer
present told him that he might commit them upon notorious
evidence: Accordingly he sent warrants to distrain upon
Mr. *Shuttlewood* for 20*l.* and 20*l.* on the owner of the
house, and 5*s.* a piece on others.   Mr. *S.* conveyed away his
cattle, but the rest paid the money.   In 1672, while he had
the king's licence, *Gibbons* came upon him and took him
and the master of the house, and brought them before captain
C. who then refused to act, but afterwards sent out his warrants to distrain on Mr. *S.* and 20*l.* on the house, &c. but
both escaped, tho' not without damages, and heavy fines
were laid upon the hearers.   In the end of *Feb.* 1674, *Gibbons* came to Mr. *Shuttlewood's* house at *Lubenham*, and
took his and several other names, appointing them to appear
before Col. *F.* who was used to furnish him with warrants
before-hand.   They all appeared according to promise, but
were dismissed upon assurance given to appear upon a lawful
summons.   But instead of such a summons, *Gibbons* procured a warrant of Sir *T. B.* to distrain upon Mr. *S.* for 40*l.*

4

and

and the officers took away seven of his milch cows, and sold
them without his knowledge. They paid the money to the
justices, who gave receipts for it. (*Conformist's* 4*th Plea*,
p. 79—81.)

With what exemplary resignation, meekness and faith in
divine providence, Mr. *S.* bore these and other trials, the
following letter will evince, written to his wife from *Leicester*
jail *Feb.* 20, 1669.

" My dear Wife ; Myself and fellow prisoners are in good
health. I bless God I am very well satisfied with his dispensations towards me, in reference to my landlady's proceedings ;
so that I am no longer disquieted with them, nor solicitous
about them, but patiently wait God's gracious disposal of me.
Perhaps infinite wisdom foresees some inconveniency which
we are not aware of, and therefore is about to remove us. I
am loth to leave the society of my dear brethren, Mr. *Clark*
and Mr. *Southal* ; but I hope in the end God will so dispose
of us, that we shall have cause to say, it is best for us to be
where God shall carry us. I know not which way to look,
but our God is a very present help in a time of trouble, and
will let us see that it is not our forecast but his providence
which shall provide an habitation for us. Let us rather
beg an improvement than a removal of his dispensation.
Remember me to my father, children, &c. Thus in haste I
remain, &c."

He was seldom permitted to live long in quiet, and was
obliged to make frequent removes, being sometimes in *Leicestershire* and sometimes in *Northamptonshire.* But notwithstanding these troubles, he educated several persons for
the ministry, and appears sometimes to have had a flourishing
seminary, from a memorandum of his in a pocket-almanack,
" that six students were added to his academy in one year."
The following persons, among others, studied under him, and
afterwards rose to eminence in life: Mr. *Julius Saunders*,
Mr. *John Sheffield*, Mr. *Matthew Clark*, Dr. *Joshua Old-
field*, Mr. *Wilson*, father of the late Mr. *Samuel Wilson* of
London, and Mr. *Thomas Emlyn**. § He kept his academy

* In the Memoirs of Mr. *Emlyn*, it is said, " That his parents chose to
bring up their son to the ministry among the Nonconformists, and that for
this purpose in the year 1678 he was sent for academical education to Mr.
Shuttleworth, (a mistake in the spelling) at Sulby near Welford in Northamptonshire. Here he staid four years. In the year 1669 he took a journey
to Cambridge, and was admitted into *Emanuel College*, but returned again to
Mr. *Shuttlewood*." E. D.

at

at *Sulby*, near *Welford*, where he preached. Mr. *Orton* says, he has heard the old people there, speak highly of him as the first minister of that place.

Mr. *Shuttlewood*, tho' blest with a robust constitution, was of a very tender spirit; and the death of one of his children so deeply pierced him as to bring on some complaints, which he carried with him to his grave. His health was also greatly injured by the sufferings he met with, and the labours he went thro' in those rigorous times, preaching often at unseasonable hours and incommodious places; so that his useful light was extinguished at an earlier period than might otherwise have been expected. He died at *Creaton* in *Northamptonshire*, *March* 17, 1688, in the 58th year of his age; where a humble stone was erected to his memory in the church-yard, with this brief but honourable testimony to his character, *Multùm dilectus multùm deflendus*: Much beloved, much to be lamented.

He was a very able and learned man; a very acceptable and useful preacher; much valued not only in the places where he statedly resided, but in all the country round about. Both his natural and acquired abilities were consecrated to the glory of God and the benefit of the church and world. The most furious of his persecutors came to a shocking end, which had much the appearance of a divine judgment. The above *Charles Gibbons*, that notorious swearer, drunkard and persecutor, being at *Lutterworth* late at night in the winter season, was dissuaded from going home, viz. to *Kingcott*, two miles off; on which he swore " he would go home in spite " of all the devils in hell." Accordingly he went, but was found dead the next morning in a shallow stream of water not sufficient to cover his body, betwixt *Lutterworth* and *Misterton*. Dr. *Calamy* relates this from the account of a conforming minister in *Beard's Theatre of Judgments*. The author of the *Conformist's Plea* is more particular, and says (p. 82,) *Gibbons* being at *Lutterworth*, in *Dec.* 1675, very full of drink, and having given out that day many threatening speeches against several Dissenters, would not be persuaded to stay all night, tho' it was late, about 9 o'clock: but when he had gone about half a mile on his way, he fell into a ditch thro' which a little water runs, and falling asleep, (as we must suppose) he dammed up that little running of water, by which he was found drowned next morning, by a milk-maid, in a very remarkable manner, for all his body was above water except his neck and face; neither was the water

high

high enough when it was dammed up, to cover all his face."
How natural in such a case to apply *Job* xxxiv. 25—28.
' Therefore God knoweth their works, and he overturns them
' in the night, so that they are destroyed,' &c.

Mr. *Shuttlewood* educated his only son for the ministry. He was a man of considerable abilities and furni-
ture, and many years preached among the Dissenters in *London*, where he died in *May* 17, 1737, in the 71st year of his
age. He left two sons and two daughters, the youngest of
whom was married in 1744 to the late worthy Dr. *Gibbons*,
pastor of the church at Haberdashers Hall, and a tutor in the
academy at Homerton, to whom the public are obliged for the
above account. §

WORKS. It does not appear that he published any thing, but
he left several MSS which (with the papers above-mentioned) were
in Dr. *Gibbons*'s hands. Some in Latin, and some in English, on subjects of learning and divinity ; one of which appears designed for
the press. Part of it is upon the scriptures, prophecy, sacraments,
offices in the church, &c. Another is entitled, Certain propositions concerning Christ's kingdom, &c.

REARESBY [R. 140*l.*] Mr. WILLIAM GRACE, He was a
serious, humble, grave person ; well esteemed by his parish,
especially by Major Hubbart and family, for the holiness of
his life and his edifying preaching. He had a great many
children, who, with their parents, were reduced to great want.
He was nearly related to Abp. *Sheldon*, to whom applications
were made for his poor distressed family ; but no relief could
be obtained from him, unless Mr. *Grace* would conform ; to
which if he would have yielded, great things were promised :
but this did not influence him to act against his conscience.
Some time after, the Bp. recovered so much humanity, as to
take some care of two of his children.

SHANKTON [R.] Mr. RICHARD DRAYTON. *Nichols*
mentions him as inducted 1648 and ejected 1662. He was
born at *Atherston* in Warwickshire. In his younger years
he was under grievous temptations, even to despair : but when
thro' the grace of God he overcame them, he was the more
fitted for the ministry, and the better able to pity and assist
such as were tempted. When he quitted his living, he had

§ The good Dr. used pleasantly to remark it as a singular circumstance,
that the grand-daughter of Mr. Shuttlewood should be married to a Gibbons,
the name of her ancestor's grand persecutor.

nothing left to live upon but the providence of God, and the charity of good people.

SIBBESTON [R.] Mr. SAMUEL DOUGHTY. He was younger brother to the polite and politic Mr. Thomas Doughty, of Medburn, who conformed. "Probably the Son of Mr. *Samuel Doughty*, rector of *Bringhurst.*" After his ejectment he lived at *Ashby de la Zouch*, and had the king's licence to preach in his own house there, and yet was convicted by Lord *B.* and Lord *S.* 40*l.* was levied upon him, 20*l.* for his house, and 20*l.* for preaching in it. He made his appeal to the quarter-sessions, and pleaded that he had licence from the king, and that there was neither sedition nor breach of peace; but he found no relief. He afterwards complained to the king and council. The lords were sent for up to council. The king was pleased to give up his part of the fine, but he could never get it.—He was a good preacher; of a meek, humble, modest, and peaceable temper, and of an exemplary life.

SWEPSTON [S. 200*l.*] HENRY WATTS, M.A. Of *Sidney Col. Camb.* where he took his degree in 1651. He was ejected in 1662, at which time he had several children. Mr. Standish, who was sequestered in the Parliament-times, died before the Restoration. Mr. *Watts* was succeeded by Dr. *John Gery*, and maintained a very friendly correspondence with him to the day of his death; and the Dr. upon all occasions used to express a great esteem and value for him. When he left *Swepston*, he removed to *Weddington*, a little village in Warwickshire, where he lived above twenty years, upon very friendly terms with Mr. *Armstead* the public minister; whom he visited every morning about eleven o'clock, and who returned the visit in the afternoon about four; spending about an hour together each time. Mr. *Watts* constantly went to church on Lord's-day morning, and in the afternoon (when Mr. *Armstead* preached at another village, he preached to his own family, admitting a few neighbours, but kept within the number allowed by act of parliament. At length he removed to *Barwell*, in the same county, upon which Mr. *Armstead* used to say, he lost the best friend and neighbour that ever man had. When legal toleration was granted to Dissenters, Mr. *Watts*, at the request of many in the neighbouring towns, preached publicly at *Hinckley*, on the Lord's-day afternoon, and was glad of such an opportunity of exercising his ministry. Nor was he ever hindered from going by badness of road or weather, or by the infirmities of age, or any thing but sickness. He had here some hundreds of hearers, and at length settled a congregation of sober serious christians; among whom he bestowed his labours without any acknowledgment from them, except a few inconsiderable presents, and he continued with them till he was removed by death, on *Feb.* 2, 1690, in the 63d year of his age; when the people chose another pastor. He was buried in the church at *Barwell*, and his funeral sermon was preached by Mr. *Pagit*, the minister of the parish, who gave him a very handsome character; mentioning " his obliging temper and gentlemanly behaviour; his great friendliness, and usefulness in reconciling differences, to the saving great expences in law; his exemplariness in relative duties, and particularly in the management of his family, which was attended with a remarkable blessing from heaven; his great moderation and charity, which recommended him to all the gentlemen in the neighbourhood, who treated him with great respect. He added, " that he did not know any one who had more real friends, and fewer enemies than Mr. *Watts*; and that he was such a religious, conscientious, useful person, that the public had a great loss by his decease."—He had good preferment offered him in the church; and therefore many wondered at his Nonconformity, considering his increasing family; but that was not the least temptation to him to act against the sense of his own mind. He trusted providence; and God remarkably blessed and prospered him. Ten of his thirteen children lived to be men and women; and he educated them well, and comfortably provided for them in the world. § Mr. *Orton* says, that he heard much of him from his grand-father, who was born in this village.

——Mr. HUDSON. He was assistant to Mr. *Watts*.

THEDINGWORTH [V.] Mr. JOHN GREEN. § In *Nichols*'s History the entry is " *George Green*, 1690, died 1662." But in the list of those who signed the Representation in 1659, it is *John Greener*. He was a very pious man; who died in the very week in which he was preparing to quit his living, upon the Bartholomew-act.

THURMASTON [Chap.] Mr. MATTHEW PATCHET.

WANLIP [Chap.] Mr. JOHN SMITH.

WETHERLY

WETHERLY [R. S.] Mr. JOHN CHESTER. This living had been sequestered some years before he came to it, from a non-preaching parson, whose curate, at the Restoration, produced a dormant title to it. This was reckoned the most wicked town in all the county; so that several ministers said they would not have accepted of the living, had it been offered them, upon any terms. But by Mr. *Chester*'s industry in preaching, catechizing, and daily visiting from house to house, (things unknown to these people before) several of them were brought to a considerable knowledge, and a lively sense of religion, so as to delight in the exercises of it. In consequence of his great usefulness, he had the general love of the people, both in town and neighbourhood. He was not, however, free from opposition and trouble. One person being some way disgusted, took up a resolution that he would hear him no more. But coming once to church, on the report of a stranger's preaching, he was ashamed to go out, when Mr. *Chester* came into the pulpit; and it pleased God so to convince him by that sermon, that he ever after proved as true a friend as any in the parish. There were two other persons, the one an ordinary weaver, and the other a mean farmer, who, upon the turn of the times, discovered their malice, and took an oath before a bench of justices, that he prayed against the king, about the time of *Worcester* fight, naming a particular day. But it so happened, that Mr. *Chester* was then at *London*; and Mr. *Doughty*, who that day supplied his place, made oath that he did so, which all the parish confirmed, to the shame of those who had sworn so falsely against him.

After the Restoration, Mr. *Bucknall*, who laid claim to the living, came to take possession of it with the greatest violence and fury imaginable. Mr. *Chester* being from home, he demanded entrance into the parsonage-house, and the servants denying it, he fetched a smith's sledge and broke open the door, and not only turned them out, but threw out what goods he pleased into the street, and kept the rest. On Mr. *Chester*'s demanding them, he told him, that if he went to law for them, he would swear him out of his life.† Upon this Mr. *Chester* removed to *London*. The people at *Weatherby* were loth to lose so good and useful a man, as well as

† Dr. *Calamy* relates some other things of this *Bucknall*, which shew him to have been a very bad man, but which are better omitted.

much

much troubled at his meeting with such usage, and parted from him with many tears. He preached once every Lord's-day for Mr. *Jenkyn*, at Christ church, till the Act of uniformity took place, and continued in London all the time of the plague, when he was instrumental to the good of many souls. Mr. *Baxter* gives him the character of " a man of a very sober, calm, peaceable spirit; sound in doctrine and life; and a grave and fruitful preacher." He often made excursions into several parts of *Surrey*, but his settled abode was in *Southwark*, where, in the latter part of his life, he preached statedly at a meeting house in Gravel-lane, near St. George's fields. Under some illness, he retired to his son's, a physician at Guildford, where he died in *May*, 1696.

WHATTON (Long) [R. 150*l.*] SAMUEL SHAW, M. A. Of *St. John's Col. Camb.* He was born of religious parents at *Repton* in Derbyshire, in 1635, and educated at the free-school there, then the best in that part of England. He went to the university at fourteen years of age, where he was chamber-fellow with Dr. *Morton.* When he had compleated his studies, he went to *Tamworth* in Warwickshire, and was usher in the free-school in 1656. When that reverend person Mr. *Blake* died, in 1657, Mr. *Shaw* spoke an eloquent oration at his funeral, after Mr. *Anthony Burgess* had preached a sermon. They were both printed, and such as have perused them must think a conjunction of three such men, as the deceased and the two speakers, a singular happiness to that neighbourhood. From Tamworth Mr. *Shaw* removed to *Mosely*, a small place in the borders of *Worcestershire*, being invited by Col. *Greavis*, who shewed him much kindness. On his coming hither, he was ordained by the classical presbytery at *Wirksworth*; and by the assistance of Mr. Gervas Pigot of Thrumpton, he obtained a presentation from the Protector to the rectory of *Long-Whatton*, which was in the gift of the crown. He had full possession of this place in *June*, 1658, and continued in the peaceable enjoyment of it, till 1660. Fearing some disturbance, in the month of *September* that year, he got a fresh presentation* under the great seal of *England*, without much difficulty, as the former incumbent Mr. *Henry Robinson* was dead, and two more who enjoyed it after him. But tho' his title was thus corro-

* Copies of both these presentations may be seen in Calamy.

5   borated,

Sugnet, Sc.

Samuel Shaw.

from an original Picture in the Possession of Mr. Peyton.

Published by Button & Son, Paternoster Row.

borated, Sir *John Prettyman,* by making interest with the lord chancellor, found means to remove Mr. *Shaw,* about a year before the Act of uniformity passed; and introduced one Mr. *Butler,* who had no manner of title to the place. He was a man of such mean qualifications, and so little respected in the parish, that some of them told Sir *John,* that they heard Mr. *Butler* had given him a pair of coach-mares to get him the living, but they would give him two pair to get him out, and put Mr. *Shaw* in again. But he now quitted the church, as he could not satisfy himself to conform to the new terms. He was afterwards offered this living without any other condition than Re-ordination. But he used to say, He would not lie to God and man, in declaring his presbyterian ordination invalid.

When he left Whatton he removed to *Cotes,* a small village near Loughborough. Here his family caught the plague of some relations, who came from London to avoid it, about harvest-time in 1665. He then preached in his own house, and afterwards published that excellent book, called *The Welcome to the Plague,* grounded on *Amos* iv. 12, ' Prepare to meet thy God, O *Israel.*' He buried two children, two friends, and one servant of that distemper; but he and his wife survived it; and not being ill both at once, they looked after one another and the rest of the family : which was a great mercy, for none durst come to his assistance. He was in a manner shut up for three months, and was forced not only to attend his sick, but to bury his dead himself in his own garden. §

Towards the latter end of the year 1666, he removed to *Ashby de la Zouch* in the same county; and was chosen to be the sole master of the free-school in 1668. The revenue was then but small, the school-buildings quite out of repair, and the number of scholars few. But by his diligence he soon got the salary augmented, not only for himself, but his successors; and by his interest with several gentlemen, he procured money for the building of a good school-house, and a gallery for the scholars in the church. But then he had another difficulty; which was, how to get a licence without subscription to such things as his conscience did not allow of.

§ The excellent temper of mind which he expressed under this severe dispensation, is discovered in the work above mentioned, which was reprinted in 1767. An extract from it may be seen in his Memoirs, prefixed to a new edition of his *Immanuel,* 1763. The memoirs are taken from Calamy.

However,

However, he got over it; for by means of Lord *Conway*, he obtained from Abp. *Sheldon* a licence (which *Calamy* gives at length) to teach school any where in his whole province; and that without once waiting upon the Abp. As he needed a licence also from the bishop of the diocese, he got a friend to make his application to Dr. *Fuller*, then Bp. of Lincoln, who put into his lordship's hands Mr. *Shaw*'s late book, occasioned by the plague. The bishop was so much pleased with the piety, peaceableness, humility, and learning there discovered, that he gave him a licence upon such a subscription as his own good sense dictated, and said, that he was glad to have so worthy a man in his diocese upon any terms. He added, that he understood there was another book of his in print, called *Immanuel*, which he desired to see.

Mr. *Shaw*'s piety, learning and good temper soon raised the reputation of his school, and the number of his scholars, above any in those parts; having often 160 boys or more under his care. His own house and others in the town, were continually full of boarders from London, and other distant parts of the kingdom. Several divines of the church of *England*, (v. g. Mr. *Sturgess* of All-Saints in Derby, Mr. *Walter Horton* afterwards one of the canons of *Litchfield*, &c.) and many gentlemen, physicians, lawyers, and others, owed their school-learning to his good instructions. He endeavoured to make the youth under his care, in love with piety; to principle them in religion by his advice, and allure them to it by his good example. His temper was affable, his conversation pleasant and facetious, his method of teaching winning and easy. He had great skill in finding out, and suiting himself to, the tempers of boys. He freely taught poor children, where he saw in them a disposition for learning, and afterwards procured them assistance to perfect their studies at the university. He did indeed excellent service in the work of education; and his school was a great advantage to the trading part of the town.

When the liberty of the Dissenters was settled by act of parliament, he licenced his school-room for a place of worship. The first time he used it, he preached from *Acts* xix. 9. 'Disputing daily in the school of one Tyrannus.' He so contrived his meetings, as not to interfere with the establishment, preaching at noon between the services at church, and constantly attending there both parts of the day, with all his scholars, his family, and all his hearers; so that the public assembly was hereby considerably augmented; and the weekly

4   lecture

lecture was chiefly attended by him and his scholars. He
was upon the most friendly terms with the vicar of the place,
[and corresponded with Dr. *Barlow* the Bp. of *Lincoln*,] to
whom he presented his book of Meditations, which has been
generally esteemed, and read with great profit. Upon which
his lordship, who was a great reader, and a good judge of
books, wrote him the following letter.

" My reverend brother,——I have received yours, and this
comes (with my love and respects) to bring you thanks for the
rational and pious book you so kindly sent me. Tho' my bu-
sinesses be many, and my infirmities more, (being now past 74)
yet I have read all your book, (and some parts of it more than
once,) with great satisfaction and benefit. For in your meditations of the love of God and the world, (I am neither afraid
nor unwilling to confess it, and make you my confessor,) you
have instructed me in several things, which I knew not before,
or at least considered not so seriously, and so often as I might
and ought. One great occasion or cause why we love our gracious God less, and the world more than we should, is want of
knowledge, or consideration. God himself, *Isai.* i. 2, 3. com-
plains of this, and calls heaven and earth to witness the justice of his complaint. 'I have nourished and brought up chil-
' dren, and they have rebelled against me. The ox knoweth
' his owner, and the ass his master's crib, but *Israel* doth not
' know, my people doth not consider.' It is strange, and yet
most true, that the ox and ass, irrational and stupid creatures,
should know their masters, who feed and take care of them,
and yet men, rational creatures, even *Israel*, God's only church
and people, whom he had miraculously preserved and nourished, should neither know nor consider. This consideration
is our duty, and the want of it our sin; (a sin of omission) and
therefore it is no wonder if it be a moral cause and occasion of
some consequent sin of commission; so that the best men (by
reason of the old man, and the remains of corruption in them)
may, and many times do sin, and come short of fulfilling the law
and doing their duty, when they want this consideration, or such
a degree and measure of it as is required to the moral goodness
of an action. Suppose a man tempted to commit adultery, murder, perjury, or any such sin; if such a man would seriously
consider the nature of the sin he is going to commit, that it is
a transgression of the law of his God, to whom he owes all he
has, both for life and livelihood, that it pollutes his soul, that
it dishonours his gracious God and heavenly Father, that it
makes him obnoxious to eternal misery, both of body and

D d 4   soul:

soul : I say, he who considers this, as all should, would certainly be afraid to commit such impieties. Now of such considerations, you have given us many in your book, and those grounded on the clear light of nature, or on evident reason, or revelation; and it is my prayer and hope that many may read, and (to their great benefit) remember, and practise them. I am well pleased with your discourse against usury ; which (as is commonly managed) I take to be one of the crying sins of our ungrateful nation. . . . . Give me leave, (faithfully and as a friend) to add one thing more. In your second page, there is, I believe, a little mistake. For you seem to say, that *James,* who wrote the canonical epistle, was brother to *John* the apostle. Now it is, certain, that amongst the apostles there were two of that name. 1. *James* the son *Zebedee,* and brother of *John.* 2. *James* the son of *Alpheus, Mat.* x. 2, 3. who was called *James* the less, *Mark* xv. 40. whose mother was *Mary,* who was sister to the virgin *Mary*; and so our blessed Saviour and *James* the son of *Alpheus* were sisters children, cousin-germans. Now that *James* the son of *Zebedee,* and brother of *John,* did not write that canonical epistle, will be certain, if we consider, 1. That *James,* brother of *John,* was slain by *Herod Agrippa.* (*Acts* xxii. 2.) which was Anno Christi 44 * or 45. And 2dly, If it be considered, that the epistle of *James* was not written till the year of Christ 63: for so *Baronius, Simpson,* and the best chronologers assure us. They say, that epistle of *James* was not writ till almost twenty years after *James* the brother of *John* was slain by *Herod* : and therefore it is certain, he neither did nor could write it. I beg your pardon for this tedious, and I fear impertinent, scribble. My love and due respects remembered. I shall pray for a blessing upon you and your studies : and your prayers are heartily desired by and for

Your affectionate friend and brother,
Buckden, March 16, 1681. *Thomas Lincoln.*

For my reverend friend Mr. *Sam. Shaw,*
at his house in *Ashby de la Zouch.*

If such a correspondence as this, between the bishops of the church of England and the ministers among the Dissenters, had been generally maintained, it might have produced

‡ Jac. Usserius. Annal. pag. 645. Baron. Annal. Tom. 1.

much

much better effects than the great distance that has been kept up on both sides.—Mr. *Shaw* was a man of a peaceable disposition. He was frequently employed, and very successful in his endeavours, to reconcile differences. He had a public and generous spirit, and was ever ready to encourage any good designs. He was given to hospitality, and was very moderate in his principles. For the space of almost thirty years he spent himself in endeavours to make the world better, tho' with no great gains to himself. It was his chief aim to live usefully; and he thought that a considerable reward to itself. He was of a middle stature, and his countenance not very penetrating; like another *Melancton*, that could not fill a chair with a big look and portly presence; but his eye was sparkling, and his conversation witty, savoury, affable, and pertinent. He was ready at repartees and innocent jests, with a mixture of poetry, history, and other polite learning. But his greatest excellency was in religious discourse, in praying and preaching. One that knew him well, writes as follows:

" I have known him spend part of many days and nights too in religious exercises, when the times were so dangerous that it would hazard an imprisonment to be worshipping God with five or six people like-minded with himself. I have sometimes been in his company for a whole night together, when we have been fain to steal to the place in the dark, to stop out the light and stop in the voice, by cloathing and fast closing the windows, till the first day-break down a chimney has given us notice to be gone. I bless God for such seasons. If some say it was needless to do so much: I reply, the care of our souls and eternity, which only was minded there, requires more. I say, I bless God for the remembrance of them, and for Mr. *Shaw* at them, whose melting words in prayer, I can never forget. He had a most excellent faculty in speaking to God with reverence, humility, and an holy awe of his presence, ' filling his mouth with ar-
' guments: by his strength he had power with God; he wept
' and made supplication; he found him in *Bethel* (such were
' our assemblies) and there he spake with us.' I have heard him for two or three hours together pour out prayer to God, without tautology or vain repetition, with that vigour and fervour, and those holy words that imported faith and humble boldness, as have dissolved the whole company into tears. *&c.*"——In short, a mixture of so much learning and humility, wit and judgment, piety and pleasantness, are rarely
found

found together, as met in him. He died *Jan.* 22. 1696, in
the 59th year of his age. His funeral sermon was preached
by Mr. *William Crosse,* his brother-in-law. from *Luke*
xxiii. 28.

WORKS. A Funeral Oration for Mr. Blake—The Welcome
to the Plague.—a Farewell Sermon in 1663, on Phil. i. 12. which
is the 8th in the Country collection.—A Farewell to Life, on
2 Cor. v. 6.—The Angelical Life; on Mat. xxii. 30. (These two
are annexed to the Welcome to the Plague, and were all printed
together in 1666, entitled, The voice of one crying in the wilderness.—Immanuel; or, A Continuation of the Angelical life;
on John iv. 14.—The great commandment; a Disc. on Psalm
lxxiii. 25. To which is annexed, The spiritual man in a carnal
fit; on Psalm lv. 6.—A Latin grammar.—A receipt for the state
palsy: Or a Direction for the government of the nation; a Serm.
on Prov. xxv. 5.—Samuel in sackcloth; a Serm. on 1 Sam. xv. 35.
essaying to restrain our bitter animosities, and commending a spirit of moderation towards our brethren, 1660.—The true Christian's Test; or a discovery of the love and lovers of the world, in
149 meditations ; *—An epitome of the Latin grammar, by questions and answers. Adam, Abel, or vain man; Sermons on Psalm
xxxix. 6.—A Serm. on the death of Mr. Richard Chantry.——
Words made visible, or Grammar and Rhetoric ; a Comedy.—
The different humours of men; a Comedy. (These two were acted
by his own scholars for their diversion, and for the entertainment of
the town and neighbourhood at Christmas-time.) He had in the
press, a description of the heavenly inheritance; on 1 Pet. i. 3—6.
But the bookseller failing, it was never perfected.

WOODHOUSE [Chap.] Mr. CHESHIRE.

Mr. DIXY and Mr. STATHAM were silenced by the Act
of uniformity, tho' not ejected; not being then fixed in livings. They lived and died Nonconformists.

The following afterwards conformed.

Mr. DOUGHTY, of *Medburn.* —- Mr. BLACKERBY, of
Langton.—Mr. JENKIN, of *North Kilworth.*—Mr. BLACK,
of *Sadington.*—Mr. HENRY PIERCE, of *Claybrook.*

*Mr. Job Orton says, "I wish this was reprinted. It is a most serious use-
ful and entertaining book. Short chapters, and many excellent stories, and
references to the classics." J. Orton.

In.

§ In NICHOLS's *History of Leicestershire*, is a list of the names subscribed to " The humble representation of divers well-affected ministers of the gospel," in this county, which was presented to parliament, A. D. 1659, in relation to Sir *George Booth*'s rising in behalf of Charles II. for which they received the thanks of the house. The following copy of it, may be thought worth being inserted here, particularly as it shews where the ministers resided at the time. Mr. *James* has given the names both of persons and places, according the spelling in DUGDALE's *Troubles of England*, which book is *Nichols*'s authority. That author stiles these ministers " a precious pack." Nichols every where calls this paper " the *famous* representation." &c.

John Yaxley { Minister of the Gospel at *Langton*	Nicholas Kestyn, *Gumley*
WilliamSheffield, *Ibstoke*	John St. Nicolas, *Lutterworth*
Maurice Bohem, *Halloughton*	Thomas Langdel, *Bowden Magna*
William Grace, *Reavesby*	Richard Drayton, *Skangton*
Richard Muston, *Langton*	Tho. Leadbeter, *Hinkley*
Mattew Clarke, * *Narborow*	William Cotton, *Broughton*
Josiah Whiston, *Norton*	Henry Watts,.. *Swepston*
Ben. Southwood, *Kymcote*	Ambrose Bent, *Ashby-Folvile*
Samuel Shaw,.. *Low Whatton*	J. Shuttlewood, *Ravenston*
Thomas Lowrey, *Harborow*	Emanuel Bourne, *Waltham*
Henry Pearce,.. *Claybroke*	Chris. Wright,.. *Eastwell*
George Wright, *Congeston*	Tho. Jenkings,.. *New Kilworth*
Y. Dixy, ...*Margaret's, Leicester*	John Pitts, ...*Burbage*
Samuel Smith,.. *Glooreston*	John Hulls, ... *Stanton Wivile*
John Greener,.. *Thedingworth*	Paul Balguy,†.. [Boby]
John Wilson, .. *Foxton*	William Black,. *Saddington*
John Bennett,.. *Winwick*	Robert Reding, *Sagrave*
Thomas Smith,.. *CastleDunnington*	Sam. Oldershaw, *Cole-Orton*
William Barton, *Martins,Leicester*	

* By mistake printed Harborow. † Mis-spelt in the copy, and no place.

⁂ Some additions to the accounts of YAXLEY, SHEF-FIELD, HORNEBY, and SHUTTLEWOOD, received too late to be inserted in their proper places, will be found in the AD-DENDA, at the end of this volume.

MINISTERS

MINISTERS EJECTED OR SILENCED

IN

LINCOLNSHIRE.

ALLINGTON [R. 160*l*.] Mr. GEORGE BECK. He was chaplain to the Earl of Manchester for some time during the civil war, and particularly attended him at the battle of Winsby near Horncastle. This perhaps might be the chief cause of Dr. *Sanderson*'s great displeasure against him, who drove him out of the country. After the war, he was minister of *Rippingal*, three miles from Folkingham, at which Mr. Cranwel was sequestered. He was one of the Folkingham classis. About 1655 he was presented to *Allington*, by the lord-keeper Fiennes, where he succeeded Mr. Robert Clark, an eminent old Puritan. During his residence there, he was one of the Tuesday-lecturers at *Grantham*, and had a *sine cure* annexed to his rectory. He was a very popular and useful preacher, an affectionate pastor, and much beloved. His life also was unblameable. He resided some time in London, till the plague drove him away to *Tottenham ;* but it followed him, as it did many others, and he died of it in 1666.

AUTHORPE (in the Isle of *Axholme*) [R.] Mr. THOMAS SPADEMAN. Of *Lincoln Col. Oxf.* Born at Rotheram in Yorkshire. He was much esteemed for his learning, diligence and charity. He was so hearty in his affection to the old English form of government, that he refused to sign the Engagement, tho' it was generally signed by the neighbouring ministers, who afterwards conformed. And tho' he would not sign the declaration appointed by the Oxford-act in 1665, yet his known loyalty and peaceable behaviour induced the deputy-lieutenants and justices of the peace, to per-

gait

mit him to reside unmolested in the place where he had been minister. After the Indulgence granted in 1672, he was chosen pastor of a Presbyterian church in *Boston*, where he was generally esteemed for his piety and moderation. He died in 1678. He was father to Mr. *John Spademan*, who was minister first at Rotterdam, and afterwards at London [where he assisted Mr. *John Howe*.]

BAROBY [R.] Mr. ELWOOD.

BARTON [V.] Mr. ROATE.

BILLINGBOROUGH [V.] Mr. JAMES MORTON. He also had the living of *Horblin;* a small town within a mile of the other. He was of the Folkingham classis, and one of the Grantham lecturers. He died at Billingborough, in 1663. He was a tall, grave, venerable person, and was in great esteem with good people in those parts.

BOOTHBY (on the Cliff) [R.] Mr. JOHN SANDERS.

BOSTON [V.] Mr. ANDERSON, He was a very pious man, and a good affectionate preacher. His principles were congregational.

BROCKLESBY [R.] Mr. THEOPHILUS BRITTAINE. After his ejectment here he took a house at *Swinderby*, a small village about seven miles from *Lincoln*, where he kept a private school for a livelihood; for which he was prosecuted by Sir *E. L.* the Bp. of Lincoln's chancellor, before whom he appeared several times at the court at Lincoln, and was at length, by the said chancellor, committed to the common jail. The jailor sometimes giving him liberty to go into the city to dine with a friend, was severely reprehended, and strictly charged to keep him close prisoner, which he afterwards did. But God was pleased so to support and refresh him with spiritual consolations, that he was never known to be more chearful than all the time of his imprisonment, which was for several months. At length, by a *habeas corpus*, he removed himself to London, where his cause was heard; and by means of the Earl of Shaftesbury, then lord-chancellor, he obtained his liberty. He was afterwards chaplain to Col. King of *Ashby* in this county, and preached publicly till the Colonel's death. He then removed to *Roxham*, a little village about two miles from *Sleaford*, where he took a small farm, and taught a few scholars. In *Monmouth*'s time, he and Mr. *Wright* of Lessingham, and Mr. *Drake*, were committed

mitted to Grantham jail, and were to be removed to Hull ; but upon the Duke's defeat, they were set at liberty. He was exercised with lameness and great pain for the five last years of his life, but bore his afflictions with much patience, and a chearful submission to the will of God. He departed this life *Sept.* 12, 1706. He was a man of a meek and humble spirit, and of but few words.

BURTON-PEDWARDIN. Mr. LEE. He was an intimate of Col. *King,* who was generally supposed to be the first in the House of Commons that moved for K. Charles's Restoration. He was so far from owning the preceding powers, that he never paid any tax for twelve years together, till his goods were distrained by the collectors. Mr. *Lee* published one pamphlet or more, against the usurpation of the Protector *Oliver.* He was commonly called the Colonel's confessor and chaplain.

COLTSWORTH [R.] Mr. BROWN.

CROWLE [V.] Mr. ROBERT DURANT. He was a gentleman of an ancient family ; the third son of Mr. *Durant,* an eminent minister near London. He was of quick parts, and had a very liberal and religious education. The learned languages, as also the *French,* were very familiar to him. He travelled very young, and visited many of the West Indian islands. After he had a call to the ministry, he settled at *Crowle,* where he was ejected in 1662. He retained a very tender affection to the people there to his dying day. After being silenced, he removed to *Redness,* where he buried his only son. He preached there in private till 1664, when being upon a journey with Mr. *John Ryther,* (another ejected minister, afterwards of Wapping,) they were both seized on in the road, and sent to York castle, but nothing being laid to his charge, he was soon dismissed. Here he became acquainted with Mr. *Thomas Woodhouse* of Glapwell in Derbyshire, (a great supporter of godly ministers, and then also a prisoner on account of religion) who, upon the death of Mr. Fisher of *Sheffield,* recommended Mr. *Durant* to that congregation, to which, after sufficient trial, he had a call, in 1669. Longing to be in his Master's vineyard, he thankfully accepted it, leaving it to the people to give him what they pleased, tho' he had left a benefice of no small value.

His behaviour was always that of a gentleman ; and few could exceed him in a sweet mixture of humility and courteousness

teousness. He had excellent ministerial abilities. His stile was scriptural and plain; and his delivery clear and affectionate. He was fervent in prayer; usually large in confession, and particular in thanksgiving. It was his common method on the Lord's-day, to spend the morning in expounding the scriptures, wherein he discovered great skill. In the afternoon he preached on the doctrines of the Christian religion; and once every month he and his congregation kept a fast. In his visits, he endeavoured, by apt questions, to discover how far his hearers profited under his ministry, and he often took leave with prayer. His self-denial and mortification of sin were visible to his nearest acquaintance; his meekness and patience to all. His circumspection was such that envy itself could not charge him with any thing blameworthy. He could never endure railing or backbiting, but exhorted all to love, christian unity and forbearance. He had an uncommon ability in writing agreeable letters, full of a christian spirit, many of which were long treasured up. When the times grew more favourable, the congregation encreased, and erected a convenient place of worship. In *January* 1678, he administered the Lord's-supper the last time: when he concluded the exhortation with these words: "I tell you this, and remember it when I am dead and gone; 'The better any man is, the more humble he is; the better he will think of others, and the lower thoughts he will have of himself." A little before his death, taking leave of a friend, he quoted *Ps.* xci. 16, and added, "The Lord has made good this his promise to me: He hath satisfied me with length of life, and he hath given me to see his salvation." He died greatly lamented, *Feb.* 12, 1678, aged 71. When the report of his death was brought to Mr. *Lobley* the vicar of the town, he expressed his esteem for him by saying, "And is the good old man dead? I am sorry for it: he hath carried it so very well, that I wish they may get one that will tread in his steps."

DOWESBY [R.] Mr. ROCKET. A very popular preacher, who met with general applause. He died soon after Bartholomew-day.

FLIXBOROUGH [R.] Mr. JONATHAN GRANT. Of *Trin. Col. Camb.* Born at Rotheram in Yorkshire. He was for a time assistant to Mr. *Stiles* of Pontefract, and afterwards minister at *Ashley* near Kidderminster. He was present at Bewdly, at the disputation between Mr. *Baxter* and Mr.

Mr. *Tombes*, which was much to his satisfaction; and the rather, as it was the means of recovering his wife, who had been made a convert by the Baptists, and had been dipped. He was an active man, of fruitful abilities and good learning; fit for any company or discourse; and an acceptable useful preacher. He had been a prisoner in four different castles during the war. After being silenced he retired to *Thurnsco* in Yorkshire. He much frequented the meeting at Lady *Rhodes'* at *Houghton*. He was at last seized with a palsy, of which, in about half a year, he died, in 1681, aged 64.

FRODLINGHAM [V.] and BROMBY. Mr. JOHN RYTHER. Upon his ejectment he removed to *York*, and after some time, to *Allerton* near Bradford. About the year 1668, he assisted in gathering a church in *Bradford dale*, where his useful labours were much valued, and the serious impressions made by his affectionate preaching were long retained. [He was once imprisoned in York castle, being apprehended on the road, with Mr. *Durant* of Crowle.] About the year 1675, he and Mr. *Hardcastle* preached together at Shadwell chapel, and took their farewell of a people by whom they were greatly beloved. Mr. *Ryther* came to London, and preached [in Wapping] with good acceptance and success till his death. He had a son in the ministry, who, after he had been two voyages to the East-Indies, and had gone as chaplain with merchants ships to most of the principal places in both the *Indies*, during the latter part of Charles the second's, and the whole of James's reign, to avoid persecution for conscience sake; in the reign of K. William settled at Nottingham, where he spent twelve years, and there he died

§ WORKS. A plat for Mariner's: or the Seaman's Preacher, delivered in several Sermons upon Jonah's Voyage. By John Ryther, preacher of God's word in Wapping near London, 1672. The editor who is possessed of this very scarce book, can pronounce it to be a very valuable performance, well adapted to that class of readers for whom it is designed and fit to be given by Masters of ships to Seamen going a voyage. It consists of six short plain and popular discourses, with a Dedication to all Commanders and Masters of ships, and an epistle to all Seamen, by the author. A strong recommendation of it is prefixed, as "a seasonable and excellent discourse, which is cal-" culated chiefly for the tribe of Zebulon." (the tribe of mariners) by JAMES JANEWAY. *

                                        FULBECK

* A late worthy gentleman in Wapping, had intended to reprint this excellent piece, but was prevented by death. It is much to be wished that some
                                                    other

FULBECK [R.] Mr. TRISTRAM HINCHFIELD.

GATE-BURTON [R.] Mr. MARK TRICKETT. Of *Magd. Col. Camb.* where he was under the tuition of Mr. *Joseph Hill.* He was of a brisk active temper, and a holy life. His pulpit performances were much applauded. When he lived at *Thurnsco,* he used to preach at the Lady *Rhodes'* chapel at Houghton. He was afterwards a great while prisoner in York castle for his nonconformity.

GLAPTHORN. See *Northamptonshire.*

GLENTWORTH [V.] Mr. AIRES.

GRANTHAM [V.] Mr. HENRY VAUGHAN; who succeeded Mr. *Angel* in this place. He was an excellent preacher, and had an extraordinary gift in prayer. He was very zealous against those in power from 1648 to 1660, especially the Rump parliament and their adherents. It was common with him to declare, with the utmost abhorrence, against putting the king to death, in the presence of the republican officers of the army. When Sir *G. Booth* was in arms for the king's restoration in 1659, he got several ministers to spend a day in fasting and prayer, at his house, for the success of the enterprize. When *Lambert's* officers, in the same year, made a short stay at Grantham in their march into the North against *Monk,* he enraged them by his free reproofs; and they severely threatened (especially Col. Axtil) to rout him from Grantham, if they returned victorious. He often exposed himself to great danger by being over zealous in those times, and once very narrowly escaped. As he was reading in a bookseller's shop in London, with his back towards the door, a pursuivant came in and told the bookseller, that he and three more had spent four days in searching for one *Vaughan,* who the Lord's-day before preached a seditious sermon against the government, at some church in the city, which he named, but said they could not find him. The parliament's voting back the king, was not more joyful to any man than to him. Yet notwithstanding all this, soon after the restoration, he was committed to the old jail in *Grantham,* for not reading the Common Prayer. His continuance there was not long; but he was afterwards a prisoner in *Lincoln*

other public spirited person, who wishes well to so useful, but generally profane and neglected a class of men as Sailors, would carry that noble design into execution.

castle, in 1661, a long time for the same omission. He seems
to have been the person referred to by the author of *The Conformist's Plea*, who says, "He was well acquainted with
one of the Nonconformists, (and he never knew a more
loyal, and honest man) who, after many disgraces and trials,
(especially sharp to one of a generous genteel spirit) went beyond sea; and who, in a terrible storm, which broke into the
ship, asked his own soul, If he could die in and for that
cause of his sufferings; leaving his native country and his
dear relations, to preach in a strange land? whose conscience
gave him a plain and satisfactory answer, when ready as he
thought to leave his body in the deep." The author adds,
that after his return, he told him this and other particulars,
with a solemn profession, that he had nothing to do in this
world but to serve Christ. *Plea* 4th, p. 41.—He went with
his family to *Bermudas*, but meeting with discouragement
from the Quakers, he came back. However he was afterwards persuaded to make a second adventure on new terms,
and soon after he arrived there, he died in honour and peace.
Mr. *Baxter* says of him, "that he was an able, sober, godly,
judicious, moderate man, of great worth." There was
printed, A Relation of a Conference between Mr. *Tombes*
and Mr. *Vaughan*, *Sept. 5, 1653*.

——— Mr. STARKEY. Of *Peter-house*, and afterwards of
St. John's Col. Camb. of which he was many years Fellow.
At the university he was a hard student, whose candle was
always alight after all the others were in bed. This thirst
after the improvement of his mind, kept him close to his
studies all his days. His pulpit performances ever smelt of
the lamp. He was a worthy divine, and an excellent
preacher. His delivery was graceful, but not noisy; and it
appeared by him, that there is a mildness in speaking that is
as powerful as force. Dr. *Bates* once told a friend, That
tho' Mr. *Starkey* much affected retirement, he was fit for the
best auditory in England. He was fellow-labourer at Grantham with Mr. *Vaughan*, and preached the lecture, supported
by the benefaction of Lady Cambden, in the room of old Mr.
Angel, who was the first lecturer, about 1650. Mr. *Starkey*
was recommended by Dr. *Tuckney*. The stipend was 90*l.*
per ann. After being silenced, he resided in Lancashire,
where it was his constant custom on Lord's-days, to attend
the public church (the parish minister being a worthy man)
and he exercised his ministry in private, when the worship
                                                    there

there was over. He spent the latter part of his life at *New-ington-Green* near *London*, where he lived beloved, and died lamented. His funeral sermon was preached by Mr. *Timothy Rogers.* He was a man who thought much, but spoke little in company; tho' upon just occasions, he could speak as much to 'the purpose as most men. Never was he heard to censure or backbite others. He had none of that intemperance of spirit whereby some are over-heated, so as to set others, as well as themselves, on fire. His moderation was known unto all. So excellent were his ministerial qualifications, so sweet his temper, so prudent his conduct, and so innoffensive his life, that he was universally beloved. The greatest enemies to the Nonconformists had nothing to object against him but his noncompliance with their impositions.

GUNNERBY [R.] Mr. MATTHEW SYLVESTER. Of *St. John's Col. Camb.* Where, tho' his circumstances were strait, his diligence and humility, his affable and obliging carriage procured him friends, from whom he received much kindness. He left the university thro' necessity, sooner than his inclination would have led him. After some time spent in the country, where, amidst other engagements, he closely pursued his studies, (for he was remarkably studious,) he fixed in this living of *Gunnerby*, where the Act of uniformity found and ejected him. The learned Dr. *Sanderson*, then Bp. of the diocese, who was his relation, sent for him and treated him very courteously, offering him considerable preferment if he would conform, and strongly urged him to do it; but he frankly told his lordship, that he could not come into the church with satisfaction to his conscience, and therefore must be excused. And the author often heard him say, He never could see any occasion to repent of his nonconformity; which, however, he maintained with great moderation. On being silenced, he lived some time with Sir *John Bright*, as domestic chaplain, and afterwards with *John White*, Esq. of Nottinghamshire, in both which families he was an ornament to his function, and met with abundant respect. He came to London the year after the fire, and had a share in the hardships of the Dissenters, tho' he never was in prison. He cultivated a good correspondence with several divines of the established church, and was well respected by them, especially by Abp. *Tillotson* and Dr. *Whichcot.* But no man valued him more than Mr. *Baxter*, who was a good judge of men: and his esteem for Mr. *Baxter* ran as high as it was fit
it

it should towards any mortal man; perhaps herein he exceeded.
He desired to be known to posterity, as he doubtless will be,
by the character of *Mr. Baxter's friend*. Never was there
a greater harmony between two colleagues, than between
Mr. *Baxter* and him, when they both preached to the same
people [in Charter-house yard] Mr. *Sylvester*.being the
pastor, and Mr. *Baxter* the assistant: and never were people
happier in two ministers, than they who had the benefit of
their joint labours.   Mr. *Baxter* shewed his respect to Mr.
Sylvester dying as well as living, by leaving him his *History
of his Life and Times*, and other manuscripts; and if he
could have influenced, none of his friends would have deserted
Mr. *Sylvester* upon his own decease.   The desertion of so
many of them was a discouragement to him; but he looked
higher than man.   And tho' he was not admired and flocked
after, as some others were, he found that declaration verified,
' Them that honour me I will honour.'   He had to the last,
as great a share of real esteem and respect from the lovers of
God and true goodness as most men.   He often signified to
his friends his earnest desire, and it was his frequent request
to God in his family prayers, that his life and usefulness
might expire together.   He would often say " It is a happy
thing to slip out of this world into eternity."   Herein God
was pleased to answer his prayer; for when his usefulness had
been extended to the age of 71, he expired without the usual
formalities of death, on the Lord's-day evening, *January* the
25th, 1708; so that he went directly from his beloved work
to his reward.   On the Lord's-day following, Dr. *Calamy*
preached a funeral discourse to his small, but well-tempered
society [which then met at Blackfriars] on *Mat.* xxiv. 44.

He was an able divine, a good linguist, no mean philosopher, an excellent casuist, an admirable textuary, and of uncommon eloquence in pleading at the throne of grace.   He
had a soaring genius, a rich and copious fancy, and great
depth of thought: to which, had there been joined a suitable
elocution and expression, he would have been universally esteemed one of the greatest men of the age.   He well deserved
Mr. *Baxter*'s character of him, as " a man of excellent
meekness of temper, sound and peaceable principles, a godly
life, and great ability in the ministerial work."   More may
be seen of him in his funeral sermon.   He was succeeded by
Mr. *Samuel Wright*, afterwards D. D. who was more popular,
and had a large meeting-house built for him in Carter Lane.

WORKS.

WORKS. A Sermon on being for ever with the Lord.—Another before the Societies for Reformation.—Elisha's cry after Elijah's God; a Serm. on 2 *Kings* ii. 14. on the decease of Mr. *R. Baxter.*—The Christian's last Redress; on Rev. xxi. 4. at the request of the relicts of Mrs. Sarah Petit, 1707.—Four Sermons in the Morn. Ex.—Sermons on the 12th chap. of *Hebrews*, in 2 vols. 8vo.—[He also published Mr. BAXTER's History of his Life and Times, Which Dr. *Calamy* abridged, and a preface to Manlove's Immortality of the Soul.]

HARLAXTON [R. 160*l.*] Mr. RICHARD NORTHAM. He was first minister of *Hather*, four miles from Grantham, and afterwards of *Harlaxton*. He was an aged, grave, and reverend person. A solid judicious divine. His preaching was plain and practical; very affecting and aweful; for he delivered his sermons with a thundering voice. His life was unblameable. He was one of those ministers who kept up a lecture at Grantham every Tuesday, from 1647 till about 1662.

HORNCASTLE [V.] Mr. DICKENSON.

KIRTON in *Lindsey* [V.] Mr. MOSES MELLS. He was born at *Sibsey* near Boston. After his ejectment he removed to *Lincoln*, where he continued till the Corporation-act forced him away, and then he removed to *Lessingham* near Sleaford, and thence into *Sleaford* town, where he continued the exercise of his ministry to a few persons who were desirous of his labours. He was a humble, holy, heavenly person; not fearful of dangers, and yet careful to take the most prudent methods to avoid them. He had an estate of his own, and therefore was not chargeable to the people. He visibly took delight in his work; and did not labour in vain. He had a liberal heart and hand, both in spirituals and temporals. He was of moderate principles, and a most obliging carriage. He went about doing good; and when he had continued doing so in *Sleaford*, for about seven years and six months, it pleased God to give him rest from his labours.

LEE [R.] Mr. THOMAS BONNER. He went thro' many straits and difficulties. At length he went to preach at Wispington, near Horncastle, and there he fell ill and died.

LINCOLN. EDWARD REYNER, M. A. Of *Camb.* University. An eminent divine, of special note. He was born at *Morley*, near Leeds, in 1600. He feared the Lord from his youth. He greatly frequented sermons in his childhood, and constantly attended the Monthly Exercise, which was encouraged by that excellent and primitive Abp. Dr. *Toby Matthews*, at Leeds, Pudsey, Halifax, and other places. He was frequent in secret prayer, strict in observing the Sabbath, and grave in his whole deportment, giving hopeful indications of future eminence. While at the university he was very studious, and laid in a good stock of learning. But the straitness of his circumstances would not allow of his staying there so long as he had an inclination to do. Some time after his removal he taught school at *Aserby* in Lincolnshire. But Mr. *Morris*, upon whom he mostly depended, being unable, thro' losses, to give him the assistance he promised, he was again at a loss for a subsistence.. But Providence seasonably opened a new way for him, by an offer, from the Countess of *Warwick*, of the school at *Market-Rason*, in which he continued a few years, industriously grounding his scholars in the rudiments of learning and the principles of religion, and improving all his spare time for the perfecting his own studies. The Countess, after four years, bestowed upon him the lecture at *Welton* which she maintained. He was afterwards invited to *Lincoln*, by a most affectionate call of many pious people there, first to be lecturer at Benedicts, *Aug.* 13, 1626; and then to be parson at Peters at the Arches, *March* 4, 1627; where he discovered uncommon ministerial abilities, and was an unspeakable blessing to the city. He was even then a nonconformist to the ceremonies, which created him adversaries, who frequently complained of him, and threatened him; but his liberty of preaching was continued, and his moderation procured him favour with several that belonged to the Minster, who sometimes heard him in the afternoon. Sir *Edward Lake* himself, the chancellor, was often his auditor, and declared he received benefit by his preaching, till he was reproved by certain persons in power.

Dr. *Williams*, the Bp. of the diocese, in one of his visitations, which was of three days continuance, appointed Dr. *Sanderson* to preach the first day, Dr. *Hirst* the second, and Mr. *Reyner* the third. As soon as he had done, the Bp. sent him an invitation to dine with him, and before parting, presented him with the Prebend of Botolphs in Lincoln; and at the visitation, commended and repeated a good part of his sermon; which prevented any inconvenience from the inferior clergy, who otherwise could not well have endured his free reproofs. The importunity of friends prevailed with him to to accept the prebend; but when he came seriously to reflect upon the necessary attendants and consequences of this his new preferment, he was much dissatisfied; for he found he could not keep it with a safe and quiet conscience. Hereupon he prevailed with the lady *Armine* (to whom he was related) to go to the Bishop, to excuse his declining this preferment; when his lordship pleasantly said to the Lady, " I have had many Countesses, Ladies and others, who have been suitors to me to get preferments for their friends; but you are the first that ever came to take away a preferment, and that from one upon whom I bestowed it with my own hands."

Mr. *Reyner* was very laborious in the duties of his place, ' warning every one night and day with tears, teaching them ' publicly, and from house to house;' being an example of a pious, diligent, and conscientious pastor. It was a great trouble to him to find some of his people falling off to unsound principles. He prayed for them without ceasing, and conversed with them, with much meekness, resolving to let no hasty word escape from his lips; and in his sermons he laid the grounds of those truths from which they had fallen, in such a general way, as if none in the congregation had doubted of them, that none might be exasperated.—In 1639, he received letters of solicitation to take the pastoral charge of the English congregational church at *Arnheim* in Guelderland. One of them was subscribed by Mr. *Thomas Goodwin* and Mr. *Philip Nye*; the other was from Sir *Wm. Constable.* But hoping that better times were approaching in England, he sent them a denial.—About this time he had orders sent him from the Commissary's-court (others probably might have the same) in these terms;

" You are to certify of your conformity to the rites and ceremonies prescribed in the book of Common-Prayer, and these ensuing particulars, under your own hand, and the hands of six or more of your parishioners, upon Thursday after *Whitsunday*, and so quarterly for these twelve months, and so often after as you shall be thereunto required. 1st. That in reading of public prayers, and the administration of the sacraments of baptism, and the Lord's-supper, you constantly wear the surplice, with a hood, according to your degree, and that you administer the communion to none but such as receive it kneeling.—2. That you read divine prayers at seasonable hours, audibly and distinctly, without chopping, altering, or mangling, both the first and second service; and

rather

rather cut short your sermon and exhortation, than leave out any part of the appointed liturgy.—3. That when there is no sermon, you read the homilies appointed by authority, and before your sermon or homily, use the prayer, according to the canon, always concluding with the Lord's-prayer.——4. That instead of your afternoon sermon, you catechize the youth and others of your parish, and handle some head of catechism, set forth in the book of Common-Prayer.—5. That you use the ring in marriage, and cross in baptism; go your perambulation in the Rogation-week; give good example to your parishioners, by making low and humble obeisance at the sacred name of Jesus, whensoever in the gospel or lessons it is named; in standing up at the gospel, creed, and *Gloria Patri*; exhorting your people to do the same.—6. That in your preaching you set forth the reverend estimation of the blessed sacrament, exciting the people to the often receiving of the holy communion of the body and blood of Christ: That you use sobriety and discretion in teaching of the people, especially in matters of controversy; that you move them to obedience as well to the order established in the church, as also to other civil duties.—7. That you have not appointed any public or private fasts or exercises, not approved by law, or public authority; nor have used to meet in any private house or place, there to have conventicles for preachings, nor use any other form of divine service, than is appointed in the book of common prayer; nor have connived at, or approved of any such within your parish."—But the general commotions that happened soon after, saved him and many others from those rigours, to which, for want of strict conformity, they had otherwise been exposed.

In the time of the civil war he was much threatened by his adversaries, and felt many effects of their malice. Most of his goods (except his books) were plundered; and he was in danger of being pistolled in the church. When, therefore, the Earl of Newcastle's forces possessed the city and county of Lincoln, he fled away by Boston to *Lynn*, and so to *Norwich* and *Yarmouth*, and thus was preserved. In this time of his withdrawment, he was useful to many. His ministry found such acceptance, that both *Norwich* and *Yarmouth* strove for him: and for a while he divided himself between both; preaching at *Yarmouth* on the Lord's day, and keeping a lecture at *Norwich* on the week-day. This being a very great fatigue, the aldermen at both places at length chose two grave ministers to determine which place gave the first

and

and fairest call. It being decided for *Norwich*, he settled there for a few years, and had a remarkable blessing attending his ministerial labours. At length the people of *Lincoln*, by importunate letters from themselves, the mayor, and aldermen, under the seal, of the corporation, and the committee of parliament, &c. challenged him for theirs ; and obtained an order from the Assembly of Divines, then sitting at Westminster, or rather a resolution in the case, upon an appeal made to them about the matter. The people of *Norwich* were in general earnestly desirous of his stay with them ; and at the same time he was invited to *Leeds*, by the magistrates and principal inhabitants, who pressed him with the consideration of its being his native country which needed his help. He had another pressing invitation to be one of the preachers in the city of *York*. But the consideration of his former relation to *Lincoln*, determined him for that city, without any debate about means or maintenance. *October* 29, 1654, he returned to *Lincoln*, and settled in the Minster. He was now wholly free from apparitors, pursuivants, ceremonies, and subscriptions, which were the matter of his former trouble ; and yet he had not been long there before a new trouble came upon him. For some of the soldiers, from one of the king's garrisons in those parts, came foraging as far as *Lincoln*. Their malice was pointed at Mr. *Reyner* ; they accordingly pursued him, and there was none to oppose them. He fled into the library to hide himself ; but they followed him with drawn swords, swearing they would have him dead or alive : upon which he opened the doors, and they stript him of his coat, took away his purse, and led him away in triumph, till Captain *Gibbon*, one of the commanders, who had been his scholar, at *Rason*, saw and released him. But after the garrisons were reduced he remained unmolested.

His great concern now was, for a method in church matters, that should answer the most desirable ends, secure purity and order, and yet hinder animosities and dissentions. His judgment was for the Congregational way, and yet he had observed such ill success in gathered churches, that he was a little discouraged. " I find (says he) many run into errors, and are unstayed. I am not satisfied with their manner of laying the foundation of a church, as if there was none before; nor with their manner of meeting, when every member may preach, which brings in despising of preaching by their own officers, and others in public : nay, and even strangers, and soldiers are permitted to exercise, &c," He was for proceeding

ing warily; and at last, after much consideration and many thoughtful hours spent in prayer with tears, he determined upon the Congregational way, with these three cautions: " To hold communion with other churches, who separated the precious from the vile, and to take advice from them in a brotherly way: Not to admit any for members who live in places under godly ministers: And to contend for truth, and bear witness against the errors of the times, both publicly and privately, and particularly, *Antinomianism* and *Anabaptism.*"

Being thus fixed, he diligently fulfilled his ministry. He was a constant preacher at *St. Peter's* in the morning, and at the Minster in the afternoon. That his ministry might be the more effectual, he reduced his evening exercise into a catechetical way. He was a great reprover of sin, wherever he saw it, in great or small. He was conscientious in his conduct as to public affairs, and could not fall in with the practices and opinions of the times. The Engagement to the Common wealth, which was taken by a great many of the episcopal party, was what he scrupled and refused. He weighed the matter *pro* and *con*, as he did most of the great concerns of his life, and could not satisfy himself in a compliance. In the year 1658, when a confession of faith and order was agreed upon at the *Savoy, nemine contradicente*, it was sent to Mr. *Reyner* into the country for his suffrage, with an intimation that the publishing of it should be stayed till his answer was returned. His answer was to this purpose; " That he gave his free and full consent to the confession of faith; but that as to the platform of order, tho' he liked the substance of it, yet there were some particulars therein so expressed, that he was not satisfied." And at another time, when he was urged to set his hand to the design, called *The Agreement of the People*, he positively denied, and sent divers unanswerable reasons against it.

He was a very humble, meek, quiet, and patient person, giving this as his observation, in the close of his days: " I have ever found, that words spoken in meekness of wisdom, and not from an angry spirit, are most piercing to others, and most comfortable to myself." He was a great recorder of God's mercies to him and his; and to that end he wrote A book of remembrance, as he calls it, wherein he has carefully inserted many particular mercies of God in his education, in the several stages of his life, in his removes, in his

wife,

wife, his son, his church, and ministry; in preservations from adversaries, &c.

WORKS. (Published, partly by himself, and partly by his son, after his decease,) Precepts for Christian Practice. (In the 11th edition, printed in 8vo. 1658, there are added, Rules for governing the Affections; and for the Government of the Tongue.)—Considerations concerning Marriage; The Honour, Duties, Benefits, and Troubles of it.—A Vindication of human Learning, and Universities, &c.—The Being and Well-being of a Christian: in three Treatises.

—— Mr. GEORGE SCORTWRETH. He was Mr. *Reyner's* colleague, and a very fervent and affectionate preacher; but of no great natural abilities, or acquired learning. His conjunction with Mr. *Reyner* was a great happiness to him; for he much helped and continually guided him, He printed *A Word or Warning to all Slumbering Virgins.*

—— Mr. JAMES ABDY. He was a person of great gravity and good learning; a judicious preacher, a companion of Mr. *Edward Reyner* whilst he lived, and a teacher of the remainder of his flock, whom the Cathedralists had not scattered, after his decease. He was a pattern for wisdom and humility, and a zealous preacher. He died in *Lincoln* about the year 1673.

LESINGHAM [R.] Mr. HALES.

LUDBOROUGH [R.] Mr. ALFORD.

MANBY. Mr. CRAMLINGTON.

† MARHAM [V.] Mr. ARNOLD. He was well esteemed both for his ministerial abilities and fidelity, and also the holiness of his life, by the chief of his parishioners, Major Hart and Major Izard, officers in the parliament's army.

PICKWORTH [R. 90*l.*] Mr. MICHAEL DRAKE. Of *St. John's Col. Camb.* Born in the parish of *Bradford* in *Yorkshire.* He spent his time at the university to good purpose, and succeeded Mr. *Abdy* at *Lincoln*; where he was many years a laborious preacher. He was presented to *Pickworth* by Sir *William Armyn,* about 1645 where he succeeded Mr. *Weld,* a person of great note, who in the time of the war retired into the associated counties, and fixed in Suf-

† If this place be *Marham,* as Dr. *C.* has it, it is in *Nottinghamshire.*

folk.

folk.   Here he most faithfully discharged all the parts of the
pastoral office, and thereby kept up and increased that piety
which Mr. *Weld* left.   When he removed from *Pickworth,*
some months after he was silenced, in 1662, he lived at
Fulbeck, ten miles from Lincoln, in a mean habitation, where
Sir Francis Fane was his neighbour; who tho' he was an old
cavalier, and as warm for the hierarchy and ceremonies as
any man, yet treated Mr. *Drake* with great respect, and conversed freely with him.   Once he told him, He thought the
clergy of the church of England had the worst luck of any
clergy in the world; for in all other countries and religions
they were had in estimation, but here they were under contempt.   For some considerable time Mr. *Drake* went constantly every Saturday evening to Lincoln, and preached to a
few people in the house of [*John Disney,* Esq; † in the
parish of St. Peter's, at Goats in Lincoln.]   After the liberty
granted by K. James, he removed thither with his family, and
preached more publicly; yet his congregation was so inconsiderable, as to raise him but 15*l. per ann.* but it was as
much as he desired of them.   In the time of Monmouth's in-
vasion, he was confined, with many others; but it doth not
appear that he was ever imprisoned for preaching.

He was a truly excellent and amiable person!   In his
friendship, he was most hearty, sincere, and constant; in his
preaching and praying, exceedingly affectionate and fervent;
in his life very holy and unblameable; in his whole conduct
he manifested more than ordinary simplicity and integrity.
He was a man of great meekness and moderation, affability
and courteousness, humility and self-denial.   He was remarkable for his carefulness to abstain from the appearance
of evil, and eminently laborious in the gospel; an excellent
Hebrician and scripture-preacher.   He was so unexception-
able upon all accounts, that they who used to inveigh most
freely against the Dissenters, had not a word to say against
him.   While he lived at Pickworth, he was one of the Folkingham classis, and one of the Tuesday lecturers at Grantham.
[His son, *Joshua Drake,* was presented 1692, to the vicarage
of Swinderby, by *Daniel Disney,* Esq; who dying *Dec.* 21,
1727, was succeeded by his son *Joshua Drake,* on the same
patronage, who died vicar thereof *Dec.* 12, 1765.]

† The Rev. Dr. *Disney,* (late vicar of Swinderby, now of Essex street,
London,) is of this family; as likewise was Mr. *William Disney,* mentioned
vol. i. p. 280.

QUAP-

QUAPLODE near Spalding. Mr. PETIT. He died in prison for Nonconformity.

SCALBY [V] Mr. WHITE.

SCRIVELSBY-HALL. Mr. ANDREW THORNTON.

SLEAFORD. Mr. GEORGE BOHEME. Of *Cambridge* University. He was born in the city of *Colberg*, in Pomerania in Germany, 1628. Mr. *Mauritius Boheme*, who was ejected from *Hallaton* in Leicestershire, was his elder brother. The family came into England when he was young; upon what occasion doth not appear. He first settled as minister of this town, § where he continued till excluded by the *Bartholomew*-act. When he was silenced, partly that he might not be useless, and partly the better to maintain his family, he kept a school at *Walcot*, within a mile of Folkingham, which he continued many years. He was much esteemed by several neighbouring gentlemen and clergymen; who committed their children to him, and had such satisfaction in the instruction he gave them, as to recommend him to others, as the best master they knew. He for some time preached in the church after his being silenced, and was connived at, as he read some of the prayers; but he was at length forbidden by Bp. *Gardiner*, because not episcopally ordained. A worthy person writes, " That pretty country church hath not had a settled minister in it for 60 years to my knowledge: and suppose, not of 60 more before that; because it was destitute of any maintenance, till the late Sir *John Brownlow* (to whose family belong all the tithes) settled 10*l.* a year upon it, for which there is a sermon preached once a fortnight." It was hard to let the people rather be uninstructed, than that such men as Mr. *Boheme* should be suffered to preach to them. About seven years before his death he removed to his daughter's at Folkingham, and there died, *Sept.* 9, 1711, aged 83. His chearfulness in adversity, his humility in prosperity, and his even, honest, and holy deportment throughout the whole course of his life, must be owned by his very enemies, and be ever remembered by those who were educated by him. Mr. *Brocklesby*, who left his ministry in the church of England after the Revolution, and was well known in these parts, was his intimate friend, and published his *Gospel Theism.*

§ Nichols says, he became Vicar of FOXTON in this county, March 14, 1651.

STAMFORD.

STAMFORD. Mr. EDWARD BROWN. He was a great and good man; generally beloved and honoured, both in town and country, for his integrity, his great zeal, and remarkable moderation. He laboured many years in the word and doctrine, in his own house, and died in *April*, 1682.

—— ST. MICHAEL'S. Mr. JOHN RICHARDSON. Of *Queen's Col. Camb.* He was born at or near *Fakenham*, in *Norfolk*. His parents, when he was an infant removed to *Cambridge*, where he had the whole of his education. When it was compleated he first taught school at *St. Ives* in Huntingdonshire; from whence he removed to a pastoral charge at *Bottle-Bridge*, near Peterborough, where he was first beneficed; and afterwards to *Stamford*, where he laboured in the work of the ministry at *St. Michael's* church, till the Act of uniformity ejected him. When the Five-mile-act banished him hence he sojourned for a while at *Uppingham* in Rutland, [and probably afterwards] at *Stockerston* in Leicestershire; where he had the pleasing conversation of Dr. Tuckney, Mr. Woodcock, &c. But he afterwards returned to *Stamford*, and preached as he could, in his own house there, and sometimes at the houses of the pious and worthy gentry in those parts; *e.g.* Mr. *Weaver* of North-Luffenham, Mr. *Horseman* at Stretton, Mr. *Braughton*, Mr. *Blake*, &c. He also practised physic, whereby he was very useful to his friends both in town and country. Here he lived, at different times, for twenty years. Having married his daughter *Dorothy* to a person at *Kirkton*, near Boston, he resided with her for about five or six years, and there he died in *May*, 1687. His wife died about half a year before him and both of them were buried in that church.

When he was young at *Cambridge*, his aim was (like those of too many other scholars) " to come to something," (as he expressed it) i. e. to get preferment. But the reading of Mr. *Robert Bolton's* works altered his designs, and put him upon a new pursuit; for he found a power and spirit in that author's writings, which he was unable to resist, and by means of which God brought him to sound conversion. After which he maintained a course of strict and uninterrupted piety, and lived a most regular life. He was a man of prayer; eminent and constant in devotion. He would willingly let none rob him of his time for communion with God, and was restless if any company detained him too long from his retirement. He was a close student, and his

ministerial

ministerial accomplishments were truly great. He had a heavenly gift in prayer, raising and melting the affections of such as joined with him; but, he was usually short, (except on a fast-day) apprehending long prayers in ordinary were not for general edification. He was a powerful preacher, whatever subject he handled; and was well furnished for his office, particularly by his eminent skill in the scriptures. He had read the Bible through above thirty times; that is about once a year, and always with some comment or other, besides his occasional and extraordinary reading. There could not be a scripture proposed to him which he would not readily expound, and give the sense of the best expositors upon it, as if he had but lately read them. He had studied *Culverwell's Life of Faith* over and over, and he lived by the rules laid down in it. The grace of faith he had continually in exercise, and the great objects and grounds of faith he had always in view; and accordingly, he gave up all for a good conscience, and cast himself upon the providence of God, which took care of him, so that he never wanted, tho' he was never rich. When some persons asked him on his quitting the church, What he thought would become of his family, he said, He doubted not, but that the God who fed the young ravens, would take care of him and his. His greatest care was about the state of his soul, in which he was serious and deeply solicitous. He was of a very heavenly mind, frequently discoursing with admiration on the life to come, and he derived comfort from it in all cases, which he preferred to all worldly pleasures.

He was a judicious moderator of discourse, and had the art to introduce good conversation with propriety, in which he was as affectionate and zealous as if he had been preaching. He lamented his fruitless life, as he was ready (in his latter time especially) to call it. He earnestly thirsted after opportunities of doing good; and thought those most happy who enjoyed most of them. In his judgment about church-matters, he was moderate and sober; never condemning any for differing from him about conformity, whom he thought to be godly. He frequented Dr. *Cumberland's* (afterwards Bp. of Peterborough's) lecture at Stamford. At *Kirkton*, he went constantly to the church, came betimes, joined in the liturgy, and received the sacrament; his gesture of sitting being allowed him by Mr. *Rastrick*, the minister of the place, with whom he had entire friendship; who also used to go to hear him, when he preached at his daughter's (as he sometimes did in the

the evening,) or elsewhere, to his great profit and delight. He was a loyal subject, and one of those who greatly desired the restoration of K. Charles II. and concurred heartily in it. He once said to a friend, who feared the consequence, *Fiat justitia et ruat cœlum:* * " *Ruit cœlum,*" said his friend to him again, when he first saw him after *Bartholomew* 1662. He was a pious and prudent governor of his family : and God exceedingly blessed him in it. He lived to see his children well educated and well disposed of, tho' once being in a deep consumption, his life was despaired of : but upon his earnest prayer, he was restored ; as he also was another time, in a manner similar to that of *Hezekiah,* and had above twice fifteen years added to his life.

He was a loving and faithful friend to the friends and children of God, and humble in his carriage to them : but far from the hypocritical, complimental, flattering humour. He would take journeys to visit the meanest christian-friends, to advise and pray with them. He had ability to give good advice upon all occasions, to reprove faults, and compose differences. He was a person of great gravity and solidity in his whole carriage ; wise and prudent. A strict observer of the Sabbath ; suffering nothing to be done on that day that was not a work of necessity or charity. A man of unparalleled temperance in the whole course of his life. Being once to preach at *Paul's-Cross,* and, as was usual, a glass of sack being offered him before he went into the pulpit, he refused it, and pleasantly said, he did not choose to preach by the spirit of sack. He was scrupulously just, and very benevolent. It was well for the poor of the hospital [or Bead-house] in *Stamford,* that he was once their warden ; for he much improved the revenue of it, and their weekly allowance.

He was highly favoured of God, who protected him in the midst of all dangers ; and once when he was so insidiously prosecuted, that he thought he should have suffered severely, God struck the informers with sudden and visible vengeance. They died nearly at the same time, in deep despair, and after such an uncommon and miserable manner, that they were blind who could not see the apparent judgment of God on them, and their heart harder than the nether-milstone who did not tremble at it.—When K. *James's* Declaration for toleration came out, he greatly rejoiced that the silenced ministers had their opportunities for service restored them, and thought of returning immediately to his work ; but, having been weakly the winter before, he died within a week or a

* Let justice be done, and let the sky fall.

fortnight

fortnight after he had seen that Declaration, in *April*, 1687. He never printed any thing, but the Epistle prefaced to Dr. *Winter's* Life.

—— Mr. JOSEPH CAWTHORN. Of *Camb.* University, Some time after his ejectment he came to London, and preached there occasionally. He at last settled at *Stoke Newington*, where he for several years continued faithful and successful in his ministerial work, being generally respected and beloved. He and his neighbour Mr. *Joseph Bennet* (who was then at *Newington-Green*) were much concerned together in their work, with mutual endearment and respect, and with as intire confidence as could have been between father and son. Mr. *Bennet* did the last friendly office for him, in a funeral discourse, from *Psal.* xxxvii. 37. on *March* 9, 1707. He represented his text as exemplified in the deceased, and gave some account of him; particularly of his early piety, which had a constant powerful influence upon him through the whole course of his life; his settlement at *Stamford*, in very good circumstances; his nonconformity in 1662, in which he had always great peace and satisfaction, as he declared a few days before his decease; his temper, moderation and candour, which kept him from censuring others, of whom he would not speak in any case, with harshness or bitterness; his patience under a variety of hardships, in which he firmly depended on divine providence, which continually took care of him and afforded him seasonable supplies, which he would be ready to own with great thankfulness; the nature of his preaching, which was plain, practical and methodical, suited to the great ends of the gospel ministry; the manner of his life, which was holy, exemplary, and unblameable; and the manner of his exit, which was such as became one that was neither weary of life, nor afraid of death, but that had a firm faith and stedfast hope in the mercy of God through Jesus Christ.—— He had a son whom he designed for the ministry, but he proved vicious, and died young.

SWAFIELD [R.] Mr. WESTON.

SWINDERBY [V. 6ol.] Mr. JOHN BIRKET. Of both the universities. He was born at *Billingborough* in this county, and was first chosen master of the free-school at *Grantham*, in which situation he continued one whole year, and then removed to *Swinderby*, [to which place he was presented by *John Disney*, Esq; in 1650, on the death of Mr. *Thomas Billard*] where he was minister till he was ejected in 1662, [at which time he had a large and increasing family, as appears by the register of the parish, as well after as during his incumbency.] He afterwards lived in a house which he had bought in the town, and preached twice every Lord's-day to many hearers, till the Five-mile-act forced him to remove to *Billingborough* where he had not been long before lady Hussey of *Cauthorp*, sent for him, and committed her two sons to his care, whom he fitted for the university. One of these was Sir Edward Hussey, afterwards member of parliament for the city of Lincoln. He continued in that family eight years, and was greatly beloved. He afterwards set up a school at his own house in Billingborough, and had the sons of Sir *William York*, and of several other gentlemen to board with him. He was reckoned an extraordinary scholar, and was so very studious as to impair his health, and became so afflicted with the stone, that he was obliged to lay his employment aside. Being advised to remove for change of air, he went to *Auber*, a small town about four miles from Lincoln, where he died *May* 5, and was buried in that parish church *May* 8, 1684. He was a wise and judicious man, of a very pious and sober life ; of ready abilities, and an excellent preacher. He was eminently qualified for training up youth in learning and piety. Many went from him to the university. He did much good in the place where he was minister, and was highly esteemed by most of his neighbouring brethren.

TOFT [R.] Mr. LAWSON.

TOTHILL [R.] Mr. GUNVIL.

TOTNEY [V.] Mr. MARTIN FYNCH. After his ejectment he was pastor of a congregation in the city of *Norwich*. [Mr. *Harmer* of *Wattesfield* writes; " the congregational church of *Norwich* had four of these silenced ministers. First Mr. *Thomas Allen*, next Mr. *John Cromwell*, and Mr. *Robert Asty*, the former pastor, the latter teacher ; and then Mr. *Martin Fynch* ; who died *Feb.* 13, 1697, in the 70th year of his age, as appears from his tombstone. He was a man of most remarkable seriousness, meekness, prudence, and patience under that most calamitous distemper the stone, (of which he died) mingled with the greatest zeal to do good to the souls of men ; which qualities commanded the veneration of

of that great assembly, and kept matters in peace there ; which
congregation, after his death, became dreadfully broken and
divided."]   § There was a Mr. *Fynch*, probably a son of
his, who was fifty years pastor of the presbyterian church in
Norwich, and lived to be near 100 years old: a man of considerable eminence. J. O.

WORKS. A Treatise of the Conversion of Sinners to God in
Christ, &c. (a useful book).—A Funeral Serm. for Dr. Collinges.
—A Manual of Practical Divinity.—An Answer to T. Grantham
the Baptist.——Animadversion on Sir H. Vane's Retired Man's
Meditations.

WIBERTON [R.] Mr. Law.

WILBERTON.   Mr. Cromwell.

WINTHORP [V.] Mr. Horn.

WRAGBY [V.] Mr. Jackson.

The following afterwards conformed:

Mr. Samuel Male, of *Beckby.*—Mr. Richard Sharp,
of *Sedgebrook.* — Mr. William Laughton, of *West-
borough.* His heart however was with the Nonconformists.
He bewailed the unsuccessfulness of his ministry after his
Conformity, saying, he could not tell of one upon whom his
preaching had been effectual. " Now and then (said he) we
have a drunkard or other prophane person reduced from their
wickedness ; but they are such as have slipped into a conventicle, and there met with something that affected them, and
brought them to be serious."

Mr. Christopher Read, of *Bassingham*, held out long
in his Nonconformity, but at last was over-persuaded by a
gentleman, who was his friend, to accept of a living. As he
was going with him in his coach to take possession of it, he
was taken so ill as to be obliged to return ; when he lamented
the step he had taken, saying, " God has been my God all
my days and never failed me ; and must I distrust him at
last ? He could and he would have provided for me ; and
why did I tread unknown paths ?" Under such complaints
he languished and died. Dr. *Walker* gives an unfavourable
account of his introduction to the ministry, [which is rather confirmed by a letter from that neighbourhood to the
editor.]

Several

Several in this county quitted the church, and came among the Nonconformists, some years after Bartholomew-day. For instance,

Mr. JOHN SPADEMAN of *Swayton*, M. A. Of *Magd. Col. Camb.* On quitting his living in the established church, he went to Holland, and became pastor of the English church at *Rotterdam*, where he had a general reputation among foreign divines ; and was, upon many occasions, singularly useful to his countrymen who pursued their studies at Utrecht or Leyden. While he was there, he was a very hard student, and increased his fund of learning, as well as his library. He was well read in philosophy and history, a good critic, and a solid divine. He was so charitable as often to leave himself bare ; very cordial in his friendships, and such a stranger to artifice and disguise, that he appeared to all that knew him to be made up of sincerity. He left Holland to be made co-pastor with Mr. *John Howe,* and succeeded him at his death, but did not long survive him. He sunk on a sudden, when it was generally hoped he might have been a blessing to this city many years. He died *Feb.* 14, 1708. [In the title-page of his funeral sermon, which was preached by his colleague, Mr. *Rosewell,* the date is *Sept.* 4.]

WORKS. Stricturæ Breves in Epistolas D. D, Genevensium & Oxoniensium nuper editas, iterumque juxta Exemplar Oxoniense typis mandatas Londini 1707.—A Discourse of the remembrance and imitation of deceased holy rulers; preached at Rotterdam, *March* 15, 1695, N. S. the day of her Majesty queen Mary's funeral.—A Funeral Sermon for Mrs. Shower.—A Thanksgiving Sermon.—A Sermon to the societies for reformation of manners.—And a funeral Serm. for Mr. *John Howe.*

—— JOHN RASTRICK, M. A. *Kirkton* near Boston [V. *70l.*] The particular occasions and circumstances of his secession from that place, may be seen in a letter which he sent o Dr. *Calamy,* which, with his permission, was printed at the end of the Third Part of the Dr.'s *Defence of Moderate Nonconformity.* When the Dr.'s Account was published, he was pastor of a society at *King's Lynn* in Norfolk ; and met with great hardships and difficulties among the Dissenters, as well as in the established church ; tho' they were of another nature.

[His son, Mr. *William Rastrick,* succeeded him in his congregation at Lynn. In the MS. of his (mentioned in the preface,

.ace, p. xv.) there is a further account of his father, from whence it appears that he died at Lynn, *Aug.* 18, 1727, aged 78. His fun. serm. was preached by Mr. *John Ford* of Sudbury, on *Matt.* xxv. 21. He was buried in St. Nicholas chapel, where upon a black marble stone there is the following inscription, drawn up by this son of his, and revised by Mr. *Ault* of Boston, and Dr. *Duchal* of Cambridge.

H. S. E.

Johannes Rastrick, A. M. Heckingtoniæ, juxta Sleaford, in agro Licoln[d] natus; et in Coll. SS[me] Trin. apud Cantab. educatus. Olim annos 14 Vicarius de Kirkton in Hollandia in agro jam dicto; et denique (quoniam Ecclesiæ Anglicanæ, præceptis quibusdam, conscientia illæsa, obtemperare nequibat) Gregi Christiano, ab Ecclesia publica separato, in hoc oppido, annos 26 Evangelii præco indefessus. Vir eximiæ pietatis, charitatis, ac modestiæ; spectatæ integritatis, studii et industriæ, singularis, omnique fere doctrinæ genere instructus; mathematica vero imprimis peritus Comes audivit facetus, theologus vere Christianus, concionator facundus et acer, pastor vigilans et fidelis, vitii reprehensor intrepidus, atque virtutis fautor amicissimus. Peracto demum vitæ cursu, ærumnis eheu! non paucis obsito, spiritum Deo lætus reddidit, Aug. 18, 1727, ætat. 78. †

WORKS. Besides the Letter to Dr. Calamy above referred to—A Serm. at the Ordination of Mr. Samuel Savage, at St. Edmund's Bury, *Ap.* 22 1714, with an exhortation to him at the close—Two Letters to Mr. Ralph Thoresby, of Leeds, giving an account of a great number of Roman coins found at Flete in Lincolnshire, and other antiquities found at Spalding, &c. printed in the Philos. *Trans.* No. 279, p. 1156, &c. with a Supplement, No. 377, p. 344. These are mentioned by Dr. Gibson in his 2d edit. of his Cambden.]

ISHMAEL BURROUGHS, A. B. curate of *Framton.* Of *Clare Hall. Camb.* who became pastor to a church at *Wisbeach.* [He died *Ap.* 17, 1734, * aged 76 His funeral sermon was preached by Mr. *John Ford,* of Sudbury.]

WORKS. A Narrative of the Conversion of T. *Mackernesse,* of *March* in the isle of *Ely,* who was condemned for a robbery, &c. and executed at *Wisbeach Aug.* 22, 1694.

† See the Translation in the Addenda.

* Some readers have supposed there must be a mistake in the Date in this and the next article, as from hence the persons appear to have been too young to have been preachers in 1662. But it is to be observed, they are mentioned as leaving the church some years after that period.

Mr.

Mr. WILLIAM SCOFFIN, of *Brothertoft*. He became pastor of a church at *Sleaford*, and died in *November*, 1732, aged 77. § The late Mr. *Benj. Fawcett* of Kidderminster, who was a native of *Sleaford*, communicated the following account of Mr. *Scoffin*. He quitted this curacy in 1686, and came among the dissenters. This was sixteen months before the secession of his late intimate friend, Mr. *John Rastrick*, from Kirkton. After providence had fixed the former as pastor to a church at *Sleaford*, and the latter at *Lynn*, they continued their intimacy by letter till Mr. Rastrick's death. Though Mr. *Scoffin* had not the advantage of an academic education, yet his strong genius and diligent application to his studies possessed him of various learning, and, like Mr. Rastrick, he more especially excelled as a mathematician. His preaching for more than forty years at *Sleaford* was plain, judicious and methodical, well calculated to form the life of God in the souls of his hearers, and by a divine blessing was rendered effectual to that best of purposes, in numerous happy instances. Through that long period he was a bright example of self-denial and temperance, faith and patience, meakness and humility, piety and heavenly mindedness. These things, added to his peaceable and candid disposition, and a very obliging deportment, gained him high esteem and respect from the whole neighbourhood, so that some of the principal inhabitants of the town, though they never went to meeting, expressed their value for him by making him annual presents as long as he lived.— His whole income never much exceeded 30l. a year, and often fell short of that; yet such was his frugality and charity, in which he was not a little assisted by his wife's prudent œconomy, that he always kept by him, what he called the poor's box, from which he liberally administered relief to a multitude of objects. One particular way he had of increasing that little fund, was, to put into it two-pence every week, only in consideration of his spending one day in every week as a private religious fast. Though his income seemed so little capable of admitting any stated deduction, yet, of his own accord, he absolutely refused the continued payment of a small annuity, which he had long received from a certain charitable society in London, because he heard of some losses at sea, which that society, or several members of it, had sustained. The life of this excellent person, like the constant tenor of it, ended with undisturbed serenity and peace. He seemed to the last to have

no other distemper than natural decay, and his death therefore was probably the more lingering. He was apprehended
to be dying several days and nights. A person that sat up
with him one of those nights, whose veracity is unquestionable, testified at the time. and continued to bear the same
testimony more than forty years after, that at midnight the
most delightful melodious sounds for a while seemed to
hover over his bed, and gradually to diminish, as they seemed to remove towards the next room, which was his study.
He died November 1732, aged 77. The above account (the
authenticity of which, the writer says may be depended upon)
was received *Dec.* 23, 1776.

WORKS. [Two funeral sermons on the death of that truly
virtuous and religious gentlewoman Mrs. *Kath. Disney;* the former
at *Kirkstead,* (the place of her abode) on the Lord's-day, *May* 18,
1690; the other on the Tuesday following, at *Swinderby,* where she
was buried.]--A help to true Spelling and Reading; with the chief
Principles of Religion in easy Metre; a Scriptural Catechism, and
other things useful for Children.—A Help to the Singing Psalm-
tunes by the book; with Directions for making an Instrument with
one String, by which any Tune may be learned, and a Collection
of Tunes in 2 Parts.

Mr. WILLIAM QUIPP of *Morton.* His case was peculiarly hard. The following account of it was drawn up by
himself.
I. He was articled against many years ago, 1, For officiating in the churches of *Morton* and *Torksey,* without the
court's licence. 2. For omitting to officiate twice every Sabbath, and other holidays, in both the said churches. 3. For
being in the company of excommunicate persons. To which
he answered, 1. That being in orders according to the church
of England, and holding a benefice where there was no church
nor people to officiate in or to, he thought himself bound
by the laws, both of God and man (*Can.* 76.) to exercise his
ministry otherwhere. And being invited by the inhabitants
of *Morton* and *Torksey,* his old neighbours, to accept of their
cures, (at least till they could get a minister) both being
vacant for many years, by reason of the small maintenance
due to the minister, and both being under sequestration, he
accepted hereof, but refused to take a licence, because there
was a suit depending, and is still, (so far as he knows) between the archdeacon and the patron of one of the churches,
about the right. 2. That being neither incumbent nor curate,
he did not think himself liable to censure for omissions men-

tioned

tioned. And 3. That he could not possibly avoid the company of excommunicate persons upon occasion: one being collector of the assessments for four years past.

II. Again, about the year 1672, (the other cause being undetermind) he was articled against for the same things. To which were added, the abbreviation of some offices. To which he answered as before, that he was no incumbent nor curate: and further, that he thought it left to the discretion of ministers, sometimes to abbreviate the one and omit the other as they saw cause. The act of parliament put an end to these proceedings. Notwithstanding which the judge of the court taxed him with a bill of charges, tho' the cause was yet undetermined; and he refusing to pay it, was again

III. Articled against in 1679 for the same things, and for not reading the litan'y, every Wednesday and Friday weekly, and the canons yearly; not catechizing daily; not bowing at the name of Jesus, and not wearing a canonical coat. To which he answered, that these were *Statuta minorum gentium non condita intentione rigidæ observationis*, as Bp. *Sanderson de Juram. Præl.* 3. § 18. calls them: and in this case, *summum jus* was *summa injuria*. But the judge of the court soon after dying, the cause was let fall. But yet again for the same matter he was

IV. Articled against, in 1679: To which were added, his not reading the communion service at the high altar; the omission of some or other holiday within five or six years. To which he answered as before. But that answer being thought insufficient, he was by *William Stow*, surrogate, suspended, and for non-payment of court fees, charged upon him, excommunicated, and laid in jail; from whence he was not released but upon payment of 13*l*. to the court, besides his own charges. But notwithstanding this great charge and trouble, he was again

V. Articled against, in 1685, as a revolter from the doctrine and discipline of the church of England. To which he aswered, 1. That as for doctrine, it was notoriously false, and it could not be proved against him. And 2. As for discipline, he concurred in judgment with as eminent divines as any the church of England had, that it might be better, and better managed. And so the action was let fall without any compensation made for the loss of his money, and (which is more) his precious time; he being caused to attend the court winter and summer, for almost 20 years, to the neglect of his

business,

business, and danger of health and life, the ways and weather being sometimes very bad. And,

VI. Since he left Conformity, he was decreed suspended, for non-appearance at the court, tho' he had no notice given him of the day, week, month or year, when he should appear: and that suspension was openly read in the church. "Now, says he, to close: If they can truly say, that I have herein falsified, relating more than they have objected, or less than they have proved against me, then I shall be content to continue under the censure, tho' illegally passed upon me : or put my neck into this intolerable yoke, and submit to such unmerciful drivers. *William Quipp.*"

Some inferences from hence of his own drawing.

1. That the court supposes perfect conformity to be a duty; and that to be the sense of their canonical oath : and consequently, that such ministers as have made the least omission are perjured, and have forfeited their livings; and that it is in their power and at their pleasure, to take the forfeiture when they will.—2. But it is plain the thing is impossible, and therefore the law is unjust. Our late bishop *Sanderson* says, *Lex de re prorsus impossibili ferri non debet; si feratur Tyrannica est; & de jure nulla, nec quenquam obligat in conscientia.*" De Consc. Præl. 6. §. 6 —3. The court rules at will : For he that hath an unseasonable law to execute, rules as much at will as he whose will is his law.— 4. Religion, that good thing, brought down to us of these times thro' a sea of martyrs blood, is very unsafe in such hands who have an unfeasable Conformity to execute: for such may cast out the best and retain the worst. I shall do them no wrong if I say, that at present they discountenance the most conscientious, whom they fear, and favour none but such as are like themselves.—5. This rigid Conformity is against charity. We ought not to do evil to our neighbour. (and it is evil to persecute for such trifles) and there is a sanction upon it, *Psal.* xv. 3. He that doth, shall not stand on God's holy hill. We are to give no offence to, nor destroy the weak, &c. Can the church, as they call it, absolve us from these duties ?—6. 'Tis against the peace of our neighbourhoods: For the court is made the common sink, into which all malicious persons, having a spite against their neighbours, do disgorge themselves, as I have often known. As it is a truth, that without law there could be no living, so were these laws prosecuted to the utmost, there could be no
living

living neither—7. How much it is against piety, take from
the pen of a Conformist. A curse is denounced against
them that remove the land-marks, *Deut.* xxvii. 17 And it
falleth most heavy on them that remove the limits in God's
worship, (as being boundaries of the highest consequence)
and turn *may* into *must*, and *convenient* into *necessary.—Objection.* The church does not pretend to make *necessaries.*
Answer. She pretends to have power to impose such things,
and then they are necessary. For imposition destroys their
indifference.—8. And lastly, I appeal to all men of judgment,
whether this high-conformity does not look like a subtle design of some cunning men, to advance and enrich themselves,
and impoverish the country, inslave the subject, supplant the
civil magistrate, and engross all power to themselves ; for to
such base ends it serves, and not at all to the public good.
At present few or none, if wrong'd by the court, dare to appeal to the common law, knowing their extravagant power ;
and if any does, they can easily pick out of the vast body of
their law, some matter against him, and so cite him to the
court, and there keep him ten or twenty years, (as they did
me) till they have wearied him, and made him glad to submit
and pay what they list. I have oft sought peace, but could
not have it. I appealed first to Bp. *Sanderson,* and he told
me, that he would speak to his son about my business ; but
this was a mere evasion : next, to Bp. *Fuller ;* but he told
me, as a great secret, that the chancellor, Sir *Edward Lake,*
had so large a patent, as that in a manner the whole episcopal
power was taken away from him. Then to Bp. *Barlow ;*
but he was a man too reserved, and never visited in all his
time, and so left the court to do as they would. Then to
Dean *Brevint ;* and he told me I was in a mistake about
canon 122. For tho' the Bp. was not there in person, yet
he was in power, and what the court did he did. And then
to Bp. *Gardiner* for the last wrong ; but his answer was,
That if I was wrong'd I might right myself at the common
law, and so turned away from me ! And now I appeal to
all the world, if our religion, ministry, property, &c. be
not in danger under such a Conformity.

William Quipp.

I the rather publish this account (says Dr. *Calamy*) for
the sake of Mr. *Olyffe* and Mr. *Hoadly* (with whom he had
a controversy ;) and I am very inclinable to believe, had
either of them met with such treatment as Mr. *Quipp,* it
would

would have a little altered their apprehension, as to the oath of canonical obedience, the force of the canons, the constitution and discipline of the church, and the necessity of a farther reformation; and their stile in the debate about these matters.

JOSEPH FARROW, M. A. Of *Magd. Col. Camb.* His case was somewhat particular. He was not ejected in 1662, nor did he professedly quit the church, but was cast by providence into a station where he had leisure to reflect on the terms of Conformity, which by degrees became more and more disagreeable to him; so that he willingly continued in a private capacity, tho' he preached in public occasionally to the last. He was born at *Boston* of religious parents, and educated in the free-school of that town. When he left the university, he for some years became tutor to a young gentleman at *Louth.* He had the first offer of a free-school newly erected at *Brigge,* but refused it, not liking the employment. He was episcopally ordained; and after he had been chaplain to Lady *Hussey* of Cauthorp, and Sir *Richard Earl* of Stragglethorp successively, he returned to Boston, and was curate there to Dr. *Obadiah Howe* till his death, *Feb.* 27, 1683. He supplied the Dr.'s place till a new vicar succeeded him, and preached constantly with great applause. He removed from thence into the family of Sir *William Ellys* of Nocton, where he continued chaplain for nine years, with great satisfaction to himself and the whole family. He sometimes went with the family to London, where he often preached in the church with good acceptation. There he contracted a familiar acquaintance with Dr. *Fowler,* (afterwards Bp. of Gloucester) the famous Mr. *Locke;* Dr. *Tho. Burnet,* master of the Charter-house, and other persons of learning and moderation. He had also a very intimate correspondence by letters with Mr. *John Spademan* when he was in Holland, as well as a personal acquaintance and great friendship with him in England. He often preached at Nocton in the afternoon, either in the church or in a consecrated chapel in the house. He was violently seized with the palsy, about the beginning of *June,* 1692, of which he had some symptoms about a year before; supposed to be occasioned by his studious and sedentary life. He went to Newark upon Trent for better advice, where he lay about seven weeks, and died, *July* 22, 1692, aged about 40. He was buried in the chancel of that church, in the grave of the last minister,

He

He was very sober and studious from his youth; a little reserved in conversation, but when he spoke it was to the purpose. He was one of a pious life and unspotted reputation, but was never married. He had a quick fancy, a clear head, and a strong judgment. He had a considerable stock of general learning, was perfect master of the Latin and Greek languages., and had a competent skill in the Hebrew. He was well versed in the new philosophy, and the several branches of polite literature. Nor was he unacquainted with the fathers, the councils, and ecclesiastical history; but his chief skill was in the old Greek and Roman histories, most of which he had read in their own language. He had a political head, and would give surprizing conjectures about public affairs, by which he foretold the several steps of the glorious Revolution. He penned all his sermons at large, and took so much time to digest his thoughts, contract his matter, and adapt his expressions, that he used to say, he never made a sermon in less than four days in all his life. Yet he seldom made use of any books in his composures; but when he was at Boston, would sit and write upon his knee by the fire in a public room, with only a bible and a concordance. His first sermons were more rhetorical, and full of synonimous expressions; but he afterwards cut off such excrescences, (as appears by the many erasures in his notes) and aimed only at a spirit of true piety and good sense, which runs thro' and animates all his latter composures. He was dissatisfied with some of the terms of Conformity, and especially with the oaths and subscriptions required; insomuch that he once told an intimate friend very seriously, He was afraid Sir *William Ellys* should offer him a considerable living in his gift, then likely soon to fall, lest he should disoblige him by refusing it. He was so pleased with that religious and regular family wherein God had placed him, that it was thought he would never have willingly left it.

WORKS. Several Sets of Sermons; (which were thought not much inferior to those of the most celebrated preachers of the age.) He also left some valuable Manuscripts, *v. g.* A Discourse on the Rule of Faith.—Of the Obligation of following the Dictates of our own Persuasion.—Liberty of Conscience stated and defended... Short Notes concerning a Comprehension.. Some short Translations out of Greek, Latin and French, &c.

§ Mr. REDMAN, of *Claypole,* afterwards conformed. Whitaker, in his History of Whalley, mentions a Mr. Richard Redman, as minister of *Low Church,* in Walton, Lancashire.

MINISTERS

MINISTERS EJECTED OR SILENCED

IN

MIDDLESEX.

ACTON [R. 200*l.*] Mr. THOMAS ELFORD. It is probable he was ejected from this place in 1660, because in the act passed that year for confirming and restoring ministers, provision is made that no one should be confirmed in the rectory of *Acton*; which it is declared his majesty, *Aug.* 26 foregoing, had granted under his sign manual to one of his chaplains, Dr. *Ryves*, as appears from *Newcourt*, who makes no mention of Mr. *Elford*. [Probably he was only an assistant.] He was a grave divine, of considerable abilities and learning; a moderate Independent; a guide and friend to Dr. *Manton*, when he first entered into the ministry. § In 1645, *Daniel Featley* was deprived of *Acton* and *Lambeth*. His successor at *Acton* was *Philip Nye*, who was appointed by the parliament, and received 500*l.* for going to the Isle of Wight. Dr. *Grey* in his note upon a sarcasm of *Hudibras* on Mr. *Nye*, says, he rode to *Acton* every Lord's-day in a coach drawn by six horses. In 1650, *John Nye* was assistant at this church, and received half the profits, estimated at 200*l. per annum.* Mr. *Baxter* resided here some years, and some times preached in the parish church, having a licence for so doing, provided he uttered nothing against the doctrine of the church of England.

ASHFORD [Chap. to *Stanes.*] Mr. CATCH.

EDGWARE. [C. or D.] Mr. RICHARD SWIFT. He was the son of. Mr. *Augustin Swift*, an attorney, and was born at *Norwich*, in 1616. His father dying while he was young, he had not the advantage of much academical learning, but he attained to considerable skill in the languages.

6

When

When he first entered on the ministry, he was chaplain to Sir Brocket Spencer, and preached for some time in Buckinghamshire, before he came to *Edgeware*, where he was ejected for his nonconformity. He removed afterwards to Mill-Hill, in *Hendon* parish; where before he took boarders, he was in great straits; as he also was afterwards, when they all left him on account of the small-pox being in his house. But he was always of a chearful spirit, and expressed a firm trust in the providence of God. Soon after, the wife of a considerable citizen, sent him two of her sons, and stirred up others to help him, till he had a competent number. He was a man of great charity, and useful to many poor families in the parish. He put out several children to trades. It was thought he did as much good as most gentlemen of fortune in that neighbourhood. He was more than once imprisoned in Newgate, for keeping conventicles in his house; and the last time was in the height of the plague. He was a pious man, and daily employed in studying the scriptures; and yet he was led away with the *Fifth Monarchy* notions, as well as with some others that were very peculiar. He died at *Hendon*, in 1701, in the 86th year of his age.

EALING [C. or D.] Mr. THOMAS GILBERT. A Scottish divine, of useful abilities for the ministry, and of great zeal against error and prophaneness. He was presented to this living in 1654, by Francis Allein, Esq. (as appears from *Mather's Hist.* B. 3. 221,) and died in New-England. At *Charles Town*, is the following epitaph upon his tombstone, from whence some further account of him may be gathered.

" Here is interred the body of that reverend, sincere, zealous, devout, and faithful minister of Jesus Christ, Mr. *Thomas Gilbert*; some time pastor of the church of Christ at *Chedle* in *Cheshire*: also some time pastor of the church of Christ at *Ealing*, in *Old-England*: who was the proto-martyr; the first of the ministers that suffered deprivation in the cause of Nonconformity in England; and after betaking himself to New-England, became pastor of the church of Christ in *Topsfield*; and at 63 years of age departed this life. Interred *Oct.* 28, 1673."—§ Mather says of him, " Of those that are gone to the better world, we have cause particularly to remember Mr. THOMAS GILBERT, whose history is, it may be, sufficiently related in his Epitaph;" and adds the following Latin lines of his own, (incorrectly printed) with a translation:

GILBERTI

GILBERTI hic tenuam, Lectores, cernitis umbram,
  Longè hâc clara magis Stella micansq; fuit.
Sic fuit in vitâ GILBERTUS, sicq; Recessu,
  Sicce detur nobis vivere, sicq; mori!

Lo here of GILBERT but a shadow slight:
He was a star of more illustrious light.
Such GILBERT was in life, such in his death—
God grant we may so live! so yield our breath!

ENFIELD [V.] Mr. DANIEL MANNING. Of *Kath, Hall, Camb.* where he was noted for his eminent improvement of his time. He was a good scholar, and an excellent preacher: much admired and followed on account of his wit and learning and serious godliness. *Newcourt* mentions him as the ejected vicar of this parish. § He was presented to this living by Trinity College, *May* 6, 1659, and was buried here *March* 2, 1666.

*FARNHAM. Mr. GOODMAN.

FINCHLEY [R.] Mr. THOMAS GOULSTON. Of *Queen's Col. Camb.* A good scholar: a man of great modesty and humility: a constant diligent preacher, who was blessed with good success.

FULHAM [V.] ISAAC KNIGHT, B. D. He was a pious man, and of a good temper. He had not the advantage of academical learning; however he had the honour of a degree conferred upon him. § He had been minister of *Hammersmith*, and succeeded Adoniram Byfield both in the rectory and vicarage of *Fulham*, being presented to the former in 1645, by Edmund Harvy, and to the latter in 1657, by Cromwell.

GREENFORD *Magna* [R. 200*l*.] EDWARD TERRY, M. A. Fellow of *Univ. Col. Oxf.* From *Newc. Rep.* it appears that he was admitted to this living *Feb.* 27, 1661, in the room of his father, [§ who accompanied Sir Thomas Roe in his embassy to the great Mogul, and who died in October 1660.] He was many years useful at Oxford in instructing and governing young gentlemen and scholars; and of great fame for his many exercises in the college and schools; particularly for his funeral oration at the interment of Dr. *Joshua Hoyle*, master of his college, and *Regius* professor of divinity in the university, who was a member, of

great

great esteem and honour, in the Assembly of Divines, being
well versed in all the ancient learning of the Greek and Latin
fathers, and one who reigned both in his chair, and in the
pulpit. Mr. *Terry* lost his sight for some years before his
death, but took great pleasure in having others read to him.
He was a man of a very mild disposition, a blameless life, and
very charitable. After enjoying all his days an uncommon
measure of health, he was suddenly carried off; being taken
with a lethargic fit about ten o'clock at night, he died about
two the next morning, *March* 8, 1716. He was much
honoured for his work's-sake, and as a lover of peace and
truth.

.HACKNEY [V.] WILLIAM SPURSTOWE*, D. D. He
had been master of *Katherine-Hall, Camb.* from which
place he was turned out for refusing the Engagement. He
was one of the Assembly of Divines, and afterwards one of
the Commissioners at the *Savoy.* He went with the Commissioners to the treaty with K. *Charles* at Newport in the
Isle of Wight. The initial letters of his name are the three
last in the fictitious word SMECTYMNVVS, the title of
that celebrated book so often referred to, in which he was
jointly concerned with four others, (see vol. i. p. 80). He
was a man of great humility and meekness; of eminent charity, both in giving and forgiving; and of a very peaceable
disposition. He always discovered an innocent and pleasing
chearfulness in conversation, which rendered his company
generally agreeable. He was preserved in the time of the
plague, but died not long after.

He possessed a considerable fortune, and among other
proofs that he employed it to good purpose, he ordered in his
Will, six Alms-houses to be erected in the parish of Hackney
for six poor widows, of good life and conversation; which
accordingly were erected immediately after his decease, between the *Grove* and what is now called *Grove-place.* It appears from the inscription upon a stone over the gate, that it
was his intention to have made provision for the support of
these widows, but that he died without having executed this
benevolent purpose. His brother, however, Henry Spurstowe of London Esq: generously supplied this defect the
following year, by settling certain funds in the parish for this
purpose, of which his son, Henry Spurstowe of London,
Gent. caused this stone to be erected as a memorial,

* So he spelt his own name, tho' we often find it without the e final.

§ Mr. *Baxter*

§ Mr. *Baxter*, in his own Life, frequently speaks of Dr. *Spurstowe* with great respect. He mentions him among those " famous and excellent divines who attended the Earl of Essex's army, being chaplain to Mr. Hampden's regiment." And it appears from the following circumstance which Mr. Baxter records, that he was in the habit of particular intimacy with him. It being agreed by the ministers to draw up a reply to a paper of the Bishops, in answer to their exceptions against the Liturgy, he says, (B. 1, p. 334.) " This task also they imposed on me, and I went out of " town, to Dr. *Spurstowe*'s house at *Hackney**, for retire-" ment; where in eight days time I drew up a reply to " their answer." And doubtless Dr. Spurstowe was one of " the brethren," who, he says, " read and consented to it." He was a frequent preacher before the long parliament, and yet bitterly lamented the death of Charles the first, as appears from one of his meditations, written on that subject. He succeeded Dr. Calibute Downing in this living at Hackney, 1644, and was buried there *Feb.* 8, 1666.

WORKS. Besides the part he took in *Smectymnuus*—The Wells of Salvation; a Treatise on the Promises.—The Spiritual Chymist, in six decads of meditations.—The Wiles of Satan; a Disc. on 2 *Cor.* ii. 11.—And some Sermons on particular Occasions. § One at Westminster-Abbey, *Nov.* 5, 1644, on Ezra. ix. 11—14, entitled, England's eminent Judgments, caused by the abuse of God's eminent mercies—Also a Funeral Sermon for Mr. William Taylor of Coleman-street, *Sept.* 12, 1661. See *Cal. Contin.* p. 54.

.** Mr. EDMUND TRENCH. Of both universities. He was not ejected from this place, nor indeed from any; but he was rendered incapable of accepting a living in the church of England; and may more properly be mentioned at *Hackney* than at any other place; as he resided there when he began his ministry, soon after the Bartholomew-act passed. The following account of him is extracted principally from his Diary, which may be seen in the works of Mr. *Joseph Boyce* of Dublin, fol. p. 329, &c. His grandfather was Edmund, a younger son of *John Trench*, a Norfolk gentleman, converted to the faithful service of God at the age of sixteen, by the labours of the noted Mr. Furnace. His father Mr. Edmund Trench, was a man of an excellent character. An account of both is prefixed to the son's Memoirs

* The old Vicarage-house is just now pulled down, April 1802. From an inscription upon a stone, it appears to have been erected A. D. 1520, when it is supposed the old church was built, which is also lately demolished. Christopher Urswick, was then Rector, whose curious monument is preserved.

of himself. He was born *Oct.* 6, 1643, in circumstances peculiarly dangerous. He was his parents immediate care, in *London* and *Hackney* [where it is probable they had a country house] and his pious grandfather's diversion, from whom he wanted not instruction, example, and encouragement. But he saw occasion afterwards to lament the sins of his youth, which he does with all the signs of the deepest self-abasement. Towards the end of his 15th year he was sent to *Cambridge*, with Mr. Samuel Jacomb, and by him placed in *Queen's College*, under Mr. Andrew Paschall. He there got the love and good report of his tutor and others, but, as he says, was far from deserving it. He made a shift to do the exercise required, but woefully neglected his studies, being sadly addicted to expensive and forbidden sports, reading obscene books, and at length was entangled in bad company, by whom he was drawn into the commission of several vices, tho' (as he acknowledges with great thankfulness to God) he was preserved from debauchery. At the end of the year 1660, his father very seasonably removed him, when exposed to peculiar dangers, from the loss of his pious chamber-fellow, tho' without suspecting any thing amiss, to *Magdalen Hall, Oxford.* He there also got connected with very bad company; but happily the great excess of their debauchery excited his abhorrence, and drove him to seek better acquaintance. God was pleased to cast him among such as were truly pious, for whom, as he says, his parents tincture had prepared him. He thought such company would please them, and it soon grew pleasant to himself also, and proved the happy means of reviving former serious impressions, and bringing him to a true repentance and conversation. He continued for a long time in a state of deep distress on account of his sins, but enjoyed gleams of light and intervals of hope, till at length (after he had made restitution of several things which he had taken from his companions, as they did from one another) he enjoyed a more settled peace. He continued at Oxford about two years. Some time after he left it, he went to *Leyden*, where his father intended he should study physic. He here enjoyed good company and a good ministry, but saw reason to give preference to his own country, and therefore returned in about a year, *viz.* in 1664. Tho' he had made some progress in the study of physic, his inclination to divinity, which he had formerly discovered, still continued. However he did not as yet enter upon the ministry, but spent some time in retirement. He lived with his parents in London till the plague broke out, when they went into the country, and staid till after the fire. At Midsummer, 1668, they returned to *Crouched Friars.*

Soon after his father's death, Mr. *Trench* was seized with some bodily disorders, which were of long continuance, and proved the happy means of enforcing serious consideration. The account he gives of the state of religion in his soul during this period is very pleasing. Upon a calm observation it appeared that he was gaining ground. He had had some thoughts of conforming to the established church, to which he was inclined by the reasons and examples of several pious and judicious persons; but he had some scruples which he could not remove. He sent them to the worthy Dr. *Conant* for his resolution. After half a year's delay, the Dr. sent him this message: " That upon the most serious consideration he could hardly satisfy himself, and therefore would never persuade any to conform while he lived." Before he recovered from his sickness his thoughts of conformity were laid aside. "The formidable horrors of my conscience, (says he) the dread of their return by reason of some doubts I could not well remove, determined me rather to a private life; which I desired to render as useful as I might."———" I remember (says Mr. *Boyce*) when I was one day discoursing with him about ministerial Conformity, he told me, It was the *declaration of assent and consent* to *all things* contained in and prescribed by the book of Common-Prayer, &c. that he chiefly stuck at; and he could not think that declaration could be sincerely made by those whose judgments disapproved so many things therein as he did. And he was the more confirmed in his aversion to so ensnaring a declaration, from observing several of his acquaintance who had made it, tho' under the same dissatisfaction with himself, by giving a looser construction to several things than he thought the words capable of, to become less strict and conscientious in regard to other things than they were before."

Mr. *Trench* appears from his Diary to have spent about four years at *Hackney,* where he wrote down various remarks, at different times, concerning the state of his bodily health, the frame of his mind, and the most remarkable events of Providence. The first passage is dated *Hackney, Sept.* 20, 1670; the last, *Dec.* 11, 1674. These passages discover great seriousness of spirit, and uncommon tenderness of conscience in all his transactions, and an earnest desire to be useful. In one paragraph, dated *May* 22, 1673, he discovers painful suspicions concerning himself, and particularly lest he should

G g 2

have

have been chargeable with presumption in thinking of so high and holy a calling as that of the ministry, considering how great a sinner he had been, and particularly how many instances of injustice he had committed, which lay with great weight upon his conscience. However, upon having recourse to God by prayer and consulting his word and servants, " I could not find (says he) it was any sin in me who had sinned so much, and perhaps hardened some, to endeavour the reclaiming of others. I found great sinners had been, after their conversion, used by the holy God as chosen instruments of his grace.—My fear of disgracing religion seemed unreasonable, as my former sins were known to few; as they were repented of and forsaken, and as I had gained too favourable a repute among men; therefore tho' most unworthy to be honoured by God, to do him any service toward the salvation of any poor creature, yet I could not but think it lawful, yea my duty, to endeavour it to the utmost of my capacity, and thereupon resolved to reject such suggestions, as temptations to sin against my duty."

As to the wrongs he had formerly committed (having made restitution in some cases more than four-fold) he remarks, that he had found advantage by his troubles, and the scruples of his mind in regard to them. " (1.) I found, said he, much pride within me, and was hereby made base and vile in my own eyes, and willing to be so in others. (2.) I had minded too much what was less needful, and these distractions drove me to the essentials of religion, and made me mind them more. (3.) I was more convinced of my own impotency and nothingness, and of my constant dependance on God for duty and comfort. (4.) I was more sensible of the necessity and use of prayer. (5.) I better understood the condition of the scrupulous, that their troubles were not to be slighted as proceeding from weakness and folly, but to be tenderly managed; and that the withdrawings of the spirit are something besides melancholy, tho' that may be joined with them. (6.) I was warned by all to walk more circumspectly, that I might not provoke my heavenly Father thus to chasten me; and instead of controversies, especially about small and mysterious matters, to study more the practical life of faith, in nearer communion with the blessed fountain of holiness, peace and joy."—After a particular account of some of his scruples, and the manner in which he obtained satisfaction, he writes as follows concerning his entrance on the ministry.

" *Hackney,*

"*Hackney, July* 28, 1674. I had in some sincere manner, I hope, served my God, and still mourned after a public opportunity, in any tolerable circumstances, on such terms as I could come up to, like what I heard some (tho' straiter than I) enjoyed. I was willing to take episcopal orders, if I could have had them; but did not think them absolutely necessary to occasional preaching under some public minister, which I would have rested and rejoiced in; an useless life being very burdensome. I thought God called me to serve him as I could. I had enough of such testimonies as the bishops usually required. I was far from slighting the solemn investing rite, very ready to seek it of them, when judged attainable and expedient in my circumstances. I had likewise observed it ordinary, in the universities, to preach long without orders as probationers, &c. and accordingly thought myself obliged not to refuse any inoffensive opportunity of doing good, by preaching where it was wanted; particularly for our aged vicar Mr. *Thompson*, who greatly needed help, and sometimes had no better than mine."

October 5, 1675, he married Mrs. *Bridget Roberts* of Glastenbury, near Cranbrook in *Kent*, daughter to the Lady of that name. His remarks concerning this change of his condition, discover much of the true spirit of piety. The most pleasing circumstances in this new relation appear to have been, in his estimation, the piety of the Lady, and the opportunity of usefulness which was now opened for him at Glastenbury, by means of her family. In a little time he came to reside here, and writes as follows:

"*Glastenbury, May* 29, 1676. On my return I set about doing good, having seriously considered my duty to God, my superiors and others, and likewise their circumstances among whom I was to live. The family and others accustomed to the old chapel at Glastenbury, being two miles or more from the church [*viz.* at *Cranbrook*] were prejudiced against the established worship, and the next minister, the vicar of G——, especially *Th.* a drunken impertinent sot, who distasted many persons, enough inclined to conformity, and made them approve more private help. I still dealt openly, as I had done before marriage, declaring my desire of more public service; readiness to read Common-prayer, almost all; going sometimes to the neighbouring churches, joining in the liturgy, and communicating kneeling. I drew none to our private meetings, but blamed such as came from good ministers; professing I would not keep up a separate congregation, but only while

while it appeared expedient help for such as were so ill provided. I proceeded with more confidence and comfort 'because I had no trouble, nor heard of any dislike from the
neighbours most used to the church-service; and I was the
more confirmed in the moderate course I had taken, by the
impotent censures of some uncharitable persons. My prayers
were, to know my duty and to do it; pleasing God, tho' I
displeased man."——

"July 5, 1677. Troublesome, censorious, dividing spirits,
had occasioned more thoughts of those unhappy controversies
about forms and ceremonies, church-government, &c. And
I was still most satisfied, even when most serious, that the
bitter extreams of Dissenters, as well as of rigid Conformists
were very displeasing to God: that spiritual pride, narrow-
spirited mistakes, and grievous wresting of the holy scriptures,
were the evil roots of unchristian divisions and real schism.
I was much grieved at such uncharitable and love-killing
principles and practices; yet had cause to be thankful that
there was more light and love amongst those that came to
the meeting at Glastenbury, which I still endeavoured to
increase."——

"Sept. 22, 1679. I was more affected with the increasing
woeful effects of church-divisions. I openly and honestly dis-
owned and opposed the uncharitable sinful courses some took:
my desires, prayers, and endeavours were, that professors
might have more sound knowledge and humility, and walk in
the good ways of catholic truth, love, and peace. My praises
flowed from freedom from unpleasant extreams, from un-
toward wranglings about little things, and losing holy love
and the vitals of religion in unchristian irrational heats about
the less necessary variable circumstances thereof." &c.

A little before this time, Mr. Boyce (who thankfully acknowledges the good providence of God in it) was brought
into his acquaintance; being invited to preach one Lord's-
day with him to the people who then met at Glastenbury;
which he continued to do for near a year. He therefore was
able to give a full account of what the foregoing passages in
his diary refers to; which he does p. 396. He closes his account with mentioning the following instance of the admirable influence of Mr. Trench's example and persuasion to
promote religion in the family and neighbourhood of Glastenbury: "The heir of it, Sir Thomas Roberts, being newly
come to age, to engage his tenants the more effectually to the
study and practice of religion, did at his desire, call together
                                                          their

their servants and children every Lord's-day evening, and catechize them himself."—Here follow several pious remarks
in *Mr. Trench's* diary while at Glastenbury. The last is dated
May 28, 1683, and closes thus: "My work at Glastenbury
drawing to an end, my conscience witnessed that I had endeavoured to promote the essentials of religion, not our unhappy differences, with as little appearance of schism or faction as I could." After this he dates from *Brenchley, Nov.*
20, 1684, and continues his remarks occasionally to *Oct.* 11,
1688. It does not appear in what capacity he was at this
place, but he continues to express great desires after usefulness and the promoting christian catholicism, a careful attention to the frame of his mind, and to the events of providence, and a chearful hope with respect to his spiritual state.
He seems to have been for some time in an unsettled situation,
and mentions in a note *Dec.* 31, 1687, his being much per-
plexed between repeated messages from *Hackney* and *Ashford.* *Oct.* 11, 1688, he removed from *Brenchley* to *Cranbrook,* and afterwards relates what passed between him and
Mr. *B.* the minister of that parish, to whom he offered to
preach once a day *gratis,* and read the Common-Prayer in
the afternoon. But the offer being refused, he told him he
must preach once a day at home, that he might not be useless, but might do some good to those who would not hear
Mr. *B.* or Mr. *W.* On the other hand, he refused to countenance a certain nonconformist minister there, as on other
accounts, so principally for his binding his people against
all communion with the parish-churches.—About this time,
as he was going to take horse, his foot slipped, and he received a slight wound in his leg, which being neglected, and
he afterwards taking cold, was soon greatly inflamed, and
a mortification ensued, which put a period to his valuable
life, *March* 30, 1689, in the 46th year of his age. Mr. *Ch*——
preached his funeral sermon, in which he gives him a most
excellent character, for judgment, learning, and piety; and
speaks of him as an eminent example of meekness and humility, moderation and charity. The reader is referred, for particulars, to the narrative in Mr. *Boyce's* works. Let it suffice
here to transcribe the closing part of his character.

"His charity was very singular and exemplary. He devoted the 10th, and for many years the 7th, part of his estate
to charitable uses. [And tho' he had a family] he did not
stint himself to, but often exceeded, these large proportions.
He was peculiarly prudent in managing his alms to the best

advantage;

advantage; and endeavoured, at the same time, to save the
bodies and souls of men. He mingled good counsel with all
his alms, and affectionately persuaded to serious piety, which
often had a very commanding and abiding influence. He
spent much pains and cost in instructing poor children in the
principles of religion, in giving bibles and other good books,
requiring a diligent perusal of them, and calling them to an
account of their proficiency. He had many other secret ways
of charity, as appears by his private accounts, for which he
courted not the applause of men.—I shall only further mention his patience and entire resignation to the will of God.
For some years before his death, God visited him with very
sore afflictions of different kinds; but he bore them all with
a just sense of his Father's hand, and did not charge his providence foolishly. In his last sickness, under all the excessive
tortures of his pain, and frequent lancings, he still expressed
great patience; and when the extremity of his pain forced him
to cry out, he checked himself, expressing his fears of dis-
honouring God by impatience, and blessed his heavenly Father that worse was not inflicted. Nor was he peevish with
those about him, but was thankful to any one that did any
office for him, and pleased with every thing that was done.
He preached in his chair and in his bed; affectionately exhorted all that attended on him to the serious practice of religion, and suited his counsels to the particular circumstances
of those that visited him. He died with comfortable hopes of
happiness. Tho' he wished he had been more watchful and
useful, he hoped he had been sincere, and trusted that for
Christ's sake all his sins were forgiven. Tho' he had not
raptures and transports, he had a constant peaceful calm,
which continued to the last moment of his life. And for
some weeks before he died, he longed to be dissolved, and
earnestly desired, if God saw good, that he might be with
Christ." —— *Barney* Eq; married his daughter.

HANWELL [R.] Mr. AMBROSE.

HAMSTEAD [C.] JOHN SPRINT, M. A. He was
the son of Mr. *Sprint*, the author of that celebrated book,
intitled *Cassander Anglicanus*, and elder brother of Mr. *Samuel Sprint* of Hampshire. He had been incumbent here 29
years. In *Newc. Rep.* he stands thus: "Joh. Sprint, M. A.
Licentiat. 17 *Dec.* 1633. He was a man well reported of,
both for his doctrine and life. § Lord Cambden allowed him
50l. *per. an.* out of the great tythes.

HARROW

HARROW *on the Hill* [V. 100*l.*] THO. PAKEMAN,
M. A. Of *Clare-Hall, Camb.* He was first minister at *Hadham* in Essex, from whence he was ejected in 1662 † with ten children. He was in great esteem with Sir Gilbert Gerrard, and indeed with the whole parish, for his diligent preaching and great charity; for he sometimes gave money where he had a right to take it. Being eminent for his integrity, and for ruling well his own house, he soon after his ejectment had the instruction and boarding of several children of persons of quality and figure, and preached as he had an opportunity. He afterwards removed to *Old Brentford*, and continued to keep boarders there, who were instructed by Mr. *Button*, who lived next door. There he preached constantly and administered the sacrament. Mr. *Button* was at length taken up, and imprisoned six months upon the five-mile-act; but Mr. *Pakeman* escaped, and for a time kept private. He afterwards lived and preached constantly at Mrs. Methwold's in *Brumpton* near Knightsbridge; and thence removed into the family of *Erasmus Smith*, Esq; where he continued some years. In 1685, he lived with his children in the city, where he attended on Dr. *Kidder's* ministry, and sometimes received the sacrament from him, preaching occasionally at the houses of his children. At one time when he was preaching at his son's house, where not above three or four neighbours were present, the city marshal seized him and his son, and carried them before Sir *Henry Tulse* then lord-mayor, and they were forced to pay a fine. In 1687, he removed to *Stratford*, where he had an opportunity of some service. He was an acceptable preacher to the neighbours there, and administered the sacraments. He procured a person to teach the poor people's children to read, and gave money to encourage it. He died in *June* 1691 (after about a week's illness, of a fever, which appeared not very violent) in the 78th year of his age. During his sickness he said, He thanked God it had been his design to glorify him. He was eminent for his great reverence of God, especially in the pulpit; his aptness to awaken and affect young people; and his readiness for edifying discourse. He was much in pressing persons to come to the Lord's supper; often saying, that he thought all adult persons that came to hear, ought to receive. He was a grave, sound,

† Most probably a mistake for 1660. In 1662 we are to suppose him to have been ejected from *Harrow*; otherwise there seems to be no reason for his being placed here.

pious,

pious, sober, and peaceable divine : a strict observer of family. order, and conscientious in redeeming time. His funeral
sermon was preached by Bp. *Kidder*, from *Rev.* xiv. 13.

HENDON [V. 100*l.*] FRANCIS WAREHAM, M. A. Of
Bennet Col. Camb. A man of great natural wit, of polite
learning, of great pleasantness in conversation, and a very
practical preacher, but unsuccessful. § He was put into this
living by the parliament, in 1650.

WORKS. A Funeral Sermon for Mrs. Hellen Foot, wife of
Samuel Foot, Esq; in Aldermanbury-church. . A Sermon at St. Paul's
Aug. 23 1657, on James i. 18.—Another at Aldermanbury, *Oct.*
14, 1657, on *Job.* iv. 5.

HILLINGDON [R. 100*l.*] Mr. PHILIP TAVERNER.
Of *Exeter Col. Oxf.* A grave, peaceable divine, of unblameable life, but who chose to live retired. He, in conjunction
with Mr. *R. Goodgroom* and Mr. *H. Hall*, had a public discourse with some Quakers at the meeting-place at *West-
Drayton* in this county, *Jan.* 18, 1657 ; an account of which
was published. He died and was buried in this parish.

WORKS. Besides the Account of the above Dispute—A Reply to EDWARD BURROUGHS the Quaker.—Truth's Agreement
with itself in the Spirit and Letter of the Word ; or a short Catechism—After his death, A Grandfather's Advice ; directed in special to his own family.

ICKENHAM [R.] Mr. NICOLAS.

KINGSBURY [C. or D.] Mr. JAMES PRINCE. A gentleman born, and of a good family. He was young when
ejected, but in good repute both for learning and piety. He
lived and died pastor of a congregation at *Oakingham* in
Berkshire.

LITTLETON [R.] Mr. EDMUND TAYLOR.

NEWINGTON (Stoke) [R. S.] Mr. DANIEL BULL.
§ Dr. *Manton* resigned this living in 1656. In the vestry
book is the following entry. " *Sept.* 27, 1657, at a vestry
then holden, Mr. *Daniel Bull* was chosen most unanimously
to succeed Mr. *Manton* as pastor. The whole parish signed
his call, sick and poor, good and bad." He received his
appointment from Cromwell, *Nov.* 25 following.] He was
a good scholar and a very agreeable preacher, who was for
some time fellow-labourer with Mr. *John Howe* ; but fell
into some immorality, over which the veil ought to be drawn,

as

as there was satisfactory evidence of his true repentance. It was upon occasion of his fall that Mr. *Howe* preached and printed his excellent discourse upon " Charity with reference to other mens sins." Mr. *Stancliff* wrote the following account of his death in the margin of Dr. Calamy's account of him, and sent it to the author.—" His last hours and dying prayers and tears, with the chearful resignation of his soul to Christ, as offered to the worst and chiefest of sinners, in the gospel, spake him both a penitent sinner and a returning backslider. He gave up the ghost in his closet; craving any place where Christ was, tho' it was but eternally to lie at his footstool."

§ In the London Collection of Farewell Sermons, there are two by Mr. *Bull*, who is there said to be of *Newington-Green*, which must be a mistake, for *Stoke-Newington*, where the parish church is. One of these was delivered in the forenoon on *John* xiv. 16; the other in the afternoon, on *Acts* xx. 32. They are both of them plain, serious, practical and affectionate; containing some things very appropriate to the occasion. Towards the close of the latter are the following passages. Having expatiated on this observation, " that the best farewell a minister can give his people, when taken by providence away from them, is, to *commend them to God*," he subjoins these admonitions. ` " A minister's commending you to God will be to no purpose if you do not commit yourselves to him.—Take God to be your God, and give up yourselves to be his people. If you will, before you and I part, it will be the comfortablest day that ever I saw, tho' in other respects it may be the saddest. Keep in God's way, and you will be sure of his protection. —I commend you to the *Word of God's grace.* Keep it, and it will keep you. I leave it as a Depositum; if you part with it, take heed how you will answer it at the last day. Study God's word. If you never hear a Sermon more, you have enough, by the use of the Bible, to carry you to heaven."

After other suitable exhortations he adds, " Labour to keep up that christian love, which in this place hath been more eminent than any where I know. I would preach St. John's doctrine ; *Little children, love one another.* If there be any consolation in Christ, any comfort of love, &c. fulfil ye my joy, Phil. ii. 1. 2,"—He closes thus : " My dearly beloved in the Lord ; it is a sad and solemn thing for a minister to be rent from a people whom he loves as his own soul—to bid adieu to the solemn meetings wherein I have
preached

preached to you; wherein we have mingled our sighs and
tears before the Lord; wherein we have rejoiced and sat
down before the Lord at his table—to think that I must minister to you no more in these ordinances, is a heart-breaking
consideration—to think that I am now dying while I am
preaching—but this is my comfort, that like a dying father
I can commend you to the care of such a friend, infinitely
able to supply all that I could do for you.—I would
hope that I have some children that I have begotten to
Christ by my ministry, towards whom my bowels yearn—
There are many poor souls yet in the gall of bitterness and
the bond of iniquity, and if the Lord had seen good, I
would fain have seen of the travail of my soul in their salvation; but I can commend them to God, who knows them
that belong to his election. He can either restore me, or
can [convert them] by another hand.—It will be some alle-
viation of sorrow, tho' I must leave you, as to my public
ministry, that I hope I may, for a while, go up and down
among you, and converse with you. The Lord grant this
favour that I may behold your stedfastness!—If the Lord
shall take off those bands of death which the Law hath laid
upon my ministry, who in regard of conscience cannot conform, I shall chearfully return to you in this place. I now
commit you into a safe hand."

NORTHALL [V. S. 300l.] Mr. ROBERT MALTHUS
Of *Magd. Hall, Oxf.* Cotemporary with Mr. William
Pemble. Dr. *Walker* says, He was thrust into this living
upon the sequestration of Mr. *George Palmer*, in 1642.
But from the books of the commissioners for approving of
public preachers, which the Dr. quotes (P. ii. p. 33.) he appears not to have possessed it till 1654. He was an ancient
divine; a man of strong reason, and mighty in the scriptures:
of great eloquence and fervour, tho' defective in elocution.

§ The parishioners, however, petitioned Cromwell to remove him from this living, and urged among other things the
following:—" The said Mr. *Malthus* is one who hath not
only a low voice, but a great impediment in his utterance,
so that your petitioners cannot receive any benefit by him;
one who hath manifested his great indisposition to the work
of the ministry; a great reviler and opposer of such who out
of uprightness and sincerity of heart, desire to worship the
Lord; one who hath uttered invective expressions against
our army whilst they were in Scotland; utterly averse from
rendering our God praise, when several thanksgivings were
in

in the nation for signal mercies which he vouchsafed our armies, in the eminent victories given in and bestowed upon us there: one who is a great oppressor of his neighbours, and hath stirred up contentious suits amongst them; too guilty of the abominable sin of covetousness, which brings a great reproach upon the gospel," &c. Signed by *Henry Arundell, John Arundell*, and about 30 more. This petition however had no effect; probably because the charges which it contained appeared void of evidence, and the effect of a party spirit.

PADDINGTON [C.] Mr. ARNHALL, or ARNOLD.

PINNER [Chap. to *Harrow.*] Mr. JOHN ROLL. A very grave and pious man, and very useful in his place. Being in a chapel of ease he never administered the sacraments. He died at Harrow on the Hill.

SHADWELL. Mr. MATTHEW MEAD. § It doth not appear where he was born, or where he had his education. The first account we have of him is, as possessing the living of *Great Brickhill*, in Buckinghamshire. *Jan.* 22, 1658, he was appointed by Oliver Cromwell, to the cure of the New-chapel at *Shadwell*, from whence he was ejected for nonconformity in 1662; and not (as Dr. Calamy had stated) from *Stepney* church: unless it was as assistant preacher with Mr. *Greenhill*, with whom it appears, from Mr. Howe's funeral sermon for him, he had been some time associated, without specifying the time or place. In 1663 he resided in Worcester-house at Stepney, where his son Richard, the eminent physician was born, who was the eleventh of thirteen children. This son he took with him to Holland, but at what time we do not learn, and there he had his education. On the liberty granted to Dissenters, Mr. *Mead* returned, and in the year 1674, the spacious meeting-house in Stepney was erected for him, the four large pillars of which were presented to him by the States of Holland, as was frequently related by Mr. *Brewer*, who for many years preached in the same place. Here Mr. *Mead* had a very large congregation, and when he preached in the city he was very much followed.

In the year 1683, he was accused, together with Dr. *Owen* and Mr. *Griffith*, of being privy to what was called *the Rye-house-plot*, for which the great Lord Russel, among other patriots, suffered death. It is said, that on this occasion he fled to Holland for safety, tho' conscious of innocence. If this

this was fact he soon returned, and obeyed the summons to
attend the privy council, at which the king, *Charles* II, was
present, and answered the interrogatories put to him in so
satisfactory a manner, that his majesty himself ordered him to
be discharged. The above infamous accusation was brought
against him and the other ministers by Dr. *Thomas Sprat*,
Bp. of Rochester,[*] in his fabulous history of the *Rye-house-
plot*, and was repeated by Dr. *Nichols*, in his Defence of
the church of England; a sufficient answer to which may
be seen in *Neal's Hist.* Toulmin's edit. vol. iv. p. 602.
Also in *Peirce's* Vindic. of Dissenters. p. 258. This last
learned author adds, concerning Mr. *Mead*.—"This worthy
man was my guardian, and therefore I think myself bound
to pay so much respect to his memory as to take this occasion of acquainting my reader, if he does not know it already,
That he was a gentleman and a scholar, and a most excellent
preacher; And that his reputation was too well established
among those who knew him to be lessened by such reproaches as those cast upon him," by the above writers.

Mr. Mead died Oct. 16, 1699, aged 70. Mr. *John Howe*
preached his funeral sermon, on 1 *Tim.* iv. 16.

[The following is an extract from it:——"I wonder
not that there are many weeping eyes, and should much
wonder if there be not many aking trembling hearts among
you, for what you have lost, and from an apprehension, how
hard and almost hopeless it is your loss should be soon or
equally supplied. He was long in preparing and forming to
be what he was when you lost him. His station among you
in this neighbourhood, when first he undertook the pastoral
charge of this church, 'over which the Holy Ghost made
' him overseer,' required a man of as much wisdom and
grace, as any such station could well be supposed to do, considering how numerous, how intelligent, and well-instructed
a people he was to take the care of. About 43 or 44 years
ago I had the opportunity of beginning an acquaintance with
him. His excellent good natural parts, his ingenuous education, his industry, his early labours in preaching the gospel
of Christ, in his native country, in the city, and in this place;
his conjunction and society, for some years, with that excel-

---

[*] It was lately remarked, by a person who liked a pun, that the *See of
Rochester*, has been more noted for SPRATS than for HERRINGS;" alluding
to the excellent prelate of that name, who was the zealous friend of civil
and religious liberty.

lent

lent servant of God.Mr. *Greenhill ;* above all, the gracious
assistances he had from heaven, gave him great advantages,
to be a minister of Christ, ' approved unto God; a workman
' that needed not to be ashamed, rightly dividing the word
' of truth.' And his multiplied years, with the continual
addition thereby to the rich treasury of his experiences, still
improved him more and more ; so that there being no decay
of his natural endowments, and a continual increase of his
supernatural, you had the best of him at last, whereby indeed
your loss was the greater, but your obligation was also the
greater, that God continued to you the enjoyment of him so
long; and that in a serviceable state. But when he could
be no longer serviceable in his stated delightful work, it was
by the decay not of the inward but the outward man : so
that when he could preach to you and converse with you no
longer, he could earnestly and fervently pray for you to the
end. And God did not afflict you by leaving long among
you only the shadow, the outside of the man, and of such a
man ! He took little pleasure in embroiling himself, or his
hearers, in needless and fruitless controversies. The great
substantial doctrines of the gospel were his principal study
and delight; such as lay nearest the vitals and the very heart
of religion and godliness, and most directly tending to the
saving them that heard him. The subjects which he chose
to insist upon, in the course of his ministry, shewed, as to
this, his spirit and design. Having formed, from the holy
scriptures, that scheme of thoughts which satisfied him, and
gave him a clear ground whereupon to preach the gospel,
with an unrecoiling heart, he loved not to discompose it.
His judgment in things which had that reference, being constantly moderate, and unexceptionably sound ; remote from
rigorous and indefensible extremities on the one hand and
the other. Hereupon he drove at his mark, without diversion ; not so much aiming to proselyte souls to a party, as to
Christ ; and to engage men, as much as in him lay, to be
sound and thorough Christians. Hitherto tended his sermons from year to year. The great subject he had in hand,
and which he left unfinished, when God took him off from
his public work, was manifestly pointed this way, *viz. Of
the Covenant of God in Christ.* And his annual course of
preaching a sermon on *May-day* to young men, had the
same manifest scope and aim, with which his public labours
were concluded; God so ordering it, that his last sermon was
this

this year on that day †. His judgment, in reference to matters of church order, was for union and communion of all visible Christians, *viz.* of such as did visibly ' hold the head,' as to the principal *credenda* and *agenda* of Christianity: The great things belonging to the faith and practice of a Christian, so as nothing be made necessary to christian communion but what *Christ hath made necessary*, or what is indeed necessary to one's being a Christian. What he publicly essayed to this purpose, the world knows; and many more private endeavours and strugglings of his, for such an union, I have not been unacquainted with. The unsuccessfulness of which endeavours, he said, not long before his last confinement, he thought would break his heart. He having openly, among divers persons, and with great earnestness, some time before exprest his consent to some proposals, which, if the parties concerned had agreed in the desire of the thing itself, must unavoidably have inferred such an union, without prejudice to their principles; and on such terms as must have extended it much further; else it had signified little. But this must be effected, as is too apparent, not by mere human endeavour, but by an Almighty Spirit poured forth, which (after we have suffered a while) shall καταρτίσαι, *put us into joint,* and make every joint know its place in the body, 1 *Pet.* v. 10. Shall conquer private interests and inclinations, and over-awe mens hearts by the authority of the divine law ; which now, how express soever it is, little availeth against such prepossessions. Till then Christianity will be, among us, a languishing withering thing. When the season comes, of such an effusion of ' the spirit from on high,' there will be no parties. And amidst the wilderness-desolation that cannot but be, till that season comes, it matters little, and signifies to me scarce one straw, what party of us is uppermost. The most righteous (as they may be vogu'd) will be but as briars and scratching thorns ; and it is better to suffer by such than be of them. In the mean time, it is a mark of God's heavy displeasure when persons of so healing spirits are taken away. And if it awaken any of us, that will tend to prepare us for the effects of it, which preparation seems a thing more to be hoped, than prevention. But this worthy servant of Christ sees not the woeful day, whatever of it he might foresee. His removal makes to many

† This annual sermon was continued by Mr. *Brewer* to the last (as it still is by Mr. *Ford*) and attended by an amazing concourse of people.

indeed

indeed a woeful day, and that all about him did long foresee.
He was long languishing, and even dying daily. But amidst
surrounding death, as a relation told me, there was no appearance of any the least cloud upon his spirit, that obscured
the evidences of his title to a blessed eternity. Being asked
how he did, he said, "Going home, as every honest man
ought, when his work is done." He was much in admiring
God's mercies under his afflicting hand, saying, "Every
thing on this side hell is mercy ; that the mercies he received
were greater than his burthens, tho' in themselves grievous;
that he rested upon that promise, that his father would lay
no more upon him than he would enable him to bear; that
he expected to be saved only by the righteousness of Christ
imputed to him." Tho' he well understood, as I had sufficient reason to know, that Christ's righteousness is never
imputed to any but where, if the subject be capable, there is
an inherent righteousness also, that is no cause of our salvation, but the character of the saved. Having before
precautioned some about him not to be surprized if he went
away suddenly, he repeated the ejaculation, 'Come, Lord
' Jesus, come quickly;' and renewing the former caution,
by saying, "Remember what I said before ;" as he sat in
his chair, § with all possible composure, he bowed his head,
and without sigh or motion expired in a moment. The
sighing part he left to others that stay behind."

Upon his tomb-stone there is the following inscription:

H. S. E.

Quicquid Mortale fuit
Matthæi Mead, V. D. M.
Honesta inter Cattieuclanos familia orti
A Pietate, Doctrina, Facundia præclari
Qui Assiduis & insignibus Laboribus
Pro Patria, Religione, Libertate,
Invicto animo defunctus,
Vitæ tandem & Laudis fatur,
Ad Cælitum Domum quam diù optaverat,
Lassus & anhelus placidissime adscendit,
An Ætat. suæ 70: 17 Kal. Novem. CIƆIƆCXCIX.

§ The chair in which he died was made for the wife of the famous LILLY
the astrologer, and was covered with crimson velvet. It was in the possession of Mr. James late minister of Hitchin.

Et Boni Civis
Amantissimi Conjúgis   . :(
Optimi Patris
Theologi vere Christiani.
Clarum reliquit Posteris Exemplum.

Here lies all that was mortal of the Rev. Mr. *Matthew Mead*, minister of the gospel. He descended from a respectable family in the county of Bucks, and was eminently distinguished for his piety, learning and eloquence. He spent his life with an invincible fortitude in constant and uncommon labours for his country, religion and liberty : till at length, full of days, and crowned with honour, he most serenely ascended, like a weary and longing pilgrim, to that celestial rest which had long filled his wishes, *Oct.* 16, 1699; and at the age of 70 years : leaving an illustrious example to posterity, of a good citizen, a most tender husband, a most affectionate father, and a truly christian minister.

WORKS. The almost christian tried and cast, in seven sermons.—A Sermon to the united brethren, about Ezekiel's wheels. —Funeral Sermons for Mr. Tho. Rosewell, Mr. Tim. Cruso, &c. —§ The good of early obedience.—The young man's Remembrancer.—A name in heaven the truest ground of joy, on Luke x. 20. —The power of grace in weaning the heart from the world ; two discourses on Psal. 131, reprinted in 1772.—Two sticks made one; or the excellency of unity, on Ezek. 37. 19.—Spiritual wisdom improved against temptation.—A Farewell Sermon (the 11th in the London Collection) on 1. *Cor.* 1.3. *Grace be unto you, and peace,* &c.

A plain, popular discourse, which closes with the following directions for maintaining peace of mind. 1. Make religion your main business. 2. Live daily by faith in Christ. 3. Maintain constant communion with God. 4. Be good at all times, but of all best in bad times. 5. In all conditions chuse suffering rather than sin. But see that your *cause* be good : it is not the *blood*, but the *cause* that makes the martyr. Let your *call* be clear : some may suffer for the cause of God, and yet sin in suffering for want of a call. Let your Spirit be meek, as Christ's was. And see that your *end* be right : if it be self, or singularity, or schism [you can have no true peace.]—6. Be much in studying the scriptures. ʹ Great peace have they that love thy law.ʹ 7. Take heed of apostasy either in doctrine or principles. 8. Make the word of God your rule in all things, and keep close to it in matters of God's worship. There are endless discourses about the *mode*. I have no disputing time. It is good in difficult cases always to take the surest side. If I follow the traditions of men I may sin : if I keep close to the directions of God in scripture, I am sure I cannot.

9. Keep

9. Keep up the power of godliness, and do not let religion down into a lifeless formality. It is the duty of them that have grace to improve it. If you sit under the daily means and do not 'grow, do you think this will be peace in the latter end? surely not. 10. Observe that excellent rule of the apostle *Phil.* iv. 8.—And now my brethren I commend you to God, with this benediction, which I shall make my Valediction. Grace be unto you and peace from God our father, and from our Lord Jesus Christ.

SHEPERTON [R. 200*l.*] Mr. JOHN DODDRIDGE. Of *Oxf.* university. He was an ingenious man and a scholar; an acceptable preacher, and a very peaceable divine. [He was grandfather to the celebrated Dr. *Doddridge,* who says of him in a letter to a friend, " He had a family of ten children unprovided for; but he quitted his living, which was worth to him about 200*l. per annum,* rather than he would violate his conscience, &c." His funeral sermon was preached by one Mr. *Marriot, Sept.* 8, 1689; from whence it appears that he had preached to a congregation at or near *Brentford;* that he died suddenly, and was much respected and beloved by his people. Mr. *Orton* says, " that some of his sermons, which he had seen, shew him to have been a judicious and serious preacher." *Orton's Life of Dr. Doddridge,* 2d edit. p. 3.]

STAINES [V. S.] Mr. GABRIEL PRICE. An honest plain preacher, of blameless life and conversation.

WORKS. Thoughts improved; or a Christian directed in the Duty of Meditation.

STANMORE *Magna* [R. 150*l.*] SAMUEL STANCLIFF, M. A. Of *St. John's Col. Cam.* He is mentioned in *Newcourt's Rep.* After his ejectment he was pastor of a congregation at *Rotherhithe,* which he was obliged to leave thro' bodily weakness and indisposition. He died at *Hoxton, Dec.* 12, 1705. He was a man of no party, an eminent divine, and had an admirable gift in prayer.—§ He was a native of Halifax, Yorkshire, and was educated at the free-school there; to improve and adorn which, he gave an hundred pounds, which act of generosity is recorded on a column erected in the school-house, with this inscription:

" In memory of the reverend Mr. Samuel Stancliff; descended from the ancient family of Stancliff, in the parish of Halifax, in the West-riding of this county of York. Sometime of St. John's College in Cambridge, and minister of Stanmore magna, in the county of Middlesex; who departed this life the 12 day of December Anno Dom. 1705, aged 75 years.

STEPNEY [R.] Mr. William Greenhill. §O *Magd. Col. Oxf.* He was born in Oxfordshire. Where he was first settled as a minister doth not appear. In 1644, he established a society of Dissenters in *Stepney ;* was made one of the Triers in 1655; and appointed to the living of this parish the year following. *Jeremiah Burroughs* used to preach at Stepney church in the morning, at seven o'clock, and Mr. *Greenhill* in the afternoon at three; which occasioned *Hugh Peters*, in a sermon preached there, to call one " The Morning-star of Stepney," and the other, " The Evening-star."—He was one of the Dissenting brethren in the Assembly of divines ; and he was the person pitched upon to be chaplain to the king's children, the dukes of *York* and *Gloucester*, and the lady *Henrietta Maria.* He was a worthy man, and much valued for his great learning and unwearied labours. [Mr. *Howe*, in his funeral sermon for Mr. *Mead*, speaking of his connection with Mr. *Greenhill*, stiles him, " That eminent servant of God Mr. Greenhill, whose " praise is still in the churches."] § His Library was sold in 1677; so that in all probability he died about that time. The following particulars are added from *Wood's Athen, Oxon.* V. ii. p. 606.

William Greenhill, born of plebeian parents in Oxfordshire, entered a student of Magd. Coll. in the condition of a Clerk or Servitor, Ann. 1604, aged 13, and took the degrees in Arts, that of Master being compleated An. 1612, at which time, as the custom and statute is, he swore allegiance and fidelity to the King, his Heirs and lawful successors: which Oath is taken by all who take but one degree; so that if they swerve from their lawful prince, as Presbyterians, Independents, &c. have done, and adhere to another authority, they are perjured. This *W. Greenhill*, I take to be the same who had some small cure afterwards bestowed upon him, and as I have heard, the same who gave money towards the reparation of St. Paul's Cathedral in *London*, and who upon the turn of the times, occasioned by the Puritans, did express those things more openly which he before had concealed, viz. many vile matters against the bishops, orthodox clergy, the king, his cause and followers, and was never wanting in his discourses, prayers, and preachings, to advance the *blessed Cause* then most violently carried on by the said

                                    Puritans,

Puritans, he having been one himself *ab origine*, and therefore sometime brought into trouble for not observing the
customs and cannons of the church. Expressing himself
then a rank Covenanter, was made one of the *Assembly of
Divines* by the *Long* Parliament, An. 1643, and much about
the same time an Afternoon-Lecturer at *Stepney*. But leaving the Presbyterians, soon after he became, for interest
sake and not conscience, a notorious Independent, had two
Lectures more at least conferred on him in *London*, (I think
at St. *Michael's* in *Cornhill*, and at St. *Giles's Cripplegate*)
which he kept with his Lecture at *Stepney*, where, when
Hugh Peters the pulpit buffoon, did sometimes preach, he
was by him called *The Evening Star* of Stepney. About
that time, when a petition was drawn up by many Citizens of
London, to be presented to the Parliament for the speedy settling of Church-government, shewing the great mischief of
the broaching all abominable errors, &c. he was much
against it; and when 'twas brought to *Stepney* to be read in
the Church and subscrib'd, he, with *Jerem. Burroughs*,
another Independent, and the morning Lecturer, was against
the reading it, (tho' the Vicar, Dr. *Josh. Hoyle*, did order it
to be read) shewing thereby their great willingness that the
Church should be supplied with all sorts of Sectaries. Afterwards he continued very active and forward in his notorious
schisms, promoting the interest of the army then on foot,
took part with them in their diabolical proceedings, in purging the H. of Commons, their making no more addresses to
the King, applauded their proceedings against him in his
Lectures, afterwards vindicated the murder of him, and in an
high manner flattered *Oliver* the tyrant. In the latter end
of 1653, he was by the said *Oliver* appointed one of the 38
Commissioners or Tryers for the approbation of public
preachers, in which office, behaving himself very forward,
obtained one or more benifices, which had belonged to honest
men: and carrying on the cause and heaping up riches 'till
the Restoration of his Majesty, was then laid aside, especially when the act of conformity appeared: what became
of him afterwards let others seek, while I tell you what he
hath published.

An Exposition on the 28 first Chapters of *Ezekiel*, with
many useful observations thereupon, delivered in several Lectures in *Lond.*, printed in several volumes 4to. which came
out at several times----Several Sermons: as (1.) The Axe at the
root, Fast Sermon before the H. of Com. 26. Apr. 1643, on

Matt.

Matt. iii. 10.—(2.) Sermons of Christ, his last discovery of himself, &c. all from *Rev.* xxii. 16, 17.,|1656..—(3.) Sermon before the Parl. on *Ezek.* xliii. 2.—(4) Sermon on *Ezek.* xviii. 32. This is in *the Morning exercise at* Cripplegate, 1661.—(5.) The sound Christian: or, a treatise of the soundness of the heart, with several other Sermons, 1670. This book was exposed to sale by way of auction 18 Feb. 1677, so I believe he died that year.—Something of his is animadverted upon by *George Fox,* in his *Great Mystery of the Whore unfolded,* &c. p. 297.

SUNBURY. Mr. JOHN TURNER. A man of great sincerity, extraordinary humility, and profitable labours: beloved by all that knew him. He settled in *London* after he was silenced; and had a considerable meeting, first in *Fetter-lane,* and afterwards in *Hatton-Garden.* He was succeeded by Mr. *Bures.*

§ TOTTENHAM. Mr. THOMAS SYMPSON. There appears to be good authority for adding his name to the list of ejected ministers from the following memorandum—" In 1650 WILLIAM BATES (supposed to have been the celebrated Presbyterian divine of that name) was minister of *Tottenham,* upon his relinquishing the cure. *Thomas Sympson* was put in by the Lord Protector, in 1655. In 1662 (calling himself late preacher at Tottenham High-Cross) he published a sermon, entitled, " A Protestant Picture of Jesus Christ."

, TWICKENHAM [V. S.] THOMAS WILLIS, M. A. A good scholar, like his father the famous school-master of *Twickenham;* a grave divine, a solid preacher, of a very good presence; and a man zealous for truth and order in the churches of Christ; of great holiness of life, of a public spirit, of much fervour in his work, and great usefulness in the county of Middlesex. § He was appointed to this vicarage by the parliament in 1646. In the returns of the Commissioners he is commended as being diligent in observing all the commands of the parliament. He was deprived in 1661.

WOKKS. A Warning to England; or a Prophecy of perilous times, on 2 *Tim.* iii. 1.

UXBRIDGE [Chap. to *Hillingdon.*] Mr. GODBOLT. An aged divine, of great sobriety and moderation.

. WILSDON [V.] Mr. EDWARD PERKINS. A truly great man. A very ready and well-studied divine, especially in school-divinity. He was noted as an eminent tutor in *Mag-*

dalen-Hall, Oxford, and particularly for giving Mr. *John Corbet* his education. § In 1652, fifty pounds *per annum*, was voted as an augmentation of his salary.

The following afterwards conformed.

The excellent and learned Mr. EZEKIEL HOPKINS, lecturer at *Hackney*, afterwards Bishop of Londonderry in Ireland.—Mr. TIMOTHY HALL, of *Norwood* and *Southam*, [or *Southgate*,] who was preferred to the Bishopric of Oxford by K. James II. for reading his Declaration of indulgence to Dissenters.—Mr. ROLLS, of *Isleworth*, who was driven into conformity by his sufferings after his ejectment.

ADDENDA.

ADDENDA.

PAGE 108. The passage in *Hooker,* there referred to, is undoubtedly that which Mr. Baxter had excepted against in his Life (part 1. p. 41.) and is found in *Eccles. Pol.* Book I. Sect. 10. about the middle. It is as follows: " By the na-" tural law whereunto He (*i. e.* God) hath made all subject, " the lawful power of making laws to command whole po-" litic societies of men, belongeth so properly unto the same " *entire societies,* that for any prince or potentate, of what " kind soever upon earth, to exercise the same of himself, " and not either by express commission immediately and per-" sonally received from God, or else by authority derived at " first from *their consent,* upon whose persons they impose " laws, it is no better than mere TYRANNY. Laws they are, " not, therefore, which *public approbation* hath not made " so."—This passage (after a fruitless search for it in the book itself) the editor has since met with in a well-written pamphlet, entitled, *A brief confutation of the Rev. Mr. Daubeny's strictures* on Richard Baxter, *in the Appendix to his* Guide to the Church: *and of his Animadversions on* Mrs. Hannah More: *In a Letter to the Editor of* Sir James Stonehouse's Letters: *by a Layman* of the Established church. Edit. second, printed at Shrewsbury 1801. Mr. Daubeny presumes " Nothing can be said in favour of Mr. Baxter's " political principles." " Yes, (says this writer) much more than in favour of those of *Hooker.* Hooker was a favourer of democracy, without knowing it: and Baxter was per-haps the first person who detected and confuted this error. Hooker maintains the same doctrine that *Locke* insisted on afterwards."—He then, in the Note quotes the above pas-sage, with Mr. Baxter's animadversions upon it, by which he clearly proves that Mr. Daubeny was as ignorant of Mr. Baxter's political principles, as he was of other matters for which he had censured him. But tho' this is a decisive an-

1   swer

swer to *Daubeny*, the true friends to the British constitution will judge *Baxter*, in *this* matter, to be in the " error," and ascribe the superior discernment to *Hooker*, who so early asserted the grand principle which the great Mr. Locke afterwards so ably defended, in which he had *Hoadley* and other ecclesiastics of *those times* for his coadjutors, against the enemies of the Revolution by King William.

Page 254. TEWKSBURY. In a manuscript account of Mr. JOHN SPRINT, of Milbournport, communicated by Dr. Toulmin, to Mr. Thompson, it is said that " his Father was " ejected from *Tewksbury*, in Gloucestershire, and was after- " wards settled at *Andover*, in Hampshire, where he was " pastor to a dissenting congregation till his death." Whether or not he was a different person from all the four ejected ministers of this name, mentioned in this work (See the *Index*) seems to be doubtful. The account of his son, given in the above MS is interesting, but is too long to be here inserted, nor does it properly fall within the design of the present work.

Page 350. Mr. TIMOTHY JOLLIE. It is much to be regretted that the contemporaries of this excellent man did not preserve some authentic memorials of him. We cannot here insert all the particulars we have received *, but are unwilling to omit the following, respecting his Academy. Many very eminent characters were here educated; both ministers and others, who venerated his memory; among whom were the celebrated THOMAS BRADBURY, the pious and amiable Mr. SAMUEL SANDERSON, minister of a large congregation at Bedford; Mr. JOHN NEEDHAM minister of the Baptist congregation at Hitchin; Dr. NICHOLAS SAUNDERSON, the celebrated blind professor of Mathematics at Cambridge; and Dr. THOMAS SECKER †, afterwards Abp. of Canterbury; who also had a part of his education under the learned Mr. *Samuel Jones* of Tewksbury; and preached a

* From the Rev. J. P. Smith, tutor at the Homerton academy, who, it is hoped, will bring forward the whole of this article in some other publication.

† The worthy bishop of London, in his well-written *Life of Secker*, was under a mistake in asserting that he never communicated in any Dissenting church; for in a List of the members of Mr. JOLLIE's church, the name " Thomas Secker" appears along with the names of other students. This List is now in the possession of Mr. John Smith, of Sheffield, who has favoured the editor with this and other anecdotes.

probation

probation sermon in the meeting at *Bolsover*, in Derbyshire.

Page 416. This short account of Mr. JOHN RYTHER should have been cancelled; since tho' he was formerly in this living and probably turned out at the Restoration, it appears that the place of his ejectment for non-conformity, in 1662, was FERRYBY in *Yorkshire*, of which the editor was not aware till reminded, too late, by a friend. A much larger account of this worthy man and of his writings, will be found in Vol. III. under the article *Ferryby*, in the North and East riding.

Page 390. Mr. SHEFFIELD was curate of *Bowden* in 1644, and accepted *Ibstoke* 1648. *Nichols*'s History of Leicestershire; in which the whole account of Mr. Sheffield is quoted from the Noncon. Mem.

Page 391. CHURCH LANGTON. In the register, according to *Nichols*, the names of the rectors stand thus:
  " Samuel Blackerby, 1656—1659
  Richard Muston   1659
  Walter Hornby (an assistant preacher, 1659)."
For the account of the last, who had the degree of M. A. See *Merston Trussel*, Northamptonshire.

Page 391. JOHN YAXLEY. It is not to be supposed that, among so large a body of men as the ejected ministers, there were none of exceptionable characters and turbulent spirits, tho' there is reason to believe they were comparatively few. Justice obliges us to acknowledge that Mr. *Yaxley* appears to have been of this description, from the account given of him by *Nichols*, in his history of Leicestershire, who after quoting that in the *Noncon. Mem.* subjoins a great deal of additional information, of which an impartial statement shall here be given, tho' our limits do not allow of inserting the whole.

Articles against this Mr. *Yaxley* were read in the House of Lords, *July* 12, 1662. He was in London when the transactions before mentioned took place at the parsonage house at *Kibworth*, to which the following papers relate. The first of them was written by one who espoused his cause, and was at that time in the house. It is entitled " *A true narrative of the proceedings of Sir John Pretyman, Wm. Beridge, Rd. Clarke, and John Brian, at the parsonage,*
                                                              August

August 17, 1660, *attested before Justice Tho. Mallet*, Aug. 21." Signed J. D. The general purport of this paper is similar to the narrative before given (p. 350.) with some small variations, and some additional circumstances of violence and cruelty, particularly to Mrs. *Yaxley*, who is represented as driven out of the house more than half naked, and refused coming in again for the smallest article of dress. Her being shot thro' the window is mentioned, with its terrible effects, tho' nothing is said concerning the infant in the cradle.

Next follows Mr. Yaxley's Defence of his right to the living, to which he had been instituted by the Committee for plundered ministers.—A copy is then given of Sir John Pretyman's Reply; of which the following is an abstract:

"Captain John Yaxley, intruder of the church and rectory of *Kibworth* *, for these thirteen years, and upwards, did make forcible entry therein, with a party of soldiers, under Lieut. Atkinson; and did violently throw out Mr. *Joseph Forster*, clerk, and curate to Mr. *Wm. Hunt*, the true and lawful incumbent, and almost killed the said Mr. Forster after they had taken possession.—Mr. *Wm. Beridge*, the true and lawful patron, Aug. 17, 1660, in the morning, finding the parsonage door open, did with one Brian and Clark, peaceably enter the same: and finding J. D. an outlandish man, and Mrs. *Yaxley* in the house (the maids being then abroad a milking) he desired them peaceably to go out, telling them that the right was in him. Accordingly they went forth. About an hour after, Mrs. Yaxley, with about half a dozen others that had been officers and soldiers with Captain Yaxley, against his majesty, came and demanded possession from Mr. Beridge, and threw stones upon Clark (who had been formerly a servant to, and soldier under Captain Yaxley) calling them Cavalier dogs and rogues, and told them that if they would not depart they would fire the house on them; which language and actions of Mrs. Yaxley, caused Clark to discharge a pistol [at her] charged only with powder [*but thro' the glass window*]. Upon information whereof made to me (being then in bed at the other town) I came with Col. Bale to preserve the peace. Understanding that Clark had discharged a pistol, and done some injury (tho' nothing near what is suggested in the nar-

---

* Dr. Walker has it *Kibworth Beauchamp*, which is evidently a mistake. He mentions *John Yaxley*, but it is remarkable he says nothing to his disparagement. E. D.

rative)

rative) I commanded a constable to seize Clark, and bound him over to answer at the assizes : the only use I made of a constable. *Yaxley* was a captain * and in arms many years at Uttoxeter, Worcester, and against Sir G. Booth, and was with his troop a great disturber of the peace, both by day and night, searching for cavaliers, and making havock and spoil of people's goods. (He with 36 more intruding ministers petitioned that his late majesty might be brought to trial). He sent hue and cry after a gentleman in a waggon going to Nottingham, whom he supposed to be *Charles Stuart*, and procured a warrant, by which he caused the gentleman to be apprehended and examined at Quarne.

He was the chief of those that petitioned against Sir G. Booth's party. He constantly preached and prayed against the Stuarts, &c. About the time of his majesty's coming to London, he delivered in his sermon these words, " Hell is broke lose, the devil and his instruments are coming to persecute the godly ;" meaning, as his parishioners *conceived*, the king and his party.——He caused the Font to be taken out of the church, which was converted into a horse trough.—Hereby let the whole world judge what this man deserves."—Such conduct we cannot but severely condemn. It must however be observed, that neither party appears to have told the whole truth, and both seem in some instances to have exaggerated.

Page 437. *Translation* of Mr. RASTRICK's *Epitaph.*

Here lies buried, John Rastrick M. A. born at Hackington, near Sleaford, in the county of Lincoln, and educated at Trinity College in Cambridge. He was formerly Vicar of Kirkton, in the same county. And afterwards, as he could not with a safe conscience comply with certain requirements of the church of England, was an indefatigable preacher of the gospel to a christian church in this town, in separation from it.

He was a man of eminent piety, charity, and modesty : of approved integrity ; of remarkable study and industry ; and well versed in almost every part of learning, but especially the mathematics. A truly christian divine : an elo-

---

* But, N. B. He had been educated at Cambridge for the church; and many ministers on both sides took part in the war. E. D.

quent

quent and striking preacher; a faithful and vigilant pastor: an intrepid reprover of vice, and a most zealous encourager of virtue.

Having finished his course, imbittered alas! with various trials, he joyfully yielded up his soul to God, *August* 8, 1727. Aged 78.

Page 400. SHUTTLEWOOD: The account of his being apprehended, is illustrated by the following passage, in a letter of Mr. *Basil Denbigh* to Mr. *Stavely*, dated Jan. 11, 1668, (probably for 1668-9) which conveys a favourable idea of the writer.—" The other cause relates only to another poor prisoner, one *John Shuttlewood* of Stoke Golding, clerk ; who is, with some others, committed by Mr. *William Streete*, * one of the justices of peace, for the county of Leicester. My desire is, therefore, that you would be pleased to use your and my interests, that the parties above said may be speedily heard and examined, according to justice and equity, without partiality.

Basil Denbigh."

Page 402. JOHN SMITH of *Wanlip*, add : He was of the Baptist denomination. *Crosby* says of him, in his *Hist. Bapt.* vol. iii. p. 35. " He was a very lively and solid preacher, a man of an unblemished conversation, very much beloved. He was sent down into the country by the Triers, and presented to the living by —— Palmer, Esq. After his ejectment he took a small farm in Charley forest, preached frequently when he had opportunity, and lived privately till he died. Mr. *Ogle* preached his funeral sermon at Diseworth in the same county. He was forced out before the act of uniformity, because such as he were excepted in the king's proclamation of pardon.

Page 298. *Billingsley*. *Hasted* mentions a Nicholas. Billingsley among the masters of Faversham school. Nicholas Billingsly, A. M. was Rector of Betshanger, Nov. 23, 1644, and resigned July 4, 1651.

Page 139. Line 1. It should have been *South Maperton* [R.] Mr. HUGH GUNDRY; 1641: ejected for nonconformity. Bernard Banger in the room of Gundry, inst. 20 *Jan.* 1662" i. e. doubtless for 1662-3. *Hutchins* mentions no ministers at *Marshwood*, but says, " Here was formerly

* This was the person of whose name the initial letter only appeared in the first edition

a chapel

CPSIA information can be obtained
at www.ICGtesting.com
Printed in the USA
LVHW011239050221
678461LV00031B/888